AUSTRIA

FODOR'S TRAVEL GUIDES

are compiled, researched and edited by an international team of travel writers, field correspondents, and editors. The series, which now almost covers the globe, was founded by Eugene Fodor in 1936.

OFFICES
New York & London

AUSTRIA:

Area Editor: ISOLDE ANNA ZOLLES

Editorial Contributors: NICHOLAS ALLEN, FRANCES HOWELL, PETER SHELDON, DAVID TENNANT

Editor: RICHARD MOORE

Cartographers: CECIL W. BACON, ALEX MURPHY, L. A. WILLIAMS, BRYAN WOODFIELD

Drawings: KEITH HOWARD

Photographs: AUSTRIAN NATIONAL TOURIST OFFICE, PETER BAKER

FODOR'S

AUSTRIA
1984

HODDER AND STOUGHTON
LONDON   SYDNEY   AUCKLAND

All the following Guides are current (most of them also in
the Hodder and Stoughton British edition.)

CURRENT FODOR'S COUNTRY AND AREA TITLES:

AUSTRALIA, NEW ZEALAND
    AND SOUTH PACIFIC
AUSTRIA
BELGIUM AND
    LUXEMBOURG
BERMUDA
BRAZIL
CANADA
CARIBBEAN AND BAHAMAS
CENTRAL AMERICA
EASTERN EUROPE
EGYPT
EUROPE
FRANCE
GERMANY
GREAT BRITAIN
GREECE
HOLLAND
INDIA
IRELAND

ISRAEL
ITALY
JAPAN
JORDAN AND HOLY LAND
KOREA
MEXICO
NORTH AFRICA
PEOPLE'S REPUBLIC
    OF CHINA
PORTUGAL
SCANDINAVIA
SCOTLAND
SOUTH AMERICA
SOUTHEAST ASIA
SOVIET UNION
SPAIN
SWITZERLAND
TURKEY
YUGOSLAVIA

CITY GUIDES:

BEIJING, GUANGZHOU, SHANGHAI
CHICAGO
DALLAS AND FORT WORTH
HOUSTON
LONDON
LOS ANGELES
MADRID
MEXICO CITY AND ACAPULCO
NEW ORLEANS
NEW YORK CITY

PARIS
ROME
SAN DIEGO
SAN FRANCISCO
STOCKHOLM, COPENHAGEN,
    OSLO, HELSINKI, AND
    REYKJAVIK
TOKYO
WASHINGTON, D.C.

FODOR'S BUDGET SERIES:

BUDGET BRITAIN
BUDGET CANADA
BUDGET CARIBBEAN
BUDGET EUROPE
BUDGET FRANCE
BUDGET GERMANY
BUDGET HAWAII

BUDGET ITALY
BUDGET JAPAN
BUDGET MEXICO
BUDGET SCANDINAVIA
BUDGET SPAIN
BUDGET TRAVEL IN AMERICA

USA GUIDES:

ALASKA
CALIFORNIA
CAPE COD
COLORADO
FAR WEST
FLORIDA

HAWAII
NEW ENGLAND
PENNSYLVANIA
SOUTH
TEXAS
USA (in one volume)

FOREWORD

Although it is one of Europe's smallest countries, Austria manages to pack within its borders as many mountains, lakes and picturesque cities as countries five times its size. On top of which it can boast a people as welcoming and friendly as any in the world, who insist on real comforts in all aspects of life. Sports rank high and skiing highest, with innumerable ski lifts, cable cars, mountaintop lodges, luxurious resorts, highways. Though the currency has stopped appreciating, inflation is still one of Europe's lowest. Thus Austria remains the most economical of skiing's Big Three (Austria, France and Switzerland).

Austria is a country that reeks of history. Once the heart of a vast empire that stretched to the New World, Austria today is an attractive amalgam of the rich vestiges of its proud past and a balanced attitude to the modern world. Vienna, for example, contains both the Hofburg, with its Burgundian treasure, and the new UNO City, which houses the International Atomic Energy Agency, as well as the UN Industrial Development Organization and other UN offices. Austria is poised between East and West, sharing its cultural heritage with both northern and southern Europe, and yet having very obvious affinities with the lands beyond. It was Metternich who said that "Asia begins at the Landstrasse", encapsulating thus the critical role of Vienna as the meeting place of East and West for two thousand years.

But, as with most countries, the capital is only a small part of what Austria has to offer. Indeed, most visitors will see only a part of the rich variety, geographical and cultural, that is available. Whether you are looking for a quiet holiday in the green depths of the countryside, exciting skiing, music and drama festivals, churches, museums and galleries, or the chance to extend your skills in a "hobby holiday", or to improve your health at one of the numerous spas, Austria can supply exactly what you want.

*

We would like to thank the Director of the Austrian National Tourist Office in Vienna and his staff for their considerable help and interest, and Director Norbert Burda of the London office for his unfailing courtesy and assistance. We welcome Frau Isolde Zolles to our team and thank her for her help with this edition. We have also had the considerable expertise and enthusiasm of Nicholas Allen to assist us in our task.

*

All prices quoted in this Guide are based on those available to us at time of writing, mid-1983. Given the volatility of European costs, it is inevitable that changes will have taken place by the time this book becomes available. We trust, therefore, that you will take prices quoted as indicators only, and will double-check to be sure of the latest figures.

We would like to stress that the hotel and restaurant listings in this Guide are *not exhaustive,* we do not profess to provide a complete listing for accommodations or for eating places. We select those we feel would interest our readers, and change that listing year by year, so as to include new establishments that we have found or exclude those we feel may not any longer be such as our readers would appreciate.

We really do welcome letters, telling us of your experiences or correcting any errors that may have crept into the Guide. Such letters help us to improve our coverage, and also give us that essential "consumer's eye view," which is so helpful to all compilers of travel guides.

Our addresses for such letters are

in the US: Fodor's Travel Guides, 2 Park Avenue, New York, NY 10016;
in the UK: Fodor's Travel Guides, 9–10 Market Place, London W1, England.

CONTENTS

CONTENTS

MAP
OF
AUSTRIA

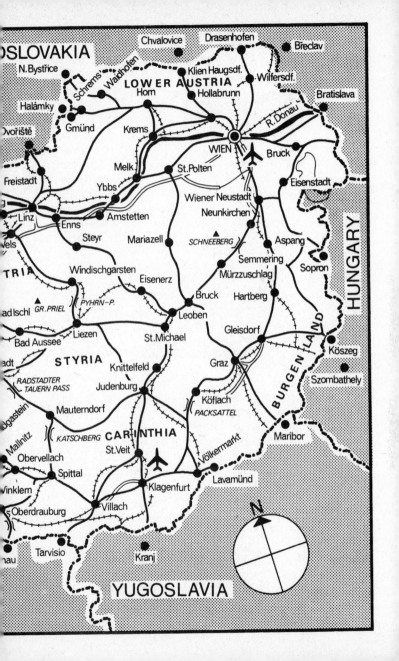

EUROPE AND
DON'T MISS

Now you can sail the legendary QE2 to or from Europe—and fly the other way, free! That means you can begin or end your European vacation with five glorious days and nights on the last of the great superliners. And get a free British Airways flight between London and most major U.S. cities. (Specially reserved flights of the Concorde are open to QE2 passengers at incredible savings.)

Only the QE2 offers four top restaurants and five lively nightspots. A glittering disco, a glamorous casino, and a 20,000-bottle wine cellar. The famed "Golden Door" spa, with saunas and Jacuzzi® Whirlpool Baths. And your choice of yoga, aerobic dance, jogging, swimming, hydrocalisthenics and massage.

• Regular crossings between England and New York, some also calling at other U.S. ports. Sail roundtrip at big savings.

• Cunard's choice European tours—varying in length, attractively priced, either escorted or independent—all include a QE2 crossing.

• Big discounts at all of Cunard's London hotels—including the incomparable Ritz.

• Enchanting QE2 European cruises, which may be combined with a crossing.

For all the facts, including any requirements and restrictions, contact your travel agent or Cunard, P.O. Box 999, Farmingdale, NY 11737; (212) 661-7777.

CUNARD

Certain restrictions apply to free airfare and Concorde programs. See your travel agent.

The QE2:
The Magic.

British Registry

$$\underset{\text{GETTING THERE}}{Q}\underset{\text{Is Half The Fun.}}{\overset{\text{UEEN}}{\underset{\text{LIZABETH}}{E}}2}$$

FACTS AT YOUR FINGERTIPS

Planning your trip

WHAT IT WILL COST The continuing low inflation rate combined lately with a rising dollar and pound, make Austria one of Europe's best buys, though Vienna is one of the more expensive capitals. Generally, prices directly concerned with tourism (hotels, ski-lifts and restaurants) have, despite high taxes, increased less than in other major tourist countries.

Vienna and Salzburg lead the list of expensive cities in Austria, followed by Innsbruck. Expensive resorts include Kitzbühel, Seefeld, Badgastein, Bad Hofgastein, Velden, Saalbach, Zell am See, Pörtschach.

Farther down the ledger, there are many old and attractive towns and cities (Graz, Linz, Krems, Hallstatt, Feldkirch, Dürnstein, Kremsmünster to mention a few) which offer almost as much history and notable architecture in attractive and comfortable surroundings, but at much lower cost.

A TYPICAL DAY FOR TWO (MODERATE)

Double room, half board, tax and service charges	schillings	1000
Lunch or dinner at tourist restaurant, with a bottle of wine		550
Transportation, excursions, sightseeing		450
Sports and refreshments		400
Evening entertainment (Operetta, concert or disco)		500
10% for contingencies		300
		3200

Other costs It will cost about 30 schillings to have a shirt laundered; from 60 to dryclean a suit, and from 55 a dress; a shampoo and set for a woman will cost her around 170, a manicure from 60; a man's haircut (without shampoo) from 60 schillings.

Opera tickets cost from 80–1,000 schillings (Salzburg Festival up to 2,000), more for special performances; theater tickets from 50–600.

SOME BUDGET IDEAS You can cut your vacation costs considerably by making a European-type, stay-put vacation, selecting one area or place and remaining there for at least a week at a time.

Many hotels, from inexpensive on up to first-class establishments, offer special all-inclusive weekly rates, although not all extend such offers during the high

LANGUAGE/30

For the Business or Vacationing International Traveler

In 24 languages! A basic language course on 2 cassettes and a phrase book ... Only $14.95 ea. + shipping

Nothing flatters people more than to hear visitors try to speak their language and LANGUAGE/30, used by thousands of satisfied travelers, gets you speaking the basics quickly and easily. Each LANGUAGE/30 course offers:

- approximately 1½ hours of guided practice in greetings, asking questions and general conversation
- special section on social customs and etiquette

Order yours today. Languages available:

ARABIC	GREEK	JAPANESE	RUSSIAN
CHINESE	HEBREW	KOREAN	SERBO-CROATIAN
DANISH	HINDI	NORWEGIAN	SPANISH
DUTCH	INDONESIAN	PERSIAN	SWAHILI
FRENCH	ITALIAN	PORTUGUESE	SWEDISH
GERMAN	TURKISH	VIETNAMESE	TAGALOG

To order send $14.95 per course + shipping $2.00 1st course, $1 ea. add. course. In Canada $3 1st course, $2.00 ea. add. course. NY and CA residents add state sales tax. Outside USA and Canada $14.95 (U.S.) + air mail shipping: $8 for 1st course, $5 ea. add. course. MasterCard, VISA and Am. Express card users give brand, account number (all digits), expiration date and signature.
SEND TO: FODOR'S, Dept. LC 760, 2 Park Ave., NY 10016-5677, USA.

season. Most of these also include Visitor's Cards, which entitle the tourist to reductions of 20–30% for all local recreational facilities, including swimming pools, ski lifts, etc. The Visitor's Card scheme is operated by the regional tourist offices, whose addresses you can obtain from the National Tourist Office nearest you.

Even some of the top resorts, such as Kitzbühel and Zell am See, are getting on the all-inclusive bandwagon, and most cities, including Vienna, Salzburg and Innsbruck, offer special weekend rates, often combined with an Austrian Airlines flight.

Budget areas Particularly easy on the pocketbook, and still not over-run with tourists are Burgenland, the areas of Waldviertel and Weinviertel in Lower Austria, the smaller lakes, such as Klopeiner See, in Carinthia, the southeastern areas of Land Salzburg (Pongau and Lungau), East Tyrol, almost forgotten since history and politics cut if off from the rest of Tyrol, and the green mountains and rolling vineyard hills of Styria.

Bungalows, Apartments In many localities there are vacation apartments and bungalows available, and if your German is up to it, many farmers throughout the country offer room and board in their own Alpine-style farmhouses, which, of course, are the original models of every balconied inn and luxury hotel in Austria. For lists of these, consult the Austrian National Tourist Office.

Among the larger firms handling villa rental is *Inter Home Ltd.*, which have over 10,000 apartments in 14 countries, including in many parts of Austria. Their address in Britain is 363 Richmond Rd., Twickenham, Middx.; and in Austria, Griesgasse 2, A–5020 Salzburg. They have a special line in chalets in the Alpine areas, which means that you can combine a relaxed, do-it-yourself holiday with skiing and other winter sports. For more modest accommodation, *Pego Holiday Homes*, Sägeweg 12, A–6700 Bludenz.

Off-season travel is recommended if you are willing to pass up the big events, which necessarily take place in the main season, and are free to take your trip at any time of the year. It is cheaper—transatlantic ship fares (where there are any left!), airplane fares and hotel rates are lower out of season. Lower hotel charges off season are very frequent in Austria, especially on full board terms, sometimes amounting to as much as 33 1/3% and even more. Even where prices are the same, you get better accommodations: the choicest rooms in the hotels and the best tables in the restaurants have not been pre-empted and train compartments are not jammed full.

WARNING: Other Nasty Taxes The tax situation becomes more complicated when it comes to beverages: there is, *in addition* to the Value Added Tax, a beverage or refreshment tax, which also applies to ice cream and coffee; then there is an alcohol tax added to beer, wine and liquor; and, finally, champagne gets hit with still another champagne tax. Thus drinking anything but water in Austria (which fortunately is very good) can be an expensive pastime. All these taxes are *included* automatically in the price.

WHEN TO GO Austria has two main seasons. The summer season starts at Easter and ends about the middle of October. May, June, September and October are the pleasantest for traveling about (except in Vienna), sufficiently warm, and there is less competition for hotel rooms and restaurant tables; also prices tend to be lower.

June through August are the most crowded months, when the main festivals take place. The Vienna Festival is from mid-May to the end of June; the Schubertiade in Hohenems, Vorarlberg, is in mid-June; the Carinthian Summer Festival is in July and August; and the Salzburg, Bregenz and Mörbisch Festivals are in late July and August. Less international, the Bruckner Festival in Linz and St. Florian is in September; and the Styrian Autumn Festival is from the beginning of October to mid-November.

The water-sports season also, obviously, has its peak in July and August when the beaches of the Carinthian lakes, Bodensee (Lake Constance) in Vorarlberg, and Neusiedlersee in Burgenland are positively swarming with swimmers. The waters of the Salzkammergut lakes are cooler, but they have just as much sailing and boating. Water-ski contests are a regular feature on the principal lakes, and on Wörthersee in Carinthia you can see occasionally night water-ski jumping with torches. The summer season in the principal lake resorts is very lively as it is also in the principal spas, such as Bad Hofgastein, Badgastein, Bad Ischl, and Baden near Vienna. In all these places, however, you have to make your reservations well in advance. Even the smallest resort features an open-air swimming pool; most better resort hotels have one, many two, indoor and outdoor pools.

The winter sports season starts in December and lasts until the end of April. You can ski in Austria as late as the middle of June and on the highest glaciers throughout the year, but if you want to do that you must be prepared to cope with rather high altitudes. Reservations are a "must" in the main resorts during the peak season.

Climate The traditional four seasons. Generally speaking Austria has moderate Central European climate. However, as the altitude and general geographical situation varies tremendously from one part of the country to another, it is always wise to check up locally. This is especially true in the winter, when road conditions can be very dangerous.

Average maximum daily temperatures in degrees Fahrenheit and Centigrade:

Vienna	Jan.	Feb.	Mar.	Apr.	May	June	July	Aug.	Sept.	Oct.	Nov.	Dec.
F°	34	37	46	59	66	73	77	75	68	57	45	37
C°	1	3	8	15	19	23	25	24	20	14	7	3

SPECIAL EVENTS that attract visitors to Austria include the many holidays which Austrians celebrate with their traditional gaiety. **New Year** is of course a time for merriment, and in some fashionable winter resorts, such as Zürs in Vorarlberg and Seefeld in Tyrol, its beginning is celebrated with such unusual features as torchlight ski races; Vienna offers the *Fledermaus* in both Opera Houses, a choice of superb concerts, and the Kaiserball in the Hofburg—the first of the glittering balls. The Three Magi singing is observed almost everywhere in the countryside and special masked processions can be seen around Twelfth Night and in mid-**January** in some localities of Styria where they are known by the name of Glöcklerlauf, as well as in the Pongau area of Land Salzburg where they are called Perchtenlauf.

Carnival, or Fasching, celebrations get under way immediately afterwards and continue, crescendo, for the next six weeks. They include hundreds of balls in Vienna, culminating in the grand gala Opera Ball and the Philharmonic Ball; mummers' parades with old woodcarved masks in several localities in Tyrol, masked dances and parties everywhere.

On the first Sunday of Lent, burning discs are sent rolling down some hills of Vorarlberg while on the top of them bonfires are lit. Spring trade fairs open in Vienna in **March** and in Graz in **April.** Easter is celebrated everywhere, with a music festival in Salzburg, and on Good Friday the Vienna Philharmonic gives its traditional Joseph Haydn concert in the Eisenstadt Church in Burgenland, where the composer is buried.

The first weekend of **May** is most energetically celebrated at Zell am Ziller, in the Ziller valley of Tyrol, which is thronged with visitors to the Gauderfest. The many attractions of this festival include Preis-Ranggeln (a folk type of wrestling), cockfighting, folk dancing, the serving of a special beer and a tremendous outburst of Gemütlichkeit.

May also marks the beginning of the season for three famous trips that can be made until October—the exploration of the largest ice caves in Europe, at Werfen and on the Dachstein above Halstatt, and the trip over the Grossglockner Alpine road (but if your heart is set on the latter, it's safer to plan it nearer the middle of its season, for late spring or early fall snowfalls have been known to close the road within the theoretically accessible dates). Corpus Christi sees colorful processions throughout Austria. Particularly picturesque are those of the Lungau region of Land Salzburg and the water processions with gaily decorated boats and barges on the Traun and Halstätter lakes. The Vienna Festival begins during the second half of May and lasts through mid-June.

On Midsummer's day (**June** 21) great bonfires burn almost everywhere throughout the country, offering a particularly picturesque view in the mountains of Tyrol and in Wachau in Lower Austria.

At the height of the season, in **July** and **August,** the Salzburg Festival, the world's most prestigious, attracts a cosmopolitan audience. In the same months, opera and operettas are performed on water stages at Bregenz on Lake Constance, and at Mörbisch on Neusiedler Lake in Burgenland. Classical plays are presented at Forchtenstein Castle in Burgenland, and in the courtyards of the Dominican Convent of Friesach and Porcia Palace, Spittal/Drau, both in Carinthia, where the up-and-coming musical and literary festival of the Carinthian Summer is shared by Ossiach and Villach. Also shared is the Festival Week of Old Music, Renaissance and baroque music at the Wilten Stiftskirche and the Silver Chapel of the Hofburg in Innsbruck. Concerts in the Abbey Churches of Garsten, Kremsmünster, St. Florian and Schlierbach in Upper Austria.

In **August,** Klagenfurt holds its Wood Fair. During the summer, Styria and Tyrol hold many brass band and folk festivals.

In **September,** musical interest shifts to Linz, where the Bruckner Festival is accompanied by an exposition of modern art. There are trade fairs in Vienna and Innsbruck. Many villages have their own harvest or grape festivities throughout this month and **October.** The Graz music and drama festival called Steirischer Herbst (Styrian Autumn) takes place from early October to mid-November.

The 15th of **November** is St. Leopold Day (for Leopold III, one of the early rulers of Austria, later proclaimed a saint), and there is a picturesque folk and religious festival in Klosterneuburg near Vienna where St. Leopold is buried. Similar celebrations in November include the festival honoring St. Martin, patron saint of Burgenland, held throughout this province on November 6 and 13; and parades on horseback in Land Salzburg and Upper Austria on 6 November honoring St. Leonhard, patron saint of cattle and horses.

St. Nicholas Day, the 6th of **December,** as in many countries of Europe, is the real beginning of the Christmas season. If you choose to go to Oberndorf, near Salzburg, for the midnight mass on Christmas Eve, you can hear *Silent Night, Holy Night* sung in the Memorial Chapel where it was sung for the first time.

HIGHLIGHTS Unless you travel on a packaged tour, with a fixed itinerary and schedule which you can't modify, it's most unlikely that you will follow unchanged any detailed plans you make in advance. Nevertheless it is advantageous to rough out your trip. This gives you an opportunity to decide how much you can comfortably cover in the time at your disposal. If you travel in the peak season, you will often have to make reservations. Finally, poring over the folders any travel agency will give you in profusion is as much fun as the winter gallop through the seed catalogs.

Vienna, of course, comes first on any "cities worth visiting" list. Here the newcomer must see at least: St. Stephen's Cathedral; the Opera, so beautifully rebuilt; Karlskirche (St. Charles Church), built by Fischer von Erlach and one of the main masterpieces of the Austrian baroque; the Hofburg, which used to be the court palace of the Habsburgs, and now houses a number of museums and collections; the Imperial Crypt under the Kapuzinerkirche where most of the Habsburg emperors together with other family members are buried; the Spanish Riding School; the baroque National Library, also built by Fischer von Erlach; at least four of the capital's art museums—the stupendous collections of the Kunsthistorisches Museum, one of the best in the world, the Belvedere Palace and its art galleries, the gallery of the Academy of Fine Arts, home until 1987 of the most important pieces of the *Schatzkammer* (Treasury), which is under renovation, the Albertina Graphic Arts collection of drawings and engravings by Dürer, Michelangelo, Rembrandt, and others; and last but definitely not least, the famous Schönbrunn Palace. Save some time for the old-fashioned cafés, the fabulous pastry shops, the wine gardens in Grinzing and Sievering, and the musical afternoons in the Stadtpark.

At **Salzburg,** the principal sights are the Hohensalzburg fortress, the cathedral, St. Peter's Abbey, Mozart's birthplace, the catacombs, the nearby "pleasure castle" of Hellbrunn—and the famous Salzburg marionettes. The Getreidegasse with its lovely guild signs, the Residenz palace, the Mirabell, the Franziskaner church and the Festspielhaus should also be seen.

At **Innsbruck,** capital of the Tyrol, you can see Maria Theresa street with its arch of triumph, the Golden Roof in the middle of the old town, the Imperial Palace, the Imperial Church, and the Silver Chapel, St. Anne's Column, and a museum of Tyrolean folk dress and furniture. You can also visit the popular resort center of Igls, a thousand feet above Innsbruck, or take the most scenic rides by cable cars, one from Innsbruck to Hafelekar, and the other one from Innsbruck to Patscherkofel.

Graz, the capital of Styria, is a fascinating old world town which offers a fine street of old buildings in the Herrengasse, and behind the Herrengasse perhaps the most complete Altstadt unspoilt in such a large city, the castle hill with clock tower, the cathedral and the mausoleum, the outstanding architecture of the Landhaus with a unique collection of weapons, the excellent museum of Joanneum, and the fine Eggenberg Castle with its hunting museum and baroque halls.

Klagenfurt, the capital of Carinthia, offers an interesting Landhaus, outstanding historic collections in its provincial museum, the dragon monument, and, of course, the Wörther Lake nearby.

In **Bregenz,** the capital of Vorarlberg, you should not miss the old town on the hill, the view from Pfänder (reached by cable car), and if you happen to be there during the festival, the performances on the unique water stage.

The principal sights in **Linz,** the capital of Upper Austria, include the old town with the Landhaus and the view from Pöstlingberg.

Eisenstadt, the capital of Burgenland, has Eszterhazy Palace and the tomb of Joseph Haydn. At **Melk,** Lower Austria, there is the famous baroque Abbey.

The **outstanding excursion** in Austria is the trip along the Grossglockner Alpine Road to the country's highest mountain. Not far behind when it comes to displaying mountain scenery are the trips up the Zugspitze for what has been called the **finest panoramic view** in Europe, the trip over the Silvretta Pass from Vorarlberg to Tyrol (or vice versa), and to the lakes in the Salzkammergut region, below the imposing Dachstein glacier. The two-hour trek through the Werfen ice caves, the shorter walk through the Dachstein ice caves reached from Hallstatt, and the view from Kanzelhöhe above the Ossiacher Lake in Carinthia (reached by cable car) are also something special. An outstanding excursion, which will take a full day, is the river-boat trip on the Danube from Passau to Vienna, or at least the section of it through Wachau with castles and vineyards on the steep banks. The greatest waterfall in Austria is that of Krimml which drops 1,250 feet in three leaps.

The country's **Number One Spa** is Badgastein. Bad Hofgastein, in the Gastein valley, has developed into a fine spa. Bad Ischl retains the flavor of imperial Austria and harbors the Emperor's Villa, Lehar's Villa (both museums now), and the famous Zauner pastry shop. An old-established favorite among spas is Baden bei Wien. Both Baden and the nearby green mountain resort of Semmering are again attracting increasing crowds of tourists. Also popular is Bad Hall; if you go there you can visit nearby Kremsmünster Abbey and see the Tassilo chalice, one of the finest examples of early Christian goldsmith work in the world. An increasing number of resorts—among them, Therme Loipersdorf, Gars/Kamp, Bad Tatzmannsdorf—now offer health and beauty programs.

Fashionable **lake resorts** include Velden and Pörtschach on Wörthersee in Carinthia; Zell am See in Land Salzburg; St. Wolfgang, where the original White Horse Inn is located, and St. Gilgen, on the Wolfgangsee, near Salzburg. Popular lake resorts are also on the Carinthian Millstättersee, Ossiachersee, Weissensee, Klopeinersee, and Faakersee; Gmunden and other localities on Traunsee; most of the small places on Mondsee; and Bregenz on Bodensee.

If you want to get into the Tyrolean valleys and mountains to glimpse the picturesque peasant life, two excellent bases are Mayrhofen and Ötztal.

TRAVEL AGENTS When you have decided where you want to go, your next step is to consult a good travel agent. If you haven't one, the American Society of Travel Agents, 4400 MacArthur Blvd. NW, Washington, D.C. 20007, or the Association of British Travel Agents, 55–57 Newman St., London W1P 4AH, will advise you. Travel abroad today is complex in its details. As the choice of things to do, places to visit, ways of getting there, increases, so does the problem of *knowing* about all these questions. If you wish your agent to book you on a package tour, reserve your transportation and even your first overnight hotel accommodation, his services should cost you nothing. If, on the other hand, you wish him to plan for you an individual itinerary and make all arrangements down to hotel reservations and transfers to and from rail and air terminals, he will make a service charge on the total cost of your planned itinerary. This charge may amount to 10 or 15 percent, but it will more than likely *save* you money on balance.

Some suggested travel agents in the US who specialize in Austria:
American Express Co., American Express Plaza, New York, N.Y. 10004.
Europacar Tours, 3 East 54 Street, New York, N.Y. 10022.
Maupintour, 408 East 50 Street, New York, N.Y. 10022.
Thomas Cook, 380 Madison Avenue, New York, N.Y. 10017.
University Travel Co., 129 Mt. Auburn Street, Cambridge, Mass.

In Canada:
Thomas Cook Inc., 2020 University St., Montreal 110, Quebec; and 92 Adelaide St., Toronto, Ontario.
Sunflight Vacations Ltd., 1470 Don Mills Rd., Don Mills, Ontario.
UTL Holiday Tours, 1253 McGill College Ave., Montreal, Quebec.

In Great Britain:

Blue Sky Holidays, Blue Sky House, London Rd., East Grinstead, West Sussex RH19 1HU.

Cosmos Ltd., Cosmos House, 1 Bromley Common, Bromley, Kent BR2 9LX.

Swan (Hellenic) Ltd., 237 Tottenham Court Rd., London W1.

Thomson Holidays Ltd., Greater London House, Hampstead Rd., London NW1.

A Sampling of US-based tours:

Globus Gateway, 105–14 Gerard Place, P.O. Box 482, Forest Hills, NY 11375, has a 9-day tour of Austria for which land costs are about $400; their general European tours also make Austrian stops for a few days each.

Cosmos, 69–15 Austin St., Forest Hills, NY 11375, which prides itself on bargain tours, has 8- and 15-day Austrian adventures with land costs round-trip from Munich running approximately $240 and $370 respectively.

Britain-based tours:

Cox & Kings Ltd., 46 Marshall St., London W1, offer fabulous special interest holidays to many destinations, Austria among them. These tours are geared towards particular areas of interest, such as painting, ornithology, or architecture; guest lecturers (usually experts in the field) lead the tours. The 15-day Austria tour focuses on botany and wild flowers and costs about £395 for a single room booking.

W. F. & R. K. Swan have one of their *Art Treasures Tours* that spends 15 days in Salzburg, Danube and Vienna and other major cultural centers for about £728. This tour is guided by an expert, too.

The Austrian National Tourist Office can be of great help with information, brochures, and advice at no charge. Its offices are located—

In the US: 545 Fifth Ave., New York, N.Y. 10017.
200 East Randolph Drive, Suite 5130, Chicago, Illinois 60601.
3440 Wilshire Blvd. 906, Los Angeles, Calif. 90010.
1007 N.W. 24th Ave., Portland, Oregon 97210.

In Canada: 2 Bloor St. East, Suite 3330, Toronto, Ontario M4W 1A8.
1010 Ouest Rue Sherbrooke, Suite 1410, Montreal, Quebec H3A 2R7.
736 Granville St., Suite 1220, Vancouver, British Columbia V6Z IJ2.

In Great Britain: 30 St. George St., London W1R 9FA.

 YOUTH HOSTELS AND CAMPING If you are a member of a Youth Hostel organization at home, affiliated to the International Youth Hostels Federation, you can take advantage of the excellent Austrian Youth Hostels, all of them in or near delightful holiday centers.

Camping information can be obtained from the *Austrian Camping Club,* Schubertring 8, A–1010 Vienna 1, or from ÖAMTC (Austrian Automobile Club), Schubertring 3, A–1010 Vienna 1.

The nightly charge in youth hostels is between 50 and 80 schillings. Those members who are older than 30 are admitted only after 7 P.M. if there is enough space. Any young person can become a member. During the season particularly, accommodation is heavily booked, and it is advisable to write to the *Austrian Youth Hostels Association (Österreichischer Jugendherbergsverband),* Gonzagagasse 22, A–1010 Vienna 1, for their booklet, enclosing an international reply coupon.

Ample information about this type of travel can also be obtained from: *American Youth Hostels, Inc.,* 1332 I St. NW, 8th Floor, Washington, D.C. 20005, or *Canadian Hostelling Association,* 109–150 Metcalfe St., Ottawa, Ontario. In England the addresses are: *Camping Club of Great Britain and Ireland,* 11 Lower Grosvenor Place, London SW1 and *Youth Hostels Association International Travel Bureau,* 14 Southampton St., London WC2.

 STUDYING IN AUSTRIA Students may choose to visit Austria any time between July and September to attend one of the three-week German language courses for foreigners given at Mayrhofen under the auspices of the University of Innsbruck. Similar courses are given by the Universities of Vienna, Graz, Klagenfurt, and Salzburg in their respective cities. Salzburg also has international summer art and music courses. The Summer School of the University of Vienna offers a 3–6 week program of social sciences for English-speaking students at Strobl on Wolfgangsee.

In the US there are two basic sources of information on all kinds of student travel and foreign study. *The Council on International Educational Exchange,* 205 E 42 St., New York, N.Y. 10017 deals with summer study, travel and work programs, and travel services for high school and college students, and provides information on charter flights. The Council's *Whole World Handbook* is the best single listing of work and study possibilities abroad. The *Institute of International Education,* 809 United Nations Plaza, New York, N.Y. 10017, provides information on study opportunities abroad and administers scholarships and fellowships for international study and training. Its *Handbook on International Study* is a very complete directory of full-time foreign study programs.

Student tours are organized by a number of tour operators in the United States, that include Austria. Write to: *Harwood Tours,* 2428 Guadalupe St., Austin, TX 78705, or *University Travel,* 44 Brattle St., Cambridge, Mass.

The American Institute for Foreign Study has a program, which includes an academic year at the University of Salzburg. For details contact the Institute at 102 Greenwich Ave., Greenwich, Conn. 06830; or in Britain at 37 Queen's Gate, London SW7 5HR.

For full information on courses in Austria, write to the *Austrian Committee for International Educational Exchange (ÖKISTA),* Turkenstrasse 4, A–1090 Vienna, and ask for their booklet *Sommerkurse in Österreich.*

HOBBY HOLIDAYS The Austrian National Tourist Office has a series of programs for those who find that a change is as good as a rest. From archeology to Wine Seminars the range is wide and full of interest. Further details of the offers listed below can be had from your nearest branch of the Austrian National Tourist Office as listed earlier this section.

Art Courses, held in the Convent of Geras in Lower Austria. The classes are in painting, sketching, oil and watercolor, and from beginners to experienced; there is expert instruction in picture restoration, too. Pottery and wood carving also have their place in this lovely setting. Other courses are held at Bernstein (Burgenland), Kötschach-Mauthen (Carinthia), and Traunkirchen (Upper Austria), Seeboden (Carinthia) and at Waidhofen on Thaya (Lower Austria). A wide variety of courses is available at Drosendorf (Lower Austria). The Salzburg Summer Academy, started by Oscar Kokoschka, and held in the fortress, is internationally known and is taught by major Austrian artists.

Engine Driving Unlikely as this is for a holiday hobby, it is wonderfully catered for in Austria. There are several centers. The narrow-gauge Zillertalbahn in the Tyrol has a 1916 engine, and the run goes from Jenbach to Mayrhofen, lasting about 30 minutes. On the Mur Valley line from Murau to Tamsweg, and on some days further on to Mauterndorf, there is a coach bar and sometimes a brass band too. It is however expensive if you wish to play driver. A really old-time engine (1909) does the run on the Montafon line in Vorarlberg, from Bludenz to St. Anton or from there to Schruns. On this run you can pay just to ride on the footplate. There is a fourth line (in Carinthia) near Treibach-Althofen where amateur driving is sometimes permitted. There are steam-engined trains in Waldviertel from Gmünd to Litschau, in Styria the so-called "Flascherlzug" from Stainz to Wohldorf; in Burgenland you find old-timers between Oslip and Schützen, and in Carinthia between Rosenbach and Ferlach and in the Gurk Valley (summer months only). Most steam trains do not have regular schedules—check at the local tourist office.

Music There are choir and chamber music courses throughout the summer at the Convent of Geras as well as the art courses. Not far away, at Castle Breiteneich, near Horn, they hold classes in the construction and restoration of woodwind instruments. At Mauterndorf in Lungau, there are choir weeks, with courses for prospective choir masters as well as courses in Renaissance music and chamber music for strings. The International Summer Academy in Salzburg, with courses during the Festival time, is the best known of all the summer music programs, and offers known artists as instructors.

Wine Seminars Held at Donnerskirchen in Burgenland for one week at a time, June to August. The whole field is examined; how to stock your cellar, how to taste and distinguish wines, theoretical topics and tours of vineyards.

More than 60% of Austria's wine comes from Lower Austria and this attractive province is ideal for a wine lover's holiday. Dürnstein, where Richard the Lionheart was imprisoned, offers a 7 days' stay, bed and breakfast, conducted tour of the host's vineyard, wine-tasting, a *heuriger* evening, and other offers.

 TRAVEL DOCUMENTS Generally there is a delay in getting a passport, so give it priority in your plans. **US residents** may apply in person to US Passport Agency in Boston, Chicago, Detroit, Honolulu, Houston, Los Angeles, Miami, New Orleans, New York, Philadelphia, San Francisco, Seattle, Stamford (Conn.), Washington, D.C., or at their local courthouse. Certain large post offices also handle passport applications. If you can submit a previous passport issued no more than 8 years before, you may apply by mail. You will need 1) Proof of citizenship, such as a birth certificate, 2) two identical photographs, in either black and white or color, on non-glossy paper and taken within the past six months; 3) $35 for the passport itself plus a $7 processing fee if you are applying in person (no processing fee when applying by mail) for those 18 years and older, or if you are under 18, $20 for the passport plus a $7 processing fee if you are applying in person (again, no extra fee when applying by mail); 4) proof of identity such as a driver's license, previous passport, any governmental ID card, or a copy of an income tax return. Adult passports are valid for 10 years, others for five years. When you receive your passport, write down its number, date and place of issue separately; if it is later lost or stolen, notify either the nearest American Consul or the Passport Office, Department of State, Washington DC 20524, as well as the local police.

If a non-citizen, you need a Treasury Sailing Permit, Form 1040D, certifying that all Federal taxes have been paid; apply to your District Director of Internal Revenue for this. You will need to present: 1) a blue or green Alien Registration Card; 2) passport; 3) travel tickets; 4) most recently filed Form 1040; 5) W-2 forms for the most recent full year; 6) most recent current payroll stubs or letter; 7) check to be sure this is all!

To return to the United States, you need a re-entry permit if you intend to stay away longer than one year. Apply for it at least six weeks before departure in person at the nearest office of the Immigration and Naturalization Service, or by mail to the Immigration and Naturalization Service, Washington, D.C.

British subjects: Passport forms are obtainable from your travel agent or local head post office. The application should be sent to the Passport Office for your area (as indicated on the guidance form) or taken personally to the issuing post office. Apply at least 5 weeks before the passport is required. The regional Passport Offices are located in London, Liverpool, Peterborough, Glasgow and Newport (Gwent). The application must be countersigned by your bank manager or by a solicitor, barrister, doctor, clergyman or Justice of the Peace who knows you personally. You will need two photos. The fee is £11.

British Visitor's Passport. This simplified form of passport has advantages for the once-in-a-while tourist to Austria and most other European countries. Valid for one year and not renewable, it costs £5.50. Application must be made in person at a head post office and two passport photographs are required—no other formalities.

Visas Citizens of the United States, Great Britain, and Canada do not need visas to visit Austria. Citizens of other nations should get in touch with the nearest Austrian consulate or tourist association representative for the latest developments on this requirement.

Health Certificates Not required for entry into Austria. Neither the United States, Canada nor Great Britain require a certificate of vaccination prior to re-entry. Because of frequent changes in law, we suggest you be vaccinated anyway, before you leave. Have your doctor fill in the standard form which comes with your passport, or obtain one from an airline, or travel agent. Take the form with you to present on re-entering.

 AIR TRAVEL Some Useful Hints The great majority of travelers today will cover some part of their journey by air. The huge pressure on the airlines, especially at the peak holiday seasons, creates problems that the traveler of only a few years ago never knew. Here are some suggestions that should make your trip just a little easier.

Health Pointers Sleep well before you leave.
Plan to arrive at your normal bedtime.
Go easy on the food and alcohol on board.
Wear loose comfortable clothes—women should avoid traveling in tight foundation garments.
Wrap yourself in a blanket to sleep—the body temperature drops.
Take it easy for 24 hours after arrival (especially after a big time change): no important meetings immediately.

Baggage Handling Don't pack valuables—jewelry, important papers, money and travelers' checks—in your checked baggage. They should be close to you at all times.
Lock each item and put name and address labels both inside and outside.
Ensure that the check-in clerk puts the correct destination on the baggage tag and fixes it on properly.
Check that he puts the correct destination on the baggage claim tag attached to your passenger ticket.
Keep your baggage weight within the free allowance—excess weight can prove very expensive. Leave some room for purchases on the trip.
If, by unlikely chance, your baggage doesn't appear on arrival, tell the airline representative immediately, so they have the details necessary to start their tracing system straightaway.
One final important point to remember. You may not use either portable radios or television sets on board aircraft, since they interfere with the plane's communications system. Calculators, portable tape recorders and hearing aids are OK. CB radios are either forbidden or severely regulated in Europe; it's not worth the trouble to take one.

WHAT TO TAKE There is really only one supreme rule—travel light. This makes more sense than ever now that any journey may suddenly be made more complicated by strikes of baggage handlers at airports. If you realize that what ever you take you may have to carry yourself, then you will be surprised to find how much you can leave at home!

For transatlantic travelers by air there are new regulations that should be noted carefully. Your baggage will now be subject to a size allowance, not a weight one. First-class passengers may have two pieces of baggage, provided that the total of the height, width and length does not exceed 124 inches (316 cm.). Economy-class passengers may also have two pieces of baggage, but the total sum of their height, length and width must not exceed 106 inches (270 cm.) and neither of the two must exceed a total of 62 inches (155 cm.). All other passengers (i.e. non-transatlantic ones), are still bound by the weight limitations of 66 lb. in First Class and 44 lb. in Economy.

It's a good idea to pack the bulk of your things in one bag and put everything you need for overnight, or for two or three nights, in another, to obviate packing and repacking at brief stops. Motorists will find it advisable to be frugal as well. You should limit your luggage to what can be locked into the trunk or boot of your car when making daytime stops.

Take what you would wear for the same sort of activities you plan to indulge in if you were staying in England or the northern United States. Remember, however, that if you are going to investigate any high altitudes (and it's pretty hard in Austria not to), you will find evenings chilly even in midsummer, so a warm sweater or two is a good thing to have. If you are going in for sports, the same sort of sports clothes you wear at home will be appropriate. If you plan to spend much time in cities or at the better resorts, and go to topnotch places, you will find Austrians dressier than Americans or Britons, and you had better take evening clothes—even in the summer, for gala performances at the midsummer festivals are apt to be formal.

MEDICAL SERVICES The *IAMAT* (International Association for Medical Assistance to Travelers) offers you a list of approved English-speaking doctors who have had post-graduate training in the US, Canada or Great Britain. Membership is free; the scheme is world-wide with many European countries participating. Office calls are $20, house and hotel calls $30, night and Sunday calls $35. For information apply in the US to 736 Center St., Lewiston, N.Y. 14092; in Canada, 123 Edward St., Toronto, Ontario M5G 1E2. A similar plan, with an initial membership fee of $6 per person or $10 per family, is *Intermedic*, 777 Third Ave., New York, N.Y. 10017. Intermedic's fees are: $20–$30, $30–$40, and $40–$50 respectively. Intermedic is affiliated with Carte Blanche. In Austria IAMAT has 12 doctors, Intermedic has 4.

Europ Assistance Ltd. offers unlimited help to its members. There are two plans: one for travelers using tours or making their own trip arrangements, the second for motorists taking their cars abroad. Multi-lingual personnel staff a 24-hour, seven-days-a-week telephone service which brings the aid of a network of medical and other advisors to assist in any emergency. Special medical insurance is part of the plan. Worldwide cover is divided into 3 zones, with a range of subscriptions from £5.65 for personal cover for up to 5 days (in Zone 1) to £20 for 13–23 day coverage (in Zone 3). Write to 252 High St., Croydon, Surrey, England CR0 1NF, for details. This service is only for residents of Great Britain.

For British travelers, free medical care (or reduced cost treatment) is available in many European countries, but you have to be prepared with documentation in most cases. One month before leaving Britain, obtain from your local Department of Social Security a Form CM1. Fill this in and return it; you will then get Form E111 to take with you.

HEALTH ON THE MOVE It is most unlikely that you will have any health upsets resulting from food or water while in Austria. Drinking water, for instance, is not only safe everywhere, but also delicious, from cold mountain sources. A few tips, however, apply to any country.

Before You Leave Pack a good supply of any prescription drugs you need. Always carry a few essential medical supplies including your favorite anti-constipation tablets and headache pills.

Take spare spectacles or your lens prescription.

Sun Bathing The sun in the Alps can be deceptively strong, so go easy the first few days and always use a good quality cream or lotion.

Rabies The epidemic of rabies raging through parts of Europe has reached Austria, affecting mostly the states of Salzburg, Tyrol, parts of Styria and Carinthia, but it is spreading fast. Affected areas are marked accordingly on all roads. If you go walking in the woods in these areas, it is advisable to carry a strong stick, preferably a stout walking stick with a metal pointed end. Dogs and cats, two each per person, are allowed into Austria if their owners can produce a valid vaccination certificate against rabies with an officially certified German translation. But even so they should not be allowed to run loose at any time.

Getting to Austria

FROM NORTH AMERICA

BY AIR There are direct flights by Pan Am from New York to Vienna stopping en route at Frankfurt. Although Austrian Airlines have traffic rights for this route they were not operating it as we went to press. But check with your travel agent. Otherwise, connections can easily be made in London or a number of Continental cities such as Frankfurt, Paris or Zürich. For Salzburg, it is better to fly to Munich, Germany, rather than Vienna; likewise for the Alpine region of Western Austria as there are good road and rail links to the major Austrian resorts, only two hours or so from the airport. For Vorarlberg, Zürich, Switzerland, is most convenient. The coach from the Vienna airport to the city air terminal costs A. Sch. 75. The airport is also linked to the city by rail with an hourly (more frequent at peak periods) service taking around 35 minutes for the run. Operates from early morning to mid-evening. Single fare costs A Sch. 65.

As we have already mentioned there are new baggage regulations in force on the transatlantic routes. Your baggage will now be subject to a size allowance, not a weight one. First-class passengers may have two pieces of baggage, provided the total of the height, width and length does not exceed 124 inches (316 cm.). Economy-class passengers may also have two pieces of baggage, but the total sum of their height, length and width must not exceed 106 inches (270 cm.) and neither of the two must exceed a total of 62 inches (155 cm.). Additional baggage can be taken but at extra cost, working out at around $60 to $80 per item.

AIR FARES There are now basically three classes of air travel: first, economy and charter. On regularly scheduled airlines, charter group passengers sit in economy-class seats, of course, but they may be paying much less for them than their neighbors who are traveling as individuals. But the service will be the same. On purely charter-flight lines, the amenities may be more sparing, the flight time longer and the delays sometimes irritating, but any annoyances should be offset by the considerable reduction in the actual cost of the flight. Only you can decide what type of trip you want, and only your travel agent can advise you on the most economical rates and times to travel, as well as on the bewildering possibilities available of 14- to 21-day, or 45-day excursion fares and the many versions of Advance Booking and other schemes.

Budget-minded travelers may want to fly to Britain from one of a dozen American cities utilizing the very low budget and stand-by fares now on offer and then proceed to Austria by surface transportation or by air. But remember that the internal fares for Europe are absurdly high, so you should look for some package deal.

Children between the ages of 2 and 12 travel at half the adult tariff, but are entitled to a full luggage allowance. Infants under 2 not occupying a seat and accompanied by an adult are charged only 10% of the full fare. Although they are not entitled to a free luggage allowance, their food, clothing, and other supplies needed in flight are not weighed. Most airlines provide special bassinets if notified in advance. Students and military personnel are entitled to certain additional reductions at specified seasons of the year.

Airline tickets can be bought on the instalment plan. A down payment of as little as 10% secures the reservations, and the balance can be paid off, after your trip, during the next 12 months. Hotel accommodations and other expenses of a trip can be added to the same instalment account, if desired. Interest charges make this arrangement more expensive.

FROM BRITAIN

 BY AIR There are daily flights by Austrian Airlines DC-9 jets and British Airways jets from London to Vienna. Flying time is under 2½ hours. Austrian Airlines, in association with BA, also flies from London to Salzburg, but less frequently. Stopovers en route to Austria for travellers from the United Kingdom are permitted only on the full first or economy class fares.

The scheduled services from London to Vienna offer both Business (Club) Class and Economy, the former being around £210 one way, the latter £205 return with no stopovers and restricted numbers. There are currently no APEX (Advance Booking) fares on this route but there are occasional charter flights costing around £170 return. Details in most newspaper advert columns or in various London weekly magazines such as *Time Out, Where to Go* etc. Many "bucket shop" agencies offer reduced rates for these tickets.

 BY TRAIN There are direct services from the Channel ports (Calais, Ostend and the Hook of Holland) to Austria. A convenient route is the "Ostend-Vienna Express" which leaves London (Victoria) at around 9.45 A.M. (15 minutes earlier on Sundays) and arrives in Vienna before 10 A.M. the next morning. Sleeping cars, couchettes and day cars from Ostend; buffet or snack bar service much of the way. For the Tyrol take the "Rhein Express" from the Hook of Holland connecting with the overnight ferry from Harwich. Leaves London around 8 P.M. and arrives in Innsbruck almost 24 hours later. Dining car most of the way. From Calais the "Arlberg Express" goes via Paris and Switzerland to Austria stopping at St. Anton, Innsbruck, Kitzbühel, Salzburg, Linz and Vienna. Leaves London around 2 P.M. arriving in Innsbruck at midday the next day and Vienna that evening. Couchettes to Innsbruck. Buffet service in Austria.

 BY CAR Car ferry routes across the Channel increase steadily to keep pace with the growing demand of people traveling abroad with their cars, but only a few are of specific interest to travelers making for Austria. These are the Dover or Folkestone routes to Ostend or Dunkirk operated by *Sealink,* with crossing times of 2¼ to 4¼ hours; Dover or Felixstowe to Zeebrugge by *Townsend Thoresen,* 4 to 5 hours; and Sheerness to Flushing, 8 hours by *Olau Line.*

The reason for choosing these ports of entry is that they are all attached to the continental motorway network, by using which on arrival after a night crossing one can be in Austria by lunch time the next day; or, with two drivers pushing it, the same evening. But travel is meant to be part of the holiday.

For motorists coming from north of London Sealink run a day and night service from Harwich to Hook of Holland, 6½ and 7½ hours. It is of course possible to reach Austria via France and Switzerland, which brings into play the shortest Channel crossings from Dover to Boulogne or Calais, or Folkestone to Boulogne, or the quickest of all, the Hovercraft Dover to Calais and Boulogne by *Hoverspeed,* both taking around 40 minutes. It is also possible to go to Hamburg direct by *Prins Ferries* from Harwich, which reduces the motoring but increases the cost. *North*

Sea Ferries also run services to Rotterdam and Zeebrugge from Hull every night.

All car ferries now have drive on/off loading, and there are no longer any air car ferries operating.

Complete tariff information from *Continental Car Ferry Centre,* 52 Grosvenor Gardens, London, SW1; from the AA and the RAC.

Car-Sleeper Train Expresses Although there are no longer any direct services from the Channel or North Sea ports to Austria there is a useful route from Brussels to Salzburg and Villach (for the Carinthian Lakes) before going into Yugoslavia. This leaves Brussels mid-evening on Thursdays from late June to mid-August arriving in Salzburg around 7 A.M. the next day, Villach about three hours later. Return is on Fridays. There is also a service from s' Hertogenbosch in Holland to Salzburg and Villach.

FROM THE CONTINENT

BY AIR The flag carrier of the country, *Austrian Airlines (AUA),* maintains a frequent all DC–9 twinjet operation linking Vienna to almost all Western and Eastern European capitals and to the Middle East, along with the flag carriers of the different countries concerned. There are also flights to Salzburg, Graz, Linz and Klagenfurt from Frankfurt, Zürich and Vienna in the summer months and an all-year-round service between Linz and Frankfurt.

BY TRAIN With Austria a crossroads of Europe, it is not possible to enumerate all the express rail services from the Continent. We list, therefore, only the more direct and famous of the International Expresses:

Alpen Express, best from Scandinavia, leaving Copenhagen in the afternoon and reaching Innsbruck about 18 hours later. Convenient from north Germany also.

Austria Express from Hook of Holland links Rotterdam to Salzburg in 14 hours, and continues to Klagenfurt with a connection to Graz. May be taken in Germany as far as Cologne, but passes other points after midnight.

Prinz Eugen links Frankfurt with Vienna in about 7½ hours.

Mozart, the fastest between Paris (leaving 7.45 A.M.) and Vienna (arriving 10.45 P.M.), also very convenient from Stuttgart and Munich in Germany; in Salzburg and Linz, Austria.

Arlberg Express from Paris, overnight to Switzerland, reaches Innsbruck, stops Salzburg and Linz, may be boarded in Basel or Zürich. Immediate connections for Bregenz at Feldkirch.

Johann Strauss connects Frankfurt and Vienna; it leaves Frankfurt at about 7 A.M. and reaches Vienna before 3 P.M.

Adria Express runs only in summer and connects the Italian Adriatic beach resorts from Ancona to Venice with Vienna.

Rosenkavalier, the fastest between Munich (leaving 7 A.M.) and Vienna (arriving 11.55 A.M.). Weekdays only.

Tirol Express which runs from Copenhagen via Hamburg, Hanover and Munich to Innsbruck with through carriages to Bischofshofen (for Kitzbühel and Badgastein).

Romulus, fastest express between Rome (departure 8.23 A.M.) and Vienna (arrival 6.50 P.M.).

Transalpin from Basel and Zürich to Vienna offers the fastest service. Runs for the most part during daylight hours, and advance seat reservation is advisable. This is Austria's best train. Total running time about 10½ hours.

Wiener Walzer is another fast train connecting Basel and Zürich with Vienna and running through Austria mainly by night; seat reservations are advisable.

For more extensive routings, consult your local travel agent. Extra trains are run during the winter sports season.

 BY BUS *Europabus,* the service operated by the European railroads, sometimes combining bus and rail for long trips, has recently extended its service to and in Austria, using up-to-date comfortable luxury coaches, equipped with radios and snack bars. There are routes from London to Innsbruck, with connecting services. The adult rate, London to Innsbruck, is about £100 one way, £180 return, including dinner and bed. Tours within Austria are also available.

Europabus have an office in Belgium at: Epervier 50, Place Brouchère, Brussels 1000; in London: Sealink Travel Ltd., P.O. Box 29, Victoria Station, SW1V 1JX.

In the US, Europabus offices are at: 11 East 44 Street, New York, N.Y. 10017; 10880 Wilshire Blvd., Los Angeles, Calif. 90024. In Canada, at 88 University Avenue, Toronto, Ontario.

There are direct bus connections from the airport in Munich to Innsbruck and Kitzbühel.

 BY CAR Once on the other side of the Channel the quickest route to Austria is from Ostend through Belgium to Cologne. The northern ring road round Brussels is now complete, so you can remain on E5 to the junction with A61 just beyond Aachen. A61 joins E12 south of Heidelberg, from where there is a choice of routes according to which part of Austria you wish to reach.

From Flushing, drive 59 kms. towards Bergen-op-Zoom then turn right for Antwerp and join E39 for Aachen.

From Dunkirk, motorway throughout via Lille to join E5 at Liège. Or, if you prefer France, N43 goes all the way from Calais to Metz, whence one can join the autoroute for Strasbourg, Basel, Zürich and Feldkirch into Austria's Vorarlberg, where the rather expensive toll tunnel under the Arlberg releases visiting motorists from the need to go mountain climbing. But allow time for the stretch between Feldkirch and Innsbruck which is severely overcrowded. Reaching Austria from Germany is just a matter of getting onto the correct autobahn and motoring on. The newly completed Frankfurt–Regensburg–Passau motorway is now the fastest route to Vienna. Cross the border at Schärding where you join the fast 137 road to the autobahn near Wels. Equally, winter brings no particular difficulties to drivers in Austria where many people use motor caravans to reach the ski resorts. The motorways are always open, including the Brenner into Italy.

If, by chance, you want to cover the Passau-Vienna stretch by Danube steamer, you can have your car driven from Passau (in Germany) to Vienna; in Passau contact *Lermer,* Neuburgerstr. 64; or *Graswald,* Schmiedgasse 10.

Arriving in Austria

CUSTOMS The following is the official list of duty-free items you may bring in with you, but there is no necessity to worry about them unduly. Overworked Austrian customs officials are not especially interested in counting to see that you may have 402 cigarettes with you instead of 400.

Travelers over 17 years of age may bring in the following items duty-free: 400 cigarettes and 80 cigars or 500 grams of tobacco if arriving from non-European countries (200 cigarettes or 50 cigars or 250 grams of tobacco from European countries), 2 liters of wine, 1 liter of liquor (0.75 liter from European countries), about 10 oz. of eau de cologne, about 2 oz. of perfume, $100 worth of souvenir items. In addition, tourists are not liable to duty on the following articles brought in for their own use: personal jewelry; 2 cameras, 1 movie camera (each with 10 rolls of film); 1 pair of binoculars; 1 musical instrument; 1 record player; 1 portable radio; 1 portable TV set; 1 tape recorder; 1 portable typewriter; sports equipment including 2 hunting guns with 100 cartridges (guns need a certificate from the Austrian Consul) and food provisions for two days.

At the end of your stay you may take out up to $400 worth of goods (for real art objects you need an export permit). For goods of additional value, you can get export forms from the shop of purchase or from the Austrian National Bank in Vienna.

MONEY The unit of Austrian currency is the Schilling, divided into 100 Groschen. In these days of inflation and fluctuating rates of exchange, you would be wise to check regularly on the dollar or sterling rates—both while planning your trip and while on it. A little forethought can save you money. At presstime (mid-1983), the rate of exchange was about 10 schillings to one US dollar; the £ was AS25.

Foreign currency and Austrian schillings (AS) may be brought into Austria in unlimited quantites. Any amount of foreign exchange may be taken out, plus 15,000 schillings. Foreign currency may be exchanged at any Austrian bank and exchange offices at the following railway stations: Vienna Westbahnhof, and Süd-Ostbahnhof, Linz, Salzburg, Innsbruck, Kufstein, and Villach. Vienna airport also has a currency exchange office, and the exchange counter at the Reisebüro City on the Stephansplatz is open on Sundays.

Travelers' checks are the best way to safeguard your travel funds. In the US, *Bank of America, First National City,* and *Republic Bank of Dallas* issue checks only in US dollars; *Thomas Cook* issues checks in US dollars, British pounds and Australian dollars; *Bank of Tokyo* in US dollars and Japanese yen; *Barclay's Bank* in dollars and pounds; and *American Express* in US and Canadian dollars, French and Swiss francs, British pounds, German marks and Japanese yen.

Note: Britons holding a Eurocheque Encashment card can cash cheques in Europe for up to £50 at any bank participating in the Eurocheque scheme. Ordinary British cheque cards, which before 1983 automatically allowed the holder to cash cheques in Europe, are no longer valid.

Two helpful tips about cash Always carry a few single dollar bills, they will save you changing small travelers' checks, as well as coming in handy for last minute airport shopping.

A very good idea indeed is to stock up with small denomination money for the countries you are going to visit. This will help see you through any airport tipping and the taxi or airport bus on arrival.

Staying in Austria

HOTELS Austrian hotels are officially classified from one to five stars according to strict government standards and inspection. In order to give our readers a clearer picture, in regard to price as well as quality, we have employed our own classification, dividing hotels into four categories. These are geared to peak-season rates (where applicable) and for the more expensive rooms with private bath facilities. By an active program of modernization, the problem of the lack of baths or showers is gradually being overcome, and all rooms in the three higher categories can be taken to possess private facilities unless otherwise stated. Only in the inexpensive category will the number of showers, if any, be mentioned. Most of the better resort hotels insist on half or full board in season; the rest of the year they are delighted to offer any terms at all.

Many summer and winter resort and spa hotels are open only seasonally. In summer resorts the peak season is July and August, with pre-season beginning June 1 and the post-season lasting until the middle or end of September. In the skiing centers the peak season is from Dec. 20–Jan. 6, and from Feb. 1–March 15. The peak-season prices at fashionable resorts are 25 to 50 percent higher than those of other months.

Except in Vienna and Salzburg, there are few *deluxe* hotels, but numerous *first-class* in all major resorts, usually with swimming pools, often indoor and outdoor, saunas. The *moderate* in the country areas or smaller cities and towns are on the whole more than adequate; food, service and cleanliness are of high standard. The newer *inexpensive* have private showers, while the older are increasingly adding. In the countryside and occasionally in the towns, various local terms are common: **Gasthof,** German for a country and small town type of a good-size hotel combined with a fairly large eating and drinking establishment. In bigger cities they are usually old, often colorful but unpretentious; in the resorts, **hof** forms frequently part of the names of even *deluxe* modern establishments. **Gasthaus,** a country inn (but found also in the cities), smaller in size than Gasthof, but usually with at least a few beds; the emphasis is on the eating and drink services. **Frühstücks-pension,** a guest house usually offering rooms with breakfast, and occasionally a small evening snack. **Kurhaus,** literally a "cure house" or spa establishment, often offering in addition to baths and other cure facilities such amenities as restaurants, cafés, and musical entertainment. In some smaller spas a hotel wing or annex is also attached to the Kurhaus. The ever-more-popular *Kurhotel* offers its guests a wide range of cures under medical supervision, from therapeutic baths to slimming.

The expression *garni* means simply bed and breakfast.

Farmhouse Holidays are extremely pleasant, picturesque and economical, especially for families with children. There are about 4,000 farms which take part in the scheme. Most of them provide only bed and breakfast, which leaves you free to enjoy the day as you please. It is the kind of holiday that is better spent with a car, though this is by no means essential.

The Austrian National Tourist Office will provide you with a list and brochures; very often advance booking is not necessary. There are three approximate price categories for bed and breakfast per person: I being from AS 100 up, II 90–100, and III up to 90.

HOTEL RATES

(in Austrian Schillings)

Category		Vienna, Salzburg, top resorts	State capitals, major resorts	Country, small towns
(L) (Deluxe	single	800–1500	600–850	—
	double	1400–2000	1000–1350	—
(1) Expensive	single	650–850	450–850	350–450
	double	1900–1400	650–900	500–700
(2) Moderate	single	480–600	320–500	180–350
	double	800–950	450–800	220–550
(3) Inexpensive	single	300–400	200–300	120–200
	double	450–750	400–500	180–350

Pensions may charge 10–20% less in their respective categories. Off-season charges are 20–40% less, but many resort hotels keep open only during the slightly cheaper pre- and post-season months.

Service and all taxes included.

All rooms with bath or shower, except in Inexpensive category.

Castle-Hotels To accommodate travelers in search of something different, Austria has converted many of its famous old castles into hotels. Some historic and atmospheric ones are:

Palais Schwarzenberg in Vienna; Schlosshotels Mönchstein, Sankt Rupert and Fondachhof in the city of Salzburg; Schloss Fuschl nearby on Fuschlsee; Schloss Pichlarn in Irdning and Rabenstein near Frohnleiten, both in Styria; Schloss Velden, Schloss Seefels and Schloss Leonstein, all on Wörthersee in Carinthia; Schloss Itter near Hopfgarten in Tyrol; Schlosshotel Igls near Innsbruck; Schlosshotels Lebenberg and Münichau in Kitzbühel, also in Tyrol; Burg Bernstein and Schloss Drassburg in Burgenland.

More details of these and others will be found in our hotel listings.

Romantik Hotels and Restaurants A German organization which now has 13 Austrian members. These are inns of historical interest but with modern comfort and at reasonable prices, they appear in our hotel listings.

 RESTAURANTS Eating in Austria ranges from extremely expensive to good, wholesome food at wholesome prices wherever you are—in Vienna, or smaller towns in the country. For deluxe restaurant meals, count on paying at least 300 schillings per person without wine; 180 schillings in an average restaurant; less if you take the set-menu meals which are offered particularly at noon (the main meal in Austria). A bottle of wine costs about 90–150 schillings (more, of course, for special vintages), but the open wines are very good and cost about 25–35 schillings per ¼-liter carafe. A glass (half liter) of beer varies from 10 to 20 schillings depending on the establishment; coffee varies from 20 to 40 schillings; whiskey about 55–90; schnaps from 15 to 30; a cocktail in a first-class bar will cost at least 90 schillings. Mineral water, apple juice, Coca-Cola, and similar drinks cost about 17 schillings, all inclusive of taxes.

The sign to watch for at a restaurant's entrance is a shield displaying the letter "G" meaning that the restaurant is a member of the *Bund Österreichischer Gastlichkeit* (Association for Austrian Hospitality), a countrywide organization of restaurants and coffeehouses of all categories; the organization has been set up with the purpose of maintaining and watching over good quality in Austrian culinary establishments. It also sponsors several culinary festivals during the year, in Vienna as well as in Salzburg, Innsbruck, Graz, Linz, Carinthia and Vorarlberg.

Lunch is served usually between 12 noon and 2 P.M. and dinner between 6 and 9 P.M., except in late-hour restaurants, where it is served much later.

 SPAS There are some thirty full-fledged spas in Austria and about twice as many more places referred to as health resorts. Some of them are internationally famous, with large modern sanatoria, clusters of first-class hotels, and well laid out parks. Others are lesser affairs, with, perhaps, a small sanatorium and one or two comfortable hotels. They are all delightful places to spend a holiday, even if—or especially if—there is nothing at all wrong with you.

If you go to an Austrian spa for a cure, the best course is first to consult your own doctor to select the place most suitable for you. Have him write a note for a local doctor, to give him the background on your particular case. In the spas, it is the law that no one may take the cure without a certificate from a local doctor, regardless of the credentials you may have brought from physicians at home. In all of them, large or small, you can be sure that all cures are under medical supervision. For more information on spas see individual regional chapters.

TIPPING Almost all hotels (among the few exceptions are smaller country inns) now include service charges in their rates. For restaurants this includes 10% service and all the various taxes; it is nevertheless customary to tip about 5% of your bill. You tip the hotel concierge only for special services. Give the hotel porter 10 schillings per bag. When you take a taxi, no tip is included in the fare; 10% of the fare is the usual. If the driver has been helpful in other ways, give him 15%. The railway station porters charge 10 schillings a bag. Hat-check girls get 7–15 schillings, depending on the locale. Washroom attendants get about 5 schillings.

 CLOSING TIMES Most stores open at 8.30 or 9 A.M. and close at noon or at 12.30 P.M. for a one- to two-hour lunch interval, and then stay open until 6 P.M.; in most villages opening time is 8 A.M. and lunch hour from 12 to 2 P.M. Foodstores open at 6.30 or 7 A.M. and close at 6.30 P.M., with a two- to three-hour lunch break. At the Südbahn and Westbahn stations, as well as in the 3rd District, Landstrasse 3, foodstores remain open every evening, including Sundays, till midnight. Most of the stores in the 1st District of Vienna (the center) do not observe the lunch interval and stay open without interruption from 9 A.M. to 6 P.M. On Saturdays shops are open from 9 A.M. to noon. The usual office hours are 8 A.M. to 5 P.M., Sat. closed. Banking hours at main offices (larger banks) in Vienna are 8–3, branch offices 8–12.30; 1.30–3, Thurs. till 5.30 P.M., closed Sat. Barbers and hairdressers close Monday, but stay open on Sat. afternoon.

The legal holidays are New Year's Day, January 6, Easter Monday, May 1, Ascension Day, Whit Monday, Corpus Christi Day, August 15, October 26, November 1, December 8, Christmas Day, and December 26.

 CASINOS Austria has currently ten casinos, all run according to international rules by the *Spielbanken A.G.*, under government license. They are as follows:

Baden, near Vienna, open from 4 P.M. daily.
Badgastein, open from 5 P.M. daily in summer and winter seasons.
Bregenz, open from 4 P.M. daily.
Kitzbühel, open daily in summer (from 7 P.M.) and winter (from 5 P.M.) seasons.
Linz, open from 4 P.M. daily.
Riezlern/Kleinwalsertal: open 25 Dec. to March daily from 5 P.M.; April to Dec. daily from 7 P.M.
Salzburg *(Hotel Winkler)*, open from 4 P.M. daily.
Seefeld in Tyrol, open from 5 P.M. daily.
Velden/Wörthersee, open from 5 P.M. daily. Openair roulette on two tables in summer.
Vienna *(Cercle)*, open from 7 P.M. daily.

All the casinos have an entrance fee of 60 schillings of which 50 schillings is returned to you in the form of a complimentary chip. The two exceptions are the *Cercle* in Vienna which is double (120 schillings, with two 50 schilling chips) and the Riezlern one, where German currency holds sway and the entrance fee is DM

5, of which 4 is returned as 2 DM2 chips. The casinos have roulette, black jack and baccarat.

SHOPPING We deal with specific shopping points in several other places in this book, but here are a few general hints that may be of use.

Wherever possible carry your purchases home with you, especially if they are valuable or fragile.

Find out all about customs regulations. You could be stung for a small fortune and turn a bargain into a very expensive commodity indeed.

If you are shipping goods home, be very sure you have understood the terms, how the shipment will be made, when it should arrive . . . and *get it all in writing*.

This is the time to warn you about those duty-free, tax-free shops. While they *can* offer bargains, especially in liquor, cigarettes and perfume—because of the huge taxes these attract in the normal shops—the "DUTY FREE" signs can often be unpleasant hoaxes. Some airport shops charge up to 50%, sometimes even 100%, above the prices charged for exactly the same goods in selected shops in town. Cameras, radios, calculators are among the goods which fall into the "Think Twice" category.

If you make expensive purchases, it may pay to take advantage of a value-added tax (Mehrwertsteuer) exemption offered tourists, although it's a complicated procedure—the minimum purchase per store is 2,000 schillings, purchases may not be used in Austria and hence must be shipped home, and the store (usually marked *Tax Free Shop*), which does the tedious paperwork involved, must inform the Finance Ministry of the transaction. Customs clearance is required upon departure, when the tax, which has been paid, is refunded.

POSTAL SERVICES Postage is about the same as in most European countries. For the first 20 grams (about ¾ ounce) letters cost 4 schillings for all domestic destinations; 6 for destinations abroad. Regular-size letters (20 grams) and postcards are forwarded within Europe automatically by airmail (with no extra charge); minimum airmail charges for letters (up to 10 grams) to US and Canada 9 schillings. Postcards to Austrian destinations 3, abroad 4, airmail postcards to US and Canada 5.50. Increases in postal rates are likely.

Cables, telegrams, and wireless messages are sent from post offices. In addition to being available in post offices, stamps are sold in tobacco shops (Tabak Trafik) and it is often easier to buy them there, as post offices can get very busy.

TELEPHONES Telephone numbers in Vienna consist only of numerals (six to seven digits). Coin-operated street telephone booths in Vienna are numerous. Direct dialling everywhere within Austria as well as to most countries in the world; otherwise dial 00 for long-distance operator.

Calls within Austria are 33% cheaper between 7 P.M. and 8 A.M. on weekdays and from 1 P.M. on Saturday to 8 A.M. Monday.

If you are calling Austria from abroad omit the 'O' preceding the area code.

Note You are warned not to make long-distance phone calls from your hotel room without checking very carefully what the cost will be. Hotels frequently add several hundred percent to such calls. This is an international practice, not one confined to Austria. For overseas telephoning, Austria is six hours ahead of New York, one hour ahead of Britain.

ELECTRICITY Austrian voltage is mainly 220, so most British 200-volt appliances can be used on it, but American 110–120 apparatus cannot. However, most hotels where sockets for electric razors are available have them adapted for both currents. Austria has the European 50-cycle circuit. Therefore, American 60-cycle electric clocks, phonographs, and other appliances with timing devices will not operate satisfactorily without being converted by an electrician.

DRINKING WATER You may drink the water safely anywhere in Austria. Vienna's water is famous, though the water piped from the mountains south of the city is blended with water from the Danube meadows. There are also excellent table waters from the country's many mineral springs: Gasteiner, which comes from the famous spring and is gaseous; Preblauer, clear thin and almost still; Kalsdorfer, Güssinger, and two especially popular ones, Römerquelle and Vöslauer.

PHOTOGRAPHY Austria is a highly photogenic country, with picturesque scenery at every turn. Should your supply of film seem to evaporate (because of all the extra pictures you take), you'll be able to replenish it locally, wherever you happen to be; however, since the 1978 luxury tax of 30% was slapped on film, it is quite expensive.

Warning Don't leave already exposed film in your pockets or in any hand luggage while passing through airport X-ray machines. The process can sometimes fog the film and you may find a whole trip's photographs ruined. It is worth investing in a product called *Filmashield,* a lead-laminated pouch. It stores flat when not in use and holds quite a lot of film—or, indeed, your camera with half-used film in it. It is available in many countries. Any trouble in finding it, write to *SIMA PRODUCTS,* 4001 West, Devon, Chicago, Illinois 60646, for the nearest distributor.

CONVENIENT CONVENIENCES are to be found in all railway stations, very often in larger city parks (for instance, Stadtpark in Vienna), in almost all the new underground passages (where they are clearly marked). In addition, all larger department stores have such "conveniences", although often hidden away and necessitating inquiries as to their whereabouts. In smaller towns (aside from railway stations) the only solution is a Gasthaus, hotel or coffee house, all of which are generally understanding.

WINTER SPORTS (for further information, see the *Sports* chapter following). **Skiers** are in luck almost anywhere in Austria. If fun and games (and après ski) comes first with them, they will probably put Kitzbühel at the top of winter sports resorts for its "ski circus", which permits almost indefinite following of trails without ever a repeat. St. Anton and St. Anton's higher twin, St. Christoph, are first in popularity from the standpoint of serious skiers. St. Anton is the more fashionable of the two; St. Christoph more reasonable but no place for novices. Seefeld, Kühtai, Obergurgl, Zürs, Lech, Bad Gastein, Bad Hofgastein, and Zell am See are also fashionable winter sports resorts. Saalbach, Maria Alm, Mariazell, Tauplitz, Radstädter Tauern Pass and Semmering are other good ski centres.

All-year skiing terrains reached by cable cars and with all facilities are on the high mountain plateaus on Wurmkogel above Hochgurgl, Rettenbachferner above Sölden in the Ötz Valley, and Spannagl above Hintertux (all in Tyrol), on Kitzsteinhorn above Kaprun, Sport Gastein, and Weissee above Uttendorf (all in Land Salzburg) and on Dachstein, the highest peak of Styria.

For up-to-date snow data, check with the Austrian National Tourist Office, which provides all its branches with twice weekly reports via Telex. In New York you can get this information also by dialing 679–8295, or from any Lufthansa office.

The *American Skiers Best Friend* network offers special assistance in some 16-odd ski resorts.

Ski Bargains Good facilities and terrain, at much lower prices, can be found, particularly in East Tyrol, Styria, Lower Austria, Carinthia, and parts of Salzburg and Upper Austria. Most ski areas offer a weekly pass for use on all lifts, cable cars and usually swimming pools, at 20–30% reductions. Consult the local tourist office. In addition, many ski resorts, including several of the more expensive and fashionable ones, offer all-inclusive weekly rates, sometimes also including ski schools and lift facilities. For a complete list, write for the special booklet prepared by the Austrian National Tourist Office.

Skiing holidays for students in some of the finest winter sports areas of Austria, from Dec. to April, are organized by the *Büro für Studentenreisen* (Office for Students' Tours), Schreyvogelgasse 3, Vienna 1; information also from *ÖKISTA*, Türkenstrasse 4, A–1090 Vienna, and its partner *OS-Reisen*, Reichstratstrasse 13, Vienna 1.

Skating and tobogganing are two winter sports that you can indulge in nearly everywhere in Austria. Skates and shoes are easy to pack but a toboggan you will have to hire—the hotel porter will see to this—or to buy. They are not expensive; an ordinary toboggan will cost about 400 schillings.

In the bigger places you will be able to go for **sleigh rides,** and this can be great fun on a moonlit evening after dinner. A rather more gentle sport is **ice shooting,** a form of curling. The rules are slightly different from those of Scottish curling and you may not use a broom, but the principles are the same. Styria is the stronghold of this sport, but it is played in most parts of the country.

MOUNTAIN CLIMBING *Österreichischer Alpenverein* (Austrian Alpine Club), with headquarters at Wilhelm-Greil-Strasse 15 in Innsbruck, owns and maintains 275 of the 700 mountain refuges, which are sometimes more like mountain inns than huts; one-fourth situated between 2,500 and 3,000 meters. Total capacity 26,000 beds in small rooms and dormitory. ÖAV branches in all major towns for details about climbs, guides, use of huts etc.

Owing to the large numbers of British enthusiasts who have become members of the Austrian Club, there is a UK Branch of the *Austrian Alpine Club,* 13 Longcroft House, Fretherne Road, Welwyn Garden City, Herts., and British visitors should make their enquiries there.

The maximum fee charged by mountain guides is 950 schillings per day for glacier and light-to-medium rock-climbing tours, whereby the guide takes care of his own food. For heavier tours and for longer engagements, a lump-sum rate is usually agreed upon. It is usual to give the guide a good tip at the end of the tour.

Hut charges are on two scales. If you are a member of the Austrian Alpine Club, your hut charges will automatically be 50% less. Membership can be obtained by foreign applicants at any of the other Austrian Alpine Club sections. Various Austrian alpine clubs operate the other two-thirds of the mountain huts.

The mountain climbers' schools, *Alpenschule Glockner-Heiligenblut* in Carinthia, *Hochgebirgsschule Glockner-Kaprun* in Land Salzburg, *Hochgebirgsschule Tyrol* and *Alpinschule Innsbruck,* both in Tyrol, and *Bergsteigerzentrum Steiermark* which offers mountain climbing courses in the Dachstein range and in Gesäuse Alps (both in Styria); the base for the school is in Öblarn in Styria. All organize climbing courses and guided tours for beginners and more advanced climbers. In most Alpine areas, specialist guides are available.

Some of the important climbing centers are:

Tyrol—*Kufstein* for the Kaisergebirge, *Mayrhofen* for the Zillertaler and Tuxer Alps, *Seefeld* for the Wettersteingebirge and Karwendel, *Sölden, Obergurgl* and *Vent* for the Ötztaler Alps, *Fulpmes* and *Gries in Sellrain* for the Stubai Alps, *Innsbruck* for Nordkette and Karwendel.

Vorarlberg—*Gargellen Galtür* for Silvretta range, *Gaschurn* for Rätikon and Verwall ranges.

Vorarlberg and Tyrol—*St. Anton* and *Lech* for the Arlberg.

Carinthia—*Heiligenblut* for the Glockner region, *Greifenburg* for Kreuzeck group, *Oberdrauburg* for Kreuzeck group and Gailtaler Alpen, *Flattach* for Goldberg group, *Pflüglhof* in Maltatal for Hochalmspitze, Ankogel, and Sonnblick.

Land Salzburg—*Neukirchen* for the Grossvenediger, *Krimml* and *Mittersill* for the Hohe Tauern, *Böckstein* for the Ankogel group, *Kolm-Saigurn* for the Sonnblick.

Styria—*Ramsau* for Dachstein, *Altaussee* and *Tauplitz-Klachau* for Totes Gebirge, *Gstatterboden* for Ennstaler Alpen, *Prebichl* for Hochschwab.

East Tyrol—*Lienz* for Lienzer Dolomiten and Schrober group, *Matrei* for Granatspitz group, and Grossvenediger, *Hinterbichl* for Dreiherrnspitze and Grossvenediger.

Austria also provides 40,000 km of well-maintained and sign-posted mountain paths through Europe's largest reserve of unpolluted air. A paradise for ecologists and a pleasure for all lovers of superb landscape.

CAMPING There are the following camping organizations: *Österreichischer Camping Club* (Austrian Camping Club), Schubertring 8, A–1010 Vienna I, and the camping section of the *Austrian Automobile Club* (ÖAMTC).

A camping booklet issued by the Austrian National Tourist Office and available to travelers at frontier crossing points, gives detailed information on existing campsites in six languages. There are about 400 sites in operation at this writing, with new ones in the offing. Most of the campsites in the brochure belong to one or another of the various organizations, although a few are privately owned. Charges per person and per day vary between 15 and 45 schillings, depending on the quality of the camp. There are about 77 winter camping sites throughout Austria. Some mountain roads are either altogether forbidden, or not recommended, for trailers.

SWIMMING AND BOATING No resort or larger village is without outdoor **swimming** pools, many of them heated; almost all pools demand the wearing of swimming caps. Swimming facilities exist also on many lake and river beaches.

Small **sailing** boats may be hired on all the lakes of the Salzkammergut region and on the large Carinthian lakes in the south. You can rent a rowboat on any of Austria's 100-odd lakes. Information can be obtained from the Austrian National Tourist Offices, and from *Österreichischer Segel-Verband* (Austrian Yachting Association), Prinz Eugenstr. 12, A–1040, Vienna IV.

Water skiing and sail skiing are popular on the Wörther See, Millstätter See, and Ossiacher See in Carinthia; on Traunsee, Attersee, and Wolfgangsee in Salzkammergut; at Zell am See in Salzburg province; and on Bodensee (Lake Constance) in Vorarlberg.

Kayaking on the Enns River between Schladming and Gesäuse (extremely difficult through Gesäuse) and on most of the Mur, which is very easy below Graz. Boats can be rented at Gröbming and Aich-Assach for the Enns run. Also on Danube, Traun and Steyr.

GLIDING From May to September you can glide or learn to glide at one of Austria's schools, located at Zell am See, Niederöblarn (Styria), Graz-Thalerhof (also Styria), Wiener Neustadt, just outside Vienna, and Spitzberg bei Hainburg (Lower Austria). The schools at Zell am See and Wien-Donauwiese also offer passenger flights in 2-seaters.

There are a number of gliding clubs, in addition to those mentioned above, which offer hourly passenger rides, although no instruction. Write to the *Austrian Aero Club*, Prinz Eugenstr. 12, Vienna IV, for further details.

FISHING Well-stocked lakes in Upper Austria are the Traunsee, Attersee, Hallstätter See, and Mondsee; the Danube, Steyr, Traun, Enns, Krems, and Alm rivers also provide good fishing. Tyrol is another good fishing region; try the Achensee, Traualpsee, Walchsee, Plansee, and nearby streams, also the Inn and Drau (East Tyrol) rivers and the Zillertal streams. Styria provides some of the best trout fishing in Austria, as do the lakes in the Styrian Salzkammergut. Carinthian lakes and Lower Austrian streams and rivers also abound in fish. Fly-fishing is perhaps the best form of fishing available, from the innumerable mountain streams. An excellent guide, *Fishing in Austria,* is obtainable from all Austrian Tourist Offices; it will give you the licenses available and their cost.

WALKING Wanderkarten or walking maps (scale 1:20,000 up to 1:50,000) are available in every town: they mark the local trails in red and often describe the walks. The local Alpen or Wandervereins have marked the walks by means of painted daubs in specific colors, often with numbers too. You can follow the daubs on fences, stones, trees and houses.

USEFUL ADDRESSES *Austrian National Tourist Office,* Margaretenstr. 1, A–1050 Vienna. *American Express* and *Wagons-Lits/Cook* have offices in Innsbruck, Salzburg, and Vienna. The *American, Canadian, British,* and *Australian Embassies* are located in Vienna; *British Consulate,* Innsbruck; *American Consulate,* Salzburg. Students who wish to live with Austrian families should contact the *Austrian Committee for Educational Exchange,* Türkenstr. 4, Vienna 9.

Traveling in Austria

See also the **Route Planning** sections in each chapter.

BY AIR There are flights between the major Austrian cities of Vienna and Salzburg, Graz, Linz, Klagenfurt and Innsbruck, but before you think of flying, check the time it would take to go by rail and also the schedules, as they vary considerably from season to season. Most domestic flights are operated by *Austrian Air Services* using 17-passenger metro turboprop equipment. Innsbruck is linked to the outside world by *Tyrolean Air.* This company and air taxis operate to some of the ski resorts in winter. There are helicopter flights from St. Anton to St. Christoph in Tyrol over the Arlberg ski terrain that can be combined with ski tours in the higher mountain regions.

BY TRAIN The Austrian railroad system is extensive, and except for remote mountain villages there are few places not served by the network. All important lines have been electrified, but you still have a choice of *types* of trains, which we list below.

Regionalzug. This is the slowest. Use only for very local services especially in country areas.

Eilzug (E-Zug) Semi-fast trains stopping at many stations. Shown as "E" in all timetables.

Schnellzug (D-Zug) Faster still. This train stops only at bigger places.

The **Express** (marked by **Ex** on timetables). These are international trains, such as the Arlberg, Tauern, and other expresses. Reservations.

The **Triebwagen.** Along with express trains, this is the best and quickest means of getting about. The Triebwagen is a very modern, comfortable and fast streamliner composed of a few coaches only. They run between most big cities in Austria, and stop only for brief periods at really big stations. They are very popular with the Austrians, and if you are getting on at a terminus, it is best to reserve a seat.

Städteschnellverbindungen (Inter-City Express Trains). The fastest trains, connecting Vienna with the various principal cities, for instance: Vienna-Graz (2½ hrs.), Vienna-Linz (1 hr. 55 mins.), Vienna-Salzburg (3 hrs.), Vienna-Innsbruck (5 hrs.), Vienna-Bregenz (8¼ hrs.), Vienna-Klagenfurt (4 hrs.) and Vienna-Villach (4½ hrs.), Vienna-Krems (1 hr.). All these operate on the "interval" system, leaving every one or two hours.

Reduced Fares Anyone traveling extensively in Austria would do well to investigate special tickets and discounts offered by the Austrian Federal Railway system. For example, it might be worthwhile to buy a railroad pass valid for one particular province or for the whole of Austria. Private railways, buses operated by the Federal Railway and Lake Constance boats allow a 50% discount to holders. Passes for 15 days or one month are also available. There are also special reductions for groups of students. A discount of 25% is offered during the international fairs in Vienna, Graz, Innsbruck, Klagenfurt, etc.

There is a 50% reduction for senior citizens against *Senioren Karte,* price 120 sch. Those under 26 are entitled to the *Austria Ticket Junior* (see below). Children up to 6 years travel free, provided they sit on your lap; half rate from 6 to 15 years.

For a reduced rate you can buy a *Kilometerbank,* a book of two or five thousand kilometers, first or second class. You mark in journeys as you make them (no limit to the number of journeys or the number of people using the Bank) and the conductor marks off the kilometers. It is valid for a year and available without formality at ticket offices.

Budget Note For anyone planning on extensive traveling and sightseeing, it is best to purchase either a *Trans Austria Ticket* or an *Austria Ticket Junior* which are unlimited travel rail tickets. The *Trans Austria Ticket* is good on all state railways for 9 days, 16 days, or one month periods. Cost in 1st and 2nd class respectively is 1950, 2640, and 4200 sch. (1st class), or 1300, 1760, and 2800 sch. (2nd class). The *Austria Ticket Junior* (available for those under 26) is valid for 9- or 16-day periods in 2nd class only, and costs 950 sch. and 1350 sch. respectively. These junior tickets entitle the purchaser to unlimited travel not only on state railways, but on post buses and buses run by the Federal Railway, many cable railways, and other smaller railways besides. Several steamer discounts are also included. *These tickets are only obtainable within Austria.*

A **Eurailpass** is a convenient, all-inclusive ticket that can save you money in 16 countries of western Europe. It provides the holder with unlimited travel at rates of 15 days for $260; 21 days for $330; 1 month for $410; 2 months for $560; 3 months for $680; and Youth Pass (under 26), 1 month for $290, 2 months $370 (2nd class travel).

May be purchased and used *only* if you live outside Europe and North Africa. The pass must be bought from an authorized agent *before you leave for Europe.* Apply through your travel agent; or the general agents for North America: French National Railroads, Eurailpass Division, 610 Fifth Avenue, New York, N.Y. 10020; or through the German Federal Railroad, 11 West 42nd Street, New York, N.Y. 10036 and 45 Richmond Street, W., Toronto M5H 1Z2, Ontario, Canada.

BY BUS Austria has a nation-wide bus and coach system although frequencies are not as great as in some other countries. But their safety record is one of the highest in Europe. The Post Buses (bright orange-yellow for easy recognition) reach to even the remotest areas. And they all carry passengers. Out of season there is usually no problem in getting a seat. But in peak weeks (winter as well as summer) prior reservation is essential. Many of the buses duplicate railway routes but take longer. The main cities also have excellent bus (streetcar as well in some cases) networks reaching out into the surrounding country. Always well worth checking on this when you are in the city. As with the trains, the buses are kept spotlessly clean and in excellent mechanical condition.

Europabus tours of Austria, lasting from two to seven days, are frequent and take you through the most scenic areas. *Austrobus* of Vienna runs fast bus services between Vienna and Venice in Italy, Opatija-Zagreb in Yugoslavia, Prague-Karlsbad in Czechoslovakia, and Cracow in Poland; most of these bus lines take you through large portions of Austria. Information from Austrian tourist offices.

BY CAR EEC tourists can bring their cars to Austria without any other documents than their ordinary registration papers and their national driving licenses. Green Card insurance is, however, recommended for them, and is obligatory for others.

Tourists' cars must be equipped with first-aid kit, a set of spare bulbs, and a red warning triangle. In the case of breakdown or accident the triangle must be placed 55 yds behind the car and not more than 1 yd from the edge of the road.

Tourist-owned vehicles must not remain in Austria for more than one year and may not be driven by Austrian residents of whatever nationality. The country's minimum driving age is 18, and children under 12 must ride in the back seat. It is compulsory for front-seat passengers to wear seat belts if the car is so fitted.

Parking is a problem in all towns and resorts. Parking zones, with various time limits, are clearly indicated and strictly policed. In major towns, parking coupons must be fixed to the windshield; obtainable at tobacco shops (*Tabak Trafik*) but expensive. Streetcars have the right of way at intersections without traffic lights, regardless of the direction from which they are approaching.

Speed limits There is a speed limit of 130 kph (85 mph) on all autobahns; on other highways and roads 100 kph (65 mph); in built-up areas 50 kph (31 mph); for cars with trailers weighing more than 750 kg. (about 1,650 lb.) 80 kph (49 mph).

Fuel Gasoline (petrol) prices: 10.60 sch. per liter for regular and 11 for premium. Motor oils vary between 50 and 88 sch. per liter. Prices liable to change.

Maps The numerous detailed maps supplied free by the *Austrian National Tourist Office* and regional tourist offices are perfectly adequate. For perfectionists, maps are sold at low cost by the Austrian Automobile Club. Particularly useful is the annually revised map of Austria showing the condition of roads (*Strassenzustandskarte*); also excellent is the more detailed 1:200,000 road map of Austria in 8 sections, printed on 4 maps.

Car Hire For those who do not wish to bring their own cars to Austria, hire firms, both local and international, will provide self-drive and chauffeur-driven cars for collection at airports, stations or hotels in the larger towns. Approximate charges for a car without chauffeur are from 280 to 860 sch. per day, depending on type of car, without fuel, plus 2.80 to 9 sch. per kilometer; insurance extra. On a weekly or monthly basis the charges are considerably lower.

You can pick up a rental car on arriving in Austria by train at the following stations: Bregenz, Dornbirn, Graz, Innsbruck, Klagenfurt, Leoben, Linz, Salzburg, Vienna (both West and South stations), Villach and Zell am See. Just contact any rail ticket office, travel agency selling rail tickets, or the conductor on an express train up to two hours prior to scheduled arrival of train, to make the arrangements.

Because of VAT at 30% it is usually cheaper to rent a car in Germany or Switzerland and bring it over the border, provided of course that this is convenient.

Tolls There are several toll roads in Austria, mostly over or under mountains. The magnificent Grossglockner Alpine road, for example, is a toll road (about 200 sch. a car), as well as the Brenner Autobahn (120 sch.), which makes it look no longer like a mountain pass. Other important toll roads are Felbertauern, Gerlos in Land Salzburg, and the (180 sch.) Tauern Autobahn.

Some other charges are: Arlberg tunnel 140 sch.; Flachau-Rennweg, 200 sch. (return ticket 330 sch.); Flachau-Zederhaus, or Flachau-St. Michael, 130 sch. (return 220 sch.); St. Michael-Rennweg (Katschberg tunnel), 90 sch. (return 110 sch.). There are considerable reductions during winter months.

Tunnel Ferries The Austrian State Railroads run a car-ferry service through a tunnel from Böckstein near Badgastein in Salzburg to Mallnitz in Carinthia, and vice versa, now mainly of local interest because of the new road over the Tauern range. Count on the tunnel car-ferry service only in the daytime. During the trip you remain in the car together with all other occupants. One-way charge for passenger car with up to 6 occupants is 160 sch.

Automobile Clubs *Austrian Automobile Club* (Österreichischer Automobil-Motorrad- und Touring-Club), headquarters in Vienna, Schubertring 3, with border offices on the main roads entering Austria, as well as its provincial affiliates, will gladly give any information you may need on motoring.

At Vienna's Schwechat Airport they are open daily until 8 P.M., also for emergency repairs. Provincial automobile clubs: *Carinthia:* Domgasse 5, Klagenfurt; *Salzburg:* Schrannengasse 5, Salzburg; *Styria:* Girardigasse 1, Graz; *Tyrol:* Tschamlerstrasse 10, Innsbruck; *Upper Austria:* Gürtelstrasse 20a, Linz; *Vorarlberg:* Bahnhofplatz, Dornbirn.

If you need information on road conditions, traffic situation, breakdown service or border formalities call the Information Service of the club in Vienna, tel. 72–21–01 (preceded by 0222 when calling from outside of Vienna but within Austria) between 6 A.M. and 8 P.M. The Austrian Automobile Club also operates a central service for objects lost by motorists; write or call.

The American Automobile Association, in addition to providing various services to motorists is also an accredited travel agency and can book your holiday. Write to AAA World-Wide Travel, 8111 Gatehouse Road, Falls Church, Virginia 22042.

Kilometers into Miles This simple chart will help you to convert to both miles and kilometers. If you want to convert from miles into kilometers read from the center column to the right, if from kilometers into miles, from the center column to the left. Example: 5 miles=8 kilometers, 5 kilometers=3.1 miles.

m		km	m		km
0.6	1	1.6	6.2	10	16.0
1.2	2	3.2	12.4	20	32.1
1.8	3	4.8	18.6	30	48.2
2.4	4	6.3	24.8	40	64.3
3.1	5	8.0	31.0	50	80.4
3.7	6	9.6	37.2	60	96.5
4.3	7	11.2	43.4	70	112.2
4.9	8	12.8	49.7	80	128.7
5.5	9	14.4	55.9	90	144.8

62.1	100	160.9	372.8	600	965.6
124.2	200	321.8	434.9	700	1,126.5
186.4	300	482.8	497.1	800	1,287.4
248.5	400	643.7	559.2	900	1,448.4
310.6	500	804.6	621.3	1,000	1,609.3

Roads All roads are paved and well-maintained, but most of the secondary country roads are narrow and winding. The West Autobahn A1 from Vienna to Salzburg cuts from that town across the southeastern corner of Germany, the route taken by drivers in a hurry; border guards usually just wave you on. Adequate and scenically lovelier is the E17, which can only be reached from Salzburg by crossing through Germany via Bad Reichenhall and the Steinpass. It rejoins the Autobahn shortly after its re-entry at Kufstein.

Now named A12, the Autobahn continues west past Innsbruck, then narrows over the Pack mountain pass to Levanttal to connect through the Arlberg tunnel with A14 in Vorarlberg to the Swiss and German frontiers.

Though the South Autobahn has been completed only from Vienna to Grimmenstein, plus a section near Graz, it is the quickest link with South Styria; but Carinthia would be better reached on E14 to Salzburg and down to Villach, where the South Autobahn is now along the Wörthersee to the Italian frontier.

The North Autobahn leads only a few kilometers from Vienna to Stockerau.

The Brenner Autobahn (A13), an outstanding feat of engineering with a series of daring bridges, runs from Innsbruck south to the Brenner. The quickest north/south connection is the Tauern Autobahn (A10) from Salzburg to Spittal in Carinthia. The Felbertauern road, another important north/south all-weather link crosses the main Alpine ridge between Land Salzburg and East Tyrol through a 3½-mile tunnel, with a one-way toll of 190 sch.

In winter there are heavy snowfalls, particularly in western Austria, and snow tires are essential, even though salt is used on main roads, in fact obligatory when the signs are out. The Austrian Automobile Club (ÖAMTC) broadcasts tape-recorded telephone messages on the current road conditions in all of Austria; dial Vienna 1590 in case you understand German; if you don't, call Vienna 72–21–01, ext. 7. Eighteen ÖAMTC posts throughout Austria will rent chains up to 60 days to any automobile club member.

The ÖAMTC road patrol and breakdown services cover most of the main roads all the year round, Sundays and holidays included, from 8 A.M. till dusk.

 BY BOAT This is a delightful and leisurely way of traveling "by armchair" to and from Vienna, through some 300 kilometers of Austria's most beautiful scenery, past romantic castles and ruins, relics from the fabulous periods of Austrian history, medieval monasteries and abbeys and lush vineyards. One of the high spots, especially in the springtime when the fruit trees are in bloom, is the Wachau near Vienna.

The trip from Passau to Vienna takes two days (including overnight stop in Linz—on board if you wish) and can be made June 28 to September 25. In leaves Passau at 3 P.M. and arrives in Linz at 8 P.M., from whence it departs at 10 A.M.

to arrive in Vienna at 8.15 P.M. The return upstream takes longer and you should check the times.

One-way fare is 442 sch.; cabins for two cost 280–560 sch. extra for the trip in either direction; meals are extra. The immaculate white-painted Mississippi-type craft each carry about 1,000 passengers on their three decks. As soon as you get on board, hire a deck chair, give the steward a good tip and ask him to place it where you will get the best views. Be sure to book cabins in advance.

A combination ship-train day tour can also be arranged. For details, inquire at the *Danube Steamship Company (DDSG)* ticket office in Vienna, Mexikoplatz 8 (at the ship landing on the main course of the Danube), tel. (0222) 26 65 36.

In fact, Vienna is, as it has always been, a gateway to Eastern Europe. From Vienna, river cruise lovers may enjoy a 14-day trip along the Danube to the Black Sea and back, on Austrian, Soviet or Romanian ships. From the Soviet ships you change in the Danube delta to a Soviet Black Sea ship to continue to Yalta. From April 22 to September 24 a Czech hydrofoil runs daily between Vienna and Bratislava, leaving Vienna at 9 A.M. and returning at 5 P.M. Visas obtainable on board; an extra passport photograph necessary. A Hungarian steamer makes the trip to Budapest in 10 hours; a duty-free shop is on board. Both are in summer only.

It is possible to travel to Hungary by train, but be sure to obtain your visa before leaving Vienna as *visas cannot be obtained at the border by train passengers.*

 ON HORSEBACK Austria is rich in opportunities for the visitor who is interested either in extended tours on horseback, or in just enjoying a happy few hours in some of the best riding country anywhere. Just about any interest in equitation can be satisfied, from visiting the superb stud farms to long cross-country rides. Several hotels specialize in equestrian holidays.

A holiday with a difference can be had if you take to the road in a gipsy caravan! Arranged in Burgenland by the *Blaguss-Burgenland* agencies; the central one is at Hauptstrasse 12, A–7100 Neusiedl am See, with branches in Rust, Podersdorf, Mörbisch, Illmitz and at A–1040 Vienna Wiedner Hauptstrasse 15.

Information on accommodations and riding facilities can be obtained from the various provincial tourist offices *(Landesverkehrsamt)*. The Austrian National Tourist Office also have a very detailed booklet called *Equestrian Sports in Austria.*

Leaving Austria

 CUSTOMS ON RETURNING HOME If you propose to take on your holiday any foreign made articles, such as cameras, binoculars, expensive timepieces and the like, it is wise to put with your travel documents the receipt from the retailer or some other evidence that the item was bought in your home country. If you bought the article on a previous holiday abroad and have already paid duty on it, carry with you the receipt for this. Otherwise, on returning home, you may be charged duty.

Americans who are out of the United States for 48 hours and have claimed no exemption during the previous 30 days are entitled to bring in the following items duty free. These values have recently been changed under the customs law, which became effective November 1982. Americans are now able to bring in $400 worth of purchases duty-free (up from $300). For the next $1,000 worth of goods beyond the first $400, inspectors will assess a flat 10% duty, rather than hitting you with different percentages for various types of goods. For persons returning to the USA from its territories (Virgin Islands, American Samoa and Guam), the duty-free allowance is $600 (up from $200). For the next $600 worth of goods above the first duty-free $600, there will be a flat duty of 5%. The value of each item is determined by the price actually paid (so keep your receipts). All items purchased must accompany the passenger on his return; it will therefore simplify matters at customs control if you can pack all purchases in one holdall. Every member of the family is entitled to this same exemption, regardless of age, and the allowance can be pooled.

Not more than 200 cigarettes, or one carton, may be included in your duty-free exemption, nor more than a quart of wine or liquor (none at all if your passport indicates you are from a "dry" state or under 21 years old). Only one bottle of perfume that is trademarked in the US may be brought in, plus a reasonable quantity of other brands.

Do not bring home foreign meats, fruits, plants, soil, or other agricultural items when you return to the United States. To do so will delay you at the port of entry. It is illegal to bring in foreign agricultural items without permission, because they can spread destructive plant or animal pests and diseases. For more information, read the pamphlet "Customs Hints", or write to: Quarantines, US Department of Agriculture, Federal Buildings, Hyattsville, Md. 20782 for Program Aid No. 1083 "Travelers' Tips".

Antiques are defined, for customs purposes, as articles manufactured over 100 years ago and are admitted duty-free. If there's any question of age, you may be asked to supply proof. The US embassies in London, Paris, Bonn and Rome have special customs advisers in case you have any questions about this or any other customs matter.

Smaller gifts may be mailed to friends (but not more than one package to one address). There should be written notation on the package "unsolicited Gift, value under $50". Duty-free packages, however, cannot include perfumes, tobacco or liquor.

If your purchases exceed your exemption, list the most expensive items that are subject to duty under your exemption and pay duty on the cheaper items. Any article you fail to declare cannot later be claimed under your exemption.

Canadian Residents, in addition to personal effects, and over and above the standard exemption of $300 per year, may bring in the following articles duty-free: a maximum of 50 cigars, 200 cigarettes, 2 pounds of tobacco and 40 ounces of liquor. Gift parcels may be sent as described above, but the duty-free value is $25.

British subjects There is now a two-tier allowance for duty-free goods brought into the UK, due to Britain's Common Market membership. *Note.* The Customs and Excise Board warn that it is not advisable to mix the two allowances.

If you return from an EEC country (Belgium, Denmark, France, W. Germany, Greece, Holland, Ireland, Italy, Luxembourg) and goods were bought in one of those countries, duty-free allowances are:

300 cigarettes (or 150 cigarillos, or 75 cigars, or 400 g tobacco); 1.5 liters of strong spirits (over 38.8 proof), or 3 liters of other spirits (under 38.8 proof) or fortified wines, plus 4 liters of still table wine; 75 g perfume and .375 liter toilet water; gifts to a value of £120.

If you return from a country outside the EEC, such as Austria, *or if the goods were bought in a duty-free shop on ship, plane or airport* the allowances are less:

200 cigarettes (or 100 cigarillos, or 50 cigars or 250 g tobacco); 1 liter of strong spirits (or 2 liters of other spirits or fortified wines) plus 2 liters of still table wine; 50 g perfume and .25 liter toilet water; plus gifts to a value of £28.

DUTY FREE One final word of warning. Don't be fooled into thinking that just because something is labeled "duty-free", it has to be a bargain. Very few duty-free shops are anything like as philanthropic as you think. Compare all prices carefully, remembering, where you can, what it would cost round the corner at home. If you have been on a budget holiday, don't go and throw your money over the moon on the way home.

THE
AUSTRIAN
SCENE

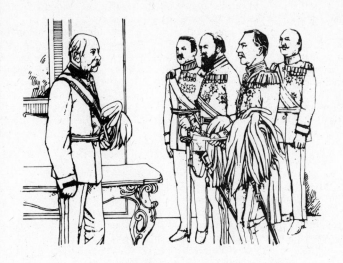

AUSTRIA'S HISTORY

The Ups and Downs of Empire

From time immemorial the history of Austria has been largely a pageant of peoples in motion along the great highways of Europe that intersect here. Not only Austria's history, but the character of its inhabitants was determined by its geography, by its situation astride natural highways. Along them came the peoples of many races, marching, fighting, trading and settling, each leaving behind some trace of their passage.

Of all these highways the greatest, of course, was the mighty River Danube. The Celts, whom Roman legionaries found in possession when they slowly pushed northward through Alpine passes and along the Danube valley about 100 BC, had probably been supreme in the area for about seven centuries. As the legionaries advanced, they consolidated their new territories by the erection of successive Roman forts and built those imperishable roads which brought the new civilization from the south. The fortified settlements were defended against the increasing waves of the migrating North and East European peoples. The vine was transplanted to the banks of the Danube; baths and arenas were built. Above all, the Romans established stable laws. Some local inhabitants became Romanized and a number of them received Roman citizenship, and some Celto-Roman towns flourished in the newly established Roman provinces, which replaced the old Celtic state formations; but in the countryside, where the Germanic tribes had already begun mixing with the Celts, the Romans were able to rule only by the law of the sword. Carnuntum, about 46 kilometers east of Vienna, became the Romans' capital city in this region. By the second century AD, it was big enough to have an amphitheater that accommodated 13,000 persons. Where Vienna's Innere Stadt (Inner City) stands today, the Romans built the fortified settlement of Vindobona, in which Marcus Aurelius died in AD 180.

Migration of the Nations

From then on, the far-flung Roman Empire was steadily weakening before the onslaught of the Germanic tribes, themselves driven westward by the even more formidable Huns. Their great primitive force and systematic relentlessness gradually overcame the resistance of the highly civilized but increasingly vitiated Romans, more occupied with civil wars than the defense of the frontiers. Before AD 400 the invading waves were battering down the walls the Romans had built. Within 80 years the latter had vanished from Austria.

From the northeast came the West-Goths, the Vandals, and Attila, "Scourge of God," with his terrible Huns. Teutons and Slavs, Franks, Burgundians and Avars flowed over the plains of the Danube, intermingling, and leaving their traces on following generations. These Dark Ages are the period that is imperishably enshrined in the great Nibelung saga. The climax of Kriemhild's revenge is supposed to have taken place in West Hungary, but much of the Nibelung story happened in the Austrian section of the Danube valley.

The Magyars of Hungary devastated the area until they were flung back by the Franks and Bajuvars (Bavarians) from the west. A bishop was established in Salzburg early in the eighth century AD and Salzburg became the center of the missionary activity among the pagan tribes to the east and to the southeast. Charles the Great (Charlemagne) conquered the lands of present-day Austria towards the end of the eighth century.

The Creation of Austria

At Christmas in AD 800 Charlemagne was crowned emperor by the pope in Rome. But Charlemagne's mighty empire, which stretched from the Pyrenees to the primeval German forests, lasted only as long as his life. Following his death it was divided among his descendants, the eastern part becoming the Holy Roman Empire of the German Nation.

Owing to constant rivalries and shaken by the Avar invasion, this empire only revived under a new dynasty in 962, when Otto the Great was crowned Holy Roman Emperor by the pope. The rivalries continued—particularly between emperors and popes—but the empire, basically a kind of confederation of German princes, nevertheless remained a historically continuous unit until 1806, being ruled for most of that period by the Habsburgs of Vienna. The simple imperial diadem, probably first used to crown Otto the Great, is still one of the most valued possessions in the Imperial Treasury in Vienna, where it lies alongside other priceless insignia.

When Emperor Otto II conferred upon Count Leopold of Babenberg in 976 the newly created eastern province of the Reich—Oesterreich (Austria), came into being as a separate country.

Under the Babenbergs, Austrian peasants and merchants alike prospered and the church accumulated vast wealth. It was also a period of considerable cultural attainment, the writing of the legend of the Nibelungs and the poetry of Walther von der Vogelweide being but two aspects. The Babenbergs were an interesting dynasty. Leopold "the Holy" was very religious, as one might expect, and founded several of the oldest monasteries in Austria. Another Leopold, "the Virtuous", quarreled over a question of honor with Richard the Lionheart during a crusade, and imprisoned him at Dürnstein Castle when the latter attempted to travel through Austria in disguise; since he harmed a crusader, Leopold—in accordance with the church laws of the time—was excommunicated by the pope and died of an injury received in an accident before he was able to make peace with the church.

Under the greatest Babenberg, Heinrich Jasomirgott (so called from his favorite oath, *Ja, so mir Gott helfe*—Yes, with God's help), the growth of trade and barter made Austria prosperous and the country acquired the rank of a Duchy. The last Babenberg was killed in battle in 1246. After an interregnum of 32 years, Austria was awarded to the House of Habsburg, who ruled it until the dissolution of their realm in 1918.

The Years of Terror

The interregnum before Habsburg rule was firmly established was known as the "Years of Terror." They were first marked by a quarrel between the pope and the Emperor Friedrich II over the allocation of the Babenberg domains, which resulted in Friedrich's excommunication. When the pope conferred them on a candidate of his choosing, the emperor divided them instead between two of his own nominees. Friedrich's premature death, which left the empire in a state of chaos, prompted Ottokar, King of Bohemia, to seize Austria. He occupied

Viénna and defeated Béla, King of Hungary (who had cherished similar ambitions).

Ottokar ruled Austria uneasily from 1252 to 1278. In the meantime, in 1273, Count Rudolf of Habsburg was elected emperor—recognized by the pope, although not crowned by him. Ottokar refused to recognize him, and Rudolf marched into Austria. Ottokar was defeated and killed at the battle of Marchfeld in 1278.

The Habsburgs

In 1278, therefore, began the 640-year rule of the House of Austria, of the Habsburgs, a period which included the rule of 20 emperors and kings. The name is derived from Habichtsburg, or Hawks' Castle, the original castle of the family, located in the Aargau region of Switzerland, and still called Habsburg today. But the Habsburgs acquired their vast territorial possessions and power only gradually. The marriage of Maximilian I to Maria of Burgundy, heiress to Burgundy and the Netherlands, in 1477 (Maximilian ascended the throne only in 1493, after the death of Friedrich III) represented the beginning of the famous Habsburg policy: "Let others wage war, you, happy Austria, grow by marriages." In 1496 Maximilian's son, Philip, married Joan of Castille and Aragon, thus bringing Habsburgs into Spain and into international politics on a large scale. After Maximilian's death, his grandson, Charles (son of Philip and Joan), inherited the vast Habsburg possessions, becoming Charles I of Spain as well as Charles V of the Holy Roman Empire.

Charles V (or Quint) left the greatest impress on Europe of all the emperors—naturally, for his domains were vast and he hoped to make them vaster still. Becoming king of Spain in 1516, in that country's Golden Century, he controlled also Spain's vast possessions overseas, the Netherlands and Burgundy (he himself was born in Ghent, now in Belgium), and in 1519 he was elected Holy Roman Emperor, the first ruler to claim that the sun never set on his dominions. Alarmed by this concentration of power, France tried to gain control of Italy, but François I was defeated at Pavia and sent as prisoner to Spain. To the unceasing conflict with France was soon added the struggle with the German protestant princes, yet Charles V personally led a successful expedition against Tunis in 1535, but failed against Algiers in 1541. The bitter obligation in 1555 to recognize the right of German princes to dictate the religion of their subjects led to his abdication, and he retired to a Spanish monastery.

Right at the beginning of his reign, in 1521, Charles V divided his possessions with his brother Ferdinand, who had married Anna of Hungary and Bohemia in 1515 (in a double marriage ceremony with Louis II of Hungary and Bohemia, Anna's brother, and Maria of Habsburg, sister of Ferdinand and Charles V). Thus were established the foundations for the two lines of the Habsburg family: the Austrian line and the Spanish line. When, in 1526, Louis II of Hungary and Bohemia fell in battle against the Turks, Ferdinand inherited the crowns of Bohemia and Hungary in accordance with the previously made treaties.

Wars, Revolts, Riches . . . and Napoleon

The westward drive of the Turks during the 16th and 17th centuries naturally involved Austria in a series of Turkish wars, during which the Turks twice laid siege to Vienna, but finally were totally defeated. These were periods for heroism and the emergence of colorful military figures, outstanding among whom was Prince Eugene of Savoy. His services had at one time been refused by Louis XIV of France because the prince did not conform to the Sun King's idea of how an officer should look. After driving the Turks back to Belgrade, Prince Eugene and the Duke of Marlborough defeated the armies of Louis XIV in the War of the Spanish Succession. In his long career he played a decisive military and political role in the reigns of three emperors and left a considerable cultural legacy to Austria. The Belvedere Palace, among others, was built for him.

The 200-year struggle with the Turks was not Austria's only military problem. The Thirty Years' War was another disastrous one, which ended with the humiliating Treaty of Westphalia, in 1648. This marked the turning of the tide against the Habsburgs, though the House was still to know its ups as well as its downs.

Unable to re-establish a strong imperial power in Germany, the Habsburgs turned east and south, till their domains encompassed, at different times, parts or all of what are today Poland, Czechoslovakia, Hungary, the Ukraine, Rumania, Yugoslavia and Italy.

Surprisingly, domination over so vast a territory and such a heterogeneous mixture of races brought few revolts in its wake. But one was led by Ferenc Rákóczy, who exploited the War of the Spanish Succession to conduct a series of uprisings in Transylvania against Vienna.

It was the misfortune of the Habsburgs that their rich domains were a tempting prize. Any pretext was good enough for foreign monarchs to help themselves to some of it whenever they were able. The extinction of the Spanish line in 1700 provided the first occasion; the death of the last male Austrian Habsburg, Charles VI, and the accession of his daughter Maria Theresa as ruler of Austria, the second. These led to the War of Austrian Succession, soon followed by the Seven Years' War.

Maria Theresa was one of the great queens of history, easily ranking beside Catherine the Great and well above Victoria. She instituted a program of major reforms at home, transforming a gaggle of feudal states into a single, centrally administered nation. Trade, education, the church, all found themselves being swept by the maternal broom. And mother she undoubtedly was, not just of her nation, but of her family which numbered sixteen children guaranteeing the continuity of the Habsburg-Lothringen line.

This was a time of great cultural expansion, the period of high baroque in art and architecture, the age of the great composers Gluck, Haydn and Mozart, a golden era.

Maria Theresa's reforms were well founded, but her son and successor, Joseph II, who had been emperor since the death of Franz I in 1765, went too far too fast. A revolt, particularly threatening in the Netherlands, was only avoided by the wide compromise of his brother (and successor) Leopold II.

Then came Napoleon, who piled humiliation upon defeat by placing most German princes under his own authority. Franz II assumed the title of Austria in 1804. Following Habsburg tradition, he gave his daughter, Maria Louisa, to Napoleon as his empress. After his cataclysmic Russian campaign, Napoleon's enemies were heartened and began the effort that finally was to defeat him. At the Battle of Leipzig in 1813 the allied armies were led by an Austrian general, Prince Karl Schwarzenberg.

With the final defeat of Napoleon, it seemed as though the House of Habsburg had regained its ascendancy. The Congress of Vienna in 1814, held in the Hofburg, was not only a political event of the first magnitude, but also a social one. It was in a very real sense a "dancing congress," for the elite of Europe, freed from the fear of the Corsican Ogre, rejoiced in no uncertain fashion.

The Treaty of Vienna of 1814 returned to Austria the territories in Italy lost during the Napoleonic wars, including Lombardy, and in addition gave her Venice. She had now regained the dominating position in the German Confederation. This revival of Austrian power was presided over by the authoritarian Prince Metternich, organizer of the so-called Holy Alliance among the principal European nations which guaranteed peace in Europe.

Enter Bismarck

It was the year 1848 which was fatal to Metternich, a year of upheaval throughout Europe, when people in many parts of the continent, particularly in the central European capitals, sought to liberate themselves from oppressive regimes. These revolutions, motivated partly by nationalistic tendencies and partly by anti-authoritarian efforts, were accompanied by the emergence on the scene of two important figures in the history of Austria: Bismarck, later the Iron Chancellor, who strove towards the union of all German princes—except the Habsburgs—in one country under the leadership of Prussia, and a delicately handsome young man who acceded to the Austrian throne in that fateful year, and who was to occupy it almost until its final collapse in 1918—Franz Josef. His reign was to be marked by successive disasters at home and abroad, mostly due to the persistent efforts of half a dozen nationalities striving for an autonomous status, although in economic and cultural fields Austria had never been richer and happier; thus to most Austrians this has remained the golden Franz-Josef era.

Bismarck's name is connected with the year 1848 because it was then that he refused to do what he most wanted to do—unify Germany. The reason was that he wished unification only under the domination of Prussia. When the proposal to bring the many Germanic states into a single nation was made at Frankfurt, Bismarck opposed it because it would have been achieved under liberal non-Prussian auspices, and also because a union in which Austria was included would almost inevitably accept the leadership of this greatest of German states. Catholic Austria, Catholic Bavaria, the Catholic Rhineland—these would form a mighty bloc against which a Lutheran Prussia would be impotent. It was not Bismarck's aim to submerge Prussia in a German Empire; it was his aim to submerge Germany in a Prussian Empire. He had to knock Austria out of the German lineup before he could hope to achieve this.

He was aided by a weakening of Austria through the aftermath of 1849, a year in which there were nationalist revolts all over the empire, particularly in Hungary and Lombardy. The French helped the Italians and in 1859, after an unsuccessful war with Napoleon III in North Italy, Austria had to cede Lombardy to France which in turn ceded it to the Italian Kingdom of Piedmont in exchange for Nice.

In 1866 Bismarck concluded an alliance with the newly established Kingdom of Italy and attacked Austria. Whereas the Italians were thoroughly defeated by the Austrians, the Prussians crushed the Habsburg armies at Sadowa in Bohemia. After this defeat the Hungarians became restless again but the Habsburgs regained the loyalty of Hungary by setting up the dual monarchy, sharing power between Vienna and Budapest and sacrificing the Slavs to the new arrangement.

But Bismarck's objective had been attained. Austria had been read out of the German Confederation. By means of the successful Franco-Prussian War, during which Prussia was able to rally to its banners all the German states, Bismarck achieved his aim. As a result of the French defeat the German Empire was constituted and William I, King of Prussia, was proclaimed emperor in the Hall of Mirrors at Versailles in 1871, after the occupation of Paris by the Prussian armies.

Austria remained outside this new German empire. But if Austria could not be tolerated as a rival within Germany, she was still desirable as an ally, and therefore Franz Josef was readmitted to the good graces of Germany with the signature of the Triple Alliance in 1882.

The Fall of the Empire

Despite its political troubles Austria had entered upon the romantic epoch conjured up in most minds by the word "Vienna." This was the period of lightheartedness, of a gaiety no doubt frivolous, of imperial balls and Strauss waltzes, and of an aristocracy that combined court ceremonial with laissez-faire.

Then came the 1914 war and, with it, disaster. The Archduke Franz Ferdinand was assassinated in Sarajevo on June 28, 1914. He was the heir to the throne of Austria and his death was the signal for the start of the First World War. At the end of the war, in 1918, Franz Josef's successor, Karl I, who had ruled for only two years, renounced his throne and, a day later, the Republic of Austria was in being.

Only the German-speaking part was left to Austria, and not even all of it. The little Austrian Republic of seven million inhabitants was only the rump of Austria-Hungary which was left when all the prime joints had been cut off. Magyars, Czechs, Slovaks, Poles, Croats and other unwilling subjects of the Habsburgs were no longer part of the Austrian hegemony.

Economically, the break-up was a debacle. The succession states possessed railroads which ran nowhere in particular; they had been built for the days when the flow from what had become Yugoslavia, Poland, Czechoslovakia, Hungary, had been to and from Vienna. Produce was cut off from its markets, ports from their hinterlands. Austria's situation was the worst of all. She had been bereft of her assets and left with her liabilities. Her problems seemed insoluble; and indeed, her early years were bitter—financial chaos, hyper-inflation of a type never previously known, but which has since been experienced by many peoples, and economic collapse.

Hardly had the League of Nations' loans set Austria somewhat on her feet again than she was rent by internal conflict. After the Social-Democrats left the coalition government in 1920, the Catholic Party dominated the federal and state governments, with the exception of Vienna. Under

Chancellor Dollfuss, who took office in 1932, this one-party rule was transformed in 1934 into a full dictatorship, following a five-day civil war conducted by the private military units of both parties. Dollfuss also feared the Nazis, who had already proclaimed their plans to incorporate Austria into Nazi Germany. The Nazis also attempted to start a civil war in 1934, a few months after the parliament was dissolved. Although unsuccessful, they managed to murder Dollfuss. Schuschnigg, his successor, was unable to resist the increasing pressure from Hitler for long. In March 1938 German troops occupied Austria without resistance and without any country lifting a finger in Austria's defense. Austria was incorporated into the Third Reich in March 1938, and within 18 months the world was once more plunged into war, and this time on a truly global scale.

Occupation

Austria was occupied at first by Soviet and then also by US, French and British forces in May 1945. Subsequently, a provisional (all-party) government was established in Vienna under Russian supervision by a Socialist, the late Dr. Karl Renner, who later became the first President of the Republic. Because it had no parliamentary sanction and contained many more Communist ministers than the strength of that small party warranted, with no ministers from the Western-occupied provinces, the Western powers delayed recognition of the Renner administration until it had been completed by the inclusion of personalities from the West and all arrangements made for free and democratic elections. These were held in November 1945. The resulting parliament consisted of 85 representatives of the Volkspartei (Conservatives), 76 Socialists, and 4 Communists. The Nazis were disfranchised en bloc for this constitutional election.

Britain, the United States, and Russia had earlier promised (in the Moscow Declaration of 1943) to restore a free, independent, and democratic Austria. A Four Power Declaration of July 4, 1945, declared that Austria (with its eight states and the city of Vienna) had been restored to its 1937 frontiers. The same declaration divided the country into four zones. Russia was allotted the state of Lower Austria (Vienna, which lies within it, received quadripartite occupation), the Burgenland (which has a long common frontier with Hungary), and that part of the state of Upper Austria which lies on the left bank of the Danube (with its long common frontier with Czechoslovakia). The zone allotted to the Americans consisted of the state of Salzburg, and that part of Upper Austria lying on the right bank of the Danube (which both have common frontiers with Western Germany). The adjoining French Zone (bordering on Switzerland and Italy) consisted of the states of Tyrol and Vorarlberg. The British Zone (southern Austria) consisted of the states of Carinthia and Styria, the former having common frontiers with Italy and Yugoslavia, and the latter sharing a common frontier with Yugoslavia and Hungary. Thus the approaches to Austria from the Western democracies were controllable by the Western Powers alone, those from the European communist dictatorships only by the Russians.

Vienna was anomalously situated within the Russian Zone but under a special Four Power occupation statute. Although it was divided into four sectors of occupation, there were, in contrast to Berlin, no barriers between sectors and no restriction of movement from one to another for Austrians or foreigners.

Vienna was the seat of the Allied High Commission for Austria, a genuinely quadripartite body. Vienna's "Inner City"—the first district—was called the International Sector. It fell under the jurisdiction of the Allied Commission's "chairman of the month," British, French, American, or Russian. When the chairmanship passed from one nationality to another, a colorful ceremony complete with band music, marching, flag ceremonies was held.

For almost ten years the Western powers sought a peace treaty for Austria, but it was not until April, 1955, when the Soviets suddenly reversed their position, that the Austrian State Treaty became a reality. The treaty was signed in the Belvedere Palace in Vienna, on May 15, 1955, the ratification was completed by June 27, and the official end of the occupation came on October 25, although most of the troops and equipment were withdrawn considerably earlier.

For a while, the Austrians forgot everything else but the long-overdue return of their freedom. The Danube was lovelier than ever, the coffeehouses livelier than ever, and there was a new jauntiness and exuberance everywhere. Then came the inevitable reaction and soberer second thoughts about the immense task of reuniting a country so long divided.

Austria Today

Present-day Austria is a democratic, federal republic, called the "Second Republic" with a legislative body similar to those of the Western democracies. Its Nationalrat is the Lower House, its Bundesrat the Upper House. This body is freely elected by the whole nation. The Upper House has only veto rights. Head of State is a President chosen by the electorate for six years; the head of the government, called the Federal Chancellor, is appointed from the majority party by the President of the Republic.

The roots of the present organization of the Austrian federal system go deep into history. The country is divided into nine federal states, or Bundesländer: Burgenland, Carinthia, Lower Austria, Upper Austria, Salzburg, Styria, Tyrol, Vienna and Vorarlberg. Each state has its own government, with the governor elected by the state parliament. State dealings with the federal government are through the governor, while "local" affairs such as building, the affairs of young people, conservation, etc., are the business of the state parliament. There are similarities with the political organization of the United States in the way the system works.

Austria holds a quietly respected place on the international scene. The former Secretary General of the United Nations, Kurt Waldheim, for instance, was once Austrian Foreign Secretary. Austria lends active support to the work of the UN, sending medical teams and even troops (to Cyprus) to assist the cause of world peace. The country has also handled its rather difficult position of outpost of the West in Europe with skill.

In June, 1979, to illustrate the focal nature of Austria's situation, the signing of SALT 2 was held in Vienna, when the city became a genuine halfway house between East and West.

CREATIVE AUSTRIA

Music in the Soul

Two main factors have combined to make Austria the treasure house of the arts that she is today. First, of course, was the creative urge that drove so many of her young people to devote themselves to one or other of the arts, particularly music. Secondly there was the reverence of the people at large for those who could create beauty. In some countries, although you find instinctive national pride in warlike achievement, wealth, invention and great industries, appreciation of the arts has to be learned. In Austria it is the artist who always ranks first.

For centuries it was the great feudal landlords who lavished much of their wealth on becoming patrons of the arts and in such cases the desire to be known as art patrons played no role at all; they were moved by genuine devotion to the arts. Foremost among them were the ruling Habsburgs, several of whom were composers and poets themselves and some of whom also actively participated, especially during the baroque period, in private performances of the court theater, the predecessor of today's world-famous Burgtheater.

First nights at the theater or opera are harder to get into here than in almost any other country and Viennese audiences probably are the most generous in the world. After the empire dissolved in 1918, impoverished Austria was certainly not in any condition to find the money to subsidize the Opera House and Burgtheater on the old imperial scale, but ways of preserving the old traditions *were* found. There is no more persistent grumbler in the world than the Austrian—"a grumble a day keeps bad temper away" is his motto. And no one more dislikes paying taxes. But you will never hear a word against the subsidizing of art. The most significant example of his willingness to adhere to the "man cannot live by bread alone" principle was the way in which the whole country rallied round to rebuild both the Burgtheater and the Opera House after they were devastated by air raids in World War II.

The Country of Musical Giants

What other nations say with words, the Austrians say with music. And through what masters of the art have they said it, from Gluck, Mozart and Schubert to Bruckner, from Strauss to Lehar! Beethoven and Brahms, two other musical giants, were born in Germany but spent most of their lives in Vienna and have therefore become very much a part of Austrian musical history; Mahler too, though born in Bohemia, composed most of his symphonies here. Nowhere but in Austria could they have composed in quite the way that they did. Their works breathe the spirit of the quiet lakes, the rushing rivers, the baroque churches, the elegant, involved courts, above all the involvement with the human spirit which is as brilliantly explored in the music of Mozart as it is by the words of Sigmund Freud.

In the beginning there were the minstrel-poets, such as the famous Walther von der Vogelweide, who sang his loveliest ballads at the 12th-century court of the Babenbergs, and became the first individual German poet of importance. (He appears, by the way, in Wagner's *Tannhäuser.*) From the outset, the court liberally encouraged music. As early as the 15th century, Maximilian I created a court orchestra, and soon every overlord had not only his own little orchestra, but his personal composer too. The cathedrals had the same—religious music has always loomed large in Austria.

Before the 17th century, the great Dutch composers were summoned to work at the Austrian court, to be followed by the Italians. (Four Habsburgs were themselves composers of music of the baroque period.) Then came the true Austrian music, which only gradually differentiated itself from that of Italy. Its first great exponent was Gluck (1714–87), who became Court Composer under Maria Theresa. Both *Orfeo ed Euridice* and *Alceste* were first performed in Vienna.

Josef Haydn, the first great classicist, spent much of his active life as composer and conductor to Prince Eszterhazy in his palace in Eisenstadt. At the age of eight he came to Vienna as one of the Court Choristers, but after his voice broke, he had to spend eight wretched years as a music teacher. He originated chamber music, the string quartet and the sonata.

Wolfgang Amadeus Mozart (1756–91), who more than any other artist set baroque Salzburg to music, was composing minuets at five years of age. He was perhaps the most purely inspired of all composers, a genius no superlatives can properly describe. Though he played before the Empress Maria Theresa as a boy, his prolific work was not appreciated by the Austrians (certainly not to the extent it was in Bohemia and England); he died at the tragically early age of 35, and was buried in a pauper's grave, all trace of which was lost forever.

Ludwig van Beethoven (1770–1827) was born in Bonn on the Rhine but lived most of his life in Vienna, where he learned and composed most of his music. Therefore he belongs as much to Austrian as to German musical history, inasmuch as one can even consider these two as separate. Together with Haydn and Mozart, Beethoven is one of the three great representatives of classical music. However, through his numerous compositions, especially through his nine symphonies, Beethoven gradually and increasingly changed into Romantic tonality, entering the Romantic period with a grandeur that many of his successors strove to emulate but few equaled.

Franz Schubert's music (1797–1828) reflects the soul of Vienna and the Vienna Forest as Mozart's does that of Salzburg. Like Haydn, he was a Court Chorister as a boy. He, the light-hearted, jovial dreamer, the "good mixer," beloved of all the friends of his pleasant Biedermeier age, for whom he composed and played at informal musical evenings in their houses, was also in strong contrast to the rough, afflicted, and melancholy Beethoven. Schubert also died tragically early, at the age of 31, of typhoid, leaving behind well over a thousand compositions of various kinds. His *Unfinished Symphony* (the 8th), although today probably his most popular orchestral work, only came to light some 50 years after Schubert's death.

The Viennese Waltz

In 1825 a son was born to the popular Austrian conductor Johann Strauss *Vater*. Johann Strauss *Sohn* started his career apprenticed to a carpenter, but the Waltz King was soon to set the world dancing to his rhythms. At 19 Strauss was himself conducting, and before long his intoxicating melodies had caught the ears of the world with their insouciant stories of the gaiety and beauty of Vienna and the Austrian countryside. As conductor he personally introduced them to audiences all over the world, including that at the famous giant outdoor concert he conducted in Boston in 1872 on the occasion of the anniversary of the

Boston Tea Party. His *Blue Danube Waltz*, most popular throughout the world, has become the unofficial Viennese anthem.

He composed and conducted for a wealthy-self-indulgent, sensuous city. The Congress of Vienna—*"qui danse, mais qui ne marche pas"* —had made Viennese sophisticated gaiety world-famous, and had established the city as the dancing capital. *Fasching,* the season of Prince Carnival, was given over to court balls, opera balls, masked balls, Chambermaids' and Bakers' balls and a hundred other gatherings.

Presiding over the brilliant picture of dazzling evening gowns and colorful uniforms, towering headdresses, feathered fans, flirtations, *chambres séparées,* "Wine, Women and Song," *Die Fledermaus, Blue Danube,* hand-kissing and abandon, was the baton of Strauss. His mantle fell onto the shoulder of Franz Lehar (1870–1948) whose deathless *Merry Widow* stood for "Vienna" throughout the world for a generation—with constant popular revivals. Oscar Straus (1870–1950), no relation, Leo Fall (1873–1925), Robert Stolz (1880–1975) and Emmerich Kalman (1882–1953) likewise maintained the Viennese operatic tradition.

Brahms, Bruckner and Mahler

Two sober contemporaries of Strauss dominated the world of serious music—Brahms (1833–97) and Bruckner (1824–96). The first-named was greeted as Beethoven's successor; he set to music many aspects of the Austrian landscape, such as the lakes of Carinthia and the Salzkammergut. In addition to four symphonies, concertos, and a large number of smaller orchestral pieces, he wrote hundreds of compositions for piano, organ, violin, voice and choir. Bruckner was organist to the Saint Florian Monastery and the Cathedral in Linz, where he wrote most of his religious music, including his three Masses, and later the Imperial Court Chapel organist in Vienna, where he composed most of his nine symphonies.

Gustav Mahler (1860–1911) has gone down in music history as one of the last of the great symphonic composers, the creator of a new musical language, the forerunner and early patron of Schönberg and his followers. But the Viennese remember him in particular as the director of the State Opera, the man who was responsible for a whole decade of Viennese musical history at the turn of the century. During the summer he wrote his great symphonies at his modest retreats in the Salzkammergut and Carinthian lake districts, while during the season he restricted himself to his duties as director and conductor in Vienna, admired for his fanatical devotion but feared for his stern discipline.

Contemporary Music

One of the best known among the modern atonal composers is Arnold Schönberg, who was born in Vienna in 1874, emigrated to America in 1933, and died in Los Angeles in 1951. Schönberg, an atonal expressionist, is considered to be the master of the "new music"; his style is called the twelve-tone system. The most successful pupils of Schönberg were Anton von Webern (1883–1945), a very individualistic composer whose works often consist of only a few musical sentences, and who exercises considerable influence on the present musical generation; and Alban Berg (1885–1935), a master of atonal expressionism, whose opera *Wozzeck* is well known. His music, with its expressionistic intensity and high degree of emotional content, also appeals to those whose tastes are more traditional.

Perhaps the best known among contemporary Austrian composers is Gottfried von Einem (b. 1918). Of particular note are the dramatic *The Death of Danton* and *The Trial*, and perhaps his most famous opera *The Visit of the Old Lady*. The music of Theodor Berger (b. 1905) shows impressionistic tendencies, whereas Rudolf Wieshappel (b. 1921), a Styrian, was an outstanding music critic, and followed a new individualistic path with his opera.

With all its enjoyment of and deep respect for the great music it has produced, Vienna is free from pompous solemnity. The same people who will listen with reverence to Brahms, Beethoven and Mozart will reward with round after round of deafening applause a brilliant presentation of the works of the Strauss constellation, Lehar and the other operetta composers, provided that the interpreter can put across that passionate heartbeat of Vienna which the compositions demand. (Performances by non-Austrians that pass as brilliant abroad are sometimes greeted with pale and watery smiles in Vienna.) Nor does appreciation of the highest in music deter the Viennese from taking a rollicking delight in an occasional evening in the *Heuriger* winegardens, with their traditional *Schrammel* quartets and their sentimental variations on the eternal themes of Vienna, lilac time, the new wine, and the effect of their combined assault on two hearts that beat as one.

Two highly characteristic examples of the spontaneous Austrian musical genius are the universally known song, *Silent Night,* which was first sung in 1818 at the Christmas midnight mass in Oberndorf near Salzburg; and the continued existence of the Vienna Boys' Choir after over 500 years. No visit to musical Vienna is complete without hearing this amazing choir, which has numbered Haydn, Schubert and many other famous musicians among its members. They can be heard at their brilliant best in the celebration of Mass in the Hofburg chapel.

Opera

The thread that runs through all Austrian musical life is the love of opera. This "exotic and irrational" art form, as Dr. Johnson called it, crystalizes all that is dearest to the heart of such an essentially musical nation. It all began, as we have seen, with Gluck, but from the days of Josef II, the conscious policy of establishing a German opera to challenge the Italian tradition took firm root. Mozart's great masterpieces, *The Marriage of Figaro* and *Cosi fan tutte,* were staged at the old Burgtheater on the Michaelerplatz. *Fidelio,* Beethoven's only opera, and one of his finest works, appeared first at the Theater an der Wien. Wagner added his luster to the scene, as did many other celebrities, Verdi among them.

But the reborn glory of Austrian opera came with Gustav Mahler's tenure of the office of Director (some said Dictator) of the Vienna Opera. "The whole building was shaken, as if by an earthquake of immense strength and long duration," wrote a member of the orchestra. "From where he sat, Mahler seemed to dominate the whole musical life of Vienna." Mahler managed to institute a whole new style of staging, lighting and production. He never tired of telling his musicians that regard for detail was next to godliness. And his control of singers rivaled that of Handel for its despotic ebullience. A tenor who annoyed him by singing off key found himself chased off stage and had to take refuge in a lavatory with Mahler pounding on the door and yelling "and what's more you're a coward."

With the arrival of Richard Strauss on the operatic scene, the long contest between the opera and the operetta for supremacy was decided in favor, at least in the eyes of enthusiasts, of opera. *Der Rosenkavalier* was a triumphant celebration of the great days of Maria Theresa's Vienna, and still holds the pride of place in the repertory.

A long line of works from many pens has passed across the Austrian operatic stage since then; all Strauss's operas, which are now among the finest productions in theaters around the world as well; Alban Berg's *Wozzeck;* the operas of von Einem and Wellesz.

But it is the tradition of production and performance that is of even more value to the musical world in general than any individual work. The long tradition of brilliant personalities who have influenced opera in Austria has included Schikaneder, Mahler, Weingartner, Schalk, Karl Böhm, Bruno Walter and Herbert von Karajan among many others. It has been a history with its scandals and triumphs, but in almost every decade for well over two centuries, the cause of music has been well served. In September 1982, Lorin Maazel became the first American conductor to take charge of this great heritage.

Baroque is a State of Mind

The most important clue to the Austrians is their baroque—not its architectural technicalities, but its spirit. When you understand that, you will no longer be a stranger in Austria. John Ruskin thought it about the lowest thing in architecture, Sacheverell Sitwell took the lead in rehabilitating it. Hermann Bahr, who often deplored its influence on the Austrian character, said that its message was that all life is an unreal dream, a theater. Of its lessons was born the famous Viennese Gemütlichkeit—easygoing good nature. The high position occupied by the theater, music and other arts in the general estimation, the love of good talk and the exchange of ideas with strangers, the welcoming of foreigners—all these qualities are somehow or other related to the baroque.

It is best understood if we cast back to how it became predominant in Austria. The Habsburg realm had just emerged, as Austria is used to emerging, from very bad times. For the 16th century had witnessed the long and painful struggle between Catholicism and Protestantism for the soul of Austria. The latter was everywhere triumphant—there were only four Catholic priests in the whole diocese of Vienna—when in 1550 the emperor called on the aid of Ignatius of Loyola, founder of the Jesuits, to send missionaries of his order to Austria to stop the rot. The successful counter-reformation set the seal of Catholic culture in Austria. In 1679 the Plague had ravaged Vienna, filling the streets with vast mounds of unburied corpses. Four years later, the unbeatable Turks did the same to Austria, and were checked only after a long siege and many assaults had enabled them to break through Vienna's strongest defenses. But that check was turned into the greatest victory of Austria's history and brought later a vast expansion of her realms. Of that victory was born Austrian baroque.

The baroque came from Italy. It was transformed and molded by the joyous spirit of the liberated Austrians. Gone at last were the years of the red death, of bitter religious strife and invasion. The Catholic Church had its own triumph to celebrate, the people their emergence from a century of tribulation. Over the country swept the new flamboyant, triumphant, joyous and extravagantly ostentatious art form. Now it was that Austria became truly international, as she flung wide her doors to foreign artists, sculptors, painters, furniture designers, builders, to playwrights, composers and scenic artists. Now was the country transformed by this dramatic style into a vast theater, and life became a dream—the gorgeous dream of baroque, with its gilded saints and cherubs, its soaring, twisted columns, its painted heavens on the ceilings, its joyous patinated domes. From this theater, from this dream, the spirit of Austria has never really departed.

Architecture

Architecture in Austria—except for modern architecture—means baroque. Despite Vienna's cathedral, Saint Stephen's, combining important elements of the Romanesque and Gothic with later baroque additions, and such isolated examples of pure Gothic as Vienna's classic Saint Maria-am-Gestade and Stift Heiligenkreuz in the Southern Vienna Woods, baroque swamped all other styles. Here and there you will find buildings that have survived this proud and intolerant art form, such as the Renaissance Schloss Porcia at Spittal, the Landhaus in Graz, the Gurk Cathedral, or the Lindenhof at Millstatt. Usually the baroque architects and decorators obliterated the work of less exuberant and more contemplative ages. Baroque itself was here and there superseded by its immediate off-spring, playful rococo—there is a charming example in the attractive little Wilten Church, in Innsbruck. In general, Austria has fine examples of rococo as interior decoration. Baroque originally came from Spain and Italy, but soon acquired a specifically Austrian character.

Preoccupation With Site

The first consideration for a baroque architect—Fischer von Erlach, father (1656–1723) and son (1693–1742), Lucas von Hildebrandt (1668–1745) and Jakob Prandtauer (1658–1726) were the greatest—in building a palace or a church, was the site, the area at his disposal had to "frame" his building. The Romanesque designers of Saint Stephen's, the Gothic architects, had no such obsession; they demanded only an open space in which to build a thing of beauty. But Fischer von Erlach chose for the Karlskirche in Vienna a position on which all surrounding roads seemed to converge. Placed there and nowhere else, the eye would be led directly to his masterpiece. He placed Schönbrunn Palace even more precisely, as you will best appreciate if you approach it from the top of the Schloss Allee. The middle of that avenue is exactly in line with a spot in the mathematical center of the main gallery, and with the exact center of the ornamental Gloriette on top of the hill behind Schönbrunn. You can check this yourself by standing in the center of the great gallery and looking straight up the axis of the Schloss Allee.

Primarily an architectural style, the baroque spirit influenced all the arts, so that in addition to baroque sculpture, paintings, frescos, and general interior decoration, you have baroque furniture, music and even baroque weapons and suits of armor. With all its flamboyance, it insisted on a precise balance of construction and ornament. Where you find broken and irregular lines, a deliberate seeking after the unbalanced, a frivolity that refuses to be controlled, the style is no longer baroque, but rococo.

In revolt against its extravagance came the simple, homely and very charming Biedermeier period (from approximately 1818 to 1848). The era of Franz Josef produced a medley of neo-everything—the Emperor Forum, the fanciful Burgtheater and the Opera, the Parliament, the Rathaus and the Votivkirche all stand with their heavy ornament and dependence on past themes in close kinship with the Victorian era, but they present a unity that city planners are now trying to preserve in the face of redevelopment.

Different, but no less ornate, was Jugendstil (Art Nouveau), which Joseph Olbrich and Otto Wagner were leading exponents of till 1914. Other 20th-century architects introduced simpler designs; among them the same Otto Wagner as well as Adolf Loos and Josef Hoffmann.

Foremost among modern architects are Clemens Holzmeister, who has worked with many church designs as well as such notable foreign assignments as the government quarter in Ankara; Roland Rainer who designed the Vienna Stadthalle; Karl Schwanzer, architect of the Museum of the 20th Century; and many even younger designers, notably the Windbrechtingers, Ottokar Kuhl and Work Group 4. The "Objekte" fantasy schemes of Hans Hollein, Walter Pichler and others have also attracted much attention with their lighthearted work.

Painting

As elsewhere in Europe, painting in Austria began during the Romanesque period in monasteries with illuminated Bibles and other manuscript decorations; the eighth-century Cutperch New Testament, the Giant Bible of Admont and the St. Peter Antiphonary are the best examples of this art in Austria. Of particular interest are the Romanesque frescos dating from about 1080, recently uncovered in the towers of the west wing of the former Lambach Monastery in Upper Austria. The 13th-century frescos in the Cathedral of Gurk are among the most important of the Romanesque period anywhere.

The advent of the Renaissance north of the Alps was closely connected with the reign of Maximilian I (1493–1519), who made his court a center of learning and art. It was at his suggestion that the famous tomb was built in the Innsbruck Hofkirche. The figures that stand watch over it have characteristics of both the fading Gothic era and the incipient Renaissance. Unfortunately, the emperor's body is missing, resting in the simpler setting of the Georgekapelle of Wiener Neustadt.

At the beginning of the Renaissance, Austria held a leading position in painting; the principal Austrian representatives of the Danube School were Max Reichlich, Wolf Huber and Rueland Frueauf the Younger, who was responsible for the Leopold Cycle in Klosterneuberg (1501).

Lukas Cranach and the two Regensburg artists Albrecht and Erhart Altdorfer, who painted the St. Florian altar (1518), are also counted as members of the Danube school, which was most remarkable for its use of landscape in the presentation of religious motifs.

Austrian baroque, particularly renowned for its architecture and sculpture, became famous also for its painters, such as Johann Michael Rottmayr (1654–1730), who was preferred by the greatest baroque architect, Fischer von Erlach; Franz Anton Maulpertsch (1724–96), the master of the high baroque period, whose work combined a mastery of color with an intensity of feeling that was unsurpassed in his period; Martin Johann Schmidt, called Kremser Schmidt (1718–1801), in the late baroque; and Paul Troger (1698–1762) and Daniel Gran (1694–1754).

The best known artists of the Biedermeier period were George Ferdinand Waldmüller (1793–1865), master of *genre* and open-air painting, and Rudolf von Alt, the great master of watercolor. Hans Makart, the colorful painter of interiors, Anton Romako (1834–89), an inspired portraitist and *genre* painter, and Franz von Defregger (1835–1921), the painter of Tyrolean rural life and of Andreas Hofer's fight against the French occupier, mark the second half of the 19th century.

Modern Art

Modern painting in Austria begins with the founding of the Vienna Sezession group in 1898 under the leadership of Gustav Klimt (1862–1918), a sensitive, spiritual, symbolistic artist. His work has become internationally popular through the vast number of poster reproductions that are now on sale. His paintings are very decorative, using as they do a heavily patterned impasto, indeed he was as excellent a designer as a painter. His later work led directly into Expressionism.

The main representatives of the early Expressionism are Egon Schiele (1890–1918), who died too young to develop fully his great talent, and Oskar Kokoschka, (1886–1979), born in Lower Austria in the town of Pöchlarn (which traces its origin back to the Nibelungs). Kokoschka's individualistic synthesis of line and color brought him world recognition.

The hard and impressive Albin Egger-Lienz (1868–1926), artist of World War I, was born in the same Tyrolean village as Defregger and also preferred rural and historic themes. Leading among the later Expressionists were Anton Faistauer (1887–1930), who painted the monumental frescos of the Festspielhaus in Salzburg; and Anton Kolig (d. 1950), who belonged to the circle of Carinthian artists.

Considered by many to be the greatest modern Austrian artist, the late Carinthian, Herbert Boeckl (d. 1966), developed from Expressionism into his own highly individualistic style. Among other artists who have followed their own chosen paths are the late Styrian, Rudolf Szyszkowitz, also a forceful graphic artist, and Werner Berg, whose melodious but sharply characteristic canvasses portray the people and the landscape of Carinthia, where he paints, works and lives on his farm.

Of increasing international importance is the Viennese school of painting known as Fantastic Realism. A close relative of Surrealism, particularly in terms of excellence in technique, the Fantastic Realist offers in sumptuous colors and painstaking exactness his personal world of fantasy, dreams and imagination. Leading exponents of this school are Ernst Fuchs, Wolfgang Hutter, Anton Lehmden and Rudolf Hausner; and, independent within the younger generation of artists, Karl Korab.

The main characteristic of the art world in Austria today, as elsewhere, is the multiplicity of styles, none of them predominant, in all fields. In some cases, an artist's work bears distinct traces of both abstract art and naturalism, as is the case with Max Weiler, Mario Decleva and Peter Bischof; in other cases, artists who twenty years ago were prominent figures in the field of abstract art, such as Josef Mikl or Wolfgang Hollegha, have more recently tended again towards realism. Friedensreich Hundertwasser, whose work figures in collections all over the world, is perhaps the best-known Austrian artist abroad, though the endless repetitions of his maze-like themes have reduced his impact.

Sculpture

The finest example of early plastic art in Austria is the Tassilo Chalice in the Kremsmünster Abbey, ascribed to the year AD 769. The Verduner Altar in the Klosterneuburg Abbey (called after the artist, Nicholas of Verdun), the portal figures in the Gurk Cathedral, and the Kreuzgang (cloisters) in the Millstatt Abbey are some of the best examples of Romanesque sculpture. Michael Pacher was a Gothic painter and worker in wood of great genius; his winged altar in the parish church of St. Wolfgang on Wolfgangsee is a fine example of Gothic woodcarving.

Austria's greatest sculptor was Raphael Donner (1693–1741), creator of the fountain on the Neuer Markt in Vienna and the priceless Pietà in the Gurk Cathedral. Also notable is Balthasar Permoser (1651–1732), whose statue of Prince Eugene is in the Austrian Baroque Museum, housed in the Lower Belvedere, which is, indeed, a treasurehouse for sculpture of the period and worth a visit.

Contemporary Austrian sculpture represents great artistic individuality. Fritz Wotruba (1907–75) is the giant among modern sculptors, and his interpretation of the human figure continues to inspire contemporary artists. The design of his Holy Trinity Church in the 23rd District of Vienna, completed after his death, is a remarkable example of sculptured architecture. The most outstanding among the younger generation are Rudolf Hoflehner and Johannes Avramidis, both of whom have received several top international prizes. Karl Prantl, the founder of the sculptors' symposium at St. Margarethen, has gained international acclaim, while, among the most provocative sculptors working today, are Gerhardt Moswitzer and Bruno Gironcoli.

Literature

After the medieval Minnesingers and religious plays and after the Jesuit-sponsored dramas and the comedies of Josef Stranitsky in the baroque centuries, Austrian literature entered its classical epoch during the first half of the 19th century. The greatest dramatist of this period was Franz Grillparzer (1791–1872), known particularly for his presentation of themes from Habsburg history. Other prominent writers of this era were the novelist Adalbert Stifter (1805–68), who was also a painter, the poet-dramatist Ferdinand Raimund (1790–1836), who knew how to blend everyday reality with the world of fairy tales, and Johann Nestroy (1801–62), the satirical and humorous depicter of life in Vienna. The most outstanding poets of the period were two aristocrats: Anton Alexander Count Auersperg, with the *nom de plume* Anastasius Grün (1806–76), and Nikolaus Niembsch von Strehlenau (1802–50), with the *nom de plume* Nikolaus Lenau, a lyric poet, who was inspired by his travels in Hungary and farther afield.

The end of the century brought a new trend, represented particularly by the dramatists Karl Schönherr (1869–1943) and Arthur Schnitzler (1862–1931), by the novelist, playwright and critic Hermann Bahr (1863–1934), and by the poet-dramatist Hugo von Hofmannsthal (1874–1929), the librettist of Richard Strauss's opera *Rosenkavalier* and creator of *Everyman*, performed every year during the Salzburg Mozart Festival. Von Hofmannsthal and Schnitzler are considered as most closely reflecting Viennese life during this period. Schnitzler, in particular, reflects the influence of his compatriot Sigmund Freud (1856–1939). Long before other prominent exponents of the stream of consciousness technique such as James Joyce, Marcel Proust and Virginia Woolf, Schnitzler made use of the internal monologue in his short story *Leutnant Gustl,* dramatized and successfully performed in Vienna in 1978.

Rainer Maria Rilke (1875–1926) was one of the greatest lyrical poets in the German language, exploring mysticism and beauty of expression with equal, restless sensitivity. Peter Rosegger (1843–1918) celebrated his native Styria in naïve style.

The present century begins with the Expressionist-influenced dramas and novels of Franz Werfel (1890–1945) and Franz Kafka (1883–1924), and the biographies and psychological novels of Stefan Zweig (1881–1942). Josef Weinheber (1892–1945), a master of rhyme, Karl Kraus (1874–1936), brilliant poet and satirist, and the novelist Robert Musil (1880–1942) also belong primarily to the early 20th century. These writers not only reflected the breakdown of Empire in their works, but also evolved new literary forms that had considerable impact on writers in other countries.

An Austrian writer whose work has attracted more attention in recent years than during his lifetime is Ödön von Horváth (1901–38); his plays, in which he criticized contemporary society, represent a continuation of Austria's long tradition of popular comedy and are among the most frequently staged productions in the German-language theater world today.

Heimito von Doderer (1896–1966) is another important novelist in a later generation. Among his younger contemporaries, the list of poets is headed by women—Christine Lavant (1915–73), Christine Busta (b. 1915) and Ingeborg Bachmann (1926–73), whereas the historic dramas of Fritz Hochwälder (b. 1911) have become known far beyond the borders of Austria. Among the youngest prominent novelists is Herbert Zand (b. 1933). Elias Canetti's work has achieved an international success and he won the Nobel Prize in 1981. Born in 1911, he lives in England and is widely translated.

Considerable attention has been aroused by the work of the novelist and playwright Peter Handke (b. 1942), inspired mainly by the idea of "anti-theater." Within a few years of publication, his *Insulting the Audience* had been played in virtually all European countries and prompted more heated discussion on modern theatrical form than there has been since Brecht. Further proof of the continuation of the Austrian theater tradition in the young generation of writers is the work of Wolfgang Bauer (b. 1941), who also uses elements of the Vienna popular theater as well as dialect.

The contemporary Austrian writer has contributed widely to the literary scene, particularly in Europe. The rich heritage of individualism, the inherent sense of the theatrical, the delight in word-play, all of which are integral elements in the Austrian artist's makeup, have been combined with many other historical and cultural facets to produce a lively and provocative avant-garde movement.

FOOD AND DRINK

Schlagobers Supreme

In the course of centuries, Slavs, Turks, Italians, Magyars and, of course, Germans, all flourished within the immediate homeland of the Habsburgs. It might be reasonable to suppose that Austria, the inheritor of the remnants of the Empire, would have a cuisine composed of all these varied and exotic elements, fused into one great big cosmopolitan gastronomic United Nations. But it doesn't work out like that. It is true that you will encounter Hungarian restaurants, Balkan restaurants, Italian restaurants, even Russian restaurants in Vienna and other important cities of Austria, but during their long residence in Austria, the various exotic schools of cooking have become Austrianized. Asperities have been smoothed away, exaggerations toned down, and the gamut of tastes brought into harmony with the lighthearted temperament of the people who produced the Viennese waltz and the operetta, and whose own great contribution to the meal comes with the dessert course, in the appropriate form of rich and luscious pastries, and in the beloved and universal Schlagobers or whipped cream.

This means that the visitor to Austria, while he will be able to enjoy a wide range of international dishes, need not fear that his palate or his stomach will be attacked by fiery or pungent concoctions. He will be able to order without fear anything he discovers on the menu. He may find it advisable to watch his weight, however, because Austrian food is filling, rich, and copious. The portions may strike visitors from countries of less hearty eaters as enormous. But if the new arrival, eating his first meal, is under the impression that he is being so well served because he has stumbled on the one substantial repast of the day, with perhaps a little minor help on a couple of other occasions, he will be quite wrong. Austrians not only eat a lot at one time, they eat a good many times during the day.

Pastry Shops

In case of a feeling of faintness between meals (and in case any time is left between meals), one can always dart into one of the *Konditorei* or pastry shops so numerous in Austria, or the milk and *espresso* bars, now fairly widespread, for a life-preserving snack. The pastry shop *is* thoroughly Austrian. Other countries have pastry shops, but they aren't the same and they don't play so important a role in the daily life of the citizen. A visit to a famous pastry shop, like *Demel's* on the Kohlmarkt in Vienna, or *Zauner's* in Bad Ischl, is a must. Both of these shops achieved their fame as imperial court caterers and so far have succeeded in preserving their quality in spite of contemporary difficulties in finding proper personnel to carry on this highly individualistic trade requiring painstaking precision and diligence. Many pastry shops do not confine their temptations to pastries alone. They also offer sandwiches, vegetable soufflés, mushrooms stuffed with a herb and cheese mixture, in fact all manner of heavenly tidbits.

All-Purpose Coffeehouses

To savor the atmosphere of the coffeehouses you must take your time. In Vienna you have a wide choice of these establishments; set aside an afternoon, a morning, or at least a couple of hours, and settle down in one of your choice. You can read (many coffeehouses carry not only Austrian papers and magazines but a few English or American ones) or you can catch up on letter writing. There is no need to worry about outstaying one's welcome, even over a single small cup of Mokka. If the waiter dusts an adjoining table it's not a hint to leave—the table probably *needs* dusting. If he brings a glass of water, it is just because he thinks you *want* water. The decline of the coffeehouse has fortunately been halted, and even reversed. They represent a way of life that is once more sought-after: many coffeehouses are being refurbished and new ones are opening.

The Austrian coffeehouse has a lengthy history. When the Turkish invaders were driven out of Vienna in 1683 they left behind some mysterious brown beans. A former Austrian spy in the Turkish camp learned how to use them. Thus was coffee introduced to Austria, and the first coffeehouse established. This was a momentous moment, for a substantial part of Austrian social life revolves around the coffeehouses. They are scattered all over the nation. They are the club, pub and bistro all rolled into one. They are the places where one meets business associates, relaxes over the paper and generally finds a home from home. Though less than in the past, Austrians by and large are rather reluctant to invite strangers to their homes and prefer to meet them in the friendly, but uncommitted, atmosphere of the coffeehouse.

Coffee is not just coffee in Austria. It comes in many forms and under many names. Morning coffee is generally Melange (half coffee and half milk), or with little milk, a Brauner. The usual afterdinner drink is Mokka, very black, and most Austrians like it heavily sweetened. But that is just the beginning. Some restaurants, notably those specializing in Balkan cookery, serve Turkish coffee (Türkischer), a strong, thick brew. There is usually considerable sediment in the bottom of the cup, which should not be stirred, and the coffee is often served with a square of Turkish Delight.

More delightful to Western eyes are the coffee-and-whipped-cream combinations (Kaffee mit Schlag), but these are tastes that are easily acquired and a menace to all but the very thin. The coffee may be either hot or cold. A customer who wants more whipped cream than coffee asks for a Doppelschlag. Hot black coffee in a glass with one knob of whipped cream is an Einspänner (one-horse coach). Then you can go to town on a Mazagran, black coffee with ice and a tot of rum, or Eiskaffee, cold coffee with ice cream, whipped cream and biscuits. Or you can simply order a Portion Kaffee and have an honest pot of coffee and jug of hot milk.

The Restaurant Scene

As in any large cosmopolitan community, you can dine in Vienna in an atmosphere of luxury with perfect service and delicious food, including not only the best of Austrian cooking but beautifully prepared foods from other lands. In Vienna, you can also find a tasty meal for a comparatively modest sum. In the larger cities, such as Graz and Innsbruck, there is a similar selection of eating places, although on a smaller scale and with lower prices generally. Out in the country, you may enjoy good, modest meals at still lower prices.

The one thing that is common to restaurants throughout the country, whether they are pricey Viennese ones or simple country inns, is that they have a great deal of character, friendliness and atmosphere. This is partly due to the fact that the Austrians have preserved a lot of ceremony and the niceties of social etiquette in their lives, with the result that the rate of change has been much slower in Austria than in many other parts of Europe. But something of a revolution has been taking place in Vienna and to a lesser extent outside. Many new restaurants are opening and new ways of presenting old dishes have been developed with varying success. This makes for a more interesting restaurant scene. Consult the restaurant guides (first and foremost *Gault Millau Österreich*) and restaurant columns in the daily papers.

One of the hardest things to do in an Austrian restaurant is to get the bill. Often it takes several repetitions of "Zahlen, bitte" to bring the *Ober* (headwaiter) with his pad and bag of change. You tell him what you ate; he will add a 10 percent service charge, a 10 percent government tax on all alcoholic drinks except beer, and sometimes a small item for music and the like. He expects a small additional tip, the size of which varies from just a few schillings rounding up the bill in the regular restaurants to about 5 percent in the fancy evening restaurants. Some tip only the headwaiter, others only the waiters who serve the food and drink.

Austrian Specialties

One of the best food buys in Austria is soup, which is consistently good—and inexpensive. Austrian soups range all the way from the highly seasoned Gulyassuppe, full of paprika and onions, to mild consommé with a poached egg. Particularly popular with Austrians and visitors is the Leberknödlsuppe, a meat broth containing liver dumplings. It contains less calories for the weight-conscious than the many other delicious noodle soups.

Having no seacoast, Austria is naturally not fish country, except for the freshwater varieties. Carp, Fogosch, pike and, best of all, succulent crawfish (when in season, which is rather short) and various trout from the native lakes and rivers are the best bet. Carp is an insipid-tasting fish to those used to the lively savor of the deep sea. Pike and Fogosch come from the Danube and the lakes on the Hungarian border and are often excellent when grilled or fried, much like pike and bass. The crawfish (called Krebs) look like tiny lobsters and make a delicious thick soup in many restaurants. Or they are served cold to be laboriously picked from their shells and dipped in mayonnaise.

Austrian brook trout and rainbow trout are delicious. The most popular way of serving them is "blue", the whole fish boiled in a court bouillon and accompanied by drawn butter. Or try it Müllerin—sautéed in butter to a crisp brown. Wonderful! In summer try cold smoked trout for a delicate entrée.

Schnitzels and Other Meat Dishes

Veal and beef dominate the Austrian kitchen, though the various types of schnitzel can also be pork. Wiener Schnitzel is usually veal steak, well beaten, dipped in flour, egg and crumbs and fried, usually in deep fat, to golden brown crunchiness. Natur Schnitzel is fried as it is, without egg or crumbs. Holsteiner Schnitzel is the same, plus a fried egg on the meat and crossed anchovy strips on the egg. Pariser Schnitzel is dipped in flour and egg and fried. There are many other types of schnitzel and related veal specialties. One of the best is Cordon Bleu: cheese and ham are rolled in a piece of veal, the whole is dipped as above and fried. Paprikaschnitzel is also good.

Pork is highly popular and also less expensive than veal. There's plain roast pork with potatoes or Knödeln (dumplings like doughy cannonballs); special cuts like Schweinscarré, or a long tender strip from beside the backbone called Schweinsjungfrau ("pig's virgin," if you must be literal), and such specialties as pig's shank, kidneys, and a great variety of smoked pork dishes.

Austrians don't care much for lamb, but it is now more widely available than a few years ago. However, venison (Rehrücken) and numerous other game dishes (wild boar, hare, pheasant, quail, partridge) are popular and usually served with cranberries.

For American and English tastes, beef is often cooked too long. Austrian cooks do a splendid job with stewing beef but steaks are often too well done, although quality has improved recently. If you want a rare steak, it is a good idea to tell the waiter the exact degree of rareness desired (*Englisch* denoting rare in Austria, true blue, in fact).

Austrian Tafelspitz (boiled beef) is famous, and deservedly so. It is prepared by being put into boiling water and simmered for about two hours, until it is well cooked. With it come various sauces, a bland sauce, like a thin hollandaise, flavored with chives; and more tangy sauces of grated horseradish, or horseradish and apple which are combined raw and allowed to fuse into a delicious form of TNT. Röstkartoffeln (roasted sliced potatoes) are usually served with the beef, and sometimes a number of other vegetables.

At the other end of the taste gamut is Gulyas (goulash), of Hungarian origin, made with beef—or best of all, venison. Highly seasoned, it is usually served with potatoes. Reminiscent of the New England boiled dinner is Bauernschmaus, a tasty meat dish of the folksy type. It varies from restaurant to restaurant but usually includes ham, a piece of salt pork, sausage, sauerkraut, and a large dumpling.

Sausages and Chicken

Austrian sausages are excellent. If you want to try a sampling of a number of different varieties, you can order a sausage platter, and you will be given a generous selection of cold sliced sausages. Frankfurters, named after a Viennese butcher, are excellent and are called Wieners almost everywhere—*except* in Vienna. There are also fine cheeses, the best of which is the Vorarlberg Farmhouse "Bergkäse" from the villages of the Bregenzerwald.

Austrian cuisine offers two superb chicken dishes: Backhuhn or Backhendl, young, medium-sized chicken breaded and fried in deep fat until it is golden brown; and Steirisches Brathuhn, roast chicken, usually turned on a spit. Vienna is believed to be the home territory of the Backhendl, while Styria, where the best chickens in Austria are raised, is the home of the Brathuhn, also called Poulard.

The Knödl is an Austrian institution. It leads both rice and potatoes in popularity, but not by much. There is an infinite variety of this dough dish. One group includes the homely hearty unsweetened type, the dumpling, which appears with meat or goes into soup. Then there are the smaller, more delicate sweet ones, eaten as dessert, flavored with jam, poppy seed, cottage cheese, and other unusual ingredients.

Vegetables and Bread

Although Austria is not famous for vegetable cookery, it has several delightful specialties. Puréed spinach (Spinat) is cooked spinach, chopped and flavored with butter, salt, garlic, perhaps a bit of flour, and a little cream. Rotkraut (red cabbage), made sweet-sour and flavored with caraway seed is also good. Mushrooms, fried to a delicious crispness in the manner of Wiener Schnitzel, are not uncommon in better restaurants. Stuffed green peppers and stuffed cabbage in tomato sauce are contributions of Hungarian and Balkan cooking to the Austrian menu.

A fairly good green salad, generally lettuce with a vinegar and oil dressing, usually somewhat sweetened, is served almost anywhere. If you don't like sugar in your salad dressing, say so when you order. A popular alternative, which may or may not please English and American palates, is a Gemischter Salat, a dab of several cooked and raw vegetables—not mixed greens as in the States and England; these dabs are neatly arranged in a ring on a plate—a bit of kraut, chopped beets, shredded lettuce, etc. Slaw, or cabbage salad, is popular, with a vinegar dressing.

Bread is crisp and excellent, perhaps the best in the world. It will pay any visitor making a long stay to go to a Bäckerei (bakery), sample some of the fine breads, and see which ones suit their particular taste. Incidentally, bread and sweet cakes or pastries are not generally made in the same bakery, as they are in the States or in England. You buy fine Torten, which are extremely rich cakes, only in pastry shops, never in bakeries.

Also, let no unwary visitor look at his pocket dictionary and order Kuchen, expecting to receive a beautiful piece of iced, many-layered cake. What he will probably get is a sort of coffee cake or sweet roll, which often turns up as dessert in Austria. Semmels and salt sticks and the like are commonly served with meals, along with dark bread of various types. Wholemeal bread is to be found in every bakery. At the corner of St. Peter's Cemetery in Salzburg, go and watch the baker baking sour-dough rye bread by hand and see how bread should be made.

All About Desserts

And now the desserts—those fabulous desserts! It is impossible to choose the best, for there are so many wonderful sweets, but perhaps the best known is Strudel. There are many kinds of strudel, most of them made with fruit, a few with cheese. There are apple strudel, cottage cheese strudel, cherry strudel, strudel made with fruit and nuts, strudel made with fruit and nuts and raisins—and a most delicious Pannonian variety with apples, raisins and poppy seeds, available only in Burgenland.

Palatschinken, thin dessert pancakes, are a distant relative of the French crêpes. They are rolled around a stuffing of fruit, jam, nuts, or other delicious tidbits. Salzburger Nockerl is one of the most famous Austrian desserts. It is a delicious soufflé of eggs, sugar, butter, and a bit of flour. Pick your restaurant carefully for this tasty item and don't hurry the chef. It's worth waiting for.

Kaiserschmarren, meaning imperial fluff, is a thicker pancake than the Palatschinken at the beginning of its preparation, but as it is shredded during the cooking process before it becomes quite firm, and is dusted with sugar and served with stewed fruit (mainly plums called Zwetschkenröster), it doesn't look anything like a pancake when it is finished.

Torte is an Austrian specialty and may be very good or very poor. The most famous is the Sachertorte, created at the Sacher Hotel in Vienna nearly a hundred years ago. It is a very rich chocolate cake baked in one thick layer that is coated with apricot jam and iced with more chocolate. The use of this renowned name has been the subject of a much-publicized trial, which came to a decision worthy of Solomon, that the original article should be spelled as one word, those others using the similar recipe must use two words.

Other names in the Torte world are Dobosch, hazelnut, Linzer, Malakoff. If these rich desserts are too much for the visitor, he may want to try Guglhupf, a fine-textured sponge cake, good with coffee. A popular specialty is the Krapfen, which used to turn up during Fasching (the Carnival season) and is now available all year. It is a relative of the jam-filled doughnut of the United States, but better, because it is fluffier and crisper.

Characteristic Viennese confections are Marillenknödel and Zwetschenknödel made from apricots and plums from which the stones are removed and replaced by lumps of sugar, after which the fruit is wrapped in a light potato-flour dough and boiled. Then there are the yeast dumplings filled with plum jam (Powidl) rolled in poppy seeds and sugar—order just one, the size may surprise you. And Powidltaschkerl (more difficult to pronounce than to eat), thin potato dough triangles enclosing again plum jam, this time rolled in breadcrumbs with hot butter and sugar.

Vienna's Heuriger

Now what do you drink with all that food? Water is excellent almost everywhere, even in Vienna—though no longer exclusively from mountain sources but supplemented by groundwater from the Danube meadows, probably better than what you have at home.

As almost everyone knows, excursions into the suburbs to drink the new wine are an important pastime in Vienna. The place where this is done, a Heuriger, is a hallowed institution of Viennese life. Words are a trifle confusing here. Heuriger wine is last fall's pressing. But a heuriger is one of the hundreds of wine houses with which the suburbs of Vienna are dotted. They serve new as well as old wine, and mostly have gardens for fine-weather drinking.

Technically a heuriger is the private wine tavern of the owner of the vineyard. The suburbs of Grinzing, Sievering, Nussdorf, Heiligenstadt, Kalenbergerdorf, Ottakring, Neustift, and Pötzleinsdorf, where there seem to be more heurigers than homes, are also the site of extensive vineyards. The gentle slopes of the Vienna woods and the Kahlenberg and Kobenzl hills are carpeted with them. A heuriger is identifiable primarily by a green branch hanging above the doorway. Some have small signs as well. The green branch, or its wrought-metal replica over the more elaborate places, is a code meaning "this year's wine served inside." The heuriger owner is supposed to be licenced to serve only the produce of his own vineyard, a rule long more honored in the breach than in the observance. It would take a sensitive palate indeed to differentiate among the various vineyards.

Heurigers open and close by some complex rules of season that few foreigners have penetrated. The daily papers contain a list of those that are currently open. Best advice for the stranger in town is to take the streetcar, or a taxi to the Grinzing terminus and just walk up the street, looking into open doors and lantern-lit gardens, cocking an ear to the strains of light music till you find an attractive place. The interiors are all much alike; plain wooden tables and benches, few decorations, fewer luxuries. Some food is always served with the wine, customarily ordered by the liter carafe. Almost all offer some form of mild entertainment, varying from an aged zither player to teams of folk singers extolling the glories of Vienna and its wine in a dialect so thick that not even visitors with fluent German can catch much of it. It's an institution of considerable charm and homely joy, the favorite Saturday afternoon or Sunday evening goal of thousands of Viennese. Here of an evening the entire family may go, bearing its own food or buying a plate of cold cuts and cheese at the wine house. It is all folksy and friendly, and in summer it is especially delightful, for then you sit in the patio or garden.

A word of warning: Heurige tastes as mild as lemonade, but it is surprisingly potent and leaves headaches in its wake, if it is of inferior quality. Austrians accustomed to the heurige eat almost constantly while drinking it, and many dilute it freely with soda water (Gespritzt).

Austrian Wines

In the last ten years there has been a revival of interest in wines of a finer quality. Many growers such as Jamek of Joching or Prager of Weissenkirchen have devoted time and money to the improvement of their wines. There is now a wide range of excellent wines, white especially, which will stand comparison with the whites of other great wine-producing countries. The standard of the wine lists in many restaurants has improved beyond recognition. Austrian wines now travel and efforts are being made to promote them abroad. White grapes to note are Grüner Veltliner, which is dry and fruity; Rheinriesling—one of the finest dry wines; Welschriesling, which is widely grown in Styria and produces a refreshing dry wine; Gewürztraminer, with a heavy bouquet and particularly good from Klöch in southeastern Styria; Muskat-Ottonel, which has a strong muscat flavor and ranges from dry to sweet, from Burgenland; and Weissburgunder, which is milder and heavier than the French equivalent.

Austrian wines tend to be thoroughly fermented and therefore drier than their German cousins. Red grapes of note are Blaufränkisch, which produces excellent red wines from table wines to top quality wines; Blauer Portugieser, an old Austrian grape producing heavy and fiery wine; and St. Laurent, a new blend producing a light, dry wine. These are but a few of the red and white wines available. So-called ice-wines (Spätlese, Auslese) made from grapes harvested after the first frost, have been produced on an increasing scale in recent years. They are very sweet, almost like liqueurs, and drunk in small quantities (e.g. with hors d'oeuvres).

Though bottled wine is of course superior, carafe wine (offener Wein), which is ordered by the quarter liter (ein Viertel), is as good as any in Europe and well worth its price. The Austrian version of champagne is called Sekt (as in Germany); the driest Henkell, Hochriegl and Schlumberger brands are palatable.

Austrian beers are very good and cheap. Among the best brands are Puntigamer, Reininghaus and Gösser, produced in Styria, Stieglbräu and

Augustiner Bräu of Salzburg, Ottakringer of Vienna, and Adambräu of Innsbruck.

Many of the Austrian distilled drinks are of considerable potency: there are various fruit brandies, such as Kirschwasser (from cherries); Himbeergeist (from raspberries); Obstbranntwein (from pears and apples); Wacholder (from juniper berries); Slivovitz (plum brandy), which the Austrians have retained as a reminder of their former Croatian and Bosnian territories, from which it originally came; an Austrian vodka; and Marillenschnapps (apricot) in the Wachau which can be superior to Hungarian Barack (apricot brandy). An excellent distilled drink is Löwenherz, a clear brandy made from the Wachau wines. Some of the changes Austrians ring into other ordinary mild drinks can be potent, too. The popular bowle (pronounced bole) consists of a few bottles of wine poured over fruit (peaches, raspberries, strawberries) or herbs and filled up with iced champagne immediately before drinking; it is considered unsmart, however, to soak the fruit first in brandy, which results in a delicious but highly dangerous combination.

If you prefer to stick to less authoritative beverages, you have a wide choice. There are excellent table waters, Römer Quelle being the most popular, and a variety of locally-produced fruit drinks, the favorite of Austrians being Apfelsaft (apple juice), Traubensaft (delicious alcohol-free grape juice) and Himbeersaft (raspberry syrup).

SPORTS IN AUSTRIA

Summer and Winter Paradise

The Austrians are great sports lovers, and go in en masse for a greater variety of sports than any other European nation. In the summer they go mountain climbing, canoeing, sailing, swimming, gliding, hunting, fishing, water skiing, horseback riding, bicycling, and play football (soccer), basketball, and tennis. In the wintertime skiing, of course, is the main attraction, and every Austrian, young or old, may be seen getting about with astonishing speed and skill on his *Brettl*. Ice skating is also very popular, particularly in the larger cities; in all, this small country has around 250 skating rinks, including those of Vienna. In country villages the older people gather in the evenings to "shoot on ice"—an Austrian version of curling—and there are hundreds of ice "shooting" alleys all over the country; the younger, more energetic folk race toboggans when not on a pair of skis. Ice sailing on the frozen lakes is as popular as sail surfing in summer. In addition to ski jumping and other skiing competitions, ice hockey is the favorite spectator sport in the winter.

Skiing

Without doubt skiing is the queen of winter sports, and for the true enthusiast, more interested in the slopes than in the bar, Austria is probably the finest place in the world to learn or to practice this far from gentle art. Not only does Austria offer the best teachers, the best skiers, and some of the best skiing terrain, but she does so at the most reasonable prices. Here, the distractions of fireside and fashion are not permitted to intrude upon the pursuit of skiing as a pure sport. This does not mean, however, that you will be required to rough it, for although other countries may offer more incidental luxuries, none can surpass Austria in terms of modern technical facilities in uphill transportation.

The winter resort season runs from about December 15 through March, but the determining factor is, of course, the snow. The season starts with the falling snow and ends as it melts slowly into the valleys. In the higher areas, there is skiing from November to May. Numerous cable cars and chair lifts are supplemented in the high mountains by some 2,800 T-bars taking skiers to ideal ski terrains located at 8,000 to 10,000 feet, where skiing goes on through the summer; in some of these areas, there is permanent snow and skiing all year round. Among these are Ramsau/Dachstein in Styria; Kaprun in Salzburg; Hintertux and the Gefrorene Wand in the Tyrol, and the Neustift/Stubaital glacier region, also in the Tyrol.

In most resorts, prices are higher during the Christmas-New Year's season and during February and March, when hotels are crowded, particularly if snow conditions are good. Advance reservations are essential at that time.

Highlights of Austrian Skiing

The Kitzbühel Ski Circus is a maze of marked slopes and trails (one slope is floodlit at night), which make it possible for you to follow new combinations day after day without ever repeating your itinerary. If you take lessons at the local ski school, you can try for a souvenir in the form of the handsome Golden Ski Book, awarded to anyone who completes 20 of the 30 runs pictured in it. The Kitzbühel ski school, in addition to regular courses for beginners and advance skiers, also offers special racing courses for those who would like to become skiing champions. These courses are conducted by former Austrian Olympic champions.

The Schmittenhöhe Spaziergang, above Zell am See, offers a spectacular promenade along the tops of mountain peaks at an average height of 6,500 feet. This one is not for novices.

The longest marked ski run in Austria served by a lift is the Angertal descent at Badgastein, which requires a 5½-mile run for a drop of 4,628 feet. Only moderately difficult.

The longest single slope descent in the eastern Alps is at Werfen, with a run of 8,000 feet, a pretty fast ride all the way. Not for beginners.

For jumping, whether you prefer to watch it or try it, the outstanding places are the Hochkönig, reached from Werfen, where jumps of 300 feet have been made; Tchagguns, in the Montafon valley of the Vorarlberg, where there are two good jumps, often used for international competitions; Villach, in Carinthia, where there is a big stadium to accommodate spectators of its jumping contests; Mitterndorf, in Styria, whose "flying skis" jump is one of the world's longest; and Innsbruck, whose Berg Isel jump attracts many championship events.

All the accepted winter sports centers in Austria have at least one ski school (often supervised by the state). Even expert skiers can learn new tricks at the best of them. And there are well over a hundred schools for children to get started in the sport. In addition, there are ski-kindergartens where you can leave children over three years between 10 and 4; they will receive lunch and be well looked after.

No one may set himself up as a ski instructor unless he holds a state diploma. To get this he must pass a rigorous two-year course conducted by the Ministry of Education at St. Cristoph on the Arlberg. At St. Christoph he learns the teaching methods founded by the late Hannes Schneider, perhaps the world's most famous ski instructor, which are acknowledged to be tried and true for learning to ski. These are the methods of the famous "Arlberg School," nowadays more accurately described as the "Austrian School," whose famous skiing technique, called *Kurzschwingen* ("short and fast swinging") or *Wedeln* ("wagging"), has re-confirmed Austrian supremacy in this field. Most ski instructors speak English, and many schools are directed by former champions. The cost of ski instruction varies widely, depending on whether you want private lessons or will settle for group work, as well as on your degree of skill. Prices are reasonable.

There are over 3,500 ski lifts, chair lifts, cable cars and cable railways dotted all over the country, and they seem to multiply like rabbits every year. There is hardly a skiing spot, however small, which cannot boast at least one ski lift. As a rule, lifts and cable cars form a network (Schischaukel, Schizirkus), so you can ski in one village in the morning, lunch in a distant valley, and return in the afternoon without going twice down one slope. In spite of its small size and limited economic resources, Austria has made great strides in the comforts of uphill ski transport.

Skis, boots and sticks may be hired anywhere in Austria for a moderate fee. For beginners especially, it is wise to put off buying your skis until you have decided on your ski school and taken the advice of your instructor. Skis come in a variety of materials (fiberglass, plastic, wood or a combination of these). They can be of various lengths and the more of a novice you are the shorter your skis should be; average skiers should see eyeball to the tips of their skis. Prices will start from about 1,700 sch. without bindings (good safety bindings are essential, don't try to save on this item), and sticks (usually aluminum and waist-high). Ski clothes in Austria are of good quality and fairly economical.

Austria seems to have been designed by nature expressly for skiing. If you are already an expert, it is sufficient to state that literally anywhere in the Tyrol, Vorarlberg, and most parts of Carinthia, Salzburg, Styria, Lower Austria and Upper Austria you will find ski slopes of every type and gradient you could wish for. But for many visitors skiing is a closed book, while others, limited to a fortnight's skiing holiday once a year, have just emerged from the *Skihaserl* or novice stage and like to have their annual skiing in easy stages. The Austrian State Tourist Department has a wealth of pamphlets and booklets on every aspect of winter sports, with voluminous listings of all the facilities available.

Ski-rambling and powder-snow skiing have become very popular in recent years. For both you must be in good shape physically, and you will need special bindings on your skis. Because of the dangers involved (avalanches, sudden changes of weather etc.) it is advisable to hire an experienced guide for such tours.

The following winter sports resorts are warmly recommended to enthusiasts—*Vorarlberg:* Schruns, Tschagguns, Gargellen, Zürs, Lech, Oberlech;

Tyrol: St. Anton, St. Christoph, Sölden, Hochsölden, Obergurgl, Vent, Seefeld, Mayrhofen, Kitzbühel;

Salzburg: Zell am See, Saalbach, Saalfenden, Maria Alm, Badgastein, Bad Hofgastein, Obertauern (Radstädter Tauernpass);

Styria: Mariazell, Tauplitz-Tauplitzalm, Mitterndorf, Schladming-Ramsau;

Carinthia: Heiligenblut, Gerlitzen plateau, Mallnitz, Turracher Höhe;

Upper Austria: Obertraun (Dachstein plateau), Windischgarsten;

Lower Austria: Semmering, Lackenhof, Hochkar.

Each one of them is a recognized center, in the midst of ideal skiing country, and each has one or more of the famous skiing schools, plenty of ski instructors, good hotels, and population of sympathetic inhabitants who won't laugh when you fall down. For most of them you are their bread and butter—and "the customer is always right."

Economy skiers will find equally good terrain, more than adequate facilities and much lower prices in such areas as *Lower* and *Upper Austria;* at Abtenau, Altenmarkt and Flachau in *Land Salzburg;* in *East Tyrol;* at Katschberg and Turracher Höhe in *Carinthia;* and almost anywhere in *Styria.*

Skiing in the Neighborhood of Vienna

If you plan a winter holiday in Austria and are not going to a winter sports resort but are staying in Vienna, you can still go out for a day's skiing. In fact it is not even necessary to have a car as there are many special day excursions by bus and by train to nearby skiing centers, all of which are about an hour to an hour and a half from the city. Assuming you have your own ski equipment with you, such a round trip would cost you something in the region of 180 sch., but this will not include your lunch and only limited lift fees.

The centers to book for are: the Semmering, due west of Vienna; the village of Spittal, a much bigger center ten minutes by road farther on; then there is the Schneeberg for really good skiers and reached by means of a cog-wheel railway. West of Vienna there is Mariazell, Türnitz, Hochkar, Lackenhof and Annaberg which is one of the best skiing areas easily accessible from Vienna. For unlimited use of ski lifts at these centers, expect to pay between 120 and 200.

One good tip is to go with one of the many Vienna Ski Clubs on a weekend excursion as this will save you money. These clubs are generally run by the better sports equipment shops and they will also hire you any equipment you may need.

Cross-Country Skiing

Although downhill skiing has long held the limelight, and provides most of the glamor of the sport, of recent years cross-country skiing has become more and more popular. It has a lot to recommend it. Not only does it enable you to appreciate the stunning beauty of the mountain landscapes, unfolding around you at a steady rate, but it is one of the most healthy of all sports. The calm rhythm of cross-country skiing has extremely good effects on the body, especially on the constitution of those who are cooped up for most of the year in the city.

There are more than 400 tracks now laid out in Austria, a total of over 5,500 km. of marvelous available skiing in Carinthia, Salzburg, Styria, Vorarlberg and Lower and Upper Austria.

Mountain Climbing

In Austria mountain climbing is a highly organized sport. The sweeping Alpine ranges of towering peaks and shimmering glaciers are a great challenge to lovers of this sport. In summer, over 400 mountain railways, cable cars and chair lifts take you up to the heights, so you don't waste time and effort on the lowlands (for that matter, there are many bus lines that will take you above 7,000 feet, a good boost on your way up). Many hundred high-perched mountain hotels and refuges, the latter belonging mostly to one or another of the various clubs, let you make overnight stops high up among the peaks. The efficient Austrian Mountain Refuge Service makes climbing as safe here as it can be anywhere.

Good guides are most important, and Austrian guides, like skiing instructors, are subject to strict state control. They train for four years and then take a stiff examination which allows them to become full-fledged guides. At present there are over 700, about 400 in Tyrol alone.

Every Austrian guide carries a brown book, a kind of passport. On page three details of all the ascent routes with which he is thoroughly familiar are entered and certified. On the succeeding blank pages, the dates and routes of all the climbs he has led are entered and counter-signed by the other members of the party. So when you engage a guide, have a look at his "passport" to see how experienced your man is.

There are more than 40 mountain climbing schools. The principal ones are: Hochgebirgsschule Tyrol and Alpenschule Innsbruck, both in Innsbruck; Bergsteigerschule Heiligenblut in Carinthia at the foot of Grossglockner, Austria's highest mountain; Bergsteigerschule Dachstein in Ramsau at the foot of Dachstein, the highest mountain of Styria; Hochgebirgsschule Glocknergruppe at Kaprun in the Salzburg province. Between June and September, these schools operate tours of various degrees of difficulty, suited for the beginner or seasoned climber. Arrangements have to be made at least about four weeks in advance. The charges include food, simple mountain hut accommodations, guide-teacher fees and insurance. Some of the schools also provide climbing equipment, or some of it, whereas others do not; check in advance by letter.

In many schools sponsored by such organizations as the Austrian Alpine Club only members of this or associated clubs can take part in the various activities, so it will pay you to make sure beforehand that you are eligible. Of course you can become a member of the Austrian Alpine Club which has special branch organizations abroad; for instance in England where the address is *Austrian Alpine Club,* Longcroft House, Fretherne Road, Welwyn Garden City, Herts. The same goes for the Tourist Association *Friends of Nature* with branches in Great Britain (Edinburgh and Liverpool) and the United States (San Francisco).

These clubs also own a large part of the more than 700 mountain huts spread over the Austrian Alps. The huts are of vital use in emergencies, and in normal circumstances are primarily for the convenience of club members—you cannot be sent away by a host, even if the hut is crowded. The Austrian Alpine Club owns some 275 huts and the "Friends of Nature" 170; another 180 are owned in Austria by the German Alpine Club.

Fishing

Fishing is cheaper and more plentiful. All you need is an official state license to fish and permission from the owner of the stream. Much of the fishing belongs to the Gemeinde, the local rural authorities, so the Bür-germeister, the mayor, is the proper person to approach. Many hotels have their own fishing and will allow their guests to fish free of charge, but you should hand over your catch when you get back.

Rainbow and stream trout are found in abundance in all Austrian rivers and mountain streams. Fishing for trout and most of the salmonides is generally permitted in Austria only with artificial flies. The use of artificial or live spinning bait is reserved for larger fish such as trout, chub, salmon, char, pike, zander, sheathfish, and the huck. Fishing with natural bait is usually limited to waters with adjoining nurseries and to large rivers, and ground fishing and trolling to the larger lakes. The Austrian State Tourist Department publishes an excellent booklet with details on fishing areas, costs, etc.

Pike lurk in large number in the large Austrian lakes. The best method is to troll for them from a boat, and specimens of from 10 to 15 pounds are not uncommon. The land-locked salmon (Huchen), which, unlike the usual salmon, does not go to the sea to spawn, is found only in the tributaries of the Danube—such as the upper reaches of the Rivers Drau, Mur or Enns—and the Melk and Pielach. The fish is regarded as a delicacy and is a great fish to fight with, great in two senses as it can grow to over 40 pounds. Standard salmon flies and large spinning bait are most effective.

Upper Austria and Tyrol are favorite fishing regions. You will find an abundance of fish, too, in the Carinthian lakes and Lower Austrian streams. For trout, your best bets are the streams and Salzkammergut lakes of Styria.

Camping and Canoeing

If your idea of a holiday is the great outdoors, or if your purse is a slender one and your vacation must be cheap, then you should certainly consider camping in Austria. Unrivaled Alpine scenery, hundreds of lakes, mountain streams, and dense woodlands, for the most part off the beaten track and yet easily accessible by train and bus, offer you a wide choice.

Facilities at the various camping grounds vary considerably. First-class camps are equipped with running water, electric light points, canteens, and the like. Other camps have running water, car parks, and canteens. Still another group offers only the bare site itself and available water (stream or lake, usually). Almost all are equipped with complete sanitary facilities. Canteens sell food you can cook yourself or readymade snacks. In many camps cooking equipment can be borrowed, but the demand often far outruns the supply. It's best, therefore, to bring your own utensils with you. Recently a number of camps have also been equipped for cold-weather camping and are open also in winter.

The Tyrol Water Sports Club's handbook called *The International River and Camping Guide to the Eastern Alps* covers in detail all the navigable rivers and lakes of eastern Switzerland, southern Germany, western and central Austria, and northern Italy, and is plentifully illustrated with large-scale maps for river navigation. Here are a few of the runs:

The Danube: No great skill is required to canoe down the Danube from the German frontier to Vienna. The river is broad, the scenery delightful.

The Inn: requires no special experience, especially going downstream. The best stretch is from Mötz to Innsbruck. If you enter farther upstream, at Landeck say, you will have to leave for a few miles at Imst, where the river is unnavigable.

The Ziller: a tributary of the Inn. The Ziller valley is considered to be one of the most beautiful in Austria, and the trip from Mayrhofen at the head of the valley down to the Inn is a delightful experience.

The Traun: a wild mountain stream, draining the Altaussee and Grundlakes, and entering the Danube just below Linz, passes through some ideal mountain scenery. There are 22 locks.

The Ager: draining the Atter lake, flows into the Traun above Wels. Canoeists should enter the river at Kammer-Schörfling. The length of this stretch is only 35 km., and there are 15 locks.

The Enns: the favorite among experienced canoeists. Starting at Radstadt, you have a clear run to the Gesäuse, a fissure where the torrents have worn through solid rock. The Gesäuse is unnavigable, and the trip continues at Hieflau, a few kilometers on. It is no accident that world championship kayak races have been held on the Enns in past years.

Gliding and Archery

Another Austrian specialty, in whose development this country has been a leader, is gliding. The atmospheric conditions peculiar to the Alps offer unique advantages for the glider. The gliding grounds at Innsbruck and Kufstein particularly, specialize in "föhn flying"—gliding in the warm, dry wind or föhn that blows from the south over the Alps and presents special problems to the glider at the same time affording him an unparalleled view of the Alps as he soars in and out among the peaks. It is an unforgettable experience.

The Zell am See Alpine Gliding School is located in Salzburg province (season from March to mid-Dec.); the Union Alpine Gliding School at Niederöblarn near Gröbming, Styria (season from April to Nov.); there is another school on the Spitzerberg near Hainberg in Lower Austria (season Feb. to Dec.), this one is about 42 km. from Vienna; and the Wien-Donauwiese just outside the Vienna city limits. About 40 well-equipped glider fields are dotted throughout Austria.

The Austrian Archery Association (Österreichischer Bogenschützenverband), with headquarters in Bad Goisern, Upper Austria, presently comprises ten archery clubs, with training sites in Vienna, Salzburg,

Panoramic view of Vienna from the
terrace of the Upper Belvedere.
The ornate classical façade of
the Parliament Building

The Anton Pilgram pulpit (1515) in
St. Stephen's Cathedral, Vienna, with
its brilliantly carved faces

A view across the Inn Valley from a cablecar
on the Patscherkofelbahn, with Igls
in the distance below

The Europa Bridge, carrying part of the
Brenner Autobahn across a deep valley
in the Tyrol

Innsbruck, Reutte in Tyrol, Kammern and Weiz in Styria, Bad Goisern in Upper Austria, Krems and Ternitz in Lower Austria. Foreign guests are welcome at all clubs. Courses of a week's duration for guests take place in Bad Goisern two to three times each summer. In Kammern, in Styria, the European archery championess, Anni Berner, takes care of the training of guests.

Wind Surfing

Wind surfing is popular on the warm Carinthian lakes and also on the Neusiedler Lake within easy reach of Vienna and indeed on the Old Danube in Vienna itself. If you are a beginner, there are regular courses with about 8 hours of tuition, which is allegedly enough to learn the art of wind surfing and they cost about 800–1000 sch. A complete outfit costs between 11,000 and 14,000 sch. but you can hire all that is necessary quite cheaply.

Golf

The gold season starts in Austria in late March. Although all 17 of the golf clubs in Austria are private clubs, all of them welcome visitors on a "green-fee" basis as readily as publicly owned courses elsewhere as their membership is rather limited. Only seven courses can boast 18 holes, among them is the Vienna Golf Club in the Prater Park, the one at Seefeld near Innsbruck, which provides a tough test of golf amongst magnificent mountain scenery, and the Innsbruck Ring just outside the city. Perhaps the smartest course in Austria is that designed by John D. Harris at Enzesfeld; it is a major tournament course and is part of a "smart set" country club.

Sailing

Although Austria is land-locked and to a large extent a mountainous country, there is a widespread interest in sailing among Austrians. Excellent facilities for sailing are to be found on the Lake of Constance (538 sq. km.) and the Neusiedler Lake (320 sq. km.), an hour's drive south of Vienna, and on the lakes of the Salzkammergut such as Mondsee, Traunsee and the Wolfgangsee, as well as the Wörthersee in Carinthia. Modest facilities exist even in Vienna, on the Old Danube. If you plan to go sailing in Austria, it is important to have at least an "A" license, for although there is no strict enforcement of licenses to sail on the Austrian lakes, it is virtually impossible to rent a good sailing boat without one. If you are a beginner, there are excellent sailing courses which run from Monday to Friday. If you are staying in Vienna you will be able to hire a sailing dinghy on the Old Danube or on the Neusiedler Lake for about 80–100 sch. an hour. You will find little difficulty in hiring the smaller boats as there are over 40 yacht clubs in the country and plenty of choice. Further details can be obtained from the *Austrian Sailing Association* at Prinz Eugenstr. 12, Vienna 1040 (tel. 65 84 95).

A large number of the better resort hotels have outdoor tennis courts and in all towns municipal or private courts can be rented by the hour.

Special-Interest Holidays

Several travel agencies offer special-interest package tours which include accommodations, breakfast and transfers, as well as a program of visits or instruction or whatever. Subject-matter might be music, with trips to places associated with the many great composers who made their home in Austria; wine, with tastings in the various grape-growing regions; or sport, including practical courses in golf, tennis, skiing, fishing, yachting, hunting and mountaineering. For detailed information on these and other holidays, just contact the Austrian National Tourist Office. (See also page 13.)

**THE
FACE
OF
AUSTRIA**

PRELUDE TO VIENNA

The Pleasures of Formality

We have subtitled one of the earlier chapters in this book *Schlagobers Supreme,* and this could be taken as the theme for this look at the atmosphere of Vienna, for the visitor may well have the sensation that he is lapped in lashings of rich, delicious, cream. The ambience of the city is predominantly ornate and fluffy; white horses dancing to elegant music; snow, frosting the opulent draperies of Maria Theresa's monument, set in the formal patterns of her lovely square; a marble Johann Strauss, playing madly among a susurration of green trees; rich decorations, secretly filling the interior courtyards of town houses that present a severe face to the outside world; the transformation of stark Greek legends by the voluptuous music of Richard Strauss; the tangible, geometric impasto of Klimt's paintings; the stately pavane of a mechanical clock; all these will create in the visitor the sensation of a city that likes to be visited and admired . . . and which is well worth admiring and visiting.

An Eagle's-Eye View

Before exploring Vienna, it is a good idea to see it whole. No one can pretend that it is easy to climb the 345 steps of the south steeple of St Stephen's Cathedral, but it is worth it as it affords a magnificent view right in the heart of town. For the less intrepid, there is an elevator to the top of the much lower north tower. An elevator likewise shoots up to the observation platform of the Donauturm, while small planes take off for regular sightseeing tours from Vienna airport. The Big Wheel in the Prater affords one of the best and most readily accessible panorama views of Vienna. But the most romantic view is from the last projecting spur of the nearby mountains of the Vienna Woods.

Immediately below flows the Danube—not, unless you are particularly lucky, exceptionally blue and too well-regulated to be romantic. Over a hundred years ago, a first artificial bed was cut to improve water transport and contain the spring floods which, however, still caused heavy damage when the snows melted abruptly. So a second channel through the broad inundation flats was completed in 1981, and the excavation soil was heaped into a 14-mile-long, 200-yard-wide island, used as a wild-life sanctuary. This second bed, though mainly intended for water sports, also raised the groundwater level needed for Vienna's water supply in the extensive meadows round the Alte Donau (Old Danube). The latter is a cut-off branch of the River Danube forming a shallow (about 2-meters deep) lake some seven kilometers long and 300 to 500 yards wide. It is one of the favorite recreation spots of the Viennese. The area is now a national park, its recreation area comprising the popular bathing beach of Gänsehäufel. The Winterhafen has been enlarged to deal with the increased water transport when the Rhine-Main-Danube canal has been completed.

The great city spreads across an extensive plain which continues over the Marchfeld toward the frontier of Czechoslovakia, marked by the rivers Thaya and March, less than 50 miles away. Upstream, to the left, lies the beautiful monastery of Klosterneuburg with its green-patina cupolas, on an eminence above the Danube.

A little higher up, on the opposite bank, is Korneuburg, with Kreuzenstein Castle atop a low hill. Behind Klosterneuburg rise the tree-clad heights of the Vienna Forest, coming to an end in the Lainzer Tiergarten, a natural wildlife preserve round the Empress Elisabeth's Hermes Villa, open to the public during the summer months. Below the wooded Tiergarten stands Maria Theresa's baroque palace of Schönbrunn, with its formally laid-out gardens and the ornamental structure of the Gloriette behind. Through the flat country farther to the right the Danube flows on to Bratislava (Pressburg to the Austrians). From that city a spur of the Lower Carpathians runs off to the northeast.

Where the Danube flows through the gap between the Alps and the Carpathians across a broad basin, there Vienna grew up, astride the natural highway from the North Sea to the Adriatic. No political changes have been able to rob her of the importance she derives from this geographical position. Just south of Bratislava, some 65 km. from Vienna, begins the Hungarian Great Plain. Thus from these Viennese observation posts you are actually looking into two countries behind the Iron Curtain, both of which, of course, formed part of the Austro-Hungarian monarchy before World War I.

Legacy of Imperial Prosperity

Vienna does not really lie on the Danube; only the northern outskirts of the city touch it. The heart of Vienna, the Innere Stadt (Inner City) or First District—in medieval times, the entire city of Vienna—is bounded by the Ringstrasse (Ring) which forms almost a circle, with a narrow arc cut off by the Danube canal–dug in 1598–diverted from the main river just above Vienna and flowing through the city to rejoin the parent stream just below it. The Ring follows the lines of what, until an imperial decree ordered their leveling in 1857, were the defenses of the city— ramparts, moats and *glacis*. About 2 km. beyond the Ring runs the roughly parallel line of the Gürtel, which until 1890 formed the outer fortifications, or Linienwall.

In the 1870's Vienna reached the zenith of its imperial prosperity. This was marked by such gigantic undertakings as the cutting of a new channel (with the overflow meadows) for the Danube, the building of the Great Exhibition of 1873, and the construction of the 90-km. water conduit from the natural underground reservoir in the Styrian mountains to the south of the city, which provides it with the most delicious ice-cold water to be found anywhere in Europe.

This same prosperity found its expression in the series of magnificent buildings erected around the Ringstrasse when the fortifications were leveled—the Opera House, National Art Gallery, and National Museum of Natural History, the "New Wing" of the Hofburg, Parliament, the Rathaus, the University, and the Votivkirche. By the time the Gürtel took the place of the outer fortifications, there was not quite so much money available and, although many open spaces were laid out as parks, it has no noteworthy buildings.

Most of the older buildings are, naturally, to be found in the small area of the Inner City, including many baroque palaces of the nobility. It was only after the invading Turkish hordes had been repulsed in 1683 that the area immediately beyond the Ring—the so-called "Inner Suburbs"— now numbered Bezirke (Districts) II to IX—began to develop, and the nobility to build summer residences here.

Of recent years many tall, functional, buildings have ringed the older, architecturally superior, districts. Notable among these is the United Nations City, situated in the Donau Park, overlooking the Danube. These high buildings, few in number by the standards of most modern cities, give an air of almost irrelevant modernity to a city whose heart beats with the pulse of history.

The Man That Hath not Music in His Soul . . .

You will discover for yourself the facets of Vienna which most appeal to you. But here are a few aspects of the city that may help you to explore the atmosphere of one of the world's most attractive capitals.

Wherever you turn, you will find how deeply music is engrained in the Viennese, indeed in all Austrians. Vienna has the most enormous variety of musical events to offer, and events of an amazingly high standard. Performances by the Vienna Boy's Choir in the Hofburg Chapel on Sunday mornings are events to remember. You will have an inkling of the world of art that gave birth to Mozart and Schubert (both of whom were connected with the choir in their day) when you hear the purity and immediacy of the boys' singing in its proper setting.

You will gain another insight into the way that music is looked upon if you attend a performance at the Opera. Be careful to dress as formally as your traveling wardrobe will allow, for opera is treated solemnly there, the intermissions becoming a kind of solemn processional rite. In the simple elegance of its auditorium, with its ranked boxes, you will find just as much intensity of attention as at the Metropolitan or Covent Garden, but somehow of a different quality, as if the audience were more ritually aware of participation in a theatrical tradition. For music in Vienna is a vital part of the great heritage of the city.

For yet another look at the importance of music in Vienna it is worth visiting the museum of musical instruments in the Hofburg complex. This is a collection of interest to the specialist as well as to the amateur. The pianos that were played by the great composers who graced Vienna's musical life, Beethoven, Brahms, Schumann and Schubert, are there. Pianos painted and carved, embellished with sphinxes and lyres, pianos that look like thrones and pianos that look like cathedrals, even pianos that look like pianos. One of the finest organs in Vienna is at the Augustinerkirche. Every Friday in summer at 8 P.M. there is a concert given by international organists. It lasts an hour or so and is completely informal with a minimal charge on the door.

The Importance of Serendipity

We mention a little later in this chapter some of the dishes that will give you a taste of Vienna, but we cannot pass by the importance of dropping in to a coffeehouse at some point in your wanderings to sample the relaxed life of the city that goes on there. It is an ideal way of drinking coffee and atmosphere at the same time. The coffeehouse is the club, meeting place, gossip center and home-from-home for many Viennese. Coffee has a long and honorable history in the city. The Turks never managed to conquer Vienna, though, heaven knows, they tried hard enough. But they did leave one legacy, for the first beans to be used are believed to have been captured from the Turkish camp after the second siege was lifted. The old-fashioned coffeehouse is not so common in the capital now; you are more likely to find one of them in Graz, Salzburg or Innsbruck. But you will still find a few as you wander round the streets of the Inner City. Don't be shy of walking in, ordering a mokka and sitting quietly to enjoy the coming and going of the regulars.

Serendipity is very much a force in Vienna. One of the most unexpected and delightful sights is that to be seen on a bright day in late winter, when the touch of frost is still in the air, but the sun holds a promise of warmth. Then it is in, say, the grounds of the Belvedere, that you will see elderly Viennese, men and women, standing in the shelter of the palace wall, dressed in their sober clothes, with their faces to the sun, enjoying the respite from the winter's chill. Another is to see the troops of schoolchildren, brought from other parts of Austria to learn more of their nation's great heritage, weaving their way in orderly but excited lines through subways, museums and squares. It is a kind of microcosm of the way their mothers and fathers behave, for, though the Austrians are a formal, tidy, orderly people, they manage still to get a great deal of fun out of life.

EXPLORING VIENNA

Splendors of the Past

by
RICHARD MOORE

Vienna (Wien) is a triple capital. It is the capital of the Federal Republic of Austria and at the same time the capital city of two of the nine federal states that go to make up the country, Lower Austria and Vienna itself. Once the heart of an empire that reached across most of the known world, Vienna is now the chief city of a comparatively small nation and has a population of 1,580,600.

A glance at the map will show you that, though Vienna was once placed centrally in the heart of the Austro-Hungarian territories, since the modern partition of Eastern Europe it is positioned in the extreme eastern tip of present day Austria. In fact it is less than 50 miles from the Iron Curtain and is actually further east than Prague. Vienna's geographical position and rich history both greatly influence what the visitor to the city sees and feels, however subconsciously.

Romans and Huns

Vienna came into being at the point where two main routes of trade and tribal migration crossed. One of these highways was the Danube, a certain means of passage through an uncertain landscape, the other was the route from the Baltic down to the Adriatic. Its position sets it as a meeting ground, a place of parley between the lands to the west and the more oriental lands to the east. In fact the East can almost be said to begin at Vienna.

Where people had lived since the Stone Age there grew up a Celtic settlement, called Vindomina which, in turn, gave way to a Roman garrison, Vindobona. These early "towns" were sited on the little plateau roughly in the angle formed by the Graben and Rotenturmstrasse today. This area was raised above what is now the Danube Canal, though in those days it was a main turbulent branch of the Danube. In the first centuries of the Christian era, the Romans planted vines and created a focus for their activities on this far rim of their empire.

After the Romans had pulled back to defend their heartland, the region became the prey of various Germanic tribes. It was in Vindobona that the *Nibelungenlied* sets the wedding of Etzel (Attila) and Kriemhild, festivities that lasted for seventeen days with a crowd of guests so great that they could not all be lodged in the city. Which was hardly surprising, for in those days, only a century or so after the Romans had left, the place must have been just a ruined shell of its former self.

Babenbergs and Habsburgs

Tradition has it that Charlemagne visited the city at the end of the 8th century, a fairly safe bet, since he seems to have popped up all over Europe. The history of this period is a trifle unfocussed and possibly includes the reign of a character called Samo, a mysterious Frankish merchant with twelve wives and forty-seven children. But the picture clears with the arrival of the Babenbergs. Margrave Leopold III became Lord of Vienna in 1135, and the town was designated for the first time in documents as *civitas,* a city, in 1137. However, it was only under the first Duke, Heinrich Jasomirgott, that Vienna became the Austrian capital.

The Babenbergs were, by and large, a civilized clan, especially Leopold VI (1194–1230), under whom the Babenberg court in Vienna became a culturally brilliant center. The city expanded and, with Leopold the Glorious at the helm, defensive walls were finally fixed at the point where they would stay until they were demolished by Franz Josef in 1857.

If the Babenbergs began the expansion of Vienna, it was left to their successors, the Habsburgs, who took formal possession in 1278, to transform it over the next six and a half centuries into one of the great cities of the world. The history of the Habsburg dynasty and the history of Vienna became inextricably intertwined, and, as we explore the city, evidence of this interdependence will constantly appear. Not that, in the earlier days of the Habsburg dynasty, Vienna was the only city to have eminence; others, Graz, Linz and Innsbruck for example, even Prague, came to the fore from time to time, but in the end it was Vienna that won out.

To symbolize briefly the next few centuries—Vienna was afflicted with two great scourges, the Turks and the Plague. They were both deadly and both, also, were the cause of some of Vienna's greatest monuments, built in redemption of vows made in the direst moment of danger.

With the defeat of the Turks, who had kept Vienna behind her protecting, encircling walls, the city was able to expand, and after centuries of confinement within medieval boundaries, was able to build in spreading safety.

This was the supreme period of baroque Vienna, the years when the major buildings of the Hofburg, the Karlskirche (plague-inspired), the palaces of Schönbrunn and the Belvedere all appeared, along with many hardly lesser gems. With that strange promptness that often marks important periods in human affairs, native artists and architects, equipped to realize contemporary needs, were suddenly to hand. As if out of thin air Fischer von Erlach and Hildebrandt, Rottmayr, Troger and Daniel Gran materialized to embody the imperial spirit of an upsurging age in that singularly ebullient style, the baroque. What forces were behind the sudden arrival of a totally indigenous, artistic powerhouse, capable not only of conceiving such huge works of art, but of successfully carrying them out, is one of those puzzles that will remain unanswered. But it is very clear that the challenge to recreate on Austrian soil such imperial concepts as Versailles and to provide settings fit for the triumphal Habsburgs, fuelled the inspiration of those artists chosen for the task.

The baroque mold into which Vienna was cast, superseding the Gothic, is still very obvious as you walk around the Inner City, but subsequent ages also left their impression, especially the middle 1800s. It was in 1857 that the young Emperor Franz Josef commanded that the old circle of fortifications which had for so long acted as corset to the city, should be torn down; an act that gave the signal for the great surge of construction along the Ring. It was a really remarkable experiment in town planning, in many ways even more remarkable than the efforts of Baron Haussmann at exactly the same time in Paris. In a flurry of archeological enthusiasm and technical skill, buildings modeled on ancient Greece, Renaissance Italy and Gothic France began to rise along the new wide boulevards.

At the end of the 19th century another artistic wave broke over Vienna. Otto Wagner's buildings marked the city with the spirit of a new age. The Post Office Savings Bank on Georg Coch-Platz (of all prosaic names for a great building this one has to win a prize) is one of his finest, while the Secession building (Friedrichstrasse 12), designed by Joseph Olbrich with doors by Klimt, carried modernity a stage further with those touches of fantasy that characterize Jugendstil, the Austrian version of *art nouveau*.

Exploring Vienna

Before setting off around the city, a few general points. It is a good idea to plan your route for the day. Opening times of the major museums and other buildings you may wish to see are very variable, some open for a very short time only. The Prunksaal, for example, the main hall of the National Library, which is one of the glories of Vienna and indeed of the world, is open only from 11 to 12 in the morning from October to May, though during the rest of the year it is open from 10 to 4. Arriving at a museum you particularly wanted to see and finding that it shut half an hour before is intensely irritating, so it is wise to check up in advance. Among their many helpful pamphlets the Vienna Tourist Board have one giving the latest times when "Kultur" can be imbibed. We give some of the opening times in this book, but it is always as well to make sure they haven't changed.

Another extremely useful Tourist Board publication is called *Introducing Vienna,* which currently costs 15 schillings. To explain. All the major buildings in the city have been equipped with small metal shields on their façades, shields which are decorated with flags in summer and which give basic information in German about the building. *Introducing Vienna* is a catalog of these shields, in English, keyed to the number in a circle which is on all the shields. This excellent system has, in fact, turned Vienna into a wonderfully captioned art gallery.

Don't forget during your explorations that there are hundreds of cafés around the city which are ideal for rest, recuperation and the comfortable study of your guidebook. A half hour spent over an icecream or a coffee will set you up for further forays and give you a breath of genuine Viennese life at the same time.

One last tip. Carry a lot of 10 schilling pieces with you. In most of the important churches and in many other buildings around town there are coin-operated tape machines that give you a commentary on the main points of interest in English and several other languages; all you have to do is press the right button. The other reason for carrying 10 schilling coins is that the entry fee to museums and galleries is either 10 or 20 schillings and it's handy to have them ready. You are going to be surprised at how many 10 schilling coins you can get through!

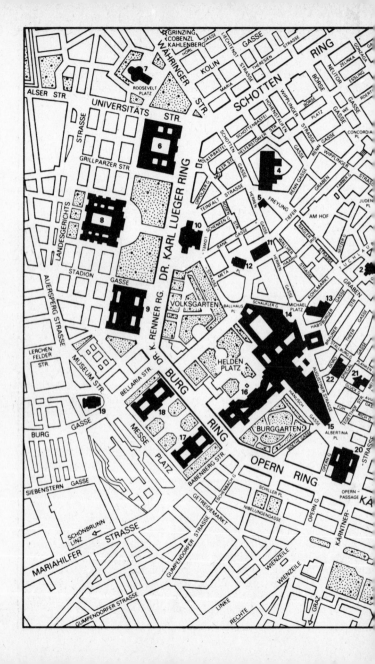

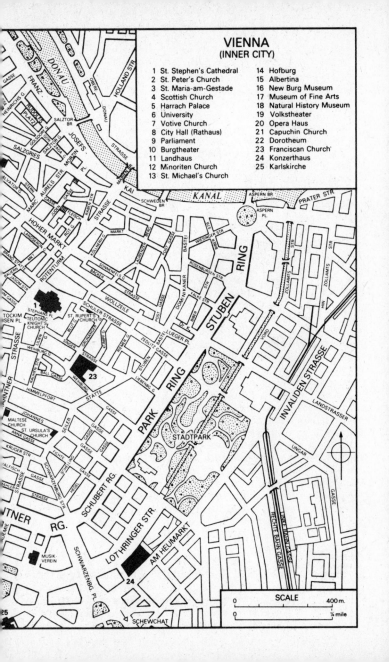

VIENNA
(INNER CITY)

1 St. Stephen's Cathedral	14 Hofburg
2 St. Peter's Church	15 Albertina
3 St. Maria-am-Gestade	16 New Burg Museum
4 Scottish Church	17 Museum of Fine Arts
5 Harrach Palace	18 Natural History Museum
6 University	19 Volkstheater
7 Votive Church	20 Opera Haus
8 City Hall (Rathaus)	21 Capuchin Church
9 Parliament	22 Dorotheum
10 Burgtheater	23 Franciscan Church
11 Landhaus	24 Konzerthaus
12 Minoriten Church	25 Karlskirche
13 St. Michael's Church	

SCALE

0   400 m.

0   ¼ mile

The Opera

As good a place as any to start exploring the city is at the Opern-Passage, a large subterranean crossing under the Ring just by the Opera that leads to the vast subway station extending as far as the Karlsplatz. Here you will find the most convenient office of the City Tourist Information, and here you can stock up with the pamphlets mentioned above, as well as maps and all the information you will need as to "What's On."

Above ground you will find the Opera House itself. It is a focus for Viennese life, and one of the chief symbols of resurgence after the cataclysm of World War II. The building was originally constructed in the middle of the 19th century, its first season being launched with a performance of Mozart's *Don Giovanni*. During the last war it was almost totally destroyed, but the Viennese made it one of their first priorities when the hostilities ceased to rebuild their beloved Opera, restoring the auditorium, but incorporating many up-to-the-minute technical improvements in the stage region. The theater was reopened in November, 1955 and this time the chosen work was that great "resurrection" opera by another of Vienna's musical pantheon, Beethoven's *Fidelio*.

From September through June there are guided tours of the building every afternoon; five times daily in July and August. The auditorium is plain when compared with the red and gold eruptions of London's Covent Garden or some of the Italian opera houses, but it has an elegant individuality which shows to best advantage when the stage and auditorium together are turned into a ballroom for the great Opera Ball. The performances are sumptuous, with a lavish buffet in the intermissions and stately patrols through the fine long halls. If you secure a ticket you would be well advised to go sober-suited.

Grouped around the Opera are several famous haunts, the Hotel Bristol, the Café Mozart and most renowned, Sacher's. Sacher's is firmly ensconced in Viennese legend and, of course, the home of the celebrated chocolate cake, the Sachertorte, about which there raged a famous law suit. When you cross the road behind the Opera to reach Kärntnerstrasse, you will be introduced to one of the basic facts of Viennese life. One does not jaywalk. You will see throngs of people patiently waiting at pedestrian crossings for the lights to change, even when the street is totally and completely clear of traffic, with apparently nothing in sight as far as the Wienerwald.

Kärntnerstrasse

Stretching ahead from the back righthand corner of the Opera is Kärntnerstrasse and the beginning of a pedestrian precinct that runs through the heart of Vienna's Inner City shopping area. It has openair cafés down the middle in summer and is generally attractive to wander down and to window shop. It is hotly disputed if the introduction of this pedestrian mall has changed one of Europe's smartest shopping streets for the better.

A little way down on the right, modestly tucked between shops, is the plain façade of the Malteserkirche, Church of the Knights of Malta, one of the few Orders remaining from the days of the Crusades. The interior is Gothic and some 600 years old, its plain walls decorated with plaques bearing the arms of the Grand Masters of the Order. The present Order is recognized diplomatically in about 40 countries, it numbers some 3,000 members around the world and the present Grand Master is, technically at least, a Head of State. It is, in fact, one of the biggest and one of the least known charitable organizations in the world today.

One of the delights of wandering around Vienna is to be able to compare the architecture and atmosphere of the city's many churches. Around a dozen will appear in the following pages and that in no way exhausts the possibilities. It is interesting to trace the changing styles over the centuries from the simple, almost severe interiors of churches such as this one, to the enormously elaborate baroque decorations of those built (or at least ornamented) in the early 18th century.

The Imperial Vault

A few yards further on, on the left hand side of Kärntnerstrasse, is a short turning that leads directly into the Neuer Markt. On the left of this square, opposite, is the Kapuzinerkirche (Church of the Capuchins), again at least 600 years old. The façade has been restored to its original 17th-century design, while the simple white interior sets off the warm browns of the marquetry work behind the high and side altars.

Below this church lie the bodies of the imperial house of Austria in the Kaisergruft, the Imperial Vault. Perhaps this is the wrong way to approach the Habsburgs in Vienna for the first time, starting with their tombs, but it does give you a chance to get their names in sequence as they lie in their serried ranks, their coffers ranging from the simplest through positive explosions of funerary conceit with decorations of skulls and morbid symbols to the lovely and distinguished tomb of Maria Theresa and her husband, designed while the couple still lived. To pass by these long lines of imperial dead is to take a short journey through history and art, and impresses one with a sense of exactly how the Habsburg centuries unfolded.

The Capuchin monks guide the groups of visitors among the tombs of 138 Habsburgs, from Ferdinand II in 1633 to Franz Josef in 1916, and of the Countess Fuchs. A well-deserved honor for this dearly-loved surrogate mother to the children of Maria Theresa, having been the

Empress's own governess to begin with. Only one coffin was ever taken away. In 1940, after Germany defeated France, the remains of the Duke of Reichstadt, the son of Napoleon and Marie Louise, were transferred to Les Invalides in Paris upon the personal order of Adolf Hitler, who was hoping to appease the French with the gesture.

In the center of the Neuer Markt is the baroque Donner Brunnen, the Providence Fountain, the work of Georg Raphael Donner, one of the leading 18th-century artists of Vienna. The original lead figures are in the Baroque Museum in the Lower Belvedere—and, one has to admit, look better there than the copies do here. Providence stands in the middle and the four figures at the corners represent four Austrian rivers, the Traun, Enns, Ybbs and March. These four figures are among Donner's most attractive works; the poise of the young man with the trident, leaning over the basin, is particularly lifelike.

The narrow sidestreets to the right of Kärntnerstrasse contain a wealth of baroque palaces and houses including (back, before the Malteserkirche) the 17th-century Annakirche decorated by Daniel Gran; the Kremsmunster Court in Annagasse; the baroque wing of the Hofkammerarchiv (Household Records Office) which backs on to the simpler 19th-century wing in the Johannesgasse, next to the 17th-century Ursulinenkirche. The Ministry of Finance's offices are housed in a masterpiece of the baroque, Prince Eugene of Savoy's Winterpalace, designed by Fischer von Erlach—the staircase, with sculptures by Giovanni Guiliani, is breathtaking—and extended by Lukas von Hildebrant, who likewise inspired the former Monastery Zur Himmelpforte (At the Gate of Heaven) after which the street is named.

Weihburggasse leads past the hotel Kaiserin Elisabeth, where many famous people have stayed over the decades, Wagner and Liszt among them. On the other side of the road are two famous restaurants you might wish to return to one evening, the Three Hussars and, not quite so fancy but with loads of atmosphere, the White Chimney Sweep, and also an excellent British Bookshop where you can stock up on reading material (and don't be put off by the closed door, it's almost certainly open for business).

Franziskanerplatz is a charming, small square, with a fountain topped off by an exceptionally urbane Moses in the middle. To one side is the former residence of Countess Fuchs, governess of Maria Theresa. It has been restored by the artist Leherb. On the façade of the Gothic-Renaissance Franziskanerkirche (Franciscan Church) is a statue of St. Jerome, lion in attendance and golden cardinal's hat on his head. The interior of this church is a cheerful one, with a most dramatically conceived backing to the altar, containing a painting of *The Immaculate Conception* by Rottmayr.

Kärntnerstrasse opens into Stephansplatz at Stock-im-Eisen (Trunk-in-Iron), a treetrunk into which every 16th-century apprentice black-smith drove a nail before leaving Vienna.

St. Stephen's Cathedral

Stephansdom (St. Stephen's Cathedral) is the focus for the pride of the Viennese in their city. It shared with the Opera and some other major buildings the fate of having been very heavily damaged in World War II, and of having risen from the fires of destruction like a phoenix. And like the phoenix, it is a symbol of regeneration.

Now that the work on the subway is finished—in this part of the city at least—it is possible to prowl around the cathedral to your heart's content, without being sent flying by raucous traffic. It sits now in the middle of a wide piazza, the space round it seeming larger than it actually is. To one side of the great building, close to where Kärntnerstrasse meets the square, you will see the outlines of two buildings superimposed on each other in colored stone on the paving. Two chapels used to stand here, one dedicated to Mary Magdalene and the other to St. Virgilius. The deep delving for the subway, which went right up to the foundations of the cathedral, revealed not only some Roman remains and lots of bones, for the area had once been a graveyard, but also the Virgilkappelle almost complete, as it had been when encased in the crypt of the Maria Magdalena Kappelle. It is now cocooned in the subway ticket hall below Stephansplatz and can be visited. It is a severe vaulted chamber which seems like part of the catacombs. As you go in there is a small collection of pottery from different periods found around the city during various excavations. If the chapel is closed, you can look down into it through a large window in the ticket hall.

A first St. Stephen's was built by Duke Heinrich Jasomirgott in 1147 and, following a fire, replaced by a Romanesque basilica during the reign of King Ottocar of Bohemia.

The Great West Front thus dates from the late 13th century, with the soaring Riesentor (Giant Doorway) flanked by two small towers (Heidentürme) on either side. There are a lot of attractive details in the carving here, Samson wrenching open the lion's jaws, a griffin, and all sorts of mythical beasts.

Continuing round to the left, you will pass by the unfinished north tower—unfinished, that is, when compared with its brother on the south side. It was decided not to rival the sky-piercing south spire and to leave the north tower a mere stump, called the Adlerturm. Inside is one of Vienna's traditional treasures, Die Pummerin, the Boomer; a huge bell weighing around 22 tons and measuring 10 feet across. The original Boomer was cast in 1711 from cannon captured from the Turks. In the south tower until 1945, it crashed down into the nave during a fire and

ST. STEPHEN'S CATHEDRAL

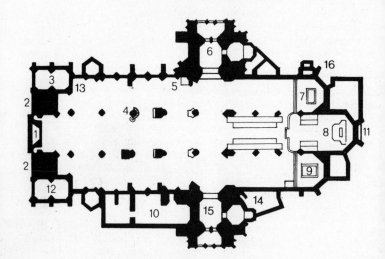

1 Riesentor
2 Heidentürme
3 Chapel of the Cross
4 Pulpit by Anton Pilgram
5 Lift to Pummerin and Entrance to Catacombs
6 Adlerturm (North Tower)
7 Wiener Neustadt Altar
8 Baroque High Altar
9 Tomb of Frederick III
10 New Sacristy
11 "Our Lord of the Toothache"
12 Chapel of Elgius
13 Altar Canopy by Hans Puchspaum
14 Sexton's House (Entrance to Alte Steffl)
15 Alte Steffl (Belfry)

was replaced in 1952, in the north tower. The new Boomer was carried in solemn procession from St. Florian in Upper Austria, where it had been cast as part of Upper Austria's contribution to the rebuilding and refurnishing of St. Stephen's. You can visit the bell by an elevator.

The northwest door is another masterpiece of medieval work. As it used to be the women's entrance to the cathedral (the southwest door was for men only) it features mainly female saints and incidents from the life of the Virgin.

Next on the circumambulation comes the openair pulpit named after the monk Capistranus who, in 1450, preached from it to rouse the people of the city to a crusade against the Turks. The elaborate group above the simple pulpit was added in 1737 and shows the saint (he was canonized in 1690) spearing a symbolic Turk to a flourish of flags and cherubs. Close by this spot the body of Mozart rested briefly in 1791 on the way to his burial. He died not far away in a house on Rauhensteingasse (Number 8, although the original house is no longer there).

Further round the east side of the cathedral is the torso of the Man of Sorrows which is irreverently known as *Our Lord of the Toothache*, because of its agonized expression. Nearby are more carvings, especially a 1502 scene of the events on the Mount of Olives.

You are now at the base of Alte Steffl, Old Steve, the dominating feature of the Vienna skyline. It is 450 feet high and was built between 1359 and 1433. If you feel fit enough, you can climb the 345 steps to take advantage of the stupendous view from the top of the tower section, not of the spire itself, of course. From that vantage point you can see out over the city to the rising slopes of the Wienerwald.

To the right of the southwest door stands the statue of Duke Rudolf IV, who ordered the Gothic enlargement of the cathedral, holding a model of the building in his right hand. Both he and his wife, Katharine, who balances him on the other side of the door, are attended by heralds carrying their coats of arms. The arch continues upwards with statues of saints, while four scenes from the life of St. Paul fill in the tympanum.

Inside the cathedral there are many easily identifiable things to see and a great deal of atmosphere to absorb. The fabric was extensively rebuilt after the terrible damage of 1945 when the cathedral was caught in the crossfire of the two locked armies, and suffered not only gunfire but blockbusters and incendiary bombs into the bargain. It is difficult now, sitting quietly, drinking in the shadowed peace, to tell what was original and what parts of the walls and vaulting were reconstructed. One of the things that has helped towards this merging of the new with the old is that many of the treasures of medieval carving were rescued. Among these is the pulpit sculptured by Anton Pilgram between 1510 and 1515, with the vivid heads of the early fathers, Augustine, Gregory, Jerome and Ambrose, and with Pilgram's own carved face peering out from behind a shutter under the stairs. All the way up the intricate balustrade are delightful animals symbolizing sins.

There is another self-portrait bust of Pilgram under the organ support, like a huge bracket, on the wall of the north aisle. This one dates from the same time as the pulpit (1513) and is a masterpiece of early portraiture, akin to the work of Dürer.

The Apostelchor (Apostles' Choir), the south choir, contains the tomb of Frederick III, another masterpiece, this time the work of Nikolaus of Leyden who took 45 years to complete it, from 1467 to 1513. With carvings representing Good and Evil (protective spirits and animals) all round, the monumental marble block on top depicts the emperor in his coronation robes.

The Marienchor (Virgin's Choir) contains the tomb of Rudolph IV, the founder of both the cathedral and of Vienna University whose small statue was on the southwest door. Apart from some lovely medieval figures on the wall here, the thing that draws the eye is the Wiener Neustadt altar which dates from 1447. A riot of wood carving, gilt and color, it was brought to St. Stephen's from the Cistercian Monastery of Wiener Neudstadt in 1884. It represents the three figures of the Virgin and the saints Barbara and Catherine, with the Coronation of the Virgin above and scenes from her life in the wings. Resting on the top of this reredos are the remains of an altarpiece dedicated to St. Andrew (c. 1420).

The central, early baroque, high altar (1647) is a turmoil of black marble with a picture of the cathedral's patron saint being stoned to death.

There is much else to see; the Catacombs, where the internal organs of the Habsburgs rest, all except their hearts (one has the impression that the Day of Resurrection is going to be an extremely busy one among the various crypts of Vienna); in the Catacombs can be seen the vestiges of the original basilica which was burned down in 1258, thus opening the way for the construction of the present building; the Eligius Chapel, to the right of the main entrance, with some exquisite sculpture, especially the statue of St. Ludmilla with her palm leaf, and a Virgin and child; and the Kreuzkappelle (Chapel of the Cross), on the other side of the west door, with a baroque wrought-iron grille and the tomb of Prince Eugene of Savoy.

On one of the pillars of the nave is a stone plaque telling of the various contributions of other parts of the country to the reconstruction. Each province took responsibility for a particular section of the work. There may be other church interiors which have more striking architectural features, but there are very few that represent the investment of more civic pride than does St. Stephen's.

Teutonic Knights and Mozart

Under the very shadow of the cathedral is the House of the Teutonic Knights, at Singerstrasse 7. The church of the Order is small and deceptively simple, dating back to the middle of the 14th century. It is a perfectly maintained, white interior with the arms of the past Masters on the walls.

Danzig lies in the Baltic area which was the realm of the Order in the Middle Ages—and realm is not too strong a word, for although the High Master of the Order was not actually a king, he was an unchallenged monarch. At the height of their power in the 14th century, the Teutonic Knights tried to build a Kingdom of God on earth in the lands bordering the Baltic—Danzig, East Prussia, Livonia and Estonia. With military dictatorship, theocracy and colonialism all working in a strange unison, the Knights forged a history that is too little known.

On the second floor above the church is the Treasury of the Order. Usually under the guardianship of a very frail old priest is a multifarious collection of items from the Order's long history. Coins and documents, especially a charter of Henry IV of England, with a fine seal; silver and gold table decorations of fine craftsmanship—a salt cellar decorated with "adders tongues", actually fossilized teeth which were supposed to detect poison in food; a stag with antlers and earrings of coral; a complicated astronomical clock, with jewels and filigree work; weapons and ceremonial dress; medieval paintings. From the window of the last room, the one that contains the paintings, there is a fine view down into the beautifully kept courtyard of the building.

Continue a little way down Singerstrasse, turn into Blutgasse and then right into Domgasse. Here, at Number 5, Mozart lived from 1784–87 and composed *The Marriage of Figaro*. It is now a commemorative museum. In the block formed by Domgasse, Blutgasse, Singerstrasse and Grünangergasse there is a grouping of old houses, called Fähnrichshof, that has been restored.

Much restoration of facades has taken place in Vienna. Many buildings have been washed and countless houses have had their frontages repainted. The face of old Vienna is much brighter than ever before.

A Basilisk and the Old University

The Viennese are essentially apartment dwellers, but apartment dwellers with a difference. Their apartments are inward looking. The whole of the old city consists of high buildings, some with very thick ancient walls, built round central courtyards. These "castles" close up tight in the evening as the citizens pull up their metaphorical drawbridges and prepare for the night's siege. In the daytime one can peek into some of these inner courtyards to see the great variety of architecture they represent, but remember that they are integral parts of private houses, so peek politely.

Across Stephansplatz from the North Tower of the cathedral is the 17th-century Archiepiscopal Palace which houses the very interesting Diocesan Museum. A small lane runs through the buildings here down to Wollzeile, named after the wool merchants and weavers who once lived and worked in the neighborhood.

The next street parallel to Wollzeile, Bäckerstrasse (starting at the small square, Am Lugeck, where there is a statue of the inventor of printing, Gutenberg) has many such houses, Number 14 being especially interesting with a Renaissance courtyard, dating from the end of the 16th century. Keep your eye roving over the façades as you walk along; you will surprise all sorts of carving and interesting decorations.

Sonnenfelsgasse, the next down on the left, also has many lovely houses, especially Number 15, with a fine gateway. This is now the area of the University. The square, Dr. Ignaz-Seipel-Platz (also known as Universitätsplatz) is named after one of the first Chancellors of the Austrian Republic, who lived from 1876–1932 and was not only a politician but also a Catholic priest and expert on international law, an unusual combination. He was enormously influential in forming modern Austria and steered his country through the chaos of the 1920s.

The 1627 façade of the University Church of the Assumption (Jesuitenkirche) takes up one side of the narrow square. It was originally built in the early 17th century, but was given its present sumptuously ornate interior by the architect Andrea Pozzo between 1703 and 1705. An abbé, Pozzo was also a great fresco painter and he brought his talent to the ethereal ceilings here, as well as to the twisting columns and the dramatic altar with its high-flying crown.

Down one of the other sides of the square is the great Ceremonial Hall of the Old University (now called the Akademie der Wissenschaften—Academy of the Sciences) built in the 1750s by a French architect, Jean-Nicolas Jadot de Ville-Issey, a court architect to Maria Theresa. It is very much a neo-classical building and clearly the work of an artist working in the disciplines of French symmetry. The opposite side of the square is taken up by the Alte Universität, where the original University was housed, ruled by the Jesuits. This building is from 1623–27.

Curving round behind the University Church is Schönlaterngasse (Street of the Beautiful Lantern), once part of Vienna's medieval *Quartier Latin*. Number 7 is the Basiliskenhaus, one of the earliest houses in the area, parts of it dating from as early as 1212. In those days the house was a bakery and a basilisk, a small fire-breathing and very deadly type of dragon, was living in the well, poisoning the water and turning anyone who came near to stone. A young baker's apprentice, clearly well versed in the classical myths, managed to kill the unpleasant lodger by showing it a mirror and so turning it to stone, in its turn.

Just along from the Basilisk House is Alte Schmiede (The Old Smithy), a commercially run place containing a reconstruction of a medieval blacksmith's workshop, with a restaurant and art gallery.

On the other side of the Basilisk House is an arched gateway leading into the quiet close of the Heiligenkreuzerhof. This was once the city residence of the Cistercian monks from Heiligenkreuz (Holy Cross), which lies not so many miles from Vienna, close to Mayerling. Many of the great monastic foundations of the Middle Ages had their urban headquarters, in much the same way as the great families maintained a city palace so as to be near the corridors of power, and this was one such. The small, closed-in square, really a large courtyard, contains a baroque chapel of St. Bernard.

Schönlaterngasse leads to the main Post Office next to the church of the Dominicans, after whom a remaining bastion of the old fortifications is named. Adjoining Rotenturmstrasse is Fleischmarkt, once the center of the meat trade, the butcher's quarter, but also meeting place of the Greek merchants, a fact still commemorated in the names Griechengasse and Griechenbeisl (Greek Tavern), the latter an atmospheric old restaurant. Part of the ancient city defenses can be seen here at Number 9 (a 13th-century tower, best viewed from the courtyard of Number 7). Number 9 Fleischmarkt has an attractive sculpture of the Virgin on its façade.

St. Rupert and the Romans

Just above the point where Fleischmarkt intersects Rotenturmstrasse, lies Hohe Markt. Apart from the attractive clock with its moving figures, this square is notable as the place where you can see part of the Roman foundations that have been unearthed. In the basement of No. 3 there is a small museum, with sections of two Roman houses which were revealed during drainage work in 1948. Further excavations have made this quite an interesting place to visit, with the Roman central heating (hypocaust) and other remains, as well as excellent maps of the area.

Rotenturmstrasse slopes down from the cathedral to the Danube Canal at Franz Josefs Kai. "Kai" is the same word as "quay", and this was the stretch of the bank where, in the old days, the fishing boats and the merchants' vessels tied up. Turn left, and two blocks along you will come to the Church of St. Rupert (Ruprechtskirche) standing high above the embankment. On street level is the site of the hotel which, during World War II, was the Gestapo headquarters, demolished in postwar disgust.

St. Rupert's is an old church, parts being from the 11th century, but it was almost certainly built on the site of a gateway of Vindobona, and no doubt some of the Roman masonry was used in the first foundations, laid, so legend says, around 740. St. Rupert was the patron saint of the Danubian salt merchants, and you will notice the carved bucket that accompanies his statue outside the church. The building is often locked, indeed you may only get in by going to a service on Sunday. The nave and tower are pure, simple Romanesque, and the remainder Gothic. There are some attractive modern decorations, including some very contemporary windows in yellow and blue, which harmonize surprisingly well with the ancient stones.

This, then, is the heart of the Roman settlement. A little beyond St. Rupert's is another memory of those early days in the name of the street that runs up from Franz Josefs Kai—Marc Aurelstrasse, called after the Roman philosopher-emperor. If you walk up this sloping street (it has no particular points of interest) and along its continuation, Tuchlauben, and then turn right down Bognerstrasse, you will reach . . .

Am Hof

Am Hof is yet another impressive square. In the center stands the Mariensäule (Virgin's Column), erected originally in 1646 after the delivery of the city from the Swedes during the Thirty Years' War. That column was removed and the present one put up in 1667. Around the base are the figures of War, Hunger, Plague and Heresy, all very real dangers during so many of Vienna's long centuries.

Am Hof is so called from the fact that the Babenbergs had their palace (castle might be a better word) here, before the center of power was moved under the Habsburgs to the Hofburg. The site of this court was to one side of the square, where Number 7 now stands. It was, naturally, the scene of intriguing events in medieval times. Vienna was on the route to the Holy Land, and many crusaders, among them Barbarossa, stayed here. Walter von Vogelweide, the famous Minnesinger who features in Wagner's opera *Tannhäuser,* was a figure of the Babenberg court in the 1190s when it was a center for art and poetry.

On the opposite side of Am Hof is the Church of the Nine Choirs of Angels, the Kirche Am Hof. The façade is a wonderful example of the early baroque style, designed by Carlo Carlone in 1662. From the deep central balcony Pope Pius VI blessed the city in 1782 and, on August 6th, 1806 heralds proclaimed the end of the Holy Roman Empire of the German Nation. This façade, with its windows, statues and recessed wings, is more like the varied front of a palace than of a church. The interior seems simpler than it is, with its octagonal pillars, grey and white coloring and very high ceiling. The generally subdued effect provides a muted background for the paintings, and of these the finest is probably the ceiling fresco by Maulpertsch, in one of the side chapels to the left.

Back in the square, notice the attractive house, Number 38, painted in tones of ocher, a simple yet very pleasing façade. Number 83 has an interesting sculpture of the Virgin. In the corner of the square is a façade that is anything but simple, it is an ornate building which looks as if it started life as a triumphal arch and carried on from there. You will be surprised to find that it is the headquarters of the Fire Brigade but, to be fair, it was once the City Armory, was "baroqued" in the early 1730s and is surely the most unlikely fire house to be found anywhere.

In the tiny streets behind the church, Schulhof and Seitzergasse, you can see the Gothic walls of the choir. You will find a fine old restaurant, Stiedl's Gösser Bierklinik (Steindlgasse 4) nearby. We enjoy the way they cook game in season so much that we have never dared find out just what a "Beer Clinic" might be. Around the corner, at Schulhof 2, is the Uhrenmuseum (Clock Museum), containing over 3,000 timepieces of every description, from the 1440s to today. The prize exhibit is an astronomical clock of 1769 by Rutschmann.

Take Parisergasse into Judenplatz where there is a rather clumsy statue of the German dramatist Lessing. This was the medieval ghetto of Vienna and must have witnessed many scenes of human misery. The plight of the Jews in the days before the Enlightenment was not a happy one. In 1421 two hundred and ten were burned alive, and for the next two centuries Jews were constantly humiliated. It is a part of Viennese history that is remembered today with pain.

There are interesting houses here, in and around the Judenplatz. Number 4 is another Mozart House; at the corner of the square, on Number 12 Kurrentgasse, two pillars support a flying lion and a fish; Number 2 has an attractive Gothic bas relief; and Number 11, which continues through to become Wipplingerstrasse 7, is the former Bohemian Court Chancery, built by Johann Bernhard Fischer von Erlach from 1708 to 1714, though changed later. Walk around this building into Wipplingerstrasse and there you will see two really superb frontages facing each other across the street. The front of the Bohemian Chancellery is the original Fischer von Erlach one, with sculptures by Mattielli, and what sculptures they are! Across the road, its statues protected from the pigeons by nets, is the Alte Rathaus, the Old Town Hall. It had been the Guildhall for centuries before it received its lovely façade in 1699.

Go through one of the short, arched passages into the Alte Rathaus' central courtyard. Against one wall is the Andromeda Fountain, by Georg Raphael Donner. This is a gentle work of bas relief, with Andromeda (whom legend says was an Ethiope, though she certainly isn't in this version) and the dragon in the foreground, and with Perseus about to swoop down for the kill. The work is normally dated 1741, but since Donner died in the February of that year, it must almost certainly be placed a little earlier.

From another corner of the courtyard an archway leads to Salvatorgasse. Turn left and walk a short way along to the Church of Maria am Gestade.

St. Mary on the Banks (St. Maria am Gestade) is one of the finest Gothic churches in Vienna. It used to stand on the edge of the river, as

its name shows, but it is now quite a bit inland from the water. It was
built on Roman foundations and also on a 12th-century church, which
accounts for the rather strangely angled nature of the floor plan of the
present building. The church as it now stands is late 14th century though
restored after the damage caused during the Turkish sieges. The tower
is seven-sided and culminates in a lacey crown. Inside, the feeling of the
nave is pure unadulterated Gothic (it is worth comparing this church
with the mock-Gothic of the Votivkirche). In a small chapel to the right,
halfway up the nave, are two superb parts of a triptych by the Master
of Maria Stiegen (1460); they show the *Annunciation* and the *Coronation
of the Virgin* and are of a quality rarely seen in public outside the most
prestigious galleries. Also worth remarking are the figures high up
around the nave and some of the stained glass.

St. Peter's Church

Leading out of Stephansplatz is the Graben, another attractive shopping street and part of the pedestrian mall. The Pestsäule (Plague Column) shoots up from the middle of the Graben like a geyser of whipped
cream. It was erected between 1682 and 1693 to commemorate the
deliverance of Vienna from the Black Death which had raged in the city
in 1679. A huge number died and the Emperor Leopold I vowed this
memorial while the plague still held sway. Among the sculptors who
worked on the column was Johann Bernhard Fischer von Erlach whom
with his son, we will meet constantly around Vienna. It is worth sur-
mounting the overall effect of swirling upward movement to look more
closely at many of the excellently sculpted details. This is one of the most
exuberant baroque monuments anywhere (especially in its cleaned and
regilded state) and as such deserves close inspection.

Just past the column, on the right, is a short turning leading to Peter
skirche (St. Peter's Church). Mind the traffic; frustrated by not getting
into the Graben it's fairly fierce. St. Peter's was built at the very beginning of the 18th century, but the site had held several churches before
that. There is a panel on the outside showing the first Christian temple
in Vienna being founded by Charlemagne, a quite possible legend. True
or not, the site was long hallowed by the time the present structure was
begun. It was finished by the middle 1730s and so is exactly contemporary with the more imperial Karlskirche.

The main architect was Johann Lukas von Hildebrandt and the interi-
or is probably the best example of church baroque in Vienna, certainly
the most theatrical. The fresco on the dome is by Rottmayr but is a bit
difficult to see clearly unless the light is coming from the right angle. It
shows the *Coronation of the Virgin,* a favorite subject for ceilings as it
calls for lots of clouds and flying angels. The pulpit is an especially fine
one with a highly ornate canopy and opposite the pulpit is what can only
be described as a religious tableau. Its subject is the martyrdom of St
John Nepomuk, who was thrown into the River Moldau, and here, like

a scene on stage are the gold figures of the saint and his brutal attackers and the silver waters of the river, frozen as it pours under the bridge.

The decoration of the high altar with its double grove of soaring pillars and the *trompe l'oeil* above is especially remarkable. As you leave the church, notice the florid ornamentation of the organ and its gallery.

A turning on the left at the end of the Graben, Kohlmarkt, will lead you directly to Michaelerplatz and the Hofburg.

The Hofburg

The Michaelerplatz, the starting point for visiting the Hofburg is worth exploring on its own account. The Michaelerkirche (St. Michael's Church) takes up one side of the strangely shaped square. It is an amalgam of periods, from Romanesque and Gothic through baroque and neo-classical, but the chief effect is Gothic. The interior has some very old frescos and fine carvings. The floor of the nave is indented with tombstones and the high altar seems almost a baroque afterthought. Near the altar is the tomb of the great 18th-century poet, Pietro Metastasio, who lived in a house on the Michaelerplatz for about 40 years, dying there in 1782.

To the right side of the church, in the Michaeler Passage (go through the arch marked No. 6), is a 16th-century carving of the *Agony in the Garden,* with the Betrayal and Crucifixion shown simultaneously in the medieval manner.

Facing St. Michael's across the square is the flat green façade of the Loos House. The Café Griendsteidl, a famous literary haunt, used to stand here, much frequented by such writers as Schnitzler and the young Hofmannsthal. It was pulled down in 1910 to make way for the present building, the work of Adolf Loos and the cause of a storm of protest. The windows of Franz Josef's private apartments looked straight out on the new building and, staunch conservative as he was in his tastes, he actually went to law to try and get the "monstrosity" demolished; he called it "the house with no eyebrows". He lost the case. The building was a landmark in undecorated architecture.

Easily eclipsing the Loos House is the great entrance gateway to the Hofburg, the Michaelertor, and the façade on either side. It is flanked by two well-muscled fountains symbolizing imperial sea and land power. Passing through the triple arch is a main roadway with side walks on each side. Here, under the oval dome, are the entrances into the Imperial Apartments (on the left). These rooms are interesting to visit for the glimpses that they give into the lives and characters of the last Habsburgs, especially of Franz Josef and his wife. Her exercising equipment and other personal effects bear mute witness to the attractive woman who was stabbed by an assassin in Switzerland.

The Hofburg is like a nest of boxes, courtyards opening off courtyards and wings (trakts) spreading far and wide. A large part of it still houses the offices and conference rooms of the Austrian Government and cannot be visited by the public. This great complex was built at several periods and, rather than demolish existing buildings, they were partly adapted and swallowed in each new scheme.

Once through the first, covered courtyard, you are in the In der Burg, with its statue of Franz II. In the left wall is the gateway to the Schweizerhof, the original nucleus of the Hofburg. This gateway is a splendid one, built in 1552, as the inscription at the top says, at the direction of Ferdinand I. It is painted a reddish-brown, black and gold, and gives a fine Renaissance flourish to the façade. The disused moat runs on either hand. Through the Schweizertor lies the Schweizerhof's courtyard with the Hofburgkapelle in one corner. In this Court Chapel, from September to June, high mass is celebrated on Sundays and holidays by the Hofmusikkappelle, made up of the Vienna Boys' Choir, Opera singers and musicians from the Vienna Philharmonic Orchestra. Needless to say, it is a musical experience of the first order, but obtaining tickets is not easy so plan well in advance.

The Imperial Treasury

The Imperial Treasury, whose entrance is normally in this courtyard, is closed for major restoration and modernization until at least 1987. Exhibits not affected can in the meantime be viewed in the Neue Hofburg, while the most important pieces are to be displayed in the Museum of Fine Arts (Kunsthistorisches Museum) on Burgring 5. As we go to press the details of what parts of this great collection will be on view in the temporary quarters are uncertain. We will, therefore, describe some of the highlights in the hope that they, at least, will still be able to be seen.

Among the items of historic significance are a wealth of heraldic objects—tabards, those short tunics that heralds used to wear emblazoned with their masters' coats of arms; staves of office, borne by chamberlains and other officers of the court; huge keys, fit for the castle of a sleeping princess; hoods for falcons; in fact all the panoply of a vast and anciently organized court. The time span covered by the multitude of items, both sacred and secular, is impressive, too. From the Imperial Crown, encrusted with roughly shaped gems and thought to date from about 962, through to objects less than a century old, the collection includes treasures covering some thousand years.

The heart of the Treasury's riches is the Burgundian Treasure, and especially those parts of it connected with the Order of the Golden Fleece. This most romantic of medieval orders of chivalry (which is still in existence) passed into the hands of the Habsburgs when, by marriage, they became Dukes of Burgundy. The Burgundian Treasure encompasses robes, vestments, paintings and jewels and spans several centuries, but of all its evocative pieces the most striking are the church vestments. These form a full set for the celebration of mass; copes, altar cloths,

HOFBURG

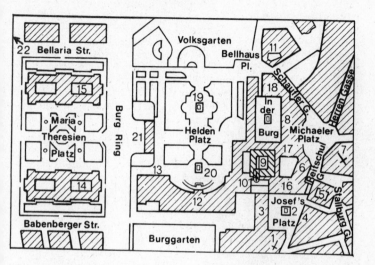

1 Augustinerkirche
2 Josefsplatz
3 National Library
4 Pallavicini Palace
5 Palace Stables
6 Riding School
7 Michaelerkirche
8 Imperial Apartments
9 Schweizerhof (entrance
   to Imperial Treasury)
10 Chapel
11 Federal Chancellery
12 Neue Hofburg (entrance to

Museums of Ephesus, Armor
and Musical Instruments)
13 Museum of Ethnology
14 Museum of Fine Arts
15 Museum of Natural History
16 Ballrooms
17 Michaelertrakt
18 Amelientrakt
19 Statue of Archduke Karl
20 Statue of Prince Eugene of
   Savoy
21 Burgtor Archway
22 To Volkstheater

dalmatics and so forth. They are covered with the most delicate and brilliant "needle paintings" of angels, scenes from the bible and saints. These embroideries date from the years before 1477 and rank with such works as the *Très Riches Heures* of the Duc de Berri as masterpieces of medieval creativity.

Here and there in the collection are various objects made of "unicorn" horn—actually narwhal horn. They are touching reminders of that mixture of faith and fantasy that characterized the Middle Ages, for not only was the horn considered a symbol of Christ, but the legend that a unicorn could only be captured by a virgin added to its rarity. One extremely long *ainkhürn,* nearly 8 feet, suggests that the virgin officiating at the hunt must have been of quite staggering purity.

Part of the collection's historical relics tells the sad story of the son of Napoleon and Marie Louise, the King of Rome. Among the more poignant items is the cradle presented by the City of Paris in 1811, no everyday cradle, but more of a cradle-throne from which the baby-king could hold court. It is a happy, elaborate piece of furniture, and not unlike a car from a very aristocratic carousel.

It is to be hoped that the temporary exhibitions will find room for a few of the large number of reliquaries, each one containing its fragment of bone, tooth, wood, hair, clothing or other relic of saint or martyr. These reliquaries are often of extremely rich workmanship, encasing their freight of holy detritus in objects of earthly beauty.

And while on the subject of relics, one of the most fascinating is the Holy Lance, supposedly the lance which pierced Jesus' side into which has been embedded a Holy Nail, wrenched from the Cross. Of great historical interest, too, is a saber, perhaps presented by one legendary hero, Haroun al Raschid, to another, Charlemagne; and a mantle from around 1133, embroidered with two heraldic lions, preying on a couple of prostrate camels, a superb relic of the Norman kings of Sicily.

The Neue Hofburg Museums

Return to In der Burg and turn left, go through the vaulted corridor and out into the openair again. This is the Heldenplatz, the Square of the Heroes. There was a plan, when the Hofburg was being extended in the 1880s, to build two huge sweeping wings, facing each other. Only the wing on the left was actually constructed, the Neue Hofburg. In the center of this great sweep stands the statue of Prince Eugene of Savoy on his rearing steed, while over to your right is the Archduke Karl. High above the Neue Hofburg are still the four flagpoles, empty now, that once flew the flags of the occupying powers after World War II. The far side of the Heldenplatz from where you entered is bounded by the Burgtor, dedicated now as a war memorial.

The flight of steps up to the center of the Neue Hofburg will lead you to three museums, the Collection of Weapons, the Ephesus Museum and the Collection of Musical Instruments.

The Ephesos (Ephesus) Museum is the newest of the three, and employs the most modern techniques for display. By a clever use of metal scaffolding poles the large sections of masonry rescued during the archeological digs at Ephesus have been placed in exact relation to each other, to give a sense of the scale and form of the original buildings. One of the main features of the exhibition is the remains of a large frieze (dating from the middle of the 2nd century AD) from the mausoleum of Lucius Verus, rather in the fashion of latterday Elgin Marbles. It tells of the conquest of the Parthians, confused in movement and without the elegance of its Greek original, but full of vivid details. Also on display are large relief maps, expertly made of wood, which, with other models, help the understanding of the terrain that yielded up these fine if fragmented sculptures.

Above the Ephesus Museum is the Collection of Musical Instruments, already mentioned in the *Prelude to Vienna* chapter. It is worth visiting, especially if you are interested in early keyboard instruments. On our last visit we had the delight of hearing Beethoven's piano being tuned, and its clear bell-like notes followed us round the galleries like Papageno's magic chimes. The instruments come in all shapes and sizes, a harp in the form of a harpooned fish, a table clavier with drawers and inkwells, one with a curved keyboard, another with the black and white notes reversed. But it is the associations that haunt many of the pianos which makes them so interesting. Mahler's piano, one belonging to Brahms, to Clara and Robert Schumann, Hadyn's . . . the list is endless. When Mozart called Vienna "Piano Land" he wasn't exaggerating.

The Collection of Weapons (Waffensammlung) is one of the best in the world. The ranks of suits of armor, contained in a maze of rooms, are accompanied by all manner of weapons—swords, crossbows, early guns and pistols, and all backed with fine Flemish tapestry. Many of the pieces are from the most renowned craftsmen of Spain, Italy and Germany. From the Middle Ages up to the 17th century, the possession of the latest fashion in arms and armor was comparable to owning the latest motor car today, with a similar balance between the utilitarian and the artistic. Here, too, are exotic items captured from the Turks.

Not infrequently, as you walk through the rooms, you will see a suit of armor that seems to embody a sense of menace, to have a brooding, threatening life. One can easily understand what a place of terror a medieval battlefield must have been.

There is a fourth museum in the Neue Hofburg, the Museum für Völkerkunde (Ethnographical Museum). The entrance to this one is at the other end of the Neue Hofburg, by the Ring. It is a very rich collection of pieces from all over the world, illuminating societies and cultures not only thousand of miles, but centuries apart. Among the treasures are the robes and head-dress of Montezuma, miracles of feather work. It gives yet another sidelight on the Habsburgs to realize into what remote corners of the world their empire reached.

The Riding School and the New Gallery

If you return to the Michaelerplatz, you can begin to explore the range of buildings that runs to the right, along Augustinerstrasse. The first one, tucked in to the right, is the Winter (or Spanish) Riding School. This is one of the few parts of Vienna known throughout the world, for the elegant white Lippizaner horses have become a kind of trademark for the city. For the last 300 years they have been perfecting their *haute école* riding demonstrations, to the sound of baroque music. The Winter Riding School was built between 1729 and 1735, and once again the architect was Fischer von Erlach.

The breed was started in 1580 and proved themselves in battle as well as in the complicated "dances" for which they are famous today. While it is easy to see them rehearsing, obtaining a ticket for full performances needs planning well in advance.

Across the road from the Riding School (entrance under the colonnade) is the Neue Galerie (New Gallery) in the Stallburg (Palace Stables), which is where the Lippizaners live. You will have to climb two long flights to reach the pictures as there is no elevator. The New Gallery collection is of paintings from the mid-1800s to just after World War I. The rooms are utterly plain, painted white, with the paintings displayed on simple colored screens. The general effect is to show the pictures to the very best advantage. The artists represented range from Millet and Corot, through Delacroix and Courbet (some fine landscapes) to Monet (a luminous garden), Renoir and van Gogh, and end with two fine canvasses by Munch. Along the way there are several German and Austrian contemporaries of these better-known artists, notably Böcklin (with a remarkably pneumatic *Sea Idyll*) and a group by Lovis Corinth, showing his strikingly bold style. There are rarely more than one or two pictures by any single painter, so that the total effect is of an easily assimilable collection of thoroughly representative works. A delight to wander through and highly recommended.

The National Library and the Augustine Church

The colonnade opens into the Josefsplatz, probably Vienna's loveliest square, with a statue of Josef II in the center. The entrance to the National Library, or rather to that part of the National Library that the public most frequently visits, is at the far left corner of the square. As we mentioned before, the Prunksaal (Grand Hall) of the Library is open for only an hour a day in winter (11–12) though from 10–4 in summer, so plan ahead.

This is one of the grandest baroque libraries in the world, in every sense a cathedral of books. It was created by Fischer von Erlach the younger from the designs of his father, while the frescos in the dome are the work of Daniel Gran and are superb examples of the difficult art of *trompe l'oeil*. The books around the central space under the dome were bought in 1738 from the library of Prince Eugene of Savoy, which contained thousands of priceless items. They are mainly in uniform red bindings. Behind the high ranks of shelves there are hidden bays that open like doors, increasing the shelf capacity tremendously, giving space for scholars to work and preserving the design of the interior. This Library has a higher proportion of manuscripts of textual or artistic importance than any comparable library outside the Vatican.

Opposite the National Library, across Josefsplatz, are the Pallavicini and Palffy Palaces, both built by great families who needed to be near the court. A little further along, at the corner of Augustinerstrasse and Lobkowitz Square, is the baroque Lobkowitz Palace, built at two periods, with the top floor being by Fischer von Erlach, senior, in 1709. It was here that Beethoven's *Eroica* was first performed.

Turning right out of Josefsplatz you will come to the Augustinerkirche (the Augustine Church) which nestles into the side of the Hofburg as befits a court parish church. It was built soon after 1330 and has a fairly severe interior following heavy restoration in the 1780s. The severity is relieved by two main features, the lovely organ case, painted in gold and white, and the tomb of the Archduchess Maria Christina, the favorite daughter of Maria Theresa. This eye-catching monument is the first thing you see, straight ahead, on entering the church. It is in the form of a white pyramid with mourning figures walking towards an engulfing black doorway. It was by the great Italian sculptor Canova, who first arrived in Vienna in 1797.

In the little crypt of the Chapel of St. George (1337) are the hearts of the Habsburgs in their urns. This is the third place of burial for the scattered remains of the imperial family. But the Augustine Church is not only a place of death, for it was the scene of some famous marriages over the centuries (Napoleon—by proxy—to Marie Louise, and Maria Theresa to Franz of Lothringen), and it is also the place to hear some of the most beautifully performed church music in Vienna.

The Albertina and the Burggarten

The farthest point of this triangular section of the Hofburg contains the Albertina (continue along Augustinerstrasse to the right), called after its founder, Duke Albert of Saxe-Teschen, husband of Maria Christina (she of the Canova tomb). At the risk of sounding lyrical, it must be said that the Albertina is one of the greatest collections of graphic art in the world. It contains well over a million items dating back to the 14th century. Not only does it house the founder's own collection, but a multitude of works collected by Prince Eugene together with many later additions. The fragility of many of the works makes them difficult to display and some are on view in exact replicas. But the Albertina frequently mounts exhibitions of originals which are always worth visiting. The most popular part of the collection are the works of Dürer, and especially his *Praying Hands*.

Up the steps by the entrance to the Albertina and round the corner of the ramp lies the Burggarten, an attractive small park which contains the only open-air statue of the Emperor Franz Josef in Vienna. It is somehow fitting that the man who held such a paternal position in the hearts of his people should have this quiet monument rather than a floridly monumental one. It stands in a small Japanese-style thicket. There are two other monuments in the Burggarten, one to Mozart, an 1896 conception of the composer, with too many cherubs and an over-romanticized statue; the other, large and impressive, to Goethe.

The Academy of Fine Arts and St. Charles's Church

Facing Goethe, across the Opernring, is Schiller. His statue stands in the center of the Schillerplatz, and behind him you will find the Akademie der Bildenden Künste (Academy of Painting and Fine Arts). This art school, founded in 1692, is the oldest art academy in the German-speaking countries. It was created the "Arts Authority for the Nation" in 1812, and was the responsibility of Metternich from 1818 to 1848. Hitler's anti-semitism may have been partly due to his inability to pass the entrance exams, a failure he attributed to the Jewish professors. The main galleries here are being redesigned, so the paintings are on view in temporary galleries on the second floor. While there are many interesting works to see, a *Conversation Piece* by de Hooch, a serene portrait by Rembrandt, eight views of Venice by Francesco Guardi, a Memling *Crucifixion*—the one masterpiece that dwarfs all the others is the *Last Judgement* by Hieronymus Bosch, one of his best works. It is a triptych which tells the story of the Fall of Man, from the beginning in the Garden of Eden on the left-hand panel, to the tortures of Hell on the right-hand one. The Judgement itself and the sins of mankind fill the central section. This is a painting which terrifies by the subconscious depths which it reveals in its intricately painted detail.

From the Academy, Nibelungenstrasse and Friedrichstrasse lead to Karlsplatz, a huge square above the main subway interchange where, outside Josef Olbrich's Sezession, Marc Anthony is seated in a bronze quadriga drawn by four lions. Dominating the Karlsplatz is one of

Vienna's greatest buildings, the Karlskirche (St. Charles's Church), dedicated to St. Charles Borromeo. It was begun in 1716 by Johan Bernhard Fischer von Erlach and completed after his death by his son, Joseph Emmanuel. The church was, from the first, a slightly disturbing mixture of styles and now with a large reflecting pool in which sits a very fine but totally inappropriate statue by Henry Moore, the effect is of even more artistic confusion, bordering on the bizarre.

The church was another outcome of the plague of 1713, being vowed by Karl VI, whose name, Charles, was thus linked with Charles Borromeo. The front of the church is flanked by two great columns, inspired by Trajan's column in Rome. They are out of keeping with the building as a whole, but were conceived with at least two functions; one was to carry scenes from the life of the patron saint, carved in imitation of Trajan's triumphs, and thus help to emphasize the Imperial nature of the building; and the other was to symbolize the Pillars of Hercules, suggesting the right of the Habsburgs to their Spanish dominions which the Emperor had been forced to renounce.

The interior of the church is based on a central oval shape, faced with chill marble. One is overwhelmingly conscious of a symmetrical and almost musical balance in the way the whole design interacts, leading the eye always upwards to the great dome, where Rottmayr's superb frescos open a new heaven.

The high altar is illuminated by stiff shafts of gilt sunlight and cloaked with a penumbra of plaster clouds; not surprisingly it bears a close affinity to the Plague Column. The altar pieces are by Prokop, Ricci and Gran. One of the many impressive features of the interior is the way that the light floods in, always controlled and serving to heighten the effect of the overall design.

Next to the church is the City Museum, with exhibits showing the history of Vienna. Above the subway, the two restored entrances to the city railway by Otto Wagner, once derided, but now considered attractive examples of Jungendstil.

Across Karlsplatz is the Musikverein, home of the Vienna Philharmonic. In the glittering Great Hall and the two smaller auditoria, some of the best concerts in Vienna are held. In its library are original scores by such composers as Beethoven, Brahms, Mozart and Schubert.

Herrengasse and the Scottish Church

From Michaelerplatz, in the opposite direction to Augustinerstrasse, Herrengasse is lined with interesting buildings, mainly government offices in former palaces. Number 5 is the early 18th-century Wilczek Palace, adjoining the Ministry of the Interior which is housed in a 16th-century palace restored in 1811. Number 9, the 17th-century Mollard-Clary Palace, contains the Museum of Lower Austria, which gives a good idea of the history of the province as well as of its natural history. The neo-Classical Landaus, Number 13, seat of the Provincial Government and Diet of Lower Austria incorporates an early 16th-century chapel by Anton Pilgram, the sculptor of St. Stephen's.

A left turn (Landhausgasse) leads to the Minoritenplatz, Vienna's quietest and most aristocratic square. The 14th-century Minoritenkirche (Church of the Minor Friars, now Mary of the Snow), damaged during both Turkish sieges, was restored in the Gothic manner in the late 18th century. The eight pillars inside divide the nearly square interior into three naves with a floor of plain tiles. There are frescos of heraldic devices on the walls. There is also a large and not entirely successful mosaic copy of Leonardo's *Last Supper* to one side, and a fragment of a fresco of St. Francis.

Among the surrounding palaces, number 1 is the Haus-, Hof- und Staats-archiv (Household, Court and States Archives), whose collection of documents is second only to the Vatican's. Some of this embarrassment of riches is displayed in the fireproof wing of the Bundeskanzleramt (Federal Chancellery), which now also houses the Ministry of Foreign Affairs. It was from this former Court Privy Chancellery, built by Lukas von Hildebrant on the Ballhausplatz, that the great imperial chancellors determined the fate of Europe. Minoritenplatz 3 is the 17th-century Dietrichstein Palace. Number 5, in the Starhemberg Palace, is the Ministry of Education. It was here that the defender of Vienna against the Turks in 1683 died. Most magnificent is the Liechtenstein Town Palace, which goes through to Bankgasse. This is another palace-lined street and is located between the Burgtheater and the Herrengasse. The Batthyany Palace, the Renaissance Portia Palace and Lukas von Hildebrandt's Kinsky Palace follow one another down it to the Schottenkirche, founded by Duke Jasomirgott in 1155. The Duke had the Babenberg drive to embellish his court and obviously thought that solid scholarship would help. The monks who gave the foundation its name were actually Irish, not Scottish in the modern use of the word for, in medieval Latin, Ireland was called *Scotia maior*. The church was frequently rebuilt and took its present shape only in the late 1880s. On one side of the various courtyards of the vast Schottenhof, last remodelled in the 1830s, is the Abbey whose Benedictine monks still teach in Austria's oldest High School.

The square beside the church is called Freyung, commemorating the church's right to grant asylum for three days. Opposite the church is the 17th-century Harrach Palace, and, beyond the Austria Fountain whose figures represent the Empire's main rivers, is the vast, imposing Schönborn Palace, a joint enterprise by Fischer von Erlach and Lukas von Hildebrant (now the Mexican Embassy). Higher up on the Schottengasse is the Melkstiftkeller, an atmospheric beer cellar.

Between Freyung and Herrengasse is a huge building known as the "Alte Börse". A stunningly beautiful shopping arcade links the two streets and inside they have restored the Cafe Central, favorite haunt of Lenin, T. Herzl and Karl Kraus, with a lovely staircase. This complex is worth a visit.

The Museum of Fine Arts

Across the Burgring from the Heldenplatz and Burgtor is the Maria-Theresien Platz, a formal garden where the focus is a statue of the Empress. It dates from 1880, assembling in one large group below the seated empress, her husband, eldest son, ministers, generals and others who made her reign glorious—Haydn and Mozart among them.

To the left is the Kunsthistorisches Museum (Museum of Fine Arts) and to the right the Naturhistorisches Museum (Museum of Natural History). If natural history interests you, you will be happy to wander in the seemingly endless rooms of stuffed animals on the first floor, like some vast immobile zoo, containing the whole of animal creation in glass cases. The ground floor has prehistoric relics, including many finds from the early Hallstatt civilization. Here, too, is the tiny bulbous *Venus of Willendorf,* some 20,000 years old, carved from limestone and thought to be one of the oldest pieces of sculpture in existence. We warn you, though, you'll have to search for it among much else on display. The Natural History Museum also has collections of meteorites and fossils.

Cross the geometrical gardens to reach the Museum of Fine Arts.

Downstairs are the collections of Egyptian, Greek and Roman art. They are well worth visiting as are the many medieval and Renaissance treasures—including Cellini's glorious gold salt cellar—but space forces us to examine just the painting collection on the first floor.

It is, perhaps, invidious to try to select from the incredible wealth of pictures in the Museum of Fine Arts any for special attention, but, on the other hand, a brief selection might help you to steer around the maze of galleries. The rooms are numbered in two sequences and round two courtyards running clockwise from I–VII (Roman numerals) and 1–13 ordinary numbers; anti-clockwise from IX–XV and 14–24. Room VIII links the two sequences. The rooms with the Roman numerals are the large ones; the smaller, outside rooms, have normal numbering. As you might expect, the large rooms have all the big-scale paintings—some of them striking, some merely pompous; the smaller rooms contain most of the jewel-like pictures, also many of the best portraits. If you suffer from museumitis or are short on time, do the sequences of smaller rooms first. If you have enough time to—take two bites at visiting the Kunsthistorisches Museum, we would heartily advise it.

Room I has the main collection of Titians in it, a fine cross-section of portraits and larger compositions; Room II contains Tintoretto's grave signors; Room V is illuminated by the daring lighting of Caravaggio, especially his *David with the head of Goliath;* Room VII will give you an unexpected view of Vienna, because it contains the 18th-century city-scapes by Bellotto, in which the baroque town comes alive; this room also has the famous canvas of *Napoleon crossing the Alps* by David; if you wish to keep your room sequence in order you will have to go back to Room I and then into the small Room 1. This room has works by Mantegna *(St. Sebastian)* and Giorgione; Room 2 has more Titians and some fine portraits by Lorenzo Lotto; Room 5 a pair of tiny Peruginos, *St. Jerome* and the *Baptism of Christ,* both gentle and reflective; Room 6 has a serene *Madonna* and a *Holy Family* by Raphael as well as a magnificent *Portrait of a Cardinal* by Sebastiano del Piombo; Rooms 7–9 contain treasures of paintings by Andrea del Sarto, Parmigianino and Corregio, Bronzino and Poussin; with Rooms 11 and 12 one is reminded just how this great collection was formed, for here are the portraits of the Habsburgs, many of them by Velazquez and famous from innumerable reproductions; Room 13 completes the sequence on this side with Canaletto and Guardi.

Room VIII is by itself between Rooms 1 and 14 (we apologize for the broken-backed system of continuity!). It contains some really lovely 15th-century works, mainly by Memling (especially an *Adam and Eve*), Rogier van der Weyden and their contemporaries. Apart from the trip-tyches by these two artists there is a fine *Baptism of Christ* by J. Patinir, an Antwerp painter noted for his fantastic scenery, and this is no exception with a blue landscape leading one's eye into the far distance. There is also a *Michaelsalter* by Gerard David. With Room X you enter the world of Pieter Brueghel the Elder, with its landscapes vividly changing with the seasons *(Winter, the Hunters)* and its throngs of animated peasants. Room XII has Van Dyck's urbane diplomatic portraits; Room XIII shows Rubens at his most monumentally mythical; Room XIV shows Rubens at his most monumentally religious; Room XV has one Rembrandt.

Room 14 (off Room IX) begins the last of the four sequences, but it is in Room 15 that the first fascinations lie on this side, for here are the two great portraits by Dürer, *Kleberger* and *Maximilian I,* both of them merciless in their psychological revelation. Rooms 16 and 17 contain work by Altdorfer and two Cranachs of great power; Room 18 shows seven detailed portraits by Hans Holbein of figures from the court of Henry VIII of England, and two excellent examples of the portraiture of Clouet; Room 19 has a group of landscapes, including a Brueghel, as well as the fantasies of Archimboldo; Room 22 has three highly con-vinced portraits by Frans Hals; and with Room 23 we come to the main Rembrandts, portraits of depth and vision, especially the self-portraits; Room 24 finishes the long, rewarding round with the *Painter and Model with trumpet,* by Vermeer.

The Ring

There are two ways of exploring the Ring. To walk along it all the way from where it begins by the Danube Canal, at Aspernplatz, to where it returns to the Canal after its curving flight. Or, and this is the way we recommend, to explore it whenever you happen to cross it on other missions. While it is a pleasant sequence of boulevards, the succession of rather pompous buildings can be a bit overpowering.

There are three points on the Ring we would suggest seeing by themselves. Firstly the Stadtpark, which can be added to your visit to the Karlskirche. It is a romantic park, once dedicated to health cures and now chiefly delightful for visiting an openair café or restaurant, listening to an orchestra playing Viennese music in summer, or looking at the statues of composers, dotted around. The most famous of these is, of course, Johann Strauss himself, fiddling away under the trees and ignoring the symphonic clicking of cameras.

The second stretch of the Ring is that which runs from Maria-Theresien Platz and the great museums along to Rooseveltplatz. This is the part of the Ring that was built up in the secure days of the 1870s and 1880s, where the Parliament Building, the City Hall (Rathaus), the Burgtheater and University all stand, mixtures of Greek revival, Roman and Gothic styles, with a fair measure of Renaissance to hold them together. It makes a pleasant walk, with the Rathauskeller or one of the openair cafés to refresh you *en route*.

At the end of the walk is the Votivkirche, built in 1856–79 to commemorate the escape of the young Franz Josef from the knife of a Hungarian assassin. The Emperor's brother, Maximilian, who died tragically in Mexico, pledged the Votivkirche in thanks. As is often the case with imitative architecture, its mock-Gothic looks tawdry and isn't helped by some truly dreadful modern stained glass. Continuing repairs to the crumbling standstone might prove financially as well as technically impossible.

On this side of town, at Fürstengasse 2, you can find the Palais Liechtenstein (this is the second one, the other is mentioned on page 122), which houses the Museum of Modern Art. The palace was built at the end of the 17th century and is a very large, attractive place, with well-kept grounds and some superb frescos based on the story of Hercules. The collections of modern works assembled in the network of rooms is in strong, sometimes violent, contrast to their faded elegance. As so often with museums of modern art, where time has not yet had a chance to winnow the wheat from the chaff, there is a lot of very forgetable stuff on display, but there are also many pieces that are magnificent. It is well worth while taking time to explore the maze of rooms, as some of the very best works are the most deftly hidden. Among the modern masters

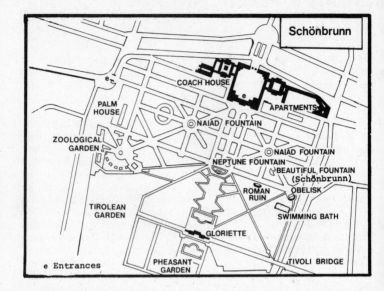

represented are Derain, Ernst, Leger, Magritte, Picasso, Lichtenstein, Warhol and many others.

Across the Danube Canal

On the other side of the Canal from the Inner City you will find two parks, the Augarten, once Imperial private gardens but opened to the public first in 1775. A part of the main Augarten Palace, built for the widow of Leopold I, is used by the famous Augarten Porcelain Factory (started in 1717), and another part as the home of the Vienna Boys' Choir, an integral part of the Hofmusikkapelle.

The other park is the Prater, the leisure grounds of Vienna, with the wheel (famous from *The Third Man*), a Planetarium, side-shows, some of the Vienna Fair grounds, a racetrack, golf course and so on. There are parts, such as Krieau, which are not recommended for idle strolling unless you happen to be an expert in judo.

On the far bank of Danube, beyond the Prater, is the Donauturm, the 826-foot TV tower, with rotating restaurant at 541 feet, and observation platform at 492 feet. Next to the Donaupark is UNO-City, a vast complex of highrises round the International Congress Center seating 1,600 in nine halls. Three UN organizations moved in 1979 into what Austria hopes will turn Vienna into the third most important center for the United Nations. The building costs of 8.5 billion Schilling seem somewhat disproportionate in comparison with the token rent of 1 Schilling a year, and it does not have very much to offer to the sightseer. It is really just a glorified office block, without the interesting features of, for example, the United Nations Building in New York.

The Belvedere and Schönbrunn

Where Kärtner and Schubert Ring meet, a large square embraces the Hochstrahlbrunnen, a fountain spurting a jet of water high in the air, illuminated at night, and the huge Russian War Memorial, whose proletarian realism has been guaranteed by the peace treaty with Russia —however dearly the Viennese would like to remove it, as it blocks out the lovely Schwarzenberg Palace, designed by Hildebrandt (outside) and both Fischer von Erlachs (inside). One wing is still occupied by the Schwarzenberg princes, the other is a luxury hotel. On the left is the Rennweg. Number 6 is the entrance to the Belvedere, the country palace built for Prince Eugene, which consists of two main buildings, one here at the foot of the hill and the other at the top—the Lower and Upper Belvedere—with wide formal gardens in between. The whole complex was masterminded by Hildebrandt and is considered to be one of the most splendid pieces of baroque architecture anywhere.

The Lower Belvedere contains the Museum of Austrian Baroque, and what better building to house it! This was the home of the Prince and the long sequence of lovely rooms now forms the perfect background for the works of art, many of which were created at the time the Belvedere was being built; paintings and sculptures by Daniel Gran, Maulpertsch, Kremser Schmidt, Troger and Georg Raphael Donner. Donner's original lead figures for the Providence Fountain are here. The State Treaty was signed in the Belvedere in 1955 and there is a huge painting of those who took part—it makes an amusing study.

The climb up through the gardens is rewarded by a fine view over Vienna from the terrace at the top. The Upper Belvedere was used by the Prince for balls and banquets, and is still used by the Government for such functions. But its main interest lies in the collection of paintings by 19th and 20th century Austrian artists, especially those of Hans Makart, Ego Schiele, Boeckl and Gustav Klimt. For those who have seen Klimt's work only in reproduction a surprise is in store, for the originals have a richness and incised patterning that gives them an almost three-dimensional quality. These more modern works are on the ground and top floors (with the Klimts and Schieles mostly at the top), while the middle floor contains a lot of mid-19th-century paintings that will, to a non-specialist, seem rather drab.

The University Botanic Gardens run parallel to the gardens of the Belvedere, while across the Gürtel can be found the Army Historical Museum and the Museum of 20th Century Art.

Schönbrunn is only a few minutes by subway from Karlsplatz, a little longer by tram up Mariahilferstrasse, main artery leading west, flanked by department stores. You could see the palace and its grounds in a morning, or spend a whole day wandering through the many delights it offers. It was the favorite residence of the Habsburgs from the time that it was built (1695–1749). Maria Theresa made it her main home, her daughter Marie Antoinette grew up here and carried her memories of Schönbrunn with her to France and to Versailles. Franz Josef was born and died here and preferred to live here above anywhere else. It was also the residence of the last Habsburg Emperor, Karl I, till 1918.

The main gates lead into a wide courtyard, the Ehrenhof (Parade Court), bordered by the palace and its wings. To the right is the Coach House, Wagenburg, where there is an outstanding collection of ceremonial state coaches, sleighs, hearses, fast private coaches, with the most splendid of all being the Imperial Coronation Coach.

Beside the Coach House is the rococo Schlosstheater (Palace Theater) now home of a drama school and where performances are sometimes given in summer.

Of the over 1,440 rooms in the palace, only about 45 can be visited, but those are of great richness and variety. Among the most interesting are: the apartments of Maria Theresa; the gold-and-white stuccoed Little Gallery and Great Gallery (also called the Gallery of Mirrors); the private apartments of Franz Josef and his wife, with the simple iron bedstead on which the Emperor died on November 21, 1916; the Great Ceremonial Hall; the Blue Salon, with its Chinese wallpaper; the pure rococo Million Room, so called because it cost a million florins to decorate it with valuable Persian miniatures framed in Chinese rosewood paneling; the Gobelin Salon, with the great Flemish tapestries; the Napoleon Room, which was his study during his two days stay here, and where the Duke of Reichstadt, his son, died at the age of 21 of tuberculosis.

Other rooms can be visited from time to time.

Behind the palace lies the large formal park, containing several fountains, including the one called Schöner Brunnen (Beautiful Fountain) which gave its name to the palace. Also in the gardens is one of the oldest zoos in Europe (founded in 1752) and probably the only baroque-style zoo anywhere.

On the rising ground at the other side of the park is the colonnaded hall, the Gloriette, surmounted by an Imperial Eagle. It was originally hoped to build the palace on this eminence, but it proved to be impractical. From here there is an extraordinary view across Schönbrunn and its grounds to the city beyond.

ARRIVING IN VIENNA By Plane You can change your money and reserve your hotel room at the airport. The airport bus takes you downtown to the City Air Terminal behind the Stadtpark, beside the Hilton Hotel, in about 30 minutes; the buses leave every 13 minutes. Fare—75 sch. There is now direct fast-train (S-Bahn) service from the airport (underground) to the Terminal at the Hilton. A taxi from the airport would be very expensive.

By Train You will end up at either *Westbahnhof* (West Station) if coming from Germany, Switzerland or western parts of Austria, or at *Südbahnhof* (South Station) if coming from southern parts of Austria or Italy. Both are new and have all sorts of facilities, including restaurant, café, food shops, money exchange, etc. In each of these two stations there is a Room Information Office *(Information-Zimmernachweis)*. Both will make room reservations (if rooms are available) as well as provide you with other information.

By Boat Freudenau Harbor near the Reichsbrücke on the main course of the Danube, is only a short taxi ride from the U Bahn station on the Praterstern; slightly longer to the city center (taxis wait at the arrival of the ship). Also several streetcar lines. During summer all the information needed can be obtained from the Vienna Tourist Association hostesses on incoming ships and at the landing stage.

HOTELS Vienna is divided into 23 districts, indicated on the basic postal code of 1000; the center two digits are changed—1st District (Inner City) is 1010, down to 23rd which is 1230. From Easter through October it is advisable to make reservations in advance, as the tourist season is extended each end by large international conventions. The room reservation offices listed under *Useful Addresses* are helpful in case of emergency.

Unless you are motorized, and particularly if you plan to spend only a short time in Vienna, you will probably want to stay in the Inner City (1010), at the center, within walking distance of the most important sights and museums, the best restaurants and nightclubs, the Opera and the concert halls and the most fashionable shops. Besides, the best way to enjoy the sights of Vienna is by walking and this is done more easily if the base is not too far away. The Inner City has hotels of all categories. Some of the numerous hostelries (largely in the medium and lower categories) in the Mariahilferstrasse-Westbahnhof (West Station) area are also within reasonable walking distance from at least a part of the Inner City, whereas from the others the center can easily be reached by a short streetcar ride.

If you are motorized, don't mind riding on the subway, streetcars and buses, or have enough cash to hire taxis and chauffeur-driven cars, you may want to stay in the green districts of Vienna, in some hotel in the Schönbrunn area or in a small pension located near the vineyards of Sievering, Grinzing, or Kahlenberg. During the Vienna Fair in September, you might have to move further afield to nearby towns such as **Tulln** (try *Zur Rossmühle*) or **Stockerau** *(Lenaustuben),* with hourly commuter trains to Vienna.

Following is our selection from about 250 hostelries available in Vienna. All listings are alphabetical and represent no particular order of preference. All rooms with baths or showers unless otherwise stated; color television in the two top categories.

DELUXE (L)

Ambassador, Neuer Markt 5 (tel. 527511). On the square with the famous Donner Fountain, flanked on the other side by Kärntnerstr., the world-famous, elegant shopping street in the heart of Vienna. A favorite of diplomats, it has a long tradition of catering to important personalities, including Theodore Roosevelt and Mark Twain. The red brocade walls in the suites and in the public rooms, including the restaurant, glitter from chandeliers. 103 airconditioned rooms at the lower price range in this category.

Bristol, Kärntnerring 1 (tel. 529552). Along from the Opera, one of the venerable Vienna hotels. Founded in 1894, it has preserved its inimitable personality—a fine blend of tradition, elegance and Viennese *savoir-faire.* 128 rooms, several plush suites; elegant restaurant and pleasantly comfortable bar.

Hilton, next to the City Air Terminal, 1030 (tel. 752652). Just beyond the Ring. 620 airconditioned rooms and 8 penthouse suites; one of the more attractive Hiltons. Finest food in *Prinz Eugen* restaurant, one of the best restaurants in the city and much frequented by the Viennese themselves; *Vindobona* wine cellar, bar, café, health club with sauna.

Imperial, Kärntnerring 16 (tel. 651765). Near the Opera. The almost 100-year-old palace of imperial fame and elegant appearance is the top hotel in the city. Old tradition and modern comfort are reflected in antique furnishings and up-to-date facilities. A large painting of the old Emperor Franz Josef presides over the palatial stairway. Visiting heads of state and other leading dignitaries stay here. All 160 rooms are spacious and have baths with heated floors. Elegant restaurant and café with Viennese music, cozy intimate bar.

Modul, Peter-Jordanstr. 78, 1190 (tel. 471584). In the Heurigen suburb, modern in green surroundings. There are 40 rooms and 3 apartments.

Palais Schwarzenberg, Schwarzenbergplatz 9 (tel. 784515). A small exclusive hotel in a wing of the baroque palace, still owned by Prince Schwarzenberg; 43 rooms with authentic period furnishings, most overlooking the garden. Uniquely quiet location off the very center of the city; large parking area in the Palace courtyard; excellent restaurant and bar.

Sacher, Philharmonikerstr. 4 (tel. 525575). Behind the Opera, filled with old tradition. Original oil paintings, sculptures and *objets d'art* decorate its halls and rooms. Its treasures of the old days include a tablecloth with embroidered signatures of most of the famous crowned and "decrowned" heads of state of seven decades. A portrait of the redoubtable Frau Sacher looks over the bar. Husband Eduard Sacher, a famous chef, left as his legacy the recipe for *Sachertorte,* the world-famous chocolate cake.

Vienna Intercontinental, Johannesgasse 28 (tel. 7505). Overlooking the City Park. 500 rooms, streamlined modern comfort, extensive convention facilities. Several restaurants and bars. 250-car underground garage.

FIRST-CLASS (1)

Amadeus, Wildpretmarkt 5 (tel. 638738). Near St. Stephen's. 29 rooms with refrigerator. Bed and breakfast.

Am Parkring, Parkring 12 (tel. 526524). 65 airconditioned rooms on 11th to 13th floor, overlooking the City Park.

Astoria, Kärntnerstr. 32 (tel. 526585). Entrance from Führichgasse. Old tradition with 100 modernized rooms, good restaurant.

De France, Schottenring 3 (tel. 343540). Near Votivkirche. 150 rooms (ask for quieter courtside rooms), French restaurant and bar.

Erzherzog Rainer, Wiedner Hauptstr. 27, 1040 (tel. 654646). Near Karlsplatz, 85 rooms, most with bath, fine restaurant; street-side rooms are noisy.

Europa, Neuer Markt 3 (tel. 521594). In heart of the city. The best of its 100 airconditioned rooms are in the corners of the building. Evening musical entertainment in the restaurant, and a really dry martini in the little bar upstairs; large café on the ground floor.

Grinzingerberg, Ettingshausengasse 10, 1190 (tel. 323051). In Grinzing; view of Vienna and Vienna Woods, 26 rooms and apartments, pool, sauna and free shuttle-bus to and from city.

Kaiserpark Schönbrunn, Grünbergstr. 11, 1120 (tel. 838610). 41 rooms.

König von Ungarn, Schulerstr. 10 (tel. 5265200). Near St. Stephen's. 33 rooms, maintains old traditions, newly restored.

Kummer, Mariahilferstr. 71, 1060 (tel. 573695). 108 rooms, 100 baths.

Mailbergerhof, Annagasse 7 (tel. 520641). In center of city. 35 rooms, bed and breakfast. An old house, with lovely arcaded courtyard.

Mate, 1170, Ottakringerstr (tel. 436133). 60 rooms, garage, indoor pool.

Novotel Wien West, Autobahnstation Auhof, 1140 (tel. 972542). 116 rooms.

Opernring, Opernring 11 (tel. 575518). Across from the Opera; 35 rooms, bed and breakfast; personal touch.

Parkhotel Schönbrunn, Hietzinger Hauptstr. 10, 1130 (tel. 822676). Next to Schönbrunn Palace, 356 rooms, most with bath, indoor pool, sauna, famed restaurant.

President, Wallgasse 23, 1060 (tel. 573636). 77 rooms with wallsafes.

Prinz Eugen, Wiedner Gürtel 14, 1040 (tel. 651741). Opposite South Station and near Belvedere Palace. 106 rooms, some with terrace and fine view.

Römischer Kaiser, Annagasse 16 (tel. 527751). Central. Romantic Hotel, 26 rooms in a baroque palace; bed and breakfast.

Royal, Singerstr. 3 (tel. 524631). Near Graben and St. Stephen's. 66 spacious rooms, on the top floor with terrace; some elegant suites.

MODERATE (2)

Albatros, Liechensteinstr. 89, 1090 (tel. 343508). Near US Embassy, 70 rooms, airconditioned, garage and indoor pool.

Alpha, Boltzmanng. 8 (tel. 311646). Next to US Embassy. 70 rooms, garage.

Am Stephansplatz, Stephansplatz 9 (tel. 635605). Across from St. Stephen's Cathedral. 66 rooms, majority with bath. Front rooms offer magnificent view of the cathedral.

Arabella, Auhofstr. 62, 1130 (tel. 827106). 30 rooms, bed and breakfast.

Austria, Wolfengasse 3 (tel. 526724). Near the main post office. 55 rooms, most with bath; bed and breakfast; in a quiet side street.

Franzenshof, Grosse Stadtgutg. 19, 1020 (tel. 242237). 43 rooms, 23 with bath.

Graben, Dorotheergasse 3 (tel. 521531). Just off Graben. 46 rooms, half with bath.

Kaiserin Elisabeth, Weihburggasse 3 (tel. 522626). Near St. Stephen's, an old hotel with 75 rooms, 58 baths, home atmosphere. Excellent value for money.

Kärtnerhof, Grashofgasse 4 (tel. 521923). Near main post office. 44 rooms, 32 baths; recommended as budget find.

Mariahilf, Mariahilferstr. 121B, 1060 (tel. 573605). 75 rooms, 15 baths.

Regina, Rooseveltplatz 16, 1090 (tel. 427681). Near University and next to Votivkirche. 127 rooms, most with baths; indoor and outdoor restaurants.

Ring Hotel, Am Gestade 1 (tel. 637701). In quiet corner of the Inner City, next to historic Maria am Gestade church. 25 small apartments, behind period-style façade.

Savoy, Lindengasse 12, 1070 (tel. 934646). 43 rooms.

Stefanie, Taborstr. 12, 1020 (tel. 242412). Across the Danube Canal. 150 rooms, most with bath.

Strudlhof, Pasteurgasse 1, 1090 (tel. 312522). Near US Embassy. 48 rooms, bed and breakfast.

Tigra, Tiefer Graben 14 (tel. 639641). Central. 45 rooms, bed and breakfast.

Tourotel, Kurbadstr. 8, 1100 (tel. 681631). 256 rooms, pool, cure facilities.

Viktoria, Eduard-Kleingasse 9, 1130 (tel. 822676). Not far from Schönbrunn Palace. 39 rooms, 13 baths; indoor pool.

Wandl, Petersplatz 9 (tel. 636317). Near Graben; 137 rooms, 95 baths; facing the baroque St. Peter's church.

Westbahn, Pelzgasse 1, 1150 (tel. 921480). 63 rooms, 27 showers.

Westminster, Harmoniegasse 5, 1090 (tel. 346604). Near US Embassy. 75 rooms, 60 baths.

Wimberger, Neubaugürtel 34, 1070 (tel. 937636). 110 rooms, 34 baths; well-known restaurant and café.

INEXPENSIVE (3)

Estate, Kleine Stadtgutg. 14, 1020 (tel. 241353). 40 rooms, 20 baths.

Gabriel, Landstrasser Hauptstr. 165, 1030 (tel. 726754). The only place in this category where all 31 rooms have showers.

Goldenes Einhorn, Am Hundsturm 5, 1050 (tel. 554755). 21 rooms, 4 showers. Old type of family-run *Gasthaus.*

Goldene Spinne, Linke Bahngasse 1A, 1030 (tel. 724486). Near city air terminal; 43 rooms, 13 baths.

Graf Stadion, Buchfeldgasse 5, 1080 (tel. 425284). Not far from Parliament. 47 rooms, 6 showers.

Kugel, Siebensterngasse 43, 1070 (tel. 933355). Near the Messepalast. 37 rooms, 26 showers.

Post, Fleischmarkt 24 (tel. 526687). Opposite the main post office. 105 rooms, 55 baths.

Schweiger, Schikanedergasse 4, 1040 (tel. 564215). In a quiet side street. 53 rooms, 12 showers.

Schweizerhof, Bauernmarkt 22 (tel. 631931). Central. 55 rooms, 45 showers.

Terminus, Fillgradergasse 4, 1060 (tel. 577386). Near Academy of Fine Arts and the Opera. 51 rooms, 14 baths.

Wolf, Strozzigasse 19, 1080 (tel. 422320). Not far from Parliament. 53 rooms, no private showers.

SUBURBS

Am Spitz (I), Am Spitz 2, 1210 (tel. 383184). In Florisdorf across the Danube, but near public transport.

Gloriette (I), Linzerstr. 105, 1040 (tel. 921146). Not far from Schönbrunn; ask for a quiet room.

Jagdschloss (M), Jagdschlossgasse 79, 1130 (tel. 841355). All 51 rooms with bath or shower, worth the moderate price range. Private garden; beyond Schönbrunn, convenient if motoring.

Mate (M), Bergsteiggasse 22, 1170 (tel. 428355). Good streetcar connections to downtown.

PENSIONS

Pensions in Vienna are numerous and only a trifle less costly than the corresponding hotel categories. Those classified top category are often overpriced for the type of accommodations offered. The service personnel may be of lower quality. The entrances can be a problem: pensions are often located on the top floors of large buildings, the lifts are sometimes out of order, stairway lights switch off automatically—usually when you are catching your breath between floors— the building doormen might well be out, so it is necessary to carry a key.

The pensions in the outlying districts, however, are usually located in separate buildings of their own and have acquired more the character of hotels rather than old-fashioned pensions.

EXPENSIVE (P1)

Sacher Appartments (no relation of hotel), Rotenturmstr. 1, next to St. Stephen's (tel. 633238), and *Wiener,* Seilergasse 16 (tel. 5248160), are tops; followed by *Arenberg,* Stubenring 2 (tel. 525291); *Pestalozzi,* Pestalozzigasse 3 (tel. 751551); *Neuer Markt,* at Seilergasse 9 (tel. 522316); all these in the Inner City. *Barich,* Barichgasse 3, 1030 (tel. 721273); *Museum,* Museumstr. 3, 1070 (tel. 934426); *Rothensteiner Appartments,* Neustiftgasse 66, 1070 (tel. 934643); all three reasonably close.

MODERATE (P2)

Some of the best are in the suburban districts. Most rooms still with baths or showers. *Sportpension Milanohof,* Neuwaldeggerstr. 44, 1170 (tel. 461497), small; *Kurpension Oberlaa,* Kurbadstr. 6, 1100 (tel. 683611); indoor and outdoor pools. *Cottage,* Hasenauerstr. 12, 1190 (tel. 345116), is closer to downtown.

Among those in the Inner City are *Christina,* Hafnersteig 7 (tel. 632961); *City,* Bauernmarkt 10 (tel. 639521); *Geissler,* Postgasse 14 (tel. 632803); *Nossek,* Graben 17.

INEXPENSIVE (P3)

Of some 20 available, try from *Astra,* Alserstr. 32 (tel. 424254), and *Auer,* Lazarettg. 3 (tel. 432121), both 1090, near the General Hospital; also *Austria,* Garnisongasse 7, 1090 (tel. 422136), near Votivkirche; and *Bettina,* Hardtgasse 32, 1190 (tel. 343267).

SEASONAL HOTELS

An excellent bargain are the student homes operating as seasonal hotels July to September. Single, double rooms, all with baths or showers.

All (M) with restaurants are—*Academia,* Pfeilg. 3a, 1080 (tel. 431661), the most luxurious, T.V., invalid chairs. *Avis,* Pfeilg. 4, 1080, 72 rooms. *Haus Burgenland 1,* 1090, Wilhelm Exnerg. 4, 1090 (tel. 439122), fitness room, sauna, 72 rooms. *Haus Burgenland 2,* Mittelg. 18, 1060, fitness room, sauna, no restaurant, 87 rooms. *Haus Niederösterreich,* Untere Augartenstr. 31, 1020 (tel. 353526), fitness room, sauna, T.V., 102 rooms. *Panorama,* Brigittenauer Lände 224, 1200 (tel. 3515410), a little far out, thus the cheapest for the usual fitness room, sauna, T.V., 442 rooms.

All (I) are—*Europahaus Wien,* Linzer Str. 429, 1140 (tel. 972538), 22 rooms. *Haus Döbling,* Gymnasiumstr. 85, 1190 (tel. 3381710), sauna, T.V., 537 rooms. *Haus Dr. Schärf,* Lorenz Müllerg. 1200 (tel. 347631), sauna, T.V., 130 rooms. *Josephstadt,* Buchfeldg. 16, 1080 (tel. 435211), sauna, T.V., 40 rooms. *Österreichische Studentenförderungsstiftung,* Alserstr. 33, 1080 (tel. 433231), sauna, 59 rooms.

RESTAURANTS First-class restaurants in Vienna can be quite expensive; for a full dinner, accompanied by a good bottle of wine, you will pay as much as in West European capitals. But in simpler restaurants, particularly in the suburbs, you can still find good food at relatively low prices. If you have your main meal at noon (as the Viennese do) you can take advantage of the luncheon specials.

Most restaurants serve meals only between 12 and 2.30 P.M. and between 6 and 9 P.M. An increasing number of restaurants stay open late, but do reserve. Most are closed one day a week, usually Sunday, also holidays.

You might like to read the chapter on *Food and Drink* for some suggestions on Viennese specialties.

EXPENSIVE (1)

Balkan Grill, Brunnengasse 13, 1160 (tel. 921494). Near West Station. Spicy Balkan specialties. Particular attraction is Genghis Khan's Flaming Sword, shashlik, served on a flaming sword, with a musical flourish. Viennese and gypsy melodies. In summer an attractive garden.

Belvedere Stöckl, Prinz Eugen Str. 25, 1030 (tel. 784198). The terrace in the garden is pleasantly fresh in summer.

Bristol Hotel (see *Hotels*). Comfortable dining under sparking chandeliers; specializes in after-Opera "bites".

Caesarea, Seitenstetteng. 4 (tel. 638982). Jewish restaurant near synagogue in romantic old part of Vienna.

China-Restaurant Ming Court, Kärntnerstrasse 32, 1010 (tel. 521775). The best of many Chinese eateries in the city.

✗ *Drei Husaren,* Weihburggasse 4 (tel. 521192). Just off Kärntnerstr., near St. Stephen's. Candlelight, antique-style furnishings, soft music creating an elegant atmosphere. Very good selection of wines and first-class bar. Dinners only. Closes for 4 weeks July to Aug.

Imperial, (see *Hotels*), choice Viennese and international specialties. Very good selection of drinks in the intimately arranged bar. Viennese music in the café during late afternoons, evenings in the restaurant.

Europa Hotel, (see *Hotels*). The accent is on tasty Viennese dishes. Discreetly modern and comfortable furnishings. A good spot to relax after a morning's sightseeing or shopping. One entrance on Kärtnerstrasse.

Feuervogel, Alserbachstr. 31, 1090 (tel. 3410392). Near Franz-Josefs-Bahnhof. Small 50-year-old evening tavern serving Russian and Ukrainian food.

Grotta Azzurra, Babenbergerstr. 5 (tel. 561144). Near Hofburg. Good Italian food, prices range considerably. The owner comes from Capri, hence the marine décor.

Hauswirth, Otto Bauergasse 20, 1060 (tel. 571261). In 6th District, just off Mariahilferstr., with several large rooms and pleasant courtyard garden in summer. Go to the back room for piano music in the evening. Imaginative modern cooking.

Kervansaray, Mahlerstr. 9 (tel. 528843). Near the Opera. Turkish specialties, from Kapama to Dönerkebab, fresh fish from the Bosphorus, including lobsters flown in every day (the owner has another restaurant in Istanbul). Turkish décor, no music. Upstairs is a fish restaurant called "Hummer Bar" under the same management. It is very expensive.

Palais Schwarzenberg, (see *Hotels*), in its small but elegant dining room, this restaurant does much to revive belief in old Vienna. Excellent cuisine, wines and service.

Prinz Eugen, in the Hilton Hotel (see *Hotels*). One of the best and most creative restaurants in all Vienna. Pleasant wine tavern *Vindobona;* fine café.

Sacher, (see *Hotels*). The main restaurant sparkles as it did in the red-plush era of the Habsburgs, as do the folklore-inspired, alcoved dining rooms on the upper floor. One of the plusher spots to eat Tafelspitz (garnished boiled beef) and, of course, its own creation, Sachertorte (chocolate cake).

Salut, Wildpretmarkt 3, 1010 (tel. 633581). French specialties in small attractive rooms, sidewalk tables in summer. Closed Sun.

Schubert-Stüberl, Schreyvogelg. 4 (tel. 637187). Near Burgtheater, pleasant, with quiet summer garden, grill and game specialties.

Stadtkrug, Weihburggasse 3, less sumptuous than *Drei Husaren* opposite, but by no means the poor man's hussar.

Steinerne Eule, tel. 932250. Gourmet restaurant with cosy little rooms.

Steirereck, 1030, Rasumovskygasse (tel. 733138). On Danube Canal. One of Vienna's best restaurants, lightly cooked Austrian dishes, with the emphasis on freshness. The cheese is the best in the city. Really Austrian atmosphere.

Wegenstein "Zum Weissen Schwan", Nussdorferstr. 59, 1090 (tel. 341650). One of the best, if not *the* best, restaurants for game in Austria. Top people come here to enjoy bear's ham, suckling wild pig, roast quail and snipe; small outdoor courtyard, wood-paneled rooms in a typical old Viennese house. Closed Sat. and Sun.; dinner reservations a must (tel. 34–16–50).

MODERATE (2)

Alte Schmiede, Schönlaterngasse 9, 1010, on premises of old smithy, preserved as museum, next to an art gallery, upstairs a coffee-snack bar with art books and newspapers, and a good restaurant in the cellar.

Altes Haus, Himmelstr. 35 (tel. 322321). In the wine-growing suburb of Grinzing, where every house is a wine tavern and this one is actually more a wine tavern with food than a restaurant in the proper sense. Try chicken, grilled and skewered meats and Topfenstrudel (strudel made with cream cheese). Open evenings only, musical entertainment.

D'Rauchkuchl, Schweglerstr. 37, 1150 (tel. 921381). Near West Station. More than a dozen house specialties with emphasis on grills, trout and Fiaker Gulasch; very good wines. Medieval décor reflected also in the dress of the waiters.

Eckel, Sieveringstr. 46, 1190 (tel. 323218). Small house with wood-paneled Stuben and garden. Great cooking such as sweetwater crayfish (in season), trout, game, Backhendl. Fluffy, hot soufflé-type desserts such as Pfannkuchen Marie-Louise, covered with chocolate sauce, ground nuts and whipped cream. A family-run establishment; closed Sun. and Mon.

Falstaff, Währingerstr. 67, 1090 (tel. 422741). Opposite the Volksoper. Large, atmospheric rooms and long menu with spicy grill dishes as specialties. Excellent Munich Pschorr beer on tap. Crowded with Volksoper visitors for after-theater dining.

Figlmüller, Wollzeile 5, 1010, and Grinzingerstr. 55, 1190; giant schnitzels and excellent wines.

Gösser Bierklinik, Steindlgasse 4 (tel. 633336). In a narrow street near Am Hof. One of the oldest inns in the city (1566) with numerous atmospheric rooms. Trout and other sweetwater fish, fish soup and wild boar.

Gösserbräu, Elisabethstr. 3 (tel. 562166). Near the Opera. A large cellar-restaurant with hearty, popular type of Austrian fare.

Griechenbeisl, Fleischmarkt 11 (tel. 631941). Near the main post office. Claims to be the oldest tavern in Vienna, having been established around 1500. It still retains its antique décor in a series of small rooms, with musical entertainment.

Crowded with tourists in the season; prices are high for the food, but you get atmosphere, good Austrian wines and original Pilsener beer on tap.

Marhold, Fleischmarkt 9. A good bet if you fail to get into Griechenbeisl, which is next door. This is another ancient spot, but a bit cheaper than its neighbor, and with not quite so much atmosphere.

Oswald and Kalb, Bäckerstr. 14, 1010 (tel. 5270793). Evenings only, very popular with the young. Closed Friday and Saturday.

Rathauskeller, Rathausplatz 1 (tel. 421219). A vast establishment in the basement of the Rathaus (City Hall), with a series of vaulted dining rooms. Evenings, Viennese music in the large *Grinzingerkeller,* where a huge, carved wooden barrel presides over long tables of tourists.

Sailer, Gersthoferstr. 14, 1180 (tel. 472121). Near Türkenschanzpark. Modern Austrian specialties, marvelous wines. Paneled dining room, cellar and atmospheric garden in summer. Closed Sat., Sun., hols.

Weisser Rauchfangkehrer, (White Chimneysweep) Weihburgasse 4 (tel. 523471). A series of rooms in Alpine Stuben style with hunting décor. Excellent Austrian dishes and good wines with piano music after 8 P.M. Very popular with Viennese and foreigners living in Vienna.

Zum Grünen Anker, Grünangergasse, 1010. Highly recommended fresh Italian dishes, salads; remarkable Italian wines. Very good value.

Zum Laterndl, Landesgerichtsstr. 12 (tel. 434358). Near US Consulate and University. Small tavern frequented by students. Good food, open or bottled wine. Closed weekends.

INEXPENSIVE (3) (see also Wine Taverns below)

Alter Ratskeller, Wipplingerstr. 8, 1010 (tel. 631441). More genuine than the one on Rathausplatz.

Gösser Bierhaus, Wollzeile 38, 1010 (tel. 524839). Large beer restaurant with simple but good food.

Stadtbeisl, Naglergasse 21 (tel. 633323). Small, cozy and usually crowded at noon.

Stadtkeller, Singerstr. 6 (tel. 521268). The daily specialties are at bargain-basement prices.

Weisshappel Stüberl, Petersplatz 1, upstairs (tel. 526212). Near Graben. Small and simple, but owned by the large meat store downstairs, so you can count on good meat dishes. Closed Sun., hols.

Zum Guten Tropfen, Schmalzhofgasse 11, 1060, pleasant garden in summer.

Zum Hochstrahlbrunnen, Prinz-Eugenstr. 2, across from Schwarzenberg Palace and near the most important concert halls. Historic premises in existence since early 18th century. Open from morning through midnight (Sun. until 3 P.M.).

PANORAMIC VIEW

Donauturm (2). A 2-floor establishment on the Danube Tower in Donaupark. Expensive international cuisine in the rotating tower, moderate café-restaurant on lower floor. Rustic *Park Tavern* at foot of tower.

Fischerhaus (1), on the Höhenstr. (tel. 441320). Reached only by car. Good view of Wienerwald and parts of the city from the outdoor terrace. Rustic furnishings. Closed Mon.

EXCURSION DINING

Burg Greifenstein, tel. 02242 2349. In the castle above the village of Greifenstein on the Danube, not far from Klosterneuburg. For splendid view of the river, dine on the terrace. Knightly décor, and limited fare, mostly from grill but good wines and moderate prices.

Holdrichsmühle in Hinterbrühl (tel. 02236 6274). Near Mödling, on the edge of Wienerwald, south of Vienna. Very fine fare from trout to *Milchrahmstrudel* (strudel with sour cream) at reasonable prices. Rustic style. It was here that Schubert composed his song of the Lindentree, "Am Brunnen vor dem Tore"; the painter Waldmüller also liked to work here.

Marchfelderhof, in Deutsch Wagram (tel. 02247 2243). 8 miles beyond the UN City, on the site of Napoleonic battle. The menu is immense and so are the portions, but prices are reasonable. Though describing itself as the most original restaurant in Austria, it is actually fantastically overdecorated. Reservations necessary, English spoken.

Stiftskeller Klosterneuburg, the historic monastery tavern (go down into the cellar section). The specialty is chicken, with excellent white wines from the estates of the Abbey.

Taverne am Sachsengang, tel. 02249 2901. A little beyond Gross-Enzersdorf, about 16 km. from the center of Vienna; cross the Danube and then take the road No. 210 to the east. Game and sweetwater fish, candlelight atmosphere, lots of parking space, also rooms available.

Tulbingerkogel Berghotel, tel. 02273 7391. On the Tulbingerkogel hill in the Vienna Woods (30 minutes by car). Viennese cuisine. Wachau white wines and Vöslau reds. (Also some rooms, with shower and WC.)

A LITTLE SOMETHING (see also **Pastry Shops** below)

Al Cavallino, Dorotheergasse, 1010. Pizzeria, Neapolitan pizza, salad bar, Italian wines.

Am Lugeck, Lugeck 7, on the way from St. Stephen's to the Danube Canal. Quick bite in the simpler ground-floor premises, more elaborate restaurant fare a few stairs below.

Carrousel, Krugerstr. 3 (tel. 527297). With summer sidewalk tables and sometimes music afternoons and evenings, café, snack bar and restaurant service.

Demel, the famous pastry shop at Kohlmarkt 14 offers at lunch time also magnificent snacks of delicate meats, fish and vegetables. Try stuffed mushrooms or vegetable-cheese combinations. Gorgeous coffee and hot chocolate.

Goldener Spatz, Maysedergasse, 1010 (tel. 522104). Specializes in a large variety of pancakes, sweet and otherwise.

Perle Josephinum, Währingerstr. 33, 1090, are open until midnight.

Reiss Champagner Treff, Marco d'Avianog, 1, 1010, Austrian and French champagne with tidbits; favored by young businessmen.

Rôtisserie Palffy, Josefsplatz 6, in Palffy Palace, entrance directly from the street. Grill dishes, very fast service. Open 9 A.M. until midnight and closed Sun.

Stibitz-Zum Schwarzen Kameel, Bognergasse 5, near Graben, in existence since 1618. A real old-time Viennese delicatessen with attached small restaurant.

Trzesniewski Buffet, a hole-in-the-wall at Dorotheergasse 1, just off Graben, is filled with mouth-watering, spicy canapés to eat on the spot or take away.

Zu Ebener Erd, 1070, Burggasse (tel. 936254). Lovely old Viennese house serving delicious Viennese cuisine.

WINE TAVERNS

These are evening institutions intended primarily for drinking, but you can always get at least a bite and often a full dinner. They vary in class from simple to more ornate, and in originality from genuine to pseudo. One of their prominent features is the *Weinheber* (wine siphon), placed in front of you on the table, instead of any other wine container. This should remind you that the wine was drawn straight out of the barrel. Nowadays, however, this is a strictly symbolic gesture, since the wine is usually poured into the Weinheber straight from—the bottle.

Some call themselves city Heurigers which, of course, is only for advertising purposes, since no real Heurigers can exist in the city. The Viennese call this kind *Nobel-Heuriger* (stylish Heuriger), defining it justly for what it is: a wine tavern arranged in pseudo-Heuriger style.

Wine taverns in Vienna are many and even an old habitué can always discover a new one. Here are some of the better known ones.

Antiquitäten-Keller, Magdalenenstr. 32, open from 7 P.M. to 1 A.M.; classical music.

Augustinerkeller, Augustine Strasse 1, tucked in under the building which houses the great Albertina collection, and so handy for lunch after sightseeing in the Hofburg. Simple and busy, but excellent value for money.

Bären Keller, Kärtnerstr. 61; beer buffet, steak and equipment to grill it yourself.

Feuchter Stock, (Damp Upper Floor) Jasomirgottstr. 5 (tel. 633430). A Nobel-Heuriger with restaurant service, atmospheric decor, Schrammel music. During the summer everything moves outdoors to the City Park next to the Kursalon and calls itself *Weingärtl.*

Melkerstiftskeller, Schottengasse 3 (tel. 635530). Hidden at the back of a small courtyard, the entrance leads down and down, into one of the friendliest and most typical of all wine cellars. Excellent food and wine plus a hard-working clientele. Connected with Melk for a long way back. Evenings only.

Piaristenkeller, Piaristengasse 45, 1080 (tel. 429152). Colorful, with restaurant service and zither music.

Thomaskeller, tel. 527446. In the Postgasse just off the Wollzeile, in the cellars of the Dominican Monastery. One of the nicest cellars, serving excellent open wines from Haugsdorf and good basic Austrian specialties. Relaxed.

Urbanikeller, Am Hof 12 (tel. 639102). A deep, centuries-old wine cellar with antique decor. Music in the evening.

Zwölf-Apostelkeller, Sonnenfelsgasse 3, not far from St. Stephen's. Frequented by students and deep below street level.

HEURIGERS

The Heuriger is a temporary, very simply-arranged wine tavern, attached to the premises of a vintner. When he has drawn off the new wine, he hangs an evergreen branch over his door, inviting passers by to try his beverage.

In summer an array of Heurigers open in the Vienna area, extending from Nussdorf and Grinzing to Gumpoldskirchen and Bad Vöslau. When they open, they usually place a notice in the daily newspapers.

The easiest to get to (if you don't have a car) are located in Grinzing, Sievering, and Nussdorf, which can be reached with streetcars 38, 39, and D (the latter becomes 36 on Sun.) respectively. Also in these areas there are Nobel-Heuriger, which are permanent wine taverns, usually offering also good food.

CAFÉS

The old-fashioned Viennese type of café, with its marble tables, newspapers, sidewalk terraces in warm weather, is an institution of long tradition that has strengthened its position here and there by adding buffets or partial restaurant service and espresso machines. All of the Viennese cafés offer pastries.

Here we can mention only a few of Vienna's 15,500-odd cafés, ranging from small espresso bars to the venerable club-like institutions located on and inside the Ring.

Except for those belonging to the famous hotels mentioned previously, some of the most typical old-fashioned cafés in Vienna are—*Raimund,* where men of letters meet, at Volksgartenstr. 5, across from the Volkstheater; *Mozart,* with very pleasant summer lunches on the street terrace, at Albertinaplatz 2 near the Opera: *Prückel* with restaurant service, Stubenring 24, across the street from the Stadtpark; *Tirolerhof,* Führichgasse 8 across the square from Albertina, sometimes afternoon music; the 100-years-old *Schwarzenberg* on the Ring corner at Schwarzenberg Square; *Frauenhuber,* Himmelpfortgasse 6, all with restaurant service; *Ritter,* Mariahilferstr. 73; *Haag,* at Schottengasse 2, with a garden; *Museum,* corner of Friedrichstr.-Operngasse.

Palais Auersperg Wintergarten in the baroque Auersperg Palace; the winter garden with palm trees and bar; also with pleasant garden next to the restaurant.

Café Laudon, Laudongasse 24, a Café-restaurant with tradition, popular with the chess set.

Among the better modern cafés is *Café Europa,* on the ground floor of hotel of the same name, with large windows facing the Kärntnerstrasse where you can watch the pretty shoppers.

The most important downtown coffeehouses are *Café Central,* Freyung, 1010, a historic place where Stalin and Trotsky used to play chess, and which reopened in 1982 (closed winter though); *Café Hawelka,* Dorotheergasse, 1010, just off Graben, a meeting place for artists, always crowded; *Café Sacher,* behind the Opera House, famous for its cake and its elegance; and *Café Landtman* on Schottenring, which is a distinguished meeting place for civil servants through its location near the Rathaus, Parliament and headquarters of leading political parties.

Cafés with music—*Kursalon* (also restaurant) in the City Park, large and popular outdoor café during the warmer months with a band playing Austrian light music in the late afternoon and evening. *Volksgarten*, afternoon and evenings, with dancing. Hotel cafés—*Imperial, Hilton, Sacher, Parkhotel Schönbrunn* and *Intercontinental*.

PASTRY SHOPS

In this field, *Demel* is a must (see page 138). Other top pastry shops include: *Gerstner,* Kärntnerstr. 15; *Heiner,* Kärntnerstr. 21, with a nice upstairs room, and at Wollzeile 9; *Lehmann,* Graben 12, and Mariahilferstr. 137; the ubiquitous but less scrumptious *Aida* chain is in the Inner City at Opern Ring 7, Stock-im-Eisenplatz 2, near St. Stephen's, and at Wollzeile 28—many would claim they serve the best coffee at the lowest prices.

 SPECIAL EVENTS The outstanding event of the winter season is *Fasching,* carnival season, which lasts from New Year's Eve until Mardi Gras. Hundreds of balls are given from Jan. to Feb., often 40 of them a night during its height. The first is the *Kaiserball* in the Hofburg on New Year's Eve, but the greatest and the most glittering is the *Opernball* in the Opera; white tie and grand gala evening gown are the requirements here. The stage and the orchestra are transformed into a huge dance floor.

Other top balls are *Philharmonikerball* in the Wiener Musikverein building, *Campagnereiterball* (Riding Club) in Pallavicini Palace, and *Jägerball* (Hunter's Ball) all of them very exclusive: invitations and, of course, formal attire are needed; at the Jägerball you can only wear a festive dirndl and a salon type of Styrian hunting suit.

There is a wide variety of other balls from those organized by various university departments, intellectual clubs, and artists to the informal dances of plumbers and chimney-sweeps. Vienna Fasching season is much more formal than its Munich and Cologne counterparts.

February is usually the month for skiing in Vienna's outskirts and, together with Jan., the month of ice skating competitions.

March brings the *Spring Trade Fair* and the *Viennale,* a film festival of growing importance.

Art exhibits are often concentrated in April, which also marks the start of a long series of *conventions.*

Heurigers begin mushrooming with the warmer May weather.

The most prominent summer event is the *Festival of Vienna,* which takes place annually from about May 20 to June 20. There is a series of performances in all Vienna theaters, and a series of concerts given by famous local and foreign orchestras, choirs, and soloists in the various halls of Musikverein and Konzerthaus, as well as in several other palaces and gardens.

Palace and park concerts (including those in the Rathaus and Schönbrunn Palace), operetta programs continue through July and August, which are the best months for Danube trips. The *Youth and Music in Vienna Festival* occurs in July.

The *Autumn Trade Fair* is the feature of Sept. when the principal theaters re-open their doors. Others stay open all the year.

Grape harvests and wine tasting Oct.; this is also the month to get that pheasant —at least garnished with dumplings and cranberries.

Opera runs from Sept. 1 to June 30, with various high points, but closing only on Good Friday, Christmas Eve, and one night before and the night of the Opera Ball.

Some of the best church music can be heard in Dec., at the end of which Vienna, with the Strauss introduction played by the Philharmoniker at their traditional Jan. 1 concert, plunges with music on her lips and in her heart into the New Year.

 HOW TO GET ABOUT By Train Travelers with one eye on the budget would find it advisable to get acquainted with Vienna's public transport system. There are streetcars (trams), buses, a *Stadtbahn* (City Railway), which is partly elevated, partly underground, and partly at ground level. This latter is limited in its coverage, but very practical between Schönbrunn Palace, Karlskirche, City Park, Wien Mitte at the City Air Terminal, Schweden Platz and some other stops along the Danube Canal, and the Volksoper. There is also a *Schnellbahn* (Fast Railway) serving primarily the northeast and southeast suburbs, including the airport.

Of the *U-Bahn* (subway), the U1 runs from Reumannplatz in the 10th District via Stephansplatz, Praterstern, to the Vienna International Center and Zentrum Kagran on the other side of the Danube. The U2 rings the Inner City from Schottenring to Karlsplatz. And the U4 covers Heiligenstadt (Vienna 19), Schwedenplatz (Danube Canal), Karlsplatz, Schönnbrunn and Hütteldorf. You will find the U-Bahn easy to use, with clear colored plans to facilitate travel.

By Streetcar and bus In most busy areas, such as would be frequented by a tourist, the streetcars tread on one another's heels. The start at an incredibly early hour of the morning and continue, usually, to between 11 and 12 at night. At each streetcar stop there is a sign which tells what cars stop there, where these cars are going and at what hours the first and last trips of the day are made.

Special city buses, marked "S", operate in the Inner City weekdays 7 A.M.—8 P.M. and Sat. until 2 P.M.

If you can't figure out the system yourself, your hotel porter or desk clerk can steer you to the right stop and tell you how to proceed.

Tickets for buses, streetcars and Stadtbahn cost AS 15 if bought singly; AS 10.50 if bought in advance in blocks of 10 at a *Tabak Trafik* (tobacco store). With a single ticket, cars and means of transport can be changed if continuing in same direction. Some streetcars have automatic ticket machines in the first car (marked by a yellow sign). They swallow 5 and 10 schilling coins, so have them handy.

Taxis in Vienna charge according to the meter, and they are comparatively cheap; luggage costs 10 schillings per case. A tip of 10% is the usual. Taxis can be taken at the stands, which are numerous in the Inner City, or ask a hotel doorman to help. For radio-directed taxis dial 31 30, 62 82, or 43 69.

Horse Cabs You can still get a *Fiaker,* the Vienna horsecab, on Heldenplatz, Stephansplatz and in front of Albertina (at the time of writing—their stands change according to the requirements of new traffic rules or road construction), or even order one for a longer ride or a special occasion.

By Car The speed limit within the city limits is 50 km. (about 31 miles) per hour. Honking is forbidden unless absolutely necessary. Priority at intersections not otherwise marked is always to the car on the right. Streetcars (trams) have the right-of-way even when approaching from the left.

Parking: During the daytime it is quite difficult to find parking space in the inner city. In many streets in the center permitted parking time is limited to 1½ hours. In some of these areas special parking tickets are required, available at a Tabak Trafik (tobacco shop) or bank—they come in 3 colors: red for ½ hour, blue for 1 hour, green for 1½ hours, and cost 5 schillings per 30 minutes. Parking is forbidden on all streets with streetcar tracks from November to April. There are several large underground parking garages, including Am Hof square near Graben, Karlsplatz, Neuer Markt on Kärntnerstr., beside the Opera (there is an underground connection between the garage and the Opera), behind the Cathedral, Franz Josefskai, and on the Ring in front of the Rathaus. The last two tend to be less full. (Note, incidentally, that Kärntnerstasse—though spelt with *two* "n"s—is often referred to as "Kärtnerstrasse".) Many shops give a free hour's parking in one of these for every 300 schillings spent.

Road information: Call up 1590 for recorded road information messages provided by the Austrian Automobile Club, and if you don't understand German, call 72 21 01, extension 7, for the information in English.

Car Hire: A variety of self-drive cars can be rented from *Carop Mosel Union,* Mollardgasse 15, and at airport; *Auto-Ring International,* Schwedenplatz 2; *Hertz,* Rotenturmstr. 5; *Avis,* Operngasse 3. *Inter-Rent Austria,* Kärntnerring 6, mostly VWs, will deliver the car to your hotel. A number of firms provide you with chauffeur-driven cars ranging from Cadillac to Volkswagen bus and with drivers who speak several languages; among them: *Hellmut Schwarz,* Kempelengasse 12; *Franz Mazur,* Leebgasse 35; *Mosel,* Hörlgasse 6.

 SIGHTSEEING Heading your list will be such tried-and-true favorites as St. Stephen's, the Kunsthistorisches Museum, the Hofburg and Habsburg Treasury (transferred to Kunsthistorisches Museum until at least 1987), Schönbrunn, the famous Ringstrasse, Vienna Woods, and "Beautiful Blue Danube". The city offers a wealth of other attractions, including ample opportunities for sightseeing excursions.

Wiener Rundfahrten (Vienna Sightseeing Tours), Stelzhammergasse 4, offer twice daily (in summer three times a day) sightseeing tours of the city, Kahlenberg and Klosterneuburg, and Heiligenkreuz, Mayerling and Baden; one-hour tours, 10 and 11.30 A.M., departure from the Opera.

Vienna by Night tours are operated by the same firm, as well as by a number of travel agencies offering sightseeing tours: *Cosmos,* Kärntnerring 15; *Cityrama Sightseeing,* Scholzgasse 10.

From April to Oct. the *Danube Shipping Company (DDSG)* provides sightseeing boat trips along the Danube Canal and the main Danube stream within the city limits. The starting point is at Schwedenbrücke on the Canal; several tours a day; the shortest is a one-hour quickie.

The caves at Hinterbrühl near Vienna, which were used during the war for the production of the Heinkel jet fighters, can now be visited; here also is the largest (6,200 square meters) underground lake in Europe.

A unique attraction of Vienna are the performances of the **Spanish Riding School** in Hofburg's baroque and chandeliered manège. Courbettes, levades, and caprioles are performed to the sounds of Mozart's music. The white stallions, called Lippizaner (until 1918 the stud farm was in Lippiza near Trieste, at that time within the borders of Austria; now it is at Piber in Styria) are trained according to the 400-year-old classical method. Most performances take place on Sun. mornings and Wed. evenings from Sept. to Dec. and from Mar. to June. In July and Aug. the horses are in the Lainzer Tiergarten. Training can be observed Tues. to Sat. 10–12. Advance reservations (*at least* two months in advance) are absolutely necessary. Write to *Spanische Reitschule,* Hofburg, 1010 Vienna.

On summer Sundays there is a special trip around the Ring, to Belvedere, Prater and Schönbrunn with an old-timer (1909) trolley. It begins at 9 A.M. at Karlsplatz.

All buildings of historic interest are marked by explanatory **shields** (in summer festooned with red-white banners); a guide in English to these shields can be bought for 15 schillings.

In most churches of importance there are coin-operated (10 sch.) **tape machines** which will give you an excellent commentary on the history and architecture of the building in English.

 MUSEUMS AND GALLERIES At present there are over 50 museums and galleries in Vienna. Entrance charges are minimal; for extensive museum visiting, a 7-day ticket, valid for the State museums and issued at their ticket offices, is recommended. Sun. usually free; small charge for guided tours.

Important Note. Visiting hours differ from museum to museum and also in some cases between the winter period (Oct. 1 to April 30) and the summer period (May 1 to Sept. 30). Some are open daily, others only certain days and half days; many are closed Mondays. As these can change from season to season, best check on the spot with the hotel desk or the city tourist information office.

Kunsthistoriches Museum Museum of Art History (also referred to as the Museum of Fine Arts), Burgring 5, entrance Maria-Theresienplatz.

This building houses 5 sections; Egyptian antiquities, among the most important collections in the world; Greek, Etruscan, and Roman antiquities, *The Youth from Magdalensberg, Athlete from Ephesus, Artemis from Larnaka;* plastic arts and *objets d'art;* collection of coins; and the famous gallery of paintings, one of the best in the world. The gallery owns some 10,000 paintings, but not all are exhibited. Among those on display, particularly well represented are Titian, Tintoretto, Veronese, Velazquez, Pieter Breughel, Rubens, Dürer, and both Cranachs.

The new and excitingly displayed **Ephesus Museum** is housed in the Hofburg, entrance in the Heldenplatz. Exhibits from the dig at Ephesus with plans and models.

Österreichische Galerie (Austrian Gallery) in Belvedere Palace. Contains— Museum of Medieval Austrian Art located in the Orangerie at Lower Belvedere; Museum of Austrian Baroque in Lower Belvedere; Austrian Gallery of 19th and 20th Century in Upper Belvedere. The baroque Belvedere Palace was built by Lukas von Hildebrandt. *Sound and Light* performances take place in Belvedere on summer evenings.

Schönbrunn Palace The Imperial apartments can be visited daily. Only some 40 of over 1,400 rooms are on display. Many of them have not been changed since the times of Maria Theresa. Baroque and rococo interiors with crystal chandeliers, furniture from precious woods, gilded wall and ceiling decorations, miniature paintings, Chinese porcelain and cabinets, the *Million Room* (its décor cost a million florins).

Wagenburg in Schönbrunn. Fine collection of various types of state coaches and sleighs, ranging from baroque and rococo to Biedermeier, and of the industrial period under Franz Josef.

Albertina Collection of Graphic Arts, Augustinerstr. 1 near the Opera. Engravings, watercolors and drawings from Middle Ages to present day, among them particularly those of Dürer, and also of Raphael, Rembrandt, Rubens, Leonardo da Vinci, Michelangelo, Correggio, Fragonard, etc. Only a small part on display; rest available on request in the reading room for study purposes. The largest collection of this kind in the world; contains over 600,000 items. Collection of papyrus scrolls in ancient Egyptian, Greek, Latin, and Arabic, most from one find at Fayum in Egypt.

Gallery of the Academy of Fine Arts Schillerplatz 3. Upstairs from main entrance to Academy. About 150 paintings on display, among them Hieronymus Bosch, Titian, Cranach, Rubens, Rembrandt, Tiepolo, Van Dyck.

Museum für moderne Kunst in the Liechtenstein Palace, Fürstengasse 1. A brand new collection of modern art of the last 30 years, housed in one of Vienna's great buildings. Open daily 10–4, except Wed. 2–7 and Sun. 10–1.

Museum des XX. Jahrhunderts 20th-century Gallery, Schweizergarten 3 near South Station and Belvedere Palace. A very representative collection of modern paintings and sculpture since the turn of the century.

Neue Galerie in der Stallburg Reitschulgasse 2. Impressionist paintings and sculptures of 19th and early 20th centuries. A really lovely collection. Open Tues., Wed., Thur., 10–3; Sat. and Sun., 9–1.

Naturhistorisches Museum Museum of Natural History, Burgring 7, entrance from Maria-Theresienplatz. Fossils, meteorites, prehistoric finds from Stone Age (*Venus* from Willendorf, about 20,000 B.C.) and from Hallstatt period (*Golden Dagger* and other fine weapons from Hallstatt smiths), botanical and zoological section. You can park your offspring in the children's room, nurse in attendance.

Kaisergruft Imperial Crypt, under Capuchin Church, entrance at Tegetthoffstr. 2. Guided tours daily. Most of Habsburg emperors and other members of the family are buried here.

Herzgrüfterl der Habsburger Small Crypt with the Hearts of the Habsburgs, in Loretto Chapel of Augustine Church, Augustinerstr. 7. The hearts of the Habsburgs who died between 1619 and 1878 are here in 54 urns.

Hofburg Imperial Apartments in the Amalien and Reichskanzlei wings. Apartments and reception halls of Emperor Franz Josef and Empress Elisabeth. The **Schatzkammer** (Treasury) is closed for modernization. Items from this rich and historically fascinating collection are on view in the Neue Hofburg and the Kunsthistoriches Museum. The excitingly displayed **Ephesos Museum** is also housed in the Hofburg, entrance in the Heldenplatz. It exhibits the finds from the dig at Ephesus with plans and models. The same entrance will take you to the **Collection of Weapons and of Old Musical Instruments.** Ornamented suits of armor in Gothic, Renaissance, and baroque styles and old weapons from the same periods; among some 1,400 guns are many masterpieces of artistic craftsmanship. The oldest among the instruments in the musical collection originate from the 16th and 17th centuries.

Heeresgeschichtliches Museum Army History Museum, in the Arsenal near Südbahnhof. The history of the Austrian Army. Every hall dedicated to a historic period during the life of a leading personality: Prince Eugene, Maria Theresa, Radetzky, Franz Josef. Very interesting for Austrian history in general. This is one of the few museums open on Mon.

Bundessammlung Alter Stilmöbel State Collection of Antique Furniture, Mariahilferstr. 88, near Westbahnhof. Furniture in styles ranging from baroque to Biedermeier. Also Habsburg throne from 19th century.

Feuerwehrmuseum Fire Brigade Museum, Am Hof 10. Historical fire fighting equipment and curiosities, and romantic lanterns with which the watchmen in St. Stephen's tower warned a city of fires, can be seen Sun. and holidays from 9–12.

Uhrenmuseum Clock Museum. Schulhof 2, off from Tuchlauben. An interesting collection of old and ancient clocks and timepieces. Daily except Mon., 9–1.

Historisches Museum der Stadt Wien Vienna City Museum, at Karlsplatz. History of Vienna; art works from Vienna.

Sammlung der ehemaligen Hoftafel und Silberkammer Collection of Former Imperial Tableware and Household Silver, Hofburg. Entrance in the Michaelerplatz gate.

Choir Museum in Musikverein building, Dumbastr. 3. Choral archives of Vienna Men's Choir, with original score of *The Blue Danube*.

Museum für Völkerkunde Ethnological Museum, Neue Hofburg, entrance from Heldenplatz. Collections from Mexico, including *feather crown and shield of Montezuma,* from Brazil, Peru, Argentina, and Africa.

Österreichisches Museum für Angewandte Kunst Museum of Applied Arts, Stubenring 5. Old ceramics, china, furniture, glass paintings, collection of textiles, Oriental rugs, East Asian artistic tapestries.

Österreichisches Museum für Volkskunde Museum of Austrian Folklore, 8th District, Laudongasse 17. Austrian folk dress, including some other areas of the old Empire, woodcarved Fasching masks, embroideries, etc. In the 18th dist. is the Sobek Sammlung in **Gayermüllerschlössl,** a Biedermeier villa with furniture and clock collection.

Dom- und Diözesanmuseum Museum of Religious Art, Rotenturmstr. 2, next to St. Stephen's. Religious paintings from Gothic, baroque, and Biedermeier periods. Fine products of goldsmith's art.

Tabakmuseum Tobacco Museum, Mariahilferstr. 1, 1070. A most interesting collection of smoking paraphernalia.

Technisches Museum Technical Museum, Mariahilferstr. 212, near Schönbrunn. Railway and Post Museums attached.

Sigmund Freud Museum, 1090, Berggasse 19.

Composer Museums Johann-Strauss-Museum in the apartment at Praterstr. 54, 2nd District, where Strauss lived and wrote *The Blue Danube*. Other museums connected with composers include the **Haydn Museum,** Haydngasse 19, which is the house where he died; the **Mozart Erinnerungsraum,** Domgasse 5; the **Beethoven Erinnerungsraum,** Molkerbastei 8, where he once lived; the **Schubert Museum,** Nussdorferstr. 54, souvenirs in his birth-house, and the **Schubert-Sterbezimmer,** Kettenbrückengasse 6, where he died.

 LIBRARIES There are about 20 major libraries in Vienna, containing not only publications but a multitude of manuscripts, handwritten musical scores, ornamental engravings, drawings, old maps and photographs. Here are just two that will be of general interest.

Österreichisches Staatsarchiv Austrian State Archives, is not, strictly speaking a library at all, but one of the most important state archives, next to the Vatican, in Europe, located at Minoritenplatz 1 (between Hofburg and Burgtheater); Mon. to Fri. 9–6. Contains many old state documents and treaties from earliest times of Habsburg rule; many personal items, such as private correspondence of Maria Theresa, and also of Napoleon, husband of Marie Louise, daughter of Franz II.

Österreichische Nationalbibliothek Austrian National Library, with the main building at Josefsplatz 1, built by Fischer von Erlach and with famed cupola baroque fresco by Daniel Gran. Library is divided into 8 sections—Books, Periodicals, Manuscripts, Maps (all located in the main building); Portrait collection in Neue Burg; Papyrus Scroll Collection, mentioned under Albertina, and Music Collection, handwritten and printed scores, in Albertina; Theater Collection, manuscripts, stage model drawings, portraits of actors, in Hofburg. Admission times vary from section to section.

PARKS AND GARDENS The average Viennese loves to do most of his warm-weather walking in the **Wienerwald** (Vienna Woods), romantic locale of Johann Strauss' famous waltz and of many a song and poem. The Wienerwald is not a park, but a range of low, wooded hills, criss-crossed by pathways and roads and framing Vienna on the western side. Among Vienna parks proper—most of them of the natural variety and a few of them formally laid out—the visitor has a wide selection through which to stroll.

Stadtpark Along the Park Ring, with small artificial lake, various statues—among them one of Franz Schubert and the famous one of Johann Strauss. Bandstandmusic late afternoons and evenings in summer.

Volksgarten Next to Burgtheater, on site of old city wall fortifications. Several monuments, including an attractive one to the Empress Elisabeth and another to Grillparzer. Theseus Temple, occasionally used for exhibitions, and Tilgner Fountain with bronze fauns and nymphs.

Burggarten A small, lovely park next to Neue Hofburg. Mozart Monument, statue of Emperor Franz Josef.

Belvedere Park The main part between Lower and Upper Belvedere and a smaller part with an artificial lake between Upper Belvedere and Südbahnhof. Formally laid out in Italian terrace style. Many garden sculptures, wrought-iron gateway by Arnhold and Konrad Küffner made in 1728.

Botanischer Garten Rennweg 14, also next to Belvedere (the other side), is part of Museum of the Botanical Institute of the University; admission to the garden April 15–Oct. 1, 9 A.M. till dusk. Many rare plants. Permission from superintendent to visit interesting hot-houses.

Schönbrunn Park A formally laid-out park in baroque style belonging to Schönbrunn Palace. The Neptun Brunnen and Schöne Brunnen fountains, which gave the palace its name; Gloriette, a colonnade from the top of which there is a beautiful view of the entire Schönbrunn area and beyond; Zoo, Botanical Garden, Palm House, Tiroler Garten.

Türkenschanzpark Next to School of Agriculture, bus from the corner of Schottenring and Liechtensteinstr. The largest rambling wooded variety of park in the city, located on site where Turks built their fortifications during siege of Vienna, hence the name.

Prater Subway U1 from Karlsplatz. Very large natural park area (over 10 square km. altogether), once hunting grounds and pleasure park of the emperor, opened to public as early as second half of 18th century. At present includes various sports establishments (stadium, swimming pool, golf course, race track, etc.), Trade Fair exhibition area, and so-called Volksprater. Latter is actually an elaborate amusement park with the famous giant Ferris Wheel as an outstanding feature and several taverns, cafés, dancehalls inside and nearby. Particularly crowded on Sun. afternoons.

Lainzer Tiergarten A natural game park, formerly imperial game preserve, with deer, boar, and even mouflon, similar to the Rocky Mountain bighorn. The park is very large and it takes several hours to walk across it. In the middle is the Hermes Villa, built originally in the 19th century for the Empress Elisabeth and used today for exhibitions. Cars and other transport vehicles are not allowed and one must walk only along marked paths. There are several entrances. Open 8 A.M. until 1 hour before dusk, April 1 to Oct. 31. Closed Mon. and Tues.

Donaupark Danube Park, laid out between the Danube and the so-called Old Danube for the International Garden Show of 1964. One of its most outstanding features is the 826-foot observation tower (Donauturm) with a rotating café-restaurant offering a magnificent view of Vienna. There are several other cafés and restaurants and a water stage on a small lake.

 ENTERTAINMENT Opera With a pre-season beginning in Sept. and the Festival in June, opera performances go on continuously from Sept. 1 to end June. The yearly program represents a happy selection, with equally superior production, from different periods and composers, unlike some of the leading world opera houses which tailor their programs according to the nationality of their singers. Evening dress and black tie are not compulsory, but they are recommended for first performances and for better seats. You should always dress quietly, anyway, since the Viennese take opera very seriously.

In summer some chamber opera performances are given in the *Schlosstheater* of Schönbrunn.

Operas of a lighter type and operettas are presented magnificently at the *Volksoper,* a bit out, on the corner of Gürtel and Währingerstr, but which is significantly cheaper than the Opera. Thus the tradition of Johann Strauss and Franz Lehar is continuing in the city that gave them their great successes. Operettas and musical shows are also performed at *Theater an der Wien,* Linke Wienzeile 6 and *Raimundtheater,* Wallgasse 18 (near the West Station).

Theater Visitors with sufficient command of the German language should take advantage of the unique attraction offered by Vienna in the field of dramatic arts at the *Burgtheater.* Vienna is one of the leading centers in the cultivation of German theatrical arts and for a German-language actor to play at the Burg means supreme achievement. Closed in summer, but similar performances are given in the Messepalast by the Wiener Sommertheater.

Thanks to this tradition, it is logical that there are many other drama theaters in the city. Among the most important are—*Akademietheater,* Lisztstr. 1 (in Konzerthaus), classical and modern plays; *Theater in der Josefstadt,* Josefstäd-terstr. 26, the old theater of Max Reinhardt, classical and modern plays; *Volks-theater,* Neustiftgasse 1, dramas, comedies, folk plays; *Kammerspiele,* Roten-turmstr. 20, modern plays.

There are also a number of small theaters, such as the new *Künstlerhaus, Atelier Theater am Naschmarkt, Theater der Courage,* and *Tribüne.*

Simpl, Wollzeile 36, has a long tradition of poking fun at Austrian and world politics and life in general, but this type of entertainment calls for knowledge of local affairs and dialect.

The *Vienna English Theater,* Josefsgasse 12, 1080, is the Continent's only English-speaking theater. It is housed in an attractive theater, with a friendly atmosphere. The plays are often performed by visiting companies from Britain, maintaining high standards. For visitors who do not feel up to coping with an evening of German theater, this provides a perfect alternative.

Music Vienna is one of the greatest cities in the world for music. The two great orchestras of the capital are the *Vienna Philharmonic* and the *Vienna Symphony.* In addition to their performances, there is an abundance of concerts by soloists, choruses, and chamber music groups.

The most important concert halls in Vienna are in the building of the *Gesell-schaft der Musikfreunde* (popularly called *Musikverein*), Dumbastr. 3, the home of the Vienna Philharmonic, and in the *Wiener Konzerthaus,* Lothringerstr. 20. Both of these contain a number of auditoriums for concerts of different types, and your ticket may be marked with the name of the particular hall in which the concert is being given. Don't hunt vainly for a building with that name. If your ticket is for the *Grosser Musikvereinssaal,* the *Brahmssaal* or the *Kammersaal,* go to the *Musikfreunde* building. If it is for the *Grosser Konzerthaussaal,* the *Mozart-saal* or the *Schubertsaal,* you will find it in the *Konzerthaus.*

Concerts are also given in the small *Figarosaal* of the Palffy Palace and the *Hobokensaal* in Albertina.

In addition to the Vienna Festival, held late-May and June, there are special summer concerts in the Arkadenhof (Arcade Court) of the Rathaus, in Belvedere garden and Volksgarten, and in many palaces, the most notable being held in Palais Schwarzenberg, Schloss Schönbrunn; but of particular interest are the candlelit baroque concerts given in 18th-century costumes and powdered wigs in Palais Pallavicini, Josefsplatz.

Schubert fans can enjoy occasional piano concerts in the house of his birth, Nussdorferstr. 54.

Church music of high artistic value can be heard during Sunday morning Mass in the following churches in the downtown area—in the Cathedral of St. Stephen, in the Franciscan Church, Karlskirche, Augustinerkirche, and in Hofburgkapelle where the famous *Wiener Sängerknaben* (Vienna Choirboys) sing at 9.25 A.M. from mid-Sept. to late June, and on Wednesday evenings in Palais Palffy, April-June and Sept.-Oct. (tickets available in ticket and travel agencies). Programs published on first of month on church door and in the Saturday papers. There are Wednesday evening organ concerts in St. Stephen's from early May to end Nov.

Try to hear brass band music. Vienna has some of the best bands in Austria, and you can hear them on various squares and in different parks throughout the summer.

Getting Tickets Operas are almost always, and better concerts usually, sold out in Vienna, so it is advisable to buy your tickets several days in advance.

For State theaters (Oper, Volksoper, Akadamietheater, and Burgtheater) you can get tickets in the city ticket office located in a courtyard near the Opera, with entrances from Goethegasse 1 and Hanuschgasse 3. Each of the theaters mentioned has its own ticket counter in this office.

The sale of tickets begins one week in advance for the State theaters, but there is such great interest in opera performances that the tickets may be sold out a couple of hours after the sale is open (people begin waiting in line several hours earlier). Tickets, if any remain, can also be purchased within one hour before the beginning of the performance at the evening ticket office of the theater concerned. Tickets for theaters other than the four mentioned can be purchased during the daily business hours 8 to 10 days ahead or within one hour before the performance at the respective theater ticket office.

You can buy tickets also at the various ticket agencies and, even more important, particularly for the opera, you can order tickets from them in advance and they will see to it that you get them.

Some of the principal travel agencies (such as *Cosmos*), and hotel desks will also perform this service. Some of the more strategically located ticket agencies are—*Flamm*, Kärntnerring 3, *Förstl*, Kärntnerring 12, *Delarue*, Führichgasse 4, all near the Opera; *Lienerbrünn*, Augustinerstr. 7, and *Kartenbüro*, Schauflergasse 2, both near Hofburg; *Weihburg*, Weihburggasse 3 and *Am Graben*, Graben 28, both near St. Stephen's. The fee charged by the agencies is generally 20% of the ticket price (hotel porters usually charge more) but most of these organizations have a tendency to ignore the existence of cheap seats. Budget tourists would do well to go to the city ticket office themselves.

Films The majority of movie theaters are still small and old-fashioned. There are some notable exceptions, among them—*Künstlerhaus* and *Gartenbau* in the 1st District, *Apollo* in the 6th District, and a few others. Foreign films are dubbed in German. The *Burgkino,* at Opernring 19, shows films of artistic merit in the original language (mostly English); the *Schottenring kino* on the Schottenring presents new releases in English only.

NIGHTLIFE Although the various night establishments of Vienna are plentiful, the city cannot boast of a real nightclub tradition. The average Viennese prefers to go to the opera, theater, and concerts for serious entertainment, and for an evening of merriment to a wine tavern or a Heuriger, where he joins in the community singing of folksongs. The Viennese love to dance, but the dancing is done mostly at the numerous balls during the season, in a few cafés with weekend music, and in dance-bars.

The prices in the Viennese nightclubs have gone up considerably in the last few years. Champagne is obligatory in some of the floor-show nightclubs and they will often insist that you take French champagne, or perhaps a whole bottle of Scotch, either of which will cost you more than in a better nightclub in Paris. Drinks at the bar in the same type of places are usually also very high and the hostesses employ the hard sell approach both at the bar and the tables.

Also watch out for the entrance tickets: in some of the places which charge an entrance fee because they have a show, they will try to charge it also long after the show is over; don't say that we have not warned you! Keep in mind, however, that these remarks apply primarily to some striptease clubs, and not at all to the dance bars frequented by the Viennese.

The leading night spots for dancing, frequented by the Viennese better class, are *Eden-Bar,* Liliengasse 2 near St. Stephen's, and *Splendid Bar,* in Jasomirgottstr. 3.

An interesting spot for dancing is *Trummelhof,* Cobenzlgasse 30 in Grinzing, with several sections, including a cellar. Some are primarily for eating, others for drinking, but mostly for dancing.

Other dance bars—*Chatanooga,* Graben 29, and *Scotch,* Parkring 10, where the accent is on youth and jazz; *Steckenpferd,* Dorotheergasse 7, disco; *Magic,* in the Volksgarten; *Atrium,* Schwarzenbergplatz 10, frequented mostly by students and offering 50 types of beer; *King's Club,* Plankengasse 6, disco; *Take Five,* Annagasse 3A; *Queen Anne,* Johannesgasse 12; *Lords Pub,* Karlplatz 1.

Fledermaus, at Spiegelgasse 2, is a mixture of literary cabaret and soul singing or whatever else is available for the sparse, but usually good quality program, with a lot of time for dancing in between; it guarantees no striptease and no girls (you have to bring your own).

The floor-show nightclubs cater primarily to the foreign customer and the out-of-towner, except the *Casanova,* Dorotheergasse 6, which is almost a revue theater. The others are mainly striptease and among the best is *Eve,* Führichgasse 3, which usually offers piquant shows devoted primarily to visiting firemen.

Next is *Maxim,* Opernring 11, also with considerable space and time for dancing between the acts. Regular shows, including dance acts, acrobatics, striptease, magicians and other international nightclub fare, are at *Moulin Rouge,* Walfischgasse 11.

CASINOS Although it's less than half an hour's drive to the casino in Baden, Vienna has a casino of its own called *Cercle Wien,* located in the Esterhazy Palace on Kärntnerstr. It is open daily from 7 P.M. for roulette, baccara, and black-jack. Mon. to Fri. from 8–9 novices can learn roulette for free under expert tutelage until the game becomes serious (and expensive) at 9.

 MONEY All Vienna banks change foreign money into Austrian schillings. The rate for travelers checks in dollars is slightly higher than the rate for greenbacks. There is no black market: the official rate is the real rate. Banking hours: 8–3 at main offices (larger banks); 8–12.30 and 1.30–3.30 at branch offices; Thurs. till 5.30 P.M.; closed Sat.

American Express is open 9–5.30 Mon. to Fri. and 9–1 on Sat. During these hours you can also change your money there.

Other exchange offices in Vienna where you can also change your money after regular banking hours are located at the Westbahnhof (daily from 7 A.M. to 10 P.M.), Südbahnhof (daily from 6.30 A.M. to 10 P.M.), and at Schwechat Airport (daily from 6.30 A.M. to 11 P.M.).

If you want to purchase foreign currencies, including that of your own country, with Austrian schillings, you have to show proof (money exchange receipt, remittance receipt) that you possess schillings on the basis of imported funds; in addition, you will lose some money because of the purchase exchange rate which is higher. It is much simpler to take your schillings across the border (you are allowed to take out up to 15,000) and have them changed in Germany, Switzerland, or Italy.

 MAIL AND CABLES The business hours of Vienna post offices vary, but most in the Inner City are open weekdays 8–7, Sat. until 12. Smaller offices close from 12–2. A few of the conveniently located post offices in the center of the city are: Central Post Office at Fleischmarkt 19, between St. Stephen's and the Danube Canal, open 7–7 for regular services; Krugerstr. 13, off Kärntnerstr. near the Opera, open 8–7; Wallnerstr. 7, around the block from Hochhaus, not far from Hofburg, open 7–7.

Post offices offering a 7-day, 24-hour service for registered, air, and express mail (a small extra charge for the late service) are: Central Post Office, late at night the telegram counter takes care of all services; the Central Telegraph Office at Börseplatz 1, off Schottenring; the post office at Westbahnhof and at Südbahnhof.

Stamps can be bought in tobacco shops.

Continuous 7-day, 24-hour telegram and cable service is provided by the Central Telegraph Office at Börseplatz 1 and by all post offices with continuous mail service. The telegram counters in the other post offices are open during the regular business hours. Telegrams and cables can also be sent by phone (dial 10), or via radio by Radio Austria, tel. 119, at any hour of day or night.

 SHOPPING The finest shops in Vienna line Kärntnerstrasse from the Opera to St. Stephen's Cathedral, then run left through the Graben and again left, following Kohlmarkt to the Imperial Palace. Almost all the small side streets within and adjoining this roughly outlined square form part of one of the best shopping districts in Europe. Part of this area is now a pedestrian precinct, with cafés in the open air in summer.

Shopping City Süd, an exit from the South Autobahn, groups a large number of attractive shops, offering goods at reasonable prices.

Vienna's Flea Market, with everything from junk to fine antiques, is next to the market area at Kettenbrückengasse, 1050, weekends and primarily in summer. The following list is of shops dealing with typically Austrian merchandise.

Austrian Jade *Burgenland,* Opernpassage 4, and Wildpretmarkt 6.

Blouses *Gretl Sieder,* Kärntnerstr. 2; *Hilde Kral,* Kohlmarkt 7; *Rositta,* Kärntnerstr. 17; *Gertrude Sikl,* Stephansplatz 6.

Books British Bookshop, Weihburggasse 8.

Candles *Metzger,* Stephansplatz 7; *Jos. Altmann,* Heidenschuss 1 and Mariahilferstr. 51, 1060. *Allegro,* Augustinerstr. 12; *Marius Retti,* Kohlmarkt 8–10, housed in a bold building in aluminum which won an American architectural prize.

Ceramics *Krolop* (Gmunden ceramics), Kärntnerdurchgang, a few shops around the corner from Kärntnerstr. 10; *Pawlata,* Kärntnerstr. 14.

Crystal *Lobmeyr,* Kärntnerstr. 26. Best crystal, tableware and gift articles—they made the crystal glass chandeliers for New York's new Metropolitan Opera.

Dirndls and Trachten for Women *Lanz,* Kärntnerstr. 10; *Tostmann,* Schottengasse 3A; *Gill,* Brandstätte 6; *Loden-Plankl,* Michaelerplatz 6; *Modell-Dirndl,* Tegetthofstr. 6; *Resi Hammerer,* Kärntnerstr. 29–31.

Handcrafts, Gifts and Souvenirs *Österreichische Werkstätten,* Kärntnerstr. 6; *Souvenir in der Hofburg,* Hofburg arcade; *Boutique Gretl,* Bognergasse 7, especially for enamel clocks; *Venuleth,* Kärntnerstr. 16, Graben 17 and the lobby of Hotel Intercontinental; *Niederösterreichisches Heimatwerk,* Herrengasse; *Tiroler Werkkunst,* Mariahilferstr. 89, 1060.

Jewelry *Heldwein,* Graben 13; *A. E. Köchert,* Neuer Markt 15; *Paltscho,* Graben 14; *Jul. Hügler,* Freisingerstr. 4 and Kärntnerstr. 53; *Juwel,* Kohlmarkt 1 and Kärntnerstr. 12; *Carius & Binder,* at No. 17; *Horwath,* at Kärntnerstr 29–31; *Kunz,* Neuer Markt 13.

Men's Trachten *Loden-Plankl* Michaelerplatz 6; *Collins Hüte,* Operngasse 12, for Alpine-style hats.

Petit Point *Jolles Studios,* Fassziehergasse 5, 1020; *Berta Smejkal,* Opernpassage 13 and Kohlmarkt 9.

Porcelain *Augarten,* Schloss Augarten, 1060, Stock-im-Eisenplatz 3–4 and Mariahilferstr. 99; *Ernst Wahliss,* Kärntnerstr. 17; *Rasper & Söhne,* Graben 15 and Mariahilferstr. 22; *Rosenthal Studio-Haus,* Kärntnerstr. 16; *E. Bakalowits,* Spiegelgasse 3; *Albin Denk,* Graben 13.

Wrought-iron and Weinhebers *Karl Zach,* Habsburgergasse 5 and Bräunerstr. 8; *Hamerle,* Annagasse 7; *Reckzügel,* on the Stephansplatz.

SPORTS It is perhaps a surprise to discover that Vienna, a center of arts and sciences of long tradition, is also extremely active in sports. The probable explanation is the average Austrian's love for nature and outdoors. Vienna possesses over 100 sports fields and about 400 recreation grounds, not even counting the two main establishments which are the large *Stadium* in Prater (it can accommodate about 90,000 spectators) and the unique *Stadthalle* (city con-

.vention and recreation hall) on Vogelweidplatz near Westbahnhof, a large, modern construction containing a main hall (capacity: 17,000 spectators), used for sporting events as well as for concerts and conventions; it also has an artificial ice skating rink for performances, another ice rink for training, a hall for various ball games, a gymnasium, several bowling alleys (for European as well as American-type bowling), and various conference rooms.

Winter Sports The Austrian national winter sport is skiing, but in Vienna the snow usually does not stay long at a time. With sufficient snow, there is very good skiing in various sections of Wienerwald, especially on the Hohe Hand Wiese slope, which is within the city limits (in the 14th District), and which even boasts a 400-meter-long ski lift; in case there is not enough snow, the ten so-called "snow guns" present here produce it artificially. There is also "grass-skiing" here in summer.

Otherwise the Vienna skiing grounds are on Semmering, Schneeberg, Hochkar, Türnitz, Annaberg, Josephsberg, and Raxalpe, about 2 slow driving or riding hours from the city, and in Mariazell which is a little farther.

Ice skating is also very popular in Vienna. There are more than 50 ice skating rinks, among them some artificial ones. The artificial openair skating rink of *Eislaufverein* (Ice Skating Union) is at Heumarkt 2 between the Konzerthaus and the Intercontinental Hotel. You can rent skates for a small fee.

Hiking and Climbing The Austrian national summer sports are hiking and mountain climbing and both of these are practiced by Viennese to a very large degree. Wienerwald—which can be reached by several streetcars and buses—offers any number of walks, light and hard, as short as half an hour and as long as the 220-km. path to Mödling. Pathways are well marked.

The nearest place for rock climbing is Hohe Wand (primarily for training) but the Styrian Alps are only a few hours' drive from the city. Consult the *Österreichischer Alpenverein* which has several branches in Vienna, including Walfischgasse 12, and Renngasse 4, both in the 1st District.

Swimming There are many open-air swimming pools and several bathing establishments on the Danube. One of the best in the open is the Stadium pool in Prater, and the most popular among the Danube bathing establishments is Gänsehäufel Island near Kaisermühlen on the Old Danube (cross Reichsbrücke and turn right). But perhaps the prettiest is the Krapfenwald pool in Grinzing, near the Cobenzl and overlooking the city.

The best among the indoor establishments are the Stadthallenbad next to Stadthalle and the Dianabad complex just across the canal, which replaces the old turn-of-the-century Dianabad, which in turn replaced the site where *The Blue Danube* was first performed.

Tennis There are many open-air tennis courts. Larger ones are in Prater, in the Eislaufverein in Heumarkt (in summer), in Pötzleinsdorf and Hietzing. There are several tennis schools, among them those at Döblinger Hauptstr. 48, 19th District, at Bergmüllergasse 8, 14th District, and in the suburb of Mauer, Kaserngasse 3, which also has indoor courts. The number of courts and schools is constantly increasing. Any problem finding somewhere to play, just ask your hotel concierge.

Horseracing and Riding For turf fans, there are spring, summer, and fall events at the two racetracks in Prater; flat-racing at Freudenau and trotting at Krieau. You may also watch trotting races at the spa of Baden, about 29 km. south of Vienna. A polo ground is near the Freudenau racetrack. Horses for riding are available at various riding schools such as *Wiener Reitinstitut,* Barmherzigengasse 17, 3rd District, *Reitverein St. Stephan,* Weingartenalle, 22nd District, and *Reitschule Kottas,* in Freudenau. In the immediate environs of Vienna are *Reitschule St. Leopold,* in Klosterneuburg-Weidling; *Reitclub,* in Grossenzersdorf; and *Dressur und Springreitschule Laxenburg,* Wienerstr. 7 in Laxenburg, a riding school specialized in dressage and jumping up to tournament standard.

Golf For golf, you also have to head out to Prater. *Golf-Club Wien* is located at Freudenau 65A, at the end of the Prater Hauptallee. The course is open from April to Dec.; 18 holes, total length (out and home) 5,510 meters which is about 6,020 yards. The clubhouse has a restaurant, closed Mon. Guests are welcome. Fees on weekends and holidays are a little higher than on workdays.

Hunting For hunters, there is neighboring Lower Austria and Burgenland as well as in the nearby areas of Styria. The famous *Internationaler Jagdorden St. Hubertus,* International St. Hubert Hunting Order, has its headquarters at Maria-hilferstr. 109, 6th District. For hunting possibilities, inquire here or at the Austrian National Tourist Office, Hohenstaufengasse 3 (tel. 561666).

Rowing The Danube offers many possibilities for rowing. There are about 20 sets of boathouses and numerous rowing clubs. Boats can be rented near the Wagramerstrasse bridge on the left bank of the Old Danube. For further information inquire at the *Österreichischer Ruderverband,* Austrian Rowing Association, Prinz Eugenstr. 12, 4th District (tel. 657307).

Sailing Sailing boats can be rented on the Old Danube, where there is also a sailing school. *Union Yacht-Club* and *Wiener Yacht-Club* have their boathouses here. The *Vienna Festival Regatta* takes place each June during the Vienna Festival and the Vienna Championship in the fall.

Bowling (American style). A large bowling establishment with 32 alleys, belonging to the Brunswick firm, is located at the Hauptallee in Prater. In Stadtalle there is also a hall with 12 modern, automatic alleys.

Gliding The gliding school *Wien-Donauwiese* is located just outside Vienna and can be reached by bus or streetcar. The gliding season is April to Nov. Programs for beginners, advanced flying and for flying instructors. Passenger flights are also available.

Camping At present, there are five campsites in the suburbs of Vienna: at Strandbad Rodaun and Breitenfurterstr. 269, Atzgersdorf in the *south;* two on

Hüttelbergstr. at Nos. 40 and 80, in the *west;* and at Wagramerstr. Süssenbrunn, in the *east.* For further information, inquire at *Österreichischer Camping-Club,* Schubert Ring 8, 1st District (tel. 72990).

USEFUL ADDRESSES Embassies and Consulates
Australian Embassy, Concordiaplatz 2, tel. 63 98 51. *British Embassy,* Reisnerstr. 40, tel. 73 15 75; *Consulate,* Wallnerstr. 8, tel. 63 75 02. *Canadian Embassy,* Obere Donaustr. 49, tel. 23 32 03; visa section at Tuchlauben 8, tel. 63 72 24. *South African Embassy,* Reisnerstr. 48, tel. 73 56 32. *US Embassy,* Boltzmanngasse 16, tel. 34 66 11; *Consulate,* Kärntnerstr. 42, tel. 34 66 11.

City Tourist Information *Fremdenverkehrsstelle der Stadt Wien,* Vienna City Tourist Office, with office in Opernpassage, tel. 43 16 08, open daily 9–7 for information on the city of Vienna but no room reservation.

For room reservation you may apply to the following offices:
Information-Zimmernachweis at Westbahnhof (West Station), tel. 83 51 85, open daily from 6.15 A.M. to 11 P.M.
Information-Zimmernachweis at Südbahnhof (South Station), tel. 65 21 68, open daily from 6.15 A.M. to 10 P.M.
Tourist information and room reservation office at the airport, open from 9 A.M. to 10.30 P.M.
Tourist Information at Novotel on Westautobahn all year; Rasthaus Föhrenberg on Südautobahn, from April to end of Oct.; 9 A.M. to 7 P.M. both.

General Travel Information For general holiday information on all of Austria inquire at the offices of the *Fremdenverkehrswerbung,* the Austrian National Tourist Office, Margaretenstr. 1, 1050 (tel. 561666). Current events (theater performances, concerts, etc.) are given in German and English by telephone (dial 15 15) on a 24-hour basis.
For information on motoring, contact *Österreichischer Automobil-, Motorrad- und Touring Club* (ÖAMTC), the Austrian Automobile Club, Schubertring 3, tel. 7 29 97, and Schwechat Airport, open daily (including holidays) until 8 P.M., for emergency repairs also, tel. 95 40.
For information on Austria as well as on other countries: *Cosmos* (international travel agency), Kärntner. Ring 15, tel. 52 26 61; *Österreichisches Verkehrsbüro* (Austrian tourist agency), Opernring 11, tel. 57 96 57; *American Express,* Kärntnerstr. 21, tel. 52 05 44. *Wagons Lits/Cook,* Kärntner Ring 2, tel 65 76 31.

Shipment Service *P.I.E. Transport,* an American firm with a branch in Vienna at Akademiestr. 3 (near the Opera), tel. 52 74 40. Under the friendly management of Herr Matz, they will ship anything for you.

Guides Inquire at Vienna Guide Service, Montecuccoliplatz 1, 1130, Vienna, or contact *Sektion Fremdenverkehr* (Tourist Section) of Chamber of Commerce.

Buses from Vienna Buses to nearby areas in Lower Austria leave from *Österreichisches Verkehrsbüro* (Austrian tourist agency), Friedrichstr. 7, and from other points.

Danube Travel If you wish to travel on Danube ships elsewhere in Austria, inquire at the *Danube Shipping Company (DDSG)*, with the main office at Hintere Zollamtsstr. 1, 3rd District, tel. 72 21 51. The Vienna ticket office of the same company is at the landing stage at Mexikoplatz 8, tel. 24 34 20.

International Organizations *Austro-American Society,* Stallburggasse 2, tel. 52 39 82. *Austro-American Institute of Education,* Operngasse 4, tel. 52 77 20. *British Council,* Schenkenstr. 4, tel. 63 26 16.

Lost and Found Fundamt (Police), Bräunerstr. 5, tel 52 46 17; Fundamt (Railways), Westbahnhof, tel. (first dial) 56 50 (then dial) 29 96.

Escort Service and Baby Sitters For these services, as well as for interpreters, translators or help in driving, contact the Meeting Center of the *Österreichischer Akademischer Gästedienst* (Austrian Student Society Service), Mühlgasse 20, 1040, tel. 57 35 25. They have 2,400 students (male and female) on their rolls who are willing to help you.

Emergencies If you need a doctor and don't speak any German, try *American Medical Society of Vienna,* Lazarettgasse 13, tel. 42 45 68, or call your embassy. In case of an accident, call 133 for Police Accident Squad, and 144 for ambulance service. British tourists receive free emergency hospital in-patient treatment, if documented before leaving Britain with Form CM1 from local Social Security Office, plus passport.

LOWER AUSTRIA

Castles, Abbeys and Vineyards

Lower Austria, or Niederösterreich (as it is called in the German original), is the largest of the nine federal states composing the present-day Federal Republic of Austria. It borders on Upper Austria to the west and Styria to the south. Tiny Burgenland, another federal state, is sandwiched in on the southeast along the Hungarian border. To the north and east is the frontier of Czechoslovakia. The Blue Danube (actually rather a muddy brown most of the year) flows through the heart of Lower Austria from west to east, its banks and surroundings studded with medieval castles, baroque abbeys and steep vineyards, especially in the beautiful Wachau section. South of the Danube is the area of slowly rising Alpine foothills, deeply cut by mountain streams and reaching their highest elevations from 5,900 to 6,500 feet in the Schneeberg, Raxalpe, Göller, Ötscher and Hochkar mountains, all near and on the border with Styria. Northwest of the Danube, the woody slopes of the Waldviertel stretch towards the Bohemian hills, while the northeastern section is rich agricultural land.

There are about 550 castles and fortresses in Lower Austria, some preserved, some reconstructed and others in ruins, since this area, particularly in the Danube valley, was the passageway between east and west

Europe and was thus fortified as the defense line of the Germanic Holy Roman Empire. The history of abbeys and other monasteries parallels that of the castles; for the purpose of defense, they were often built as fortresses. The romantic appeal of times gone forever lingers about them all.

The main skiing area is in the southern part of Lower Austria, particularly in the range of mountains bordering Styria. Skiing facilities exist also in some places in the Waldviertel region north of the Danube. Technical installations have improved greatly during the past few years and this is becoming an increasingly popular, but still inexpensive, winter sports area, with the emphasis on cross-country skiing. In general, good snow conditions can be expected between December and March, but in the highest spots one can usually ski until the end of April.

Hotel facilities in general are geared primarily to the needs of budget-minded Viennese vacationists. Although some hotels have few rooms with bath, they are very clean and generally comfortable and range from the moderate category to the inexpensive countryside Gasthaus type. Exceptions are the large, first-class hotels in resort centers such as Semmering and Baden, well fitted to the needs of top international clientele.

Prices throughout the province are about 25 percent lower than those of similar hotel categories in Vienna and in the large tourist centers of Tyrol and Salzburg. In the smaller places you will usually take your meals where you are staying, although any roadside Gasthaus will provide you with a good, if limited, menu.

Route Planning

Railways and roadways follow almost identical routes, but fast train service is provided only on the main railroad lines: Vienna–St. Pölten–Melk–Amstetten–Upper Austria, Vienna-Wiener Neustadt–Semmering, Vienna–Eggenburg–Gmund in Waldviertel. The latter, however, provides only a couple of fast trains daily in each direction. The other two are main international lines to the west and the south and provide many fast trains daily. Secondary railway lines reach most of the places of interest, but service is slow and trains must be changed often; they are not recommended to anyone wishing to cover more than a few dozen kilometers daily. One exception is the street-car type of train from Vienna (near the Opera) to Baden, which operates almost every half hour between 6 A.M. and 10 P.M.

Travel **by bus** is usually more interesting, and sometimes faster, than by train. Lower Austria has an excellent network of buses. In Vienna inquire at the Niederösterreichisches Landesreiseburo, Heidenschuss 2, or Strauchgasse 1, both in the Inner City, or at any tourist office, and at the post office in smaller towns. Most of the buses in the countryside are run by the postal administration. Daily sightseeing tours in summer (in winter two or three a week) to Heiligenkreuz–Mayerling–Baden, Klosterneuburg, Wachau, and Semmering are available from Vienna. For details of exploring **by boat,** see our *Facts at Your Fingertips* section. River travel is one of the most exciting ways of seeing the region.

From Vienna the best way to visit Lower Austria is **by car.** You can make daily trips leaving in the morning and returning in the evening and, in a week or so, can superficially cover the most important points. Routes 7, 2, and 4 (the last two forking after the embryonic North Autobahn past Stockerau) take you north to the Czech border and, with the use of side roads, will enable you to cover the Thaya valley area. Route 3 will take you to Krems; combined with 34, 38, and 37, it will enable you to cover Kamp valley. From Krems you can continue on a very scenic road along the left bank of the Danube through the Wachau and Nibelungengau to Persenbeug, where you can cross the bridge to Ybbs and return to Vienna on the West Autobahn, A1; if you want to drive along both banks in the Wachau, follow the left bank road as far as Emmersdorf, cross by ferry and bridge to Melk, and return along the right bank on an older but also good road to Mautern; there you can either cross the bridge back to Krems, take 32 to St. Pölten and the autobahn, or drive back to Vienna via Tulln and Klosterneuburg. Route 1 and the West Autobahn are the main roads west from Vienna and will take you to St. Pölten, Melk, Pöchlarn (off the road), Ybbs (off the road), Amstetten to Upper Austria. From St. Pölten take 20 to Annaberg, Mitterbach and Erlauf Lake, from the vicinity of Ybbs 25 to Lunzer Lake, and from Amstetten 121 to Waidhofen and other localities in the upper Ybbs valley. Semmering is reached by 17, proceeding south of Vienna, and Raxalpe and Schneeberg by side roads branching off 17. The South Autobahn A2 is complete from Vienna to Grimmenstein, whence 54 continues to Mönichkirchen and the Wechsel mountains.

Exploring Lower Austria

Lower Austria derives its name from the fact that for many centuries it was the "lower" (in the sense of the Danube's course) part of the Archduchy of Austria. The Archduchy of Austria eventually imposed both its name and its capital, Vienna, on the entire territory of today's Austria, but at the same time Vienna also remained the official capital of Lower Austria and therefore the Lower Austrian state government has its offices there. Many Lower Austrians no longer agree with this accommodation and would prefer to see the tradition-filled and vineyard-framed Krems become their capital, since nowadays Krems represents the spirit and the face of Lower Austria much more adequately than Vienna. A change, however, is unlikely.

Vienna Woods and Baden

Wienerwald, the Vienna Woods, is not a natural park or forest, as frequently thought of thanks to the impressions received from Strauss musical motifs and Viennese poetic references, but a geographic name given to a large range of rolling, densely wooded hills, extending from Vienna's doorstep to the outposts of the Alps in the south. Wienerwald is criss-crossed by country roads and hiking paths, dotted by forest lodges and inns, ornamented by quaint little villages and market towns. Throughout the year it is the weekend playground of the Viennese and, particularly in summer, thousands of them swarm on foot and by car through its forests and meadows.

Wienerwald reaches its northernmost point at Burg Greifenstein, a medieval castle soaring on a steep rock above the Danube and the tiny village of Greifenstein. A few miles down the Danube is Klosterneuburg, an old market town characterized by its remarkable 12th-century Augustine Abbey: its originally Romanesque church has a beautifully hand-carved wooden choir and oratory; in the Leopold Chapel is the famous Verduner Altar (1181) by Nikolaus von Verdun (Werden) decorated with 51 biblical scenes in medieval enamel, medieval stained-glass windows and a 12th-century candelabrum; in the great marble hall there are ceiling frescos by Daniel Gran; in addition, there is a library of 230 old manuscripts and 140,000 volumes, a museum and treasury. Klosterneuburg is actually located just outside the northwestern boundaries of Vienna.

The panoramic Höhenstrasse (High Road), disclosing beautiful vistas of Vienna and the north section of the Vienna Woods, takes you from Klosterneuburg over the Leopoldsberg, Kahlenberg and Cobenzl elevations to the western suburbs of the city.

The eastern edges of the Viennese Woods are skirted by vineyards beginning at Klosterneuburg, which is also an important wine center, with the Abbey being the biggest and the best wine producer. The vineyards then follow southwards through the renowned wine villages of Nussdorf, Grinzing and Sievering, all of them within the city limits of Vienna. South of the city, the wine belt resumes at Perchtoldsdorf, a picturesque market town with many wine taverns, the 13th-century Gothic parish church and an imposing defense tower completed in 1511. Perchtoldsdorf, called locally "Petersdorf", is a beloved wine drinking excursion spot of the Viennese. In the nearby town of Mödling, founded in the 10th century, there are even more buildings of historical interest, including the Gothic parish church, a Romanesque 12th-century charnel house and the Town Hall with a Renaissance loggia. Near Mödling is the Romanesque Liechtenstein castle, which received its name from the Styrian minnesinger, Ulrich von Liechtenstein (1199–1275).

A few kilometers east of Mödling, already in the plain, and about 16 km. south of Vienna, is Schloss Laxenburg, a complex consisting of a large baroque Neues Schloss (New Castle), a small 14th-century Altes Schloss (Old Castle), and an early 19th-century neo-Gothic castle—now a good restaurant—in the sizeable lake. The large park is populated by many birds as well as small game, such as roe deer and hare. According to the taste of the period, the park is also decorated with statues, cascades, imitation temples and similar structures. The Altes Schloss was built in 1381 by Duke Albrecht III as his summer residence, and several Habsburg emperors resided in the Neues Schloss, which now, of all unlikely institutions, houses the International Institute of Applied System's Analysis. Opposite is the large baroque Convent of the Charitable Sisters.

Back in Mödling we follow the Weinstrasse (Wine Road) through the lush grape-growing country to Gumpoldskirchen, one of Austria's most famous wine-producing villages and the home of one of Europe's pleasantest white wines. Vintner houses line the main street, many of them with large wooden gates, typical of this area, leading into the vine-covered courtyard-gardens where the Heuriger (wine of the last vintage) is served by the owner and his family at simple, wooden tables (sometimes to the tune of merry or not-so-merry melodies played by an accordion player). Gumpoldskirchen also has an arcaded Renaissance Town Hall, the market fountain made out of a Roman sarcophagus, and the castle of the Teutonic Knights who own some of the best vineyard sites in the area.

Baden

We can proceed on the same Wine Road to the famous spa of Baden, which can also be reached more quickly from Vienna via the autobahn, by the local Vienna–Baden streetcar-type of train, or by the main railroad.

Since antiquity, Baden's sulphuric thermal baths have attracted the ailing and the fashionable from all over the world. The Roman Aquae Pannonae revived under the Babenbergs in the 10th century; but only with the visit of the Russian Tsar, Peter the Great, in 1698, began Baden's golden age, highlighted by the visits of Emperor Franz II, who spent the twelve summers before his death in 1835 in the spa. And in Baden, Mozart composed his *Ave Verum,* Beethoven passed 15 summers and composed large sections of the *Ninth Symphony* and *Missa Solemnis;* Franz Grillparzer wrote his historical dramas and Josef Lanner, Johann Strauss, Karl Michael Ziehrer and Karl Millöcker directed and composed their waltzes, marches and operettas.

The loveliest spot in Baden is the huge and beautiful Kurpark, where one can listen to one of the many public concerts, attend operetta performances in the outdoor Summer Arena (in winter, theater performances are given in the Stadttheater), just sit peacefully under the old trees, or walk through the upper sections of the Kurpark for a view of the town from above. The old Kurhaus, enlarged, renovated, and with a new Kongresshaus (Convention Hall) with all the latest equipment for simultaneous translation and other gadgetry accompanying convention centers, is now known as the Kur-Kongress-Haus.

The baths themselves are built right over the sites of the 15 springs, which pour forth the sulphuric thermal water to the tune of 8 million liters (1,760,000 gallons) a day. The water is about body temperature and is reported to be particularly good for the therapy of rheumatic diseases and partially disabled persons. In addition to the six bath establishments proper, there are also two outdoor thermal water swimming establishments, the larger one with five pools and a water temperature of 32 degrees C. (89.6 degrees F.).

West of Baden, the quiet and soft Helenental Valley takes you to Mayerling, scene of the tragic death in 1889 of Archduke Rudolf, Emperor Franz Josef's only son, and his young mistress. The reasons and mystery of the Mayerling tragedy are still impetuously discussed and disputed by the Austrian public, press and historians at the slightest provocation as well as providing a torrid subject for movie-makers and novelists in many other parts of the world. The site of the hunting-lodge where the double death took place is marked by a Carmelite convent, built by the bereaved Emperor.

Nearby in the heart of the southern section of the Vienna Woods is Heiligenkreuz, a Cistercian Abbey with a famous Romanesque and Gothic church, founded by Leopold III, the "Holy", in 1135.

The vineyards immediately south of Baden produce some of the best red wine in Austria. Here is the small green spa of Bad Vöslau, resting on a hillside, with a lovely open-air thermal swimming establishment at the foot of the hill, and a large and unique forest of pine trees, freshly and healthily smelling of tar, beginning in the Kurpark above and extending to the top of the Harzberg hill. The latter can be reached in a half-hour walk; from here there is a fine view of the Vienna Woods, Schneeberg and Wechsel mountains.

From Wiener Neustadt to Semmering

South and southwest of the Vienna Woods lie the highest mountains in Lower Austria, the Semmering, the Schneeberg, Rax and Wechsel groups. In winter the high plateaus of Schneeberg and Rax and the undulating ridges of Semmering and Wechsel are covered with a thick mantle of snow and provide ideal skiing conditions.

To reach these winter sports and mountain air resorts, you follow the South Autobahn or the main railroad to Wiener Neustadt, originally built in the 12th century as a fortress town for the protection against invasions from the east. The remains of the 12th- and 13th-century town walls can still be seen near the large and pleasant city park; the most prominent among them is a Gothic tower, called Reckturm, which is said to have been built with part of the ransom money exacted for Richard the Lionhearted. As there are several other sites in Austria which claim the same financial source, it would seem that the vast sum wrung from the people of England was put to good use.

Wiener Neustadt is usually thought of as an industrial city, but it still has a number of historic artistic treasures, in spite of the heavy destruction through air raids in 1943, when 52,000 bombs (about 1½ bombs for every inhabitant) demolished 3,982 of about 4,000 buildings existing at that time. The city has been rebuilt, however, more along functional lines though, of course, the entire face of the city had been altered. Some of the damaged historic buildings could be repaired, such as the fine 13th-century late Romanesque and Gothic parish church, with later interior baroque and rococo additions (tomb of Cardinal Khlesel by Bernini; rococo choir, twelve apostles and unique Annunciation group by the late Gothic sculptor Lorenz Luchsperger). In addition to several other interesting churches, there is also a beautiful 14th-century sculpture by Master Michael (who also designed St. Stephen's tower in Vienna) located in a small park on Wienerstrasse. Wiener Neustadt is also the seat of the Austrian Military Academy, installed by Empress Maria Theresa in the 13th-century castle (open to visitors). It was completely burned out in 1945 and rebuilt between 1949 and 1952. In the west wing of the Military Academy is the 15th-century Georgskapelle, a Gothic church with the grave of Emperor Maximilian I, called the "Last Knight", under the high altar.

For the Wechsel Mountains, continue on the autobahn or by train to the market town of Aspang, a summer resort in the Pitten Valley, whose heights are guarded by a line of castles, particularly the notable 11th-century Seebenstein castle-fortress (later rebuilt in Renaissance style). From Aspang, Route 54 winds up to Mönichkirchen (3,300 ft.), the summer and winter resort center in this area.

Schneeberg and Raxalpe

Schneeberg and Raxalpe lie west of Wiener Neustadt. The village of Puchberg, a mountain resort in summer and winter, is the departure point for Schneeberg. A small, cog-wheel railway crawls 4,000 feet up the crest of the mountain to a point nearly 6,000 feet above sea level. Puchberg has a modern Kurmittelhaus, where water cures and other medical treatments are administered. If you want to lose weight or improve your blood circulation, this is the place to try it.

Immediately southwest beyond Schneeberg lies the Raxalpe. Reichenau, a pleasant summer resort in the valley of the river Schwarza, and next-door Hirschwang, which is the valley station of the Rax cable car, are the best departure points for the 6,500-foot plateau of Rax. Both can easily be reached by bus from nearby Payerbach, another summer resort and a station on the main railroad line south of Vienna, which in this section makes a steep climb from Gloggnitz, an old town in a deeply cut, scenic valley, up to the Semmering mountain pass.

The Semmering resort center lies around the pass, mostly on the steep slopes on the Lower Austrian side, the other side of the pass being in Styria. Semmering is now largely the preserve of rest homes belonging to health insurances and large firms; but some hotels and pensions, romantically perched high up on the side of the mountain that gives the place its name, remain from the luxurious past. In summer there are facilities for swimming, sunbathing, tennis and, of course, easy walks through the refreshing woods as well as harder mountain excursions. Skiing, ski competitions, ice skating, and tobogganing represent the main activities of the winter season. Semmering is also a Höhenluftkurort (a place for high climatic cures) for respiratory and allied ailments.

Höllental, northwest of Semmering, is the wild mountain valley of the River Schwarza that once cut the high mountain plateau into two parts, which today are called Raxalpe and Schneeberg. The road through Höllental leads over the Ochssattel Pass to St. Aegyd in the Göller mountain area, an unpretentious winter and summer resort, which, however, can be reached much more comfortably through the Traisen Valley from St. Pölten.

Marchfeld and Weinviertel

Marchfeld is the fertile plain to the east of Vienna between the Danube and the river March, which has given it the name and which marks the border between Lower Austria and Slovakia. Marchfeld is the granary of Austria, the wide grain fields being interspersed by woods and lush meadows. Pheasant, partridge and quail, as well as other small game, prefer such terrain and for centuries this region has been a hunter's paradise.

Marchauen Nature Preserve is a haven for wildlife, including Austria's only cormorant colony; the Safari Park Gänserndorf, open for cars, contains 340 species of large animals, among them 40 lions. Numerous baroque castles and sumptuous hunting lodges, now house museums; open April to October. One, Schloss Marchegg, on the Slovakia border, is today an important hunting museum. To the east is Schloss Obersiebenbrunn, given by Charles VI to Prince Eugene, who entrusted Hildebrandt with the construction of a charming garden pavilion. To the south on Route 49 are Schlosshof, once owned by Empress Maria Theresa, and Niederweiden, which was the hunting castle of Prince Eugen. Schloss Orth, on the Danube, once a fortress dating from the 12th century, now houses a fishing, honey-making and bee museum, with a 30-million-year-old bee fossilized in a piece of amber. Eckartsau, an 18th-century hunting castle with an imposing stairway and ceiling frescos by Daniel Gran, was given by Archduke Franz Ferdinand, assassinated in 1914 by the Serbs, to his nephew Emperor Charles. He signed his abdication here in 1918.

Across the Danube from Marchfeld, on the southern bank, lies the Roman town and military camp of Carnuntum, presently partially excavated; in addition to the remainders of the old Roman houses, the sites to visit are the amphitheater and the Heidentor (Heathen Gate), standing alone far out amidst the fields. The objects found during the excavations can be seen in the Museum Carnuntinum in Bad Deutsch-Altenburg, a nearby spa. The town also has a 13th-century Romanesque basilica and an African Museum in the Schloss Ludwigsdorf. In the summer Roman plays are performed in another amphitheater on the road to Petronell, where there is a Danube Museum in a baroque castle whose one-time owners are buried in a remarkable 12th-century Romanesque circular chapel.

Another few miles to the east is Hainburg with interesting medieval walls and gates, a castle-fortress on an elevation in the town, the ruins of the Rothenstein castle on a hill outside the town, the baroque parish church and many Gothic, Renaissance and baroque houses. 8 km. south of Carnuntum is the Castle Rohrau, home of the Counts of Harrach and Austria's only private art museum. It has more than 200 paintings, mostly Italian and Spanish, but is open to the public only in summer, as is Haydn's birthplace, a modest, thatched building in the village, which was restored and extended for the composer's bicentenary in 1982.

The Weinviertel

North of Vienna, between the Danube and the border of Czechoslovakia, lies the Weinviertel, the Wine District. Though other regions of Lower Austria are even more noted for their wines, the local dry whites are pleasing even to a discriminating palate. A string of medieval castles, often in ruins, and many colorful old market towns can also be found in this area.

Across the Danube, beside the short North Autobahn, Korneuburg is a small town with a picturesque main square dominated by the Gothic Town Hall tower; the Augustine Church is a remarkable example of rococo style. On a hill a bit beyond Korneuburg is Kreuzenstein, a 12th-century castle-fortress, destroyed by the Swedes in the Thirty

Years' War, restored in the 19th century, and presently a museum and showpiece for old Austrian castle atmosphere. 32 km. to the north at Ernstbrunn, 13th-century St. Martin's contains an altar piece by Kremser Schmidt, while the huge 17th-century castle, in a beautiful park, houses an Empire museum. To the west is Hollabrunn, one of the main towns in this area, surrounded by wooded hills; while 5 km. to the north is Schöngrabern, home of an important Romanesque church with notable reliefs on the outside of the apse and frescos within. Farther west lies the charming little town of Eggenburg, with medieval walls, Gothic churches, Renaissance and baroque houses, and the Krahuletz Museum, with important prehistoric finds from the area.

On the way to Eggenburg you pass Kleinwetzdorf and "Heldenberg" (Heroes' Mountain). The latter is a formal garden and the incredible burial place of Field Marshall Radetzky. There are innumerable statues and busts, including all the Habsburgs and Babenbergs and countless generals; Radetzky is buried in a crypt along with two barons who paid for the honor of occupying the same tomb as the Field Marshall.

Some of the best wine in the Weinviertel is produced north of Eggenburg and Hollabrunn in and near the Pulkau Valley. Here particularly is the wine town of Retz, renowned also for its Gothic Dominican church, several Renaissance and baroque buildings, among them a castle with fine interiors, and a windmill. Important wine-producing villages are Pulkau, with a Romanesque charnel house and the Gothic Heiligenblut Church (whose winged main altar is a masterpiece of carving); Röschitz, with the Ludwig Weber Cellar (wall reliefs made of loess); Haugsdorf, with "cellar streets" lined by wine press houses, (typical for this area); and Mailberg, with the baroque castle and church of the St. John's Order of Knights.

East on the Thaya River is the small 13th-century town of Laa, with partially preserved walls and an old fortress. East and south of Laa, the fortress ruins of Falkenstein and Staatz still seem to be powerful enough to dominate the countryside around them. The village of Falkenstein and the nearby market town of Poysdorf also produce good wines. Massive 15th-century Schloss Asparn on the Zaya houses the Museum of Lower Austria's Prehistory; in the park are models of habitations from the Ice Age to the Celts.

Southeast are the oilfields near the town of Zistersdorf, which is also surrounded by vineyards. Not far away is Dürnkrut, where in 1278 the famous battle was fought which established the supremacy of the Habsburgs in Austria for the next six and a half centuries.

Along the Danube through the Wachau

If you have time, you should see this part of Austria from the deck of a Danube paddleboat steamer. When the weather is fine and warm, the trip downstream is highly rewarding. The slower trip upstream against the swift-flowing current is even better, allowing more time to take in the magnificent scenery, the charming wine-growing villages, and the fairyland castles perched precariously on the rocky crags on the river bends. If you cannot spare the time for this leisurely inspection, and go by car, be sure to cross over to the north bank of the Danube and follow the river along the scenic road through the Wachau and Nibelungengau.

Traveling by boat upstream from Vienna, you leave the Kloster-neuburg Abbey and Greifenstein castle at your left and enter the area of the fertile Tullner Feld (Tullner Plain), on the south bank, named after the town of Tulln, which is known primarily for its flower cultivation. It was here that Kriemhild met Etzel (Attila) in the *Niebelungen Saga*. The Danube spreads out here in several natural canals among thick river woods, abounding with game. At the end of Tullner Feld, the river Traisen flows into the Danube, rushing from the high mountains on the Styrian border.

Near the confluence of the Traisen with the Danube is the old market town of Traismauer, with a Renaissance castle, a tower gate, remains of the town walls and many old houses with bay-windows and arcaded courtyards. Farther up the Traisen are Herzogenburg, with the famed Augustine Abbey, founded in the 12th century, but whose architecture is partially from the great baroque masters Fischer von Erlach and Jakob Prandtauer; it has a valuable library and a rich museum of Gothic altars, as well as a wine tavern serving its own wines; and Pottenbrunn, a moated castle with a tin-soldier museum, open in summer only. Still further is St. Pölten, the most important city and the key railroad and road junction in this district.

The old center of St. Pölten shows a distinct baroque face and contains many artistic treasures. The originally Romanesque cathedral has rich baroque interiors and more than a dozen paintings and frescos by Daniel Gran. The rococo Franciscan church has four altar paintings by Krem-ser Schmidt. The so-called "Institute of English Maidens" in Linzer-strasse is one of the finest baroque buildings in the city; the ceiling frescos in its church are by Altomonte and there is also a painting by Lukas Cranach from 1516.

Farther up the Traisen Valley is Lilienfeld, the seat of a medieval Cistercian abbey, founded in 1202 and built in Romanesque style with later baroque additions; a small gallery of paintings, and a valuable library (1704) with several hundred manuscripts and early prints and 30,000 books are also part of the abbey. Still farther upstream is the small industrial town of Freiland, where the river Türnitz, coming from the winter sports resort of the same name, flows into the Traisen. Higher up near the source of the Traisen and the Göller mountain is St. Aegyd, a quiet year-round resort surrounded by mountains and forests.

Krems and the Wachau

Back on the Danube we continue upstream to Krems, one of the most important cities in Lower Austria and the Austrian wine trade center; the steep vineyards above and near the city produce some of the best Austrian wines. Krems also marks the beginning (when traveling upstream) of the Wachau section of the Danube. It is a delightful old town, founded in 955 or earlier, with partially preserved city walls, a 15–16th century Rathaus with a Renaissance oriel, a parish church that is one of the oldest baroque buildings in Lower Austria, a city museum located in the former Dominican Romanesque and Gothic church, a very interesting wine museum in the adjoining former monastery, the Gothic–Renaissance Palais Gozzo on Hoher Markt, where open-air plays are staged during the summer, the former Minorite Church in the Stein section of the city (converted into a museum of the work of Kremser Schmidt, the famous Austrian baroque painter), the former Imperial Toll House, also in Stein (Steiner Landstrasse 84), with splendid Renaissance façade and frescos, and many other Renaissance, baroque and rococo buildings, some of them hidden away in the narrow streets on both sides of Obere and Untere Landstrasse, which you enter through the majestic 15th-century Steiner Tor, and others located in the western suburb of Stein, once a town in its own right.

Across the Danube from Krems, in a commanding position on a hill, stands Göttweig, another great abbey, this time Benedictine, founded in the 11th century, but the present baroque buildings are from the 18th century, built to the plans made by Lukas von Hildebrandt; it has a nice tavern with its own wines, and a beautiful view of Krems and the Danube valley from the terrace.

Our next stop in the Wachau is Dürnstein, famous for its wines, for its quaint old houses and streets, and for its baroque reddish church tower which is considered the most beautiful of its kind in Austria. Dürnstein is also known for its castle, now mostly in ruins, where Richard the Lionheart was imprisoned for 13 months; according to the story, it was beneath its battlements that the faithful Blondel played. He had wandered all over the area, trying to find the castle where his king was imprisoned and finally was rewarded by hearing his master's voice.

Farther upstream on the same bank are: the charming Weissenkirchen, with a Gothic walled church and the beautiful Teisenhofer patrician house, with a 16th-century arcaded courtyard, presently housing the Wachau Museum. Weissenkirchen also has the Prager and Jamek vineyards, the latter of which has the finest restaurant in the Wachau region. St. Michael has a fortified church; Spitz is another famous wine village. On the other bank, the Aggstein fortress, partially in ruins, is perched upon the top of a 1,000-foot cliff, in a commanding position over the Wachau. At its foot lies the village of Aggsbach, and straight across the

Danube on the left bank, the market town of Aggsbach-Dorf, connected by a small ferryboat.

Farther up on the right bank comes Schönbühel Castle. Right beyond it on the same bank is the town of Melk, dominated by its impressive baroque abbey, one of the most beautiful in Austria. Originally a 10th-century fortress, and the seat of the Babenberg family who preceded the Habsburgs, it was given to the Benedictines in the early 12th century, but its present baroque buildings were planned by Jakob Prandtauer in the 18th century. Its library is one of the finest, with some 80,000 volumes and 1,850 old manuscripts dating from the 9th century. This huge and richly endowed complex, though full of art treasures, is also important as an integral part of Austrian history, which can be sensed on every hand. Unfortunately, Melk is in a bad way, physically, with all sorts of decay attacking the fabric of the massive buildings. It may be that you will not be able to visit parts of the complex that have been closed off for repairs. Restoration of the West Front has been completed and the result is magnificent.

The church in the village of Mauer, just north of Melk, has a richly carved altar.

Beyond Wachau the Danube Valley is called Nibelungengau because the Nibelungs are supposed to have settled here, at least for a while; their romantic arrival by ship is enacted every year at the June solstice in a pageant performed at the medieval river town of Pöchlarn; then, both banks of the Danube in this section are ablaze with bonfires and fire-works. This is the area which is supposed to have witnessed some of the events of the *Epic of the Nibelungen,* the great saga that has inspired many versions, mainly that of Wagner's *Ring.* The original story was concerned with the mythical hero Siegfried, his faithful and brave Nibelungs, his marriage to the Burgundian royal daughter Kriemhild and his assassination by Kriemhild's relatives; in revenge Kriemhild then married the King of the Huns and brought about the conflict between the Burgundians and the Huns. Kriemhild and her brothers, kings of Burgundy, stayed in Bechelaren (Pöchlarn) when they travelled to Attila's court in West Hungary.

Crowning a hill on the left bank is the two-towered Maria Taferl pilgrimage church, in the summer resort village of the same name, and at its foot is the bright little market town of Marbach, also a small summer resort. 5 km. northeast of Maria Taferl is the castle of Artstetten, burial place of Franz-Ferdinand and his morganatic wife Sophie, both of whom were assassinated in Sarajevo in 1914 (which of course was to lead to World War I). Nibelungengau ends at the 17th-century Persenbeug Castle, the birthplace of Karl I, the last Austrian Emperor. Across the river and connected by a dam bridge is Ybbs, with remains of medieval walls and towers and a pretty Renaissance fountain on the main square.

The natural beauty of the Danube Valley is marred here by a large hydro-electric power station on the river.

The Erlauf and Ybbs Valleys

At Pöchlarn, the small Erlauf River, coming from the Ötscher mountains in the south, joins the Danube. Not far up the Erlauf Valley are the towns of Wieselburg and Pürgstall, both with interesting churches and castles. Wieselburg is also known for its beer and for its country fair taking place in late June. Nearby is Scheibbs, another small old town with partially preserved walls, a tower gate and a cluster of Renaissance houses around the Gothic parish church, standing on the main square next to the 16th-century castle, which has a beautiful arcaded courtyard.

Farther upstream in a rising side valley is Gaming, noted for the former Carthusian monastery, once the largest in the Order's German province. Dissolved by the "liberal" Emperor Josef II in 1782, it is presently in a fair stage of dilapidation but still interesting to visit. In its upper course, skirting the mountain of Gemeinde Alpe and Ötscher, the Erlauf flows through two Erlauf lakes, one natural and one artificial. In this area there are several small summer and winter resorts saddled on wooded and meadowed mountain backs, such as Puchenstuben, Gösing, Annaberg, Josefsberg and Mitterbach, the latter actually on the Styrian border and only three miles from Mariazell, the well-known Styrian resort with the famous pilgrimage church. All these places can also be reached by the main road from St. Pölten.

From Erlauf Lake, a side road takes you to the upper Ybbs Valley to Lunz and Lunzer Lake, nestled among fir-treed slopes. This unpretentious summer resort, whose meadows are covered with white narcissi in late spring, can be reached more easily either by road or train from Gaming and the lower Erlauf Valley. A few miles down the Ybbs River is Göstling, from where a mountain road takes you up to the Hochkar Plateau and a chair lift close to the peak of Hochkar (5,930 ft.).

The most picturesque town in the lower Ybbs Valley is Waidhofen, with rows of 15th- and 16th-century gabled houses with bay windows and arcaded courtyards; the parish church with winged main altar and several other interesting churches; the high and impressive castle tower; and the massive "city tower", built in 1542 in memory of the city's victorious repulsion of the Turks, with the clock dial still showing the hour of the Turkish defeat—11.45 A.M. A landmark seen miles around is the majestic baroque pilgrimage church of Sonntagberg, crowning a 2,300-foot hill not far from Waidhofen. A few kilometers to the northwest is the historic Benedictine Abbey of Seitenstetten, founded in 1112, with frescos by Kremser Schmidt and a priceless collection of paintings and engravings; to the northeast is the small town of Neuhofen, which likes to call itself the "cradle of Austria", since the oldest known spelling of Österreich (Austria)—Ostarrichi—was found here in an old document dated 996. In its further lower course, the Ybbs passes by Amstetten, and flows into the Danube near the town of Ybbs.

Waldviertel

Waldviertel is the hilly and forested region north of Wachau and Nibelungengau marked by two main rivers: the Kamp, curving through its heart, and the Thaya, winding up and down its northern section. Many a romantic castle is hidden away off the beaten path on wooded hills above the bends of the Kamp and the Thaya. The best departure point for exploring Waldviertel is Krems.

Heading towards the Kamp River, which flows into the Danube some miles below Krems, we reach its vineyard-terraced lower valley near the sunny wine town of Langenlois, with rows of Renaissance and baroque houses painted blue, pink and yellow. Farther upstream the vineyards disappear and the Kamp rushes its way through soft and tranquil green hills and through several dams and artificial lakes providing the local hydro-electric power station with energy and the summer vacationers with water sports.

Traveling up the river, some of the most interesting spots on its bank and nearby include: the quiet resort town of Gars with an 11th-century fortress; the imposing Rosenburg castle-fortress with a large tournament courtyard, Gothic chapel and a collection of weapons and furniture; the romantic town of Horn, with five medieval wall towers, several churches of note and a cluster of Renaissance houses; the Benedictine monastery of Altenburg, with a cupola fresco by Paul Troger, an important Austrian baroque painter, and a crypt with grotesque paintings representing the Dance of Death; the Renaissance castle of Greillenstein, again with works of Troger; the quiet dammed lake of Dobra, framed by woods, with the still powerful medieval Dobra fortress ruins; Ottenstein castle, above the largest of the artificial lakes, with the 12th-century massive chief tower; and Rastenberg castle-fortress, in a side valley nearby.

Zwettl, on the upper course of the Kamp, is a small market town with partially preserved walls, including six towers, located in the center of Waldviertel. About 3 km. out of town is a beautiful Cistercian monastery with a Romanesque canonical house, one of the oldest of its kind in existence. A score of country roads spread out of Zwettl like a spider's web over the surrounding rolling dales and hills.

To the southwest, above the upper Kamp River, is Rappottenstein, an excellent example of a medieval castle-fortress. To the west are the towns of Weitra, with medieval walls, and Gmünd, right on the border of Czechoslovakia, with a Renaissance face and an interesting glass museum showing the development of glassmaking from the Middle Ages through the 19th century.

To the north are Litschau, dominated by the round medieval fortress tower and Heidenreichstein, one of the most remarkable "water" castles in Austria. "Water"—or moated—castles were surrounded by a water surface (natural or artificial) for defense purposes whereas the "hill" castles used steep, often rocky and inaccessible, slopes for protection. The most interesting places to the northeast along the Thaya River are the baroque town of Waidhofen (not to be confused with Waidhofen on the Ybbs river described earlier); Drosendorf, with well-preserved medieval walls; the dreamy castles of Karlstein and Raabs; Fischer von Erlach's Riegersburg, which provides a suitable setting for a Baroque Museum; and 12th-century Hardegg, all on small hills above the river, their images mirrored in the water below, and observing life, and the lack of it, in the small towns at their feet.

PRACTICAL INFORMATION

HOTELS AND RESTAURANTS
AGGSBACH Hotel *Post* (3), 36 rooms, 15 showers, outdoor pool, sauna, tennis, excellent restaurant.

AMSTETTEN Hotels and Restaurants In Ybbs valley. Both (3)—*Hofmann,* 50 rooms, 35 showers, next to station, dance-bar with farmhouse ceiling; *Reisenberger,* 20 rooms, 15 showers, a little less expensive. Both have good restaurants.
See also Benedictine abbey at **Seitenstetten; and Ötscher** mountain.

BAD DEUTSCH-ALTENBURG Hotel On the Danube. *Kurhotel,* 160 beds, 6 baths, cure facilities (3).

BADEN Hotels All (1)—*Clubhotel Baden-Schloss Weikersdorf,* Schlossgasse 9–11, in Doblhoffpark, large, 101 rooms, own cure facilities, pool, sauna, tennis courts; *Gutenbrunn,* Pelzgasse 22, 86 rooms, quiet, indoor pool and cure facilities, terrace restaurant, café; *Herzoghof,* Theresiengasse 5, across from Kurpark, 86 rooms, many with balcony, annexed to thermal springs and bath establishment; *Parkhotel,* Kaiser Franzring 5, facing the Kurpark, 90 rooms, most with balcony overlooking the park, restaurant and heated outdoor café terrace; *Sauerhof,* 87 rooms, slightly more expensive, large park with tennis court, indoor pool and sauna.
Krainerhütte, 8 km. west of Baden, in the green and quiet Helenental, off the road and surrounded by trees, 68 rooms, very good food and trout as specialty.
All (2)—*Papst,* Renngasse 8, near Kurpark, 28 rooms; *Josefsplatz,* Josefsplatz 12; and *Schlosshotel Oth,* Schlossgasse 23, 42 rooms, in spite of its name, a new establishment with garden café, wine tavern.
Cholerakapelle, a bit closer to Baden than *Neue Krainerhütte,* in the same valley and on the road, noted for its restaurant.
Restaurants Both (2)—*Stadtkrug,* in the Kongresshaus in Kurpark, with very nice terrace facing the park, also café; *Krebs,* Palffygasse 2, near station.

Sauerhof zu Rauhenstein, Weilburgg. 11–13. Very charming Schönbrunn-yellow Biedermeier palace with period-furnished rooms, excellent cuisine.

BAD VÖSLAU Hotels A small spa about 5 km. from Baden. *Kurhotel Neydharting* (2), modern, uphill in the green section, at edge of Kurpark, small, quiet.
Stefanie (3), is on the main road next to the thermal swimming establishment, restaurant and café.

DÜRNSTEIN Hotels *Richard Löwenheart,* Richard the Lionheart, (1), 46 rooms, a Romantic Hotel in a former convent, very atmospheric period furnishings, historic vaulted dining rooms and garden terrace overlooking the Danube, very good food with game and Danube fish specialties, excellent local wines.
Schloss Dürnstein (1), a baroque castle-hotel on rocky terrace overlooking the Danube, fine food and good wines, heated pool and sauna.
Both (3)—*Gasthof Sänger Blondel* with comfortable restaurant; *Neue Welt,* with rustic *Wachauerstüberl.*

ENGELSTEIN Hotel A castle pension in Waldviertel.
Riding in hilly surroundings with escort, or ring practice. Reserve 4 weeks in advance, *Pension Burg Engelstein,* Post Gross-Schönau.

GARS AM KAMP Hotel *Kamptalhof* (2), 40 rooms, pleasant garden restaurant and wine tavern.
In the nearby castle of Rosenburg there is a medieval-style tavern.

GLOGGNITZ Hotel *Sclosshotel Kranichberg* (1) is a castle hotel with a lovely location. Beautiful rooms, admirable for groups.

GÖSING Hotel On the railway line from St. Pölten to Mariazell, *Alpenhotel Gösing* (2), in a beautiful isolated position 3,000 ft. high facing the Ötscher Range, mountain-lodge style with balconies and terraces, good restaurant, indoor and outdoor pools, sauna, hunting and fishing facilities.

GUMPOLDSKIRCHEN Restaurants *Weinstadl,* wooden rustic interiors, grill specialties, open evenings only; *Rathauskeller,* with old tradition, general Austrian fare and good local wines; *Haus an der Weinstrasse,* on the highest spot of the "Wine Road", halfway between Gumpoldskirchen and Mödling, with outdoor terrace and good view.
Many Heurigers.

KLOSTERNEUBURG On right bank of Danube, just before Vienna. **Hotels** *Schlosshotel Martinschloss* (1), 50 rooms, in a baroque castle on the edge of town, large park, heated pool, hunting facilities.
Both (3)—*Buschenreiter,* indoor pool; and *Alte Mühle.*
Restaurant *Stiftskeller,* historic restaurant of the Abbey, most interesting in the cellar section. There are many Heurigers in the area.

KREMS Hotel *Parkhotel* (2), near railroad station. Modern, very comfortable.

Restaurants *Bacher* is over the bridge in Mautern, on the other side of the Danube. Frau Wagner, the owner, was voted cook of the year in 1983. Also south of the river below Stift Göttweig is *Schickh*, like Bacher first-class and with superb wines. With *Jamek* in Weissenkirchen just beyond Dürnstein, these form a trinity worthy of pilgrimage.

Both (3)—*Alte Post*, in a 16th-century house with a lovely, arcaded Renaissance courtyard, used in warm weather as restaurant garden, period-style restaurant rooms, good local food and wine; *Goldenes Kreuz*, also a good restaurant.

Large campsite on the bank of the Danube.

LACKENHOF Skiing resort. Hotel *Jagdhof* (1), 20 rooms/bath, sauna.

MARIA TAFERL High above the Danube, in the Nibelungengau. **Hotels** Both (2)—*Krone*, with rooftop swimming, garden terrace with view of Danube; *Kaiserhof*, also with pool.

Rose (3), heated pool.

MARKHOF Hotel Near Schönfeld-Lassee in Marchfeld area, an estate about 32 km. east of Vienna devoted to horsemanship. Guest rooms and a *gemütlich* tavern, swimming pool. Bridle paths through open fields and pine forests; new indoor ring. Latest attraction—four Lippizaners; English owned and run. Inquiries from Reitzentrum Markhof bei Schönfeld-Lassee, A-2294 Marchegg.

MELK Hotels Several small hotels and old inns in the romantic old town section. Both (2)—*Stadt Melk*, 16 rooms, attractive restaurant; and *Goldener Ochs*.

Weisses Rössl (3), with garden restaurant.

The famous Abbey has a tavern serving their own wines.

Large campsite by the Danube.

MÖNICHKIRCHEN Hotels Both (2)—*Alpenhotel Lang*, with good food, especially game, in historically decorated dining rooms, dance bar, indoor pool, tennis; *Thier*, new, 69 rooms, indoor pool; *Pension Reidinger* and *Hechtl*, all rooms with bath or shower, both a little less pricy.

NEUHOFEN Hotels Both (2)—*Ostarrichi*, pool and pleasant restaurant, with garden; *Kothmühle*, about 3 km. from town, attractive dining room.

PUCHBERG At foot of Schneeberg mountain.

Hotels Both (2)—*Forellenhof*, with indoor pool and sauna; *Puchbergerhof*, rustic-style, good food and attentive service.

Both (3)—*Almboden*, garni; *Schneeberg*, small, at upper end of cog-wheel railway at 5,900 ft.

RAXALPE A high mountain plateau averaging 6,000 ft., NW of Semmering. Railway stop at Payerbach, road to Hirschwang or Prein.

Hotels Both (3)—*Berghotel Raxalpe,* 80 beds, about 5,000 ft., at upper station of the aerial cable car from Hirschwang.

Ottohaus, 60 beds, 5,500 ft., about 2 km. from upper cable car station, reached only by walking, or skiing in winter.

REICHENAU Hotels All (3)—*Kurhaus Thalhof,* 30 rooms, restaurant, musical entertainment in season, own farm in wooded area, hunting and fishing; *Goettler,* with indoor pool; and *Flackl.*

Alpenhotel Knappenhof (3), in quiet location on south slope of the Raxalpe. Very large campsite on the right bank of the River Inn near Reichenauer Brücke.

ROSENAU Hotel *Schlosshotel* (1), 20 rooms with bath, golf course, tennis.

ST. PÖLTEN Hotels *Pittner* (3), 90 rooms, 17 baths, centuries of tradition, consult the old guest books for imperial visitors of the past, high level of Viennese cuisine in the atmospheric dining rooms, particularly *Krebsenstüberl.*

SEMMERING Near mountain pass of same name, on main road and railway south of Vienna.

Hotels *Dr. Hermann Stülinger* (1), 37 rooms, indoor pool, cure facilities. *Hotel Panhans* (1), reopened 1983 after restorations with former grandeur intact. Beautiful location; indoor pool.

All (2)—*Belvedere,* 22 rooms, 14 baths, *Gartenhotel Alpenheim,* 22 rooms, 18 baths; both with pools. *Haus Wagner,* 17 rooms.

Both (3)—*Daheim, Haus Mayer.*

STEINAKIRCHEN AM FORST Hotels In the vicinity is *Schloss Ernegg* (2), a 16th-century castle, 22 rooms, open May to Sept.; hotel car service from Amstetten, on Vienna-Linz rail line, but must book. Lovely castle park, hunting and fishing, pool, 9-hole golf course nearby.

TULBING Hotel *Berghotel Tulbingerkogel* (1), 50 rooms/bath, lovely location. The cuisine is famous.

WAIDHOFEN-THAYA Hotel *Gasthof Haberl* (3), excellent value, good local food and wines. Family run with spacious and well-appointed rooms. Very good.

WIENER NEUSTADT Hotels *Corvinus* (1), newly built by the city walls, modern hotel run by Alba group. Equipped for seminars. Bar, all rooms with mini-bar, and a remarkable restaurant.

All (3)—*Bader,* on main square; *Forum,* Kochgasse 2.

Goldener Hirsch, off the main square behind the Town Hall, small but comfortable, several restaurant rooms, including the colorful cellar section, good food. *Zentral,* on main square.

Restaurants Good restaurants are *Porsche,* in Neunkirchner Allee, the main road to Semmering, at the Volkswagen-Porsche workshop; and *Witetschka,* at Allerheiligenplatz 1.

YBBS Hotel *Royal-Hotel Weisses Rössel* (2), on the bank of the River Danube, restaurant terrace overlooking the river.

CASTLES AND ABBEYS

AGGSTEIN Castle, mostly in ruins, on hill on right bank of Danube. First built in 12th century, last rebuilt in 1606, beautiful view of the Wachau; those interiors still standing are open to public April 1 to Oct. 15.

ALTENBURG Benedictine abbey in town of same name. Founded in 12th century, rebuilt in baroque style in 18th century; under the library a unique crypt with grotesque paintings representing the *Dance of Death;* cupola fresco in the church is important work of baroque painter Paul Troger.

BREITENEICH, near Horn, is Lower Austria's oldest Renaissance castle. Summer courses in woodwind instruments, with chamber orchestra concerts.

DÜRNSTEIN 12th-century castle in ruins on left bank of Danube above town. It was the prison of Richard the Lionheart from Jan. 1192 to March 1193.

ECKARTSAU Castle mansion some 13 km. from Orth farther down left side of Danube valley. Present baroque construction mainly built in 18th century as hunting castle; 2 wings from the end of the last century; grand ceiling fresco in Great Hall, other frescos, paintings, wall decor.

FALKENSTEIN Castle in imposing location above village of same name near Czech border. Probably built in 11th century, largely in ruins, but marks of past magnificence still visible. To visit, get key at forester's house in village.

GÖTTWEIG Benedictine abbey on hill near right bank of Danube. Founded in 11th century, present baroque buildings from 18th century, constructed according to the plans of Lukas von Hildebrandt; tavern with wines of own production, beautiful view of Krems and Danube valley from the terrace.

GREILLENSTEIN Castle about 8 km. west of Altenburg. Originating from the 13th century, except for the gate tower and a rare medieval judgment chamber completely reconstructed during 17th century. Very interesting baroque interiors and ceiling frescos by Paul Troger in the family crypt.

HARDEGG Castle on Thaya River in town of same name right on Czech border. Built around 1200, partially rebuilt at the end of the last century.

HEIDENREICHSTEIN Castle in town of same name in northern Waldviertel. First built in 12th century, rebuilt in 15th and 16th centuries, one of the most remarkable Austria water castles.

HEILIGENKREUZ Cistercian abbey, some 16 km. west of Baden. Founded in 1135; Romanesque church, built in 12th and 13th centuries, with late Gothic and baroque additions; stained glass windows from 1300; altar paintings by Rottmayr and Altomonte; cloister from 1220, with 300 small, red marble columns; gallery of old German and Austrian baroque paintings; baroque library.

HERZOGENBURG Augustine abbey in the town of the same name about 13 km. up the Traisen Valley near the right bank of the Danube. Founded in 12th century; present architecture partially by great baroque masters Fischer von Erlach and Jakob Prandtauer, frescos and paintings particularly by Altomonte. Baroque library and museum with rich collection of Gothic winged altars. Wine tavern with wines of own production.

KLOSTERNEUBURG Augustine abbey in town. Founded in 12th century, since then various parts rebuilt several times; church originally Romanesque, beautifully handcarved wooden choir and oratory, large organ from 17th century; Leopold Chapel with world-famous enameled Verduner Altar by Nikolas von Verdun (Werden) in 1181, stained glass windows from 14th and 15th centuries, and Romanesque candelabrum of 12th century; great marble hall with Gran's ceiling fresco; library with 230 old manuscripts, 140,000 volumes; also abbey museum and treasury.

KREUZENSTEIN A few km. from left bank of Danube, almost straight across from Greifenstein. First built in 12th century, destroyed by Swedes during Thirty Years' War in 17th century, reconstructed and refurnished in the corresponding style by Count Johann Wilczek at the end of the last century.

LIECHTENSTEIN Castle near Mödling some 16 km. south of Vienna. Built in Romanesque style during 12th century, partially destroyed during Turkish wars and rebuilt in same style. Romanesque chapel constructed in 1165 still exists in original form.

MELK Benedictine abbey, largest in Lower Austria, on right bank of Danube. Originally a fort in 10th century; given to Benedictines in early 12th century; present unique baroque buildings from 18th century by Jakob Prandtauer; one of the most beautiful existing baroque churches; library with 1,850 old manuscripts, from 9th century on, many old prints and 80,000 volumes.

ORTH Castle fort near left bank of Danube below Vienna in center of village of same name. Originally built in 12th century; today it houses a fishing museum and an apiary museum, with a 30-million-year-old bee in amber.
See also **Eckartsau.**

PERSENBEUG Castle, in town of same name on left bank of Danube. Present baroque building from 17th century, the original castle was probably from the 9th century.

POTTENBRUNN Moated castle near St. Pölten, noted for its ponds, parks and stairway; also offers a unique tin soldier museum, the figures illustrating actual historical battles. Open March 15 to Nov. 15, daily except Mon.; from 8 A.M. to 4.

RAABS Castle in town of same name on River Thaya. First built in 11th century, later rebuilt, present style mainly from 16th century. Renaissance library, baroque chapel.

RAPPOTTENSTEIN Castle about 14 km. SW of Zwettl. First built in 12th century, additions and renovations through 16th century. Fine medieval castle fortress, with Austria's best-preserved torture chamber.

RIEGERSBURG Baroque castle in the Waldviertel, many rooms with original furnishings. Open mid-May to mid-Oct., tours conducted in English.

ROHRAU 8 km. south of Carnuntum, the birthplace of Haydn. The castle houses the Count Harrach collection, Austria's only private art museum, with over 200 paintings, mostly Italian and Spanish baroque. Open spring to fall.

ROSENAU Baroque palace housing freemasonry museum.

ROSENBURG Castle near Gars on the lower Kamp. Probably first built in 12th century, rebuilt in 17th century, destroyed by fire in 19th century and rebuilt according to the previous model; 13 towers, large tournament courtyard, Gothic chapel, collection of weapons and furniture.

SCHALLABURG A few km. south of Melk, is considered Austria's finest Renaissance castle; terracotta sculptures line the arcaded courtyard.

SCHÖNBÜHEL Perches on the rocky right bank of the Danube downstream from Melk. Originally built in 12th century, rebuilt in the 19th.

SEEBENSTEIN Castle above place of same name about 14 km. south of Wiener Neustadt. Built in 11th century, rebuilt in Renaissance style around 1600.

SEITENSTETTEN Benedictine abbey about 24 km. SW of Amstetten. Founded in 1112, early Gothic and late Romanesque church from 13th century with baroque additions of 17th century, present monastery building from 18th century. Frescos by Kremser Schmidt, Altomonte; library of 300 old manuscripts, 70,000 volumes; picture gallery, Brueghel, Altomonte, Gran, Kremser Schmidt; collection of engravings.

STAATZ About 13 km. SW of Falkenstein. Castle ruins in magnificent position on lonely rocky hill springing up from almost flat countryside, powerfully dominating surrounding area; village of same name is huddled in shadow of cliff. Built in 12th century or earlier, destroyed by Swedes in 17th century during Thirty Years' War. Today a complete ruin. You can walk up from main road.

ZWETTL Cistercian abbey about 3 km. from town of same name. Church first built between 12th and 14th centuries; mainly Gothic, acquired baroque additions in 18th century, including most of the altars with notable exceptions of a late Gothic wing altar and some Gothic window glass paintings from 15th century; 13th-century monastery; Romanesque canonical house, one of the oldest of its kind in existence; baroque library with 420 old manuscripts, 35,000 volumes. Stift Zwettl has been restored and looks magnificent.

See also **Rappottenstein.**

SPECIAL EVENTS

BADEN Jan. and Feb. some balls during the *Fasching* season, sometimes stretching into March, when concert performances are given in the spa hall.

Then the summer season opens in May with balls and concerts. Many people come here for vacation, since the summer season in this Biedermeier-style town becomes the nearest away-from-Vienna social center. Open-air operettas and concerts, balls, Kurpark festivities and garden parties take place June-Aug.

CARNUNTUM In July and August plays (sometimes Roman comedies) in the Roman amphitheater at Carnuntum.

KLOSTERNEUBERG Nov. 15, nameday of St. Leopold, the patron saint of Lower Austria, a picturesque folk and religious fete is held here.

KREMS Danube steamer trips between here and Melk through the Wachau begin in late April. Austrian wine fair takes place here in May. Summer solstice festivities and outdoor plays in summer. The Krems country fair, with a wine fair and a very colorful folk costume parade on the last day, is in late Aug. and early Sept.

MELK Danube steamer trips between Krems and here through the Wachau begin in late April. Summer plays begin in July.

SEMMERING Dec. the winter sports season begins; the old year ends and the new one begins with a night torchlight skiing race. Jan. and Feb. are the main winter sports months, skiing, skijumping, toboggan competitions.

SPITZ IN WACHAU June, *Summer Solstice* festivals along the Wachau. *Apricot Village Fair,* end July.

WIENER NEUSTADT Trade and industrial fair in mid-Aug.

YBBS Summer solstice festivities on the Danube.

SPAS

BAD DEUTSCH-ALTENBURG Large Kurpark stretching to the Danube. The sulphuric thermal water is for various rheumatic illnesses and skin diseases.

Museum Carnuntinum contains Roman antiquities discovered during the excavations of nearby Carnuntum, an old Roman settlement.

BADEN This is the most important spa in Lower Austria, with its 15 sulphuric thermal springs, one of which, called the Roman Spring, has been in use for about 2,000 years. Baden waters are considered to be beneficial for various types of rheumatic afflictions and skin diseases.

BAD VÖSLAU This is a smaller and more modest spa than Baden, with radioactive thermal water, which offers drinking and bathing cures for rheumatic illnesses and physical and nervous exhaustion.

CASINOS

BADEN Roulette, baccara and black-jack are played here from 4 P.M. daily, including Sundays and holidays.

SPORTS

BADEN There's a large open-air swimming and sunbathing establishment, which uses thermal waters and can accommodate in its various sections up to 10,000 people. You can also relax in deck-chairs in special 'silent meadows' where not even a whisper is allowed.

There is also, for the active, an indoor and outdoor riding ring at *Reitstall Baden,* Leesdorfer Hauptstr. 76, with instruction available, but country rides only with an escort.

ENZESFELD About 40 km. south of Vienna. Riding, boarding stall for private horses and horses for hire. Indoor and outdoor rings, jumping track and about 24 km. of bridle paths. Instruction in all phases. Inquire at *Country-Club Schloss Enzesfeld.*

Golf: a 9-hole course.

GARS AM KAMP Saddle horses for hire from the local riding club or at Hotel Kamptalhof; excursions and instructors for beginners; inquire at Bürgermeisteramt (Mayor's office).

GLOGGNITZ Horseback riding, with country rides and teachers for beginners; inquire at Gloggnitzer Reitverein, Enzenreith 39.

HOLLABRUNN Saddle horses and horse-drawn coaches from the local riding club; one to two-week riding trips through Waldviertel arranged for not less than 4 riders; also riding for beginners.

MÖNICHKIRCHEN Chair lift, 4 ski lifts, ski school and skating rink.

ÖTSCHER Mountain in the center of large skiing area, near the Upper Erlauf and Ybbs Valley, reached by road or railway from St. Pölten, Pöchlarn, and Amstetten, all on main Vienna–Linz line.

Very long 2-part chair lift, 9 ski lifts, ski school at Mitterbach; 13 ski lifts and school at Annaberg; 6 ski lifts and school at Puchenstuben; cable car, chair lift, 5 ski lifts, school at Lackenhof; 5 ski lifts, skating rink at Lunz; 2 chair lifts, 11 ski lifts, ski school at Göstling and on Hochkar mountain; ski lift and school at Opponitz; 5 ski lifts, skating rink at Waidhofen on Ybbs; 3 ski lifts at Ybbsitz. This fast developing area has skiing terrains for all degrees of skill.

PUCHBERG Ski jump, ski school, skating, curling and horse sleighs. Haflinger horses (mountain breed) available for scenic rides from the local riding club.

RAXALPE Cable car from Hirschwang. Easy, medium and difficult ski runs. Ski lifts at Prein and Payerbach. Skating, curling rinks, horse sleigh rides at Payerbach. Jan. and Feb. main winter sports months, skiing, skijumping, toboggan competitions.

REICHENAU Ski school and ski lifts, skating, curling rinks and horse sleigh rides.

ST. PÖLTEN Riding instruction and horses for hire from the riding club.

SCHNEEBERG Mountain range, north of Semmering. Local railway and road from Vienna to Puchberg, departure point of cog-wheel railway up the mountain. Ski tours, easy, medium, and difficult runs. Together with Hohe Wand area, there are 3 chair lifts and 6 ski lifts.

SEMMERING This is one of the best known winter sports resorts in eastern Austria. 2 chair lifts, from Semmering to Hirschenkogel and from Maria Schutz to Sonnwendstein; 6 ski lifts, 2 ski jumps, ski school, skating rink, horse sleighs. Ski slopes for beginners and ski runs of all degrees of difficulty, including the internationally known Erzkogel downhill from Sonnwendstein.

SPITZERBERG Near Hainburg, 45 km. from Vienna. There's a gliding school here, with dormitory accommodations, 110 beds. Season is from March to Dec. Inquire at *Bundessportschule Spitzerberg, A-2405 Bad Deutsch-Altenburg*, Lower Austria.

SPITZ IN WACHAU There's a ski lift on the Jauerling mountain near here.

TÜRNITZ and UPPER TRAISEN Rivers area. Reached by road or railway from St. Pölten on main Vienna–Linz line.

Chair lift, 6 ski lifts and ski school at Lilienfeld. Chair lift, 6 ski lifts and ski school at Türnitz and the Eibl mountain. 6 ski lifts at St. Aegyd. Slopes for all degrees of skill, except for Göller mountain area, which is only for very experienced skiers.

WECHSELGEBIET East of Semmering area. On secondary railway and roads from present end of the South Autobahn to Styria; principal localities Aspang, Mönichkirchen and St. Corona. Ski slopes for beginners, easy and medium ski runs, ski tours possible. Chair lift, 4 ski lifts and ski school at St. Corona; skating and curling rinks at Aspang.

WIENER NEUSTADT Riding school with indoor riding ring. Saddle horses and horse-drawn coaches for country rides: inquire at *Reitverein,* Bahngasse 29. There's an 18-hole golf course.

ZWETTL North of the Danube there are ski lifts at Gross Pertholz and Harmanschlag, both near the Czech border in the area W of Zwettl.

USEFUL ADDRESSES
BADEN *Kurdirektion,* Hauptplatz 2/10.

BAD VÖSLAU Informationsburo, Schlossplatz.

BURGENLAND

Puszta and Papa Haydn's Skull

Burgenland, the land of castles and fortresses, corn and wine, is a narrow, fertile belt of vineyards and rich agricultural land running along Austria's eastern frontier with Hungary, touching north on Czechoslovakia and south on Yugoslavia, broken up by the foothills and mountains of the Leitha and Rosalien ranges. Shaped rather like a kidney bean, the state is 65 km. broad at the widest point, and narrows in the center to a "waist" barely three kilometers across. Only 24 km. from Vienna, it is easily reached by frequent bus and train services, and even the most remote parts are accessible in two or three hours.

Although small in size, its scenery is interesting because much of it is quite in contrast to that in the rest of Austria. The face of Burgenland is strongly marked by the large and strange Neusiedler See—a very shallow salt-water lake, the remainder of a prehistoric sea which at one time covered all of the Pannonian Plain. There are myriads of birds in its reeds and on its shores, the most noted among them the famous Rust storks, faithfully returning to their chimney nests every year. On the eastern side of the lake, the landscape turns into the real Hungarian type of *puszta* (steppe), with typical water wells made of tree trunks and the red *"puszta* sun" sinking into the plain in the evening.

Burgenland is the vegetable garden of Vienna and the source of copiously-produced inexpensive wine, some of it of considerable quality. In many places you will see bunches of drying corn cobs adorning the colorful farm houses, for corn, next to wine, is the main agricultural produce of this state, although other kinds of grain are also grown in large quantity.

Its hard-working, industrious population of small farmers, foresters, vintners and craftsmen is descended from German (88 percent), Croatian (10 percent) and Magyar (2 percent) ancestors, and Burgenland itself looks back on a history as hectic and unsettled as that of any other corner of Europe.

Most hotels are small and range from the modest provincial type to the simple village Gasthof; a few exceptions, particularly some spa and castle hotels, belong to higher categories. Prices on the whole are considerably lower than in the regions more frequented by foreign tourists. However, new hotels are being built and many private rooms are available.

Route Planning

The best point of departure **by train** for the northern part of Burgenland is Vienna; for the southern part, Graz. Except for the Vienna–Budapest (from Westbahnhof) mainline, with only a few stops in Burgenland, train communications are only of the local and slow type. At Parndorf the sections for Eisenstadt and for the area east of Neusiedler See branch off (sometimes necessary to change as only a few trains are direct). From Wiener Neustadt there is a local line to Sauerbrunn and Mattersburg. Both this line and the line from Eisenstadt traverse Hungarian territory at Sopron to southern Burgenland (these are the so-called "corridor" trains with locked cars through Hungary). At Friedberg, on the Styrian–Lower Austrian border and on the secondary railroad line between Graz and Vienna, there is a local line for Oberwart, Rechnitz, and Bad Tatzmannsdorf. During the spa season (April–October), a special daily direct train runs in both directions between Bad Tatzmannsdorf and Vienna (over three hours one way).

Various **bus companies** (inquire at travel offices) cover almost the entire province from Vienna and its southern part from Graz. In addition there are bus services between Neusiedl and Eisenstadt and the eastern Neusiedler See area; between Wiener Neustadt and Eisenstadt and Lockenhaus; between Eisenstadt–Mattersburg–Lutzmannsburg; between Oberwart–Schlaining–Reichnitz–Güssing, and some others.

In summer there are **motorboat** roundtrips on Neusiedler See between Neusiedl, Podersdorf, and Rust and between Mörbisch and Illmitz.

If you go **by car** from Vienna, you can obtain a bird's-eye view of northern Burgenland in a day or day and a half; the same time will be used for the main sights of southern Burgenland from Graz. From Vienna take Route 10 to Parndorf and the Hungarian border; branching off at Parndorf, use a combination of 304, 51 and 52 to make the Austrian part of the circle of Neusiedler Lake and to reach Eisenstadt. From Eisenstadt continue on the Autobahn, otherwise 331, to Mattersburg; from there it is very near to the Castle of Forchtenstein and to Sauerbrunn. To return to Vienna, proceed either to Wiener Neustadt or return in the direction of Eisenstadt and take Route 16.

From Graz take Route 65 and 307 to Heiligenkreuz on the Hungarian border; from there north on 57 to Güssing. Oberwart (side road to Schlaining), Bad Tatzmannsdorf, Bernstein, Oberpullendorf (side road to Raiding), and on to northern Burgenland or back along the Hungarian border on 56.

Exploring Burgenland

It is no mere coincidence that the many castles, fortified churches, battlemented villages, and isolated farmsteads have been built on high, strategic ground. Beginning with the Celts in the 4th century BC the area has been fought over by Romans, Huns, Goths, Lombards and Slavs. Then came the Bavarians, Hungarians, Austrians and, in the 16th and 17th centuries, the Turks to continue the game of battledore and shuttlecock. In 1648 the area now known as Burgenland finally fell to Hungary, and remained a Hungarian province until the end of World War I. In 1921 it became one of the nine present-day Austrian federal states, except for its capital of Ödenburg (Sopron) and the surrounding area which voted in a plebiscite to remain in Hungary; this accounts for the "wasp waist" in the center of the province.

In 1924 the small town of Eisenstadt at the foot of the Leitha mountains, 40 kilometers southeast from Vienna, was made the provincial capital. With less than 11,000 inhabitants, it is best known as the place where Josef Haydn lived and worked for most of his life in the service of the Esterhazys.

The composer's home has now been turned into a museum, and one room contains relics and mementos of the Burgenland's other gifted son, Franz Liszt (he was born in Raiding in 1811). The body of Josef Haydn lies in an elaborate tomb of white marble, built by his grateful master, Prince Esterhazy, in the crypt of Eisenstadt church. Until the summer of 1954, it was a headless body that lay in this tomb. Haydn's skull could be seen—and handled, if you felt so inclined—in the Musikverein Museum in Vienna. How it came to be there is a long and complicated story.

Ten days after the composer's death in Vienna, a group of young phrenologists persuaded the prince's secretary and an accomplice, a prison warder, to steal the head from the temporary grave in Vienna, and "lend" it to them for a few weeks. In the dead of night the two ghouls, after bribing the cemetery guards, accomplished their mission. It was not until some time later, when the remains were transferred to the final resting place at Eisenstadt, that the theft was discovered.

On his deathbed the secretary confessed to his crime, but refused to part with his treasure—the phrenologists had returned the head to him—unless Prince Esterhazy paid his "heavy expenses," which included a "costly black casket." This the prince refused to do, and the secretary bequeathed the skull to the Musikverein. But the skull had disappeared again. This time it was the doctor attending the accomplice who was the culprit. Finally, it was sold to a famous Austrian professor, and on his death his widow loaned it to the Vienna Pathological Museum.

The Musikverein now claimed the skull, and after a lengthy and costly lawsuit finally managed to secure its "legacy". Since 1895, therefore, the skull had been sitting in a glass case on top of a grand piano in the Musikverein Museum. But the Musikverein finally yielded to the entreaties of those who felt that Haydn's head should be restored to his body. During the Vienna Music Festival in June 1954, the skull was taken in triumphal procession, by way of Haydn's birthplace at Rohrau, to Eisenstadt and placed at last in his coffin with the body from which it had been separated for 145 years.

On the other side of the church where Haydn is entombed, there is a unique structure called the Kalvarienberg, an artifically made "indoor" Calvary Hill, representing the Way of the Cross with life-like, life-size figures placed in cave-like rooms and chapels along an elaborate path. At its highest point, the path reaches the platform of the belfry, offering a beautiful view over the town and this section of Burgenland. The magnificent wooden figures were carved and painted by Franciscan monks, with the aid of simple peasants, more than 250 years ago. Another main point of interest is Eisenstadt in the gracious, sweeping Esterhazy Palace, the home of the famous Hungarian aristocratic family.

A few kilometers to the east of Eisenstadt you come to the picturesque towns of Rust, Oggau, and Mörbisch, strung along the western shores of the great, shallow Neusiedler Lake. On nearly every cottage roof you will see the nests of young storks, and occasionally the parent birds standing majestically and motionless beside the chimney stacks. Medieval Rust, once an imperial free town, is known in particular as the "stork capital". Worth visiting is the Gothic Fischerkirche, with interesting frescos and stained-glass windows. Here organ concerts by candlelight are given on occasion. The three parishes are famous, and justly so, for the fine, strong wines made from the small, exceptionally sweet grapes, which have been grown in the district for over 1,000 years.

Near St. Margarethen, on the road between Eisenstadt and Rust, you pass by a giant quarry, already used by the Romans and the source for many 19th-century buildings in Vienna, including the Opera. Today it is a unique outdoor sculptors' workshop—a number of sculptors from all over the world come here during the summer to work in stone cut in the quarry; their finished works remain in this huge atelier until they are sold, thus making the quarry a vast, naturally set, open-sky exhibition hall.

Mysterious Lake Neusiedl

The 32km.-long Neusiedler See, one quarter of its huge expanse in Hungary, is nowhere deeper than seven feet, while the size of the lake varies erratically. When the wind blows steadily in one direction for several days, the shallow waters are swept up to one end of the lake, leaving the other end high and dry. Once a century, so the story goes, the lake dries up altogether. Where the water comes from no one knows. The one small stream that runs into the lake is only a thin trickle, but it is believed to be fed by underground springs. The water in the lake itself is salty, containing up to 1.8 percent of salt.

On the farther side of the lake lie vast salt marshes and the ancient villages of St. Andrä and Frauenkirchen, famous for their basket weaving.

North of Frauenkirchen, also known for its pilgrimage church, is Halbturn with a baroque castle-palace, built by Lukas von Hildebrandt and used by the Empress Maria Theresa as a summer residence; there is a ceiling painting by Maulpertsch in the middle hall and a lovely park. West of Frauenkirchen is Podersdorf, a very good place for swimming; the shore here is free of reeds. To the south is the area known as Seewinkel, with Illmitz and Apetlon and the vast natural wildlife sanctuary with its forests of reeds, hundreds of different types of birds, small steppe animals, and millions of flowers. These lonely, rather desolate marshes hold a collection of flora and fauna unsurpassed anywhere in Europe, and the area is now an international sanctuary, with a Biological Station partially supported by the World Wildlife Fund. Here also begins the real *puszta* (Hungarian type of steppe), with a few windmills and the typical Hungarian-type of well, with long wooden poles for drawing water.

East of Illmitz and St. Andrä, right near the Hungarian border, is the small village of Andau, the famous crossing point during the Hungarian anti-Communist revolution of 1956, and it is from here that you can see the Iron Curtain with its grim and inhuman barbed wire fences and watchtowers.

Above the lake, in the northeast corner of Burgenland, lies Kittsee, with a baroque castle and noted ethnographical collection. At the end of the village, a little before reaching Bratislava (Pressburg), the capital of Slovakia, you come to a small cluster of houses, the most easterly settlement west of the Iron Curtain—Chicago.

About 1900, many Burgenlanders emigrated to the United States and regularly sent back their savings to the old country for investment in land and houses. At one time the inhabitants even worked out everything in American dollars rather than in Austrian schillings, so great was the flow of dollars to Burgenland. One émigré, returning to his native land, was astonished at the rapid building progress, and, so the story goes, exclaimed: "Why, you work nearly as fast as back in Chicago!" This particular settlement was promptly called Chicago, and Chicago it is to this day.

Traveling south again to Eisenstadt, you cross the Leitha range, where you can still see, on the Zeilerberg above Winden, where cavemen and great bears lived, according to experts, cheek by jowl as next door neighbors in the Stone Age, 7,000 years ago. All through this area, strip-farming makes many-colored ribbons of the hillsides in summer, and the forested areas are lush and green. Northwest of Eisenstadt is the famous baroque pilgrimage church of Loretto, visited each summer by up to 100,000 pilgrims. Bronze Age graves, as well as the burial places of Celts and Illyrians were discovered nearby a few years ago. A settlement dating from Roman times is presently in the process of excavation; finds include an old Roman wine press, proving the great age of the surrounding vineyards.

Southwest of Eisenstadt, just before the "waist" you reach the little market town of Mattersburg. Nearby is the village of Neustift an der Rosalia and the mighty, fairyland Castle of Forchtenstein, formerly the stronghold of the highly independent Mattersburg barons. First built in the 13th century and then rebuilt in the 17th century, it is definitely not to be missed. Burgtheater actors perform Grillparzer plays there in the summer months. The small spa of Sauerbrunn is also near Mattersburg.

Bernstein is German for "amber," but this charming little hilltop village is not in any way connected with the warm yellow stone. In Roman times, however, the association was much closer. The "Amber Road" from the Prussian quarries to Rome ran straight down the province, through the Roman settlement at Parndorf in the north, where recent excavations have revealed mosaic floors, skirting Neusiedler Lake and passing quite close to the village of Bernstein. Bernstein, however, has its own specialty: "Bernstein Jade," more correctly called "Serpentine Stone." Much darker than the Chinese gem, almost a jet green, the Bernstein Jade is found in Europe in substantial quantities only in Burgenland. There is a small local industry making ornaments. The north–south line of mineral springs also runs through this area, and less than 16 km. south of Bernstein is Bad Tatzmannsdorf, the most important spa in Burgenland. On the edge of the Kurpark is an open-air museum where old barns, farmhouses and stables have been restored. Near Bad Tatzmannsdorf is the medieval town of Stadtschlaining, with the castle-fortress Burg Schlaining, and farther east is the 13th-century castle-fortress Burg Lockenhaus, with Romanesque frescos in the chapel and a Gothic arcaded Knights Hall.

The whole of the southern part of Burgenland is divided into small-holdings of a few acres each, tilled by industrious small farmers, with the castles of the nobility of the Middle Ages dotted picturesquely all over the countryside. In one way, at least, these ancient strongholds are unique. All of them are built on top of extinct volcanoes. The huge system of fortifications of the castle-fortress of the once proud and mighty Counts of Güssing, in the extreme south, is a good example.

PRACTICAL INFORMATION
HOTELS AND RESTAURANTS

BAD TATZMANNSDORF Hotels Both (1)—*Hotel Batthyany* and *Kurhotel/Dependence*.
All (2) with cure facilities—the balconied *Parkhotel, Zum Kastell* and *Kurhotel* are best, followed by *Pension Sonnenhof* and *Krone*.

BERNSTEIN Hotel *Hotel Burg Bernstein* (2), 13th-century castle-hotel, 24 rooms, most with bath or shower. Swimming pool, lovely flower beds, own hunting grounds, historical collections including a torture chamber, a ghost also available; reservation advisable in summer.
Youth Hostel.

DONNERSKIRCHEN Restaurant *Gasthof Engel* is renowned for its food and wine.

DRASSBURG Hotel *Schloss Drassburg* (2), 28 rooms, excellent castle-hotel, indoor and outdoor pools.

EISENSTADT Hotels *Burgenland* (1). Every possible appointment and amenity. Underground garage, conference facilities, good restaurant.
Parkhotel (2), 28 rooms, bed and breakfast.
Both (3)—*Eder,* with garden restaurant; *Haydnhof,* 20 rooms, 3 showers.
Horsedrawn gypsy wagons with modern comforts and accommodations for 4 people can be rented through *Burgenland Tours,* Hauptstr. 19.
Restaurants Many colorful wine restaurants, taverns and wine gardens in nearby St. Georgen.

FORCHTENSTEIN Hotels *Wegscheidler* (2), 30 rooms, 9 showers.
Both (3)—*Sauerzapf, Wutzlhofer.*

ILLMITZ-APETLON On Neusiedlersee. **Hotels** All (3)—Several inexpensive Gasthöfe and pensions, such as *Mann Martin,* for riding enthusiasts; and *Trauben-mühle,* garni.

At **Apetlon,** attractive vacation bungalows (3) and apartments at *Vogelparadies.*

JENNERSDORF Hotel *Raffel* (2), 33 rooms with bath/shower, W.C. Famous restaurant serves memorable Pannonian cuisine, both rich and plentiful.

LOCKENHAUS Hotel *Burgpension Lockenhaus* is in a beautifully located castle. "Robber baron" meals cooked on an open fire are a specialty. Lots of atmosphere—including resident ghost.

MÖRBISCH AM SEE On Neusiedlersee. **Hotels** Both (2)—*Gasthof Steiner,* 58 rooms; *Seehotel,* on small island in the lake, connected by road across the water, boating, sailing, Hungarian cuisine, good local wines, terrace café, music.

NEUSIEDL AM SEE On Neusiedlersee. **Hotels** Both (2)—*Wende,* 106 rooms, indoor pool, sauna, with beauty farm. *Neusiedler Csarda,* a small riding pension. All (3)—*Frischmann, Maut-Hotel, Rittsteuer;* and breakfast-pension *Fischbach.* Horsedrawn gypsy caravans, with modern comforts and accommodations for 4 people, can be rented through *Burgenland Tours,* Hauptstr. 12.
Youth Hostel.

PAMHAGEN Hotel *Feriendorf Pamhagen,* 60 rooms with bath. Indoor and outdoor tennis, lake, surfing.

PODERSDORF On Neusiedlersee. **Hotels** *Seewirt Karner* (2), 25 rooms. All (3)—*Martinshof, Reeh, Strandhotel.*
Campsite.

PURBACH AM SEE Hotels *Am Spitz* (3), 20 rooms, 12 showers, on the lake, at the end of the picturesque "Kellergasse" street, with wine cellars. Excellent food and wine. *Türkenhain* (2), a large vacation apartment complex with sports facilities, on the lake just outside Purbach.

RUST On Neusiedlersee. **Hotels** *Seehotel Rust* (1), 80 rooms with bath. On the lake; sauna.
All (3)—*Arkadenhof* and *Sifkovits* serve good local food and wines in their restaurants; vacation bungalows tucked among the reeds directly on the lake at *Feriendorf Romantica.* Also *Seehotel Rust,* 80 rooms/bath, sports facilities.
Restaurants *Storchennest Rust,* with "Puszta Nights"; *Alte Schmiede; Storchmühle,* in nearby Oslip; the 15th-century *Eselmühle* in nearby St. Margarethen, all offer good grill dishes and gypsy music.
Seebadrestaurant, a large restaurant built on piles on the lake, fish specialties, very good Rust wines, plus *Storchenespresso* (miniature island for dancing).
Youth Hostel.

ST. ANDRÄ Near Zicksee. **Hotel** *Ferienparadies Seewinkel* (3), vacation apartments, with indoor pool and riding facilities.
Campsite.

STADTSCHLAINING Hotel *Burg Schlaining* (P3), a small pension, garni, in the castle-fortress above the medieval town.

WEIDEN AM SEE On Neusiedlersee. **Hotels** Both (3)—*Haus Carinthia*, 30 rooms, garden; *Seepark Weiden*, a series of low bungalows directly on the lake, sport facilities.
Vacation bungalows and apartments.

SPECIAL EVENTS
EISENSTADT Early May, *Haydn Days* chamber music festival. Late August, Burgenland Wine Week.

FORCHTENSTEIN German drama performances in castle moat.

ILLMITZ-APETLON *Puszta Nights* in Illmitz. Wine seminar in summer.

LOCKENHAUS Chamber music festival 1–15 July.

MÖRBISCH AM SEE Operetta performances on a romantic water stage in July and Aug. with special bus service provided from Vienna.

RUST Passion plays, Sun. from June to Sept. in St. Margarethen.

SPORTS
ILLMITZ-APETLON Lake swimming and boating; riding facilities. Bicycling through the wine areas, and there's an international wildlife sanctuary nearby.

MÖRBISCH AM SEE Swimming, lake beach, sailing school.

NEUSIEDL AM SEE Lake swimming, sailing school, riding at the *Neusiedler Csarda* riding-pension nearby. Ice sailing during the winter months, ice skating. Motorboating, rowing, wind-surfing and sailing. Sailing season opens late May. Fishing for pike and carp—apply for permission to the Gemeinde (town administration) where you wish to fish. Tennis courts.

PODERSDORF, PURBACH AM SEE, RUST, ST. ANDRÄ and **WEIDEN AM SEE** all have water sports—swimming and sailing.

USEFUL ADDRESSES
BAD TATZMANNSDORF Go to the *Fremdenverkehrsverein* or *Kurkommission* for information.

EISENSTADT *Südburg*, government sponsored travel office for Burgenland, at Pfarrplatz 47; and *Abteilung Fremdenverkehr* (tourist section) of Burgenland State Government, in Esterhazy Palace.

NEUSIEDL AM SEE The town hall has a section for local tourist information.

SALZBURG

A Lot of Night Music

Salzburg first appeared in history about 500 BC as a gathering place for Alpine Celts, whose settlement was called Juvavum or Petena, while the general area was named Noricum. The Romans, arriving about 40 AD, built roads (their routes are still being followed) to Wels, Augsburg, Regensburg, and to the lakes to the east. In the fourth century St. Maximus arrived to Christianize the people, and incidentally dug the catacombs under the Mönchsberg that are still high on the list of tourist attractions.

In the eighth century, St. Rupert built St. Peter's Monastery in front of the catacombs, as well as the cloisters on the nearby Nonnberg, and started Salzburg on the way to greatness. In 798, 21 years after the founding of the monastery, the city became, as an awe-struck German account puts it, the *Residenz der mächtigen Fürsterzbischöfe von Salzburg*—the see of the powerful bishop-princes of Salzburg. They were indeed powerful. They dominated all the other bishops of the German-speaking world and Salzburg was referred to as the German Rome—the *German* Rome, not the Austrian Rome. The proper adjective is important, for Salzburg, which even today is only barely within Austria's frontier, was not to become a part of that country for another thousand years.

The setting of Salzburg is perfect. It lies on both banks of the Salzach River, at the point where it is pinched between two mountains, the Kapuzinerberg on one shore, the Mönchsberg on the other. All about are enchanting mountain vistas.

Salzburg's many fine buildings are a complement to their surroundings and form a blended harmonious whole. Salzburg is architecturally a city of a single style, the baroque. Perhaps nowhere else in the world is there so unanimous a flowering of this school. Salzburg is a riot of baroque, which is quite proper, for baroque is itself riotous. Its exuberance is propitious to the wholesale display it gets in Salzburg.

It was in 1077 that the great fortress, now the chief landmark of the whole of Land Salzburg (the State of Salzburg as distinguished from the city), was started by Archbishop Gebhard. This huge pile, sitting 500 feet above the city, on the end of the Mönchsberg, became not only the seat of the archbishops who were both spiritual and temporal leaders of western Austria, but also a siege-proof haven during the countless wars that swept the area. Frequently enlarged, the fortress is one of the most impressive sights, both from inside and outside, in Europe. A cog railway up the face of the Castle Hill will take you there the easy way, but the hardy will find the zigzag climb far more exciting.

It was natural that when the Protestant Reformation occurred, the reaction of the mighty Catholic Bishops of Salzburg should be strong. It was so strong, and so successful, that large numbers of Protestants were forced to leave this region—and thus linked the history of Salzburg with that of America. Some of the Pennsylvania Dutch (who, in reality, were not Dutch but Germans) came from Salzburg. Other emigrants from this area helped to found the city of Savannah, Georgia.

In 1816, after the Napoleonic Wars, and as one of the conclusions of the Congress of Vienna, the present territory of Salzburg (city and State) became a part of the Austrian Empire and has remained with Austria ever since.

The Mozart Festival

To most people, Salzburg today means the city of Mozart. It is at the time of the Mozart Festival, held annually in July and August, that it receives most visitors and this is without doubt the single greatest drawing card of a city which, nevertheless, does not lack other attractions. So let us consider the Festival season first.

Wolfgang Amadeus Mozart was born in the city of Salzburg in 1756, and into the 35 short years of his life he crammed a prodigious number of compositions—the mere cataloging of them is the subject of a ponderous work, impressively entitled *Chronologisch-thematisches Verzeichnis sämtlicher Tonwerke Wolfgang Amadeus Mozarts,* the work of one Ludwig von Köchel. His great labor is amply recognized by the fact that his name is perpetuated in the numbering system of Mozart's works, for the "K" which precedes each number stands for "Köchel". It is true that Mozart began early. He started to play the piano at three (to become the outstanding pianist of his time, despite small hands that seemed quite incapable of playing the chords he wrote himself); he was writing compositions at six which already prefigured the musical style he was to develop later and in the same year played before Empress Maria Theresa, among others, in Vienna; and he began giving public concerts at the age of seven. It is on record that at the age of eight, George III of England heard him play and "tried him with hard questions." One wonders who prepared the hard questions for George III to ask.

Although Mozart was the wonder child of Europe, his native city did him no particular honor in his lifetime. It is making up for it now. Ever since 1925, on the initiative, among others, of the theatrical director Max Reinhardt, the poet Hugo von Hofmannsthal and the stage designer Alfred Roller, the last week in July and most of August have been given up to Salzburg's internationally famous Festival, which, though it is not devoted exclusively to Mozart, is nevertheless dominated by veneration for this native of the city who stands at the very top in the hierarchy of music. The world's greatest musicians, conductors, singers and instrumentalists come here yearly to take part in the Festival performances.

The heart of the Festival is the Festspielhaus, where most of the operatic performances and the big orchestral concerts are given. The new Festspielhaus is a grandiose, modern construction, decorated with works of art by the leading Austrian artists, among them the painters Oskar Kokoschka, Wolfgang Hutter, Karl Plattner and the sculptor Rudolf Hoflehner, and designed by the architect Clemens Holzmeister. It has space for 2,300 spectators and an especially large stage. Still in use for the performances is the section of the previous Festspielhaus, now also a part of the new Festspielhaus complex, which was originally built in 1607 as a court riding school and stable. But it was a stable for highly superior horses; in their winter manger they could have entertained themselves by looking at Rottmayr's ceiling paintings. Thus it was not too difficult to convert the building to its present uses.

Other performances are given in the Landestheater. Some concerts and sacred music, such as masses, are presented in the cathedral, where there is a fine locally-designed 4,000-pipe organ, or in the Abbey of St. Peter's, but the finest church music is at the Franziskanerkirche, where masses are performed on Sundays with orchestra and choir. Chamber music concerts are usually given in the hall of the Mozarteum, where a summer music school is conducted, attended by students from all over the world. The Residenz is the scene of serenade concerts held by candlelight, attended by audiences of which the great majority have bought standing-room tickets—somewhat of a misnomer, since the initiated listener prefers to sit somewhere on the wide expanse of marble floor or even to lie full length, head pillowed on a coat, eyes closed, listening in blissful repose to the strains of the music. Finally, one of the great features of the Festival, and one which has nothing to do with Mozart, is the performance in the square before the cathedral of the morality play *Everyman,* written by Hugo von Hofmannsthal. The cathedral provides a perfect backdrop for the spectacle; and as the play is so timed that Death makes his climatic appearance after dusk has fallen on the great Domplatz; the spectacle closes with shattering dramatic effect.

Often during the Festival the visitor has half a dozen different performances to choose from in a single day—all of them of a quality that no one would want to miss. But if you find a spare moment, you can complete your homage to Mozart by visiting the house where he was born, at Getreidegasse 9, only a block back from the river on the west bank. It has now been converted into a museum.

It is the tourist who comes to Salzburg outside the Festival season who will have most time to explore its many fascinating attractions. But even for busy Festival visitors, making the acquaintance of the town is not too difficult, for most of its sights are compactly located in a comparatively small area.

Some Festival Advice

Although Salzburg has a seemingly high number of hotels, inns and pensions, they are not always sufficient for the Festival crowds. It is unwise to come to Salzburg without a reservation expecting to be able to find accommodation on the spot. If you haven't time to write individual hotels and wait for replies, try the Stadtverkehrsbüro, Auerspergstr. 7. This office is also a clearing house for placing visitors in rooms in private houses, if you are willing to accept this sort of accommodation. Students who want to take a summer course at the Mozarteum music school and attend the Festival incidentally, can find living quarters through the school if they register early.

If you can't find a place to stay in Salzburg, you can do what many do—find a place nearby. If you have a car, it's fairly simple. Lake resorts nearby are Fuschlsee, Wolfgangsee and Mondsee, served by buses from Salzburg. Or you can stay at the famous Bavarian resorts Berchtesgaden or Bad Reichenhall, nested among high Alps across the border in Germany and reached in 25 minutes and by bus in 50 minutes (frequent service during summer) as well as by train. However reserve also here in advance.

The same thing is true for Festival performance tickets—don't arrive without any and expect to be able to pick them up when you reach Salzburg. The demand is always greater than the supply, and tickets are dealt out parsimoniously each year to representatives in different countries. Get them through your travel agent or at the official Austrian tourist agency office in the country you come from, and be sure to order them well in advance of your trip. *Otherwise, the only tickets you will get will be those sold by hotel concierges at considerably increased prices.*

You can get standing room in Salzburg for the serenade concerts, and sometimes for sacred music or special performances where there is more or less unlimited space, like outdoor concerts, but that's all you can count on without advance booking.

And now, what to wear. If you come at Festival time, bring evening clothes. For the important first night performances evening dress is *de rigueur,* and you will notice that the Austrians particularly dress up. At other times, dress is more informal, and during the skiing season, of course, sportswear is general. Remember that Salzburg is in the mountains and the evenings are apt to be cool even in summer. If you like to walk, this is good country for it.

The Left Bank

The Number One sight of Salzburg is certainly the Festung Hohensalzburg, the 12th-century fortress that dominates the town (especially at night during the Festival, when it is floodlighted) from one end of the Mönchsberg on the left or west bank of the Salzach. Since at least from a distance the castle hill appears to be standing alone, one usually forgets that it still is, although at the very end, a part of Mönchsberg ridge. You reach it by a cogwheel railway which starts behind St. Peter's cemetery. Its prize exhibit is a later addition, St. George's Chapel, which missed being 15th century by only two years. One year later, in 1502, the fortress acquired the 200-pipe barrel organ, which plays daily during the summer at 7, 11, and 6. From the Festung there is a marvelous view.

Not far from the fortress is the Nonnberg Convent, which was founded by St. Rupert in about the year 700. The church is from the late 1400s and contains, among other riches, a lovely ornate gilded altar backing. Each evening during May at 18.45 the nuns sing a 15-minute service called "Maiandacht". Their beautiful singing helps create an atmosphere of calm that one hadn't thought possible in Salzburg.

The other end of the Mönchsberg can also be scaled mechanically, this time by a lift from the Gstättengasse. On this side the only attraction is the view, which is marvelous indeed.

You can cover the lower-level sights of the left bank fairly readily in a single walk, starting from the Ferdinand-Hanusch-Platz on the river, between the Museum and Staats bridges. Go up the Hagenauerplatz, which brings you into the Getreidegasse just opposite Mozart's birthplace, and follow it westward until you come to an open place, in which

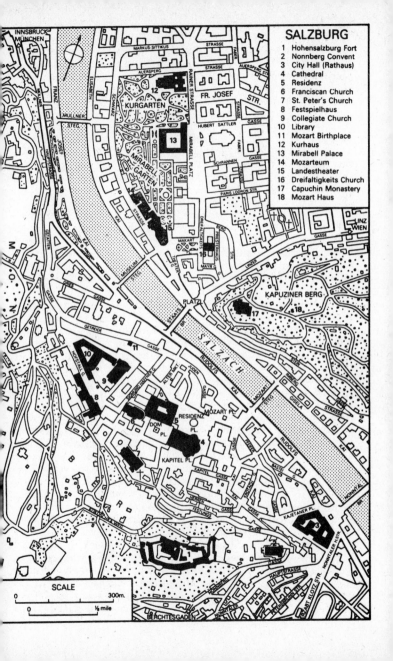

SALZBURG

1 Hohensalzburg Fort
2 Nonnberg Convent
3 City Hall (Rathaus)
4 Cathedral
5 Residenz
6 Franciscan Church
7 St. Peter's Church
8 Festspielhaus
9 Collegiate Church
10 Library
11 Mozart Birthplace
12 Kurhaus
13 Mirabell Palace
14 Mozarteum
15 Landestheater
16 Dreifaltigkeits Church
17 Capuchin Monastery
18 Mozart Haus

stands the Bürgerspital Church (which you can pass up if you don't feel
in the mood for minor attractions), and the above-mentioned Mönchsberg lift. Doubling around to the left, you are in Sigmundsplatz, which
contains a somewhat bewildering tribute to the equine race, the
Pferdeschwemme, a series of frescos of prancing horses spread out behind a statue dedicated to the same animal. This watering trough was
designed especially for the archbishop's horses, which shows they were
almost as well treated as Caligula's. Salzburg's love for the horse does
not end with this display, nor with the stable ceiling paintings by the
same master who performed a similar service for the bishop-princes in
their Residenz. When you come to the Kapitelplatz, you will find a Little
Pferdeschwemme there (this one was intended for the horses of the
church dignitaries to drink at), while in a nearby fountain the same noble
beast, in multiple examples, spouts jets of water from the nostrils.

   Another half-turn left and you pass through Sigmundsplatz and then
Hofstallgasse, by the old university building, now no longer a university,
but with a library containing 13,000 books and many valuable manuscripts, to Universitätsplatz, for the Kollegienkirche. This is an outstanding example of baroque, not only for Salzburg, but for all Austria—or
all Europe, for that matter. This one you should enter, as the interior is
worthy of the exterior. It was built by Fischer von Erlach for the University, which is to the right.

   On emerging, swing around the corner to the right. Straight ahead,
crossing the Hofstallgasse brings you to the Festspielhaus, which pre-
sumably you will visit some other time for the performances there, so you
might as well swing left again to the Abbey of St. Peter, one of the oldest
Benedictine abbeys in German-speaking countries, founded in 696, again
by St. Rupert, and its oldest parts date from 847. It is in Romanesque
style, with a Gothic cloister, and of its many art treasures, a 1420 Virgin
is most highly prized. A favorite visit here is to the catacombs, starting
in the interesting old cemetery where St. Virgilius is buried (a resounding
name behind which hides this bishop's real name, O'Farrell—he somehow reached Salzburg from Ireland in the eighth century—and helped,
in his days, to make his contemporaries forget that he was crazy, a fact
which was evident from his belief that the earth was round).

   From St. Peter's (unless you propose to take the car up to the Festung
Hohensalzburg from here), cross the Kapitelplatz, with its Neptune
Fountain, to what used to be the Prince Bishops' Palace. Across the way
is the 17th-century cathedral, which you see from the rear. Circle around
it into the Dom Platz. The Cathedral Square is a complete concept. It
is not difficult to see why Max Reinhardt chose it as the setting for
Everyman. In the center rises the Virgin's Column, and at one side is
what is considered to be the first early baroque building north of the Alps
and one of the finest. Its façade is of marble, its towers reach 250 feet
into the air, and it holds 10,000 persons. It is not all that usual to find

fine modern art allied to superb old buildings, but the Cathedral of Salzburg is an exception. Pay special attention to the three great doors, cast in bronze. The one on the right symbolizes Hope, the one on the left Faith, and the center one by Giacomo Manzù is, of course, Charity. Manzù whose strange episcopal figures, wrapped in their copes, seem to conjure up a world of religious myth and mystery, was a natural choice to bridge the gap between baroque and modern.

Across from the Cathedral, the Franciscan Church is a mirror of architectural history: originally built in the eighth century, it was destroyed by fire in the 12th; Romanesque style from the 13th, Gothic additions in the 15th, followed by Renaissance and baroque. Its finest possession is a carved Madonna (1495) by Michael Pacher.

On the other side of the cathedral from the Kapitelplatz is the Residenzplatz before the Renaissance Residenz Palace (so called because it was the town residence of the Prince Bishops), with its state rooms, ceiling frescos by the same Rottmayr who performed for the edification of the horses, and fine furnishings. The 40-foot-high Residenz Fountain in the square before the Palace is lighted at night, and sometimes, in fine weather. The serenade concerts otherwise held inside the Residenz are given about the fountain in the open air. Across the square from the palace rises the Glockenspiel Tower, containing a carillon of 35 bells, which performs at 7 A.M., 11 A.M., and 6 P.M. The tunes are taken from the works of Weber, Haydn, and you know who.

Pass from the Residenzplatz into the Alter Markt, and you find yourself in the old marketplace, where there are some fine baroque buildings and the 16th-century St. Florian Fountain. You now emerge at the river again, about where you started from, near the city hall.

The Right Bank

The right bank of the Salzach is rather less crowded with places not to be missed than the left, which contains more of the oldest buildings of Salzburg. You can start to explore it very conveniently just opposite the point where the west bank walk began, in the Platzl, to which the Staatsbrücke (State Bridge) leads. The famous physician and philosopher, Paracelsus von Hohenheim (1494–1541), the scion of a well-known Swabian-German family of that period, who was the first to introduce the use of chemical drugs in medicine, lived here; his neighbors considered him a sorcerer. You can see his house today, at No. 3. Take Schwarzstrasse out of the Platzl and only after two or three short blocks you will find yourself passing the Landestheater and the Mozarteum, in the garden of which is a little summerhouse in which Mozart finished composing *The Magic Flute*. It is called Zauberflötenhäuschen, a mouthful meaning "the little Magic Flute house."

You are now opposite a large park, originally the private garden of the Schloss Mirabell, which is in a way the Taj Mahal of Salzburg, since it was built in 1606 for his love, Salome Alt, by Wolf Dietrich, who did not abstain from passion simply because he was a bishop—perhaps because he was also a Medici. You may cut across the park to inspect its interior, not neglecting, on the way, the Dwarf's Garden, with its statues of the bishop's favorite midgets, or the delicate wrought-iron gate. Of the splendors inside, the most admired is Rafael Donner's marble stairway, known as the Angel Staircase, though the figures on it are not angels but cupids.

While the south portion of the park about Schloss Mirabell is still called the Mirabell Garten, the north part is now called the Kurgarten, since it encloses the very modern Kurmittelhaus, where all kinds of cures can be taken, as well as the Kongresshaus, Salzburg's convention hall.

Returning along the Mirabellplatz on the other side of the castle, you see the baroque Holy Trinity Church (Dreifaltigkeitskirche), the first one built in Salzburg by Fischer von Erlach around 1700, and you are back at your starting point, with the east bank (lower level) seen—unless, of course, you care to walk back from the river a few blocks up the Linzergasse to visit the Sebastianskirche and its 16th-century graveyard, where Paracelsus and Wolf Dietrich are buried (the latter in a magnificent tiled mausoleum).

Between Schloss Mirabell and the Holy Trinity Church, in Dreifaltig-keitsgasse, is the marionette theater, where the famous Salzburg marionettes, known round the world, have their home. They have done a great deal of touring, including trips to the United States, and films have been made of them, but this is where you see, during the summer, the puppets of Professor Hermann Aicher at their best. His family has been making and exhibiting marionettes for 200 years.

The upper level on this side of the river is provided by the Kapuzinerberg, up which you climb for the view and the walks in the woods on top, since it is not, like the Mönchsberg opposite, provided with a castle to visit. You do, however, begin your climb by passing the Stations of the Cross which lead to the Capuchin monastery that gives the hill its name. If you don't feel up to climbing, from the same point at which you would otherwise start upwards, you can stroll southwards along the Steingasse, at the foot of the slope, and enjoy its lovely old houses.

Excursions from Salzburg

The favorite trip on the outskirts of Salzburg is to what is described as Lustschloss Hellbrunn (the Hellbrunn Pleasure Castle), built in the early 17th century for Bishop Marcus Sitticus. It is the paradise of a mad fountain designer. Some of the fountains operate mechanical figures, others balance balls on water jets and others merely spout water. Wear your old clothes, as one of the pranks of the merry fountain makers is to drench you suddenly from concealed spouts as you are sitting quietly at a table minding your own business. Hellbrunn has a number of other attractions, including the Stone Theater, a natural formation, where the first operatic performance on German-speaking territory was staged in 1617. The interior of the castle, which can be visited with a guided tour, has some fascinating rooms; especially the music room. The *trompe l'oeil* decorations are especially effective.

A pleasant drive if you have a car is to the north, via Maria Plain (a pleasant village with a pilgrimage church) and Bergheim to Oberndorf (you can get there also by a local railway), much visited because of its one claim to fame—here *Silent Night, Holy Night* was composed by Franz Gruber, and written by Father Mohr, the village priest. Its birthplace, the old St. Nikolas Church, was destroyed by flood in 1899; on the site is a memorial chapel, and here, and in the new St. Nikolas Church, there are special Christmas midnight masses.

Schloss Leopoldskron is an 18th-century rococo palace, built by Archbishop Leopold Anton Firmian, later owned by Ludwig I of Bavaria, and still later by Max Reinhardt. Its large grounds, including a small lake, are now being developed as a pleasure park. You can walk there in half an hour.

Other points are the Gaisberg, served by regular sightseeing buses from Salzburg, and the Untersberg, a mountain whose approaches can be reached by bus and whose top can be reached by a daringly constructed aerial cable car. The spa and casino of Bad Reichenhall, Berchtesgaden, and Königsee, all in Germany, also make a pleasant half-day excursion.

PRACTICAL INFORMATION

HOTELS It is difficult for a Salzburg hotel not to have a good location, but if you really want a room with a view, you will find some of the better ones on the slopes of the Kapuzinerberg or the Gaisberg, behind it, while the one that is the very top is on the Mönchsberg, across the river. The city offers numerous hotels of all price categories, with the accent on the upper categories. Salzburg is as expensive as Vienna. Rates during the summer season (June 1–Sept. 30) and especially during the Festival may be as much as 50% higher than during the rest of the year. Many hotels also offer pension terms, but Salzburg has many good restaurants.

Deluxe (L)

Bristol, Makartplatz 4, in center, 74 rooms, half-board only, April to Oct.
Gastschloss Mönchstein, on the Mönchsberg in a magnificent location above Salzburg, an exclusive castle-hotel of 12 elegant suites, superior service.

Goldener Hirsch, Getreidegasse 37, in the main shopping street, 800-year-old house, an inn since 1564, arched corridors and vaulted stairs, antique and rustic furniture, modern appliances ingeniously hidden, 50 rooms, outstanding food and service.

Kobenzl, 11 km. out and 2,700 ft. up on Gaisberg mountain (there's a bus) 27 rooms, pool, garage and large parking lot, restaurant, crisp mountain air and fine view over Salzburg, open March to Sept.

Mirabell, Auerspergstr. 4, at the Mirabell Park, 100 rooms, 70 with bath or shower, restaurant, bar, airconditioning, teleprinter service available, direct passage leads to the glass-enclosed swimming pool of the Kurhaus next door.

Österreichischer Hof, Schwarzstr. 5–7, near Landestheater and Mozarteum, 110 rooms, panoramic apartments on 4th floor, beautiful location on right bank of the River Salzach, rooms overlooking river offer a fine view of the fortress and the old city.

Schlosshotel Klessheim, a section of the Klessheim Castle in Siezenheim on the outskirts of the city, 25 rooms, 16 baths, in a large park with golf, tennis, pool, half-board only, and open July and Aug. only.

First-class (1)

Cottage, Joseph Messner Str. 14, 86 rooms, indoor pool, sauna.

Fondachhof, castle-hotel at Gaisbergstr. 46, in a large park at the foot of the Gaisberg, 30 rooms, antique furnishings, heated pool and sauna, open April to Oct.

Kasererhof, Alpenstr. 6, in Nonntal near river, 58 rooms, quiet location, garden restaurant.

Maria-Theresien Schlössl, Morzgerstr. 87, 17 rooms, pleasant.

Schlosshotel St. Rupert, Morzgerstr. 31, 30 rooms, most with bath, restaurant serves very good food, located in lovely area outside city in direction of Hellbrunn Castle, open April to Oct.

Winkler, Franz Josefstr. 7, 103 rooms.

Moderate (2)

Auersperg, Auerspergstr. 61, most of the 60 rooms with baths, between the main station and the Kapuzinerberg.

Bayerischerhof, Elisabethstr. 12, near railway station, 50 rooms, some with view of the Gaisberg.

Drei Kreuz, Vogelweiderstr. 7A, 20 rooms.

Europa, Rainerstr. 31, next to railway station, 94 rooms in a 15-story box sticking out above the roofs of Salzburg. The roof café and restaurant offer a fine view of Salzburg and the Alps.

Flughafen, Innsbrucker Bundesstr. 105, 15 rooms, outstanding airport restaurant.

Gablerbräu, Linzergasse 9, near main bridge, 50 rooms, 26 baths.

Humboldt, Egger-Lienzg. 3, 100 rooms, bed and breakfast, July to Oct.

Johann Strauss, Makart Kai 37, 30 rooms, 20 baths.

Kasererbräu, Kaigasse 33, not far from Mozartplatz, small, furnished in old Salzburg style.

Mozart, Franz Josef Str. 50, 33 functional rooms.

Pelz, Gaisbergstr. 40, 30 rooms, bed and breakfast, June to Sept.

Pitter, Rainerstr. 6–8, near railway station, 220 rooms, restaurant, café, beer cellar, musical entertainment, garden in summer.

Reiter, Mirabellplatz 8, 16 rooms, bed and breakfast.

Stein, at main bridge, the Staatsbrücke, 80 rooms, 40 baths, good restaurant, roof terrace café.

Stieglbräu, Rainerstr. 14, 50 rooms, large restaurant divided into several sections, garden in summer, parking.

Wolf Dietrich, Wolf-Dietrich Str. 7, 30 rooms, pool.

Inexpensive (3)

Blaue Gans, Getreidegasse 43, 40 rooms, 20 showers.

Elefant, Sigmund-Haffnergasse 4, 34 rooms with baths.

Emminger, Reisenbergerstr. 16, 25 rooms with bath.

Germania, Faberstr. 10, near Mirabell Garden, 30 rooms, 10 baths and showers, open summer only.

Markus Sittikus, Markus-Sittikussstr. 20, near main station, most of the 35 rooms with baths.

Neutor, Neutorstr. 8, 54 rooms.

Many more hotels and Gasthöfe (3) are available in Salzburg and suburbs. In the vast majority you'll get a clean room and an honest price.

PENSIONS Presently Salzburg has a better selection of pensions than any other city in Austria. They are of all categories and are usually well appointed.

Expensive (P1)

Haus Arenberg, Blumensteinstr. 8, is under the Kapuziner Berg.

Fuggerhof, Eberh.-Fuggerstr. 9, 13 rooms, with heated pool.

Haus Ingeborg, Sonnleitenweg 9, 11 rooms, with heated outdoor pool, closed in winter.

Dr. Wührer's Haus Gastein, Ignaz-Rieder-Kai 25, on bank of Salzach, 13 rooms, well-appointed.

Moderate (P2)

Astoria, Maxglanerhauptstr. 7, in suburb of **Maxglan,** 35 rooms.

Am Dom, Goldgasse 17, 15 rooms, central, comfortable.

Am Eschenbach, Hellbrunnerstr. 21, good for a sumptuous breakfast.

Helmhof, Kirchengasse 29, 18 rooms, 13 baths and showers, heated pool.

Koch, Gaisbergstr. 37, 13 rooms.

Inexpensive (P3)

Haus Wartenberg, Riedenburger Str. 2, 30 rooms, half with showers, good Italian restaurant *Camino* on the premises.

Adlerhof, Elisabethstr. 25, near station, 25 rooms, some showers, restaurant.

Goldene Krone, Linzergasse 48, 35 rooms, 12 showers.

Youth Hostel

The *Jugendgästehaus Nonntal,* Josef-Preis-Allee 18, not far from the old town, 400 beds, full board as well as private cooking facilities, is open the whole year.

Out of Town

Doktorwirt, Glaserstr. 9, in suburb of **Aigen.** Quiet, family-run, 35 rooms, 28 baths and showers. *Doktorschlössl,* next door at no. 7, 45 rooms, 20 showers, shares outdoor pool with *Doktorwirt;* summer only.

At **Anif,** 8 km. south, *Schlosswirt,* Romantic Hotel, near valley station of Untersberg cable car, 30 rooms, Biedermeier-style furnishings, good restaurant, garden, closed in winter. *Friesacher,* 30 rooms, tennis; both (I).

Zistelalm, over 3,000 ft. up the Gaisberg, is the most restful of hotels in this category, offering mountain air with good food and comfortable lodgings, 40 beds, 12 baths, about 14 km. or a 15-minute drive, up the Gaisberg road.

 RESTAURANTS Salzburg is plentifully supplied with good restaurants. It's wise to make reservations at the more frequented places. During spring or fall, special gastronomic weeks are sponsored by the *Bund Österreichischer Gastlichkeit,* an association of Austrian restaurants, with all members offering specially selected dishes. The hotel restaurants are all up to standard.

Expensive (1)

Alt-Salzburg, Burgerspitalg. 2, excellent Tournedos Mozart and Spezialbecher mixed grills.

Dachgarten Restaurant Europa, atop the Europa Hotel, splendid view.

Das Beisel, Neutorstr. 28, pleasant atmosphere, good service—and admirable Austrian cuisine.

Flughafenrestaurant, at the airport, for grills, game and fish.

Glockenspiel, Residenzplatz, 2 stories, both with terrace, the place to relax while wandering around the old town, perhaps at lunchtime, café and restaurant

Goldener Hirsch, is the best of the hotel restaurants, excellent food, particularly game, also good wines and mixed drinks.

G' würzmühl, a bit out of town on Leopoldskronerstr. 1, broiled specialties including steak.

Jedermann Grill, Franz Josef Str. 7, specializes in Tafelspitz and Braumeisterschnitzel.

Österreichischer Hof, has 3 restaurants, all good—*Red Salon,* the regular hotel restaurant—*Salzach Grill,* small and attractive, with riverside terrace—and *Sa*

zach-Keller, in the cellar, tastefully arranged, better in the evening than for a leisurely lunch, as they throw you out promptly at 2 P.M.—last two both (2).

Zinnkrug is on the 4th floor on the right bank and its windows look across the Staatsbrücke to the illuminated Festung. Food is good, often with fresh lake fish, friendly service. One of the nicest restaurants.

Moderate (2)

Brasserie, Kaigasse 7, interesting mixture of French and very Austrian cuisine.

Festungsrestaurant, at the fortress with fine view from the outdoor section, folklore evenings mid-June to early Sept. on Tues., Thurs., Fri.

Friesacher, at Anif, resembles a Viennese heuriger; big garden.

Hotel Schlosswirt, also at Anif, is on a small lake and close to a fairytale castle. Rooms with period furnishings; very good restaurant.

Mundenhamer Bräu, Rainerstr. 2, a beer restaurant with good local food.

Paracelsus, Kaigasse 8, authentic menu and good local atmosphere.

Schlossstube Mirabell, Mirabellplatz 4, delicious Apfelstrudel.

Stadtkrug, Linzergasse 20, particularly for fresh mountain trout.

Stieglbraü, Rainerstr. 14, in hotel of the same name but with completely separate, rambling restaurant halls in modernized Salzburg style.

Stiftskeller St. Peter, in St. Peter's Abbey, traditional *Peterskeller Teller* with good white Praelaten wine from the Abbey's own vineyards.

Weinhaus Moser, Wiener Philharmonikerstr. 3, good wines, game specialties.

Weisses Kreuz, Bierjodlg. 6, noted Balkan food.

Zum Mohren, Judengasse 9. Cosy cellar offering excellent food and friendly service.

Inexpensive (3)

Augustiner Bräu, Augustinergasse 4, where the Augustinian fathers have their beer on sale, in winter several large halls, in summer a pleasant shady garden.

Bärenwirt, Müllner Hauptstr. 8, genuine Salzburger fare.

Hofwirt, Schallmooser Hauptstr. 1, wide choice.

Sternbräu, a vast brewery restaurant, with entrances at Getreidegasse 25, and Griesgasse 23, self-service garden and a semi-covered restaurant garden with music on Fri. and Sun. evenings; own butcher and sausage shops.

Stieglkeller, Festungsgasse 10, the seat of the Stiegl brewery, on the way to the fortress, very popular, excellent beer and low prices.

Cafés and Pastry Shops

Bazar, Schwarzstr. 3, glassed-in terrace, frequented by old and young, by chess players and newspaper readers and also, in Festival time, by performers.

Another old landmark of Salzburg is *Café Tomaselli* on Alter Markt with sidewalk tables and an attractive upper floor terrace.

The *SchatzKonditorei* in a passage leading off the Getreidegasse just before the Mozart house has delectable pastries. Best are the handmade Mozart Kugeln which can be taken away or mailed.

You can enjoy an excellent view of the city and its surroundings from the café of *Hotel Europa,* from *Café Winkler* on Mönchsberg, and from the roof terrace café of *Hotel Stein.*

Among other cafés there are *Mozartkugel* in Hotel Österreichischer Hof; *Pitter* in hotel of the same name; *Wernbacher,* Franz-Josefstr. 5.

HOW TO GET AROUND Salzburg is served by a large number of bus lines. It is also, by the way, an open-carriage city; if you like leisurely promenades behind a horse, this is the place for it.

Taxis are expensive and hard to get just before curtain time during festivals (reserve in advance with hotel porters).

Driving in the city is a problem, so park your car on the edge of the city center and proceed by bus or on foot; a city bus runs between the center and the Nonntal parking lot. In Mönchsberg there is a huge garage with a long passage leading directly to the lobby of the Festspielhaus.

Sightseeing trips in the city and surrounding areas start from the Mirabellplatz. The most scenic are to the Grossglockner and the Dachstein ice caves.

An aerial cable railway, over 2 km. long, takes you to the Untersberg mountain, to an elevation of 5,825 ft. Its valley station is at St. Leonhard, on the road to Berchtesgaden. Each of the two cabins can transport 50 people, and 700 people can be taken to the top in one hour.

If you want to rent a car you may try *Hertz* or *Avis,* both at Porschestr. 7 and the airport; *Nölli,* Gyllenstormstr. 7; *Wiechenberger,* Langmoosweg 21; *Inter Rent,* opposite the main station.

MUSEUMS Admission times vary from season to season. You will be fairly safe if you keep to the week-day schedule of 9–12, 2–4, Sat. and Sun. mornings. But to be sure, check with the city tourist office or your hotel porter.

Fortress Hohensalzburg Cog-wheel cable car operating daily every 10 minutes between 7.30 A.M. and 7 P.M. (in summer until 9 P.M.). Conducted tours.

Rainer-Regiments-Museum The historic memorabilia of one of the oldest Austrian Army regiments, located at the Fortress.

Catacombs Church of St. Peter. Conducted tours daily.

Residenz City palace of Salzburg archbishops since 12th century. Present building dates from early 17th century. Conducted tours through State Rooms. Various art exhibitions take place in the Residenz Gallery.

Festspielhaus Conducted tours through auditorium and stage. Closed because of rehearsals in July and Aug.

Mozart Museum Mozart's birthplace. Mozart's clavichord, Hammerklavier, his first violin, family pictures, exhibition of staging of Mozart operas, etc. Open weekdays.

Mozarteum Music Academy. Two concert halls, Bibliotheca Mozartiana (about 1,500 works by Mozart in addition to several thousand other books and musical works), some Mozart letters; *Zauberflötenhäuschen* (tiny house in which Mozart is supposed to have composed *The Magic Flute*) has been in the garden since 1950. Open weekdays; conducted tours only July and Aug.

Rupertinum Salzburg Landessammlung, Wiener Phiharmonikerstr. 9. Modern paintings.

St. Sebastian's Cemetery Linzergasse 41. Wolf Dietrich's mausoleum, tomb of Paracelsus, and Mozart family grave.

Hellbrunn Castle-Palace Building dates from early 17th century, oldest baroque park in Europe with fountain water plays, natural rock theater, fine garden sculptures, Monatsschlösschen with folklore museum. Conducted tours from Easter to late fall. Bus H from Salzburg.

Haus der Natur A museum-like, 80-room natural history exhibition in its variegated forms, historic, geographical, biological development. Open daily 9–5.

Carolino Augusteum The City Museum dealing with the history of Salzburg. Open daily 9–5.

 ENTERTAINMENT The great annual event is, of course, the *Festival,* from the last week in July to the end of Aug. Details can be obtained from the *Salzburger Festspiele,* Postfach 140, 5010 Salzburg; tel (06222) 425.41.

Warning. Festival performance tickets—don't arrive without any and expect to be able to pick them up when you reach Salzburg. Demand always exceeds supply, and tickets are dealt out sparingly to representatives in different countries. Get them through your travel agent or at the official Austrian tourist agency office in the country you come from, well in advance. *Otherwise, the only tickets you will get will be those sold by hotel concierges considerably above the official top price of 2,000AS.*

You can get standing room in Salzburg for the serenade concerts, and sometimes for sacred music or special performances where there is more or less unlimited space, like outdoor concerts, but that's all you can count on without booking.

This is the period when Salzburg is swamped with visitors. Thus it is advisable to plan an off-season visit to Salzburg if you want to go, not for the Festival, but for the city and its surroundings. From the viewpoint of weather, May to Oct. are the best months unless you plan a visit in winter, in which case, mid-Dec. to Feb. is the best time for skiing and for enjoying the winter scenery.

In addition to the traditional *Mozart Festival,* Salzburg has a number of other seasonal musical events: late Jan. there is a *Mozart Festival Week; Castle Concerts* in Mirabell castle from April to Oct.; an Easter Festival of Music; chamber music concerts in the Mozart Haus from June to Aug. and further musical events during the *Salzburger Kulturtage* (Culture Days) in Oct. Concurrent with the Mozart Festival is the *Szene der Jugend* ("Youth Scene") festival, taking place at Petersbrunnhof, in churches and in the university aula. Includes avant-garde theater, cabarets, workshops.

An important event in Salzburg is also the celebration of *Fasching* (carnival) beginning with a long series of balls in early Jan. and lasting until Shrove Tuesday, and crowned on one of the weekends by a gaudy parade presided over by the Fasching Prince and Princess, duly elected every year. Of particular interest among the balls are several given in folk dress and attended by folklore dance and music groups.

Special all-inclusive arrangements (hotel, food, theater or concert ticket, sightseeing tours), conveniently priced, are available in Salzburg for weekly or shorter stays on such occasions as Christmas, New Year, Mozart Week, etc. For further details, inquire from the *Stadtverkehrsbüro Salzburg,* Auerspergstr. 7.

The famous *Marionette Theater* is not to be missed by young or old.

NIGHTLIFE *Stieglkeller, Festungsrestaurant* and *Sternbräu* have folklore shows on some days of the week during summer (see *Restaurants*). A number of wine taverns have local atmosphere and musical entertainment, among them: *Bacchus Stuben,* Rudolfskai 16; *Paracelsus Weinstube,* established 1541, Kaigasse 8; *Höllbräu Kerzenstübl,* Judengasse 15; *Steirische Weinstuben,* St.-Julienstr. 9, which also serves the best chicken in Salzburg.

Discos: *Chez Roland,* Gisela Kai; *City,* Schallmooser Hauptstr. 1; *Golden Black,* Dreifaltigkeitsg. 3; *Old Grenadier,* Ursulinenplatz 2; and *Scotch Dancing Club,* Franz Josef Str. 5. *Copersucar,* St. Julienstr. 3, Brazilian band and samba shows: *Mexicano Keller,* Getreideg. 43, Mexican way; *Casanova,* Linzergasse 23, striptease towards midnight, not earthshaking.

The mortality of nightclubs is greater in Salzburg than in Vienna; better inquire from the city tourist office or from the hotel porter (however, keep in mind that he probably gets a percentage from the places reserved by him and therefore your bill will run that much higher).

CASINO Located at the Hotel Winkler on Mönchsberg. Roulette, baccara and black-jack are played according to the international rules, daily after 5 P.M. Passport required, knowledge of German advisable and you must be over 21.

SPORTS Gaisberg mountain in the outskirts of Salzburg (the top is only 16 km. from the center of the city by a good mountain road) offers excellent **skiing** terrain. There are 4 ski lifts and a chair lift on various slopes of the mountain and a ski jump at Zistelsalm. There is a ski school on Gaisberg, and skiing equipment, including boots, can be rented from the Hintner sports store.

Ice skating rinks are located in Volksgarten and in Rupertgasse 11. **Tobogganing** on Gaisberg.

Swimming Among the various pools are—the indoor pool in Kurhaus (Paracelsusbad); AYA-Bad on Alpenstr.; Waldbad Anif on the busline to Hallein; Kreuzbrückl in the suburb of Maxglan; and the pools in Volksgarten (Franz-Josefs-Park) on the way to Aigen; in the park of Klessheim Castle near the golf course; and in the grounds of Leopoldskron Castle. The nearest Salzkammergut lakes (Wallersee, Trumersee) are only 21 km. away, but very cold.

Many **tennis** courts are available in the city, the best being those of the Salzburger Tennisklub in Volksgarten. Tennis courts are also available in the park of Klessheim Castle, where a 9-hole **golf** course is open from April to Oct.

Gliding is another feature of the Salzburg area; starting and landing sites on Gaisberg, at Koppl and at the airport of Maxglan; for further information inquire at Aero-Club-Landesverband, Mozartplatz 8, Salzburg.

For **horseback riding**, go to the riding school at Innsbrucker Bundesstrasse 75E, or to a similar establishment at Hellbrunner Allee 67, near Hellbrunn. Riding and jumping tournaments are held from time to time.

Soccer (football) and **handball** matches are very popular, and the more important ones take place at one or the other of the three main sports fields.

Camping There are 9 campsites in and around Salzburg, the largest ones at Bayerhamerstrasse 14A, in the city; on the Gersbergalm, in the Maxglan section near the airport; and at Schloss Aigen. The Gersbergalm site and Kasern in the city are equipped for winter camping.

 SHOPPING Salzburg stores are open from 9 A.M. to 6 P.M., some of them closing for an hour or two at lunchtime. All of them are shut Sat. afternoons. The best shopping streets are in the heart of the old city particularly Getreidegasse, Judengasse, Griesgasse, Schwarzstrasse and Linzergasse and the several historic squares such as Waagplatz and Residenzplatz. Salzburg specialties include dirndls and Lederhosen, petit point, leather goods, jewelry, handsomely decorated candles, and sports equipment and clothing, particularly ski and mountain boots.

One good shopping tip is to take a short bus ride out to the main railway station and visit the *Konsum Markt,* a 2-floor department store, with some good handcrafts at less than the downtown prices.

Candles *Johann Nagy,* Linzergasse 32. *Hans Nagy,* Getreidegasse 48.

Dirndls and Trachten for Women *Lanz,* Schwarzstr. 4 and Imbergstr. 5. *Wenger,* Münzgasse 2. *Seifert,* Judengasse 8.

Handicrafts, Gifts and Souvenirs *Salzburger Heimatwerk,* Residenzplatz 17. *Hans Schmidjell,* Münzgasse 2.

Petit Point *Slezak,* Markart Platz 8. *Fritsch,* Getreidegasse 42–44, *J. Ennsmann & Co.,* Getreidegasse 31 and 21, Neutorgasse 32.

Toys *Neumüller,* Rathausplatz 3. *Spielwarenhaus Böhlein,* Makartplatz 4.

Wood Carvings *Johann Lackner,* Badergässchen 2.

Wrought Iron and Weinhebers *Hans Schmidjell,* Münzgasse 2. *Gebrüder Roittner,* Getreidegasse 7–8. *Siegfried Kopfberger,* Judengasse 14.

MAIL AND TELECOMMUNICATIONS All these services are handled by the post offices. The main post office at Residenzplatz 9 is open daily from 7 A.M. to 3 A.M. during the Festival time, from 7 A.M. to midnight during the rest of the summer (June 1 to Sept. 15), and from 7 A.M. to 10 P.M. during the rest of the year. The post office at the Markartplatz is open on weekdays from 7.30 A.M. to 7 P.M. except during the Festival when it is open also Sun. and holidays from 8 A.M. to noon. The post office at the railway station never closes.

USEFUL ADDRESSES *Stadtverkehrsbüro,* the official city tourist office, has its headquarters at Auerspergstr. 7, tel. 71511, and an attractive information center, in traditional Salzburg style, at Mozartplatz 5. In addition it maintains an information office at the main railway station, also open all year, and 4 additional summer offices; *Informationsdienst Salzburg-Mitte,* at AGIP service station in Münchener Bundesstr., and *Informationsdienst Salzburg-West,* at BP service station in Innsbrucker Bundesstr., *Informationsdienst Salzburg-Ost,* Sterneckstr., and *Informationsdienst Salzburg-Süd,* Alpenstr. 47.

Landesverkehrsamt, the official Salzburg State Tourist Department, has its offices at Mozartplatz 1 (tel. 0662 43264), and shares the above-mentioned information center at Mozartplatz 5 with the city tourist office.

Sightseeing flights: carried out with Cessnas by ÖFAG-Flugdienst at the airport. For bus sightseeing tours: *Autoreisebüro Salzkraft,* Mirabellplatz 2, and *Albus,* Markartplatz 9.

American Express, Mozartplatz 5 (tel. 0662 42501); *Wagons Lits-Cook,* Münzgasse 1 (tel. 0662 72755).

Children carrying a statue in the Corpus Christi procession in Natters, near Innsbruck. The Hohensalzburg fortress rises above the Mirabell Gardens, Salzburg

**The meeting place of the Rivers Steyr
and Enns, in the town of Steyr,
Upper Austria**

The lower stage of the mighty
Krimml Falls, the highest in
Europe

A typical cobbled street in the
medieval town of Solbad Hall, in Tyrol

LAND SALZBURG

Sports and Spas in the High Alps

The shape of the Bundesland Salzburg (Federal State of Salzburg), or briefly, Land Salzburg, makes it look as if its boundaries had been drawn by drunken surveyors on the instructions of crazy mapmakers. But it was not the mapmakers who were mad; it was the country itself. The land had thrust itself upward into such weird and fantastic shapes that rivers, roads and boundaries were forced to follow them. The landscape is softer in the narrow neck of Land Salzburg, to the north and northeast of the city of Salzburg; here, blue lakes dream peacefully among the round-shouldered mountains covered by forests; here too is the beginning of the Salzkammergut region, most of which, however, lies across the state border in Upper Austria. The country here is so delightful that visitors to the Salzburg Mozart Festival often stay on the shores of its nearer lakes, not because a crowded capital has forced them to commute to the festival performances, but because they prefer to stay in these surroundings, even though it does mean frequent trips to and from Salzburg.

Land Salzburg offers all types of accommodations, from the tops in luxury at Badgastein to the most modest countryside Gasthof and mountain lodge. Except for Badgastein, Bad Hofgastein, Zell am See, St.

Gilgen am Wolfgangsee and a few castle hotels, the accommodations are mostly moderate and low-priced, and in the country spots, you often get more for your money than you do in the large cities and more fashionable spots.

Weather Matters

This is mostly high mountain country, which can be quite capricious when it comes to weather. The Hohe Tauern on the southern border is the highest mountain range in Austria, a sort of arbitrator between the southern and northern winds. If they decide that the weather should be nice, violent opposition may be raised by the Steinernes Meer and Dachstein groups, closing the region toward the north. The consequence is that war clouds may roll down from the mountains at any moment.

For the sightseeing tourist, the best time to come is late spring to early fall and, for winter scenery, the weeks from the end of January until early March are usually the clearest.

Almost all of Land Salzburg is excellent skiing country. The season usually begins in the second half of December or the first half of January and lasts until mid-March, in the high spots until May. On some very high elevations such as Kitzsteinhorn (above Kaprun and Weissee), reached by cable cars and glacier lifts, and in the new Sport Gastein area above Badgastein (reached by toll road), there is skiing all year round. Budget skiers should investigate the up-and-coming ski possibilities of Abtenau, Altenmarkt, Radstadt, Filzmoos, Flachau and Maria Alm.

For the rock climber, early summer—unless a lot of snow piled up in the winter—and late summer and early fall are the most advisable.

Many colorful folklore events take place during the Christmas and Fasching season and in the summer period, but not always on the same day of the year and some of them not even every year. It is advisable to check with the government or the local tourist office.

Route Planning

Land Salzburg is the meeting point of three main **railway** lines, all of them also international train routes. On the main line from Switzerland, Germany, and Innsbruck to Vienna, the fast train stops in this province are Zell am See, Schwarzach-St. Veit, Bischofshofen, and Salzburg; the medium fast trains stop also at Saalfelden, Bruck-Fusch, Taxenbach-Rauris, St. Johann im Pongau, Werfen (occasionally), Golling-Abtenau, and Hallein. A medium fast train takes about 2¼ hours from Salzburg to Saalfelden (several daily trains). At Schwarzach-St. Veit the main line for Carinthia and Italy branches off with fast train stops at Bad Hofgastein and Badgastein. The fast train ride from Salzburg takes about 2 hours and several daily trains are available in both directions. The third main line parts for Styria at Bischofshofen with the fast train stop at Radstadt and sometimes also in Eben in Pongau. A direct fast train covers the Salzburg–Radstadt section in about an hour (several daily services). A local, narrow-gauge railroad connects Zell am See with the Upper Pinzgau as far as Krimml, making the trip in 2 to 2½ hours; six daily trains in both directions.

Tamsweg and the rest of the Lungau district, as well as Lofer on the other side of the province, can only be reached from Salzburg and Radstadt by road; a regular bus service covers these routes.

Steam locomotive fans can enjoy the summer schedules of the narrow-gauge lines running between Mauterndorf and Murau (Styria), and St. Georgen and Voecklamarkt north of Salzburg.

In summer there is a direct bus Salzburg–Grossglockner. The Salz-kammergut lake area is reached from Salzburg by **postal buses** or special excursion buses.

Salzburg **airport** is relatively small, but modern, and is open to inter-national jet traffic, including regular flights (Austrian Airlines) from London. Zell am See airport and a small airfield near Badgastein have been adapted for small aircraft traffic. Air taxis can be taken from Salzburg to these airports and round sightseeing flights can be made from all of them.

For the **motorist,** Land Salzburg offers many dramatic and dazzling roads, especially in the mountains, as well as many fast and modern autobahns. All the routes described below use Salzburg as their starting point.

To reach the Grossglockner and the southern areas of the province, there are two principal routes. The first is the more scenic and meander-ing, whilst the second is much more direct. Both, however, end in the magnificent climb up the Edelweissspitze. The first route leaves Salzburg heading southwest and cuts across the narrow strip of Germany at Bad Reichenhall, re-entering Salzburg at Unken. From here it continues south through the whole of the province, via Saalfelden and Bruck and on to the Grossglockner toll road. This then climbs to the Edelweissspitze and into Carinthia through the Hochtor tunnel, which, at 8,200 feet, marks the highest point of the road and is on the Salzburg-Carinthia border. The second route takes the Tauern autobahn south from Salz-burg and continues past Bischofshofen and runs on to Bruck. From here the two routes merge.

To reach the eastern parts of the province, the most direct route is to drive to Bruck on the Tauern autobahn and then take the 311, from where this all-weather road continues east to Mittersill—where you can either turn north or south to reach the Tyrol and the East Tyrol respec-tively—and Neukirchen am Grossvenediger and finally to the Gerloss pass on the Salzburg-Tyrol border. The final part of this road is particu-larly spectacular, reaching 5,350 feet.

The southeastern part of the province is reached again by the Tauern autobahn to Bischofshofen. Turning right here on 308, the road continues to Radstadt—and into Styria—and from there climbs dramatically up the Radstädter-Tauern pass to Tamsweg in the extreme southeast of Salzburg.

The Salzkammergut lake area, due east and north of the capital, is reached by the 24 km of the A1 autobahn. This then continues into Upper Austria.

Exploring Land Salzburg

The narrow northern corridor which Land Salzburg thrusts upward between Bavaria and Upper Austria is the beginning of the Salzkammergut lake country. North of the city of Salzburg are the lakes of Wallersee, visited chiefly for scenic reasons, though there are a couple of interesting old churches on its shores, and a group of three connected lakes, with the principal town of Mattsee lying between two of them. The Gothic basilica of its 18th-century abbey was remodelled in a baroque manner in 1766, but the notable 15th-century frescos and atmospheric cloisters have been preserved. The abbey museum contains splendid monstrances, and the library some very valuable early printed books.

To the east, the lake nearest to Salzburg, Fuschlsee, is close enough to the city (about 24 km.) to be a weekend resort for Salzburgers, and the place where many festival visitors choose to stay in preference to the city itself. A few kilometers farther southeast is the romantic Wolfgangsee, most of whose shores are within the borders of Land Salzburg, but whose chief attraction, St. Wolfgang of the White Horse Inn fame, is in Upper Austria.

At the western end of Wolfgangsee is St. Gilgen, which again is near enough to Salzburg so that it is possible to commute. This accounts for the fact that it possesses many modern villas belonging to members of the international set who are apt to be found in Salzburg at festival time. There is precious little local color left to St. Gilgen, since the foreign invasion has deprived it of the real thing, leaving it simply a pleasant resort on a beautiful lake, with a nice beach, and the comfortable surroundings of such resorts the world over. Its chief claim to fame is that Mozart's mother was born here.

The chief attraction of Strobl, at the eastern tip of Wolfgangsee, is its delightful setting. If you wish a quiet vacation, this is a place to go. North of Wolfgangsee, a very narrow strip of Land Salzburg reaches the southern bank of Mondsee, whose main localities, however, are all within the borders of Upper Austria.

The great bulk of shoe-shaped Land Salzburg lies to the south and southwest of its capital. This is mountain country, with much higher mountains than those of the lake region, the sort of towering rocky peaks that come to mind with the words "the Alps." The mightiest range stretches across the southern boundary of the state and continues eastward into Styria, where a frontier is drawn on the other side of the range and becomes the northern border of that state. Wherever you draw the line on the map, south of the range for Salzburg, north of the line for Styria, it has to translate the hard fact of the geography of this region—that there is a wall rearing itself from west to east right across the center of Austria.

However, the exploration of this country has been simplified by dynamite: the Pass Lueg and the tunnels of the Tauern Autobahn go straight through the mountains, while along the other three roads, snaking and climbing above them, the magnificent scenery compensates for the steep gradients.

The Tennengau

The territory south of Salzburg is blocked off before the higher mountains are reached by the Tennen range, from which the district gets its name of the Tennengau. If we start down into it on the left bank of the Salzach River, we pass by Schloss Anif, a moated castle, which can also be visited conveniently as an excursion from Salzburg.

The first place of any size to which we come is Hallein, second largest town in Land Salzburg (though it has only slightly over 13,000 inhabitants), which is a spa, with brine baths, now a winter sports center. It is an old town, with a history going back to Celtic and Roman times, and with some medieval structures still standing, like the town wall. The parish church is 15th century, and Franz Gruber, composer of "Silent Night, Holy Night" was buried here.

The most interesting sights of Hallein are not in the town proper, but in the mining settlement of Dürrnberg above it. Here you may visit, from May 1 to Sept. 30, a salt mine—a weird trip to another world, a cleverly-lighted land of subterranean lakes and dark caves into which you descend wearing a heavy white overall that serves as a portable sled for chuting into the depths. At the very end comes a fast ride on a gravity-pulled "train" that will delight the young and alarm their elders. Not an excursion for the timid as, except for stairs from the first descent, you have to continue chuting.

An unusual underground museum not only shows you what salt mining was like in Celtic and Illyrian times, but displays prehistoric finds from the region as well. Above ground, you may be lucky enough to witness that curious pastime, for miners, of the local sword dance, but if that isn't scheduled at the time of your visit, you can always see the town's 16th–17th-century church, to which pilgrimages are made for its 17th-century statue of the Virgin on the 18th-century altar. The church is all of marble, for this is marble country; Hallein possesses a flourishing marble industry today.

The main road south passes a little to the west of the small summer resort of Vigaun to Kuchl, an interesting old market town whose Gothic rock church, on the Georgenberg, occupies the site of the Roman temple of the fifth-century settlement of Cucullae. A curious feature of this church is its outside pulpit.

Golling is a more frequented center, itself a summer resort, and the jumping-off point for winter sports regions in the mountains near it. Mountaineers also start in a variety of directions from this point, while speleologists can explore the great Tantalhöhle network of caves in the Hagengebirge mountains.

Just south of Golling, a branch road leading eastward, that eventually reaches Gosau and the Hallstättersee, goes through the small summer resort of Unterscheffau, and then through Oberscheffau (near which the Lammer River roars spectacularly through a rocky gorge), to Bad Abtenau, with its Gothic church, frequented chiefly in summer but as of lately also a winter sports place.

Werfen

The Tauern Autobahn by-passes Golling and as you plunge into the Pass Lueg Tunnel you leave Tennengau and emerge into the Pongau, whose first point of importance is Werfen. The approach is signaled some distance before you reach it by the Hohenwerfen Castle perched high above the town and consequently visible for miles. It was first built in 1077, but the present building, dating from the 16th century, replaced the original one, destroyed in the Peasants' Rebellion of 1525, and was itself restored in 1935 after a bad fire.

Werfen is visited in the summer by climbers and in the winter by skiers—it has a ski descent of nearly 8,000 feet, one of the longest single-slope drops in the eastern Alps—but its great attraction is ice. It is the starting point from which to visit the Eisriesenwelt (the Ice Giants' World), the largest known complex of ice caves, domes, galleries and halls in Europe. It extends for some 42 kilometers, and contains fantastic frozen waterfalls, natural formations suggesting statues, and other wonders. It's about a 3½-hour climb to the Dr. Friedrich Öld-Haus, where the tours begin, but it is possible to drive to the resthouse a little more than halfway and thence to take the cable car to the cave entrance.

Radstadt

A town since the 13th century, Radstadt still possesses its old walls from that period, with the addition of towers built three centuries later at the corners. It has a fine Gothic parish church, two other interesting churches in the baroque style, law courts in neo-classical style, two castles in Renaissance style and some fine old town walls. If it seems surprising to find so much architectural importance tucked away in a small mountain town the explanation is that Radstadt lies at the entrance to the Radstädter Tauern Pass, an important north–south way through the mountains which has been used since Roman times, lately of lesser significance because of the Tauern Autobahn, tunneling through the mountains.

Radstadt is itself a highly picturesque town and it is surrounded by some of the most impressive scenery in Austria. The Radstädter Tauern Pass is very popular with Austrians as a high-altitude summer resort, a paradise of pure mountain air and of gentians and Alpine roses blooming beside minute lakes, and is even more popular in winter as a skiing resort.

After Untertauern, you are really climbing through magnificent scenery, and over a road whose original bed was laid down by the Romans. At Obertauern you are at the mouth of the pass. At the summit of the pass itself, which is at an altitude of about 5,900 feet, is the Cemetery of the Unknown. It is the resting place of the bodies recovered here in the early days before the development of organized mountaineering.

Once across the pass, you are in the southernmost, and for that matter, the easternmost, part of Land Salzberg, the Lungau. The southward road passes through Tweng to Mauterndorf, a thousand-year-old market town. It has old buildings, old traditions (its Samson Procession), and a splendid castle-fortress watching over it, which is open to the public.

From Mauterndorf you can exercise one of the few choices which permit you, in these mountainous regions, to make a return trip by an alternative road instead of retracing your path. Take the eastern road to Tamsweg, capital of the Lungau and an ancient Roman town of which some remnants still remain. A minor summer and winter resort near the Preber Lake, Tamsweg possesses a museum, the baroque Künberg Castle and a 16th-century town hall, and the early 15th-century pilgrimage church of St. Leonhard is nearby, notable especially for its fine windows and Gothic carved confessional chairs and paintings.

Returning from Tamsweg, you start back by the same road, but just outside of town turn left, to the west, passing through Unternberg, and below the Schloss Moosham, a restored 13th-century castle which can be visited and is now a museum.

St. Michael goes back to the 13th century, but it was wiped out by fire in the 17th, so its buildings go back no farther than that. The settlement prospered from the old mines once worked here (now exhausted), which were also arsenic mines. Among the few surviving relics of the pre-fire days are the 13th- and 14th-century frescos in the Gothic parish church, and the nearby Ägydius Church, outside of the fire area, which dates from 1278.

The Pongau

Back in the Pongau, Bischofshofen (with three fine churches) is important chiefly as a point of departure: as a rail and road junction and as the entrance to skiing country which has long been a traditional training ground of champions. The Hochkönig, which can be reached from this side as well as from Werfen, has a jump where leaps of more than 300 feet have often been made. Here Sepp Bradl, the championship skier born and raised in this country, trained two generations of champions. Mühlbach, at the foot of the Hochkönig, is a favorite ski center, and the whole Mitterbergalpe region beyond it is wonderful skiing country. Austria's most important copper mine is also in this district, at Mitterberghütten.

From Bischofshofen, the main route passes through St. Johann im Pongau, a highly popular place in both summer and winter. In summer, visitors come for fresh air, folklore, and to take the bus excursion to the Lichtensteinklamm, the deepest, narrowest, most spectacular gorge in the eastern Alps, with a tremendous waterfall at one end. In winter, this spot is particularly favored by non-champion skiers, for its location, on the floor of a cup whose sides are formed by mountains all about it, provides an almost endless variety of good runs down into town.

At Schwarzach is the railroad junction where the traveler by train has to make up his mind whether to continue westward along the master trail or to turn southward to what is the goal for many tourists who get this far, Badgastein (on a line that later tunnels through the mountains and continues through Carinthia to Trieste). Schwarzach is not particularly interesting for its own sake, though like every mainline town from now on it can serve as a center to reach skiing and mountaineering resorts. Only 15 minutes away by bus is St. Veit im Pongau, a summer and winter resort, while beyond that is the pleasant mountain village of Goldegg, on a small lake, with a 14th-century castle, often used for historical exhibitions.

The idiosyncracies of fashion have made Badgastein the main center, but smaller Bad Hofgastein is no less attractive and has the advantage of being somewhat cheaper. It may appeal more to those who prefer relaxation among beautiful scenery to lively entertainment. As a spa, its advantages are the same, for the Badgastein waters are piped here, so that precisely the same cures are available. It is a minor resort only because it is so close to Badgastein; alone it would still draw many visitors, and it has plenty of facilities for them. There is a Gothic parish church with three old altars, a 16th-century castle, and a number of old houses with corner turrets dating from the valley's gold mining days.

Badgastein

In the Middle Ages, the riches of Badgastein came from the gold mines, long since worked out. But it has a new and more profitable gold mine in the tourist industry, which Frederick, Duke of Styria, must be credited with founding, in the 15th century. The story is that he was dying of a gangrenous wound, when he was told of a miraculous spring in the Gastein valley. He went to Badgastein, was cured, and royalty, nobility, the wealthy, and plain tourists have been flocking to it ever since.

The attractions of Badgastein are many. First, there are the springs, which have a temperature of nearly 120° Fahrenheit. Duke Frederick had no idea what had cured him, but today we have the answer. The springs are radioactive; even the atmosphere here increases the percentage of ultra-violet rays in the sunshine which is general in this high, yet protected, fog-free region. Even without the springs, Badgastein would be attractive, for the mountain scenery here is exceptionally beautiful. As for the setting of the town itself, it is incomparable. It clings to the evergreen-wooded slopes on either side of a rushing mountain torrent, which pours down a spectacular waterfall in the very heart of the settlement, under its Steinbrücke. A third attraction is its importance as a winter sports center, which, with the newly developing Sport Gastein area above it (reached by cable car or toll road), makes it one of the best equipped in Europe.

The cheapest way of all to benefit by the Badgastein springs is to push on into the valley to the last station on the railroad before it leaves Land Salzburg, Böckstein. Here the hotels have no thermal baths of their own, but guests staying here may use the Badgastein Municipal Spa Establishment. Böckstein also has a very special sort of cure all its own.

The Pinzgau

We now resume our exploration of the main westward route, which we left to enter the Gastein valley. Beyond this point, we are in the largest district of Land Salzburg, the Pinzgau. The next north–south passage into the mountains is the Rauris valley, entered from Taxenbach if you're driving, or from Kitzlochklamm, which is where you get off if you come by train. The principal sight here is the 300-foot Kitzloch waterfall and the gorges cut by the stream of which it is a part. The largest town in the valley is Rauris, an old medieval mining center for gold, precious and semi-precious stones and mountain crystals. Old houses from those days still remain, notably the 16th-century Vogelmeyer house. Today Rauris is a summer and winter resort.

The Sonnblick peak at the end of this valley is the chief point of interest of those who enter it. There is a meteorological observatory on top of it, but its importance for visitors is its splendid ski runs. These are not for novices, however; this terrain is strictly for experts.

Resuming our westward journey, we pass by St. Georgen with a Gothic church to Bruck, a summer resort with a pleasantly situated swimming pool, a famous view from nearby Fischorn Castle and a winter skiing center, but which is better known as the starting point for one of the most spectacular trips in Austria.

The Grossglockner Road

This is the excursion over the longest and most spectacular highway through the Alps, the Grossglockner High Alpine Highway, an engineering achievement of the first magnitude. You can do it by bus or by private car. This is a toll road and it is normally open from about mid-May until mid-November, but unusually heavy late spring or early fall snows may block it. Whatever the season, it is advisable to inquire about conditions ahead before starting out. Fog is often encountered and can be dangerous. It is unwise to attempt to drive through during the night.

There is a mystery about the Grossglockner road. Before it was built, there had been no passage anywhere between Brenner Pass and Radstädter Tauern Pass (more than 160 kilometers apart) leading over these high mountains, nor was it on record that there had ever before been a regularly used route across the barrier at this point. Yet when the engineers who built the High Alpine Highway were blasting for the Hochtor tunnel, through which it passes at one point, they found, deep in the bowels of the mountain, a Roman statuette of, appropriately, Hercules.

From Bruck you plunge into the Fuscher valley leading south, and immediately find yourself confronted by the finest mountain scenery imaginable. You pass first through Dorf Fusch, and then by the Embach Chapel. At Ferleiten, where the toll house stands, the grade becomes steeper. You are really going up now. You pass the Schleier waterfall, and notice that the trees have disappeared. You are above the timberline.

You may pause, or the bus carrying you may do so, at the Piffalpe parking place, to enjoy the view across to the Grosses Wiesbachhorn, and again, perhaps, at the Hochmais parking place. (Parking on the road except at the spots provided is forbidden.)

About now you will notice that the grass has disappeared too. The only vegetation that can exist at this altitude is moss, which you will see here and there, sparsely punctuating the otherwise unrelieved gray of the rocks. At nearly 7,000 feet you pass a gully that presents an awesome aspect of desolation. It is strewn with great boulders among which wisps of fog wreathe eerily and bears an appropriate name—the Witches' Kitchen. In the neighborhood is an old inn which has been here for 500 years, centuries before the Grossglockner road, or any passage at all through these seemingly impenetrable mountains, was ever contemplated.

There are a number of parking places and rest houses on the ascent. At the Edelweisspitze, nearly 8,500 feet up, you can sit on a terrace, sip a beer, and gaze out over an incredible view, which includes 37 peaks higher than 10,000 feet and 19 glaciers. Later, when you go through a pair of tunnels, the Mitteltörl and the Hochtor, you leave the second one to enter Carinthia. (The Grossglockner, like the Dachstein, is a great anchor post from which three Austrian federal states depend—in this case, Land Salzburg, Carinthia and Tyrol, whose borders meet here.)

At Tauerneck, the road sweeps around a curve and suddenly the Grossglockner bursts on your vision for the first time. The impact of the sight of this glittering snow-covered 12,461-foot peak silhouetted against the sky is breathtaking. The road now turns westward, heading straight for the majestic peak, and stops at the dead end of the Franz Josefs Höhe, where you can have lunch and gaze at the distant black dots moving painfully over the face of Europe's oldest, biggest glacier, the Pasterzen (they are really mountain climbers and those fine lines across the ice face on which they are clambering are actually a series of deep and dangerous ice crevasses).

The Upper Pinzgau

Returning to Bruck and exploring some more of Pinzgau, many tourists turn north on the third and last of the road and railroad paths that leave the main route, to Zell am See, the chief resort of the Pinzgau. We shall enter that region later, as we follow that track back to the city of Salzburg, so we look first at the rest of the westward trail, the part of this region known as the Ober Pinzgau.

We will simply name briefly the chief points on the route—Kaprun: A little south of the main highway, in the next of those north–south valleys, the Kaprunertal (railways stop at Fürth, from which you can enter the valley, though most excursionists to this point come from Zell am See). The reason for making this trip is to go through the gorge, past the ruins of an old castle, to the Kessel waterfall, dramatically lighted at night. The Kaprun Dam, built with Marshall Plan money, is an interesting sight. Kaprun is also a summer resort and an increasingly important winter sports center. A three-section aerial cable car takes you up over the glaciers to an elevation of 9,935 feet, almost at the top of Kitzsteinhorn; up here, you can ski all year round.—Stuhlfelden: there is a 17th-century castle here, and from it is reached Heilbad Burgwies with radioactive sulphur and iron baths.—Mittersill: summer and winter resort, on the main line. Mittersill was a great hunters' rendezvous between the wars and has again assumed this role. South of the town a mountain toll road rises up through the Felber and Amer valleys, revealing breathtaking mountain vistas, and penetrates the Hohe Tauern Range through a 5-km. tunnel at an elevation of 5,250 feet, coming out on the other side in East Tyrol.—Hollersbach: mainline resort, entrance to the Hollersbach valley, for climbing.—Neukirchen am Grossvenediger: a much-frequented main-line summer resort, with guides for climbing the nearby Grossvenediger and Wildkogel peaks, and a winter sports center as well.—Wald im Pinzgau: has a late Gothic churchyard, the gravestones are made of rare minerals. This is the point from which you go to Ronach, for Krimml: here is the last spectacle of Land Salzburg's Far West, and if it did not exist at this point, it is doubtful whether the railroad would have been continued to serve all the localities we have passed since Bruck, for Krimml's lodestone is a greater attraction than any of the intervening ones. It is the Krimml waterfall, the highest in Europe, dropping 1,250 feet in three stages. If it's sunny, the falls are at their best at noon; take a raincoat. In summer the waterfall is floodlit every Wednesday night if the weather is good. There is a notable Madonna in the parish church. This is the end of the line, for if you cross the Gerlos Pass, you find yourself in Tyrol; so we will return to Bruck and turn northward.

The Middle Pinzgau

Just north of Bruck, on Zeller Lake, four kilometers long and one and a half kilometers wide, is the most important resort of the Pinzgau, Zell am See. Its main season is July and August. It is almost as frequented, however, in the winter season, chiefly by skiers, who find this an excellent terrain.

Bathing is pleasant in Central Europe's cleanest lake, whose water in summer maintains an average temperature of 73 degrees; a theater, tennis courts, attractive promenades, and good shops cater for the many tourists. The chief architectural features of the town are the Renaissance Rosenberg Castle; the 1250 tower, originally a granary; and the Romanesque parish church, built about 1230.

Among the wealth of local excursions are short daily Alpine and longer Panorama Flights from the local airport, motor boat trips around the lake, or across it to Thumersbach, a popular health resort on the far side of the lake from the road and railroad, so that it is much quieter, and the cable-railway ascent of the Schmittenhöhe plateau. Both are remarkable for the views they afford. From the lake, the outlook to the mountains in which it is set is delightful; from the plateau (where in winter there are ski courses) there is a sweep which will impress upon you the geology of Austria as no written description could ever do; for with your own eyes you see the great hard-rock ranges of the Alps to the south and the quite different lower limestone ranges to the north.

There are a larger number of bus trips to points of great scenic beauty from Zell am See, some of which we have described already from other points, like the Grossglockner, Kapruner valley and Krimml falls excursions.

Proceeding north from Zell am See, through the Mittelpinzgau, at Maishofen the Glemm valley opens to the west. Halfway up the valley is the famous skiing village of Saalbach and, at the valley's head, Hinter-glemm. These two important winter sports centers have combined with Kaprun and Zell to form the Europe-Sport-Region. They offer a large range of sports in all seasons at an equally varied range of prices.

Saalfelden is first and foremost a summer resort, from which moun-taineers like to take off, but all around it is excellent skiing country, so that in winter it is a central point from which practitioners of this sport branch out to the nearby slopes.

Interesting sights in Saalfelden include the parish church, with a late Gothic winged altar; the 14th-century Farmach Castle; and the Christ-mas Crib Museum, located in the Ritzen Castle near the town. Off at the edge of the Steinernes Meer (Sea of Stone) is a late Gothic chapel in a cave, containing a winged altar, near the stone pulpit and the cell of the hermit who lives there.

Steinernes Meer is a climber's Mecca, but it should only be crossed by mountaineers of some experience. This is even truer of the Hochkönig, which can be approached from this side, as well as from the eastern and southern slopes, which we passed at the start of our circuit. Mountain guides are available in Saalfelden. This is also a point from which excur-sions are made to the Königsee in that part of Bavaria that thrusts its arrowhead into Land Salzburg.

St. Martin bei Lofer has a pilgrimage church dating from 1695, and is a point from which you may visit the Lamprechtsofenlochhöhle caves, with their great domes and waterfalls, the Vorderkaserklamm gorge, and the Hirschbichl Pass, a strategic route that was the scene of several battles during the Napoleonic Wars.

Lofer, an old market town, is a summer and winter resort, with peat-water baths. It is a starting point for a number of interesting excur-sions, among them the ascent of the 4,611-foot Loferer Alpe, which can be made on foot in about 2½ hours, and from which there is a remark-able view. A pilgrimage museum, featuring votive tablets from the 17th through the 19th centuries is in Maria Kirchental near Lofer.

From Lofer, the road continues through Reith and the summer resort of Unken, to the Bavarian border, at the western end of the narrow neck of the arrowhead of Bavarian territory which thrusts into Austria. You come out through Bad Reichenhall, on the border just within Bavarian territory, and on the direct road to the city of Salzburg, a few miles away.

PRACTICAL INFORMATION

HOTELS AND RESTAURANTS

ABTENAU 2,345 ft., reached by bus from Golling in Salzach Valley, on main road and railway line from Salzburg. **Bad Abtenau,** spa nearby, is closed in winter.

Hotels Both (2)—*Gasthof Galler,* 24 rooms; *Sporthotel Moisl,* 70 rooms, most with bath, indoor pool, sauna.

All (3)—*Eder,* 19 rooms; *Post,* 36 rooms, full board only; *Roter Ochs,* 45 rooms.

ALTENMARKT 2,765 ft., near Radstadt, railway and bus stop.

Hotels *Stranger* (2), indoor pool, sauna, fitness room; open Dec.–Oct.

All (3)—*Alpenland,* 17 rooms; *Barbarahof,* 13 rooms, pool, sauna, full board only; *Markterwirt,* 45 rooms, most with showers; *Sport Alm,* 25 rooms; *Urbisgut,* 35 rooms.

BADGASTEIN Top spa in Austria, and top winter sports center in Land Salzburg, 3,552 ft.

Hotels About every building is a hostelry, there are more than 100 hotels, pensions and inns of all categories. Most of them close from mid-Oct. to mid-Dec. and around April, though a few are open all year round. The following categorization is based on high-season summer and winter rates. All hotels and most pensions have thermal baths and most hotels have restaurants.

All Deluxe—*Der Kaiserhof,* former palace in a private park, all therapeutic facilities; full board only.

Elisabethpark has apartments with panoramic view from the top floor, cozy tavern and bar, nightclub entertainment and indoor thermal swimming, an art gallery and rustic furniture collection.

Grand Hotel de L'Europe is one of Europe's great hotels offering old-style luxury. Completely refurbished, it reopened Christmas '82. With therapy center, indoor pool with thermal water. All rooms with bath. Magnificent.

Parkhotel Bellevue, with annex *Alpenhof Bellevue* across the road, is the largest, with indoor thermal swimming pool and providing elegant living.

All (1)—*Bellevue-Alm,* another more distant annex (reached by chair lift or car) of *Parkhotel Bellevue,* entirely in rustic style, with only a few rooms, has outdoor grill and heated swimming pool.

Habsburgerhof, on the edge of town, balconied and modern, offers underwater therapy, indoor swimming pool and full-board terms only.

Salzburgerhof, with sauna, pool, near station.

Germania is a bit out of town in green surroundings, apartments with view, indoor pool.

Grüner Baum, out of town in Kötschach Valley, 70 rooms, 63 baths, large restaurant and tavern with bar, has heated thermal indoor and outdoor pools.

Miramonte, 30 rooms, cure facilities.

Straubinger, near waterfall, 70 rooms, has been in same family since 1610, Emperor Franz Josef used to stay.

All (2)—*Mozart,* 60 rooms, 36 baths, with wine tavern and café, near tennis courts; *Pension Haus Gerke, Krone,* near station; and *Alpenblick,* a bit out on road to Kötschach Valley, beautiful view and heated pool.

All (3)—*Moser,* 36 rooms, right next to the waterfall; and *Münchnerhof,* 32 rooms, on the way to Böckstein.

Pensions Some of the best—*Ullrichshaus* (P1), indoor and outdoor pools.

Both (P2)—*Meranhaus,* former vacation house of the Counts of Meran, in Biedermeier style, right in center; and *Jedermann,* at the waterfall.

All (P3)—*Orania, Haus Pfarrmaier* and *Villa Elisabeth* are pretty little chalets.

BAD HOFGASTEIN 2,820 ft., 15 minutes bus ride from Bad Gastein, also a fast train stop.
Hotels All (1)—*Carinthia,* 40 rooms; *Grand Parkhotel,* 52 rooms; *Norica,* 80 rooms; *Palace Gastein,* 200 rooms. All with indoor pools and cure facilities.
All (2)—*Astoria,* 50 rooms; *Kärnten,* 60 rooms; both with pools. *Kurhotel Moser,* 52 rooms; *Kurparkhotel,* 58 rooms; *St. Georg,* 24 rooms; all have a few cheaper rooms without bath.
All (3)—*Alpina, Berglift, Germania* and *Völserhof.*

FILZMOOS 3,467, ft. reached by bus from the railway station of Eben im Pongau 14 km. away.
Hotels All (2)—*Filzmooser Hof,* 27 rooms; *Hanneshof,* 46 rooms; *Priska,* 46 rooms; all with indoor pools.
Both (3)—*Alpenkrone,* 50 rooms, most with bath; *Wurzer,* 35 rooms, most with bath.

FLACHAU Hotels Both (2)—*Alpenhof,* 30 rooms; *Tauernhof,* 66 rooms; indoor pool, sauna.
Both (3)—*Forellenhof,* 25 rooms; *Pension Kofler,* 14 rooms.

FUSCHL AM SEE Hotels All (3)—*Parkhotel Waldhof* (2), 45 rooms, indoor and outdoor pools.
All (3)—*Leitner,* 42 rooms; *Seehotel Schlick,* 50 rooms; *Seewinkl,* 28 rooms; all with a few cheaper rooms without showers; outdoor pools. *Zum Mohren,* 50 rooms, 37 showers, good restaurant.

GOLDEGG Hotels *Zur Post* (2), 47 rooms, pool, sauna, cure facilities.
All (3)—*Laerchenhof,* 27 rooms; *Seehof,* 28 rooms; both with outdoor pool. *Bierführer,* 20 rooms; *Neuwirt,* 40 rooms; a few cheaper rooms without showers.

HALLEIN 1,538 ft., near Salzburg. **Hotels** *Hochbichl* (2), 64 rooms, indoor pool, sauna.
All (3)—*Bruckenwirt,* 25 rooms; *Hafnerwirt,* 18 rooms; *Kranzbichlhof,* 23 rooms; a few cheaper rooms without showers.

HINTERTHAL 2,600 to 3,300 ft., bus from Saalfelden.
Hotels Both (2)—*Club Appartments,* Alpine hunting style, 18 apartments with kitchen, private ski lift; *Wachtelhof,* 22 rooms, cellar bar.
In nearby **Hintermoos**—many accommodations (3).

HOF Hotel *Schloss Fuschl* (L), 70 rooms, 56 baths, indoor and outdoor pools, on Lake Fuschl. Former hunting castle of the prince-bishops of Salzburg; period-furnished rooms and suites; some less expensive rooms in 400-year-old adjacent hunting lodge, with hunting museum. Swimming, boating, and tennis facilities and a lakeside 9-hole golf course. Renowned elegant restaurant.
Both (2)—*Baderluck,* 40 rooms, 12 baths; *Gasthof Nussbaumer,* 57 rooms.

KAPRUN 2,578 ft., near Zell am See.

Hotels All (2)—*Sporthotel Kaprun,* 67 rooms, sauna; *Zur Burgruine,* 30 rooms, 23 showers, indoor pool; *Zur Mühle,* 70 rooms, 50 showers, indoor pool.

All (3)—*Austria,* 12 rooms; *Gletscherblick,* 14 rooms; *Orgler,* 25 rooms.

Above the village in the mountains are a number of mountain hotels and lodges, all (2), among them—*Kesselfall Alpenhaus,* about 3,500 ft. up; *Berghaus Mooserboden,* between the 2 artificial lakes of the Kaprun power works in a very scenic spot, more than 6,500 ft. up; *Krefelder Hütte* (7,540 ft.) and *Berghaus Gletcherbahn* (8,085 ft.), both in magnificent high Alpine landscapes.

KRIMML 3,516 ft., local railway and bus from Zell am See.

Hotels All (2)—*Haus Hanke,* 13 rooms, indoor pool; *Klockerhaus,* 50 rooms, 28 showers; *Post,* 42 rooms, good food.

All (3)—*Schönmoosalm,* at 4,690 ft. above Krimml, mountain inn, 7 rooms; *Krimmler Tauernhaus,* mountain inn 5,350 ft. up; *Krimmlerfälle,* 80 rooms.

LOFER 2,063 ft., and Loferer Alm, 5,041 ft., bus from Saalfelden (26 km.) and Salzburg (51 km. via Bad Reichenhall in Germany).

Hotels *Schloss Grubhof* (1), a bit outside town in a quiet scenic position, a castle-hotel with indoor swimming pool, all rooms with bath.

All (2)—*Bräu,* 28 rooms, with period rustic interiors; *Post,* 35 rooms, most with bath; *St. Hubertus,* 22 rooms.

MARIA ALM 2,700 ft., bus from Saalfelden. 13th-century church with Salzburg's highest steeple (261 ft.). Very good skiing region. **Hotel** *Norica* (2), 40 rooms, indoor pool.

MAUTERNDORF 3,500 ft., bus from Radstadt and from Unzmarkt in Styria.

Hotels *Elisabeth* (1), 40 rooms, indoor pool.

All (3)—*Post,* atmospheric, with pleasant courtyard garden; *Steffner-Wallner;* and *Neuwirt.*

NEUKIRCHEN AM GROSSVENEDIGER 2,800 ft., local railway and bus from Zell am See.

Hotels Both (2)—*Gasthof Kammerlander,* 45 rooms; *Jagdhotel Graf Recke,* 30 rooms, 18 baths.

All (3)—*Abelhof,* 18 rooms; *Gassner,* 70 rooms, 40 showers, indoor pool; and *Alpengasthaus Rechtegg,* 40 rooms, 23 showers, higher up, ski lift.

OBERALM Hotel *Schloss Haunsperg* (2), castle-hotel near Hallein and Salzburg, 8 antique-furnished rooms, tennis, large car park. *Schlosspension Kahleperg* (3), 130 rooms, full board only.

OBERTRUM At Obertrumsee, near Salzburg.

Hotels Both (3)—*Gasthof Neumayr,* 30 rooms, some with bath, known for local fish dishes, particularly trout, served in paneled Stuben with rustic decor; *Braugasthof Sigl,* 30 rooms, 19 showers, with own brewery.

RADSTADT 2,800 ft. **Hotels** *Sporthotel Stegerbräu* (2), 32 rooms, 13 showers, pools, excellent food; *Gasthof Stegerbräu* (3), 34 rooms; *Post* (3), 26 rooms.

Many inns (3) and a Youth Hostel.

A bit outside and higher up, both (3)—*Alpengasthof Seitenalm* and *Alpengasthaus Pertill,* both mountain inns at about 3,800 ft.

RADSTÄDTER TAUERN PASS Also called **Obertauern.** Highest point about 5,900 ft., one of the most important skiing centers in land Salzburg. Bus service from Radstadt and Mauterndorf, both about 22 km. away.

Hotels In all hotels, winter rates are much higher than summer ones, a number of hotels are open only for the winter season, and offer only full-board terms. Advance reservations are a must in winter.

All (1)—*Edelweiss,* 150 beds, 50 baths, leads, mostly balconied rooms, heated indoor swimming pool, restaurant with splendid view, bar and dancing; *Sporthotel Bauer, Kohlmayr, Passhotel Schütz,* and *Römerhof,* are all slightly smaller; *Kärntnerland, Perner,* and *Taurach* are a little less expensive.

All (2)—*Berghotel Pohl; Wisenegg;* and *Tauernpasshöhe.*

All (3)—many pensions.

SAALBACH 3,290 ft., the famed skiing village of Land Salzburg, bus service from Zell am See.

Hotels Rates during the skiing season, Dec. to April, are much higher than in other months. Some hotels offer full-board terms only—inquire in advance.

All (1)—*Bergers Sporthotel; Kristall; Saalbacher Hof;* and *Tambacherhof,* under same management. All have pools.

All (2)—*Panther; Bauer; Alpenhotel.*

In **Hinterglemm,** the twin village—*Kristiana* (2), recent and large, all rooms and apartments with bath or shower, indoor pool, sauna.

SAALFELDEN 2,440 ft., fast train stop on Salzburg–Innsbruck line.

Hotels *Waldhotel Bellevue* (1), 100 beds, all rooms with bath or shower, isolated green surroundings at the main road Saalfelden–Zell am See, indoor swimming pool, dance bar.

Among several modest hostelries in town—particularly, *Oberbräu* (2), a Gasthof since 1629, wooden rustic interiors in several restaurant rooms, own brewery and farm, and Gasthof *Schatzbichel,* with excellent local food.

Close to Saalfelden on main road to Lofer: *Hotel Brandlhof* (1), 75 rooms with shower. Indoor pool, indoor and outdoor tennis courts, riding hall, horses; 18-hole golf course under construction. Good restaurant. (*Note:* manager not too keen on very young children.)

Campsite.

ST. GILGEN AM WOLFGANGSEE Reached from Salzburg by bus or car, about 48 km., and the road's kept in good condition in winter.

Hotels Both (1)—*Excelsior,* on the lake, completely modernized, about 50 rooms, all with bath, radio, wall safe, private bar and other amenities, lakeside terrace restaurant, cellar tavern with music, tennis facilities, private beach for water sports, free transfers to Salzburg airport and railway station.

Billroth, about 2 km. outside town, 85 beds, terrace restaurant overlooking lake, tennis court, own park and beach.

Both (2)—*Radetzky-Hof,* 45 beds, on main square, good restaurant; and *Zur Post,* indoor pool.

Kendler (3), large, old-fashioned inn on main square, own butchery.

Campsite.

Restaurant *See-Restaurant Fischer,* spacious, good restaurant in beautiful location right on the lake shore.

ST. JOHANN IM PONGAU About 2,000 ft., fast train stop.
Hotels *Prem* (2), *Goldener Stern* (3).

At the upper end of the chair lift, the mountain hotel *Hahnbaum* (2) at about 4,000 ft., all rooms with bath or shower.

Both (3)—*Plankenwirt;* and the attractive chalet-pension *Monika.*

Campsite.

SIGHARTSTEIN Hotel *Schloss Sighartstein* (L), castle-pension, open April 15 to Oct. 15, with old castle atmosphere, presided over by the owner, Countess Palffy. Advance written reservations necessary. Located near Wallersee, about 16 km. northeast of Salzburg.

THUMERSBACH Across the Zellersee from Zell am See, reached by boat or road.

Hotels *Lohninghof* (2), 100 beds; and both (3)—*Parkcafé* and *Zieglerwirt,* both small.

Campsite.

WAGRAIN 2,749 ft., bus service from St. Johann im Pongau (13 km.) and Radstadt (48 km.).

Hotels *Alpina* (2), small, all rooms with bath, with sauna, full-board terms only.

All (3)—*Alpenhof Edelweiss,* indoor pool; *Enzian* and *Grafenwirt,* both with good restaurants; *Tatzelwurm,* with terrace café, sauna.

At **Kleinarl,** farther up the valley, there are additional hostelries (3), with *Tauernhof,* sauna, ski lift, bar, among them.

WALD Base for the Eisenerzer Alpen and the Seckauer Alpen.
Hotel *Jagdschloss Graf Recke* (2), in the hunting castle owned by Count Recke, with heated pool, hunting and kayaking facilities, open May 10 to Sept. 30, for a few weeks in Jan. and from mid-Feb. to Easter.

ZELL AM SEE With the Schmittenhöhe mountain, one of the top winter sports centers in Land Salzburg.

Hotels All (1)—*Grand-Hotel,* beautifully situated on Zellersee, magnificent summer view of the lake and the mountain from terrace, garden restaurant and café, romantic outdoor dancing in the evening, own swimming and fishing facilities; elegant winter dining hall and large windowed *Seebar;* folklore shows in the *Seekeller* tavern summer and winter.

St. Georg, a bit above the lake, rustic-style decor, all rooms with bath and radio, pool, sun terrace, bar.

Salzburgerhof, indoor pool and sauna; good food.

At 6,600 ft., reached by cable car—*Berghotel Schmittenhöhe* (1), 150 beds, 20 baths and showers, excellent skiing in winter, intensive nightlife, splendid view of the Austrian Alps. *Zum Hirschen* (1), all rooms with bath. Genuinely antique appointments, best food in the region and elegant dining rooms.

Both (2)—*Latini,* 220 beds, indoor pool and sauna; *Grand,* on the lake, with attractive garden restaurant and café.

All (3)—*Auerwirt,* simple but picturesque, in the middle of town, with an inviting tavern restaurant; *Fischerwirt,* 70 beds, pleasant, quiet and not far from lake; *Lebzelter,* next to the old tower, 115 beds, lively local color in *Felsen Keller; Neue Post,* on Schlossplatz, 100 beds, bar.

Particularly nice Youth Hostel located on the lake. Campsite.

SPECIAL EVENTS

BADGASTEIN In winter, there are Christmas and end-of-the-year celebrations; balls, parties and fireworks begin the New Year; mid-Jan. there's the *Perchtenlauf* masked processions, originating in pagan times; *Fasching* balls and amusements, and winter sports. During the summer season a series of almost daily performances (concerts, comedy, folk shows) begins in mid-May lasting through mid-Sept.—spa orchestra and local folk brass bands; and in addition there are nightclub variety shows, folk dance and music evenings in the taverns, and balls and elegant soirées in the best hotels.

BAD HOFGASTEIN Much *après ski; Perchtenlauf* masked processions every few years, mid-Jan.

HALLEIN Brass band concerts and folklore events throughout the year; special Christmas celebrations in honor of the song *Silent Night,* whose composer Franz Gruber is buried here.

KRIMML *Fasching* period, in Feb., masked groups dancing and parading.

LOFER Feb., *Fasching* period, masked groups dancing in parades.

MAUTERNDORF Music weeks throughout the summer, with special courses for children, choir and choir directors, stringed and woodwind instruments, chamber and Renaissance music.

SAALBACH *He-and-She races,* downhill *torch run* on the last of the year, mask runs on *Fasching Sunday.* Much *après ski.*

WAGRAIN Advent singing before Christmas, commemorating the carol *Silent Night,* whose author, Father Mohr, is buried here.

ZELL AM SEE Balls, parties and fireworks begin New Year; *Fäsching* is celebrated in Feb., with masked groups in dancing parades. Much *après ski.*

SPAS

BADGASTEIN By far the most fashionable as well as the largest spa in Austria, Badgastein has 18 radioactive thermal springs with 81 outlets and the natural radium inhalatorium in the thermal tunnels at Böckstein. Many types of cures are offered, but during the peak seasons social life is just as important as cures—if not more so.

BAD HOFGASTEIN Offers cures similar to Badgastein's, generally in lower-priced, quieter and less sparkling counterpart.

CASINO

BADGASTEIN Roulette and baccara daily from 5 P.M. Open Dec. 25 to end March and 1st Sat. in June to mid-Sept.

SPORTS

ABTENAU Chair lift, 9 ski lifts, ski school.

ALTENMARKT Together with nearby Flachau (3,040 ft.), 3 chair lifts, 9 ski lifts, ski school.

BADGASTEIN 6 indoor swimming pools, 3 with thermal water, 9-hole golf course.
Stubnerkogel cable car and toll road to new Sport Gastein area take you to a height over 7,300 ft., with year-long skiing in Austria's highest ski center.
In the area—3 cable cars, 6 chair lifts, 13 ski lifts, schools, ski jump, skating rink. Slopes for all, the longest is the Angertal descent, of moderate difficulty, 10 km. long dropping over 4,600 feet to the vicinity of Bad Hofgastein. Ski school with gold, silver, and bronze awards for certain runs. Big ski jump, ice skating rink, ice hockey, bobsleigh school. *Après ski.*

BAD HOFGASTEIN 2-section cable car to Kleine Scharte (6,725 ft.), 3 chair lifts, 7 ski lifts, ski school with gold, silver, and bronze awards for different runs (usually slalom), slopes for beginners, runs of all degrees of difficulty, ski tours in the Schlossalm and Gadauner Hochalm areas, ski jump, skijoring, 2 skating rinks, ice hockey, bobsleigh school.

FILZMOOS Base for mountain tours of the Dachstein group. Chair lift, 14 ski lifts (one for children), skating, ski schools.

FUSCHL AM SEE Sailboats for hire; fishing, ice skating, curling, 2 ski lifts, ski school.

HALLEIN Cable car, 1 chair lift, 1 ski lift, ski school, ski jump, skating rink, bobsleigh school.

KAPRUN Mountain guides are available, and there's a mountain climbing school in the Grossglockner Group above Kaprun offering one-week courses for beginners and for advanced climbers—for information and registration write to Hochgebirgsschule Glocknergruppe, Post Kaprun, Land Salzburg.

The 3-section cable car and underground cable railway, the first in the world, to Kitzsteinhorn (9,935 ft.) provide year-round skiing for all degrees of skill and with 2 glacier ski lifts. Also 2 cable cars (one aerial and one on ground) to Maiskogel (5,092 ft.) with excellent skiing grounds, chair lift, 9 ski lifts, ski school, mountain ski guides, bobsleigh school, ice skating rink. *Après ski.*

KRIMML Easy skiing slopes around the village, more difficult up on Gerlosplatte and Plattenkogel. *White Chamois Award* for the run from Plattenkogel to Gerlosplatte if made in 5 minutes by men and 6 minutes by women. 2 ski lifts near the village, chair lift and 9 ski lifts in Gerlosplatte and Plattenkogel areas. 2 ski schools, mountain ski guides.

LOFER Ice skating, schools, chair lift, 10 ski lifts in Lofer and on the Alm.

MARIA ALM With Hintermoos and Hintertal, 3 ski schools, 2 chair lifts, 12 ski lifts, *après ski,* bobsleighing, curling, cross country skiing.

MAUTERNDORF With nearby Fannenberg, 2 chair lifts and 5 ski lifts, one of the longest in Austria.

MITTERBERGALPE Between 4,200 and 4,900 ft., above Mühlbach am Hochkönig, with bus service (13 km.) from Bischofshofen railway station.

Together with Mühlbach—1 chair lift, 12 ski lifts, 2 ski schools, 3 ski jumps (one giant), ski guides.

NEUKIRCHEN AM GROSSVENEDIGER Cable car, chair lift to Bergerkopf (6,888 ft.), 11 ski lifts, ski school, guides, skating rink.

OBERTRUM Here, and at Seeham also on Obertrumsee, sailboats for hire.

RADSTADT 11 ski lifts, ski school, 2 ski jumps, skijoring, skating rink, mountain ski guides. *Königslehen Award* for downhill run from Königslehen, which can be super, gold, silver, or bronze, according to the performance.

RADSTÄDTER TAUERN PASS Cable car, 3 chair lifts, 19 ski lifts, 3 ski schools, ski jump, skiing possible from Nov. to May for all degrees of skill, very good terrains for beginners, 47 downhill various runs. Tours to about 20 mountain peaks, guides available. Considerable *après ski.*

SAALBACH Cable car to Schattberg (6,625 ft.) and chair lift to Zwölferkogl (6,560 ft.) in Hinterglemm.

In addition—9 chair lifts, 30 ski lifts, 2 ski schools with 150 instructors, skating rink, indoor heated swimming pool, 78 ski runs of every grade, good slopes for beginners, grass runs in summer. Gold, silver and bronze badge for selected 3-km.

run. Downhills always end at ski lifts thus forming the *Saalbach Ski Circus.* Base for mountain climbing tours.

SAALFELDEN Chair lift, 5 ski lifts, ski school, ski jump, skating rink, cross-country skiing, *après ski.*

ST. GILGEN AM WOLFGANGSEE Waterskiing and sailing schools, sailboats for hire, national and international sailing competitions on Wolfgangsee.

Zwölferhorn mountain above St. Gilgen, almost 5,000 ft. high, has become a well-known skiing center during the past years; skiing is possible from Dec. to April. Cable car from St. Gilgen to Zwölferhorn, a chair lift and a ski lift on Zwölferhorn, another ski lift at St. Gilgen. Ski school. *Après ski.*

ST. JOHANN IM PONGAU Chair lift, 6 ski lifts, ski school, skijoring, skating rink. *Hahnbaum Award* gold, silver, and bronze, for specified minimum time for Hahnbaum downhill run.

WAGRAIN 3 chair lifts, 10 ski lifts, 2 ski schools, *après ski. Tatzelwurm Ski Award* for specified minimum time on specially-designed run.

Kleinarl has 3 more ski lifts and a ski school.

WEISS SEE 7,425 ft., reached by cable car from Enzingerboden in Stubach valley, which is reached by bus either directly from Zell am See, 38 km., or Uttendorf, 17 km., on local railway Zell am See–Krimml.

Excellent skiing for experienced, serious skiers. Downhill run from Sonnblick mountain to Enzingerboden, almost 11 km. long, with drop of 5,280 ft., is one of longest and nicest in entire Alps. Skiing usually possible from Nov. to July, in some locations all year round. 2 cable cars, 6 ski lifts, mountain ski guides. Ski school open all year. Because of its quality, this terrain is often used for training by the Austrian national skiing team.

ZELL AM SEE Water-skiing and sailing schools, sailboats for hire on the lake.

A specialty of Zell am See is its *gliding* school, actually located near the southern end of the lake. The flying time is March to Dec., and instruction is given to beginners and to advanced flyers wishing to get training in Alpine gliding, the school's specialty-Passenger flights are also offered.

Cable cars to Schmittenhöhe (6,450 ft.) and to Sonnenalm (4,530 ft.); chair lift from Sonnenalm to Sonnkogel (6,000 ft.); 2 cable cars, 5 chair lifts, 12 ski lifts, ski schools, a combined German language–ski instruction school, mountain ski guides, ski jump, skijoring on the frozen Zellersee, ice skating rink and instruction, ice hockey, bob-sleigh school. Gold, silver, or bronze *Ski Club Award* for north side Schmittenhöhe downhill run.

UPPER AUSTRIA

From Salzkammergut to the Bohemian Forest

The Federal State of Upper Austria (Bundesland Oberösterreich) lies in the north-central section of Austria. To the east, it borders on Lower Austria, its historic twin; to the south, there are two other Austrian federal states, Styria and Land Salzburg. Its western border with Bavaria is defined mostly by the river line Salzach–Inn–Danube and it is at the same time the frontier between Austria and Germany; to the north is Czechoslovakia.

The Danube flows through Upper Austria from the Bavarian city of Passau in the west, almost as far east as the Nibelungengau in Lower Austria, passing by Linz, the capital. Beyond the confluence of the Enns River with the Danube, however, the right bank of the Danube is already in Lower Austria while the left bank still remains in Upper Austria. Mühlviertel is the hilly and forested country north of the Danube and it stretches as far as the Bohemian Forest (Böhmerwald), the range of wooded mountains at the triple border between Austria, Germany and Czechoslovakia. The rich, undulating agricultural land to the southwest of the Danube is called Innviertel because it slopes mostly towards the Inn Valley. But most of the scenic beauty in Upper Austria is displayed in its southern part—the Salzkammergut lake region and the adjoining, mountainous, Pyhrn District.

Vacationists flock to Salzkammergut because its lakes, streams, valleys, meadows and woods provide a perfect summer playground and the mountains attract skiiers in the winter. Not only is this an area of largely unspoiled landscapes, but it is also the realm of salt, of saltmines whose presence has shaped the country in many ways. Today, when this commodity is one of the commonest and cheapest that we buy, we are inclined to forget its importance in not-very-distant history. It was ordinarily a government monopoly, and the tax on salt was considered everywhere one of the most irksome of all, for it was applied to a basic necessity, almost as if air were taxed.

In Austria, too, salt was a government monopoly, and the Salzkammergut (Estate of the Salt Chamber) region was banned to visitors in order to prevent untaxed salt from being smuggled out. The peasants stayed locked in the valleys, citizens from other regions were, for the most part, locked out. This situation lasted until the early 19th century. The region was finally opened up because Emperor Franz Josef, in his youth, had discovered its attractions. He established his summer residence at Bad Ischl. The aristocracy flocked into the Salzkammergut and its salt-inspired isolation was ended.

Weather and Allied Matters

The visitor can find pleasure for the eye and the satisfaction of a well-spent vacation throughout most of the year. The Danube valley, however, should be avoided during a few weeks in the late fall and early spring when the fog usually descends upon it. The lake country is quite rainy during the warm season; by far the best months here are July through mid-October.

The Salzkammergut region is well equipped with hotels, with the emphasis on the moderate category. There are also a few luxurious converted castles and first-class lakefront establishments, as well as many low priced pensions, and Gasthof-type accommodations. The city of Linz is reasonably well provided with hotels. Most lake hotels are open in summer only, usually May 1–Sept. 30 (sometimes up to a month earlier or later) with high-season prices during July and August. Many hotels and pensions offer reduced full-board rates if taken on a weekly or monthly basis.

The main skiing areas of Upper Austria are the mountain groups of Dachstein and Totes Gebirge, the first partially and the latter mostly within Styria, and in the lower Höllengebirge, between Traun and Atter lakes. The skiing season in the high mountains lasts from December to May, in the Dachstein sometimes extending into June. In lower areas January to March are the most reliable months. Experienced skiers can undertake exceptionally rewarding scenic tours across the high mountain plateaus dotted with lodges, while the less experienced will find enough challenge in lower localities, among them several spas which in winter become also centers of the white sport. Mühlviertel is also being developed as a skiing area. The technical facilities in Upper Austria have increased greatly within the past years, matched by improved accommodations for guests.

This is economy country for skiers, with similar, albeit not so spectacular, facilities and terrain as in wider known resorts.

Route Planning

Three main **railway** lines cross this region. Covering the Salzburg–Linz section of the main Austrian railroad line from Vienna to the west, a very fast train takes less than two hours and a slow train over three hours. Small local trains branch off at Steindorf for Braunau, at Vöcklamarkt for the town of Attersee, at Vöcklabruck for Kammer, at Lambach for Gmunden and Haag, and at Wels for Grünau; local trains of greater importance take off at Attnang-Puchheim for Braunau and Schärding to the northwest and for Gmunden, Ebensee, Bad Ischl, Hallstatt towards the southeast. The second main line goes from Linz to Passau (Germany) via Bad Schallerbach and Schärding; about 1½ hours by fast direct train. The third main line runs from Linz to Graz, passing through Rohr (local train to Bad Hall, about 5 km. away), Kremsmünster, Klaus, Hinterstoder (station only, bus to the village), Windischgarsten, Spital am Pyhrn (about two hours by fast train). Freistadt and Aigen can be reached by the local trains from Linz. Enns is on the main line from Linz to Vienna; to get to Steyr by train, take the local train at St. Valentin a little beyond Enns.

The local **bus services** cover the region well and bus tours of the main places of interest originate in Salzburg, Linz, Bad Ischl, Gmunden and elsewhere. Inquire at the local tourist offices or travel agents.

Between Linz and Passau fast **steamer services** operate from early May to mid-September and from Linz the boats continue to Lower Austria and Vienna. In addition to the Danube shipping line, there are frequent lake ship services in summer on Traunsee, Attersee, Wolfgangsee, and Mondsee. The Hallstatt boat takes passengers to and from all the trains stopping at the Hallstatt railroad station, located across the lake from the town. Motorboat trips are also possible on all of these lakes.

Salzburg is the nearest large city to the lake region and most of the Salzkammergut area can be visited by making day trips out of Salzburg. **By road** it is about 43 km. to St. Wolfgang, 49 to Bad Ischl, 75 to Hallstatt. Via the autobahn it is about 25 km. to Mondsee, 53 to Attersee, 74 to Gmunden on Traunsee, 130 to Linz.

From Linz to the Totes Gebige area on A1 southwest to Sattledt, then turning south on to 138, using local roads where necessary, the distance is about 90km. to Almsee, 98 to Hinterstoder, 97 to Windischgarsten and 103 to Spital and Pyhrn. Route 138 continues 27 km. over the Pyhrnpass to Liezen in Styria.

It is 80 km. from Linz to Schärding (No. 128), 61 to Aigen (129, ES), 42 to Freistadt (125, E14), 20 to Enns (A1), and 40 to Steyr (A1 and 115).

Exploring Upper Austria

The Salzkammergut, which is the most frequented region of Upper Austria, lies northeast of Salzburg, and much closer to that city than to Linz. We shall therefore begin our round trip through Upper Austria by heading out from Salzburg on the autobahn, or by local bus, through pleasant rolling country to Mondsee, the largest town on the third largest of the Salzkammergut lakes. We are now in Upper Austria and enter the heart of the lake country, with the Zellersee, a small little-visited lake just to the north; the Wolfgangsee which we shall inspect on the return trip, to the south; the Attersee to the east; and the Mondsee—for the lake and the town bear the same name—confronting us.

Mondsee means Moon Lake. The name was given it by the Romans, who were impressed by the beauty of this eight-kilometer long, one and a half-kilometer wide, body of water, reflecting in its placid depths the double-toothed mountain rising above it. The water is warmer than in any other of these high-lying lakes, making it a good place for swimming.

The town of Mondsee takes pride in pointing out that its parish church, built in 1470, is the largest in Upper Austria. The claim is a trifle spurious, since it was not originally constructed as a parish church, but for the more pretentious role of the abbey church of the Benedictine monastery established here in the eighth century and closed, like so many others, by the reforming zeal of Emperor Josef II. Another part of the abbey became the Schloss Mondsee, a castle that has come down in the world. Once owned by the German royal family, it became an American summer school, an epoch in its history that was ended by the war. It contains some exceptionally fine examples of baroque art.

The Wolfgangsee, or Abersee, just south of the Mondsee, is visited most frequently from Salzburg; for the sake of following a consecutive route, we shall keep to the Linz road through the northern lakes and inspect this one as we swing back through the southern part of this region. If you approach this lake from Salzburg, therefore, simply follow in reverse the directions given at the end of this section.

With the next place of importance on the Linz road, Unterach, we come to the largest of the lakes, the Attersee, precisely twice the size of the Mondsee (sixteen kilometers by three). A boat trip is particularly interesting, for traffic on the Attersee is lovely—not only pleasure craft, but the working boats of the fishermen, the gravel boats carrying the product of the pits in the mountains, and the rafts peculiar to the lake, which may be loaded with almost anything.

Most settlements on Attersee are now summer residential areas; the railroad terminal is at Schörfling-Kammer at the north head of the lake, where trains connect with the boats making the lake circuit. The town of Attersee on the west shore is the seat of a sailing club, but the main attraction is the lake, favored especially by fishermen—the water is very clear and very cold, teeming with, besides *saibling* (char), lake trout and pickerel, and the neighboring streams with brook trout.

The Traunsee

The Höllengebirge is back at the southern end of the lake, where we started, but we had better return to that region in order to reach the Traunsee. If you actually follow this route on the ground, you can start at Weissenbach and take the good secondary road to Mitterweissenbach on the Traun River, the most important water course in the Salzkammergut. Turn left, follow along the stream, and you presently reach the Traunsee at Ebensee, where you can begin to ascend the Höllen range from its eastern end, as a cable railway starts here for the Feuerkogel, from which there is a magnificent view over the Totes Gebirge—the Dead Range (i.e. no vegetation)—to the glittering snow-clad peak of the nearly 10,000-foot-high Dachstein, at the point where the borders of Land Salzburg, Upper Austria, and Styria meet. Feuerkogel is mainly a winter sports center; although not so well known as many other skiing centers in Austria, it is well rated by the experts.

Traunsee is the second largest of the Salzkammergut lakes—about eleven kilometers long and one and a half kilometers wide—and it also has a steamer service during the summer. Moving up the lake, south to north, the following places are of interest: Traunkirchen (west shore): the famous Fishermen's Pulpit in the parish church, a pleasant walk to the old church on the top of a former small island off the shore, now joined by land. The view at sunset from the Kalvarienberg is worth the climb. Altmünster (west shore): This is the oldest settlement on the Traunsee, whose parish church dates from the 16th century. It seems to have had a particular attraction for musicians; many have lived here at one time or another, the most notable having been Brahms and Wagner—the latter composed *Tristan und Isolde* in Otto Wesendonk's villa here until his interest in Otto Wesendonk's wife deprived him of those lodgings.

Gmunden (north shore, foot of the lake) is the biggest place in the region, one much visited, and deserving of special attention. Gmunden is both an old town (important in Roman times because of the salt trade, and still the terminal port for the barges bringing salt from the mines of the Aussee, Bad Ischl, Hallstatt, and Ebensee down the Traun River and across the Traunsee) and a modern watering place. From its older days, it retains a few Gothic dwellings, a Gothic church, and several castles spread over the vicinity, of which the most famous is a double castle—a Landschloss on the shore, a Seeschloss connected to the other by a causeway on an island in the lake. The latter is the very picturesque Schloss Orth.

As a resort center, its attractions are its location—the tree-shaded promenade along the lake shore is delightful—two theaters (one open-air), a Kurhaus, regular concerts, water sports, fishing and often, in the summer, sports festivals. It is a center from which a number of delightful excursions can be made—to a fine waterfall, the Traunfall; to the 5,546-foot-high Traunstein; to the 3,300-foot Grünberg; and to a number of other points. Finally, Gmunden will provide you with an excellent souvenir of your visit; it is famous for its ceramics and it is unlikely that you will want to depart without taking a few samples with you.

Wels

North of Gmunden, the Traun River plunges through tremendous gorges, rushing turbulently to its approaching junction with the Danube. Following the valley toward Linz, you first come to Lambach, whose originally Romanesque monastery, later converted into baroque style, has some of the earliest (1080) and best-preserved Romanesque frescos in Austria, and then to Wels, which is a convenient center for trips into the Danubian hinterland to the northwest, or southward to the Almtal and the mountains beyond. Although Wels is thus used chiefly as a point from which to visit other attractions, it is not without its own. The baroque town hall, the parish church—originally Gothic, later renovated in baroque style, and also boasting a Romanesque doorway—the Renaissance Pollheimer Schloss, the Lederer Tower and Gate, and several buildings with Renaissance and baroque façades are its chief sights.

You can also see the house in which legend has it that the shoemaker-poet Hans Sachs, the original of the character in Wagner's *Die Meistersinger von Nürnberg,* lived in 1513. On Mount Wels, overshadowing the city, stands the stronghold erected for Emperor Maximilian I in 1519, and in the town itself you can inspect the City Museum's prehistoric and Roman collections.

Linz

From Wels, we come to Linz on the Danube, the capital of Upper Austria, with 208,000 inhabitants. It was only during the last few decades, after large steel works and chemical plants were erected here during the period of German rule in Austria, that the population number surpassed that of Innsbruck and Salzburg, Linz becoming the third largest city in Austria (after Vienna and Graz). Linz is also a center of river navigation (its river port has more cargo volume than any other port on the section of the Danube belonging to the West), an important junction on international railroad lines, and a key crossing point of a number of highways and main roads. In addition to being a busy industrial and trading city, it also harbors much of the charming old world in the town streets around the main square, in the shadows of the cathedral and under the castle hill. A large bridge across the Danube connects it with its left-bank suburb of Urfahr, which at one time was a market town in its own right.

Exploring Linz

The name of Linz comes from Lentia, a Roman settlement which existed here in the fifth century, and possibly earlier, since the word Lentia appears to be only a latinized form of an earlier Alpine Celtic name. However, a salt trading post existed here already in prehistoric times. As early as the sixth century, there was a Bavarian settlement; in the ninth century, Linz became a market town and later on acquired full town rights. Emperor Friedrich III resided in Linz from 1489 to 1493.

Extensive redevelopment, restoration and the creation of traffic-free zones have transformed Linz.

The center of the old town is the large, quadrangular main square with the ubiquitous baroque Trinity column in the middle; the square is lined by once patrician houses, among them the 17th-century Town Hall. Towering above one of the square corners are the two spires of the baroque Old Cathedral (nowadays called also St. Ignatius Church or Jesuit Church), with splendid interiors, including a particularly beautiful Renaissance carved choir and the Krisman-made organ. Nearby is the city parish church, originally built in the 13th century and rebuilt in 1648 in baroque style. The Victorian Cathedral is magnificent and worth a visit. Hofgasse, one of the narrow romantic streets which converge on the square from all directions, takes you to the castle, where Emperor Friedrich III lived.

Some of the gates, ramparts and walls of the original medieval schloss still exist, but the massive main building was reconstructed in 1599–1607 and later on served as military quarters for the imperial troops. Today the castle houses the most important collections of the Upper Austrian State Museum (Oberösterreichisches Landesmuseum), including prehistoric and Roman finds, historic Upper Austrian house interiors with rustic and other period furnishings, models of Upper Austrian farmhouses, rich samples of folk dress, old weapons including those of peasant rebellions, paintings, and a fine collection of carved church sculpture. The museum is splendidly arranged and is certainly worth a visit.

From the castle ramparts, now adapted as a park, there is a very good view of the Danube, of Pöstlingberg and other hills to the north. Beyond the castle park is Römerberg (Roman Hill), with the small Martinskirche, which is one of the oldest churches in Austria; it originates either from the late Roman or early Bavarian times and was rebuilt for the first time toward the end of the eighth century. Continuing on the Römerstrasse beyond Römerberg, one can get to the wooded hill of Freinberg, with fine vistas from the Höhenstrasse (high road) and good walks.

Retracing our steps on the Römerstrasse, we return to the center, passing by the theater building on a large, tree-lined street called Promenade. In front of us stands the Renaissance Landhaus (seat of the state government) built in the late 16th century, severely damaged during the great city fire of 1800. The original, beautiful arcaded courtyard with the fountain still remains. Next to the Landhaus is the Minoriten Church with late baroque and rococo interiors and some altar paintings by Kremser Schmidt. Following Herrenstrasse from Promenade we come to the neo-Gothic New Cathedral, with a 444-foot tower. On the corner of Herrenstrasse and Bischofstrasse is the Bishop's Palace, built between 1721 and 1726 according to plans made by the baroque master, Jakob Prandtauer. Continuing on Bischofstrasse we reach Landstrasse, the principal shopping precinct of Linz, which runs all the way from the vicinity of the main railroad station to the main square. Across Landstrasse in Harrachstrasse is another notable example of baroque art—the Seminary Church, formerly of the Order of Teutonic Knights, completed in 1825 after the plans of Lukas von Hildebrandt, with portal sculptures by Rafael Donner and some paintings by Altomonte and Kremser Schmidt.

Across the Danube bridge from the main square is the suburb of Urfahr, which was administratively a separate town until 1919, when it was incorporated into the city of Linz. A "must" is the view from Pöstlingberg, the hill on the left bank of the Danube, clearly defined by a twin-spired church; the top can be reached by a special streetcar from Urfahr, or by road if you are driving. On a clear day the view comprises a good deal of Upper Austria south of the Danube and a long chain of the Austrian Alps on the horizon.

The city's great industrial zone lies in the southeastern outskirts along the Danube. Closest to the city is the large freight harbor, with very modern installations and a free port section. Next are the chemical plants of Chemie Linz, founded by the Germans in 1938; they produce millions of tons of fertilizers, insecticides, pharmaceuticals and various other chemicals. Much larger are the steel works of VÖST (Vereinigte Österreichische Eisen- und Stahlwerke), also built by the Germans in 1938 and subsequent years, presently one of the major steel-producing factories in

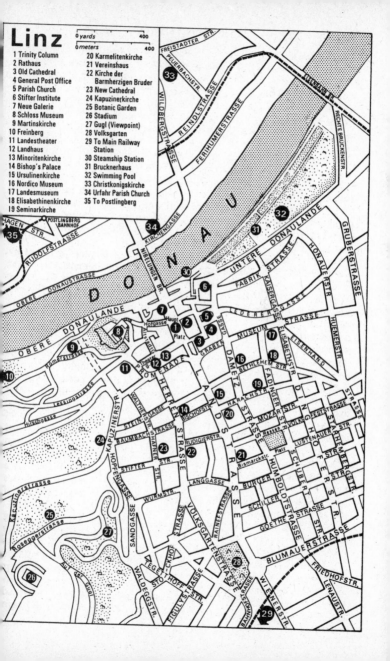

Linz

0 yards 400
0 meters 400

1 Trinity Column
2 Rathaus
3 Old Cathedral
4 General Post Office
5 Parish Church
6 Stifter Institute
7 Neue Galerie
8 Schloss Museum
9 Martinskirche
10 Freinberg
11 Landestheater
12 Landhaus
13 Minoritenkirche
14 Bishop's Palace
15 Ursulinenkirche
16 Nordico Museum
17 Landesmuseum
18 Elisabethinenkirche
19 Seminarkirche
20 Karmelitenkirche
21 Vereinshaus
22 Kirche der Barmherzigen Bruder
23 New Cathedral
24 Kapuzinerkirche
25 Botanic Garden
26 Stadium
27 Gugl (Viewpoint)
28 Volksgarten
29 To Main Railway Station
30 Steamship Station
31 Brucknerhaus
32 Swimming Pool
33 Christkonigskirche
34 Urfahr Parish Church
35 To Postlingberg

Europe. VÖST developed an entirely new method for steel-making and has since sold it to all the biggest steel producing countries.

Northern Upper Austria

Upstream from Linz comes the town of Wilhering, with its monastery and church, perhaps Austria's lovelist rococo church. Farther along, a little back from the south bank of the Danube, is Eferding, with its 15th-century Gothic parish church and interesting castle with a museum. If you have always thought of the Nibelungs as a mythical race known only to old German legends and Wagner, get that idea out of your head here. The Nibelungs existed, though not quite as Wagner describes them, and Eferding was their stamping ground. The parish church has an unusual double-corkscrew staircase, some pretty baroque altars and a cemetery with some interesting old graves. The Spitalkirche is also worth seeing.

The Danube now flows through a deeply-cut valley; after passing several castles, the boat traveler leaves it at Passau on the German side of the border, between the Danube and the Inn, which flows into it at this point. The Austrian town is Innstadt, on the east bank of the Inn, which may be followed south to Schärding, still possessing parts of its medieval walls as well as many old gabled buildings, a fine town hall, several old town gates, a baroque parish church with a fine marble high altar and a painting by Rottmayr, and a museum housed in a Renaissance building. The baroque houses in the main square are all painted in a great array of colors and are a remarkable sight.

Continuing up the Inn, we come first to the Abbey of Reichersberg, founded in the 11th century and rebuilt in the 17th; the Abbey Church has some magnificent rococo work and a lovely late-baroque pulpit. Then on to Braunau, an old town which has retained its charming medieval character. Bürgerspitalkirche and the parish church are both 15th-century Gothic (the latter is overwhelmed by its 320-foot tower). The Glockengiesserhaus (bell foundry), is a good example of an artisan's workshop from the Gothic period. The Salzburg Tower Gate is the best preserved piece of the old walls, and there is an interesting city museum in the restored Herzogsburg, one of the oldest buildings in Braunau.

The more important centers on the way back toward Linz are: Ried: home of the Schwanthaler family of baroque architects and sculptors (at Schwanthalergasse 11) and the parish church with two altars by Thomas Schwanthaler; from here you can visit the village and the castle of Aurolzmünster, about 6 km. away.—Haag: an old town lying at the foot of the hill with Starhemberg Castle.—Gallspach: site of the renowned Zeileis Institute of Radiology.—Bad Schallerbach: a spa with hot sulphur springs, whose drinking and bathing cures are recommended for a large variety of ailments. At this point, we are almost back to the Traun valley, and can return to Linz either via Eferding and along the Danube, or via Wels and along the Traun.

Linz is the most practical point of departure for visits to the Mühlviertel, the hilly region between the Danube and the border of Czechoslovakia. Two main roads roughly cover this area from Linz, with two local railroads following approximately the same direction. On or near the road to the northwestern corner of Austria are: the small town of Ottensheim with a castle (still on the Danube); farther inland, the railroad stop of Niederwaldkirchen, from where the Castle of Neuhaus can be reached by a scenic road; Neufelden with an artificial lake and the 13th-century Gothic Castle of Pürnstein in the vicinity; Rohrbach, with a baroque church and the pilgrimage church of Maria Trost nearby; Haslach, with a baroque town hall, the remains of medieval fortifications, and the Lichtenau Castle on a hill not far away; and Aigen, at the end of the railroad line, with the Abbey of Schlägl, founded in the 13th century and later rebuilt several times. The Abbey Church has some rich baroquery and paintings by Altomonte and others.

The other main road of Mühlviertel goes to Freistadt via Gallneukirchen in Gusen valley with the Castle of Riedegg, while the local railroad passes by Wartberg with three Gothic churches, Prägarten with the nearby Castle of Hagenberg, and Kefermarkt with the famed Gothic carved altar in the parish church. Freistadt is a charming town with old walls, towers, and gates (the Linzertor being particularly remarkable among the latter), a castle, a baroque and a Gothic church. If you are interested in Gothic winged altars, you should not fail to visit the church in Waldburg, which has three, and the small Church of St. Michael in Rauhenödt, which has one; both of these places are located only a few miles from Freistadt.

The Southward Route—St. Florian and Steyr

Starting our backward trip from Linz, briefly east and then southwest, we pass first through a favorite excursion trip from Linz, St. Florian. The Augustinian Abbey (rebuilt between 1668 and 1751 by Antonio Carlone and Jakob Prandtauer and standing over the tomb of St. Florian, who was drowned in the Enns in 304 for refusing to sacrifice to the Roman gods, is considered among the finest baroque buildings in Austria and one of its most important art treasures is the *Sebastian Altar* painted by Albrecht Altdorfer, one of the most important painters of the so-called Danube School. A magnificent staircase rises to the marble hall, on the ceiling of which Altomonte depicted the Austrian victories over the Turks. The library contains 120,000 volumes and there are 14 sumptuously decorated "Emperor's Rooms". In one stands Prince Eugene's superbly carved fourposter, in another the simple bed in which Anton Bruckner died in 1896. Under the church's white-and-gold organ, an

18th-century masterpiece with 7,000 pipes and 103 registers, is the grave of the great composer who was organist at the abbey and at the cathedral at Linz. During the summer, there is an organ concert daily at 4.30. Prandtauer also designed the abbey's hunting castle, Hohenbrunn, now a museum with a fine collection of porcelain. St. Florian has another claim to fame: there is a bell foundry here which cast the great bourdon bell for Vienna's Cathedral of St. Stephen, "Big Pummerin".

To the north, across the Autobahn, is Austria's oldest town, Enns, granted a charter in 1212. Finds from the original Roman town, Lauriacum, are in the Renaissance town hall and Ennsegg Castle. There is a fine view from the 200-foot Town Tower over the town's churches and old houses. 15 miles up the River Enns is Steyr, whose inhabitants are still working iron, as they have done since the Middle Ages, though less lucratively since the break up of the Austrian Empire which cut the town off from its markets. Steyr has partly recovered from its depression by adding automobile manufacture to its activities.

Fortunately, it has another string to its bow in addition to the industrial one. It is considered by some to be one of the best preserved old towns on German-speaking territory. It would be impossible to list here all the fine old buildings to be seen in Steyr. You should not miss the Hauptplatz, the center of the old city, the town hall, the central parish church (one of the largest Gothic churches in the province, of which the earliest parts date from the 15th century), or, above all, the Bummerlhaus, built in 1497, which is considered the finest Gothic private dwelling in the city. There is also the Lamberg Castle; St. Michael's Jesuit church, with its fine organ; the Schnallen tower, built in 1613, the Bezirkshauptmannschaft (District Government building), in rustic Renaissance style; and the baroque Dominican church built in 1550.

In Steyr you are still in Bruckner country. He composed his *Sixth Symphony* in the Parish House here, and there is a Bruckner room in the Mesnerhaus. Steyr is also a favorite center for boating enthusiasts, who make it their starting point for trips along either the Enns or the Steyr, which meet here.

West from Steyr is Bad Hall, a spa having the strongest bromine-iodine springs in Austria. Lying in lovely wooded surroundings, with all the amenities of a modern watering place, it caters to patients with a wide variety of maladies as well as to healthy visitors, who make this a starting point for excursions into the mountains to the south.

Kremsmünster Abbey

Not far west of Bad Hall is Kremsmünster-Markt; its Benedictine abbey was founded in 777, but the present building dates from the much later baroque period. Its great treasure is the Tassilo Chalice (named after Duke Tassilo of Bavaria, founder of this and many other abbeys), the oldest example of the goldsmith's art in either Bavaria or Austria (it is ascribed to the year 769), and the finest example of such work from early Christian times anywhere in the world, with the single exception of the Irish Cong Cross.

This monastery is the site of a famous school, which has numbered among its pupils many of Austria's greatest men. Its so-called Astronomic Tower, often called Europe's first skyscraper, contains a fine natural history collection, its art treasures include a 12th-century reliquary, and there are 100,000 volumes in its library, among them an illuminated Bible dating from the eighth century. Fish basins with arcaded passageways, built by Carlone and Prandtauer, and the Kaisersaal, with its paintings by Altomonte, are also not to be missed.

Southwest of Kremsmünster is Grünau (also reached from Traunsee) in the lovely Alm Valley. Southeast are the summer and winter resorts of Windischgarsten, with the nearby Gleinkersee, and Spital am Pyhrn, with a baroque abbey church and the Vogelgesang gorge in the vicinity.

Hallstatt

From Spital am Pyhrn, Hallstättersee, the Salzkammergut lake located in the southernmost corner of Upper Austria and squeezed between Styria and Land Salzburg, can be reached in the easiest manner by traveling a short distance (about 53 km.) through Styria. We proceed over the Pyhrn Pass (about 3,100 ft.) and then through Mitterndorf and Bad Aussee, which once also belonged to the Salzkammergut salt estate, and afterwards cross back into Upper Austria on the beautiful mountain road over the Pötschenhöhe (about 3,200 ft.). Immediately below this mountain pass are the shores of Halstätter Lake. On its west bank is Halstatt, believed to be the oldest community in Austria. More than a thousand graves of prehistoric men have been found here, and it has been such an important source of relics of the pre-Christian Celtic period that this age is known as the Halstatt epoch. The prehistoric men built on piles in the lake, for safety's sake, and Hallstatt today is also on props, for it occupies a series of terraces on the side of the mountain to which it clings precariously.

For lack of space, the bones of the dead are dug up after 10 years and, with artistically painted skulls, placed in the much-visited charnel house, next to the 16th-century parish church, which contains a splendid winged altar with nine panels.

The museum (open May through October) has, of course, relics of the Hallstatt epoch and also, as already noted, recounts the history of salt; and you may likewise visit a salt mine here. There are guided tours from April through October. It would be difficult to imagine a more impressive spectacle than these caverns, of which the largest is more than 32 km. long. Taken together, they make up the largest underground complex in Europe. The antithesis to the descent into a mine is the trip by cable car from Obertraun up to the ice caves of the glacier of the Dachstein, that mighty mountain which is the anchor post of Upper Austria, Styria and Land Salzburg, for the borders of the three states meet here.

Bad Ischl

Continuing down the Traun valley, we come to one of the most important places in the Salzkammergut—Bad Ischl. This was the place, as we have already noted in the introduction to this chapter, where Franz Josef chose to establish his summer court, and the chief amusement of oldtimers still seems to be retailing the gossip of the vanished imperial society. One of the incidents connected with the emperor's sojourn at Ischl is that it was here, for the only time in his life, that he consented to ride in an automobile (he never used the telephone, either). This single break in the tradition was explained by the identity of the person with whom he shared the car—his fellow monarch, Edward VII of England, who was no mean force himself in establishing the social popularity of the spas of Europe.

It is an easy transition from Imperial Austria to Franz Lehar, the composer of so many operettas that glorified it, and sure enough, Lehar had a villa here, which today is a museum. You may also see the emperor's villa (Kaiservilla, now owned by his great-grandson, Markus von Habsburg), and its surrounding park. It is open from May to September. Bad Ischl today is a modern spa, one of the best equipped in Austria.

The Wolfgangsee

If we continued to follow the Traun from Bad Ischl, we should quickly come to Mitterweissenbach, where we joined it at the start of our circuit; instead we shall turn west to the Wolfgangsee, named after the most famous place on its shores.

St. Wolfgang is on the north shore of the lake, where you will find yourself—literally—in the Austria of operetta. For you may stay if you like at the *White Horse Inn,* unfortunately recently given a facelift that has destroyed some of its original charm, but you *are* at the White Horse Inn, the one which was the setting for the famous operetta. It is favored over other localities on the same lake because it is on the far side from the road and therefore off the beaten track.

The fame of the White Horse Inn has dwarfed that of St. Wolfgang's more serious drawing card, the winged altarpiece of Michael Pacher, made in 1481, which is one of the finest examples of Gothic wood carving in the world. The 16th-century parish church in which it is placed possesses two other notable altars, either of which would be the prize of any other church, but they sink into insignificance before this one. Its custodians treat it with great ceremony. The "wings" are kept closed on ordinary days. On Sundays they are half opened, on important religious festivals, like Christmas and Easter, they are opened wide, exposing the fine work within. If you pay it a visit, however, it will be opened for your inspection. St. Florian, that Austrian martyr whose acquaintance we have already made, the hermit St. Wolfgang, the local patron, and others are pictured in the scene of the crowning of the Virgin, with workmanship so minute that you can see even the stitches on the Virgin's clothing.

All other localities on Wolfgangsee are within the borders of Land Salzburg and we have described them in that chapter. Only a few kilometers northwest over the Schafberg Mountain (5,850 ft.)—whose summit can be reached from St. Wolfgang by cogwheel railway—is Mondsee, where we started our round tour of Upper Austria. (However, there is no direct connection between St. Wolfgang and Mondsee.)

PRACTICAL INFORMATION

HOTELS AND RESTAURANTS

ASCHACH On the Danube. **Hotels** *Faustschlössl* (2), 60 beds in 15th-century castle with modern hotel facilities, top restaurant, music in the evening, heated pool, riding, fishing.
Zur Sonne (3), a few inexpensive rooms, good local food in restaurant.

ATTERSEE Hotel *Oberndorfer* (2), on lake with own beach, excellent restaurant with fish and game dishes, garden terrace.

BAD GOISERN Part of the Salzkammergut, sometimes difficult to decide whether this is more a spa or a winter sports resort.
Hotels *Alpenhotel Mühlkogel* (1), 60 rooms with bath/shower.
Both (2)—*Kurhotel Jodschwefelbad,* open Jan. to Oct., outside village in park, terrace and garden, cure facilities in hotel; *Post,* a little less expensive, with ski lift.
Golsermühle (3).

BAD HALL Hotels *Schloss Feyregg* (1), small exclusive castle pension with period-style furnishings.
Under the spa management and owned by the government of Upper Austria, all in or near the spa park, both (2)—*Kurhotel,* about 100 beds, with smaller annexes *Landesvilla* and *Villa Rabi; Goldener Adler,* with a new 16-room annex, most rooms with bath.
Haller Hof (3), on main square.

BAD ISCHL Fashionable spa and winter sports center.

Hotels Both (1)—*Post,* central, in old imperial style, fish and game specialties in restaurant, fishing and riding; *Kurhotel,* large and new, all rooms with bath or shower, cure facilities, indoor pool and sauna, terrace café.

All (2)—*Freischütz,* located a little outside in Rettenbach, with garden; *Golfhotel Salzkammergut,* adjacent to the golf course outside of town, all rooms with bath or shower, has indoor pool; *Goldenes Hufeisen,* 55 beds; *Zum Goldenen Schiff,* with a good garden restaurant.

All (3)—*Goldener Stern* and *Schenner,* both in center, good food; *Goldener Ochs,* colorful restaurant.

Restaurants *Café-Konditorei Zauner,* Pfarrg 7, next to Vienna's Demel the most famous pastry shop in Austria, used to serve the imperial court during summer vacations; *Weinhaus Attenger,* fine food and wonderful pastries.

BAD LEONFELDEN Newly developed health and sports center in Mühlviertel. **Hotels** Best is *Böhmertor* (3), with indoor pool, cure facilities.

BAD NEYDHARTING Hotel *Kuranstalt Schwarz* (2), 60 rooms/bath, diet restaurant, famous for mud cures.

BAD SCHALLERBACH Hotels Both (2)—Pensions *Angel* and *Parkpension* are small.

Both (3)—*Grünes Türl* and *Waldesruh* have good restaurants.

BRAUNAU Hotels Both (3)—*Post,* 50 beds, 16 baths, with pleasant Stuben style restaurant; *Gann,* 70 beds; both on main square.

EBENSEE On Traunsee. **Hotels** *Langbathsee* (2), all rooms with bath or shower; *Post* (3), larger, some rooms with kitchenette.

GALLSPACH Hotels Both (2)—*Bayrischer Hof,* at the spa park, most rooms with bath, excellent restaurant and fireside bar, fine café; *Gallspacherhof,* 70 beds, good restaurant.

GMUNDEN Main resort on Traunsee. **Hotels** All (2)—*Parkhotel am See,* 100 beds, 35 baths, veranda restaurant, heated pool, in small park on lake.

Freisitz Roith, about 50 beds, 10 baths, with own beach, fishing and riding, excellent restaurant with game dishes.

Schwan, on main square, dining overlooking the lake.

Gästehaus Grünberg, at 3,300 ft., Alpine style, reached by cable car, small but all rooms with bath, panoramic view, heated outdoor pool, good restaurant.

Pension Magerl (P2), 75 beds, indoor pool and sauna.

Both (3)—*Gasthof Ramsau,* in quiet position on lake with good restaurant; *Marienbrücke,* with garden restaurant.

Restaurants *Grillstadl* (2), a pleasant restaurant with old vaulted ceilings, on main square. *Gasthof Gold* (3), Brunnen, offers unpretentious family cooking with many regional specialties, including locally caught fish.

GOSAU Over 2,500 ft., point of departure for the Dachstein ski tours, can be reached by bus from the railway station Steeg-Gosau.

Hotels Both (3)—*Sommerhof,* all rooms with bath or shower, most with balcony, terrace and attractive restaurant; *Pension Koller,* just off main road, with panoramic view, pool, hunting facilities.

GRÜNAU IM ALMTAL 1,700 ft., can be reached from Wels by a local railway.

Hotels *Almtalhof* (2), Romantic Hotel, 25 rooms, good restaurant. *Hochberghaus* (3), in center, with new annex and attractive restaurant.

On Almsee, about 14 km. away, both (3)—*Gasthöfe Seehaus,* 26 beds; and *Deutsches Haus,* with good restaurant (try trout stuffed with mushrooms), and a few double rooms. Both open summer only.

HALSTATT On Halstättersee, the point of departure for the Dachstein plateau, but less convenient than Obertraun and Gosau.

Hotels Both (2)—*Grüner Baum,* on lakeshore, with lake fish dishes in terrace restaurant, open April to Oct. *Seewirt,* a little less expensive, with good restaurant, wine tavern and own beach.

Both (3)—*Simonyhütte;* on lake, rustic; *Gasthof Pension Gosaumühle,* 50 beds, in nearby Gosaumühle, on lake.

HINTERSTODER Almost 2,000 ft. up, in a beautiful valley under the Totes Gebirge, reached by bus from the railway station of the same name on Linz–Graz line. Hinterstoder, together with the nearby Windischgarsten and Spital am Pyhrn, has developed into a skiing center of rapidly increasing importance.

Hotels *Berghotel Hinterstoder,* 120 beds, all rooms with bath, full-board only, indoor pool.

All (3)—*Dietlgut,* heated pool; *Stockerwirt,* also with heated pool; *Stoderhof,* all rooms with bath or shower, restaurant and tavern, sauna.

LINZ Provincial capital, lying on both banks of the Danube.

Hotels Accommodation is somewhat limited but the prices are lower than in other Austrian state capitals.

Schillerpark (L), on the Landstrasse, run by Alba group. Casino, coffee shop, two restaurants, underground garage, bar, excellent staff.

All (1)—*Dumhotel,* Baumbachstr. 17, central, nearly all 50 rooms with shower. *Tourotel,* Untere Donaulände 9, 180 rooms, restaurant, nightclub, indoor pool and sauna. *Waldegg,* about 3 km from center in the suburbs on Wankmüllerhofstr. 39, convenient for motorists coming from the autobahn, 103 rooms, 2 restaurants, cocktail bar, parking.

All (2)—*Drei Mohren,* Promenade 17, across from the Landhaus, an inn since 1595 but modernized. *Lokomotive,* Weingartshofstr. 40, near main station, with sizeable pleasant restaurant. *Nibelungenhof,* Scharitzerstr. 7.

Across the Danube is *Pöstlingberg,* on the hill of the same name, reached by car or streetcar, 6 rooms with bath, excellent restaurant, cellar wine tavern, café.

Prielmayerhof, Weissenwolffstr. 33, a bit out of center, with bus stop at the door, 80 beds, wine restaurant.

Wolfinger, on main square with entrance from a historic alley-like courtyard, lined by old street lamps and crossed by open terraced corridors, white-table-cloth restaurant on upper floor, period-style wine tavern approached from the courtyard below.

Both (3)—*Ebelsbergerhof,* Wienerstr. 485, in Ebelsberg suburb, Upper Austrian specialties in restaurant, café and wine tavern; *Goldene Krone,* Hofberg 5.

Camping There's a fairly large site at Landwiedstr. 138, open May to Sept.

Restaurants All (1)—*Allegro,* Schillerstr., is a remarkably brave attempt to establish a top-level restaurant in Linz.

Kerzenstüberl, next to cathedral at Hafnerstr. 4, an evening restaurant, closed mid-Aug. to mid-Sept.

Kremsmünsterer Weinstube, an old wine-restaurant in an historic house at Altstadt 10, with good food.

Landhof, Pummererstr. 4A, with game and smoked trout; garden.

Theater-Casino, Promenade 30, at the theater, is a bit formal.

Antiquitätenstube, Le Bistro and *Herz As* are all in the Altstadt.

All (2)—*Kaufmännisches Vereinshaus,* House of the Merchants' Association, corner Landstr.-Bismarckstr., large wood-paneled hall, nice courtyard garden.

Klosterhof, Landstr. 30, formerly the library of the Kremsmünster Abbey, a vast establishment with a series of upstairs and downstairs rooms and halls with rustic and hunting décor, beer garden, hearty dishes and the good Stieglbräu beer.

Sportkasino, Brucknerstr. 40, game and fish specialties.

Stieglbierstuben, Volksgartenstr. 28, old-time interior, pleasant garden.

Zum Mühlviertler, Graben 24–6, particularly for game, fish, and a great variety of dumplings, closed weekends and holidays.

Schloss Puchenau is somewhat outside the city, on the Danube; a little formal but very good Austrian food.

Cafés and Pastry Shops *Goethe,* Landstr. 109, with buffet section.

Schlosskaffee, attached to the Castle Museum, with outdoor terrace on the ramparts and excellent view of the Danube, Urfahr and Pöstlingberg, open April to Oct.

Café-Konditorei Tautermann, Klammstr. 14–16, winner of many international cake and pastry prizes.

Café Traxlmayr, Promenade 16, best of old Vienna type.

Konditorei Wagner, Landstr. 15, this and Tautermann specialize in *Linzer Torte* and will mail it anywhere in the world.

Konditorei Wrann, on the Landstrasse, makes the best pastries in Linz.

Numerous wine taverns dot the old city section, varying in quality of atmosphere and wine.

Andreas Hofer Stüberl, Domgasse 8, offers Schrammel music and a good dose of *Gemütlichkeit.*

Styrian wines are the feature of *Steirische Weinstube,* Neutorgasse 3.

Wachau wines at *Wachauer Weinstube,* Pfarrgasse 20.

MONDSEE Hotels *Motel Mondsee* (1), near autobahn exit, all rooms with bath, refrigerator and balcony, indoor pool.

Both (2)—*Plomberg,* 40 beds, with Austria's finest restaurant. Reservation in the restaurant essential, expensive but excellent value and highly recommended. *Weisses Kreuz,* 34 beds with bath or shower. Excellent restaurant specializing in modern Austrian cuisine.

All (3)—*Leitnerbräu,* good restaurant; *Lackner,* most rooms with bath; *Königsbad,* a bit outside on the lake.

Several large campsites on the lake.

NEUKIRCHEN Near Altmünster. **Hotel** *Ferienhof International* (2), 18 rooms in Austrian style, indoor pool, sauna, sun terrace, bar.

OBERTRAUN In the Dachstein mountain group. Skiing is actually done on the Dachstein plateau, most easily reached from here by a 3-section cable car. The Dachstein Plateau, between 5,000 and 9,500 ft. high, with its ideal skiing terrain (for all degrees of skill, or lack of it) and magnificent scenery, is the top skiing center of Salzkammergut.

Hotels Both (3)—*Hotel Krippenstein,* 90 beds, all rooms with bath, perched 7,000 ft. high at upper cable car station, good food, magnificent mountain and glacier scenery, higher priced in season; *Hotel Schönberghaus,* 45 beds, 4,500 ft. high at middle cable car stop, 15 minutes walk to Dachstein ice caves.

In town, both (3)—*Dachsteinhof,* near cable car station, garden; and *Sarstein,* open June to Sept.

ST. MARTIN IM INNKREIS On a side road (No. 143), about halfway between Braunau and Schärding. **Hotel** *Schlosspension St. Martin* (2), in a castle originally built in the 11th century, swimming, tennis, riding, hunting and fishing in quiet unspoiled country.

ST. WOLFGANG On Wolfgangsee. **Hotels** Both (1)—*Weisses Rössl* (White Horse Inn), scene of the famous operetta, Romantic Hotel, most of the 60 rooms with bath, many with balcony overlooking lake, restaurant and terrace facing the lake, indoor pool, open mid-March through Oct., service bounces around like a rubber ball—sometimes very good, then very bad, mostly just in between. *Auhof,* all rooms with bath, good restaurant.

All (2)—*Haus Appesbach,* about 2 km. from town, tennis, café terrace; *Strandhotel Margaretha,* own beach, bar and restaurant; *Post,* next to the church, and its annexes, *Schloss Eibenstein,* in the castle of the same name, and *Haus Gastberger,* in the west section on the lake shore, altogether 210 beds, indoor pool; *Seehotel Cortisen,* own beach, restaurant; *Eden,* smaller, most rooms with bath.

All (3)—*Belvedere,* heated pool; *Wolfgangerhof,* also with indoor pool; *Zimmerbräu* and *Tirol.*

Up the Schafberg mountain, cog-wheel railway, *Schafbergspitze,* at 5,850 ft., 80 beds, restaurant, open summers; *Gasthof Schafbergalpe,* a bit lower down, also with restaurant.

2 large campsites.

SCHÄRDING Hotels All (3)—*Forstinger,* 50 beds, 14 baths, good restaurant with own meats; *Schärdinger Hof,* game and fish specialties; *Lachinger Hof,* rustic restaurant rooms with good fish dishes.

Restaurant You can also eat well at *Weinstuben Scheurecker.*

See also **St. Martin im Innkreis.**

SEEWALCHEN Hotel *Häupl* (1), 62 rooms with bath. First-class dining.

SPITAL AM PYHRN About 2,100 ft. high, on the railway line Linz–Graz, under the Pyhrnpass in eastern Totes Gebirge.

Hotels Among the best of the 2 dozen or so hostelries in town, both (3)—*Gasthof Alpenrose* and *Pension Vogelhändler.*

The largest mountain hotels in the vicinity, both (3)—*Linzerhaus,* about 4,600 ft., reached by cable car; and *Rohrauer Haus,* 4,420 ft., both open all year.

STEYR Hotels *Minichmayr* (2), next to main bridge, 75 beds. The restaurant is remarkable, in a dramatic setting built out over the confluence of the two rivers. The food is excellent (includes fresh local fish). Rooms recently refurbished and very comfortable. *Zu den drei Rosen* (3), small Gasthof in old patrician house.

In nearby **St. Ulrich, Restaurants** *Ulrichsklause,* with terrace overlooking Steyr; and *Mayr,* garden in summer. Both good.

TRAUNKIRCHEN On Traunsee. **Hotels** All (2)—*Am Stein,* 2 km. outside in beautiful shore position, own beach and garden, restaurant and dancing. *Post,* on main square, 100 beds, most rooms with bath or shower, balcony, restaurant and bar. *Berghof,* above lake, offers good food and fine view from its terrace.

Traunsee (3), on the lake in town, roof terrace and garden.

UNTERACH/ATTERSEE Hotel *Georgshof* (2), 25 rooms/bath, indoor pool.

VICHTENSTEIN On the Danube, upstream from Linz, about 72 km. along the right bank road.

Hotel *Schlosspension Vichtenstein* (3), 20 beds, small, room-and-breakfast pension in the castle.

WELS Hotels *Greif* (2), 140 beds, excellent accommodations, good restaurant. *Bayerischer Hof* (3), smaller.

Restaurants *Reitinger,* in the Sattledt section, specializes in chicken and dumplings, on summer Sat., grill and dancing on the terrace; try *Wirt am Berg,* for a huge selection of game, on the main highway, a Gasthaus since 1630; *Urbann,* in center, near station, is a noted café with a summer garden.

WINDISCHGARSTEN About 2,000 ft. high near Spital, this small town is an important winter resort.

Hotels All (2)—*Austria,* in quiet location with fine view, about 60 beds; *Bischofsberg,* indoor and heated outdoor pools; *Seebachhof,* outside of town, with fine restaurant; *Sporthotel,* new, with a good restaurant serving local specialties.

All (3)—*Blaue Sense;* and *Pension Sperl; Schwarzes Rössl,* 50 beds, typical Upper Austrian dishes and game in attractive surroundings.

SPECIAL EVENTS

BAD GOISERN Summer season, June to Sept. with concerts, folk music, theater, Alpine evenings, and dancing.

BAD HALL The summer season is from June to Sept. with theater and concert performances, folk music, dancing and Alpine evenings.

BAD ISCHL Summer season, June to Sept., concerts and folk music; regular theater performances are given again in the old imperial court theater, now called Lehar-Theater; operetta performances, Alpine evenings, dancing events.

GMUNDEN At "Liebstattsonntag" in April there is a famous local-costume parade, when girls in dirndls hand out or sell gingerbread hearts with messages written on them in pink sugar. High season is July and Aug. with brass band concerts, folklore shows, occasional fireworks and balls.

HALSTATT Late May to early June, Corpus Christi lake processions. High season, July and Aug., brass band concerts, folklore shows, fireworks and balls occasionally.

LINZ September sees the Bruckner Festival.

OBERTRAUN The famous Dachstein giant slalom race in May ends the skiing season in the high mountains.

ST. WOLFGANG High season is July and Aug. with brass band concerts, folklore shows, occasional fireworks and balls.

TRAUNKIRCHEN Late May to early June, Corpus Christi lake processions. National and international sailing regattas.

SPAS AND HEALTH RESORTS

BAD GOISERN This is an iodine-sulphur spa with treatments for rheumatic disorders, thermal outdoor swimming pool in summer.

BAD HALL With 11 iodine-bromine-brine springs.

BAD ISCHL Best known and most fashionable spa in Upper Austria, noted for its brine waters and treatment of heart ailments. In the old days, the emperor's villa was the social center of the empire during the summer months.

BAD SCHALLERBACH With 99.5° F. sulphuric thermal springs feeding an outdoor swimming pool.

GALLSPACH Cures from simple means provided by nature; seat of the radio-therapeutical *Zeileis Institute,* with cures for disorders of the nervous, vascular and glandular systems.

SCHÄRDING Cures using the simple means provided by nature. The sanatorium of *Hospitallers* provides cold water cures for rheumatic and nervous disorders following the system established by Rev. Kneipp before the turn of the century.

ENTERTAINMENT

LINZ The theater season lasts from Sept. to June. *Landestheater* offers opera, operetta and drama performances; *Kammerspiele Theater* produces drama and comedy—both at Promenade 39.

A rich concert season is scheduled from fall to spring, with concerts in the *Bruckner-Haus,* a beautiful piece of modern architecture on the banks of the Danube, voted one of the five best concert halls in the world by the London Symphony Orchestra.

The top musical event is the *Linzer Bruckner Festival,* end Sept. to early Oct. In summer, concerts are given in the arcaded courtyard of the *Landhaus.*

Try the nightclub in *Tourotel.* Disco dancing at *Jolly Dancing Club,* Klammstr. 3, and by candlelight at *TIK,* Landstr. 109.

SPORTS

BAD GOISERN Headquarters for the Austrian Archery Association—*Österreichischer Bogenschützenverband,* A–4822, Bad Goisern.

Also 2 chair lifts, 5 ski lifts, 2 ski jumps, ski school, toboggan runs, curling.

BAD HALL Tennis, swimming, riding and shooting facilities.

BAD ISCHL Tennis courts; a very scenic 9-hole golf course, May to Oct.

There's a mountain-climbing school, write to *Bergsteigerschule Oberösterreich,* A–4820 Bad Ischl, Kaiser Franz Josefstr. 7.

2 skating rinks, ski jump, curling alleys, cable car from Kaltenbach to Katrinalpe, 1 chair lift, 2 ski lifts, floodlit runs for night skiing.

BAD LEONFELDEN 1 chair lift, 2 ski lifts, ski school, ice skating, curling, tobogganing, horse sleighs.

EBENSEE Ski school, ski jump in the Langbathtal nearby, curling facilities.

FEUERKOGEL About 5,400 ft., above Ebensee in the Höllengebirge, reached by cable car from Ebensee.

Ski slopes for beginners, runs and trails for the advanced, 8 ski lifts, chair lift, ski tour guides, 2 ski schools.

GMUNDEN Tennis courts; skindiving school; sailing school, national and international sailing regattas on the lake, windsurfing.

Winter skating and curling facilities, ice hockey games, toboggan course, cable car to Grünberg mountain with 2 ski lifts.

GOSAU Ski guides available, 5 ski lifts, ski jump, 3 curling alleys, toboggan runs and skijoring, cable car to Zwieselalm.

GRÜNAU IM ALMTAL Ski school, chair lift to Kasberg, 5 ski lifts, ski jump, skijoring, curling and horse-drawn sleighs.

HALLSTATT Skindiving school, also in winter.
Ski guides and a cargo cable car to Wiesberghaus, ski school, cable car to Rudolfsturm, 1 ski lift, 2 ski jumps, 2 toboggan runs, skijoring and curling facilities.

HINTERSTODER A 2-stage double-chair lift, 10 ski lifts, 2 ski schools, ski jump, toboggan runs, skijoring, curling and horse sleighs.

LINZ Linz has several swimming establishments, among them—*Parkbad,* Untere Donaulände 11, with indoor pool open Oct. to April, outdoor swimming May to Sept.
Tennis courts—Ferdinand-Marklstr. 2, and in Böhmerwaldstr.
Riding and instruction at *Linzer Reiterbund,* Roseggerstr. 51; *Union-Reitclub St. Georg,* in Ebelsberg Castle across the River Traun; *Reitklub Linz,* Museumstr. 31.
Golf—9-hole course at Schloss Tillysberg near the autobahn exit Asten-St. Florian.
Good skiing terrains are in the hilly area 8–16 km. north of the city, around the villages of Lichtenberg (ski tours), Kirchschlag (5 ski lifts, ski school, ski jump) and Hellmondsödt (3 ski lifts).
Ice skating and ice hockey facilities exist in the city.
Soccer games and other field sports—there's a large stadium on the Gugl elevation holding 26,000 spectators.

MONDSEE Sailing school, windsurfing school, national and international sailing regattas. A riding estate nearby, *Fohlenhof,* offers riding tours and lessons.

OBERTRAUN Altogether, there are 7 ski lifts, 3 ski schools, toboggan runs and curling alleys.

ST. WOLFGANG Sailing school, national and international sailing regattas, tennis courts.

SPITAL AM PYHRN Ski jump, toboggan course, curling facilities, ski lift near town, cable car to Linzerhaus mountain lodge (with 3 ski lifts and a ski school); additional ski lifts at Bosruckhütte and Rohrauer Haus, two other lodges high up in the mountains. This area is ideal for beginners and experienced skiers and offers mountain ski tours of all degrees.

WINDISCHGARSTEN Renowned ski school, chair lift, 5 ski lifts, ski jump, skating rink, curling alleys, toboggan runs and horse sleighs for hire.

SHOPPING

LINZ The main shopping area in Linz is along the Landstrasse, running its entire length from the vicinity of the main station to the Taubenmarkt, with some of the side streets such as Mozartstrasse, Bethlehemstrasse and Spittelwiese. Taubenmarkt marks the beginning of the old town, Graben, Promenade, Schmidtorstrasse and Hauptplatz (main square) being the main shopping lanes; and Herrenstrasse, which runs parallel to Landstrasse, is also important.

Dirndls and Trachten for Women *Feichtinger,* Herrenstr. 9; *Elise Thalbauer,* Spittelwiese 4; *O.Ö. Heimatwerk,* Landstr. 31; *Wieser,* Hafferlstr. 3; *Resi Hammerer,* Landstr. 7.

Handicrafts, Gifts and Souvenirs *O.Ö. Heimatwerk,* Upper Austrian folklore store, with shops at Landstr. 21, and Bürgerstr. 1, articles ranging from ceramics, glass, pewter and wooden objects, folk dress, folk furnishings to entire rustic room interiors.

Toys *Sommer,* Promenade 17; *Kinderparadies,* Landstr. 64; *Kleinbahn,* Graben 32B, toy trains only.

USEFUL ADDRESSES

BRAUNAU There's a branch office of *Oberösterreichisches Landesreisbüro,* the state-sponsored Upper Austrian travel agency, at Stadtplatz 33.

LINZ City Information Main station open 8 A.M. to 7 P.M. *Landesfremdenverkehrsamt Oberösterreich,* Schillerstr. 50 (tel. 997 663021). *Oberösterreichisches Landesreisebüro,* state-sponsored Upper Austrian Travel Agency, Hauptplatz 9 (tel. 997 71061).

Danube steamers: DDSG, Untere Donaulände, passenger ship station, open early May to late Sept.

Car Hire: *Avis,* in Hotel Tourotel; *Carop,* Industriezeile 64; *Herz,* Stockhofstr. 25.

WELS Branch office of *Oberösterreichisches Landesreisbüro,* state sponsored Upper Austrian travel agency, Kaiser-Josefplatz 46.

TYROL

A Mountain Fairyland

Today, the Bundesland Tirol (Federal State of Tyrol) has a population of some 541,000 and covers an area of nearly 13,000 square kilometers. Before World War I, the Tyrol was much bigger; but the large, prosperous wine-growing area of South Tyrol was ceded to Italy under the terms of the peace treaty, and the wealthiest part of the state was lost to Austria. As a result of this political surgical operation, the East Tyrol has been entirely cut off from the main body of the state and can only be reached by passing through Italy or over the Alps through Salzburg. The Tyrolese feel very deeply the loss of South Tyrol, and have never given up agitating for the return of this rich fertile country, where they all have relatives, and many still own property. The red wine you will drink in the Tyrol (called Kalterer, Magdalener, and other names) will come from South Tyrol, and very good it is.

Italy, then, forms the long southern boundary of the state. To the north the Tyrol has another international frontier with Bavaria. To the east lies Land Salzburg and—beyond East Tyrol—Carinthia. Over to the west the great Arlberg massif marks the western limits of the Tyrol, and once you are over the pass you are in Vorarlberg.

Early Tourists

Since the early 1930's the Tyrol has been one of the most popular holiday centers for British visitors, though they have now been overtaken by the Germans as the backbone of the tourist trade, the youngest and most prosperous of Tyrolean industries. It is said that the first missionaries to come to the Tyrol were either Irish or English. As early as the middle of the 15th century, we read of the marriage between Archduke Sigismund the Wealthy and Eleanor, daughter of James II of Scotland. In 1621 Scottish troops were stationed in Hall near Innsbruck, and a few years later Tyrolean traders were opening shops in London. In 1719 Princess Clementina Sobieski, the Polish bride of the Old Pretender, was imprisoned at Innsbruck by order of the Holy Roman Emperor, and was rescued in the best film tradition by a party of Irish adventurers, one of whom, disguised as a "serving wench," managed to enter the castle where the princess was being held.

From the beginning of the 18th century a procession of what might be called "pioneer tourists" from all parts of the British Isles came singly and in small parties to discover the Tyrol as a country of great scenic beauty and as an ideal holiday center. Indeed, the Tyrol can be said to owe a great deal to British pioneering. It was the British Kandahar Ski Club that played an important part in making the Tyrol the world's most popular winter sports center: it was this club that encouraged and sponsored the late Hannes Schneider in teaching his revolutionary technique, which has made Austrian skiing world famous. During the late 19th century scores of adventurous and enterprising British businessmen came to the Tyrol and built factories, and they too can claim to have had a major share in the credit for the rapid growth of its industry. In the light of all this, it is no wonder that British visitors are made doubly welcome by their hospitable Tyrolese hosts.

The Americans discovered this area as a holiday center, only several decades later. In 1906, the railroad millionaire Morgan spent a holiday in Innsbruck, and from then on the Tyrol was much publicized and boosted as a holiday playground in the United States. Since the last war, Tyrol has become very popular with American skiers who are now coming here in droves every winter, many returning every year. Tyrol has also been selected by most US downhill and slalom champions as the training ground for these Alpine skiing disciplines.

The history of the Tyrol is full of romance. Up to the beginning of the 16th century it was a very powerful state, under a long line of counts and dukes of varying fortunes, as can be judged by some of their nicknames— "Friedl with the empty pockets," and his son, "Sigmund the rich in coin," for example.

Under Maximilian I the state reached the zenith of its power. But perhaps the best known historical figure is Andreas Hofer, the hero of the Tyrol, who led the famed rebellion against the Napoleonic occupation, defeating the French troops at the Battle of Berg Isel. Both the "Golden Roof" and the magnificent Maximilian's mausoleum are in Innsbruck, and the memorial to Andreas Hofer lies just outside the city.

Innsbruck, capital of the Tyrol, is very conveniently situated for the tourist. Even if you have already settled on a resort for your holiday, you should certainly spend a day or two in the capital first; for Innsbruck is the treasure house of the whole Tyrol, historically, esthetically and economically.

Weather Matters and Winter Sports

During each season of the year the beauty of the Tyrol's spectacular mountain scenery is defined by a different color: the fresh green of the high pastures in spring, the deep blue of the dreamy lakes in summer, the golden red of the rocky mountain faces in the fall sunsets, and the brilliant white of snowy slopes reflecting the winter sun.

Tyrol is the best winter sports area in Austria and very probably the best skiing center in the world. Here are the best skiing schools, the best skiing techniques originated here, they are constantly being improved, and are taught by the old masters and by the new ones who are growing up on every hill. Tyrol is the home country of such skiing masters of the past as Hannes Schneider and Toni Seelos, of such record holders of yesterday as Toni Sailer, Josl Rieder and Andreas Molterer, and of dozens of present-day champions. Scores of international and national competitions take place here throughout every winter season. More hotel comforts and more *après-ski* entertainment may be provided for the skiing tourist in other countries, but none equals Tyrol when it comes to real skiing. Equipment can be rented in most places. The best time for skiing in the lower areas is from early January until mid-March, but you can usually ski from mid-December until the end of March. In the higher areas skiing goes on from early December until the end of April. The best time for the high mountain skiing tours is early spring, and for glacier tours May and June. Above Hochgurgl, on Rettenbachferner above Sölden, and on Stubai and Tuxer glaciers, there is year-round skiing.

Mid-June to mid-October is usually the best time for climbers, most of the hunting takes place during the second half of the year, and you are allowed to fish for trout until the end of September. The tourist traffic is at its peak in July and August, when to arrive in a summer resort without a reservation often means to be left without a room, or at least to have a very slim chance of obtaining the type of room desired.

Route Planning

The main **railway** line of the Tyrol, coming from Vorarlberg to St. Anton am Arlberg, crossing the main part of North Tyrol, and leaving it shortly after St. Johann for Land Salzburg, is also the route of the Arlberg-Orient Express. The latter, however, makes stops only at St. Anton, Landeck, Ötztal, Innsbruck, Jenbach, and Kitzbühel. Other fast trains on this line stop also at Imst, Telfs (some), Wörgl, and St. Johann. The second most important railway line enters Tyrol from Germany at Kufstein and proceeds to Wörgl, Innsbruck, Brenner, and from there to Italy, Fast-train stops are at Kufstein, Wörgl, Jenbach, Schwaz (occasionally), Innsbruck, Matrei am Brenner, Steinach, and Brenner. A local railway line connects Innsbruck with Seefeld, Scharnitz, and continues through a short stretch of German territory at Garmisch with Ehrwald, Lermoos and Reutte. Narrow-gauge local railways connect Jenbach with Mayrhofen in the Ziller valley and with Achensee, and Innsbruck with Fulpmes.

The state and private **bus service** net is well organized; in a few mountain sections caterpillar vehicles and motor sleighs have to be used sometimes in bad weather to make the last stretch. Bus sightseeing tours, often covering also the sights of South Tyrol, originate in many localities (mostly only in summer), in addition to Innsbruck; among them Igls, St. Anton am Arlberg, Landeck, Reutte, Kitzbühel, St. Johann in Tirol, Brixen im Thale.

In summer **motorboat** roundtrips take place on Walchsee and there is frequent lake boat service between the localities on Achensee.

The best way of seeing Tyrol is, of course, **by car.** In the official travel offices in Tyrol you can obtain an attractive booklet containing suggestions for some 45 automobile roundtrips in Tyrol, including a description of the roads and traffic rules. Driving is recommended, however, only in the snow-free months unless you are an expert in high-mountain snow driving. From Innsbruck you can cover all of North Tyrol in day trips.

The main mountain passes are: Arlberg Pass (5,900 ft.) on the main road between Tyrol and Vorarlberg (the 14km. Arlberg Tunnel avoids the 16 percent climb from Tyrol, 15 percent from Vorarlberg); Finstermünz Pass (4,500 ft.) at Nauders near the Swiss and Italian borders (9 percent); Reschen-Scheideck (5,000 ft.) on the same road on the Italian border (11 percent); Brenner Pass (4,500 ft.) on the main road to Italy (9 percent on the Austrian side, 13 on the Italian); Fern Pass (4,000 ft.) between Nassereith (7 percent) and Lermoos (10 percent); Pass Thurn (4,200 ft.) between Kitzbühel on the Tyrolean side (8 percent) and Mittersill on the Salzburg side (6 percent); Zirlerberg (3,900 ft.) between Zirl (15 percent) and Seefeld (14 percent); Iselsberg (3,960 ft.) on the border of East Tyrol (9 percent) and Carinthia (10 percent); Pass Strub (2,230 ft.) between Waidring on the Tyrol side (10 percent) and Lofer on the Salzburg side (5 percent); Achenpass (3,100 ft.) between Austria (18 percent) and Germany (16 percent) on Achensee–Tegernsee road; Silvretta Pass (6,700 ft.) between Galtür on the Tyrolean side (16 percent) and Partenen on the Vorarlberg side (12 percent).

The west Autobahn re-enters Austria from Germany at Kufstein and runs southwest past Innsbruck to Telfs. From there the 171 continues comfortably west to the Arlberg. From Innsbruck the Brenner Autobahn, an outstanding example of Alpine road construction, runs south to the Brenner to connect with the Italian Autostrada to Bolzano. Among its engineering achievements is the Bridge of Europe (Europabrücke), almost 600 feet high above the Sill Valley near Innsbruck, and the 6,000-foot-long Lueg Bridge shortly before the Brenner Pass; the Europabrücke is so called because it is the key passageway between the fast highway systems of northern, central and southern Europe.

Another supermodern mountain road is the Felbertauernstrasse, between East Tyrol and Mittersill in Land Salzburg, whose most outstanding feature is the 5-km. tunnel cutting through the main range of the Hohe Tauern at an elevation of 5,250 feet, while the gradient is never higher than 7 percent; this road is now the fastest link between Bavaria, northeastern Tyrol and Salzburg on one side and East Tyrol, Carinthia and northeastern Italy (Trieste, Venice) on the other side.

Among other roads offering exceptional vistas are: the Timmelsjoch road from Untergurgl in Upper Ötz Valley to the Timmelsjoch mountain pass (about 8,200 ft., 14 percent gradient) through magnificent mountain scenery; the scenic road along Achen Lake which leads to Germany and has shortened the driving time between Innsbruck and Munich to 1¾ hours; the Gerlos Pass road from the Ziller Valley to the Krimml Waterfalls and Mittersill in Salzburg province, also in beautiful mountain landscape (highest point about 5,350 ft., maximum gradient only 9 percent); Burgital Panorama Road from Nassereith north of Imst to Holzleitensattel in Mieminger Range.

Innsbruck—Center for Touring the Tyrol

The capital of the Tyrol is one of the most beautiful towns of its size in the world. This 700-year-old town (it received its municipal charter in 1239) undoubtedly owes much of its fame and charm to its unique situation. To the north, the steep, sheer sides of the mighty Alps of the Northern Chain rise like a shimmering blue and white wall from the edge of the city; an impressive and awe-inspiring background to the mellowed green domes and red roofs of the picturesque baroque town. To the south, the mountains of the Tuxer range form a series of drop-curtains ranging from 7,000 to 10,000 feet in height.

The charming old-world town, of 117,000 inhabitants, built largely in baroque style, has remained virtually intact. The old part of the town, though the skyline has suffered from the encircling highrises, is built on the right bank of the swift-flowing Inn, which delimits its northern and western boundaries. The railway line and the smaller Sill River run around the old town to the south and east. Beyond the rivers and the railway line lie the newer, modern parts of Innsbruck for the most part either factory sections or attractive residential districts, with tree-lined avenues and large, spacious gardens. For the tourist bent on sightseeing, Innsbruck is not an exhausting city to explore. It is only a half-hour walk from one end of the old town to the other. You cannot stray far if you remember not to cross the railway or the rivers.

Innsbruck (Inn Bridge) is first mentioned in history books as a trading post in the 12th century. Owing to its commanding position on the most important trade route over the Alps into Italy and Central Europe's principal outlet to the south over the famous Brenner Pass, Innsbruck grew rapidly and towards the middle of the 13th century became a full-fledged town. In the early 15th century, Duke Friedrich (popularly known as "Friedl with the empty pockets") transferred his official residence from Meran to Innsbruck, which thus became the capital of Tyrol. Many of the beautiful buildings in Innsbruck were built by the powerful Emperor Maximilian, who loved the Tyrol and its capital city; others by Austria's famous Empress Maria Theresa, who gave her name to the principal street of the town.

Exploring Innsbruck

Any sightseeing in Innsbruck should begin at Maria-Theresien-Strasse, which runs through the heart of the city from north to south, and is the main shopping center. Within the pedestrian zone, you can see four of Innsbruck's best known sights in the space of an hour.

The first of these is the world famous view from the Maria-Theresien-Strasse toward the Nordkette range of mountains. Stand halfway down the street and face north. You will get the best uninterrupted view from the left-hand side of the road.

The second is the Roman-style Triumphal Arch, that spans the Maria-Theresien-Strasse at the southern end of the short street, and was built in 1767 by Maria Theresa. The sculptured reliefs on the southern face commemorate the marriage of her son Leopold, Archduke of Tuscany, who later became Emperor Leopold II, to the Spanish Princess Maria Ludovica in 1765, and those on the northern side are a memorial to the sudden and tragic death of Franz the First, husband of Maria Theresa, both events occurring at the same time in Innsbruck's Hofburg castle.

The third is another monument erected by the Tyrol Diet, or council, in 1706 to commemorate the liberation of Tyrol from the Bavarian army of invaders which occupied the greater part of the province during the Wars of the Spanish Succession. This is the Annasäule (St. Anne's Col-

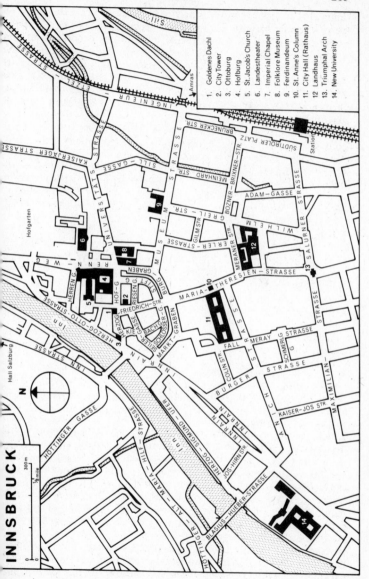

INNSBRUCK

1. Goldenes Dachl
2. City Tower
3. Ottoburg
4. Hofburg
5. St. Jacob's Church
6. Landestheater
7. Imperial Chapel
8. Folklore Museum
9. Ferdinandeum
10. St. Anne's Column
11. City Hall (Rathaus)
12 Landhaus
13. Triumphal Arch
14. New University

umn), halfway down the Maria-Theresien-Strasse in the center of the road, so called because the Tyrol was liberated on St. Anne's Day.

Next to the famous view of the Alps, Innsbruck is best remembered for that remarkable curiosity, the Goldenes Dachl (Golden Roof), which, together with the old town section surrounding it, is the fourth famous sight. To reach it, carry on past the Annasäule to the end of the Maria-Theresien-Strasse, and down the narrower Herzog-Friedrich-Strasse to the bottom, where this famous Innsbruck landmark faces you across the little square.

The shimmering golden roof covering the beautiful, ornate stone balcony is not really of gold, but is a mass of heavily gilded copper tiles. The ancient mansion was originally built as a residence for Duke Friedrich onto the back of the old Hofburg castle, and it is said that the indignant Duke had the original roof covered with costly golden tiles to give the lie to the belief that he was poor. In later days the famous balcony was used by the Emperor Maximilian and his guests as a kind of "Royal Box" from which to watch the performances of strolling players in the square below. The original building was altered and added to at the beginning of the 18th century, and only certain parts, notably the balcony and alcove below it, with the magnificent, finely-wrought coats of arms of Austria, Hungary, Burgundy, Milan, the Holy Roman Empire, Styria, Tyrol, and the Royal German emblem.

Restoration and revitalization of the old town in Innsbruck together with the repaving of the narrow lanes is transforming this lovely part.

Other Landmarks

The other sights you should not miss are the Hofburg palace, with the beautiful imperial park laid out in the English style, the Imperial (or Court) Church, with the tomb of the Emperor Maximilian, and the Silver Chapel adjoining it.

The Hofburg was originally built in the 15th century, but was later almost completely restyled and rebuilt by order of the Empress Maria Theresa in the latter half of the 18th century, and the original palace and the grounds were considerably enlarged. The banqueting rooms, especially the Giants' Hall, the paintings in the suite of reception rooms, and the elaborate furniture are of most interest.

The Hofkirche (Court Church) was built in 1553–63 solely as a great mausoleum for Emperor Maximilian I. At the beginning of the 18th century it was restyled in the baroque idiom. The emperor's cenotaph of grained marble is the largest Imperial Germanic tomb ever known to have been built. But the church and the tomb are entirely dominated by the heroic-sized armor-clad statues of the emperor's ancestors and notable kings and emperors of history, who guard the kneeling figure of the

Emperor Maximilian in bronze, a work of the Flemish master Alexander Colin of Mechlin. There are no less than 28 of them—14 to a side—some of them are ladies, all are in bronze except two, which are in copper. The legendary King Arthur of England is one of them, and another of the giants is Theoderich, the famous King of the Goths; both were sculptured by Albrecht Dürer. During those times Innsbruck was a great center of armor makers and this explains the elaborate armor suits of the statues. The remains of Emperor Maximilian, however, do not lie beneath the fabulous tomb. He is buried in the town of Wiener Neustadt, near Vienna.

The Silberne Kapelle (Silver Chapel), adjoining the Court Church, was built as a separate mausoleum in 1587 by Archduke Ferdinand (1529–95), the Regent of Tyrol, so that he might be buried beside his wife Philippine Welser, a commoner, albeit the daughter of the rich and powerful merchant family of Welsers; her cenotaph and the statue of Ferdinand were sculptured by Colin of Mechlin. The chapel owes its name to the silver altar figure of the Madonna.

Museums

The Museum Ferdinandeum, in the Museum-Strasse, has a magnificent picture gallery specializing in Gothic and baroque works by famous Tyrolean, German, Dutch, and Italian masters. But the most interesting part of the museum is the comprehensive industrial art collection of bronze, glass, enamel and iron. There is also a large collection of old coins and medieval arms. The Tiroler Volkskunstmuseum, next to the Imperial Chapel, has a very complete collection of local folk costumes and antique rustic furniture, as well as of old farm and artisan tools and utensils. Anyone interested in the dirndl and its many variations, and in old house interiors, will spend a happy hour here. There are several other museums, all of great interest, in the city.

Short Excursions

To visit Ambras Castle, a bus from the main Innsbruck station departs every half-hour for Ambras, a little village 30 minutes away. The magnificent castle, one of the finest and best preserved in Austria, was originally a Gothic castle built by the dukes of Andechs in the 11th century. It was rebuilt as a residence for the Archduke Ferdinand of Tyrol in the German Renaissance style, between 1564 and 1582. Of particular interest is the Spanish Hall, the earliest known large Renaissance council chamber on German soil, which was built in the year 1570. Unfortunately, the greater part of the archduke's personal collection of fine arts was transferred long ago to the Kunsthistorisches Museum in Vienna, but there is still a very large collection of pictures, weapons, armor, *objets d'art,* furniture, various ingenious household gadgets, and other curiosities dating from medieval times to be seen. The castle grounds are very beautiful and extensive and contain the original tilting grounds and a little cemetery set deep in the woods, where heroes of the War of Liberation were laid to rest.

There are three other short excursions outside the town you must make. Two of them are trips by cable railway up to the Hungerburg (2,800 feet) and from there right up to the Hafelekar. You can do both trips in one, taking the cogwheel railway up to the Hungerburg from the valley station directly inside the town itself, and then transferring to the Hafelekar two-stage cable car, which starts from the Hungerburg and soars right up to the dizzy height of 7,500 feet, with the second stage (change of cars) beginning at the intermediate station of Seegrube (6,248 feet). At all three stops, Hungerburg, Seegrube, and the Hafelekar terminus, there are hotels and restaurants commanding a wonderful view over the Tyrolean Alps with Innsbruck spread out at your feet.

If you are staying a few days in Innsbruck, you would enjoy the views better if you do not attempt more than one stage at a time. Start with the lower Hungerburg, and try a different altitude and perspective each day, enjoying a leisurely lunch at each halt.

The third excursion you should not miss is to Berg Isel, just outside the southern limits of the town near the Sill gorge. The Isel Hill is a large beautifully laid out park, a Field of Remembrance to soldiers of the famous Tiroler Kaiserjäger Regiment and to the Tyrolean fighters against the Napoleonic occupation and oppression. The hill became famous as the scene of several pitched battles fought during the war of Liberation in 1809, and there is a fine memorial to Andreas Hofer, leader and military commander during that war, and the national hero of Tyrol. Although Hofer defeated the French at the Battle of Bergisel, Austria had to cede this region to Napoleon at the peace treaty. Hofer continued to fight, however, using guerrilla tactics and the support of faithful Tyrolean mountaineers, until he was betrayed and shot in Mantua at the personal order of Napoleon. Seven years after the War of Liberation the hill became the rifle range of the Kaiserjäger, and became a Field of Remembrance at the end of the 19th century. Besides the striking statue of Andreas Hofer, the Provincial Cenotaph, the Tomb of the Unknown Soldier, and the little lookout tower should not be missed. The great charm of the Bergiselgrounds is that the memorials and buildings are spaced widely apart amid beautiful woods and lawns, so that the place in no way resembles a cemetery.

A fine attraction in the vicinity of Innsbruck is the Ehnbach-Klamm near Zirl (half-hour walk), where a romantic pathway was blasted through the rocks of a wild gorge.

Another excursion destination, particularly interesting for the un spoiled beauty of its mountain scenery, is Axamer Lizum which is 22 km away from the Olympic village in Innsbruck's Arzl-South district. Three chair lifts will take you to various elevations. Axamer Lizum came into the spotlight in 1964 as one of the sites of the IXth Winter Olympics and was again the site for all alpine events, except the men's downhill, in the XIIth Winter Olympics.

You will now have seen the most important landmarks and sights in Innsbruck, but the city is full of historical buildings, and the museums are veritable treasure chests of the arts.

Exploring the Environs of Innsbruck

Only a few kilometers by road up the steep hill behind Berg Isel is the village of Igls, perched a thousand feet above the city under the Patscher-kofel mountain. Igls is well known as a winter sports center and many visitors to Innsbruck prefer to make their headquarters here rather than down in the valley below in the city itself. In winter there are the obvious advantages of the skiing facilities, but in summer, too, Igls is a pleasant place, and there are frequent buses to Innsbruck, as well as a country-style tram.

In the hot summer months there is a small bathing lake, the Lanser See, at the edge of the plateau and about a kilometer from Igls, which lies well back at the foot of the Alps. But the real lure at Igls is the famous Patscherkofel cable-car railway, which runs from the village to the top of Patscherkofel mountain (6,600 feet) in less than 20 minutes. The view over the whole valley and the town of Innsbruck is just as fine as that seen from the Hafelekar station on the other side of the Inn valley, and serves to round off the tourist's bird's-eye impression of the magnificent panorama of the Alps.

There is also an intermediary station called Heiligwasser (Holy Water), which used to be a popular place of pilgrimage, and the spring water was—and still is—said to be the panacea for all kinds of complaints.

The third lift out of Innsbruck is a chair lift from near Mutters to the Stubai valley and the Mutterer Alm. Here also there is a fine view, although not the equal of the other two.

To the South: Stubaital and Wipptal

The delightful little Stubaital (Stubai Valley), less than 40 km. in length, is noted for its beautiful and striking mountain scenery. No less than 80 glistening glaciers and more than 40 towering Alpine peaks of over 10,000 feet have turned this valley into one of the showpieces of the Tyrol. Only 16 km. from the Tyrolean capital, the Stubai region is a popular summer center and offers splendid opportunities for mountain climbing and skiing on the glacier. In the winter, the valley is particularly favored by skiing parties wishing to make extensive tours along the glaciers and mountains of the Stubai Alps.

To see the whole of the Stubaital is a full day's excursion from Innsbruck. It is easily reached by car, bus, or on the narrow-gauge, single-line electric railway that serves the Stubai valley exclusively. Both the latter means of transport take different routes as far as Fulpmes, halfway up the valley and the terminus of the "Stubai valley railway," so it is a good plan to take the bus one way and return on the quaint little electric train, and you will see more of the beauties of the valley. Buses leave Innsbruck at regular intervals for the valley.

Fulpmes is noted for its historical play about Andreas Hofer and the war of liberation from the French in 1809. It attracts large crowds of tourists from Innsbruck and the neighboring summer resorts, and is quite entertaining even if you don't speak a word of German.

At Fulpmes a road branches off over the high plateau to the west to the little village of Schönberg (Lovely Hill), which guards the entrance to the Stubai valley. As its name implies, Schönberg is perched on a hill, and from the village you can enjoy a fine all-round view over the surrounding Stubai and Tuxer Alps. From Schönberg the road dips down into the Stubai valley to Mieders, less than an hour's run from Innsbruck. This is a tiny place with fewer than 90 houses.

After a longish stop at Fulpmes, the valley capital, the bus climbs up to Neustift, the old terminus. This is a good place to have lunch; the driver of the postal bus will be able to recommend the best place to patronize—he probably lunches there himself. From here the bus follows the narrow winding Alpine road into the Stubai Alps as far as Ranalt, which is just a collection of mountain farms at the foot of the great glaciers. The distance from Neustift to Ranalt is 13 km.; following a 1 in 10 climb immediately after leaving Neustift, the road ascends quite gently up through gorgeous Alpine scenery to the hamlet of Ranalt. The village is a popular starting point for mountaineers touring the glaciers crowned by the great craggy peak of the Zuckerhütl (Little Sugar Hat), a mountain nearly 12,000 feet high.

Returning to Fulpmes, the Stubai train will take you back to Innsbruck, climbing up to the high plateau at the entrance to the valley through Telfes (3,300 feet, the highest point reached by the train), then down to Mutters and Natters—where there is a little lake—and finally descending into the Inn valley at Innsbruck.

The valley of the Sill River is called Wipptal; it leads from Innsbruck to the Brenner Pass and over it into South Tyrol (now in Italy). The new autobahn crosses the valley near Innsbruck over the 600-foot high Bridge of Europe (Europabrücke) and continues along its western slopes to Brenner, while the main Munich–Innsbruck–Bozen–Verona–Rome railway line runs through the valley. There is a good bus service up to the Brenner. Although Wipptal can hardly be classed as one of the most beautiful in the Tyrol, the villages along its length are quite popular in summer, and in the wintertime cater for large numbers of winter sports enthusiasts.

Matrei is the first stop up the Wipptal. This is a well-cared-for village with typical Tyrolean-style, new-looking houses. Matrei was almost razed during World War II, and was completely re-built to harmonize, successfully, with the surroundings. Many houses are gaily decorated with multi-colored murals painted all over the outside walls. If you have a car, you can return to Innsbruck via Igls along the steep mountain backdoor road that gives you a marvelous view over the Tuxer Alps to the east, instead of by the rather dull road along the Sill.

You come next to Steinach at the foot of the Brenner Pass, a popular little resort in summer and winter, with an Alpine lake, swimming pool, and some excellent skiing slopes. The road for Gschnitztal, another small and romantic valley penetrating the Stubai range, branches off at Steinach.

After Steinach the road starts to climb steeply to Gries near the top of the pass, and parts company with the railway line that burrows through a series of tunnels into the Alps and toward the Italian frontier. Gries is a small winter sports center frequented mainly by Austrian tourists. Near Gries there are some interesting Roman remains, a reminder of the times when the road on which you are traveling was once the imperial military road from Rome to the North Sea. Shortly after passing the ruins you reach the top of the pass entering South Tyrol across the Austrian–Italian frontier.

To the Northwest: Seefeld and Scharnitz

One of the most delightful excursions from the Tyrolean capital is to travel along the length of the Karwendel railway. Starting at Innsbruck, the electric train leisurely winds in and out of the valleys and mountains, to and fro across the Austro-Bavarian border roughly in the shape of a huge letter S to Reutte, tucked away in the northwestern corner of the Tyrol. After leaving Innsbruck, the train first of all follows the Inn valley, then climbs steeply round the massive Solstein mountains, passing through several long tunnels and culverts until the line finally reaches the great Seefeld plateau on the edge of the Wetterstein range.

Seefeld, one of the Tyrol's most fashionable winter sports centers, is only 16 km. from Innsbruck. Ranking with Kitzbühel and St. Anton as far as hostelry and atmosphere are concerned, it concentrates on cross-country skiing and was the site of the competitions in this discipline during the Olympic Games.

In summer, too, Seefeld is a popular resort; it is a good base for exploring the countryside or visiting neighboring Bavaria, and is not far from Innsbruck. A remarkable feature of Seefeld is the little Wildmoos lake, which is apt to vanish suddenly, leaving a lush green meadow and a little bubbling spring to mark its location. At other times it is deep enough to swim in and, when available, is one of Seefeld's major summer-time attractions.

Dipping down the receding high ground of the plateau we come to Scharnitz, a little town on the Austro-Bavarian border. There is not much left to see of the Porta Claudia fortress nowadays, but during the Napoleonic Wars the Austrian garrison—oddly enough commanded by an English colonel, an ancestor of the poet Swinburne—successfully defied a large French army under Marshal Ney. Scharnitz is a center for summer walking tours into the Karwendel mountains and along the Isar valley.

Detour Around the Zugspitze

The electric railway then leaves Austria, traveling in a large semicircle through Garmisch-Partenkirchen, and round the mighty Zugspitze back, at Ehrwald, to Austrian territory again. Ehrwald is a winter and summer resort at the foot of the Wetterstein Alps, and the great attraction here is, of course, the famous Zugspitze. A short bus ride from the center of town takes you to Obermoos with the valley station of the Austrian aerial cable car to Zugspitze which reaches to the very top of this great mountain (about 9,800 ft.). From the summit there is a magnificent view over Austrian, Bavarian and part of the Swiss Alps. Zugspitze, which marks the Austrian-German border, is at the same time the highest mountain in Germany and its peak can be reached by cable car also from the German side.

Northwest of Ehrwald is Lermoos, in summer a health resort and in winter a popular winter sports center. Beyond, in the Lachtel Alps is Berwang, idyllic mountain village, winter and summer resort. Here you can be sure of fine powder snow from late autumn to late spring, and many skiing aces come here for serious training. 5 km. farther on is Heiterwang, another picturesque little village on a small Alpine lake.

In the center of the district known as the Ausserfern lies Reutte, a pleasant and convenient spot for a summer holiday. There are some very colorful houses with richly painted facades, and a small, interesting museum. You may swim in the three lakes in the vicinity. The largest lake, the Plansee, connected to the Heiterwang lake by a short canal, is nearly 6 km. long and is set in the heart of a beautiful forest. To the north of Reutte lies Vils, which has the distinction of being the Tyrol's smallest township, and the German frontier. To the west, over the Gaicht Pass, there are two more delightful little mountain lakes within easy bus ride of Reutte.

To the southwest of Reutte, the long, straggling Lech valley follows the course of the mountain stream across the Lech Alps right up to the mighty Arlberg and the provincial frontier of Vorarlberg. In summer this rather out-of-the-way Alpine valley is a favorite base for mountaineering enthusiasts.

Exploring the Lower Inn Region

To the east of Innsbruck the Inn valley broadens out considerably, and courses right through the Tyrol to Kufstein and the German border. Hall, a bare 8 km. from the Tyrolean capital, is very ancient, and was founded by miners from the nearby salt mines, which have now fallen into disuse. The picturesque old part of the town is built on a steep slope in the form of an amphitheater with narrow cobbled streets running straight down the hill. From the main road you cannot get a proper perspective of the fine old buildings. The old Rathaus, or town hall, was built in the middle of the 15th century and is a fine example of the architecture of those times. The ornately carved councillors' room should be seen, and also the beautifully worked mosaics which cover the Rathaus walls. The Mint Tower, which you can hardly miss, and the monastery church, the oldest ecclesiastical building of the Renaissance period to be found in the Tyrol, are all interesting examples of Tyrolean craftmanship.

Schwaz, on the right bank of the Inn, is even older than Hall and dates back to the 12th century. In the 15th century Schwaz was a rich and important mining center, whose chief sources of wealth were the silver mines burrowing deep under the towering Tuxer Alps. Many of the buildings built during those prosperous times still stand, and the market place is much as it used to look in olden times.

Jenbach, our next stop, and a main line station on the railway, is important to the tourist as the starting point for the Achen and Zillertal valleys, both very popular summer resorts.

A small cog-wheel railway takes passengers from the Jenbach railway station up the steep 1 in 4 gradient to Maurach near the head of the great Achensee lake. As the little train crawls jerkily up the Achen valley you get a magnificent view over the Alps to the right. Buses provide alternative means of transport from Jenbach, and travel all along the lake as far as the Achen Pass at the farther end of the 32 km.-long valley, stopping at the three or four lakeside summer resorts on the way. From Maurach you can take a cable car to Erfurter Hütte, a mountain lodge about 6,000 feet up in the Sonnwend mountain group.

The Achen Valley

Although you can have some excellent skiing in the Achen valley in the winter, the lake is the main attraction, and the whole valley is a very popular summer resort. The mountain lake, largest and most beautiful in the Tyrol, is nearly 10 km. long and a kilometer broad at the widest point. The great mountains of the Karwendel and Sonnwend ranges rise from its blue waters, nearly 450 feet deep in places. A small steamer plies between the different villages strung out along the lakeside, and is usually crowded with trippers at the height of the season. There is some excellent fishing in the lake and on the river, too, which flows out of the lake at the farther end and into Germany.

Pertisau, a small picturesque little village, the only one on the western shore of the lake, is the most popular place to go to, and less than a mile from the cogwheel railway terminus at the level of the lake. Located nearly 3,000 feet above sea level, Pertisau offers fair comfort, excellent bathing, sailing, tennis and fishing, and even boasts of a small nine hole golf course, all at budget prices.

On the eastern side of the lake, the road leads through Buchau to the northern end with various small settlements belonging to the commune of Achenkirch; Seehof is one of them and Scholastika another one. Although Pertisau and the western shore of the lake are more popular, the eastern side enjoys at least two hours of sunshine a day more, and the bathing is consequently warmer.

The drive, either by bus or in your own car, along Achenbach stream to the Bavarian border is very lovely. It passes through the village of Achenwald and you reach the Austrian-German frontier on the Achen Pass.

Because it lies so conveniently close to Innsbruck, 48 km. away, the lake is always crowded with weekend holidaymakers from the city during the hot summer months. If you only plan to pay a fleeting visit to the valley, you would do well to choose a weekday, and inspect the lake and its attractions at your leisure.

The Ziller Valley

On the other side of the Inn valley lies the Zillertal, biggest and most famous of the many beautiful valleys of Tyrol. You may be a little disappointed traveling along the lower reaches of the Zillertal. As far as Zell am Ziller the valley is broad and shallow, and the scenery is certainly not very inspiring. It is only from Zell onwards that the valley really starts to live up to its good name. On the way up the lower part of the valley you pass through the small Alpine villages of Fügen, Ried and Aschau, all pretty little places, and then you come to Zell am Ziller, the first of the tourist centers.

The Gauder Festival, the traditional Ziller valley May fête, takes place on the first weekend in May. Thousands of tourists from far and wide pack the little market town to watch the events, which are very colorful and most amusing. These festivals have been held at Zell for over 400 years, and the different events are based on ancient customs. Here, too, you can hear some of the best Ziller valley singing, and listen to some expert harp and zither playing. For the Ziller valley folk are famous throughout Austria for their prowess on these ancient instruments.

At Zell am Ziller the valley divides. The main valley goes straight on up to Mayrhofen, the most important resort in the valley, and to the Tuxer valley, while an offshoot climbs to the Gerlos plateau, a favorite winter sports resort, and a center for mountain climbing. The Ziller valley railway doesn't run up this branch of the valley, but buses and sleighs take passengers from Zell up to the plateau. The dominating feature at Gerlos, lying 4,000 feet above sea level, is the towering Kreuzjoch, nearly 9,000 feet high. Beyond Gerlos there is a scenic road leading over the Gerlos Pass to the village of Wald and Krimml waterfalls in the neighboring Land Salzburg.

The old Ziller steam railway sometimes makes scheduled runs between Jenbach and Mayrhofen, and can be rented—at a price—by steam-engine buffs. Mayrhofen is the main base for sightseeing tourists, and has been a favorite Tyrolean summer resort of the British for many a year. At Mayrhofen the Ziller valley splits up into four. Three of these are called gründe (grounds): the Zillergrund, Stillupgrund, and Zemmgrund. Each of these narrow, pretty little valleys striking deep into the heart of the Ziller Alps is a perfect gem, a prime example of the picture-postcard Alpine valley, rising near the top to the glittering pale blue glaciers.

The Tuxer Valley

The fourth arm leads into the Tuxer valley, highest of the four, which ends at the foot of the massive Olperer and Rifflerspitz glaciers, nearly 11,000 feet up. Frequent buses leave Mayrhofen for Lanersbach and Hintertux, the two villages in the valley. The view over the Tuxor Alps to the north is perhaps the finest of the whole.

Lanersbach is the first of these small mountain villages and at the top of the valley is Hintertux, right at the foot of the great glaciers that have made the Tuxer valley so famous a beauty spot and summer-skiing region. Nearly 5,000 feet above sea level, Hintertux is also quite popular as a spa, and has a small thermal swimming pool. Apart from the magnificent landscape that surrounds the mountain village, Hintertux is also the center of an ancient wood-carving industry.

The Rattenberg District

Back in the main Inn valley, we come to Brixlegg, with its two famous castles, Schloss Kropfsberg, built to defend the approaches to the Ziller valley, and Schloss Matzen, a 12th-century castle on the mountainside. Brixlegg stands at the entrance to the short Alpbach valley, whose main attraction is the lovely small town of Alpbach, a winter sports center, but a delightful place at any time of the year. Alpbach is also the setting for the annual Europäisches Forum Alpbach (European Forum).

Two miles farther along the Inn valley from Brixlegg is Rattenberg, a quaint little medieval town, once a famous mining town like Hall and Schwaz, and now reduced to a small place of less than 1,000 inhabitants. There are some very fine examples of Gothic architecture and the ruins of a powerful castle built by Emperor Maximilian I.

Rattenberg and Kramsach, across the Inn River, are known for fine glass workshops, owned by Sudeten German refugees from Czechoslovakia: in Kramsach there is also a school teaching the art of etching, engraving and painting on glassware—you can have your name or initials engraved on any glass within half an hour. Near Kramsach is the 17th-century Achenrain Castle with three small and charming lakes in the vicinity. Here is also the entrance to the short but lovely Brandenberg valley. About 8 km. up and high above the valley is the small village of Brandenberg, surrounded by beautiful woods.

We arrive next at Wörgl, a mainline junction, which is Austria's youngest township and a thriving market town. Here the main road and the railway divide. One route follows the Inn up to Kufstein and on to Bavaria, the other turns due east through Kaisergebirge and the Kitzbühel Alps to the famous skiing center of Kitzbühel. Just south of Wörgl is the Wildschönau district with the small skiing villages of Niederau, Oberau and Auffach, reached by a country road.

The Kufstein District

Like many other Austrian provincial towns Kufstein is dominated by a mighty castle. In this case it is the Geroldseck fortress, built by the Dukes of Bavaria in the 12th century on a spur of Kaisergebirge guarding the entrance to the Inn valley. It has withstood many sieges, and was later used as a political prison before becoming the town museum. Perhaps the most interesting feature of the fortress is the colossal "Heroes' Organ" built in one of the great towers. It is said that you can hear the organ quite clearly more than eight kilometers away on a windless day.

The great attraction at Kufstein during the hot summer months is the large number of warm water lakes in the immediate neighborhood. There are no less than eight of these. Some of them, like the Pfrillsee and

Längsee, are perched high up on the mountainside in the middle of dense forests. Others, like the Thiersee, are larger and in open country.

Thiersee is a picturesque mountain village on the lake of the same name, amidst magnificent Alpine scenery. The town is also known for its passion play, revived in 1955 and similar to that of Oberammergau in neighboring Bavaria. The passion play was started in the 17th century and still takes place from time to time in a special theater that seats 900. The play is acted by a village amateur group and non-villagers are not allowed to perform.

Up in the northwest corner, near the German border, is the village of Erl, whose ancient passion play was revived during the summer of 1959. One of the oldest of its kind in the Alpine regions, it traces its origins back to the religious plays first given there in the year 1613.

The Kitzbühel Alps

The main trunk road from Wörgl leads through the valley between the Kaiser and the Kitzbühel mountains via St. Johann in Tirol to Kitzbühel, one of the most famous winter sports centers in the world. Another road, not quite as good a surface, but considerably shorter, goes right over the Kitzbühel Alps through Hopfgarten and Kirchberg—both winter sports centers. Wheel chains are essential if you take this route while it is snowing, but for most of the year it is easily usable, clear and much less busy than the main road round through St. Johann.

Long before Kitzbühel became a fashionable winter sports resort, the picturesque little old-world town, set in the heart of the magnificent Kaiser and Kitzbühel Alpine ranges, was popular as a summer resort. In those days the main attractions were the unrivaled scenery and the attractive warm water lake of Schwarzsee just outside the town. Nowadays, of course, the accent is wholly on skiing. The town's facilities are among the finest in the world. The famous Kitzbühel Ski Circus is a carefully planned, clever combination of lifts, cable railways, and runs, beginning at the foot of the Hahnenkamm (valley station of the main cable railway) by which you can ski downhill for over 80 km. without having to climb a single foot on your own power.

Many famous people have their own villas near Kitzbühel, and the place is teeming with celebrities during December and again in February. If you want a day off there are frequent bus services to Salzburg through Germany, and the trip takes an hour each way. But there is always plenty to do and see in Kitzbühel: ski races, festivals, fancy dress balls, and plenty of local color. Kitzbühel also has quite a name as a health resort.

A few miles north of Kitzbühel is the far less fashionable winter sports town of St Johann in Tirol. Many sportsmen who cannot afford the luxury of actually living in Kitzbühel itself come here instead, enjoying the same skiing facilities as their better-off brothers.

High up in the Kitzbühel Alps, southeast of St Johann, a 15-minute bus run from St Johann station is another smaller winter sports center—Fieberbrunn, in our opinion one of the prettiest villages in this part of the Tyrol, set amid beautiful scenery, with plenty of snow and first-class skiing. Another small winter and summer resort easily reached from St Johann by bus is the village of Kössen near the German border. From Kössen you can take the bus also to Kufstein by the way of Walchsee, a beautiful lake among the mountains where all water sports are practised in the summer.

Exploring the Upper Inn Region

The Upper Inn valley from Innsbruck to the Swiss border is very beautiful, particularly the narrow mountain valleys which branch off to the south from the broad Inn up into the vast, glistening regions of the Stubai and Ötztal glaciers.

The first of these, and the shortest, the Sellrain, is only a few kilometers west of Innsbruck and is easily and rapidly reached by bus. At Zirl, the first town along the Upper Inn, the mountain road up to the high Seefeld plateau branches off over a steep mountain ridge to the north. Your Sellrain bus, though, crosses the Inn to Kematen, a small village at the entrance to the Sellrain valley, and then runs along the lovely Melach gorge to the villages of Sellrain and Gries in Sellrain. Both these places are popular skiing centers during the winter months, and are chiefly patronized by the city dwellers from nearby Innsbruck. In the summer the villages are starting points for extensive tours into the Stubai glaciers. At its end the valley climbs up to the mountain plateau at Kühtai with the renowned hunting castle of Emperor Maximilian I, converted into a hotel. Kühtai is a high summer and winter resort and at the same time a pass; the road continues from here down into the Ötz valley.

The 16-km. stretch of road from Zirl to Telfs is not very interesting to tourists. If you are traveling by car, you will find the old country road running along the southern bank of the Inn rather more diverting than the newer arterial highway which hugs the mountain cliffs all the way. Telfs, like Zirl, is another typical Inn valley market town. Traveling westwards from Telfs by car you have two choices. You can continue down the main road along the Inn or turn off towards the Mieminger plateau to Nassereith, then south to Imst where you rejoin the highway.

If you have the time to spare, the short extra trip is well worth while. From the top of the plateau, at Barwies, you have a magnificent view down over the Inn valley on your left, and to the right over the Wetterstein massif which you will miss by keeping to the Inn. If you are going to Reutte from Innsbruck by car and not via the Karwendel railway, this is the route to take. At Nassereith the road to Lermoos and Reutte branches off and climbs steeply out of the village and over the Fern Pass. The village of Nassereith is best known for its procession of grotesque masks which takes place every five years at Fasching and which has its origin in old pagan customs.

Following the main road from Telfs you pass by the village of Stams with its 13th-century Cistercian abbey. If you are interested in architecture you will most certainly want to visit it. The monastery church, originally Romanesque, has been rebuilt several times and presently is one of the largest baroque churches in Tyrol; the interior is by various masters, including Feichtmayr and Vischer. The monastery building has also been rebuilt several times, the present baroque structure dating from the early 18th century. It is now known as the "Schigymnasium", being a boarding school for would-be ski racers.

Imst, a thriving little market town, lying a kilometer or so back from the Inn River and the railway line, is an excellent center to choose for a summer holiday and base from which to visit the famous Pitz and Ötz valleys. Here is held the Schemenlaufen, another renowned masked Fasching procession. Many of the magnificently carved masks worn by the mummers—especially those of the fearsome witches—are very old and are works of art. Good specimens of these masks can be seen in the Imst museum. A great feature of these rustic carnivals is the ringing of cow bells of all shapes, sizes, and tones, and the resulting noise is quite deafening when the procession gets into its stride.

A bus from Imst will take you into the Pitz Valley, whose entrance is directly opposite Imst, across the Inn. The road rises steeply and abruptly to Arzl, a pleasant mountain village for a restful vacation.

The Ötz Valley

The Ötz Valley begins 11 kilometers (about 7 miles) east of Imst and rises in a series of great natural steps for nearly 42 km., from the Inn river to the glaciers around Obergurgl, nearly 6,400 feet above sea level.

At the head of the first stop is Ötz, a typical Tyrolean mountain village with an interesting old Gothic parish church. A kilometer farther on you pass through the tiny hamlet of Habichen; up another step to Umhausen, the oldest, and Längenfeld, the largest, village in the valley. Near Umhausen is the wild Stuiben waterfall.

We now come to Sölden, the first of the famous villages in the valley. Sölden (4,460 feet) is a winter sports center with an international reputation. The natural skiing facilities are extremely good, and by taking the chair lift up to Hochsölden (6,800 feet) you can be sure of excellent snow conditions for all the year. Hochsölden, by the way, is in no sense of the word a village, but merely the terminus of the chair lift graced by a collection of sports hotels. A modern cable car takes you from Sölden over the glaciers to an elevation of almost 10,000 feet on Gaislachkogel, to the permanent snow area where skiing is done all year; this is the highest cable car in Austria.

Tiny Obergurgl is famous for three things: it is the highest village in Austria (6,320 feet), it is the place where Professor Piccard landed in his famous balloon, and it is a magnificent winter sports district. A vast expanse of snow and ice shimmers all around you during the winter, and all year round the great peaks and glaciers of the Ötztal Alps appear to be deceptively close at hand. A high Alpine road takes you from Obergurgl to the hotel settlement of Hochgurgl (over 7,000 ft.), an excellent skiing spot, and farther up to the Timmelsjoch pass (about 8,200 ft.) through magnificent mountain scenery. From Hochgurgl, a three-stage chair lift, running up to about 10,000 feet, takes you to an area where skiing is possible all year round.

The Venter Valley burrows even deeper into the Ötztal Alps, and finally ends at Vent, a small Alpine village, lying a mere hundred feet lower than Obergurgl. It, too, is a popular winter sports center. During the summer it becomes the base for serious mountain climbers, experienced in ice and rock climbing, who wish to attempt to scale— preferably with professional local guides—the formidable Wildspitze (12,450 ft.) or other, even more difficult, neighboring peaks.

Landeck

24 km. farther west along the main Inn valley from Imst we come to Landeck, the largest and, perhaps, the least attractive town on the Upper Inn. Although the town has not the same charming atmosphere as Imst, it is a popular tourist center during the summer months, and is a convenient base from which to explore the nearby Paznaun Valley and the final stretch of the Inn Valley.

Landeck is famous for an ancient and awe-inspiring rite which takes place around Christmas time each year. At dawn the young men of Landeck set out to climb to the top of the great rocky crags that overshadow and hem in the old city on three sides. As dusk falls they light huge bonfires which can be seen for miles around, and then set fire to great discs of pinewood dipped in tar which they roll down to the valley below. The sight of scores of these enormous fiery wheels bounding down the steep slopes towards the town is a fearsome spectacle, and the more daring young bloods, clutching blazing torches and yelling at the top of their voices, race down the mountainsides on skis at breakneck speed in an attempt to beat the firebrands to the bottom of the valley.

At Landeck the river Inn turns southward along the edge of the Silvretta mountains toward Engadin in Switzerland and South Tyrol in Italy. Ried is a small village where you turn off to the west up a small precipice to Ladis, and higher up (about 4,500 ft.) Bad Obladis on the

Samnaun range, with a wonderful view over the Inn valley and down to Landeck, with the Lech Alps in the far distance.

On the same side above the Inn valley, also perched up high on the plateau, is Serfaus (4,700 ft.), an old village with interesting painted houses, a 14th-century and a baroque church; it is also reached by a branch road from Ried. Serfaus is an important winter sports center with a good number of ski lifts and the Komperdell cable car will take you also in summer up to an elevation of 6,500 feet from where you can take several interesting mountain tours or just enjoy the view.

At the head of the Inn valley, where the Austrian, Swiss and Italian frontiers meet, is Nauders, an unpretentious but delightful little winter sports center, dominated by the striking 14th-century Castle of Naudersberg. Due west of Nauders, up a steep pass to Martinsbruck, you reach the Swiss frontier post and the entrance to the Engadine. Carry straight on through Nauders for 5 km. and you are in South Tyrol, in Italy. Nauders is a good place to stay overnight if you are driving to or from Italy.

The Paznaun Valley

Another interesting valley tour, easily undertaken from Landeck by bus, is up the enchanting Paznaun valley running southwest from the village of Pians, a kilometer to the west of Landeck. This valley follows the course of the Trisanna mountain river for 40 km. into the heart of the Blue Silvretta mountains, so called because of the shimmering ice-blue effect of great peaks and glaciers, dominated by the mighty Fluchthorn at the head of the valley at Galtür.

At Ischgl the biggest village of the Paznaun, lying just over halfway up the valley, you will find excellent skiing, particularly in the small Fimber valley, which branches off the Paznaun at this point. In summer 4,500-feet Ischgl is the popular high altitude health resort. The almost 4-km.-long Silvretta cable car takes you even higher, to 7,600-ft. Idalpe.

Galtür, 700 feet higher, at the top of the valley road, a two-hour bus ride from Landeck, is the best-known resort in the Paznaun, equally popular as a winter sports center, summer resort, and as a base for mountain climbing. Although well known as a base for hardened, practised mountaineers, many of the climbs up the Blue Silvretta to the half dozen mountain rest huts belonging to the Alpenverein are very easy.

The Arlberg

Between the entrance to the computer-controlled Arlberg road tunnel, Europe's third-longest, and the railway, from which the "Arlberg Express" takes its name, at the foot of the great mountain pass, lies St.

Anton am Arlberg, to use the town's proper title, one of the most famous winter sports centers in the world and the cradle of modern skiing.

It was to this small and—at that time—unpretentious little Alpine valley town that Hannes Schneider, an unknown young ski instructor with advanced ideas, came to teach his now world famous "Arlberg School" skiing technique at the invitation of the newly founded Arlberg Ski Club. Although there have been many important modifications— notably by other Austrian instructors—to the "Arlberg technique" as originally taught by Hannes Schneider just after the turn of the century, the basic features of all skiing courses the world over are based on the fundamentals laid down by him.

At the height of the season, the little town with a population of fewer than 1,600 inhabitants, is seething with visitors. Many prominent people in public life, including royalty, come regularly every year to St. Anton for the winter sports.

The Skihaserl or ski bunny, as the beginner is referred to, will join the ski school. The nursery slopes are good at St. Anton and you will have plenty of company, often very distinguished company. Once you are past the Skihaserl stage—this may well take more than a season—you will want to get up into the Arlberg mountains and enjoy the superlative runs from the top of the Galzig and the Valluga above it. The summit of Valuga (over 9,200 ft.) reached by aerial cable car, offers also in summer a splendid view over the Alps.

Two kilometers higher up is the hamlet of St. Christoph, where a hospice was founded as early as the 15th century to succour stranded and imperiled travelers caught by snowdrifts on the pass. St. Christoph is another important, but much smaller, winter sports center, and it is here that the Austrian government holds its severe and exacting courses for would-be ski instructors.

While at St. Christoph there is not the same social round as at St. Anton, the skiing facilities are exactly the same, and are nearer to hand. In some respects, especially if you are determined to take your skiing seriously and willing to forego the distractions of high life (or cannot afford them), winter sports are more fun at St. Christoph.

East Tyrol

The present-day Austrian Federal State of Tyrol is roughly rectangular in shape, with East Tyrol tacked on to the southeastern corner like an appendix. The state is one great mass of mountains, scarred by scores of Alpine valleys, some large, but mostly small and narrow, winding in and out of the great ranges of the Alps.

The isolated position of East Tyrol is one of those strange historical accidents. In 1918, after World War I, South Tyrol was ceded to Italy. This left East Tyrol completely cut off from the rest of the Tyrol by a narrow upthrust of Italy which joins the border of Land Salzburg. East Tyrol, although separated, is an integral part, for administrative purposes, of Tyrol proper.

Geographically, therefore, to the west and south of East Tyrol runs the Italian frontier, while to the north stretches a massive, impassable barrier of the Alps, the Venediger and Glockner groups of Hohe Tauern. Except for the new Felbertauern Road and for the Drau Valley running to Carinthia, these mountains now separate it from the rest of Austria and, consequently, East Tyrol has been neglected by the international tourist in spite of magnificent mountain scenery.

Exploring East Tyrol

To reach East Tyrol from inside Austria, there is a railway coming from Carinthia that enters East Tyrol at Dölsach proceeding through Lienz and Sillian to South Tyrol (now in Italy), and from there to Innsbruck. The so-called corridor trains (cars locked while in transit through Italian territory, but without passport and customs control) operate between Innsbruck and Lienz (about four hours by autorail; connections are often bad).

To enter by car you must either travel over the Felbertauern alpine road, the only link with North Tyrol through Austrian territory, or from Carinthia. From Land Salzburg, you can take also the celebrated Grossglockner mountain road, whose Carinthian section will bring you to the Iselsberg Pass. Each of these routes will bring you directly to Lienz, capital of East Tyrol.

A town with more than 11,000 inhabitants, it is a summer resort, a center for mountain climbers, and an up-and-coming winter sports headquarters. The 16th-century Lieburg castle-palace on the main square is presently the seat of the local district government. The most interesting sights in the 15th-century parish church include four late Gothic winged altars, frescos by Josef Adam Mölk, and late Gothic tombs. Near the church is the district war memorial with chapel frescos by the famous Tyrolean painter Albin Egger-Lienz, who, as his name implies, was from Lienz, and who is also buried here.

Just outside the market town there is a small bathing lake at Tristach with a little Lido. The old battlemented Castle of Schloss Bruck, at the entrance to the Isel valley, a kilometer and a half outside the town, should not be missed. In the old days it used to be the seat of the Counts of Görz (now called Gorizia and located in Italy), and today it houses a very interesting museum with finds from the nearby Roman excavations, folklore collections, and paintings by Egger-Lienz and Franz Defregger, another Tyrolean painter. The castle was first built in the 13th century and then rebuilt in the 16th century. It is remarkably well preserved and its most outstanding features are the tower and the Romanesque chapel with late 15th-century frescos. Another point of interest are the excavations of the Roman town of Aguntum, between Nussdorf and Dölsach, less than 5 km. from Lienz. Before the Roman times Aguntum was a Hallstatt-period market town.

Lienz owes its importance as a town to the fact that it stands at the junction of three valleys. The Isel valley to the northwest, the main Drau valley to the east, and Pustertal to the west. The East Tyrolean section of Pustertal is also the valley of Drau River, but the long Puster valley crosses the Austro-Italian border and continuing through South Tyrol (while retaining the name of Pustertal) becomes the valley of the River Rienz and ends near the town of Brixen in South Tyrol. The Drau River crosses into Carinthia less than 16 km. below Lienz, but the Isel and its tributaries cover most of the East Tyrol north of Drau.

The section of Pustertal to the Italian frontier at Toblach is not very exciting. To the south of the road you get a magnificent view over the Lienz Dolomites, and the road and railway finally reach the village of Sillian, the highest in this valley, and just before the frontier. Near Sillian is the 13th-century Heimfels Castle, also once owned by the Counts of Görz; although it is slowly decaying it is still a powerful sight, and if you are at all romantically inclined, very much worth roaming through its walls and courtyards.

From Sillian you'll have to turn back to Lienz unless you want to cross the frontier of Italy and visit South Tyrol. North of Lienz, at the confluence of the Virgen and Tauern valleys, is Matrei, quite frequented as a summer resort. It has a late baroque parish church built by Hagenauer; nearby is the old but remodeled Weissenstein Castle and the 13th-century Nikolauskirche (St. Nicholas Church) with Romanesque frescos from the early 13th century, among the oldest preserved in Austria. Matrei is a mountain climbing center. If you do not wish to engage in this somewhat strenuous activity you may take the bus to Matreier Tauernhaus, almost 5,000 feet up in the Tauern valley, in order to enjoy the spectacular landscape of the Venediger range. If you drive, you can also reach this area by the new smooth and fast Felbertauern road amidst spectacular mountain scenery.

Retracing our steps back towards Lienz we come to a point where the Isel, Defereggen, and Kalser valleys meet. At the end of Kalser valley, deep under the pyramidal peak of Grossglockner, is the mountain village of Kals, one of the top mountain climbing centers in Austria. If you don't feel like climbing Grossglockner from this side, a walk into the nearby Lesach valley, up to the Lesacher Alpe, will reward you with beautiful mountain scenery and the absence of modern mechanical contraptions. Defereggen valley, a deep cut in the Defereggen Alps, is dotted with unspoiled villages, and St. Jakob in Defereggen, near its upper end, a small summer and winter resort, is one of the nicest mountain villages in East Tyrol.

If you drive (or ride on a bus) from Lienz to the Grossglockner mountain road, you have to cross the Iselsberg pass on the border of East Tyrol and Carinthia. From Iselsberg, a summer resort and winter sports center, there is a most magnificent view of the Lienz Dolomites.

There is a game reserve located between Oberassling and Bichl, 4,000 ft. up in the mountains, stocked with indigenous animals including chamois, wild boar and the golden eagle. Visitors are welcome and there is a car park and restaurant.

PRACTICAL INFORMATION

HOTELS AND RESTAURANTS
ACHENKIRCH At the north end of Achensee. **Hotels** *Post* (2), 60 rooms. All (3)—*Achenseehof,* 36 rooms, tennis court; lake. *Achentalerhof,* 31 rooms; *Imhof,* 26 rooms, all with private facilities, boats for hire.
Winter campsite for ski-campers.
See also **Pertisau.**

ALPBACH 3,200 ft., with skiing terrain up to 6,000 ft.
Hotels Both (2)—*Alpbacher Hof,* 33 rooms; *Böglerhof,* 54 rooms; both with indoor and outdoor pools.
All (3)—*Angelika,* 16 rooms; *Elisabeth,* 12 rooms; *Post,* 50 rooms, 18 baths.

ARZL In Pitz Valley, 10-minute bus ride from fast train stop Imst-Pitztal.
Hotel *Post* (3), 60 rooms, 37 baths, restaurant and wine tavern, Tyrolean interiors, heated swimming pool.

AXAMER LIZUM 4,800 ft., with skiing terrain up to 7,700 ft.
Hotels *Lizumerhof* (2), 28 rooms, 22 baths, sauna; *Kapferer* (3), 18 rooms, 6 showers.

BERWANG 4,382 ft., in the Zugspitze area. Bus service from Bichlbach on Innsbruck–Garmisch–Reutte railway line.
Hotels All (2)—*Singer,* the best, 50 rooms, excellent restaurant, sun terrace; *Alpenstern,* 49 rooms; *Berwanger Hof,* 90 rooms, 20 baths, indoor pool.
All (3)—*Alpenhof, Bergheim, Edelweiss,* and some 30 Gasthöfe and pensions.

BRIXLEGG Hotels *Brixleggerhof* and *Mehrnerhof,* indoor pool (3).

EHRWALD 3,267 ft. On Innsbruck–Garmisch–Reutte railway. Cable car to Austrian side of the Zugspitze (8,676 ft.).
Hotels Both (2)—*Alpenhof,* 53 rooms, 30 showers; *Alpenhotel-Tiroler Zugspitzbahn,* 50 rooms.
Both (3)—*Daniela;* and *Sonnenspitze,* rooms with bath higher price.
Many more inexpensive inns and pensions.
Ehrwald-Obermoos winter caravan site.

ELLMAU 2,500 ft., at the foot of Wilder Kaiser Mountain.

Hotels *Bär* (L), 56 rooms, indoor pool, sauna, best food in Tyrol.

All (2)—*Alpenhof*, 20 rooms; *Berghof*, 105 rooms; *Hochfilzer*, 60 rooms, 43 showers; *Sojer*, 27 rooms; *Sporthotel*, 60 rooms, 20 baths.

All (3)—*Alpenland*, 35 rooms; *Kaiserblick*, 60 rooms, 40 baths; *Post*, 50 rooms, 40 baths.

FIEBERBRUNN 2,500 ft., with skiing terrain up to 5,400 ft.

Hotels *Brunnhof* (2), sauna and restaurant. *Schlosshotel Rosenegg* (2), 60 rooms/bath, fine restaurant.

Many inexpensive inns and pensions.

FULPMES Main ski and sports area in the Stubaital (3,075 ft.).

Hotels All (2)—*Alphof*, 20 rooms; *Auenhof*, 27 rooms; *Cristall*, 25 rooms, indoor pool; *Hupfauf*, 30 rooms, indoor and outdoor pools; *Sporthotel Brugger*, 24 rooms, sauna; *Waldhof*, 30 rooms.

All (3)—*Alpenrose*, 33 rooms; *Atzinger*, 30 rooms; *Helzmeister*, 32 rooms; *Tirolerhof*, 31 rooms.

GALTÜR 5,200 ft. Bus service from Landeck, fast-train stop on Arlberg Express route.

Hotels All (2)—*Ballunspitze*, 43 rooms; *Berghaus Franz Lorenz*, 23 rooms; *Fluchthorn*, 50 rooms.

All (3)—*Alpenrose*, 40 rooms, most with bath; *Paznauerhof*, 30 rooms; *Wirlerhof*, 36 rooms.

GERLOS 4,070 ft. Bus service from Zell am Ziller.

Hotels *Gaspingerhof* (2), 80 rooms, 35 baths, indoor pool, tennis.

All (3)—*Glockenstuhl; Jägerhof; Hubertushof;* and 40 Gasthöfe and pensions.

HOCHGURGL 7,053 ft., situated above Obergurgl, can be reached by the Timmelsjoch High Alpine road.

Hotels *Gotthard* (1), 32 rooms, 2 pools.

All (2)—*Angerer Alm*, 45 rooms, indoor pool, sauna; *Hochgurgl*, 68 rooms; *Hochland*, 49 rooms; *Ideal*, 40 rooms; *Laurin*, 34 rooms.

HOCHSÖLDEN In the Ötztal Valley.

Hotels All (2), full board only—*Alpenfriede*, 60 rooms, 40 showers; *Edelweiss*, 30 rooms, indoor pool and sauna; *Enzian*, 52 rooms; *Schöne Aussicht*, 40 rooms.

HOPFGARTEN 2,200 ft., in the Brixental, on Innsbruck—Salzburg rail line.

Hotels Best is *Sporthotel* (2), 28 rooms. Also some 25 Gasthöfe and pensions.

IGLS Can be reached from Innsbruck by frequent bus service (6 km.) or streetcar (8 km.) or private car, parking facilities available.

The modern *Kurhaus*, with large air-conditioned hall, scheduled concerts and Tyrolean shows, buffet bar, facilities for bowling, table tennis, target shooting.

Hotels Some Igls hotels, like Innsbruck hotels, offer various reductions, special winter 6-day half-board package deals with reductions on cable cars and ski lifts, or for summer visitors who book in advance and stay at least 2 nights, a Guest Card entitling reductions on cable cars, museums, golf and tennis.

Schlosshotel Igls, with indoor and outdoor pools, sauna, is deluxe.

All (1)—*Parkhotel,* 54 rooms; *Sporthotel,* 80 rooms; *Waldhotel,* 20 rooms.

All (2)—*Agidihof,* 25 rooms; *Alpenhof,* 38 rooms; *Astoria,* 18 rooms, indoor pool; *Batzenhäusl,* 21 rooms; *Bonalpina,* 66 rooms, indoor pool; *Romerhof,* 18 rooms. Apartment hotels *Bellevue, Chalet and Quellengrund.*

All (3)—*Tirolerhof,* apartment hotel; *Gruberhof,* 25 rooms; *Romedihof,* 20 rooms; *Villa Juliana,* highly recommended guest house.

IMST Hotels All (2)—*Eggerbräu,* 62 rooms; *Post,* 45 rooms, 22 baths, indoor pool; *Stern,* 48 rooms, 25 baths, outdoor pool; *Wolf,* 15 rooms. Higher up, at about 4,000 ft., *Linserhof,* 42 rooms, 32 baths; *Terrassenhotel Linser,* 30 rooms; both with pools.

INNSBRUCK Hotels The main station is centrally located, and most of the main hotels are within easy reach. You are advised to book your rooms well in advance for the high season (July to Aug. and in the winter). However, if you arrive without having booked, inquire at the rooms reservation office in the railway station: they will find you accommodation, either in a small hotel or a private house.

Special winter 6-day half-board package deals are generally offered by Innsbruck hotels of all categories at much lower than regular rates; guests choosing this arrangement also enjoy a 20% reduction on cable cars and ski lifts. Similar low rates are granted to summer visitors who book in advance and stay at least 2 nights; in addition, they receive a Guest Card entitling them to reductions on cable cars, in museums, the Alpenzoo, golf, tennis and horseback riding.

Deluxe (L)

Europa, Südtirolerplatz 2, 130 rooms, fine restaurant, central, traditional atmosphere.

Holiday Inn, Salurnerstr. 15, 194 airconditioned rooms, indoor pool, garage, bar. Good food in the Maximilian Grill.

Innsbruck, Innrain 3, 56 airconditioned rooms, pool.

First Class (1)

Alpenmotel, Kranebitter Allee 88, 70 rooms, pool, suitable for motorists.

Central, Erlerstr. 11, 85 rooms, most with bath, pool.

Goldener Adler, Herzog-Friedrichstr. 6, founded in 1390, in the heart of the old town, where dukes and princes of yore stayed, sometimes with their mistresses and sometimes with their wives. In later years it was popular with Goethe and Andreas Hofer, now its 37 rooms are snapped up by seekers of atmosphere.

Grauer Bär, Universitätsstr. 5, 175 rooms, many with bath.

Maria Theresia, Maria Theresienstr. 31, 84 rooms, old tradition but renovated, underground garage.

Roter Adler, Seilergasse 4–6, 57 rooms.

Moderate (2)

Clima Hotel, Zeughausg. 7, 51 rooms.

Defregger, Defreggerstr. 13, 35 rooms.

Greif, Leopoldstr. 3, 66 rooms.

Happ, Philipinne Welser Str. 96, 45 rooms, most with bath.

Mozart, Müllerstr. 15, 50 rooms, most with showers, bed and breakfast.

Penz, Fürstenweg 183, 25 rooms.

Royal, Innrain 16, 23 rooms.

Sailer, Adamg. 8, 70 rooms, 30 showers.

Schwarzer Adler, Kaiserjägerstr. 2, 20 rooms, pleasant Tiroler Stuben restaurant.

Union, Adamg. 2, 60 rooms, bed and breakfast.

Villa Blanka, Weiherburgstr, 8, near Alpenzoo, 19 rooms.

Inexpensive (3)

Gasthof Koreth, 19 rooms.

Goldene Rose, Herzog Friedrich Str. 39, 30 rooms, half with bath.

Goldener Stern, Innstr. 39, 120 rooms, half with shower.

Golf, Höttinger Au 41A, across the river in Hötting suburb, 11 rooms, indoor pool, bed and breakfast.

Internationales Studentenhaus, Innrain 64, 300 rooms, no private showers, July through September.

Weisses Kreuz, Herzog Friedrich Str. 31, 26 rooms, half with shower.

Pensions

Budget tourists can obtain bed and breakfast terms at a number of simple, clean pensions, such as *Elisabeth,* Elisabethstr. 2, near the Hungerburg funicular, 17 rooms; *Stoi,* Südtiroler Platz 4, at the main railway station, 20 rooms, no private showers.

Campsites at Gasthof Seewirt in Amras (also winter camping), and Innsbruck-West near Gasthof Kranebitten.

Suburbs

You may not wish to stay directly in the town. Many visitors prefer the Hungerburg Plateau, on the top of a hill 3,000 ft. above sea level, and overlooking the town, or one of the hotels and inns perched still higher up on the Nordkette chain, both reached by funicular, the latter journey taking ½ hour. If you choose to lodge on the Hungerburg Plateau or in one of the lofty eyries 6–7,000 ft. up, you will have invigorating mountain air and a wonderful view over the Alps with Innsbruck spread at your feet.

On the Hungerburg Plateau, near the cable car station, *Bellevue* (2), 52 rooms, indoor pool; *Mariabrunn* (2), 30 rooms; both with terrace café-restaurants.

Pensions: *Alpenhof, Alpina, Hungerburg, Klamm, Zur Linde;* all small, most rooms with shower; all (3).

Much higher up the mountain you come to the *Berghotel Hafelekar* (3), a small (8 beds) mountain hotel at an elevation of over 7,500 ft.

Between the Plateau and the Hafelekar at 6,248 ft. is a pleasant hotel called the *Seegrube* (3), 20 beds, the view is excellent.

One word of caution. If you settle on one of the latter remember that the frequent commuting to Innsbruck will add considerably to your expenses.

RESTAURANTS. Once you have settled on your hotel, the next question is where to eat. All the hotels, of course, serve meals, the bigger hotels provide some of the best food in Innsbruck. But there are a number of excellent restaurants. The top gastronomic event is the Tyrolean Culinary Week, scheduled during the Innsbruck Fair in early fall, with the best restaurants in Innsbruck and in environs offering special gourmet fare—look for the letter "G" at the restaurant entrance; as with similar events elsewhere in Austria this one is organized by the *Bund Österreichischer Gastlichkeit.*

Belle Epoque (1), Mariahilfst. 6, next to the bridge. Beautiful old building on the river, excellent food and good value for money.

Domstuben (1), behind the Golden Roof. Delightful, intimate and sophisticated.

Kapeller (1), Phil. Welserstr. 96. Imaginative Tyrolean cuisine in delightful surroundings.

Moderate (2)

For a meal amid Tyrolean surroundings, try a little Gasthaus half-way down the Maria Theresienstr., the *Alt Innsprugg,* the old way of spelling Innsbruck, which is about as old as its name. Here you will sit on highly polished wooden seats—rather hard ones—in a Tyrolean *Bauernstube* and eat generous portions of hearty local specialties.

Ottoburg, Herzog-Friedrichstr. 1, near Goldenes Dachl, is a favorite among the establishments that remain mainly eating places during the day and become mainly wine taverns late in the evening. Built in 1234, it is a tower-like structure where there are many snug, intimate rooms in distinctive Tyrolean style, 2 or more on each of the 3 or 4 stories and each named after one of the Tyrol's famous men, some with music and some without. The same hearty fare and excellent red wines from South Tyrol are served in all of them.

Happ, beside the Golden Roof. Friendly.

Altes Haus Delevo, Maria-Theresienstr. 9, built by Johann Ignaz De Levo in 1736, has beer cellar, ground floor and first floor rooms with music in the evenings. Tyrolean specialties and atmosphere.

Churrasco, with a beautiful garden-terrace overlooking the River Inn, with Italian specialties.

Goldenes Dachl, Hofgasse 1, next to House with the Golden Roof.

Restaurant-Café Villa Blanca, in a quiet hilly position not far from the Alpenzoo, fine view, part of the hotel of the same name.

Schwarzer Adler, Kaiserjägerstr. 2, very good Tyrolean cuisine.

Inexpensive (3)

Stiegl-Bräu, Wilhelm-Greilstr. 25, with a pleasant garden, an atmospheric establishment with typical Tyrolean dishes.

Cafés and Pastry Shops

Munding, Kiebachgasse 16, in the oldest part of the town, has been making pastries for over 100 years.

Central (see Hotels), is a large, Viennese-style café.

Under the old-city arcades, *Café Stuben-Lamprechter* is particularly pleasant.

Schindler, Maria-Theresienstr., is elegant.

Erhart, Museumstr. 10, is small and simple but it serves very good pastries.

From the terrace of *Stadtsaal Café* at Rennweg, you enjoy a magnificent view of the Nordkette mountains.

ISCHGL 4,500 ft. Bus service from Landeck.

Hotels *Madlein* (1), 90 beds in woodpaneled rooms, most with baths, has indoor pool, best.

Both (2)—*Ischglerhof;* and *Post,* indoor pool.

ISELSBERG 3,960 ft. Bus service from Lienz.

Hotels On top or near top of the pass, all (2)—*Defreggerhof,* indoor pool, good restaurant; *Wacht,* and *Gasthof Dolomitenblick,* about two-thirds up the Tyrolean side, marvelous view of the Lienzer Dolomites. All these in chalet style, with balconies and terraces, in scenic locations.

ITTER Hotel *Schloss Itter* (1), hotel in 10th-century castle, swimming pool, sauna, open mid-Dec. to Oct.

KALS AM GROSSGLOCKNER 4,350 ft., reached by bus or car from Huben.

Hotels All (3)—A dozen or so good hostelries in Kals and the surrounding hamlets, among them *Krone* and *Ködnitzhof;* higher up are *Taurer Wirt; Groderhof;* and *Lucknerhaus,* the highest at 6,500 ft.

Campsite.

KIRCHBERG 2,745 ft. Fast-train stop on line from Innsbruck to Salzburg.

Hotels All (2)—*Sporthotel Alexander,* 50 beds, Tyrolean-style rooms, all with bath or shower; *Daxer,* Tyrolean evenings, dancing, tennis court; *Schochenhof,* all rooms with bath or shower, heated pool.

KITZBÜHEL 2,500 ft. About 1½ hours by fast train from Innsbruck.

Hotels Categories are based on seasonal rates, for Christmas and New Year period, from Feb. to mid-March, and July to Aug. Most hotels are closed in early spring, after the snow has gone, and in late fall.

Deluxe (L)

Schloss Lebenberg. Castle-hotel, 95 rooms, indoor pool, tennis courts, cure facilities.

Parkhotel, 90 rooms, 10 suites, in large park just outside town, looks like a palatial country mansion in Tyrolean style. Has been popular with jet-set for some time, music, dancing, pool.

Maria Theresia, 100 rooms, modern.

First Class (1)

Goldener Greif, 50 rooms and suites furnished in neo-Tyrolean style, in middle of old town, has been a hostelry since 1274, antique-style hall with fireplace, cozy grill and wine tavern, indoor pool, Tyrolean entertainment in *Sportklause.*

Tenne, 50 beautifully appointed rooms with bath, glassed-in terrace.

Tennerhof, Romantic Hotel, 40 rooms, out of town in beautiful natural sur-roundings with the appearance of a charming hunting lodge, Tyrolean antique furnishings, small swimming pool and own bus service to town. The superb restaurant is worth visiting even if you are not staying there.

Moderate (2)

Weisses Rössl, just outside town gate, 80 rooms, 60 baths and showers, Tyro-lean-style tavern, dancing in *Rössl* bar, tennis, heated pool, roof terrace.

Schlosshotel Münichau, 3 km. out of town, 2 restaurants, bar, lovely garden.

Klausner, 50 rooms, 40 baths, at railway station, extraordinary view of moun-tains through dining room windows.

Zum Jägerwirt, 70 rooms, 44 baths.

Schweizerhof, good family-run hotel, quiet and sunny, near Hahnenkamm cable car station.

Eggerwirt, rustic decor, good restaurant.

Tyrol, chalet-style hotel.

Pensions

Heading the list, all (1)—*Alpina,* near Hahnenkamm cable car; *Hahnenhof,* at foot of the Hahnenkamm, pleasant, heated pool; and *Bruggerhof.*

Among the mountain hotels in the vicinity, both (2)—*Ehrenbachhöhe,* 100 beds; *Hochbrunn,* 50 beds, both on Hahnenkamm, reached by cable car.

Both (3)—*Kitzbühler Horn* and *Bichalm,* reached by cable car.

In the following bed-and-breakfast pensions, you can rent small flats with kitchen and bath—*Hoffmann,* Aschbachweg 1; *Karlberger,* Hahnenkammstr.; *Alpenblick,* Wehrgasse 14; *Zum Waldschützen,* Hahnenkammstr. 34.

Campsite on Schwarzsee nearby.

Restaurant *Unterberger Stuben* (1), sophisticated modern cuisine. Considered Kitzbuhel's best.

KUFSTEIN 1,650 ft. About 1 hour from Innsbruck by fast train, on the main Innsbruck–Munich railway line.

Hotels All (2)—*Andreas Hofer;* the smaller *Goldener Hirsch* and *Alpenrose* are best.

All (3)—*Post,* 85 beds, Tyrolean music at weekends; *Auracher Löchl,* 60 beds, picturesque wine tavern, excellent food. Both near the old bridge, terraced, the best rooms on the river side.

If you don't mind walking about 45 minutes, while the hotels involved take care of the luggage, 2 attractive small Tyrolean-style hostelries in the unspoiled Kaisertal above Kufstein, both (3)—*Berghof Pfandl* and *Alpengasthof Pfandlhof.*

Youth Hostel in town and at the castle of Hohenstaffing nearby.

Campsite.

Restaurant Don't miss a visit to *Batzenhäusl,* original old colorful wine tavern at Römerhofgasse 1.

KÜHTAI Almost 6,500 ft. Bus service from Innsbruck and Kematen; when road conditions between Gries in Sellrain and Kühtai are very bad, a caterpillar motor vehicle is used.

Hotels Both (1)—*Jagdschloss Kühtai,* 96 beds, 26 baths, once the hunting castle of Tyrolean dukes, almost all public rooms are 16th-century original, bar and dancing, open Dec. 15 to end April, owned by Count Karl zu Stolberg-Stolberg.

Astoria, 84 beds, all rooms with bath, bar with dance band, indoor pool.

All (2)—*Tyrol,* 68 beds; *Mooshaus,* all rooms with shower; *Kühtaier Schlössl.* Most hotels open winter and summer seasons only.

LANDECK 2,676 ft. Fast train stop on the railway line Innsbruck-Vorarlberg-Switzerland.

Hotels *Schrofenstein* (2), 70 beds, 20 baths.

All (3)—*Schwarzer Adler,* with good restaurant; *Sonne,* with nice view of the town from restaurant; *Tramserhof,* 80 beds, high in the woods, lovely view.

Youth Hostel.

3 campsites, the largest at *Berghotel Tramserhof.*

LÄNGENFELD In the Ötztal Valley. **Hotels** Both (2)—*Zum Hirschen,* 50 beds and *Edelweiss* are the leading hotels, with many hostelries (3) and rooms in private houses as in all other places in this valley.

LANS 8 km. from Innsbruck. **Restaurant** *Wilder Mann,* excellent Tyrolean and international cuisine, very good service.

LERMOOS 3,264 ft., in the Zugspitze area, on same railway as Ehrwald.

Hotels Both (2)—*Drei Mohren,* over 100 beds and 40 baths; and *Edelweiss,* 160 beds, indoor pool.

All (3)—*Post,* 110 beds, 24 baths, indoor pool; *Tyrol,* same size, dancing in *Kellarbar* and weekly folklore shows; *Bellevue,* at the valley station of the Hochmoos chair lift.

Haus Bergheim is one of the many inexpensive pensions.

LIENZ 2,224 ft., reached by railway Salzburg-Mallnitz-Lienz line from Carinthia, and by car on the Felbertauern road, 3 hours from Munich.

Hotels Both (1)—*Traube,* 52 rooms, off the main square, period-style interiors. Exceptional restaurant with remarkable wine list. Indoor pool on the fifth floor with a stunning view. *Traube-Keller,* with dancing and wooden-lodge decor; indoor pool. Nearby, slightly less expensive *Sonne,* 55 rooms, two dining rooms, atmospheric *Tiroler Stube;* car park.

All (2) and with local color—*Garni Eck,* 15 rooms; *Post,* also on main square, music at weekends in its *Postkeller; Dolomiten,* in the western part of town; *Glöcklturm,* on left bank of the Isel.

All (3)—*Edlinger,* 14 rooms; *Goldener Fisch,* 50 rooms. 10 showers; *Haidenhof,* 35 rooms, 20 showers.

At **Oberlienz**—*Haus Stocker,* at Zettersfeld cable car station, 30 rooms, heated pool; *Pepi Stiegler,* 22 rooms, indoor pool.

Restaurants *Rose,* with garden on a charming old square, Tyrolean musical entertainment in summer; *Schloss Bruck,* at the castle, with fine view from the terrace; *Adlerstüberl,* with local color; *Altes Haus Lerche,* game and fish specialties; *Sun Valley Stüberl,* with Tyrolean music at weekends; *Enziandiele* and *Dolomiten-Keller* also have dancing.

MATREI IN OSTTIROL 3,300 ft., on the Felbertauern road, bus from Lienz.

Hotels Both (2)—*Rauter,* 35 rooms, 30 showers, heated outdoor pool, fishing facilities; *Sporthotel,* 32 rooms, 15 showers.

All (3)—Among about 2 dozen Gasthöfe and pensions are *Hinteregger,* with own farm; *Egger-Wirt,* with gemütlich restaurant rooms; *Ederbräu,* with own farm and riding facilities; *Panzl* and *Schönblick.*

About 16 km. up in the Tauerntal is the lovely mountain hotel *Tauernhaus,* about 5,000 ft., reached by bus.

Restaurant *Bacher's Grillstube,* local dishes.

MAYRHOFEN 2,066 ft., reached by local Ziller Valley railway.

Hotels Most of the hotels and inns have Tyrolean wine taverns featuring Zillertal music on weekend evenings, with pleasant garden restaurants.

All (2)—*Alte Post,* 40 rooms, 7 baths; *Elisabeth Hotel,* 36 rooms; *Kramerwirt,* 59 rooms, on market square, 6 rustic *stüberln,* 2 restaurants; *Neuhaus,* 140 rooms, most with bath; *St. Georg,* 45 rooms, half with bath; *Strass,* 66 rooms. All with indoor pools.

All (3)—*Hundsbichler,* 30 rooms; *Kristall,* 25 rooms; *Neue Post,* 85 rooms, 60 baths; *Sonne,* 100 rooms, 18 baths; *Zillergrund,* 30 rooms, 25 showers. Some 50 Gasthöfe and pensions.

MUTTERS 2,500 ft., part of the Innsbruck skiing area.

Hotels Both (2)—*Altenburg,* 40 rooms, 20 baths, rustic *stüberl;* and *Sonnhof,* 28 rooms, pool.

Both (3)—*Egger,* 25 rooms, 17 baths; and *Muttererhof,* 30 rooms, 18 baths, a rustic Tyrolean gasthof with beautiful garden, good local food and quick service.

NAUDERS Hotels All (2)—*Almhof,* 35 rooms; *Edelweiss,* 36 rooms; *Maultasch,* 58 rooms; *Regina,* 20 rooms; *Tirolerhof,* 70 rooms; all with indoor pools.

All (3)—*Astoria,* 21 rooms; *Erika,* 40 rooms; *Schwarzer Adler,* 30 rooms.

OBERGURGL 6,320 ft. Bus service from Ötztal (Arlberg Express stop).

Hotels All (2)—*Alpina,* 45 rooms; *Austria,* 30 rooms; *Burger,* 30 rooms; *Deutschmann,* 42 rooms; *Hochfirst,* 88 rooms, pool, the leader, facing glaciers; *Hochland,* 44 rooms.

Edelweiss & Gurgl (2), 100 rooms, 61 baths, pool. A traditional Tyrolean house with a very pleasant atmosphere despite its size. Famous for excellent local and international cuisine.

All (3)—*Alpenrose,* 22 rooms; *Gamper,* 30 rooms; *Sonnberg,* 35 rooms, 18 showers.

ÖTZTAL Hotels At **Habichen,** *Habicherhof* (2), 35 rooms, 24 showers, pool; *Waldhof* (3), 30 rooms, 11 showers.

At **Ötz,** all (3)—*Alpenhotel,* 50 rooms, 40 baths; *Alpenrose,* 120 rooms, 60 baths, 29 showers; *Drei Mohren,* 35 rooms, 22 showers; *Stern,* 12 rooms.

At **Umhausen,** *Johanna* (3), 25 rooms, 15 showers.

PATSCH Above Igls. **Hotels** All (2)—*Altwirt,* 26 rooms; *Bär,* 40 rooms; *Eschenhof,* 27 rooms; *Grünwalderhof,* 30 rooms, 20 baths; all with indoor pools.

At upper cable car station, *Patscherkofel,* 40 rooms, no private showers.

PERTISAU Near the south end of Achensee. **Hotels** All (2)—*Kristall,* 45 rooms, 25 showers; *Pfandler,* 55 rooms; *Rieser,* 75 rooms; *Sportalm,* 20 rooms; *Strandhotel,* 63 rooms; all with pools.

All (3)—*Bergland,* 27 rooms; *Karlwirt,* 52 rooms; *Wiesenhof,* 45 rooms, pool.

PETTNEU/ARLBERG Hotel *Gridlon* (2), beautiful rooms, some apartments. Fitness center, dances, barbecues, tennis tournaments.

REUTTE 2,800 ft., in the Zugspitze area, same line as Ehrwald and Lermoos.

Hotels Both (2)—*Glocke,* 60 rooms, 20 baths, pool; *Urisee,* 16 rooms.

Both (3)—*Goldener Hirsch,* 50 rooms, 20 showers; *Tirolerhof,* 40 rooms, 12 showers.

Near Reutte and higher up, *Ammerwald* (2), 80 rooms, 20 baths, indoor pool, ski lift, wine tavern, good restaurant, café and bar.

At **Plansee** nearby, both (3)—*Forelle* and *Seespitze* are both small.

ST. ANTON AM ARLBERG 4,277 ft., fast train stop on Arlberg Express route.

Hotels All reservations must be made in advance to avoid disappointment.

All (1)—*Alpenrose,* 40 rooms, indoor pool, central, Jäger Stuben, dancing; *Arlberg,* 60 rooms, 40 baths, Arlberg Keller Bar; *Mooserkreuz,* 40 rooms, above village, indoor pool; *Post,* 90 rooms, most with bath, below rail station, international renown; *Rosanna,* 40 rooms; *Schwarzer Adler,* 43 rooms; *Sporthotel,* 86 rooms; indoor pool; *Tyrol,* 44 rooms.

All (2)—*Berghaus Maria,* in pleasant location, 27 rooms, 18 baths; *Nassereinerhof,* 32 rooms, most with showers; *Schweizerhof,* 35 rooms; *Tannenhof,* 25 rooms.

Both (3)—*Gasthof Reselehof,* in the Nasserein section, in original Tyrolean style; *Goldenes Kreuz,* near the church.

Pensions are numerous and practically every house offers bed-and-breakfast accommodations. Rates range from (2) to (3). Among the best pensions—*Karl Schranz,* owned by the famous skiing champion; *Montjola,* in upper village.

Restaurants If you wish to avoid eating *à la carte* in the hotel restaurants, you can arrange for *en pension* terms for lunch and dinner in any of the hotel restaurants here or in St. Christoph, as well as in the mountain restaurants *Vallugagrat, Gampen,* and *Kapallstube; Rossana Stüberl* is a pleasant restaurant catering particularly to English-speaking guests.

ST. CHRISTOPH 5,904 ft., on mountain pass, a few km. above St. Anton, and reached from there by bus.

Hotels *Hospiz* (L), 80 rooms, 70 with bath, and a long tradition as the first hospice for travelers crossing the pass. Food excellent and the best wines in Austria; restaurant very expensive.

Bellevue (2), 130 beds, all rooms with bath, indoor pool.

All (3)—*Galzig,* 80 beds; *Arlberghöhe;* and *Edelweiss.*

SCHWAZ 1,765 ft., 25 minutes by fast train from Innsbruck.

Hotels In town, both (3)—*Post* and *Brücke.*

Other hotels are situated in the excursion and mountain area above the town— *Alpenhotel Grafenast* (2), 60 beds, beware of the steep twisting approach road.

Both (3)—*Gamsstein,* 40 beds, private ski lift; *Alpengasthof Egertboden,* 45 beds, in Tyrolean style, good restaurant and Tyrolean music.

SEEFELD 3,870 ft. About 30 minutes from Innsbruck by fast train; also by bus (24 km); parking facilities.

Hotels All hotels listed insist on full or half board; most have a few cheaper rooms without baths; open in season only, many December through March, but some 50 adequate inexpensive establishments remain open all year.

All (L)—*Astoria,* a little above village, chalet style, 49 rooms with balconies, indoor swimming pool with cafe-bar where you can swim and dance. *Karwendelhof,* 44 rooms, at station, chalet style, 18th-century cellar tavern, excellent dining, casino. *Klosterbräu,* behind church in former monastery, 120 rooms; tavern *Kanne,* bar, indoor and outdoor pools. *Schlosshotel,* 23 rooms with original rustic furniture, wooden walls and ceilings from old farmhouses; heated pool; open high season only. *Tümmlerhof,* chalet style in garden outside town; 74 rooms, indoor and outdoor pools; fine restaurant. *Tyrol,* 45 rooms, indoor pool.

All (1)—*Dreitorspitze,* 44 rooms, indoor pool, good food; *Eden,* 50 rooms; *Hohe*

Munde, 120 rooms; *Kurhotel,* 45 rooms, cure facilities; *Lamm,* 70 rooms, tavern with zither music. *Lärchenhof,* 52 rooms, outside town, indoor pool, sauna. *Philipp,* 70 rooms, in center, good restaurant, popular with British skiers. *Post,* 130 rooms, in center. *Schönruh,* 55 rooms, pool. *Strandhotel Seespitz,* 45 rooms, 35 baths, on small lake Wildsee, ice rink in winter.

All (2)—*Marthe,* 40 rooms, pool; *Schönegg,* 40 rooms; *Stern,* 65 rooms; *Wetterstein,* 50 rooms, chalet style, near chair lift.

All (3)—*Christina,* 20 rooms, pool; *Gasthof Schlossberg,* 20 rooms, on road to Munich; *Tiroler Weinstube,* 40 rooms.

Campsite on Wildsee.

Restaurants *Locanda* serves well-prepared Italian food; *Sir Richard,* excellent international cuisine.

SERFAUS 4,700 ft. Bus service from Landeck on Arlberg Express route.
Hotels All (1)—*Alpenhof,* in Tyrolean style; *Cervosa* and *Löwen,* with indoor pools; *St. Zeno; Furgler* and *Post* have good restaurants. *Tirolerhof* (3).

SILLIAN 3,618 ft., about 50 minutes by slow train from Lienz.
Hotels *Atzwanger* (2); and pension *Adelheid.*
Several other inns (3), and a Youth Hostel.
At nearby **Arnbach,** both (3)—*Bad Weitlanbrunn,* and *Dolomitenhof.*

SÖLDEN 4,460 ft. Bus service from Ötztal on Arlberg Express route, with the high plateau of Hochsölden (6,800 ft.) reached by chair lift, and Gaislachkogel (about 10,000 ft.), climbed by a supermodern cable car, the highest in Austria.
Hotels *Sporthotel Central* (1), all rooms with bath, indoor pool. Beautiful restaurant, wood-paneled *stuben,* silver cutlery, admirable food.
Both (2)—*Alpina,* all rooms with bath; and the large *Bergland,* indoor pool.
All (3)—*Sölderhof,* 60 beds; *Sonne,* larger, noted for good cooking; *Pension Waldcafé* and *Pension Hermann.*

STEINACH AM BRENNER In the Wipptal, 3,437 ft. About 30 minutes by fast train from Innsbruck.
Hotels All (2)—*Rose,* since 1840 in the same family; *Steinacherhof,* indoor pool, tennis, terrace café, good food; *Weisses Rössl,* roof terrace and cellar bar; *Wilder Mann,* reader-recommended for pleasant rooms, good pool.

STUBAITAL Romantic mountain valley south of **Innsbruck.** From **Schönberg,** at entrance to the valley, the view is magnificent in all directions.
Hotels Both (3)—*Jägerhof,* 160 beds, quiet, in a commanding position over the Sillertal, tennis courts next to hotel; the *Stubai,* 40 beds, all rooms with bath.
At **Mieders,** *Alte Post* (3), a little farther up the valley.
At **Telfes,** both (3)—*Tyrol;* and *Grier.*

TUXERTAL Hotels at **Hintertux:** Three hotels (2) under same management which owns a thermal source channeled into the indoor and outdoor pools—*Alpenhof, Berghof* and *Badhotel,* 200 beds.
At **Lanersbach:** *Kirchler* (2); and *Forelle* (3).

VENT 6,200 ft. Bus from Ötztal to Zwieselstein, and special bus from there on.
Hotels *Similaun* (2), 22 rooms.
Both (3)—*Post,* 36 rooms, 24 baths; *Vent,* 50 rooms, 27 baths.

WALCHSEE 2,200 ft. Bus service from Kufstein and St. Johann.
Hotels Best is *Seehof* (2), indoor and outdoor pools.
Both (3)—*Fisherwirt,* attractive garden; and *Schick,* indoor pool.
Campsite.

WESTENDORF 2,570 ft. On Innsbruck-Salzburg railway line, about 2 hours
from Innsbruck by slow train.
Hotels (2)—*Briem,* 55 rooms, 40 baths; *Jakobwirt,* 57 rooms; *Post,* 40 rooms,
20 baths.
Both (3)—Pensions *Tirolerhof* and *Veronika.*

WILDSCHÖNAU 2,800 to 3,100 ft., a plateau with the villages of Auffach,
Niederau and Oberau, all close together and reached by bus from Wörgl.
Hotels at **Niederau,** *Austria* (2), 45 rooms, indoor pool; *Alpenland* (3), 25
rooms, 14 showers, pool.
At **Oberau,** *Angerhof* (2), 33 rooms, indoor pool; *Kellerwirt* (3), 38 rooms, most
with bath, richly atmospheric.

WIPPTAL The valley leading south of Innsbruck to the Brenner Pass.
Hotels At **Matrei:** several picturesque inns with wrought-iron guild signs
hanging above the entrance, and both (2)—*Parkhotel* and *Krone,* with long tradi-
tion are best.
In the vicinity, a 2-hour walk, and considerably higher up (5,400 ft.)—*Maria
Waldrast* (3), a point of departure for mountain tours.
At **Gries am Brenner**—*Weisses Rössl* (2) with a noted restaurant.

ZELL AM ZILLER Hotels All (2)—*Gasthof Bräu,* where, if you are a guest,
they will probably let you fish for trout in their waters; *Tirolerhof* and *Zellerhof,*
both have all rooms with bath or shower.
See also **Gerlos.**

MUSEUMS

INNSBRUCK We give the admission times for those places of interest that can
only be visited during certain hours. The Hofburg, Imperial Church, and Silver
Chapel are all close together, but to explore their treasures thoroughly you must
allow a half day.

Hofburg, Hofkirche, Silberne Kapelle (Imperial Palace with the church
and Silver Chapel). Imperial Palace: reception rooms and halls, richly ornamented and furnished in baroque and rococo, frescos by Maulpertsch in large main
hall. Imperial Church: tomb of Emperor Maximilian, *The Last Knight,* with
bronze statues of his predecessors, relatives, and other famous knights. Silver
Chapel: tomb of Archduke Ferdinand II, silver altar relief, organ from 16th
century; in summer organ concerts on Wednesday evenings. Conducted tours
through these three places in summer daily 9–12, 2–5, in winter on weekdays
10–12, 2–4.

Tiroler Volkskunstmuseum Next to Hofkirche, the museum of Tyrolean folk art and craftsmanship, very interesting collection of folk dress, rustic furniture, farmhouse interiors. Fasching masks, etc. Weekdays 9–12, 2–5, Sundays and holidays 9–12.

Landesmuseum Ferdinandeum Museumstr. 15. Paintings, sculptures, a prehistoric collection, a hall devoted to the Andreas Hofer-led rebellion for the liberation from Napoleonic occupation. Weekdays in winter 9–12.30, 2–4, in summer 9–5; Sun. and holidays 9–12.30.

Armory Zeughausgasse. Built by Maximilian I about 1500 and recently restored; historical museum, closed in winter.

Stadtturm (City Tower), part of the old Rathaus at Herzog-Friedrichstr. 21. Beautiful view from top. Daily 9–5.

Kaiserjäger Museum On Berg Isel. History of Tyrolean Imperial élite mountain regiment from 1816 to 1918 and of the Andreas Hofer war of liberation. Flags, weapons, trophies, paintings, etc. In summer daily 8–6, in winter on weekdays open from 9–4.

Rundgemälde Next to Hungerburg funicular station. Huge round painting representing Battle of Bergisel. Daily 10–5.

Alpenzoo In Hungerburg section, an Alpine zoological garden, recently opened, with specimens of almost all Alpine fauna. Open 9–6.

Schloss Ambras Castle on southern outskirts of city. Fastest public transport is Bus K from main railway station. Collection of fine paintings, especially the Habsburg family portrait gallery with some pictures dating back to the 14th cent.; old weapons, etc.; nice park. Open May to Oct., daily 9–12, 2–5. Also houses **Kaiserschützen Museum** containing paintings and other souvenirs of the battles of the Imperial Rifles Regiment during World War I; open daily mid-July to end Sept., 2–6.

SPECIAL EVENTS
ALPBACH Different topics every year at European Forum, late August.

EHRWALD Folk Festivals July and August.

FIEBERBRUNN Ski carnival in Feb.

HOCHSÖLDEN Glacier ski races, end April.

IGLS Masked ski races and masked parades on last day of *Fasching* and the preceding Sun. In July and Aug., tennis, golf, dancing tournaments, fashion shows. End-of-year parties and balls in Dec.

IMST Certain years in Feb. (inquire locally) the famous *Schemenlaufen,* a procession of picturesque woodcarved masks; origin in pagan times.

INNSBRUCK The capital of the Tyrol has its own attractions as well as those of the surrounding areas; many folk-dress brass band concerts and folklore performances in front of the Goldenes Dachl, as well as other events, take place from May through Sept. Peak summer period for visitors July and Aug., as elsewhere. Towards the end of Sept. the Trade Fair. The best time for skiing and other winter sports is from Jan. to March.

KIRCHBERG *Corpus Christi* in June, a most interesting colorful religious procession, brass band concerts and folklore programs in summer.

KITZBÜHEL Hahnenkamm ski race and curling competitions in winter. Tennis, golf, and dancing tournaments, fashion shows, July and Aug. End-of-year parties and balls in Dec.

KUFSTEIN Castle plays and concerts, including musical exhibitions on the huge outdoor organ, July to Aug.

MAYRHOFEN Folk festivals in July and Aug., rides on the narrow-gauge Zillertal steam railroad throughout the summer.

OBERGURGL Glacier ski races, end April.

ÖTZTAL Folk festivals, July and Aug., in Piburgersee nearby.

ST. ANTON AM ARLBERG Skiing competitions of resort guests mark the beginning of Jan. Famed *Kandahar race* in March, held only every 5 years, according to the present rules, because St. Anton, where the race originated, now alternates with famous skiing centers in other Alpine countries.
End-of-the-year parties and balls at the end Dec.
Peak season draws the international set, much *après ski.*

SEEFELD Skiing competitions for the resort guests mark the beginning of Jan. Cycle of *Fasching* balls begins in Jan. in all fashionable resorts and particularly here, reaches its peak in Feb. Night slalom races in March. Folk festivals in July and Aug. End-of-year parties and balls in Dec.

TANNHEIM European championship of Husky Sled Racing.

WIPPTAL Folk festivals, July and Aug.

ZELL AM ZILLER First weekend in May, the gay Gander folk festival.

ENTERTAINMENT AND CASINOS

INNSBRUCK For an enjoyable evening's entertainment there is the *Tiroler Landestheater* on the Rennweg, where you can see opera, operetta, drama, and comedy. Concerts are given in the modern Saal Tirol of the *Kongresshaus.* Performances usually start at 7.30 P.M. In summer, brass band concerts of folk music performed in the park or in one of the public squares are almost a daily event. In season you can hear the real Tyrolean yodeling and zither music and see the authentic Tyrolean dances as a part of the Tyrolean folk shows, performed at *Stiftskeller, Gasthof Adambräu,* and in the *Hotel Europe.*

Under the ancient arcades along the narrow Herzog-Friedrichstr. which is a continuation of Maria-Theresienstr. and in many of the old side streets, you will find inviting wine taverns, some of them centuries old, and offering music.

In addition to those mentioned under the restaurants, the *Goethestube* of the *Goldener Adler,* where Goethe used to sip his *viertel* of the red South Tyrolean during his stays here in 1786 and 1790, has the best music, wine and food.

Tiroler Bauernkeller, Meinhardstr. 7, also has music and local specialties.

Happ, under the Arcades, a wine tavern with good Austrian specialties.

Gasthof Adambräu, Heilig-Geiststr. 16, has daily folklore shows at 9 P.M.

Innsbruck is not the place for nightclubs; there are a few bars, sometimes with music, among them *Maximilian Bar* in Holiday Inn, *Bacchus-Keller,* Salurnerstr. 18, and *Orangerie,* upstairs at Maria-Theresienstr. 10.

KITZBÜHEL Roulette, baccara and black-jack, open summer and winter seasons daily from 7 P.M.

SEEFELD Roulette, baccara and black-jack, open daily from 7 P.M. in summer, 5 P.M. in winter.

SPORTS

ALPBACH 2 chair lifts, 10 ski lifts, ski school, ski kindergarten, bobsled school, ice skating, horse sleighs, tobogganing.

AXAMER LIZUM 20 km. from Innsbruck by bus, or private car, parking facilities are available. Site of the 1964 and 1976 Winter Olympics, and part of the Innsbruck winter sports area.

Skiing terrains of all degrees of difficulty. Ski school, 2 cable cars, 3 chair lifts 4 ski lifts, including a chair lift to Birgitzköpfl (6,700 ft.) and a ski lift from there a double chair lift to Schafböden, where there is a chair lift to the top of Hoadl (7,700 ft.) and a ski lift to Pleissen (7,300 ft.).

BERWANG 5 chair lifts, 5 ski lifts, ski school, 2 toboggan runs, skating rink horse sleighs.

EHRWALD 1 chair lift, 4 ski lifts, ski school, ski jump, skijoring, 2 toboggan runs, artificial and natural skating rinks, ice hockey, 4 curling rinks, horse sleighs

ELLMAU 60 chair and ski lifts, ski schools, 20 km. ski runs.

FIEBERBRUNN 3 chair lifts, 7 ski lifts, ski school.

FULPMES Together with Mieders, Telfes, and Neustift, there are 2 cable cars, 4 chair lifts, 17 ski lifts, glacier train, ski schools, summer glacier skiing above Neustift, ice skating, curling and horse sleighs.

GALTÜR 1 chair lift, 8 ski lifts, ski school, outstanding ski runs and tours, tobogganing.

GERLOS 2 chair lifts, 12 ski lifts, ski school, sleighs.

HOCHGURGL The 3-section chair lift to Wurmkogl (almost 10,000 ft.), has opened up all-year skiing terrains; all-year skiing instruction available. Another chair lift, 2 ski lifts, ski school, tobogganing, horse sleighs. Skiing from mid-Nov. to mid-May. Slopes for beginners, runs for advanced, ski tours with or without guide.

HOPFGARTEN Ski jump, 3 curling rinks, 3 chair lifts, 6 ski lifts, ski school, 5 toboggan runs, skating, horse sleighs.

IGLS This is part of Innsbruck winter sports area, with skiing terrains of all degrees of difficulty. A cable car connects Igls with the mountain hotel on Patscherkofel where there is a chair lift to the top of Patscherkofel and another from Patscheralm.

1 chair lift, a ski lift, ski school, Olympic bobsled run and Olympic toboggan run, skating rink, curling alleys, horse sleighs, skijoring, tennis courts with national and international matches often taking place.

There's a 9-hole golf course nearby.

INNSBRUCK Innsbruck, together with Igls and Mutters on the outskirts, and Lizum and Seefeld in the immediate vicinity, is one of the top Austrian *winter sports* centers.

Skiing terrains of all degrees exist at Berg Isel and Mühlau in the suburbs of the city, at Seegrube in the Nordkette range above it, and on the Patscherkofel mountain.

Seegrube has 2 chair lifts, a ski school, a cable car to Innsbruck and another to Hafelekar near the top of the Nordkette ridge. A cable car from Tufles goes to Halsmarter; from here, a chair lift to Tulfeinalm.

Important international *jumping* contests are held on the long Olympic ski jump at Berg Isel.

The best establishment for figure and speed *skating* is the new Olympic Ice Stadium in Innsbruck, skating in summer too; *ice hockey* as well; *curling* alleys, *toboggan* runs here and in Patsch; *horse sleighs* can be hired here and in Patsch.

Innsbruck is also a first class *mountain climbing* center and the seat of the *Hochgebirgsschule Tyrol,* Innrain 67, which organizes rock and ice climbing courses and tours. Mountain guides are also available for hire. Another mountain climbing school, *Alpinschule Innsbruck,* is at Marktgraben 2.

For *swimming,* there's a large complex at Tivoli with 5 pools, and a few small lakes nearby. Also *tennis* courts.

For *riding,* you may have to join the club, but the fees are reasonable.

There's a new 18-hole *golf* course in Rinn.

Kranebitten nearby has a center for international *gliding.*

If you like *soccer* (football), you can watch in Tivoli Stadium.

ISCHGL Cable car to Idalpe (7,600 ft.) 9 ski lifts, ski school, 2 toboggan runs, ice skating and curling, horse sleighs, winter game feeding.

ISELSBERG 5 ski lifts, ski school, skating rink, 4 toboggan runs, horse sleighs

KALS AM GROSSGLOCKNER Mountain-climbing base for the Gross-glockner; chair lift and 2 ski lifts open terrain up to 6,600 ft., ski schools, ice skating, curling, toboggan runs and horse sleighs.

KIRCHBERG 5 chair lifts, 9 ski lifts, ski schools, ski jump, 5 toboggan runs, skating rink, curling, horse sleighs.

KITZBÜHEL The famous *Kitzbühel Ski Circus* runs and trails (one slope is floodlit by night) are served by 4 cable cars, 13 chair lifts, 13 ski lifts. For all degrees of skill. Many ski schools, hang-gliding school. Free bus service to all cable car stations. Ski guides for high mountain tours. Ski jump, skijoring, artificial and natural skating rinks, 2 toboggan runs, horse sleighs. Kitzbühel is also one of the centers for ice-hockey and curling competitions.

International atmosphere, frequented by international social set, a lot of *après ski* including casino.

A modern swimming pool, with double glass walls which roll into ground in summer. Swimming in Schwarzsee.

National and international tennis matches take place here quite often.

9-hole golf course near Schloss Kaps, April to Oct.

KÖSSEN 1,930 ft. Bus service from Kufstein and St. Johann in Tirol.

3 chair lifts, ski lifts, ski school, ski jump, toboggan run, hang-gliding with school.

KUFSTEIN Swimming in several small lakes nearby, Hintersteinersee and Hechtsee.

Often national and international tennis matches here.

International airport for gliders, where passenger flights can also be made.

4 chair lifts, 5 ski lifts, ski school, skijoring, ski jump, 3 toboggan runs, skating rink, ice hockey, 3 curling rinks, horse sleighs.

See also **Kössen.**

KÜHTAI Cable car, chair lift, 4 ski lifts, ski school, tobogganing, horse sleighs

LANDECK Cable car to Krahberg (7,290 ft.) with skiing from May to June, panoramic view all the time. Mountain skiing tours from here. 1 chair lift, 5 ski lifts, ski school, 2 rinks, 7 toboggan runs.

LERMOOS 3 chair lifts, 4 ski lifts, ski school directed by Olympic champion Walter Schuster, toboggan run, skating and curling rinks, horse sleighs.

LIENZ Mountain climbing center for the Lienzer Dolomites; gliding field; swimming in Tristachersee nearby; camping sites; cable car to Zettersfeld (5,400 ft.), 2 chair lifts, 5 ski lifts up to 6,900 ft., downhill runs of all grades, max. length 13 km. Chair lift to Venedigerwarte (3,300 ft.) another 2 ski lifts, ski school, toboggan runs, skating rink, 8 curling rinks, ski kindergarten.

MATREI IN OSTTIROL Mountain climbing base for the Grossvenediger. Skiing terrains between 3,300 and 6,000 ft. 2 chair lifts, 4 ski lifts in Matrei, another chair lift and ski lift at Tauernhaus. Ski school, mountain ski guides, skating rink, curling, 4 toboggan runs, horse sleighs.

MAYRHOFEN 2 cable cars, 2 chair lifts, 11 ski lifts, ski kindergarten, horse sleighs, ski school, ski jump, skating rink, 2 toboggan runs, 3 curling rinks.

MUTTERS 6 km. from Innsbruck by bus or local train or private car, parking facilities available.
Part of Innsbruck winter sports area, with skiing terrains of all degrees of difficulty. A gondola goes from here to Mutterer Alm, and a chair lift from there to Pfriemesköpfl. Ski school, ski jump, toboggan runs.

NAUDERS Cable car, chair lift, 5 ski lifts, 2 children's lifts, ice skating, tobogganing, bobsled runs, cross-country skiing.

OBERGURGL One of the top, although internationally less well-known, skiing centers in Tyrol. 3 chair lifts, 6 ski lifts, ski school, 2 toboggan runs, horse sleighs. The snow stays very long and skiing is possible until late in the spring. Slopes for beginners and runs for all degrees of skill. Guides for high mountain ski tours available.

ÖTZTAL Swimming in Piburgersee.

PERTISAU Swimming; sailboats can be hired; 9-hole golf course, June to Oct.

REUTTE Cable car at Höfen, 5 ski lifts, ski school, 7 ski jumps, skating and curling rinks, horse sleighs.
International gliding center at Höfen nearby.
Swimming in Plansee, and sailing school.

ST. ANTON AM ARLBERG This famed winter sports center with intricate system of ski runs and trails, referred to as the "St. Anton-St. Christoph Ski Circus", is served by 7 cable cars, 2 chair lifts and 18 ski lifts. The famous skiing

technique started by Hannes Schneider is still taught, together with the newest
additions.

Guides for mountain ski tours available; ski jump and toboggan run; skating,
curling facilities and horse sleighs; swimming in Moorsee.

ST. CHRISTOPH Besides a ski school, also has slopes for beginners, runs of
all degrees of difficulty, including those used for the famous *Kandahar race.*
Guides for mountain ski tours available, ski jump and toboggan run, peak season
draws the international set.

SCHWAZ 3 chair lifts, 7 ski lifts, ski school, 4 toboggan runs, skating rink, ice
hockey.

SEEFELD Swimming in Wildsee. 18-hole golf course.

Part of Innsbruck winter sports area, with skiing terrains of all degrees of
difficulty.

At the village, on Hochegg, and at Rosshütte, there are 3 cable cars, 4 chair
lifts, 9 ski lifts. Toni Seeler has his ski school here. Terrain for all degrees of skill.
2 ski jumps, 30 curling rinks, toboggan run, 2 skating rinks with *Internationale
Eislaufschule Seefeld* (international skating school). Considerable *après-ski.*

SERFAUS This is a new and important ski center, 2 cable cars, 2 chair lifts,
8 ski lifts, 2 for children, 4 ski schools, skating rink, tobogganing, curling, horse
sleigh.

SILLIAN Chair lift, 2 ski lifts, ski school, ski jump, 3 toboggan runs, curling
alleys, skating rink.

SÖLDEN There's an archery center. In addition to the chair lift to Hochsölden,
there are 5 more chair lifts, 12 ski lifts, famous ski school, skating rink, 3 toboggan
runs, horse sleighs. A toll road to the Gaislachalm and Rettenbachferner, where
there is year-round skiing. Guides for superior mountain ski tours in the area are
also available. This is one of the top skiing centers in Tyrol.

STEINACH AM BRENNER 2 chair lifts, 3 ski lifts, ski school, ski jump, 4
toboggan runs, skating and curling rinks, horse sleighs.

TUXERTAL Mountain valley above Mayrhofen, 4–5,000 ft. Ski schools, toboggan runs and horse sleighs at both Hintertux and Lanersbach, villages with only
modest, low-priced accommodations available.

At **Hintertux:** cable car, 4 chair lifts, 4 ski lifts, summer skiing on Tuxe
Glacier, outdoor thermal pool, indoor heated pool.

At **Lanersbach:** cable car, chair lift, 8 ski lifts, ski jump.

VENT 2 chair lifts, 2 ski lifts, ski school, toboggan run, horse sleighs, exception
al mountain ski tours, guides.

WAIDRING 2,500 ft., with the Steinplatte (6,000 ft.) above it.

6 ski lifts, ski school, toboggan runs, winter camping.

WALCHSEE Chair lift, 4 ski lifts, ski school, ski jump, skating, tobogganing, curling, horse sleighs.
Swimming, sailing boats can be hired, water skiing school.

WESTENDORF 2 chair lifts, 6 ski lifts, ski school, skijoring, tobogganing, curling, horse sleighs.

WILDSCHÖNAU Combined facilities. Cable car, 3 chair lifts, 23 ski lifts, ski schools, tobogganing, curling, horse sleighs.

SHOPPING

INNSBRUCK Shopping in Innsbruck means browsing leisurely through the historic streets of Maria-Theresienstrasse, Museumstrasse, Brixnerstrasse, Meranerstrasse and in and out among the arcades of Herzog-Friedrichstrasse. Everything can be found within a relatively small area. The best-known Tyrolean specialties include: Tyrolean hats, Loden cloth and handwoven materials, dirndls and lederhosen, leather clothing, wood carvings and wrought iron, glass and ceramics, mountain climbing and skiing equipment.

Dirndls and Trachten for Women *Trachten-Konrad,* Maria-Theresienstr. 7 and Herzog-Friedrichstr. 22. *Lanz,* Wilhelm Greilstr. 15.

Handcrafts, Gifts and Souvenirs *Tiroler Heimatwerk,* Meranerstr. 2. *Albrecht & Kaaserer,* Wilhelm-Greilstr. 15. *Kunststüberl Aichberger,* Riesengasse 5. *Tresor,* Salurnerstr. 15.

Leather Clothing and Furs *Felix Bernarello,* Museumstr. 16. *Schwammenhöfer,* Burggraben 1. *Obholzer,* Herzog-Friedrichstr. 32. *Leder Boutique,* Salurnerstr. 15.

Leatherware *Frechinger* Maria-Theresienstr. 22. *Elegance,* Maria-Theresienstr. 49 (Landhauspassage). *Ennsmann,* Meranerstr. 7. *Fürrutter,* Herzog-Friedrichstr. 12.

Lederhosen *Oppacher,* Mentlgasse 2.

Men's Wear and Trachten *Strobl,* Salurnerstr. 16. *Fritz Mayr,* Burggraben 5–27 (also hats). *Lodenbaur,* Brixnerstr. 4. *Lodenhaus Hubertus,* Museumstr. 26.

Petit Point *Ennsmann,* Meranerstr. 7. *Frechinger,* Maria-Theresienstr. 22.

Wrought-Iron and Weinhebers *Tiroler Heimatwerk,* Meranerstr. 2.

Wood Carvings *Tiroler Heimatwerk,* Meranerstr. 2. *Ghedina,* Maria-Theresienstr. 4.

USEFUL ADDRESSES

INNSBRUCK *Official* tourist offices: *Tourist Dept. for Tyrol,* Adamgasse 2A, tel. 207 77; *Verkehrsverein Innsbruck-Igls* for Innsbruck-Igls, Burggraben 3, tel. 257 15; *Tiroler Fremdenverkehrswerbung,* Tyrol Tourist Office, Bozner Platz 6, tel. 207 59; *Zimmernachweis,* room reservation service for city, main railway station; International tourist agencies: *American Express,* Brixnerstr. 3; *Wagons Lits-Cook,* Brixnerstr. 2.

British Consulate, Erlerstr. 17/I, tel. 56–20. *Amerikanisch-Österreichische Gesellschaft,* American-Austrian Society, Maria-Theresienstr. 38, tel. 244–07.

Car Hire *Carop,* Amraserstr. 6, tel. 31491; *VW-Leihwagendienst,* has chauffeured cars with English-speaking drivers and excursions by *VOWA,* Erlerstr. 17, tel. 20095; *Franz Rindfleisch,* Zeughausgasse 3, minibus; *Avis,* Salurnerstr. 16, tel. 20715.

KALS AM GROSSGLOCKNER *Fremdenverkehrsverband* tel. 211.

KITZBÜHEL Tourist Office at Südtirolerplatz 4.

LIENZ for city information including room reservations, *Fremdenverkehrsverband,* Tourist Association, Hauptplatz, tel. 2671.

MATREI IN OSTTIROL *Fremdenverkehrsverband* tel. 227.

SILLIAN *Fremdenverkehrsverband* tel. 280.

VORARLBERG

Alpine Meadows and a Floating Stage

Tiny Vorarlberg covers an area of slightly more than 2,600 square kilometers, and is (with the exception of Vienna) the smallest of Austria's federal states. As its name implies, the state lies "before the Arlberg," that massive range of Alps, the watershed of Europe, and forms the western tip of Austria. To the north lies Bavaria, and to the west and south Vorarlberg is bounded by the Swiss frontier.

The history of Vorarlberg goes much further back than the times of the Alemannic tribes, for remains from the Stone Age and prehistoric times have been found in all parts of the state. The Vorarlbergers claim, according to legend, that when Noah landed from the ark after the flood he found himself in Vorarlberg. Timbers from the ark are said to have been found on the top of the Widderstein Mountain.

The countryside has much in common with neighboring Switzerland, and the inhabitants of the state have close affinities with the Swiss. Both peoples are descended from the same ancient German Alemannic tribes that flourished in the 3rd century BC and both have the same characteristics of thrift, hard work, and a deeprooted instinct for democracy and independence. Indeed, after the collapse of the Habsburg monarchy, Vorarlberg could have become a part of Switzerland. In May 1919 about

80 percent of the inhabitants voted for starting negotiations with Switzer
land for an eventual union with that country, but the Peace Conference
at St. Germain decreed otherwise, and Vorarlberg became a part of th
newly created Austrian Republic.

Today, Vorarlberg is the center of Austria's important textile industry
playing a vital role in the country's export trade and bid for self-sufficien
cy.

While the seat of the Vorarlberg state government is in Bregenz, th
official capital of the state, the highest court, the chamber of commerce
and the financial administration have their headquarters in Feldkirch
and the state institute for economic promotion selected Dornbirn for th
seat of its office.

Vorarlberg is well provided with accommodations ranging from th
international first class to the low-priced regional Gasthof-types. I
smaller and less-known resorts you will often find that the bottom price
do not always represent the lowest quality when compared to the othe
areas inside, as well as outside Austria. The highest prices are charge
during the peak winter season in such renowned skiing centers as Zür
and Lech, and here, together with extras, your daily expenses may ru
as high as in any other top-priced locality in the country.

When staying in summer or winter resorts you will find that the bes
arrangement is to take en pension terms. When traveling through th
countryside or visiting a town, the exploration of local style taverns an
non-hotel restaurants will be more interesting.

Winter Sports

Similar to the neighboring Tyrol, Vorarlberg is an excellent area fo
skiing, including high mountain ski tours. Several top winter spor
centers, such as Zürs, Lech-Oberlech, Bielerhöhe, and Hochkrumbac
are located quite high and skiing is possible here from early Decembe
until the end of April and even later, particularly on Bielerhöhe. On son
of the glaciers you can ski in August. The best time for skiing in low
areas is usually between early January and mid-March. International ar
national competitions take place throughout the winter. Skiing equi
ment can be rented in most places. In several places ski lifts are lit fo
night-time skiing. Snowmobiles are banned altogether. During summ
months, many resorts—Mellau and Brand for two—offer tennis, hiki
and fitness packages.

Tobogganing is widely practised in the region and several competito
take place every year. Ice skating competitions and ice hockey games c
frequently be seen on the most important skating rinks. Horse sleighs a
often a necessity in higher areas and are therefore easy to find.

Route Planning

The main **railway** line from Vienna and Innsbruck enters Vorarlberg at Langen after coming out of the Arlberg tunnel. This is the route of both the Arlberg and Orient Express trains. It proceeds through Bludenz to Feldkirch, where it splits into two lines, the Arlberg Express route going through tiny Liechtenstein to Switzerland and Vorarlberg Express route through Dornbirn to Bregenz, continuing from there to Lindau in Germany. The shortest connection between Bregenz and Switzerland is via St Margrethen (in Swiss territory). All the localities mentioned are fast-train stops. A fast train takes about 1½ hours from Bregenz to Langen and about 3½ hours from Bregenz to Innsbruck. Small local railroads connect Bregenz with Bezau in lower Bregenzerwald, and Bludenz with Schruns in lower Montafon valley.

Narrow-gauge steam locomotives with old cars used to take passengers through the Bregenzerwald and the Montafon Valley. The line damaged by floods a year or two ago should be in operation again this summer.

State and private **bus services** connect all the towns and villages not served by the railroad. Half-track vehicles and sleighs are used in winter in the higher places when necessary. Some of the highest roads become impassable for motor vehicles in heavy snow and then you have to hire horse sleighs. Sightseeing bus tours originate in Bregenz.

If you are **driving**, the A14 Autobahn leads south from Bregenz to Dornbirn (11 km.), Feldkirch (35 km.), and Bludenz (53 km.); Route 316 continues west to the entrance to the 14 km.-long Arlberg tunnel at Langen (80 km.) and winds up to Stuben and the Arlberg pass (92 km.). From Feldkirch it is 15 km. to Vaduz in Liechtenstein. From Bludenz, very narrow roads lead south to the Bradner Tal and north into the Grosswalser Tal. Route 188 leads southeast up the Montafon valley to the Silvretta pass (43 km.). The Silvretta high mountain toll road begins at Partenen and climbs up at a maximum of 12 percent in many sharp curves to a height of 6,700 feet. If weather conditions are normal it is open for traffic from early June until late October. Shortly above Stuben the Flexen Pass (5,800 feet) road branches off for Zürs and Lech (8 and 12 km., kept open during the winter months as far as Lech) and continues to Warth (18 km.), where it meets the road coming from Bregenz through Bregenzerwald. The latter is a beautiful drive through the lower and upper sections of the Bregenzerwald mountains (77 km. from Bregenz to Warth), although the entire road is not in the best condition and the last section near Warth is quite narrow.

Exploring Vorarlberg—Bregenz

Bregenz is a picturesque little town with 24,000 inhabitants, lying at the eastern extremity of Bodensee (Lake Constance), that vast sheet of water 64 km. long and nearly 13 km. across at the widest point. The town is built on the slopes of the wooded foothills that rise gently from the shores of the lake. The old part of the town is built on higher ground and overlooks the new, modern part of Bregenz, which spread out along the lakeside, where an almost eight-kilometer-long promenade follows the shoreline. More than any other town in Austria the face of Bregenz has changed. With the opening of the new goods railway station outside the town, acres of lakeside land were redeveloped as a recreation area.

The time to visit Bregenz is during the four weeks of the Music Festival (July to August). This is a spectacle you shouldn't miss if you have any time to spare, since the Bregenz Festival takes place on the lake itself and offers a unique and memorable evening you are sure to enjoy. A vast floating stage is the setting for one of the world's most beautiful floating musical festivals. In front of the stage, the orchestra pit is built on a jetty. If it rains, performances are moved to the new Festival Hall near the lake.

Another "must" in Bregenz is a trip to the top of the Pfänder Mountain above the town. A funicular from the heart of the town will take you up in a matter of 6 minutes. From this vantage point 3,200 feet up, you get one of the finest panoramic views to be found on the Continent.

On a fine, sunny day the breathtaking view right down the entire length of the lake. At your feet lie the compact group of houses of the Old Town, and lower down, the bustling New Town of Bregenz. To the right a few miles away, lies the German frontier, with the Bavarian town of Lindau clearly seen in the foreground, and the large city of Friedrichshafen in the middle distance. To the left, you can catch a glimpse of the Rhine, 16 km. away, and beyond it lies Switzerland.

The Bregenz Forest

Directly behind Bregenz lies the Bregenzerwald (Bregenz Forest). This is the name given to a wide area of densely wooded highlands, charming valleys, and lovely alpine meadows dotted with thick clusters of red, white, blue and yellow alpine flowers, all set against a fabulous backdrop of majestic Alps.

Should you be searching for the ideal place for the family summer holiday, particularly if some of the family are very young, then you couldn't do better than to choose the Bregenz Forest. Even if you are just passing through, a day's tour of the Bregenz Forest is most rewarding.

Here you will see the Vorarlbergers as they really are. In the picturesque little villages the women still wear the handsome, stiffly starched folk dress of their ancestors, as it has been the usage for the past five or six hundred years.

The women take a great pride in their national dress, and with great justification. On festive occasions the girls carry a golden headdress shaped like a small crown, and the married women a pointed cap. Old men's folk dress is still worn by the members of local brass bands, and it differs from place to place according to the shape of the cap and the color of various parts of clothing.

In the Bregenz Forest white is the color of mourning, while in other districts the more usual black is worn at funerals and on Sundays.

At Egg—an easy name to remember—the valley branches into two. The left-hand fork leads down a country road to the villages of the lower part of Bregenzerwald, all with an old-world charm of their own: Langenegg, Lingenau, Krumbach, Hittisau, Riefensberg, and Sibratsgfäll, to name only a few.

The right-hand fork, continuing the main road through the Bregenz Forest, takes you through Andelsbuch, where the main valley of the area starts to spread out. On the other side above the valley is Schwarzenberg, which can be reached also from Dornbirn by the road over Bödele. Then, round a bend, Bezau, the best known of the Bregenzerwald villages, comes into view.

All these villages lie at about 2,000 feet above sea level, but now the winding country road climbs steeply round the spurs of the Alps to another string of villages, Mellau, Schnepfau and Au. From Au—which really is pronounced "ow"!—a side road leads to Damüls, the highest village of Bregenzerwald.

Dornbirn and Feldkirch

Dornbirn is important because it is the center of Vorarlberg's main industry—textiles. Every year an important international trade fair, with textiles a specialty, is held that coincides in time with the Bregenz Music Festival. A cable car joins the town with the 3,300-foot Karren heights, with a very fine view.

From Dornbirn, still traveling up the Rhine valley you pass through Hohenems, with its outstanding Renaissance Palace and the remains of the once very powerful Alt-Ems fortress. Further up the valley is Götzis, a small town with interesting churches and castle ruins, and known for its textile industry.

Still farther is Feldkirch, Vorarlberg's oldest town. This is the first stop on the main railway line after crossing into Austria from Switzerland. Parts of Feldkirch date from the Middle Ages and it is still a town with great character. Picturesque arcades line the busy, narrow main street, and the ancient town hall and city gates are splendid examples of 13th- and 15th-century craftmanship. The Great Castle of Schattenburg, the 12th-century former seat of the powerful valley barons, is open to the public.

At Feldkirch both road and railway turn into the Ill valley toward Bludenz, the fourth of Vorarlberg's democratic little towns. Bludenz, a mainline station, is the starting point for three of Vorarlberg's loveliest valleys, which all emerge into the deep Ill valley in this area.

The Great Walser Valley

To the north lies the Grosswalser Tal (Great Walser Valley), first colonized by Walliser highland clans from the Valais area in Switzerland (of Burgundian origin). At the entrance to the valley, which is easily accessible from the Bludenz railway station by bus, lies Thüringen, a charming little summer resort with a small lake, waterfall, and splendid view down over the Ill valley with the Rhätikon mountains in the distance.

From Thüringen, the bus climbs steeply up the gradient into the Walsertal, to Sonntag, or "Sunday village", in the heart of the valley. Be sure to get a seat on the right-hand side of the bus, or you will not be able to enjoy the magnificent panorama of Alps—the back door to the Bregenz Forest—as you go along. Beyond lies Buchboden, a tiny hamlet high up in the outer range of the Arlberg. This hamlet, Sonntag, and Fontanella, another mountain village at the foot of a spur three kilometers to the north of Sonntag, are well known bases for mountain climbers in the summer, and in winter for proficient skiers.

The Brandner Valley

Turning southwest across the Ill river from the railway station at Bludenz, we reach Bürs, a pleasant village at the foot of the 13-km.-long Brandner valley, which straggles steeply on through the narrow, sheer mountain gorge, and after about half an hour's drive from here we arrive in Brand, a mountain village at the foot of Scesaplana in the Rätikon range.

Brand (3,200 feet) is becoming increasingly popular among foreign tourists as a health resort and winter sports center. If you are fond of walking, you can climb by easy stages along the forest paths without much exertion to the beautiful Lüner glacier lake, standing 6,700 feet above sea level (about a 3-hour climb). You can shorten your walk by half if you take the cable car which brings you from Schattenlagant, farther up the valley from Brand, to Lünersee in five minutes. This cable car operates only in summer, but the chair lift to Niggenkopf (5,300 ft.) runs in summer and winter.

Anyone interested in geology should pay a visit to the tiny village chapel, which is built of a local rock called "trowel stone." This stone may be cut into shape quite easily with an ordinary saw; when exposed to the air, the masonry then shrinks slightly, hardens and becomes rather brittle.

The Montafon Valley

The third valley leading from Bludenz is the lovely Montafon, famous for its brown castle, the most attractive of Vorarlberg's many tourist-frequented valleys.

Tschagguns and Schruns, about halfway up the valley, both lie within a mile of each other, both equally well known as summer and winter sports resorts. Neither place is of the fashionable variety, but the picture postcard views over the Ferwall Alps to the east and the mighty Rätikon on the western side of the valley are unsurpassed anywhere in Austria, while in wintertime the skiing is as good here as in any of the more internationally famous centers.

Shortly before St. Gallenkirch the valley divides. To the southwest, a narrow offshoot from the main valley leads up to Gargellen (4,667 feet), a tiny Alpine village sandwiched in between the massive Rätikon and the towering Silvretta mountains. In the summer Gargellen is famous as a base for mountaineers intent upon getting to grips with the challenging Alpine peaks. Those less athletically inclined may enjoy really excellent trout fishing in the fast mountain streams. In the winter there is some very fine skiing, but to make the most of the facilities, you should have some considerable ability.

Continuing on, Gaschurn is still another popular little place for winter sports enthusiasts. This is the touring region par excellence. Local guides will take skiing parties on 2- or 3-day tours across the 10,000-foot peaks and glaciers of the Silvretta and the Ferwall, sleeping in the snug, well appointed rest huts at night. But it is not necessary to be a skiing expert to enjoy winter sports at Gaschurn, and there are plenty of facilities for beginners.

Exploring the Bielerhöhe

Less than 5 km. from Gaschurn, along the main road, is Partenen (3,470 feet), another pleasant village, particularly for skiers. One of the huge Vermunt power plants is at Partenen, and another one is above, at the lower artificial lake. A third plant is at Latschau above Tschagguns, but this one also receives its water from Partenen. The plants were opened before World War II, but enlarged after the war when the dams for the artificial lakes on Silvretta were built. Most of the current is exported to West Germany, with the rest divided between Vorarlberg and Tyrol.

Just beyond Partenen is the beginning of the Silvretta Hochalpen-Strasse, a private toll road owned by the Vorarlberger Illwerke power company, leading through 24 km. of curves and bends over the Bieler-höhe Pass (6,700 feet) and the Vorarlberg-Tyrol border to Galtür in the Paznaun valley of Tyrol. Built in connection with the giant Vermunt electricity works that collect water from the Silvretta glaciers in two artificial lakes, it is a masterpiece of high Alpine road engineering. Many curves and a narrow width make it difficult to drive; it is normally open early June to mid-October.

The Other Arlberg

Bludenz is the departure point for the Arlberg massif, that Mecca of winter sports. Passing through the narrow Klostertal valley and the small hamlet of Dalaas, the road begins the steep ascent up the Arlberg, while the railway started its slower climb to Langen am Arlberg right after leaving Bludenz. Langen is the main-line-stop for the internationally known winter sports centers on the Vorarlberg side of the Arlberg. If the Arlberg pass is closed temporarily to motorists during the winter due to a sudden avalanche, then the Arlberg tunnel with its fast approach road will soon see you into Tyrol.

Stuben (4,615 feet), at the beginning of the climb, is famous as the birthplace of Hannes Schneider, Austria's most distinguished ski exponent and pioneer of the ski teaching methods which are now taught throughout the world. Like every village on the Arlberg, it offers magnificent skiing from December until the end of April. Although not as fashionable as the resorts farther up, beyond the Flexen Pass, it is very popular, particularly with tourists who take their skiing seriously.

Just past Stuben the famous Flexen road over the pass begins. This is a veritable triumph of bold engineering. From Stuben the Alpine road looks like some gigantic caterpillar crawling along the face of the steep mountain cliffs. For much of its length the Flexen road is completely covered over by short tunnels of reinforced concrete, or complicated structures of massive wooden beams. For the short stretches where the road emerges into the sunlight, the mountain side is shored up with formidable concrete barriers, while higher up immense barricades guard against the danger of avalanches.

In summer the treeless slopes are covered with Alpine flora, and in wintertime, with eight to fifteen feet of snow on the ground, they become a winter sports paradise. Zürs itself is nothing more than a collection of large hotels. Various ski lifts and chair lifts will take you up to heights of over 8,000 feet to the start of some of the finest downhill runs in Europe.

From Zürs the valley dips down a shallow slope for a few kilometers to Lech (4,800 feet), the second of the two international winter sports resorts on top of the Arlberg. Although some people maintain that Lech is not quite as fashionable as Zürs, the fact is that there are more hotels, better technical facilities, bigger ski schools, more life, and almost as high prices as in Zürs. But there is really not much to choose between them. Zürs has the advantage of being a little higher up, but Lechs is a genuine and very pretty village.

From Lech, the road takes you to Warth am Arlberg, another small village in beautiful mountain scenery, the point of departure for many walks and climbing tours, and an up-and-coming winter sports resort. At Warth, the road splits: one route runs into Tyrol down the wild Lech Valley, eventually reaching Reutte, while the other crosses the high plateau of Hochtannberg, over the pass of the same name (5,500 ft.), to the high resort, and winter sports center of Schröcken.

This old village, framed by towering mountains, was originally settled by Walliser, as were the Grosses Walsertal to the southwest and the Kleines Walsertal to the northeast. Kleines Walsertal or Kleinwalsertal (Small Walser Valley), with its tiny villages of Riezlern, Hirschegg, Mittelberg, and Baad—all renowned summer and winter resorts—represents a sort of geographic anomaly because, thrusting itself into Bavaria from the other side of the high Alpine range above Schröcken, it can be reached from the Austrian side only by a few high mountain paths, whereas its only road communication is with Oberstdorf in Germany. For this reason, the Kleinwalsertal has an economic union with Bavaria, and the currency here is the German Mark; we therefore deal with its tourist facilities in our book on Germany.

From Schröcken, the Hochtannberg road descends along the swift flowing Bregenzer Ache to Au, and then on to Bezau and Egg in Bregenzerwald.

PRACTICAL INFORMATION

HOTELS AND RESTAURANTS

BEZAU Hotels Both (2)—*Kur-Sport-Hotel,* indoor pool, cure facilities; and *Gams.* Both with excellent restaurants.

BIELERHÖHE 6,700 ft. This area is the best for experienced skiers who wish to engage in longer or shorter tours; base for mountain climbing the Silvretta group.

Hotel *Silvrettasee* (1), 80 beds, 45 baths and showers, modern, magnificently situated above the lake, in full view of the mountains, evening tavern with dancing, indoor pool, open Dec. to Oct. Reserve well in advance in winter.

BLUDENZ 1,929 ft. Fast train stop on main line, about 1 hour from Bregenz.
Hotels Both (2)—*Schlosshotel,* 50 beds, many private baths; *Herzog Friedrich,* small, with fine restaurant in Vorarlberg style.
All (3)—*Einhorn,* some rooms more pricey, in quiet locations with good restaurant in rustic décor; *Weisses Kreuz; Arlberger Hof,* and *Post,* both near Rathaus; *Bludenzer Hof,* near railway station; *Gasthaus Zum Hirschen,* 500 years old, renovated but retains local style and décor.

BÖDELE About 4,000 ft., on a mountain plateau above Dornbirn.
Hotel *Alpenhotel Bödele,* modern, restaurant, dancing, beautiful view.

BRAND 3,400 ft. Bus from Bludenz; base for mountain climbing Rhätikon group of mountains; excellent area for ski tours.
Hotels All (1)—*Scesaplana,* beautiful mountain views, 2 pools, dance tavern, indoor tennis, fine restaurant; *Walliserhof* and *Colrosa,* both with indoor pools.
Both (2)—*Hämmerle,* hunting-style tavern; *Lagant,* all rooms with bath.
Valbona (3), dancing in bar café.

BREGENZ 1,305 ft. high on Bodensee.
Hotels *Weisses Kreuz* (1), totally refitted; garni.
All (2)—*Messmer,* small, most rooms with bath, modern, noted restaurant and café; *Central,* 80 beds, most rooms with bath and balcony; *Schwärzler,* good food; *Bodensee* (garni), most rooms with bath or shower; *Berghof Fluh,* with view of lake and forests from restaurant, wine tavern, and bar.
Both (3)—*Adler,* a good Gasthof; *Schwedenschanze,* on the Pfänder mountain above city, reached by cable car, fine view over lake, open mid-May to mid-Sept.
Pension Montfort (P2), best pension, Neugasse 5, not far from railway station.
Restaurants *Zoll,* Arlbergstr. 118, on the edge of Bregenz, is one of the finest in Austria. Fresh local food, fish dishes and cakes are superb. Very expensive but good value for money. *Gösserbräu Stadtkeller,* Anton-Schneiderstr. 1, large Stuben-type establishment with good selection of food; *Burgrestaurant* on Gebhardsberg has several atmospheric rooms and a magnificent view of the lake from the terrace; *Zur Ilge,* Maurachgasse 6, wine tavern in 15th-century house.
Both (3)—*Heidelberger Fass,* Kirchstr. 30, pleasant, spacious, wood-paneled Stuben; *Brändle-Stuben,* Bahnhofstr. 19, across from the railway station. Both have a few rooms. The rough and ready *Goldener Hirsch* in the town center will on request produce the best Backhendl in Austria.

DAMÜLS 4,684 ft., base for climbing highest peaks of the Bregenzerwald.
Hotels Best is *Hohes Licht,* indoor pool, small and (2). *Damülserhof* (2), 40 rooms with bath or shower; fitness room, indoor pool, very good restaurant.

DORNBIRN 1,433 ft. 15 minutes by fast train from Bregenz.
Hotels *Parkhotel* (1), Goethestrasse, with café, restaurant, Stübe tavern and dancing in *Alp-Bar.*
All (2)—*Zum Verwalter,* in same family since 18th century; *Katharinenhof,* garni, indoor pool; *Rickatschwende Alpen,* indoor and outdoor pools, sauna.
Gasthof Hirschen (3), good food and garden.

Large campsite.

Restaurants *Rotes Haus,* original 16th century, old tavern with period furniture, wood-carving, wrought-iron and pewter ware, located on main square next to the church; *Karrenrestaurant,* at the top station of Karren cable car.

FELDKIRCH 1,500 ft., about 35 minutes from Bregenz by fast train.

Hotels Both (1)—*Alpenrose,* with period-furnished rooms, in pedestrian zone of medieval town; and *Bären,* on main road but with soundproofed windows, airconditioning, recommended restaurant.

All (2)—*Weisses Kreuz,* most rooms with bath or shower, restaurant; *Löwen-Central,* good restaurant; *Alpenrose,* small, in quiet location.

All (3)—*Hochhaus,* café, near station, garni; *Gasthof Lingg,* good food; *Montfort* and *Hecht,* both small.

Youth Hostel, large campsite.

FRASTANZ Near Feldkirch.

Hotels Both (2)—*Motel Galina,* 90 beds, all rooms with bath, modern; *Haus Evi,* a baby-hotel with 25 beds, where you can leave your small children while traveling, doctor in the house.

GARGELLEN 4,667 ft. Bus from Schruns. Base for mountain climbing the Rhätikon group.

Hotels The following categories are based on peak season rates. *Heinspitze* (1), all rooms with bath; beautifully furnished; good restaurant.

All (2)—*Madrisa,* 110 beds, in new annex, all rooms with bath, indoor pool, restaurant, local color in tavern, bar and own orchestra.

Feriengut Gargellenhof, several small buildings, restaurant, local-type tavern.

Silvretta, 80 beds, most rooms with shower, indoor pool, nursery.

Bachmann, newly renovated, most rooms with bath and balcony, indoor pool, sauna, fireplace and bar.

All (3)—*Alpenrose,* restaurant, bar with music; *Edelweiss;* and *Alpenhaus Montafon,* about 100 beds, a type of chalet hotel with separate apartments for 4–6 people, all with kitchen and refrigerator, most rooms with shower.

GASCHURN 3,211 ft. Bus from Schruns and Blundenz. Base for mountain climbing Rhätikon and Ferwall.

Hotels Both (1)—*Sporthotel Epple,* 130 beds, most rooms with bath or shower, indoor pool, zither music in the grill restaurant; *Posthotel Rössle,* 85 beds, 23 baths, indoor pool, folk-style tavern, café with dancing, slightly less expensive.

Both (2)—*Versettla,* 40 rooms, restaurant and dance bar; *Pension Sonnblick,* indoor pool.

Restaurants *Altmontafon* (2), good grill dishes, a noted restaurant.

LECH-OBERLECH 4,736 ft. and 5,600 ft., respectively. Base for mountain climbing in the Arlberg area. Bus from Langen (Vorarlberg) and St. Anton am Arlberg (Tyrol), both on the main railway line.

Hotels Four sets of rates are applied by the top hotels—1) the highest during peak winter season, Christmas, Feb., March and early April; 2) next highest for the rest of the winter season, first 3 weeks in Dec., last 3 weeks in Jan., rest of April if still open; 3) a little lower for the summer season, July, Aug.; 4) the lowest before and after summer season, May, June, Sept.

Average opening time is early Dec. to mid-April, early May to end Sept.

Our categories are based on the highest rates, which can, in the case of the best accommodations, be up to double the lowest rates. Advance reservations are a must in winter.

First is *Post* (L), a Romantic Hotel patronized by royalty and Bruno Kreisky among others; the beautifully furnished restaurant serves excellent food; also bar with music, indoor pool, games room.

All (1), with restaurants, cafés or taverns, some with dancing and entertainment—*Post,* a Romantic Hotel, heads the list, indoor pool, bar with music, games-room; *Arlberg,* indoor and outdoor pools; *Schneider-Almhof,* 2 pools, tennis; *Tannberghof; Krone; Kristiania,* owned by Olympic ski champion Othmar Schneider, all rooms with bath, popular *Scotch Club; Hinterwies,* all rooms with bath, restaurant, bar.

Both (2)—*Haus Lech,* and *Solaria.*

Youth Hostel.

In Oberlech: Both (2)—*Sporthotel Sonnenburg,* lovely sun terrace, *gemütlich* restaurant, small bar and dancing weekly, indoor pool; *Montana,* smaller with good restaurant.

Restaurant The restaurant on the *Rüfikopf,* reached by cable car (7,700 ft.) offers spectacular mountain scenery.

LOCHAU 4 km. from Bregenz on a lovely lakeside trail.

Restaurants *Mangold* and *Messmer* can both be highly recommended, serving local as well as international cuisine.

MELLAU in Bregenz Forest. Tennis school. **Hotel** *Kreuz* (2), indoor pool, apartments, good restaurant.

SCHRÖCKEN 4,162 ft. Bus from Bezau on Bregenzerwald local railway.

Hotels Only modest but comfortable hostelries available, some fairly large.

SCHRUNS 2,263 ft. Local railway and bus from Bludenz.

Hotels Both (1)—*Kurhotel Montafon,* with cure facilities; *Löwen,* both large and with indoor pools, dance bars.

Both (2)—*Messmer,* most rooms with bath and balcony; *Krone,* with zither music in its rustic tavern.

Both (3)—*Gasthof Rhätikon* and *Gavadura,* with 2-bed and 4-bed apartments.

Located in a picturesque small alley and serving delicious cakes and torten, is *Café Feuerstein.* Antique furnishings; take a look at the upstairs room.

Campsite.

SCHWARZENBERG-BÖDELE 2,300 ft. to about 5,000 ft. Reached by bus from Dornbirn by a new road which opened up this growing skiing center.

STUBEN 4,615 ft. Bus from Langen on the main railway line.

Hotels *Hubertushof* (2), fine restaurant, indoor pool.

All (3)—*Post,* all rooms with bath/shower, *Albona* and *Mondschein,* indoor pool.

TSCHAGGUNS 2,250 ft. Base for mountain climbing in the Rhätikon. Local railway and bus from Bludenz. Actually one locality together with Schruns.

Hotels All (2)—*Cresta,* indoor pool; *Sonne,* indoor pool; *Verwall,* all rooms with bath or shower.

Large campsite.

VANDANS 6 km. from Bludenz.

Hotel *Zentral Sporthotel Kasper* (1), 30 rooms with bath. Tennis, indoor pool, fitness center; good restaurant.

ZÜRS 5,632 ft. Base for mountain climbing in the Arlberg area. Bus from Langen and St. Anton am Arlberg, both on main railway line.

Hotels The usual opening time for hotels is early Dec. to end April, early June to late Sept. The top hotels here are the most expensive in the Vorarlberg. Highest rates are charged during peak winter season, Christmas, New Year, Feb. to April. In summer, prices are lower, often a half or less of the peak winter rates.

Our categories are based on the top rates. Reserve in advance for winter season.

Both (L)—*Albona,* 60 beds, all rooms with bath; and *Zürserhof,* 170 beds, 10 apartments with all amenities and fireplace, renowned cuisine, cocktail bar, ice bar, indoor tennis court, bowling, open winter only, and full-board terms only.

All (1)—*Alpenhof,* 85 beds, all rooms with bath, indoor pool and sauna.

Alpenrose-Post, 230 beds, 50 baths, restaurant, sun terrace, cocktail bar, ice bar in winter, dance hall with evening entertainment.

Central Sporthotel Edelweiss, 120 beds, 40 baths, restaurant, café, cocktail bar, ice bar in winter, evening dancing; in winter full-board terms only.

Lorünser, en pension terms only, open in winter, 96 beds, 54 baths and showers, restaurant, sun terrace cocktail bar, ice bar in winter.

All (2)—*Flexen,* open only in winter, *en pension* arrangements only, 50 beds, Tyrolean-style restaurant, sun terrace.

Gasthof Enzian, 50 beds, open winter only, and with full-board terms only.

Mara, small, all rooms with bath.

Hirlanda (3), with full-board terms only.

SPECIAL EVENTS

BLUDENZ Sun. before *Fasching* ends, colorful masked groups and processions; 1st Sun. in Lent (and after *Fasching* ends), observation of ancient *Funkenbrennen* and *Scheibenschlagen,* burning bonfires and witches' trial; June and July, colorful folkdress brass bands playing in town square, local parades, religious processions.

BÖDELE Early March, international ski jumping.

BREGENZ There are sailing regattas in June on Bodensee, and also a yearly Bodensee Week. Mid-July to early Aug., *Bregenz Festival,* light opera and ballet performances, on incomparable water stage on the lake—city theater and city concert hall sites of other performances.

DORNBIRN *Joler Cup* toboggan race on Twelfth Night; renowned *textile fair* with several fashion shows, usually first 10 days of Aug., most important yearly event. *Hobby-fair* in mid-Apr.

FRASTANZ Early March, giant slalom race on Bazora, above the town.

GASCHURN June and July, colorful folk-dress brass bands, folk tunes in town squares, local parades, religious processions.

HOHENEMS *Schubertiade,* for three weeks in June, includes concerts, lieder evenings and chamber music, in a beautiful Renaissance castle.

LECH-OBERLECH Feb., masked ski processions, downhill runs, and *Fasching* balls. Early March, often fashion shows in skating rink.
June-July, colorful folk-dress brass bands hold forth with marching and folk tunes in town squares, local parades, religious processions.

SCHRUNS Masked ski processions, downhill runs and *Fasching* balls in Feb. June and July, colorful folk-dress brass bands hold forth in town square with marching and folk tunes, local parades and religious processions.

ZÜRS The year opens with a torchlight race of ski instructors. Feb., masked ski processions, downhill runs, and *Fasching* balls.
Early March, often fashion shows in the skating rink. Late April, giant slalom race, one of the skiing season's closing events.

CASINO
BREGENZ In the GWL department store, Römerstr. open daily from 4 P.M for roulette and baccara.

SPORTS
BIELERHÖHE To reach this out-of-the-way spot, take a bus to Galtür from Landeck on Tyrolean side, and motorsleigh or horse sleigh from there; or bus to Partenen on Vorarlberg side from Bludenz or Schruns, cable railway to Tromenir ½-hour walk through 3 tunnels, from the last tunnel the sleigh to Silvretta Pass In both cases, it is advisable to notify the Silvrettasee Hotel of your arrival; they will provide for a sleigh and take care of luggage. Hire of ski equipment available as well as ski school, ski teachers and mountain guides, suitable slopes for beginners, ski lift.

BLUDENZ Riding facilities, at *Reitclub Bregenz,* Bürs bei Bludenz. Landing site for gliders at Rungelin nearby.

Cable car to Muttersberg, ski lift, ski school, ski jump, 2 toboggan runs, skating and curling rink.

BRAND Fishing in Lünersee nearby, for lake trout and char.

3 chair lifts to Niggenkopf (5,300 ft.), 5 ski lifts, ski school, skating rink, tobogganing, horse sleighs, swimming pools, tennis courts, ski-tennis tournaments.

BREGENZ Water sports, large swimming complex on lake, sailing school, rowing and kayaking, 4 yacht clubs.

Riding facilities, riding club at Altreuteweg 1.

Fishing for salmon trout, pike, carp, tench and perch in Bodensee.

Skiing mainly on the Pfänder (3,200 ft.) reached by cable car, 2 ski lifts, ski school, ski jump, tobogganing, skating rink, ice hockey, curling rink.

DAMÜLS 2-part chair lift, 2 ski lifts, ski school, skijoring, tobogganing, horse sleighs.

DORNBIRN Riding facilities, instructors and covered riding arena, contact riding club at Neugasse. Indoor swimming pool.

Cable car to Karren (over 3,200 ft.) Together with Bödele, 3 ski lifts, ski school, 3 ski jumps in the area, skating rink, tobogganing.

FELDKIRCH Skating rink, ice hockey, curling, tobogganing, ski instructors, ski lift. Riding facilities at the *Riding School Wüstnerhof,* also offering riding excursions. Regional gliding association at Neustadt 37, Feldkirch.

FONTANELLA-FASCHINA 3,750 ft., and 4,900 ft., respectively, base for mountain climbing in the Bregenzerwald. Bus from Ludesch or Bludenz on the main railway line.

Cable car to Stein, chair lift, 4 ski lifts, 2 ski schools, skijoring, tobogganing, curling, horse sleighs.

Indoor swimming at Faschina.

FRASTANZ Riding facilities; gliding landing site.

GARGELLEN Mountain climbing school. Fishing for brook trout in the Suggadinbach.

2 chair lifts, 4 ski lifts, ski school with courses for beginners, advanced, and for those wishing to learn high mountain ski touring, slopes of all degrees of difficulty, tobogganing.

GASCHURN Fishing for brook trout in the Ill. Indoor swimming pool.

2-section chair lift to Gaschurner Sattel (6,600 ft.), 6 ski lifts, ski school, ski jump, outstanding ski tours, skating rink, curling, tobogganing, horse sleighs.

LECH-OBERLECH Particular tennis center here, with tournaments for guests. Fishing for brook trout in Lech brook. Several indoor swimming pools.

3 cable cars, 6 chair lifts, 11 ski lifts, 2 ski schools, first class terrain of a
degrees, ski tours, skijoring, skating rink, horse sleighs.

PARTENEN 3,447 ft., base for mountain climbing in Silvretta group, parts o
the Rätikon and Ferwall. Bus from Schruns and Bludenz.

Ski lift and cable railway to Tromenir, ski school, similar outstanding ski tou
to nearby Gaschurn, tobogganing.

SCHRÖCKEN 9 ski lifts in the area, ski school, toboggan runs, indoor swim
ming pool.

SCHRUNS Mountain climbing school. Fishing in Ill brook for brook trou
Indoor swimming pool.

2-stage cable car and chair lift to Sennigrat (7,540 ft.), cable car in neart
Silbertal. 6 ski lifts in the area, ski school, ski tours, ski jump, skating rinl
tobogganing, horse sleighs.

SCHWARZENBERG-BÖDELE Altogether there are 2 cable cars, 10 ski lift
ski school, ski jump, tobogganing, horse sleighs.

STUBEN Mountain climbing school. 2-section chair lift to Albona mounta
(7,753 ft.), 3 ski lifts, ski school, ski tours, ski jump, tobogganing.

TSCHAGGUNS Chair lift to Grabsalpe, ski lift on Grabsalpe, ski school, s
tours, ski jumps, toboggan runs.

At **Latschau**, 2-section cable railway to Golmerjoch, 2 ski lifts on Golmerjoc

ZÜRS Cable car to Trittkopf (almost 8,000 ft.), double chair lift to Seeko
(7,200 ft.) near Zürsersee, a chair lift from the lake to Mädlochjoch (8,000 ft
5 ski lifts in various locations.

Ski school with 40 instructors, skijoring, skating rink, curling, tobogganin
horse sleighs.

You can continue making a constant circle up and down the mountains by usi
the Lech and Zürs cable cars, lifts, including Europe's first triple-chair lift, a
then the stretch of road between Zürs and Lech (5 km. down from Zürs, sever
daily buses in both directions).

USEFUL ADDRESSES

BREGENZ Official state tourist office, *Landesverkehrsamt Vorarlberg* 690
Bregenz, Römerstrasse 7 (tel. 05574 22525). *Verkehrsverein*, city tourist organiz
tion, Weiherstr. 3; *Landesreisbüro*, officially sponsored provincial tourist agenc
Bahnhofstr. 9A (tel. 05574 22089), across the square from the railway statio

LECH-OBERLECH *Fremdenverkehrsamt Lech* A–6764 Lech.

CARINTHIA

Blue Lakes—Ancient Forests

Few regions of Europe are such well-defined geographical units as Carinthia. High mountains frame it on all sides, with only a few very narrow valleys cutting through this frame. The northern ranges lower slowly—the southern abruptly—into the center, which is composed of the Klagenfurt plain and its extensions, the principal lakes, and the undulating hills between. If you observe the Carinthian landscape from the top of Pyramidenkogel above Wörther Lake or from Kanzelhöhe above Ossiacher Lake, both of which offer excellent views over most of the state, Carinthia will appear before your eyes as a huge arena. The Drau River winds its way through the arena, passing by Gothic and baroque steeples of village churches, and together with the lower Gurk and Glan valleys forms its floor. Blue-green lakes rest comfortably between the shoulders of low forested elevations and reflect the golden white light of rocky faces of the Karawanken and Carnic Alps, the highest southern steps of the arena. To the northeast the lower, balding Koralpe and Saualpe, and to the north the heavily wooded Gurktaler Alps, close off the region toward Styria; and to the northwest the snowy peaks of the Hohe Tauern soar to the mighty Pasterzen glacier of the

Grossglockner, king of Austrian Alps (12,461 feet).

Carinthia's History

Because of this geographic compactness, it is no wonder that Carinthia became a political unit very early in history. Many Bronze Age graves have yielded rich prehistoric finds. Various Illyrian tribes lived here during the Hallstatt period. The first known state organization, however, was the kingdom of the Alpine Celts, set up a few centuries BC, with the capital in Noreia, the site of which is still unknown and disputed by historians. It lasted until the Romans conquered the area in the late 1st century BC, setting up the Roman province of Noricum. The Romans left around AD 600. The ancestors of the Slovenes, then called Carinthians or Carantanians, established a state organization in this region, with its probable center in the Zollfeld area; it was ruled by independent dukes and was, according to medieval chronicles, called Carantania.

In the mid-eighth century the Slovenes asked the neighboring Bavarian dukes for assistance in staving off Avar invasions from the east, and an alliance was born which later resulted in Bavarian lordship over Carantania. During the time of Charles the Great, Carantania, together with Bavaria, became his vassal state; thus Carinthia became a part of the Holy Roman Empire of the German Nation at its very birth and remained with it until its end. In the early ninth century, after an unsuccessful rebellion, the Slovenian rulers were replaced by Franks and in 976 Carinthia became the first imperial duchy in the present Austrian territory. In 1335 the Habsburgs added Carinthia to their possessions, ruling benevolently till 1918. Since the disintegration of the Austrian Empire in 1918, Carinthia has been a federal state of the Austrian Republic.

After the Slovenian settlement many parts of the country remained only thinly inhabited, but through the following centuries many new settlers arrived, mostly from Bavaria and also from other German areas, and the German language gradually prevailed. Numerous old Slovenian customs and also old pagan Celtic beliefs, however, have still been preserved together with a Slovenian minority in South Carinthia which in a plebiscite in 1920 voted to remain with Austria.

Weather Matters and Winter Sports

If you wish to see the province in its best festive dress of blue and emerald lakes, framed by dark green wooded hills and rocky peaks, and also do some swimming, you should come between mid-May and early October. Carinthia has the best summer weather in Austria. If you plan to come during July and August and stay even at a lesser-known resort, you will need advance reservations. Early spring or fall, when the colors are purest and the crowds not yet in evidence, are perhaps the most enjoyable seasons for quiet sightseeing.

Here, as in the rest of Austria, skiing is the principal winter sport. The skiing season in the mountain areas lasts from December to March, high up in Hohe Tauern it extends into late spring with the international Grossglockner glacier ski racing, usually in early June.

Carinthia has slopes of all degrees of difficulty, from the gentler ones for novices to real challenges for the experienced Alpine skier, with accommodations at considerably lower prices than in many other areas. Particular bargains are Katschberg and Turracher Höhe. There is winter camping for skiiers at Döbriach on Millstättersee.

The principal lake resorts are well provided with hotels of all categories, some of them luxurious. Hotels elsewhere are usually of the modest and provincial type, although you will find some exceptions in such large localities as Klagenfurt and Villach and in some mountain resorts. In the mountain areas in general, however, the picturesque Alpine-style hostelries will often give you more in return than you expect. Prices on the whole are a little lower than in such tourist-conscious provinces as Salzburg and Tyrol; during the peak summer season first class accommodations in the top lake resorts of Velden or Pörtschach, may run into about the same amount of money as in most other fashionable Austrian vacation spots. During the high season you will find it advantageous to take room-and-board terms in resort areas.

Fishing will bring nice rewards in the form of trout and grayling, if you are fishing in smaller streams; in the Drau River you can also count on huck, eel, and a number of other species. The richest variety is, of course, provided by the lakes, where you can get lake trout, pike, carp, sheatfish, zander, perch, tench, and a number of others. Licenses have to be obtained locally; inquire at the town administration.

Route Planning

Two main **railway** lines connect Carinthia with the rest of Austria: one from Vienna which enters Carinthia at Friesach and divides at St. Veit, one branch to Klagenfurt and the other to Villach, each about 4½ hours from Vienna, and connected via Pörtschach and Velden. The second line runs from Salzburg through the Tauern tunnels, enters Carinthia at Mallnitz and continues through Spittal to Villach.

On a few summer evenings you can enjoy midnight rides on an old narrow-gauge steam train through the Gurk Valley; the trip begins at 8.30 P.M. at Treibach-Althofen.

In summer the following **Europabus** routes cross Carinthia: Vienna–Wörthersee–Venice, Salzburg–Grossglockner–East Tyrol–Venice, Lienz in East Tyrol–Kötschach–Plöcken Pass–Italy. Austrian postal and private bus services connect all the important places in the province.

If you are **driving by car,** these are the mountain passes in Carinthia to watch for: Iselsberg (3,960 ft.), maximum gradient 8 percent; Grossglockner road (highest point over 8,200 ft.), 12 percent, open from about mid-May until mid-November; Katschberg (5,400 ft.), 18 percent, toll tunnel; Turracher Höhe (5,800 ft.), 23 percent; Seeberg (4,000 ft.), 12 percent, closed in winter; Loibl (4,500 ft.), 24 percent, closed in winter, but the tunnel keeps communication with Yugoslavia open all year; Wurzen Pass (3,500 ft.), 26 percent, open in winter; Plöcken Pass (4,470 ft.), 14 percent, mostly snowed-in in winter; Gailberg Sattel (3,200 ft.), 10 percent; Obervellach to Mallnitz (3,900 ft.), 9 percent.

A short route from Vienna is via Graz, with considerable sections of the Vienna–Villach South Autobahn (A2) now completed. The alternatives from Graz, Route 70 over the Pack Sattel, and 74 and 69 over the Soboth, are both scenically beautiful, but, like most roads in Carinthia narrow and winding. An exception is the Tauern Autobahn from Salzburg to Spittal an der Drau, and its continuation, Route 100, to Villach. The 18km. of the Malta Hochalm toll road are particularly scenic. The shortest connection from Vienna to Carinthia is by the old Triester strasse via Semmering, Bruck-Mur, Knittelfeld, Unzmarkt, Friesach and St. Veit.

All the important roads are plowed in winter, but if you are not experienced in Alpine winter driving you should be very careful. Snow tires or chains are needed.

The Grossglockner toll road connects West Carinthia with Salzburg; the "Parking Tower" at the Frans-Josefs-Höhe above the glacier, provides parking for about 1,000 cars at no extra charge.

The 16-km. road from Villach up the Villacher Alpe (7,100 ft.) discloses magnificent views on every curve.

Lake boats ply between towns on Wörthersee, Ossiachersee, Weissensee, and Millstättersee from mid-May until about mid-October; the services are quite frequent during the peak season months.

Exploring Carinthia

Traveling by the main road or railroad from Vienna, and after crossing Styria, our first town in Carinthia will be Friesach, in the narrow Metnitz valley. Here begins an area, extending to the Wörthersee and Villach that can be called the heart of the state and the hub of Carinthian history. The most important historic finds have been made in this area; here the main Roman settlements existed, the first churches were founded, the oldest castles and towns built.

Romantic Friesach, which is still surrounded by double ramparts and a moat, was first mentioned in the 9th century, and the market town has existed at least since the 11th century. For a long period it belonged to the prince-bishops of Salzburg and was the seat of the administrator of their estates in Carinthia. Gallant medieval tournaments used to take place here and 600 knights participated in the famous one of May 1224 and broke 1,000 lances; the Styrian Minnesinger Ulrich von Liechtenstein, who appeared dressed and equipped all in green, calling himself the "May Knight," alone broke 53 lances on his adversaries.

The town is huddled underneath the hill of Petersberg, where the once-powerful bishop's castle welcomed many a high-ranking medieval dignitary. Today it is mostly in ruins but still well worth visiting, particularly the donjon or watchtower with the Rupertus Chapel and 12th – 13th-century frescos, among which the one of Bishop Romanus from around 1130 is supposed to be the oldest in Austria; and in summer for the open-air classical plays, excellently performed by the local amateur company on a special stage set up in the upper courtyard. Next to the castle ruins stands the ninth-century Peterskirche, a small pre-Romanesque church facing Geiersberg Castle on another hill. Carinthia's two largest churches are the 12th-century, twin-spired, Romanesque parish church with Gothic interior additions, somewhat spoiled by 19th-century restoration, but with exquisite stained-glass windows; and the 13th-century Gothic church of the Dominicans' first monastery on German soil, with a 14th-century stone statue of the Madonna and other remarkable sculptures. Also of great interest in this romantic medieval town are the two winged altars and the 12th-century frescos in the church of the Teutonic Knights; the Renaissance fountain on the main square with reliefs representing scenes from Greek mythology.

If you believe that Tannhäuser was a creation of Wagner's imagination, you will be surprised to learn that descendants of his family were Salzburg administrators in Friesach and a Tannhäuser Chapel was erected in 1509 in the Dominican Church, with a red marble tomb of Deputy Dean Balthasar Tannhäuser added after his death in 1516.

A few kilometers south of Friesach, on the main road to Klagenfurt, is the village of Hirt and, in its vicinity, the climatic health resort of Agathenhof, supposed to be the largest of its kind in Europe. A little over a mile from Hirt lies Zwischenwässern, where the Metnitz River flows into Gurk and a local road branches off for the upper Gurk valley. The neo-classic Schloss Böckstein, looking rather like a country palace, is located at this crossroad. It was built for the bishops of Gurk by Hagenauer, the famed 18th-century Salzburg architect.

The Cathedral of Gurk

The upper Gurk valley road, and the small narrow-gauge railroa running alongside, first reach the small town of Strassburg with th majestic castle dominating the valley from the hill above it. Until the lat 18th century, when they moved to Klagenfurt, the prince-bishops c Gurk had their secular residence in this castle which is presently partiall in ruins.

Farther up the narrow valley is Gurk, an old village first mentione in medieval manuscripts in the ninth century. But much more interestin than its age is the twin-spired cathedral church, once the religious sea of the Gurk bishops, and one of the greatest architectural treasures i Austria. The first church was built at this site by Countess Hemma c Friesach-Zeltschach, a legendary figure from early Carinthian history who after the death of her husband and son in battle, devoted her lif and money to religion, built some ten churchs, died in the conver founded by her at Gurk, and about 900 years later was proclaimed saint.

The construction of the present prevailingly Romanesque basilica wa started around 1140 by Bishop Romanus, whose fresco-portrait is dis played in the Petersberg Castle in Friesach. It took more than half century to erect this impressive structure of three naves, separated b quadrangular pillars and ending in three apses. Beneath the cathedral crypt of 100 gracefully slender marble pillars was built to entomb th body of Countess Hemma, who died in 1045 and was canonized in 1938

Around 1200, when the construction was completed, the church wa adorned with several works of art, among them the beautifully simpl main portal and the more ornate Samson tympanum relief. Through th ensuing centuries it was further embellished with many additions i various period styles. Among the most valuable ones are: the 13th century frescos, among the most important of the Romanesque perioc ascribed to Master Heinrich, precise in design and chromatically expres sive although biblically complicated, located in the so-called Bishop' Chapel; the Gothic *Poor Man's Bible* (frescos depicting scenes from th New and Old Testaments) and painted glass windows in the 14th-cen tury vestibule enclosing the main portal; other Gothic frescos and Romanesque wall painting of St. Christopher (around 1250) near th main altar; the largest and oldest Carinthian *Fastentuch* (Lent Curtain a linen cloth still used to cover the altar during Lent), with biblical scene painted in 1458; six lively woodcarved reliefs (around 1500) representin scenes from the life of St. Hemma; a small Renaissance winged altar; th richly elaborate main altar, the chief baroque creation of Michael Höne the lovely lead 18th-century *Pietà* by Raphael Donner; and the rococ pulpit.

Weitensfeld is known for the oldest preserved painted glass window in Austria, originating from 1170. Today only its copy can be seen in the small St. Magdalen Church, while the highly valued original is in the safety of the Diocesan Museum in Klagenfurt.

Not far is Klein Glödnitz, a crossroad where one road continues to Feldkirchen and the Ossiacher Lake. Another road rises to Flattnitzer Höhe, bypassing Flattnitz, three kilometers away, and then drops steeply into the Metnitz valley to Metnitz, from where it proceeds via Grades to Friesach. Flattnitz (4,580 feet) is an unpretentious resort in an idyllic location in the middle of Gurktaler Alps, with a small lake nearby, frequented in summer by vacationists in search of mountain quiet and in winter by skiers. Metnitz has an interesting parish church and is particularly known for its octangular Gothic charnel house with outside Totentanz (Dance of Death) frescos. A finely woodcarved Gothic winged altar can be seen in St. Wolfgang Church in Grades, and another castle of the Gurk bishops on the other side of the river. If you do not wish to make the full circle of upper Gurk and Metnitz valleys (about 88 km. altogether), you have to turn back at Klein Glödnitz or Weitensfeld, returning through Gurk to Böckstein Castle crossroad.

Medieval Strongholds

The next larger town is St. Veit an der Glan, which from the 13th to the early 16th century was the capital of the Duchy of Carinthia. Architectural evidence of its medieval origin is still visible in spite of the conflagration of the early 1800's which destroyed numerous old buildings. The most outstanding structure on the picturesque main square is the Rathaus, with a richly ornamented façade and a rococo stuccoed ceiling in the grand hall. Only the main tower has remained of what was once a mighty ducal castle: it is located in the northeastern section of the town, housing the local museum.

More than a dozen castles are located in the surroundings of St. Veit. Some of them are ruins, others have been preserved in their original form or were renovated during a later period. They usually can be reached by narrow roads, but occasionally you will just have to walk. Three kilometers north of St. Veit are the two Kraig Castle ruins, the 11th-century Hochkraig and the 14th-century Niederkraig, both with mighty towers. In their vicinity is the lovely and romantic six-towered Frauenstein, built in the early 16th century and completely preserved. A few miles toward the southwest are the 12th-century Hardegg ruins and the old and the "new" Karlsberg castles; two Romanesque towers are the best parts of the old one still standing, whereas the "new" (17th-century) castle is preserved. Near St. Veit, in an easterly direction, are the ruins of the once-powerful Taggenburg, nowadays attracting visitors also for the view from the hill on which it is located and for a tavern which has been set up inside.

A little farther east is the famed Hochosterwitz, literally crowning the steep, isolated hill on which it is built. This is probably the most beautiful of all the castles in Austria. When you observe it from afar it does not look real but rather like a picture from a fairy tale, and one almost expects a dragon to appear in a puff of smoke or to hear troubadours sing. By branching off the main road at St. Donat, you may drive up (there is also bus service from Klagenfurt) as far as the first gate. From the parking lot the fortified castle lane winds up around the rocky hill through 14 tower-gates before reaching the main entrance. They all date from the 16th century, when the 13th-century castle was converted into the present stronghold by Freiherr Georg Khevenhüller, whose descendants still own it. Conducted tours through the armory and portrait gallery of ancestors; there is a restaurant. The view of the surrounding area is magnificent. If you are in a hurry and wish to return to your car in a few minutes, take the *Narrensteig* (Fool's Ascent), a precipitous footpath that begins at the castle church beside the eighth gate.

Four Hills

A couple of miles from St. Donat, back on the main road, is the hamlet of Willersdorf; from here a 6-km. road takes you up Magdalensberg (about 3,500 feet), well known for the excavations of a Celtic-Roman town. As early as 1502 a farmer, while plowing, found here the statue of the *Youth from Magdalensberg,* today one of the prized possessions of the Kuntshistorisches Museum in Vienna (copies of it were made for the Klagenfurt and Magdalensberg museums). The "Youth," probably a Roman copy of a fifth-century-BC Polycleites original, was sent by the Roman merchants of Aquileia on the Adriatic as a gift to the flourishing Celtic town on Magdalensberg, where it was installed in the temple as the image of Latobius, the local god of war. After this discovery a few other objects were found, but digging started only in the second half of the 19th century, whereas systematic excavating began only after World War II. Parts of a Celtic and Roman town have been uncovered so far, and a particularly interesting feature is what appears to be a government building with an assembly hall for representatives of various tribes and a section for archives and records. The Alpine Celts used to build their towns on hills, and the settlement on Magdalensberg appears to have been one of the most important of their federal state organizations.

Magdalensberg is also known as the starting point for the age-old Vierberglauf (Four-Hills-Pilgrimage), which takes place every year on the second Friday after Easter. The participants gather on Magdalensberg on the eve of that Friday and light campfires around the 13th-century church and the Gothic chapel on the top of the hill. A midnight

Mass is read and then everyone hurries downhill, burning torches in hand. The simple procession, with only a small cross leading it, and rather resembling a group of hikers, now proceeds across the Zollfeld on 3,350-foot Ulrichsberg, the second hill, from here down into the Glan valley and up again on the third hill, the 3,870-foot Veitsberg, and then through the village of Sörg on the Lorenziberg (3,200 feet), which is the fourth and the last hill and close to St. Veit. Masses and other religious services are performed on the top of the hills and in some churches on the way. The pilgrimage has to be completed within 24 hours, hardly a generous concession in view of the considerable amount of walking involved (about 40 km., half of it uphill). This ancient and mysterious observance apparently originates from a number of pagan rites connected with the fertility of the soil and the worshipping of sun and light. The direction taken and the time limit point to the movement of the sun: Magdalensberg is in the east, Ulrichsberg in the south, Veitsberg in the west, and Lorenziberg, reached after nightfall, in the north.

The Zollfeld

The small plain of the Zollfeld is actually a wider section of the Glan River valley, beginning shortly after St. Veit and reaching almost to Klagenfurt. Magdalensberg on the eastern side and Ulrichsberg to the west watch over this north–south passage. The Roman legionary, marching north, did so and founded the city of Virunum, which was the capital of the Roman province of Noricum and was located approximately in the middle of the Zollfeld: its sophisticated life is still reflected in the Dionysiac mosaic floor found here and today preserved in the Landesmuseum in Klagnefurt, and in the post horses depicted in a Roman relief, now immured in the south wall of the church in Maria Saal. The hoofs and wheels of nations migrating south rode and drove over Virunum and smashed to bits its way of life and its splendid buildings. But those who decided to tarry longer on Zollfeld picked up the pieces and constructed forts, churches, farmhouses, and a new period of history.

A large number of Roman stones can still be seen in the buildings in the Zollfeld area, particularly in the walls of the churches of Karnburg and Maria Saal. St. Peter and Paul at Karnburg dates from Carolingian times, but the place is better known, from ancient documents as well as through some excavating, as the site of a castle-fortress which was the seat of the earliest rulers of Carantania and referred to in those times as *Curtis Carantana* (Carantanian Court). Across the valley, on another elevation, was Sancta Maria in Solio, the earliest version of the present Maria Saal Church, founded in the mid-eighth century by Bishop Modestus, sent by the Bishop of Salzburg upon the request of Cheitmar, a Slovenian Carantanian duke, himself already a Christian and wishing to introduce Christianity among his people. St. Modestus is supposed to be entombed in a Roman sarcophagus below a ninth-century altar. The present Church of Maria Saal, built in the 15th century, is one of the best examples of Gothic architecture in Carinthia though the twin towers end in a baroque helmet. Of special interest is Christ's genealogical tree on the ceiling of the central nave.

Not far from Maria Saal, in the middle of the Zollfeld and shaded by a group of trees, lies the Herzogstuhl (Duke's Chair), a double-seated throne made with stones from the ruins of Virunum. Another stone chair, the Fürstenstein (Prince's Stone), made from the base of a Roman column, and also originating from the remnants of Virunum, used to stand in the open field near Karnburg (it is now in the Landesmuseum in Klagenfurt). The remarkable ceremony of the investiture of Carinthian rulers, one of the earliest examples of constitutional law, took place on these two chairs in medieval times.

Klagenfurt

Only about 8 km. south of Maria Saal and the Herzogstuhl is Klagenfurt (85,000 inhabitants), founded in the 12th century and the capital of Carinthia since 1518. The center of the city has a quadrangular form defined by four "Rings," streets running along the sides of the no-longer-existing walls. Exactly in the center of this quadrangle is the Neuer Platz with the city's emblem, the dragon fountain carved from a schistblock in the 17th century. The usual dragon tale was given a realistic undertone when the cranium of a prehistoric rhinoceros (now in the Landesmuseum) was found near Klagenfurt. On the same square is a statue of Empress Maria Theresa.

A block north of the dragon square is the longish Alter Platz, which is not only an old square as its name implies, but the oldest part of the city. It acquired the present form, however, only in the 16th century after the great fire of 1514. Near the west end of the Alter Platz are the Landhaus and baroque parish church. The church steeple rises 300 feet high, and at noontime you may observe the tower watchman pulling up his lunch, neatly packed in a basket and tied to the end of a rope. The arcaded twin-towered Landhaus (seat of the provincial Diet)—the front façade of which is far less impressive than its courtyard side—was built towards the end of the 16th century; in the Hall of Arms (Wappensaal), ornamented with 665 coats of arms of Carinthian estates, you can also see the Fürstenstein investiture ceremony portrayed by Josef Ferdinand Fromiller, the most important Carinthian painter of the baroque period.

Other important sights in the city include the 16th-century cathedral, which was originally built as a Protestant church; the Diocesan Museum in the Bishop's Palace with a good collection of medieval church art; and particularly the Landesmuseum with the Fürstenstein, objects from Magdalensberg, the mosaic floor and other finds from Virunum, prehis-

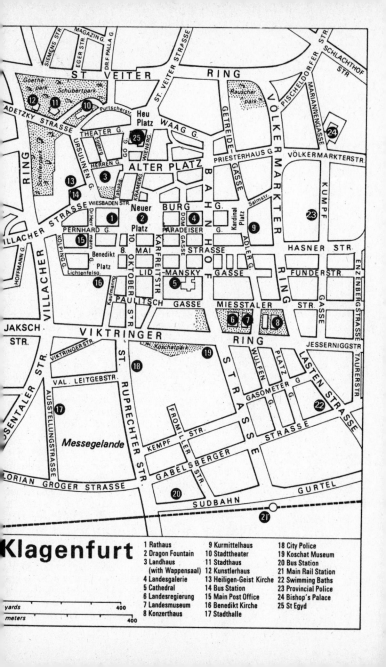

Klagenfurt

1 Rathaus
2 Dragon Fountain
3 Landhaus
  (with Wappensaal)
4 Landesgalerie
5 Cathedral
6 Landesregierung
7 Landesmuseum
8 Konzerthaus
9 Kurmittelhaus
10 Stadttheater
11 Stadthaus
12 Kunstlerhaus
13 Heiligen-Geist Kirche
14 Bus Station
15 Main Post Office
16 Benedikt Kirche
17 Stadthalle
18 City Police
19 Koschat Museum
20 Bus Station
21 Main Rail Station
22 Swimming Baths
23 Provincial Police
24 Bishop's Palace
25 St Egyd

yards 400
meters 400

toric collections, paintings and *objets d'art,* natural history collections, Carinthian folk dress, rustic house furnishings and decorations.

About 5 km. south of Klagenfurt is the village of Viktring with a moated 12th-century Romanesque church, which has suffered from rebuilding; the three 14th-century stained-glass windows, however, have retained their unspoiled beauty; worth seeing also are the two arcaded courtyards of the former Cistercian monastery, today housing a school.

Blue waters of Wörther Lake are beautifully framed by its wooded sloping shores and by the jagged chain of Karawanken mountains in the background. The Wörthersee is the warmest of the larger lakes in Carinthia, perhaps owing to the existence of subterranean thermal springs. During the summer months its banks are swarming with holiday-makers actually enjoying a pleasurable swim. In winter there is skating on the partially or totally frozen lake. Fog is a frequent visitor during fall and spring in the entire Carinthian lake area.

Wörthersee

Proceeding from Klagenfurt-See to the north shore we come first to Krumpendorf, at the end of the Klagenfurt city bus line. The center of the village is located on the main road, while the majority of small hotels, pensions, and private villas are scattered along the lake about a mile away. Krumpendorf is an unpretentious and primarily family-type resort. Midway on the north shore is Pörtschach, one of the two top vacation spots on the Wörthersee. Here you may practise skeet shooting, watch fashion shows and fireworks, take part in folklore activities. Here, as well as in other places on the lake, the water is often warm enough for swimming as early as May, which is very early indeed for an Alpine region. Pörtschach is mainly a settlement of hotels and summer villas, parts of it built on a narrow peninsula with pleasant walks.

Velden, at the western end of the Wörthersee, is the most fashionable resort in the entire province, with a more international atmosphere, and livelier and longer night hours combined with roulette and baccara in the Casino, than Pörtschach. Many visitors, however, may find this almost Mediterranean exuberance overwhelming, particularly on a Saturday night in summer.

The south shore is quieter, more modest, and more genuinely Carinthian. The road on this side is narrower. Less than 8 km. from Velden is Dellach with an attractively situated golf course, the only one in the area. Three kilometers farther, on a small peninsula, almost completely surrounded by water, is picturesque and ancient Maria Wörth, the most outstanding landmark on the Wörthersee. Although it is an unpretentious lake resort, it can boast two attractive old churches. A church existed here at least as early as the ninth century, if not earlier, but the present two churches date from the 12th century. The small one, called the Winter, or Rosary, Church, is basically Romanesque with later Gothic additions: the interior sights include the Romanesque choir with fragments of 12th-century frescos of the Apostles, a Madonna stained-glass window from 1420, and Gothic woodcarved figures. The larger parish church has a Romanesque portal, but its architecture is mainly Gothic and its interior décor mostly in baroque style. Skulls and bones can still be seen in the round Romanesque charnel house in the cemetery.

Only a little over two kilometers from Maria Wörth is Reifnitz, a lesser lake resort, from where you can take a short side road to the small, emerald green Keutschacher Lake, with the Romanesque church of St. George, a baroque castle and an 800-year-old linden tree. A winding 5-kilometer road ascends to the observation tower atop the 2,800-foot Pyramidenkogel. From the platform there is a view over half of Carinthia (on a fine day).

Around Other Lakes to the Grossglockner

Leaving Klagenfurt by Route 95 in a northwesterly direction, the first small town we meet is Moosburg, with the ruins of a Carolingian castle where Arnulf, the late-ninth-century German emperor, was born. Continuing through this area of rolling hills we leave on the left side the round-towered Renaissance Castle of Gradisch near the village of Glan and reach Feldkirchen, an ancient town that for several centuries belonged to the bishops of Bamberg. The parish church, a defense tower, and Biedermeier-style houses are the main sights. Feldkirchen is also an important crossroad. One road, mentioned earlier, goes to Klein Glödnitz and Gurk. Another climbs, at a gradient of 23 percent, 37 km. through the mountainous Nockgebiet up to the Turracher Höhe, a high pass between Carinthia and Styria, a mountain summer resort and fine skiing center, on a lovely small lake.

Only 20 km. west of Velden are the Ossiachersee and the city of Villach. Ossiacher Lake, about 11 km. long, is the third largest lake in Carinthia (after the Wörthersee and the Millstättersee), and it still retains some of that peaceful atmosphere Boleslaw II, King of Poland, came here to find in the 11th century. According to the story he stayed in the Benedictine Abbey at Ossiach for eight years as a simple brother, without revealing his identity and pretending to be mute, all in self-imposed penance for his murder of the Bishop of Cracow, and only on his deathbed confessed the truth. Though historians claim that Boleslaw's sojourn in Ossiach is only a legend, the king is commemorated by a tombstone and a fresco on the church wall—which the Polish government recently asked to have restored—facing the cemetery where many old wrought-iron crosses can be seen. Only the crypt—closed by a huge concrete slab—remains of the Romanesque abbey church, whose Gothic successor was remodeled into baroque in 1720. Fromiller is the painter of the frescos, as well as of those in the Baroque Hall of the secularized monastery, where some of the Carinthian Summer Festival events take place.

Other events of this annual festival are held in Ossiach and attract a large and sophisticated audience, due mainly to the participation of the composer Leonard Bernstein. The other lake villages, however, have remained quiet summer resorts. Near the other end of the lake is Annenheim, from where a cable car takes you to the Kanzelhöhe (4,950 ft.) and with a bit of walking and by combining two chair lifts from here on, you easily reach the top of Gerlitzen (6,300 ft.). The view is magnificent from both elevations and includes a large chunk of Carinthia, as well as the Slovenian Alps across the border. Back in Annenheim we proceed around the bottom of the lake to St. Andrä, and then by a good side road up to the castle-fortress Landskron (Crown of the Land), today only partially preserved but with still-visible lineaments of past might and stateliness. From the castle café terrace there is a fine view of the 5-km.-distant Villach framed by Dobratsch Mountain and the Karawanken.

The small city of Villach is the second largest in Carinthia (39,000 inhabitants) and an important railroad junction. Its history goes back to the times of the Romans, who used to take the waters in an early version of the present spa establishment at Warnbad Villach, just outside the city; parts of a Roman road can still be seen, but the Roman bridge and the fortress of Bilachium have disappeared. Medieval Uillah eventually became Villach, whose old section lies on the right bank of the Drau River, which makes a semi-circle around it. Stately Renaissance houses with arcaded courtyards surround the main square (with a baroque Trinity column), and also frame the narrow, picturesque streets around it, including the house where, in the 16th century, Theophrastus Paracelsus of medical fame lived as a youth with his father, who was the town physician. The churches to visit are the prevailingly Gothic parish church with a 313-foot steeple and the pinkish baroque Heiligenkreuzkirche on the edge of the city, with two towers and a cupola. Other interesting sights include the 16th-century Rathaus, the Heimatmuseum with prehistoric, folklore, and other collections, and a huge relief of Carinthia (65×31 feet) displayed in a building in the Schiller Park. Villach, together with the Dobratsch plateau above it and nearby Gerlitzen, is also a leading winter sports center.

Spittal an der Drau, in the Drau Valley, about 40 km. northwest of Villach, is the main town of Upper Carinthia and is particularly known for its architecturally superb Schloss Porcia, built in the 16th century for the Count of Salamanca, the Imperial Treasurer. This castle-palace, located in the center of town next to a lovely park, is one of the most beautiful Renaissance buildings in Austria, especially in its gracefully arcaded court stairways and open corridors, which provide a dream-like setting for performances of classical plays in the summer.

From Spittal there are only a few kilometers to the blue waters of Millstättersee, about 13 km. long and second largest in Carinthia. Millstatt, about halfway on the north shore, is the main locality on the lake to which it gave its name—or perhaps it was the other way around. The season of this lively resort culminates in the International Organ Music Week held in August. The imposing abbey with its mighty towers, many courtyards and centuries-old linden trees, was founded in the 11th century but secularized in the 18th. The twin-towered Romanesque church, originating from the same period, has become the parish church. During later periods the church was partially rebuilt in Gothic style and also received some distinguished baroque additions, but its 12th-century Romanesque portal has remained the most exquisite feature of its architectural décor. From the same period, and highly interesting for its complicated pillar ornaments, is the Kreuzgang, the arcaded court connecting the church and the monastery.

Seeboden, at the western end of the lake, is growing in importance as water sports center and many people are building summer villas here. A little beyond Seeboden, the lake road joins the main road connecting Carinthia with Salzburg and Rennweg, where you have the choice of the Autobahn tunnel or the steep climb over the Katschberg Pass. Less than halfway up the valley is the colorful old town of Gmünd, where the Malta mountain stream rushes into the Lieser. The Malta Hochalm toll road follows the waterfalls and artificial lakes, formed by the torrent, up to Austria's largest dam, where, at 6,000 feet, the glaciers of the High Tauern are mirrored in the glassy waters of a lake.

The small village of St. Peter in Holz, about 5 km. from Spittal, lies on the site of the ancient town of Teurnia, which was already Christian in Roman times. Only a little excavating was done here, but the small museum contains a well-preserved mosaic floor and some other remains of a building supposed to have been an early Christian church. A few kilometers farther up the Drau valley the Möll River flows into the Drau. If you proceed up the larger Drau valley, cut between the Kreuzeck and Gailtaler mountain ranges, the two largest localities before reaching East Tyrol will be Greifenburg and Oberdrauburg. From Greifenburg, a steep 1-km. ascent leads in a southeasterly direction to the lofty, 3,045-foot-high Weissensee, the fourth largest lake in Carinthia and considered by some to be the most beautiful. On its shores are only a few small villages, which in summer are becoming more and more lively resorts, with hotel accommodations increasing every season. Techendorf is the principal locality and here the lake, narrowing to about 350 feet, can be crossed by a wooden bridge. Neusach is at the end of the road, and to reach the other end of the lake, you walk or take a motorboat.

Both the Drau and Möll valleys are dotted with medieval castles. The well-preserved 13th-century Groppenstein near Obervellach in the Möll valley is particularly worth a visit. Also in the same vicinity, and of an even more romantic appearance, is Unterfalkenstein, which is unfortunately only a castle model, built in its present form not earlier than 1906 but few would guess it. The parish church at Obervellach has a three section altar painting from 1520 by Jan van Scorel, a Dutch disciple of Dürer. From Obervellach a steep 8-km. road branches north (right) to Mallnitz, a 3,900-foot-high mountain village and a winter sports center of increasing importance. Mallnitz is at the Carinthian end of the Tauern railroad tunnel, and here you load your car on the train if you wish to drive straight into Land Salzburg, because no road crosses the high mountain chain.

Proceeding farther up the Möll valley, the road rises steadily into the realm of the Hohe Tauern, turning sharp north at the village of Winkler, where it is joined by the road coming from Lienz, capital of East Tyrol. The ascent of the Grossglockner begins after the unpretentious summer and winter resort of Döllach (3,300 feet); bypassing a splendid waterfall the road climbs to Heiligenblut, a 4,290-foot-high winter sports center and the seat of the famed mountain climbing school. The sharply pointed spire of the Gothic church appears almost a duplicate of the conic peak of the Grossglockner in the background. The greatest treasure inside the church is the winged and richly woodcarved main altar.

At the upper end of Heiligenblut is the toll gate of the Grossglockner road, which from here on curves up to Franz-Josefs-Höhe after joining its counterpart coming from Land Salzburg over Hochtor. Franz-Josefs-Höhe (almost 8,000 feet) is so called because Emperor Franz Josef got this far in his exploration of the Grossglockner area (no roads, of course existed in those times).

South Carinthia

The swift Gail flows through small scattered villages with ancient churches and aged, often wooden, farm homes. The narrow valley is peacefully soft, with many old linden trees, but its fir-treed slopes rise steeply, particularly on the south side, and craggy peaks peer from behind them. The main town in the Gail valley is Hermagor, situated approximately in its center, and together with the nearby Pressegger Lake, comprises an invitingly modest vacation spot.

Further down, where the valley becomes wider, lies the village of Nötsch below the wild rocky face of the Dobratsch Mountain, which has a lovely alpine garden surrounding the towering peak, (also called Villacher Alpe), and a little further the village of Feistritz with a 1,000 year-old linden tree and an old Gothic church on a steep hill. A few kilometers east of Feistritz we reach the main road from Villach to Italy. The Austro-Italian border, only about 3 km. distant, is near the village of Thörl, where some very fine 15th-century Gothic frescos can be seen in the parish church, representing one of the chief works of Thomas von Villach, a famed Carinthian painter of that period.

The Gail flows into the Drau near Villach. In the vicinity is the round blue-green Faaker Lake with a tiny island in the middle, a few small but rapidly growing resorts, and the mighty pyramid of Mittagskogel watching over it from the Karawanken range. The best view of the lake and the surrounding area is from the nearby hill of Tabor (about 2,400 feet) which can be reached by a recently built road.

Proceeding along the Drau valley, called here Rosental, we come eventually to Ferlach, the centuries-old town of gunmakers. In modern times these individualistic and independent craftsmen, who pass the secrets of their skill from generation to generation, have been producing handmade hunting weapons, chiefly the excellent combination guns, adorned with artistic engravings. There is an interesting gun museum.

North of Ferlach, across the Drau, are the baroque pilgrimage church of Maria Rain and the Castle of Hollenburg with 14th-century chapel frescos and wall paintings on the gate tower and in the arcaded court. South of Ferlach on the steep Loibl Pass road, crossing the Karawanken into Slovenia (the northwestern Yugoslav republic), offers grandiose scenery which you miss if you take the tunnel; from the Small Loibl Pass, halfway up, a narrow road leads into the Bodental, perhaps the range's most beautiful high valley.

The parish church in the village of Abtei, on the Drau some 16 km. east of Ferlach, contains the *Lamentation over Christ* by Thomas von Villach, considered to be the best Gothic painting in Carinthia. To the southeast is the Seeberg Pass, over which another important road climbs into Slovenia through spectacular Alpine landscape, which begins after the small spa of Eisenkappel, which has a Gothic church and the Renaissance Hagenegg castle. A steep, narrow side road leads from Eisenkappel through a wild waterfall-filled gorge to tiny Trögern.

North of Eisenkappel lies Klopeiner Lake, supposed to be the warmest lake in Carinthia, where you can usually swim from early May until the end of September. It is crowded in summer.

Völkermarkt, across the Drau to the north, acquired town rights in the 13th century, when the Gothic church was erected; the rich frescos and tombs in the three naves all belong to the Middle Ages. The town hall is part of the 14th-century ducal castle, whose gate opens on the square with houses belonging to the baroque and Biedermeier periods. The tower of St. Ruprecht church below Kolhof Castle is the oldest and loveliest in Austria. The River Drau, which has recently been dammed in this section, forms a large artificial lake, called Edinger See and now one of the largest lakes in Carinthia, crossed by a gracious 1,200-foot bridge on the road to Eisenkappel and Seeberg Pass. To the east is Bleiburg, a 750-years-old town, dominated by a 16th-century castle and the 7,000-foot Petzen mountain on the border of Slovenia.

The Lavant Valley

The main road from Klagenfurt to Graz goes through Völkermarkt and the Lavant valley, which separates the almost twin-like Saualpe and Koralpe mountain plateaus. Of exceptional interest in this valley is the 11th-century Benedictine Abbey at St. Paul, with its basically Romanesque basilica, a small museum of paintings, drawings, engravings, and a valuable library containing manuscripts and a Gutenberg Bible. The Lavant flows into the Drau at the small town of Lavamünd with the nearby castles of Kollegg and Thürn. Higher up the Lavant valley, St. Andrä possesses two churches of note; the former Jesuit monastery has been converted into a comfortable senior citizens' home. At Wolfsberg the original Romanesque and Gothic style of the stately castle has disappeared entirely through the rebuilding in 1846–1853; the Romanesque parish church contains a baroque altar with a painting by Kremser-Schmidt. In the upper Lavant valley are the spa of St. Leonhard with radioactive sulphuric springs and a very impressive Gothic church, and Preblau, known for its mineral table water. From the Twimberg Castle ruins, and passing Waldenstein Castle, the main road curves up over the Pack Sattel into Styria.

PRACTICAL INFORMATION

HOTELS AND RESTAURANTS

BAD KLEINKIRCHHEIM Spa, and **St. Oswald,** in the center of Nockgebiet.
Hotels All (1)—*Kurhotel Ronacher,* large, with indoor pool and cure facilities; *Sankt Oswald,* all rooms with bath, serves fine food; *Pulverer,* indoor and heated outdoor pools, cure facilities, good restaurant and bar.

All (2)—*Kristall,* all rooms with bath, cure facilities; *Alte Post,* own tennis court, good restaurant; *Prägant,* large and balconied; *Trattlerhof,* 50 rooms with bath, warmly recommended for families, first-class food in cozy Stüberl.

All (3)—*Aufegger,* small; *Kolmhof; Pension Waltl;* and *Sporthotel,* in quiet location and cellar, restaurant—all offer good facilities, most rooms with bath or shower.

DELLACH Near Maria Wörth. **Hotel** *Golfhotel* (1), near the golf course, health center, chalet style, 40 rooms, private swimming facilities, open April 15 to Oct. 31, beautifully situated above the lake shore.
Campsite.

DÖLLACH Hotels Both (3)—*Schlosswirt,* chalet style, 60 beds, heated pool, tennis and game park, very good restaurant; *Post,* comfortable, old tradition.

EISENKAPPEL Hotels *Schosspark* (1), 48 rooms, pool, tennis courts; in a huge castle park, as its name indicates, opposite cure center for heart and circulatory diseases. *Obir* (2), 48 rooms.

FAAKERSEE Hotels *Karnerhof,* 250 beds, situated between Drobollach and Egg, in a marvellous isolated position overlooking the lake, beautiful country style main building with restaurant, two modern annexes, indoor pool.

There's a camp site on the lake.

At **Egg**—*Strandhotel Trink,* good food, and *Strandhotel Faakersee,* both with private beaches, are (2). Both (3)—*Tschebull,* 70 beds; and *Kanz,* 66 beds.

At **Drobollach**—*Hübner,* (2), 80 beds, own beach, tennis. Both (3)—the balconied *Schrönruh;* and *Schleicher,* heated pool.

At **Faak**—*Inselhotel* (1), 100 beds, beautiful location, lake terrace, tennis and fishing, fish and game specialties in restaurant. Both (3)—*Strandhotel Fürst,* good food; and *Strandhotel Faak.*

On the banks of the Faakersee a holiday village called *Seeleit'n* has been built. Re-erected old farmhouses serve as sleeping quarters and the old barn is a good restaurant with local hams, cheeses and cider as well as more sophisticated fare.

FELD AM SEE 4 km. from Radentheim. **Hotel** *Lindenhof* (1), 25 rooms with bath or shower; homely atmosphere, quiet location, own beach, dance bar, admirable food.

FRANZ-JOSEFS-HÖHE Near Heiligenblut on Grossglockner Alpine road.
Hotels Almost 8,000 ft. high, in magnificent situation facing the highest Austrian peak across the Pasterzen Glacier, *Franz-Josefs-Haus* (2), 216 beds, open in summer only, restaurant where prices tend to be a bit high.
Wallackhaus (3), at 7,700 ft.

GMÜND Simple winter resort.
Hotels All (3)—*Alte Mühle,* all rooms with shower; *Kohlmayr* and *Pension Platzer.*

HEILIGENBLUT 4,289 ft. high, Carinthian mountain climbing school.
Hotels All (2)—*Glocknerhof,* 75 rooms with bath or shower; the *Hubertusstube,* bar, indoor pool; a little less expensive is *Sonnenhof,* small, all rooms with bath or shower. *Senger* (2), now renovated and enlarged, with beautiful old-style rooms, fireplace; *fondue* nights Wednesdays, barbecues Mondays.
Both (3)—*Post,* 65 beds; and *Kärntnerhof,* heated pool.
Youth Hostel; campsite.

KANZELHÖHE On the Gerlitzen Plateau, by cable car from Annenheim.
Hotels All (1)—*Waldhotel Diana,* 1-room and 2-room apartments, indoor pool, riding, tennis; *Sonnenhotel Zaubeck,* 60 beds, indoor swimming pool, excellent restaurant, closed Oct. 1 to Dec. 19, April 16 to May 14; *Sporthotel Alpenrose,* indoor pool, sauna, slightly less expensive.
These comfortable hotels are located near the upper station of the cable car at 4,950 ft., they face south and have numerous terraces and balconies.

Farther up, near the chair lifts, are several lower-priced inns.

KATSCHBERGHÖHE Around the pass of the same name.
In **Katchberg, Hotels** *Alpenhotel* (2), large and modern, indoor pool, sauna.
A few inns (3), such as *Berghof* and *Hubertus.*

KEUTSCHACHERSEE Hotels *Fischerhütte* (2) offers vacation apartments in
summer, indoor pool.
Gasthof Brückler (3), at the lake, 110 beds, in lovely countryside, with grill
restaurant and wine tavern in converted barn.
Several inns and numerous small pensions in the area. Nudist beach.
Restaurant On the top of Pyramidenkogel (2,800 ft.) reached by 5–6 km. of
mountain road, is a café-restaurant.

KLAGENFURT With Wörthersee nearby.
Hotels *Musil* (L), Romantic Hotel, 18 period-furnished rooms, fine restaurant,
exceptional coffeehouse.
All (1)—*Dermuth,* close to the lake, 51 rooms, indoor pool; *Goldener Brunnen,*
27 rooms; *Moser-Verdino,* 75 rooms, excellent restaurant; *Porcia,* 45 rooms, central; *Sandwirt,* 47 rooms, 35 baths, renowned restaurant; *Europapark,* 35 rooms,
and *Roko Hof,* 70 rooms, 30 showers, are both on Villacher Str. leading to lake.
Almost on the lake, *Schloss Freyenthurn,* 17 rooms, some baths, bed and breakfast; *Wörthersee,* 40 rooms, 13 showers. In town, *Blumenstöckl,* 17 rooms; *Goldenes Rössl,* 7 rooms.
Youth Hostels at Kumpfgasse 20 and Feldgasse 7.
Campsite on Wörthersee nearby.
Restaurants In addition to hotel restaurants mentioned above, you might try
Ascot (1), Kramerg. 9 in the pedestrian mall, mostly French, but also Austrian
specialties, excellent, and less expensive daily specials. Otherwise, *Berghof,* Klagenfurt Jugenddorfstr. 4, for local specialties and fish dishes; and *Maria Loretto,*
in romantic lakeside location, for trout.

KLOPEINERSEE Hotels All (3)—*Amerika-Holzer,* with fishing facilities;
Marolt, indoor pool; *Obir, Birkenhof,* and *Klopeiner See,* all with own beaches.
In **Seelach,** both (2)—*Hormosana; Sporthotel Kleinsee,* a little less expensive,
riding facilities.
In **Unterburg**—*Krainz* (3), with own beach, café and good food.

KOLBNITZ Up the valley from Spittal an der Drau.
Hotel *Marhof* (2), 50 beds in rooms decorated in rustic style, most with bath,
large garden and swimming pool, open summer and Dec.–Jan., owned by the
same family since 1150. Also, *Sporthotel Reisseck* (2), at 7,000 ft., is reached by
funicular and a tiny railroad that leads through a tunnel; good skiing base; indoor
pool; closed May.

KÖTSCHACH/MAUTHEN picturesque mountain resort in Gail Valley at end
of Lesach Valley. **Hotel** *Kürschner* (2), 40 rooms/bath, heated pool.

Restaurant *Kellerwand,* building inconspicuous though elegantly refurbished within; Carinthian cooking with a modern imaginative touch.

KRUMPENDORF Hotels Both (2)—*Koch,* with good restaurant, outdoor pool; and *Habich,* all rooms with bath or shower.
Schloss Drasing (3), a small castle-pension, heated pool.

MALLNITZ Hotels All (2)—*Alpenhotel Alber,* large, with annex, good food in gemütlich dining rooms; *Almstube,* music; *Berghof,* wine tavern and grill bar, sauna; *Bellevue,* in quiet, sunny location; *Bichlhof,* chalet-style hotel in woods.
Both (3)—*Drei Gemsen,* fishing facilities; *Egger,* with own meat in simple but good restaurant.

MALTA *Hotel Sporthotel Maltatal* (2), 30 rooms in circular building with view over Austria's highest artificial lake; at 6,304 ft., on toll road.

MARIA WÖRTH Hotels All (1)—*Post Astoria,* indoor pool; *Linde,* lakeside terrace restaurant, fishing; *Harrich,* indoor pool and sauna; *Ebner,* tennis and good food.
In **Reifnitz,** outside town, both with small beaches—*Maria Wörth* (1), small, with sauna; *Strandhotel Sille* (2), 80 beds.
In **Sekirn,** farther down the road to Klagenfurt, *Parkhotel* (2), 95 beds, own beach.
Both (3)—*Paulitsch* and *Pension Föhrenhof,* both with pools and own beaches.

MILLSTÄTTERSEE Hotels Most hotels are open summer only; peak season is July and Aug. and our categories are based on these prices; at other times, the prices are considerably lower.
In **Döbriach,** on east side of the lake, there are several vacation apartments and bungalows (2) and (3).
In **Millstatt,** both (1)—*Die Forelle,* 100 beds, lovely lakeside café-restaurant; *Postillion am See,* 50 beds, all rooms with bath or shower, heated pool, bar.
All (2)—*Hubertushof,* 100 beds, heated pool; *Annenhof,* indoor pool, sauna; *Seewirt,* 45 beds, many rooms with shower, garden restaurant, in center near lake; *Seevilla,* 85 beds, directly on lake, terrace café; *Post* with fish specialties in attractive *Wappenstüberl.*
All (3)—*Strandhotel Marchetti,* on lake next to public swimming establishment, pleasant café and restaurant; *Zur Glocke,* in center near Rathaus, small with good grill dishes in restaurant; *Pension Silbernagel,* in wooded location overlooking town and lake, garden restaurant; *Lindenhof,* in wing of old abbey, with outdoor restaurant around an ancient linden tree.

MOOSBURG Hotel *Schloss Moosburg* (2), 14 family rooms (for 3–4 people) and larger apartments, all with bath and small kitchen, 15th-century castle in large park and woods, indoor pool, hunting and fishing, tennis, sauna, complete informality, children welcome.

OSSIACHERSEE Hotel *Strandhotel Lido* (1), 80 rooms, 40 baths, fine position near the village of St. Andrä, private beach and water sports facilities, open May to Oct. At **Annenheim,** *Haus am See* (2), 25 rooms, 12 baths.

All (3)—*Gerlitzenhaus,* 30 rooms, 15 showers, pool; *Lindenhof,* 15 rooms, 8 showers; *Marienheim,* 16 rooms.

Campsite.

At **Ossiach,** almost at the other end of the lake, historic *Stiftshotel* (2), 50 rooms, 13 baths, located on the lake in the former abbey, partially decorated in antique style, restaurant, bar, lake view from splendid baroque Hall and from most of the rooms, which are former cells, open May to Oct.

All (3)—*Schlosswirt,* 10 rooms, 5 showers; *Seefriede,* 25 rooms, 12 showers; *Strandpension,* 27 rooms.

PÖRTSCHACH Hotels *Schloss Seefels* (L), in a beautiful garden, with tennis, fishing, boating; and excellent cuisine.

Both (1)—*Schloss Leonstein,* 34 rooms in a converted castle on the main road, candlelit dining in atmospheric courtyard, summer concerts in rococo costumes, open May to Oct.; *Sonnengrund,* 41 rooms.

All (2)—*Ambassador,* 80 rooms, 52 baths; *Dermuth,* 60 rooms, 47 baths; *Joainig,* 45 rooms, 17 baths; *Österreichischer Hof,* 55 rooms, 29 baths, indoor pool; *Savoy,* 32 rooms, 25 showers; *Sportzentrum,* 35 rooms, 23 baths, pool; *Strandhotel,* 50 rooms, 18 showers; *Wallerwirt,* 50 rooms, good restaurant.

All (3)—*Karawankenblick,* 34 rooms, 24 showers; *Ulbing,* 35 rooms, 22 baths; *Waldhotel,* 23 rooms.

Restaurant In the basement of the Österreichischer Hof is the excellent French *La Boheme.* Costly but worth it. *Schifferwirt* specializes in fish dishes; reservations necessary.

SEEBODEN At west end of Millstättersee. **Hotels** Both (1)—*Bellevue,* 50 rooms, indoor pool; *Royal Hotel Seehof,* 90 rooms, indoor and outdoor pools, tennis, private park on lakeshore.

All (2)—*Klein,* 29 rooms; *Seehotel Steiner,* 60 rooms, 40 showers; *Strandhotel Koller,* 49 rooms, indoor pool.

All (3)—*Feichter,* 20 rooms; *Landhaus Gastein,* 20 rooms; *Seiz,* 28 rooms, 20 showers, pool.

Campsite.

SPITTAL AN DER DRAU Hotels *Salzburg* (2), 65 rooms, 38 showers, opposite the castle in the center.

Both (3)—*Alte Post;* and *Ertl,* with Carinthian specialties in restaurant, both have heated pools.

Youth Hostel.

Restaurant *Beim Rabl,* Bogengasse 14, in center, *gemütlich* restaurant with grill specialties.

TURRACHER HÖHE 5,800 ft. Bus from the railway stations of Feldkirchen in Carinthia and Turrach in Styria.

Hotels On the Carinthian side—*Hochschober* (2), 180 beds, indoor pool, sauna, fishing facilities and noted restaurant.

Both (3)—*Bauernstuben,* annex to small, located on the lake; and Alpengasthof Siegel, simpler.

On the Styrian side—best is *Seewirt* (2), like a small castle, excellent food, bar, attractive interiors.

Both (3)—*Bauernstubn,* annex to *Seewirt,* on the lake, café, farm-style rooms; and *Jägerwirt,* indoor pool.

VELDEN On Wörthersee. **Hotels** Our classification is based on the prices during the peak season, July and Aug. which are considerably higher than during the rest of the year.

Both (1)—*Schloss Velden,* 260 beds, 90 baths, a converted and rebuilt baroque castle dating from 1603, with antique decor in public rooms, excellent food and wines in its lakeside terrace restaurant, small rustic tavern, an impressive list of drinks in the lakeside bar, indoor and outdoor lounges, music every day during the season, private beach, tennis court, open April to Oct. In every way except price this is a luxury hotel. *Seehotel Veldnerhof-Mösslacher,* 240 beds, 87 baths and showers, many rooms with balcony overlooking lake, large garden restaurant on lake-front, 2 orchestras, tennis and water sports instructors.

Both (2)—*Yacht Hotel,* 70 beds, boasts all rooms with bath or shower and balcony, private beach, large park, 3 tennis courts. *Seehotel Hubertus,* on lake with own beach, heated pool, good restaurant and snack bar, open May to Sept.

All (3)—*Bacherlwirt,* about 60 beds, pleasantly situated a bit above town on the road to Rosegg, good restaurant with local specialties; *Carinthia,* 140 beds, own beach, heated pool, bed and breakfast; *Frank,* all rooms with shower; *Michaela,* in center, good restaurant in Carinthian-style garden terrace; *Kleines Hotel,* small as its name says; *Wrann,* 90 beds, in center but has shore swimming facilities.

There is also a large number of pensions (2) and (3) and breakfast pensions (3), as well as many Gasthöfe (3) in the environs, and rooms in private houses. The local tourist office in the center of town will advise you on these and make the necessary reservations, and can also tell you about the numerous establishments renting bungalows and small flats, a few of them with swimming pool and several of them with private lake swimming and boats.

Campsite.

VILLACH Under the Dobratsch mountain, Villach is affectionately known as the secret capital of Carinthia. **Hotels** *Parkhotel* (1), centrally located, with good food and a pleasant garden.

All (2), rooms with bath higher—*Betty,* Bambergerstr. 3; *City,* at station, 57 rooms; *Europe,* near station, 50 rooms, large café; *Post,* Romantic Hotel, 70 rooms, in a 15th-century patrician house on the main square, every modern comfort in surroundings of real beauty. Restaurant has been refurbished and is excellent value with warm, friendly service; *Trampitsch,* Ossiacherzeile 29, 40 rooms.

All (3)—*Brauhaus* and *Moser,* both near station and with garden restaurants; *Fugger,* cellar tavern; *Schloss Wernberg,* about 7 km. east of Villach, a well-

preserved 16th-century castle which, in addition to a convent, houses a sma
32-bed, pleasant pension run by nuns.

Youth Hostel. Campsite.

Restaurants *Landskron Castle,* less than 5 km. northeast of Villach, in pa
tially ruined castle, but the reconstructed part is a good international restauran
also café, large terrace and excellent view; *Bacchus-Restaurant-Weinstuben,* Kh
venhüllergasse 13, behind Town Hall, good food, beer and wine; *Steirische Wei
stube Tostenwirt,* Ledergasse 25, not far from main square, Styrian wine tave
with grill dishes, wines and music, open late.

WARMBAD VILLACH Hotels Both (1)—*Karawankenhof,* 50 rooms, 2 pool
Warmbader Hof, 125 rooms with thermal water bath or shower and balcony, ca
and top restaurant.

Josefinenhof (2), 60 rooms, 43 baths, indoor pool.

WEISSENSEE In **Techendorf, Hotels** *Sporthotel Alpenhof* (1), 60 beds, mo
rooms with shower, heated pool, sauna, tennis, cure facilities.

Arlbergerhof (3), a pension of chalet type with wooden outside balcony-corr
dors, at the beginning of the town Techendorf.

Strandhotel Weissensee is well suited to families; with its own beach, surfing ar
sailing schools, good food.

Restaurant *Restaurant-Café Moser* is near the bridge, with timber-covere
terrace overlooking the lake.

In **Neusach, Hotels** both (2)—*Enzian,* smaller, is a bit above the road; ar
Strandhotel, modern chalet style, nearby.

SPECIAL EVENTS

BAD KLEINKIRCHHEIM Masked ski races nearby, in Feb.

MALLNITZ Night ski jumping in March.

MARIA WÖRTH Ascension Day, colorful religious boat procession on Wörtl
ersee, connected with church fete (Kirchtag).

OSSIACHERSEE June, first sailing regattas. June to Aug., *Carinthian Sur
mer,* an international music and literary festival.

SPITTAL AN DER DRAU Classical plays at Schloss Porcia, July/August.

TURRACHER HÖHE Masked ski races in *Fasching,* Feb.

VELDEN June, International *Amateur Film Festival;* night torch light wate
skijumping. Parade of historic floats, late Aug. In Sept. season closes with fir
works and floating lights. International *Wörthersee Week* once a year.

VILLACH Feb., *Fasching* highlights, the Villach Carnival; Carinthian Summ
Festival, July/August.

SPAS

BAD KLEINKIRCHHEIM Indoor and outdoor thermal water swimming pools, he waters are beneficial for rheumatic, nervous, respiratory and other troubles.

WARMBAD VILLACH Indoor and outdoor thermal water swimming pools, or rheumatism, the after-effects of infantile paralysis and convalescence.

ENTERTAINMENT AND CASINOS

KLAGENFURT Operas, operettas and plays are performed in the *Stadttheater,* on Theaterplatz; concerts and plays in the *Konzerthaus,* on Viktringer Ring. *Burghofsingen,* choral groups every evening in summer.

SEEBODEN Casino open July and Aug. only, roulette daily from 7 P.M.

VELDEN Dance spots, with or without shows are lively here, particularly during the summer season. The casino is open all year, roulette, baccara and black-jack daily from 5 P.M. Open-air roulette in summer.

VILLACH Concerts all year, particularly during Carinthian Summer Festival, in the large, modern Kongresshaus.

SPORTS

ANNENHEIM On Ossiachersee. Water-skiing school, sailboats for hire, yacht club. Cable car to Kanzelhöhe, on the Gerlitzen Plateau.

BAD KLEINKIRCHHEIM Twin chair lift to Waldtratte, chair lift to Kaiserburg (6,230 ft.) 2-stage chair lift from St. Oswald to over 6,200 ft., 14 ski lifts, ski school, ski jump, skijoring, curling alleys, horse sleighs, long toboggan runs.

DELLACH 18-hole golf course operated by Kärntner Golf Club, April–Oct., over 3,000 yds.; clubhouse and parking; guests welcome.

GMÜND Ski lift, ski school, 2 ski jumps, 4 toboggan runs, curling alleys.

HEILIGENBLUT The mountain climbing school courses, carried out in the Grossglockner group, are designed for beginners, intermediate, and advanced climbers, and last from 3 days to 2 weeks, according to individual choice. You can join at any time from mid-July to early Sept. Climbing equipment is supplied by the school free of charge and you may also rent boots and necessary clothing. Write to *Bergsteigerschule Heiligenblut,* A-9844 Heiligenblut, Kärnten.
There is also a 2-stage chair lift to Schareck at 8,364 ft. (also served by another chair lift from Fallbichl at 7,280 ft.), 8 ski lifts, ski school, ski bus service, skating rink, curling, tobogganing, horse sleighs. Goldpanning in organized groups.

KANZELHÖHE 4 chair lifts, ski school, ski jump.

KATSCHBERGHÖHE 6 ski lifts, ski school, tobogganing, skating and curling

KLAGENFURT *Yacht* club on the lake. Riding facilities—12-day riding tour are organized spring to fall, by *Reisebüro Obersteiner.*

There's a regular airport, which can be used by private sports planes an gliders, at K-Annabichl.

KRUMPENDORF Lake swimming, sailing; water skiing, sailing and horseback riding schools.

MALLNITZ In the area, there's a 2-stage Ankogel cable car to Elschesatte (8,646 ft.), chair lift to Häusleralm (6,100 ft.), 7 ski lifts, ski school, 2 ski jumps 2 toboggan runs, skijoring, skating rink, curling, horse sleighs, riding facilitie

MILLSTÄTTERSEE Skindiving school. Sailboats for hire; regattas at Mil statt.

OBERVELLACH Riding facilities; landing site for gliding buffs. Cable car, sk school, 2 ski lifts, ski jump, skating, curling, tobogganing.

OSSIACHERSEE Sailboats for hire in St. Andrä.

PÖRTSCHACH Waterskiing school, regular water skijumping competition sailing school, yacht club, motorboat racing, riding facilities, skeet shooting facil ties. Bio-training possible.

SEEBODEN Sailboats for hire; landing strip for private planes and gliders

SPITTAL AN DER DRAU There's a landing site for gliding buffs. 2-stage cabl car to Goldeck (over 7,000 ft.), chair lift on Goldeck range, 5 ski lifts. Ski schoo skijoring, skating rink and ice hockey, 2 curling rinks and 2 toboggan runs.

TURRACHER HÖHE Both sides of the plateau together have 8 ski lifts, 1 chai lift, 3 ski schools, 2 toboggan runs, skating and curling.

VELDEN Waterskiing schools, regular water skijumping competitions. Ridin facilities with international riding and jumping tournament every summer. Sailin school, sailboats for hire, first sailing regattas in June.

VILLACH Riding facilities; landing site for gliding buffs, in the vicinity; motor cycle racing takes place quite often, very popular.

Ski school, 3 ski jumps, artificial skating arena, ice hockey, 2 chair lifts, 2 sk lifts. Bio-training at Warmbad-Villach.

USEFUL ADDRESSES

KLAGENFURT *Landesfremdenverkehrsamt für Kärnten,* the official touris department, Kaufmanng. 13 (tel. 04222 54428); *Kärntner Landesreisebüro,* offi cially sponsored tourist agency, Neuerplatz 2 (tel. 04222 564000); local informa tion and room reservation, *Fremdenverkehrsamt,* city tourist office, Rathaus.

STYRIA

White Horses and Hills of Iron

Styria is a romantic country, a country of virgin mountains and
Austria's largest and densest forests, rife with game. It is a country of
old folk traditions and a long historic record. Her rich deposits of iron
attracted both the Celts and the Romans who left many traces of their
presence behind. Later on Styrian iron provided the armor for the Christian armies fighting the Turks. Styria became the "Western Wall"
against the Turkish invasions and in the 15th century when Emperor
Friedrich III resided there, as well as thereafter, Graz was the strongest
fortress of Christianity and the Turks never succeeded in taking it. The
silent witness of those glorious days are the 27,000 pieces of armor and
weapons preserved in the Graz Armory, the largest remaining collection
of its kind in the world. But the "Styrian green," more than anything
else, symbolizes to the Styrian his love for nature, his old traditions, and
his home.

Styria has a very large number of low-priced but delightful and unspoiled little countryside hotels and inns of the Gasthof variety. The
capital of Graz, the Styrian lakes of Salzkammergut and certain other
localities also offer first-class accommodations, but in the countryside as
whole the stress is on the unpretentious and inexpensive type of hostel-

ry. We can indicate only a very short selection of the numerous pleasan
inns. You will find that the prices in Styria are lower than anywhere els
in Austria, with the possible exception of Burgenland. But for them, yo
will often receive a higher quality accommodation.

Route Planning

Graz is connected with Vienna and Salzburg by inter-city **train**
sleek, fast and very comfortable. The Vienna–Bruck–Graz–Leibnit
route is served by the *Laibach Express* and *Balkan Express;* and severa
other intercontinental express trains traverse Styria. The line from Gra
to Bruck, Leoben, St. Michael, Trieben, Selztal, Steinach, Schladmin
and on to Salzburg and Germany, follows the *Steiermark Express* rout
and from Selztal you may also proceed directly to Upper Austria an
Linz.

Secondary train routes link Graz with Vienna via Feldbach, Fürste
feld, Hartberg and Burgenland; Leoben with Präbichl, Eisenerz, Hiefla
Gstatterboden, Admont and Selztal; Steinach with Tauplitz, Bad Mi
terndorf, and Bad Aussee. Among the small local lines are: Feldbach
Bad Gleichenberg, Spielfeld–Radkersburg, Graz–Köflach, Kapfenberg
Aflenz–Seewiesen, Unzmarkt–Murau–Predlitz.

State and private **bus services** connect all the important places. Sigh
seeing bus tours from Graz, Leoben, Mariazell, Schladming, etc.

Sightseeing round flights by **small planes** can be taken from Gra
airport. They are of two types: a short flight over Graz and surrounding
and a longer flight over the Styrian Alps.

If you are driving **by car** from Vienna, take the South Autobahn
Wiener Neustadt, and then continue on Route 17: about 153 km.
Bruck, 170 to Leoben, 217 to Judenburg, and 233 to Unzmarkt. Fro
Unzmarkt it is around 35 km. to Murau and 58 to Predlitz on the bord
of Land Salzburg. For Graz, take Route 67 at Bruck (about 200 kr
from Vienna to Graz). From Kapfenberg, Route 20 goes to Mariazell (
km.) after crossing Seeberg Pass. From Vienna, Mariazell is more easi
reached by taking the West Autobahn to St. Pölten in Lower Austri
then Route 20.

The shorter route from Vienna to Graz is by the road through Ea
Styria, scenically very rewarding and a bit shorter than via Bruck (18
km. Vienna–Graz): at Wiener Neustadt branch off for Aspang, the
proceed via Mönichkirchen (maximum gradient 12 percent), Hartbe
and Gleisdorf to Graz. From Leoben No. 115 leads to: Trofaiach (1
km.), Präbichl (about 24 km., maximum gradient 9½ percent), Eisene
(28 km.), Gstatterboden (about 57 km.), Admont (69 km.), and conti
ues to Liezen. The A9 autobahn is only finished from Graz to St. M
chael, whence it is 75 km. on 113 over the Schober Pass (maximu
gradient 18 percent) to Liezen. From there 308 follows the Enns sout

est to Schladming and Radstadt in Salzburg, while 145 branches north-
est at Stainach to Bad Mittendorf and Bad Aussee.

Among the most scenic high Alpine roads are the short road from Bad
Mitterndorf to the Tauplitz plateau (about 5,250 ft.), open and plowed
in winter, the much longer road over the Sölker Tauern (5,900 ft.)
connecting Gröbming in the Enns Valley with Murau in the Mur Valley,
and the road to Planneralm from Wald near Steinach.

Winter and other Sports

Stryia's excellent skiing terrains will become much better known following the Alpine World Skiing Championships which were held in
Schladming in 1982. However, the area suffers from a lack of top-quality
hotels though its technical facilities are first class. There are over 500 ski
lifts, chair lifts and cable cars as well as more than 60 ski schools. If nice
bars and fancy *après ski* activities do not figure as musts in your winter
sports program, you may find that the skiing in Styria is extremely good
and the ski lodge Gemütlichkeit is real and sincere. But there are a few
places, such as Mariazell, where all the fashionable amenities of winter
resort life are available, and at even lower prices than elsewhere in
Austria. Styria also has the longest chair lift in the world at Tauplitz and
one of the biggest ski jumps in the world near Bad Mitterndorf. The
skiing season lasts from December to March, in the higher areas several
weeks longer, and many races as well as jumping events take place during
this time. All-year skiing is now possible on the Dachstein Glacier, and
there are outstanding high-mountain ski tours.

Tobogganing is extremely popular and there are frequent competitions. Many curling matches are featured. Ice hockey is played at Graz,
Bruck an der Mur, Leoben, Mariazell, and Mürzzuschlag. Skijoring is
practiced both with horses and motorcycles, and in several localities
horse sleigh rides can be taken.

If you prefer fishing, you can catch some of the best brook and rainbow
trout in Styria, particularly in the Enns River at Schladming, Gröbming,
Wörschach, Admont, Gstatterboden, in the Walster and Salza rivers
near Mariazell, in the Mürz River at Kindberg, and in several other
places. In the Lafnitz River near Fürstenfeld, you will find pike, carp,
and tench in addition to trout. The waters around Hartberg abound in
pike.

Licenses are purchased from the owners of fishing waters; for their
names, inquire at the local town administration.

In Styria mountain climbing is extremely popular and is pursued with
particular tenacity, especially among the university students, who have
produced some of the best climbers of the Alps. There are about 200

mountain lodges belonging to various climbing clubs and association
and scattered over all the mountain ranges.

Exploring Styria

The geography of Styria is largely dominated by the Mur River whic
collects its waters from most of the Styrian valleys. Its source, howeve
is in the Lungau region of Salzburg province, from where it enters Styr
at Predlitz following its long northeastern course as far as Bruck, wher
joined by Mürz—the "little Mur"—it suddenly turns southeast and ru
through Graz.

The most usual way to travel from Vienna to Graz, either by road
railroad, is via Semmering and through the Mürz-Mur valley. If drivin
the road through East Styria (Aspang–Graz) may be scenically ev
more rewarding. Another gate from Vienna to Styria is provided
Mariazell, the famous resort and pilgrimage place, located near th
northernmost point of the Styrian border with Lower Austria.

Mariazell

If you want to spend some time in a resort with a really local flave
you might try Mariazell, because this is where the Austrians, particular
the Viennese, go. In the past royalty—not only the Habsburgs b
princes of foreign countries as well—used to go there, not for soci
pleasures however, but on pilgrimages, for Mariazell has a double pe
sonality. It is not only a summer and winter pleasure resort (particular
the latter, for it has been estimated that every second Viennese learn
to ski at Mariazell) but a renowned place of religious pilgrimage. T
evening candlelight processions through the village to the basilica a
even to non-participants, beautiful and inspiring.

Mariazell began in 1157 as a cabin housing five monks, who built
church and set up in it a statue of the Virgin carved from limewood. A
time went on, curious stories began to emanate from Mariazell: the stat
was performing miracles! Its reputation grew and by the end of the 14
century Mariazell was drawing pilgrims from all parts of Europe, pa
ticularly from Slavic and Hungarian lands. Today it is the country
foremost pilgrimage church and contains Austria's national shrine, t
Chapel of Grace. The miracle-working statue is still to be seen in Mari
zell, surrounded by a splendor unknown to it in the 12th century.
stands on a silver altar designed by the great Austrian architect Fisch
von Erlach (who also created the baroque high altar) in the parish a
pilgrimage church, a 14th-century basilica rebuilt in the 17th century
Sciassia. Its fine treasury is open in the summer.

A cable car takes you from Mariazell to the Bürgeralpe, over 4,1
feet high. On the main road south of Mariazell is the Seeberg Pass (ov

4,100 feet) with a fine view of the surrounding mountain ranges of Hochschwab and Veitschalpe. The road proceeds farther south through the quiet summer and winter resort of Aflenz and by the Schachenstein Castle ruins and the 14th-century fortress at Thörl to Kapfenberg in the Mürz Valley.

From Semmering through the Mürz Valley

Taking the train from Vienna you literally penetrate into Styria through a tunnel over half a mile long underneath the Semmering Pass, while the excellent road crosses over the Pass. The first communities on the Styrian side of Semmering are Steinhaus and Spital, unpretentious summer resorts, sharing in winter a first-class skiing area. The Semmering Railway is one of the great Victorian railway achievements in the world. It has tunnels, elegant viaducts and breathtaking views.

At Mürzzuschlag we reach the Mürz River. Here is the heart of Austrian skiing, and, in a sense, of the Winter Olympics, since the first Nordic Games were held here in 1904. The main current has moved away now, but there is still a winter sports museum here in honor of past glories. The old parish church was rebuilt in baroque style and partially redecorated in rococo, and there are also several interesting old houses; see the Gutschelhoferhaus, distinguished by the fact that Czar Alexander I of Russia and Emperor Franz I of Austria slept here. Further up the Mürz Valley are Neuberg with a 14th-century Cistercian monastery reputed to possess the most beautiful cloisters in Styria, and Mürzsteg with a hunting castle that belonged to Emperor Franz Josef, currently the summer residence of the presidents of Austria.

Down the valley from Mürzzuschlag is Krieglach, known chiefly for the fact that Peter Rosegger, the famed Styrian folk poet, spent part of his life here. He was born in the nearby Alpl (about 8 km.), in the beautiful wooded mountain area that is called his Waldheimat (forest homeland) and which inspired many of his poems. His birth house as well as the Waldschule (school in the forest), founded by him, have been preserved. His grave is in the Krieglach cemetery.

Kindberg is a small summer and winter resort as well as an old town. The main square is lined with old houses, some of them from the 17th–18th century, there are two fine churches, and Schloss Oberkindberg, a 17th-century castle with four towers and valuable interiors.

Kapfenberg is a modern industrial center dominated by the 12th-century Oberkapfenberg Castle. A few 18th-century houses line the main square, among them the old Rathaus, and a kilometer or so away is the 17th-century four-towered Krottendorf Castle.

Bruck an der Mur

Bruck an der Mur lies at the confluence of Mur and Mürz and is a good center for one of the best walking areas of Austria. Most people who arrive here are too busy changing trains to notice that Bruck has marked merits of its own. Its most notable structure is the Kornmesserhaus, built between 1499 and 1505 in late Gothic style, and recently restored. Some authorities refer to it as the most beautiful late Gothic building in Austria, barring ecclesiastical architecture; the original owner was called Pankraz Kornmess, hence the name. The wrought-iron Renaissance fountain on the main square is the most beautiful of its kind in Styria. Another wrought-iron masterpiece is the late Gothic sacristy door of the 14th-century parish church, itself well worth an inspection. Maria im Walde is an interesting church, with one of the best Austrian 14th-century frescos. Another old fresco, depicting the Last Judgment and originating from around 1420, can be seen in the Church of St. Ruprecht.

A treasure of Gothic art is contained in the 14th-century St. Ulrich Church in Utsch near Bruck: a crucifixion fresco from 1390 and sculptures and glass window paintings from 1430.

Following the Mur River to Graz we pass through Mixnitz, the starting point for a highly interesting trip that takes you first to the savage Bärenschützklamm gorge, which you have to negotiate on steps and ladders, but whose raging waterfalls are worth all the trouble; then across mountain meadows that seem incongruously peaceful in the midst of such tormented scenery; and finally to the 5,650-foot Hochlantsch. You can also go a few kilometers up the side valley called Breitenau Tal to St. Erhard, where there is a 14th-century parish church with extraordinary glass window paintings from around 1400, as well as other valuable interiors.

Farther south is Frohnleiten, an old town with rich rococo interiors in its parish church. On an abrupt rock about 3 km. southwest of town is Rabenstein Castle, a medieval structure built on the ruins of a Roman fort and subsequently redone in baroque style. A couple of other castles are nearby, the 18th-century Neupfannberg in a pleasant park, and the ruins of Pfannberg.

Near Peggau, only about 20 km. from Graz, is the largest stalactite and stalagmite cave in Austria, the 5 km.-long Lurgrotte with a small underground lake, artificial pathways, electric lighting, and conducted tours of varying length.

Through East Styria to Graz

Proceeding from Vienna on the eastern route, we enter Styria just beyond Mönichkirchen, crossing the Wechsel mountain range. The first

Styrian communities are the twin towns of Pinggau and Friedberg, the first sitting modestly in the narrow valley and the second towering above it on a steep hill. Friedberg was once a fortress town, founded in the 12th century, allegedly with part of the ransom paid by Richard the Lionheart. At Rohrbach we reach the Lafnitz river and the secondary road leading west to Vorau where there is a renowned baroque abbey, whose church contains a grandiose high altar and many fine paintings and frescos and whose library, in addition to many other treasures, has an extraordinary collection of early German manuscripts. A few kilometers north of Vorau is Festenburg Castle, now partially converted into a church and belonging to the Vorau Abbey, but once a meeting place of Minnesingers.

Lafnitz river branches off from the main road at the town of Lafnitz and from here on forms the border between Styria and Burgenland. A secondary road approximately parallels it through the towns of Neudau with a castle, and Burgau, where the 13th-century fort provides a spectacular backdrop for the huge swimming pool.

But Europe's largest pool is in East Styria's main town, Fürstenfeld, founded in the 12th century as a fortress-town in the chain of the Empire's eastern defenses, later a district seat of the Knights of Malta. The architectural evidence of this period can still be seen, including fine old town houses and churches, remains of fortifications, and several castles in the vicinity. To the southwest of Fürstenfeld is Riegersburg Castle-Fortress, the most powerful Styrian castle, dominating the town of the same name below it from the top of a basalt pile of rocks. First record of its existence goes back to 1100, it was last rebuilt in the 17th century: it has seven gates, arcaded courtyards, decorated halls, a collection of armor and weapons, and a fine view over East and South Styria. It was savagely fought over in World War II.

If instead of following the course of Lafnitz river we continue from the town of the same name along the main road to Graz (the railroad line goes via Fürstenfeld) we first come to Hartberg, another old town with a castle and a baroque church but with a Romanesque charnel house and murals from the same period. West of Hartberg is Pöllau with the former abbey church, the best example in Styria of High Baroque, and with a 16th-century Rathaus with a whipping post. Nearby is the Pöllauberg pilgrimage church, one of Austria's loveliest.

Three kilometers or so upstream from where the main road crosses the Feistritz river is the 13th-century Schloss Herberstein, owned by the famous South Styrian aristocratic family of the same name, one of the most beautiful Styrian castles, last rebuilt in the 17th century, with rich internal and external decorations, a family and castle museum, and a game preserve. Nearby is Austria's largest artificial lake—Stubenbergsee. Farther up the Feistritz valley are several small summer resorts, the best known among which is Birkfeld.

Back on the main road we continue to Gleisdorf, a marketing center for the fruit grown in this fertile region. Here the main road from Fürstenfeld in the east joins our route and after crossing the low hills between Raab and Mur valleys in a westerly direction we come to Graz. North of this section are Weiz with a 17th-century church built as a fort for defense against the Turks and the vividly decorated Weizberg pilgrimage church; and Passail, an unpretentious summer resort with the picturesque gorges of Raabklamm and Weizklamm and several underground caves in the vicinity.

Graz, Styria's Capital

Napoleon's play on words, *"Ville de grace aux rives de l'amour"*, aptly describes the elegant baroque center, framed by parks and gardens, on the banks of La Mur. There was probably a Celtic settlement on the spot and almost certainly a fortress in the 9th century. However, documentary evidence only begins early in the 12th century, and it was one century later that it acquired officially the status of a town, and enclosed itself in the walls that helped it later on to escape capture by the Turks. It was the capital, not only of Styria, but of all Inner Austria—Carinthia, Carniola, Görz, Istria, and Trieste as well—from the late 14th to the early 17th century. Today it is a city of 260,000 inhabitants, spread out over both banks of the Mur. The left bank, on which the Old Town is located, is the richer in relics of the past, although there are also some interesting old buildings on the right bank, the Lend and Gries sections.

Exploring Graz

The easiest way to get an overall view of the city is to take the little cogwheel railway from the Kaiser-Franz-Josef-Kai up to Schlossberg, the steep wooded rock that dominates the town, crowned, till the Napoleonic Wars, by a large castle-fortress. From it you will be able to see all of Graz and a good part of East, South and Central Styria as well. Orientation tables, located at various points offering the best views, will help you to identify what you see. Near the top is also an open air theater where opera and drama performances are staged in summer, particularly during the Graz Festival. Only the clock tower remains of the old fortifications. It was saved during the Napoleonic Wars when the townspeople paid the French 3,000 guilders not to destroy it. Thus Styria's largest bell, the Liesl, weighing more than four tons, is still pealing forth the musical tone for which it has been famous since 1588. The *big* hand on the gigantic dials show the hours and the *small* hands the minutes, an endless source of confusion to unsuspecting visitors.

The castle hill is included in the vast park area of the City Park (Stadtpark) which forms a crescent around the eastern part of the old

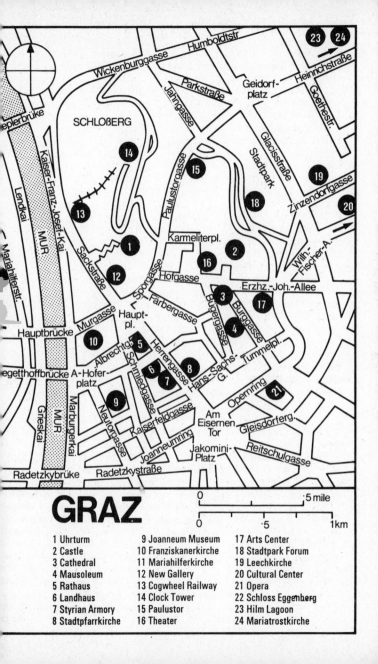

GRAZ

1 Uhrturm	9 Joanneum Museum	17 Arts Center
2 Castle	10 Franziskanerkirche	18 Stadtpark Forum
3 Cathedral	11 Mariahilferkirche	19 Leechkirche
4 Mausoleum	12 New Gallery	20 Cultural Center
5 Rathaus	13 Cogwheel Railway	21 Opera
6 Landhaus	14 Clock Tower	22 Schloss Eggenberg
7 Styrian Armory	15 Paulustor	23 Hilm Lagoon
8 Stadtpfarrkirche	16 Theater	24 Mariatrostkirche

town. From the Clock Tower you can take a pleasant pathway to the cit
gate called Paulustor and to the Styrian Folklore Museum, housed in a
old monastery, and then proceed through Sporgasse, lined with interest
ing old buildings, such as the House of the Teutonic Knights and Saurau
Goess Palace, to the main square. If you decide to return from th
Schlossberg by the cogwheel railway then you reach the main squar
walking through Sackstrasse, which also has several old palaces, such a
Palais Herberstein with an outstanding stairway and ceiling fresco
Palais Khuenburg, where Archduke Franz Ferdindand was born i
1863; and particularly the baroque Palais Attems with stucco decora
tions by Boscho, frescos by Matthias von Görz, very valuable furnish
ings, rare 18th-century tapestries and the largest private art collection i
Styria.

On the main square (Hauptplatz) stands the Erzherzog Johann Foun
tain with the statue of the Styrian Governor and the four female figure
representing the four principal rivers of Styria. The Rathaus, a structur
from the end of the last century, is of less interest; remarkable howeve
is the richly ornamented Luegg House with arcaded passageway on th
corner of Hauptplatz and Sporgasse. Artistically superior is the row c
façades in Herrengasse, which begins at the other end of the squar
among them particularly the 15th-century Herzogshof or Gemalte
Haus (Painted House) at No. 3. In the same street is the architectural
renowned Landhaus, the seat of the Styrian state parliament and govern
ment, whose main wing was built by Domenico dell'Allio, a native c
Lugano, in Italian Renaissance style. Its arcaded courtyard is magnifi
cently proportioned and the star exhibits among the interiors are th
Knights' Hall and the Council Chamber. The 16th-century courtyar
fountain is an unusually fine example of the old Styrian wrought-iron ar
Historic coats of arms of all the principal Styrian cities figure prominent
ly on an outer wall. Adjoining the Landhaus is the famous Zeughaus, th
world's largest armory; four floors stocked with 30,000 historical wea
pons and armor.

Farther down on the other side of the street is the twin-naved Gothi
parish church, built early in the 16th century, to which have been adde
a baroque façade and spire, both 18th century. Tintoretto's *Assumptio
of the Virgin* decorates the altar. Across the street from the parish churc
begins a short narrow street, called after the great architect Johan
Bernhard Fischer von Erlach because he was born in one of the house
there. From the parish church you can wander through the heart of th
old town toward the cathedral. If it happens to be 11 A.M. or 6 P.M., yo
might stop and watch the Glockenspiel on the square to which it ha
given its name.

The cathedral is 15th-century Gothic, and its most notable exterio
decoration is a fresco painted in 1485 depicting the "Divine Torments
—which turn out to be (a) plague, (b) locusts, and (c) war. Inside a

a number of details you should not miss—the high altar, the beautiful choir stalls, Raphael Donner's tomb of Count Cobenzl, and Konrad Laib's *Crucifixion*. The Diocesan Museum and cathedral treasure are also worth seeing. The treasure includes two magnificent ivory reliquaries, which were originally the hope chests of Paola Gonzaga, daughter of Ludwig II of Mantua.

Adjoining the cathedral is the baroque mausoleum in which Emperor Ferdinand II is buried. The interior, designed by Fischer von Erlach, is particularly admired. Across the square from the cathedral and the mausoleum is the Stadtburg, begun by Friedrich III in 1438 but including sections from every succeeding century. Its most notable detail is the double spiral Gothic staircase, added in 1499—unless you call the medieval Burgtor Gate attached to it a detail.

Through the Burgtor you again find yourself in the City Park. If you cross it approximately to the left you eventually come to the Teutonic Knights' twin-spired early Gothic Leech Church with a 13th-century stone relief of Madonna with Child, and beyond it to the University, noted for its creation of eminent jurists, philologists and physicians. Near the southeastern end of the City Park is the monumental Opera House and some six blocks beyond it, in the same general direction, the Technical University, founded by Erzherzog Johann and renowned throughout the country. Some 150 years ago Erzherzog Johann also founded the Joanneum, the Styrian Provincial Museum with the main building in Neutorgasse, three blocks from the Landhaus. Rather like a smaller version of the Victoria and Albert in London, this museum was designed to foster the progress of industry and the arts. Apart from some fine paintings, it also houses historical and pre-historical exhibits.

After crossing Andreas Hofer Platz, the terminal for out-of-town buses, Neutorgasse takes us to the Franciscan Church which provides an appropriate backdrop for an ancient, tiny square, and to the main bridge connecting the Old Town on the left bank with its right bank sections. Several old town houses are to be seen here, especially on Mariahilferstrasse and Griesgasse, and among the churches the twin-spired Mariahilf Church is particularly appealing. Annenstrasse, the principal business artery of the right bank becomes increasingly modern as it approaches the new railway station.

Excursions around Graz

There are many pleasant spots for short trips from Graz in the outskirts. Among them is Maria Trost, where there is a fine baroque church with two towers and famous paintings, and an attached convent. It is beautifully located on high land; Steirerhof and Zum Kirchenwirt are two fine choices for a meal; both have a few moderate rooms.

Eggenberg Castle, about 20 minutes from Graz with streetcar 1, is
magnificent 17th-century residence, with no less than 26 large rooms fo
receptions and banquets, in addition to normal living quarters. It
decorated and furnished in accord with its grandeur, and the baroqu
stucco work and mural and ceiling paintings are remarkable. In additio
it also houses the small Graz City Museum and an interesting Jag
museum (Museum of Hunting). Mouflons, deer, and peacocks roam
freedom in the large park around the castle. Open daily, Apr.–Oct., 9–
2–6. Entrance at end of Eggenberger Allee.

Plabutsch—an elevation west from the city—has lovely walks and
fine view of the western Styrian mountains.

St. Radegund-Schöckel is a health resort, wonderful for walkers–
there are 42 km. of walking paths here. There is also a swimming poo
Take the funicular, one of Europe's most modern, up the Schöckel fo
a view extending from the Alps to the Hungarian plain.

Stift Rein, near Gratwein, reached by bus, is also a popular excursio
spot with Graz citizens. The monastery church, originally Romanesqu
was rebuilt in the 18th century; one of its main attractions is the alta
painting by Kremser Schmidt, but practically every part of it is magnit
cent. Only a few km. away is the Gothic Maria Strassengel, the "daug
ter church" of the Rein monastery with the main altar by Fischer vo
Erlach and some paintings by Kremser Schmidt.

Just over 9 miles from Graz, at Stübing, is the Austrian Opena
Museum, where some 70 rural buildings from all over Austria have bee
reconstructed. Spaced out through the Mur valley the grouped house
mills and barns are all in working order and make a very interestin
excursion.

South Styria

South Styria is mostly a region of undulating hills, carpeted wit
vineyards in its middle section, becoming higher and more foreste
toward the west, and slowly disappearing onto the plain in the east. Onl
a fraction of South or Lower Styria (Untersteiermark) was left to Austr
after World War I; the bulk of it had had to be ceded to the newly create
Yugoslav State. The largest community in the present Austrian Sout
Styria is Leibnitz, dominated by Seggau Castle which since the nint
century had been a stronghold of Salzburg Prince-Bishops and later we
into the hands of the Styrian Bishops of Seckau. The castle houses
collection of Roman stone reliefs for on the grounds of Leibnitz stoo
once the Roman town Flavia Solva, founded by Emperor Vespasian
the first century. More remains from Roman times can be seen
Frauenberg near Seggau, where a Roman temple once stood and a pi
grimage church stands today. Leibnitz itself has an interesting paris
church, originally Gothic with an impressive 18th-century main alta
East of Leibnitz, on the Mur river which forms here the fronti

between Styria and Slovenia, is the small, picturesque town of Mureck, and farther down the river the larger Radkersburg. Its Gothic parish church contains a famous Black Madonna, while the 165-foot clock tower on the Rathaus rises above fine patrician houses. Both towns have old castles which are on the hills across the river and therefore across the border. North of Radkersburg in quiet green surroundings lies Bad Gleichenberg, the most important Styrian spa.

At Ehrenhausen, south of Leibnitz, begins the "Styrian Wine Road", leading across undulating hills through the wine villages Platsch, Gamlitz and Leutschach. The Austrian-Yugoslav border runs down the middle of the wine road for several miles—there is different paving on each side! The scenery is spectacular; the steep slopes of the hills are ornamented with vineyards and little wine press houses. "Klapotetz", a special type of wooden scarecrow, merrily rattle in the wind.

West of the wine region, the wooded slopes of Koralpe rise to a considerable height along the border of Carinthia. Deutschlandsberg, a summer resort at the foot of Koralpe and an old town with a medieval castle, is the main center. North of Deutschlandsberg are the towns of Voitsberg and Köflach, both defined by long history, medieval castles and coal mining, and actually already in central Styria.

If you are fond of horses, you will probably want to visit the Lippizaner stud farm at Piber, in the vicinity of Köflach. These snow-white horses trace their lineage back to 1580 when Archduke Karl of Styria established a stud farm at Lippiza near Trieste, using stallions imported from Arabia and mares from Spain. Born black, the steeds gradually turn white between the ages of two and seven. After World War I, when Austria lost Lippiza, the farm was transferred to Piber. Of course, the farm provides the horses for the famous Spanish Riding School in Vienna. From Köflach, the Pack Road, the main route between Graz and Klagenfurt, climbs to Pack Pass.

Iron Alps and Upper Mur

Leoben, a few kilometers upstream from Bruck in the Mur Valley, with a population of about 37,000, is the largest town in central Styria and the center of this important mining and heavy industry region. It also possesses a mining engineering college but industry is not its only point of interest. Leoben is an old town and the heritage of its past includes the 17th-century parish church; the baroque column commemorating the passage of the plague, which stands on the handsome main square lined with fine old buildings, including the Rathaus and the 17th-century Hacklhaus. Maria Waasen Church with brilliant 12th-century Gothic windows is worth visiting. There are many interesting old houses as well as the Massenburg Castle ruins. One unique feature is the Schwammerl ("little mushroom"), a name irreverently bestowed

on the former Customs Tower (Mautturm), the town symbol, becaus
of its shape.

In the southern suburb of Göss is the oldest monastery in Styria
founded around 1000; its most outstanding features include the Gothi
church and Bishop's Chapel with frescos from 1285, and a Romanesqu
crypt. The monastery has long been secularized and presently houses th
renowned Göss Brewery.

To the north is the Donawitz basin, an important factor in Europea
steel production. Donawitz itself is the northern suburb of Leoben an
the *Alpin Montan Gesellschaft* operates several blast furnaces and a
modern rolling mill here.

The atmosphere changes abruptly from industrial to touristic at Tro
faiach, where interest centers about summer holidays and two old Gothi
churches with 14th- and 15th-century statuary. Both elements, however
are combined again at Vordernberg, the oldest center of the Styrian iro
industry, where the Romans worked the metal from the surroundin
mines of what are accurately called the Iron Alps. There are a coupl
of interesting churches and some 17th-century guild houses that ar
worth looking at.

We now come to the most amazing place in this entire region, Eisen
erz. What is unique at Eisenerz is Erzberg, the mountain that tower
above it. Erzberg is literally a mountain of iron. The ore is 34 percen
pure iron. It does not have to be mined; it is quarried. For centuries, mer
have been chipping off pieces of the mountain. In modern times, the stu
of which the mountain is made has been pulled away in strips, so tha
now it rises in terrace after terrace, some forty of them. 5,000 feet high
it is rated as the largest ore field in Europe capable of open-face mining
Guided visits of the mine can be made.

In Eisenerz itself there are several things of interest. The St. Oswal
Church, built in 1509, is the biggest fortified church in Styria, built t
resist the onslaughts of the Turks. The Schichtturm, or Shift Tower, usec
to tell when it was time to change the shifts at the mine.

Near Erzberg, in the northerly direction, is the lovely Leopoldsteine
See, hidden among the mountains, while to the south, on the main roac
between Eisenerz and Vordernberg is Präbichl, near the pass of the same
name, a point of departure for climbing and skiing tours.

Back at Leoben, we continue upwards through the Upper Mur Valley
At St. Michael the main road leading to the Enns Valley and farther tc
Salzkammergut and Salzburg branches off. Knittelfeld is a small indus-
trial town with the dreamy Ingering Lake nearby, framed by forests
About 16 km. north is the 12th-century Seckau Abbey, another famec
Styrian monastery, with the original Romanesque style of its church stil
visible despite later additions, containing many outstanding features ol
all periods, such as the Renaissance-style Mausoleum of Archduke Kar
II as well as the modern apocalyptic frescos in the Angel's Chapel by

Herbert Boeckl, one of the most prominent 20th-century Austrian paint-ers. For five and a half centuries Seckau was the episcopal center for Styria, and the whole complex of buildings bears rich testimony to the wealth that was lavished on it. The stained-glass, wrought iron, paintings and carvings are well worth spending time to visit.

Farther up the valley is Judenburg; as its name implies it was a Jewish town several centuries ago. An old building still displays a 500-year-old sculptured head of a Jew. Judenburg has several interesting churches (especially the Parish church with a rococo pulpit and some interesting sculptures), private dwellings, remains of the city wall, the ruins of the old Liechtenstein Castle nearby with the 17th-century new Liechtenstein Castle below it. At St. Georgen the road crossing the range of Niedere Tauern takes off, reaching after less than 16 km. the old silver mining town of Oberzeiring where a former silver mine can be visited.

Back in the Mur Valley we come to Unzmarkt with the ruins of the still impressive Frauenburg Castle on an elevation across the river. Among his castles this was the one that the famous Styrian Minnesinger Ulrich von Liechtenstein liked most, and here he died in 1275. At Scheifling the main road for Carinthia leads south, but the valley itself continues toward the west.

At Niederwölz a short side road takes you to the 800-year-old Ober-wölz with medieval walls, three gates, old churches and the Rothenfels Castle perched on a red cliff. You can still see here now a medieval town was laid out.

At Teufenbach, with an old and a new castle, another side road takes you to St. Lambrecht, another famed abbey, founded in the 11th century. The twin-towered church is the largest in Styria and the Renaissance-style monastery building contains two ornate halls, one with the portraits of the emperors and the other with the portraits of the abbots. This, like Seckau, is a richly endowed abbey, full of items to interest anyone who likes church art and architecture. There are fine medieval wood carvings, rococo altars and splendid vestments.

Murau, founded in the 13th century, with remains of the 14th-century walls, several Gothic churches, the Rathaus that was once part of the fortifications, many old dwellings in the narrow streets, and crowned by Schwarzenberg Castle, is a historic jewel. But the main attraction of this area is, perhaps, the old steam-engine narrow-gauge Murtal railway, which puffs and whistles through the lovely Mur Valley between Murau and Tamsweg (in Land Salzburg). It runs only on certain days in sum-mer, and is accompanied by bright red and green cars (one of them a bar), and often also by the Murau brass band.

At Predlitz, the last village in Styria, with a remarkable wood-paneled ceiling in its church, a rough side road takes you up to Turrach, where the first blast furnaces and Bessemer converters on the Continent were put to use, and farther up to Turracher Höhe, a mountain resort with a small lake and famed for its Alpine flowers and skiing.

The Enns Upstream to Dachstein

The most spectacular entrance into the Enns Valley, which dominates northwestern Styria, is near its lower or eastern end, reached either from Eisenerz or via Altenmarkt if coming from Upper Austria. Immediately upstream from Hieflau, where the two mentioned routes join, begins the spectacular gorge of Gesäuse. The rocky faces of craggy peaks soar up on all sides, almost straight from the river bed, and the Enns cuts its way through them in a rushing, foaming, wild stream, white and green. This is one of the most splendid examples of natural mountain architecture anywhere in the Alps.

Once out of Gesäuse the Enns Valley widens and it is here that the famous Abbey of Admont is located in the town of the same name. The abbey is particularly renowned for its library with ceiling frescos by Altomonte, rococo bookshelves, some 145,000 volumes, 900 very early printed books, and 1,100 old manuscripts, besides a collection of 250,000 insects. The rocky Ennstaler Alps provide a magnificent frame for the town. On a hill near Admont is the twin-spired pilgrimage church of Frauenberg.

At Liezen the Enns Valley road is joined by the road coming from St. Michael near Leoben over the Schober Pass and through Rottenmann, one of the oldest towns in Styria, and Selztal. Stainach, located under the mighty Grimming mountain group, is famous for its Glöcklerlauf (masked procession) on Twelfth Night. In the vicinity are several castles, the lovely Putterersee, and the medieval fortress settlement of Pürgg with the Gothic parish church and 12th-century frescos in the Romanesque Johannes Chapel.

Near Stainach, the main road forks into two directions. One road climbs to Klachauer Höhe, and from there passes into Ausseer Land which is the Styrian section of Salzkammergut. The other road continues up the Enns valley along the base of the powerful Grimming to Gröbming, a very pleasant climatic resort and one of the centers of Styrian horsebreeding.

At Schladming, a picturesque old town that was the site of the Alpine Skiing World Championship in 1982, the Enns Valley narrows between the Dachstein mountain range and Schladminger Tauern. Schladming, a renowned summer and winter resort, has remains of old walls, the town hall, which was formerly a hunting castle, and a Gothic church. The nearby mountain resort of Ramsau is the principal climbing base for the majestic Dachstein (nearly 10,000 ft.), covered by glaciers on its north side, vertically cut on its south side, the highest peak of Styria, reached by a super-modern cable car.

Ausseer Land

In the high valley beyond the Klachauer Höhe are the summer resorts and first-class skiing centers of Tauplitz, with Tauplitzalm (5,500 ft.) and Mitterndorf, and the giant ski jump of Kulm nearby.

The heart of this region is Bad Aussee, with Altaussee on the lake to which it gives its name, as a secondary center. The former is a big spa, especially beneficial for such respiratory troubles as asthma and bronchitis because of its altitude and its location, which protect it from wind and fog, so that sun baths as well as brine and mud baths can be a dependable part of the cure here. You can choose between a swimming pool and lake bathing, climb mountains on foot or take a chair lift, inspect the 5,000 different Alpine flowers in the Alpine garden or the costumes in the museum, go to the Kurhaus theater or the cinema, look at the 15th-century parish church with its statue of the Virgin or the 14th-century Hospital Church, with its Gothic statues and frescos, or simply watch the pageantry of everyday life in a town where folk costumes survive in full ceremony, hunt, fish, play tennis or, in winter, ski.

Altaussee is by comparison a quieter, more reposeful place than its cousin, dominated by the endless spectacle of the Dachstein glacier, always the same and always changing with each minute variation in the light. It adds to the baths of the larger center a variant of its own, the pineneedle bath.

Grundlsee on the lake of the same name is also a quieter resort, and Gössl at the end of the lake is recommended for those who want complete peace and do not mind simple accommodations. From Gössl there is a 20-minute walk to the beginning of Toplitzsee, which you can cross by a motor raft; from the other end it is five minutes to the rustic Kammersee and the Traun waterfall pouring down a rocky cliff.

With various new ski lifts and more under construction, the district around Bad Aussee, Altaussee and Grundlsee is a winter sports center of major importance.

PRACTICAL INFORMATION

HOTELS AND RESTAURANTS

AFLENZ KURORT 2,500 ft, with the Bürgeralm, 5,100 ft. above. Base for mountain climbing in the Hochschwab. Health resort. About 20 minutes from Kapfenberg by local bus.

Hotels *Aflenzerhof* (1), 30 rooms with bath or shower. 15th-century, but new-wing rooms very comfortable.

All (2)—*Hubertushof,* 45 beds, good restaurant and bar with fireplace; *Post,* 80 beds; *Pension Vasold,* all rooms with bath or shower, indoor pool, sauna.

Gasthof Gollner (3), higher up on the Bürgeralm (5,100 ft.).

ALTAUSSEE Located on the picturesque Altausseersee, in the Styrian part of the Salzkammergut and known as both a summer and winter resort with a newly developed skiing region on Mount Loser (5,000 ft.).

Hotels All (1)—*Am See,* beautifully situated on the Altausseersee, 110 beds, 30 baths, many rooms with balcony, dining on the veranda, bar, indoor and outdoor pool, own beach, boating and tennis; *Hubertushof,* 20 rooms, in elegantly furnished former hunting lodge of Prince Hohenlohe-Schillingfürst; *Seevilla,* 30 rooms with bath, in new hotel on lake with own beach, indoor pool, sauna; and *Tyrol,* all rooms with bath.

Both (2)—*Haus Loser,* small, local-style hotel known for its praiseworthy restaurant; and *Kitzer,* with fine restaurant and pastries.

ALPL-WALDHEIMAT Hotel *Waldheimathof* (2), 60 rooms with bath or shower. Pleasant accommodations, restaurant, in lovely location at 3,300 ft.

BAD AUSSEE 2,155 ft. in Styrian Salzkammergut, becoming increasingly important spa, resort and winter sports center. It is also the home of the Erzherzog-Johann-Kapelle, one of the renowned Styrian folk-dress brass bands.

Hotels Both (1)—*Paradies,* 20 rooms with bath. A little outside town; friendly atmosphere; restaurant residents-only. And *Villa Kristina,* 14 rooms with bath; period furnishings. With large garden.

All (2)—*Wasnerin,* Styrian chalet type, above and outside the town, with magnificent view of the Dachstein; *Erzherzog Johann,* on main square, garden café, cure facilities, wine tavern and good restaurant; *Sarstein,* 11 rooms with bath, bar, some rooms in antique style.

BAD GLEICHENBERG Hotels All (2)—*Austria am Kurpark; Strandhotel Stenitzer,* and *Parkhotel;* also a few km. south in **Poppendorf** is a pension in the baroque castle, set in large park, all rooms with bath.

Hindenbergerhof (3), pool and sauna.

BAD MITTERNDORF 2,600 ft. Small spa, and base for climbing the Grimming. About 4 hours by fast train from Graz, and about 3 hours from Salzburg (via Bischofshofen), changing trains at Stainach-Irdning.

Hotels *Kurhotel Bad Heilbrunn* (1), about 100 comfortable rooms with all facilities, 8-storied building on the outskirts of town, folklore-inspired wooden interiors in its public rooms, water cure facilities, adjoining indoor and outdoor pools, pension terms only.

All (2)—*Lord,* smaller, all rooms with bath, indoor and outdoor pools; *Hubertushof* and *Schmidt* with good restaurant.

All (3)—*Seidenhof* and *Kogler,* both with good restaurants; *Speckmoser,* all rooms with bath or shower; *Schrottshammer* and *Alpenpension Kulka,* sauna.

Restaurant *Grimmingwurz'n,* country-style gourmet eatery with international and local dishes.

Kochalm campsite.

BAD RADKERSBURG Popular health resort. **Hotel** *Thermal-Kurhotel* (1), 70 rooms with bath; indoor pool, cure facilities.

BRUCK AN DER MUR Hotels Both (2)—*Zum Schwarzen Adler,* on main square, a hostelry since 1683, 88 beds, good restaurant; *Bayer,* next to Town Hall, a little more reasonable, good food.

Restaurant For typical Styrian dishes, *Restaurant Lackner* on main square. Youth hostel.

DONNERSBACH 2,260 ft. in Niedere Tauern. Bus from Stainach.

Hotels Both (3)—*Tauernhaus,* outdoor pool, game and fish specialties in restaurant; and *Grimmingblick.*

FERNITZ 16 km. from Graz. **Restaurant** *Purkharthofer* specializes in nouvelle cuisine but also has local dishes. Exceptionally pretty decorations.

FLADNITZ 2,270 ft., on the Teichalpe about 43 km. north of Graz.

Hotels *Pierer* (2), on the Teichalpe (4,000 ft.), indoor pool, sauna.

Zur Kraltaverne (3), small and friendly, with fireplace and sauna, good restaurant with own meats and Styrian specialties.

FROHNLEITEN Hotels Both (1)—*Schloss Rabenstein,* on a cliff nearby, a baroque building above the river, a section is arranged as a castle pension with 12 beds, all rooms with bath, period furnishings, open April to Oct., reservations essential; *Murhof,* at the golf course a few km. south, 34 beds, all rooms with bath, indoor pool.

FÜRSTENFELD 50 km. from Graz. **Hotel** *Hitzl* (1), 30 rooms with bath. Excellent food, first-rate service.

GRAZ One of Austria's less expensive state capitals; wide choice of hotels.

Hotels Heading the list is the tradition-filled *Steirerhof,* (1), Jakominiplatz 12, near the Opera; 98 rooms with a row of pleasant, wood-paneled restaurant rooms, including Weinstube at rear, bar at front, both with musical entertainment.

All (1), though with a few less expensive rooms without baths are—*Daniel,* at the station square, 82 rooms; functional.

Grandhotel Wiesler, Grieskai 4–8 on the river bank, 64 rooms, fine view of the old town rooftops and the castle hill from its front windows.

Parkhotel, Leonhardstr. 8, near the City Park, 58 rooms, café-restaurant.

Erzherzog Johann, Sackstr. 5, just off main square, 60 rooms, freshened-up old-fashioned face and good food in its cozy restaurant, old-style café.

Weitzer, Griesgasse 15, on the river, together with its annex *Goldener Ochs* next door, 170 rooms.

Gollner, Schögelgasse 14, 50 rooms, 17 baths, sauna in the roof, excellent room service, clean and very comfortable. Many artists from the opera stay here.

Süd, Stemmerweg 10, in Strassgang suburb, indoor pool, 26 rooms with bath or shower.

Mariahilf, Mariahilferstr. 9, not far from main bridge, Styrian specialties in its restaurant, garage.

Drei Raben, Annenstr. 43, halfway between station and downtown.

Both (3)—*Grazerhof,* Stubenberggasse 10, near the center; and *Zum Kreuz,* on the outskirts at Kärntnerstr. 451, in the same family for over 100 years, only 14 beds but good restaurant.

Youth Hostel at Idlhofgasse 74, and 2 winter campsites.

Restaurants Though the food is so good that an English tour operator organizes special cookery trips in autumn, prices are very reasonable.

All (1)—the atmospheric dining rooms of the *Steirerhof,* which has a very good selection of Styrian wines; and in the restaurant of *Wiesler,* adorned with the coats of arms of Styrian towns and retaining its old-world charm. *Victorian Steak House,* Burgg. 15, opposite the Opera. Evening restaurant with music; discothèque *Down-Stairs.*

All (2)—*Gambrinuskeller,* Färbergasse 6, offers Balkan-style dishes. *Goldene Pastete,* Sporgasse 28, for fine local dishes and wines in genuine friendly surroundings.

A piece of old Graz is *Krebsenkeller,* Sackstr. 12, in the inner courtyard of a 16th-century Renaissance house, with wide choice of food and wine.

Pfeffermühle, Hilmteichstr. 134, away from center, evening restaurant with Styrian specialties and charcoal grill, atmospheric decor.

Holzhof, Baiernstr. 20, game specialties when in season.

Stadtkeller, Andreas-Hoffer-Platz 3, with terrace overlooking the Mur.

Brandhof, by the opera, is simple and excellent with Schilcher wine—a natural rosé that only grows in West Styria.

All (3)—in the southern suburbs of the city the vast *Puntigam,* with a large garden and several halls, located in the brewery of the same name, with its own excellent beer.

Schuberthof, Zinzendorfgasse 17, near city park, is known for its hearty food.

Weisses Rössl, Lendplatz 37, with garden and good Styrian food.

Zum Kreuz, (see *Hotels*), in Strassgang south suburb, Kärntnerstr. 451, good Styrian wines and food, especially the home-made sausages during slaughter months (Sept.–March).

Cafés and Pastry Shops An inviting choice, with the *Herrengasse* offering the best. A leisurely reminder of the past is the corner café of *Hotel Erzherzog Johann.* More elegant is the café of *Parkhotel. Sorger,* with own pastries, has several branches, the most pleasant are the ones in the City Park and in Sporgasse. In summer, a pleasant café is *Hilmteich,* near the pond of the same name at Hilmteichstr. 70. *Café am Tummelplatz,* Hans Sachs Gasse 8, is a coffeehouse exuding a sense of nostalgia and with interesting vaults; meeting place of the elegant young of Graz. *Café Leinich,* Kaiser Joseph Platz 4, serves delicious pastries and homemade ice cream. Situated on a picturesque market square where farmers from the surrounding country come to sell their produce.

Taverns The local people like to have a glass of wine and listen to a song (and usually participate in singing) in the so-called evening wine taverns *(Weinstuben),* all of them also serving food: *Herzl-Weinstube,* Prokopigasse 12, is one of the most typically Styrian; a historic old place is *Kepplerkeller,* Stempfergasse 6; *Landhauskeller,* Schmiedgasse 9, with food and drink in originally-decorated Stuben such as the Ritterstube (Knights' room) and the Jägerstube (Hunters' room). *Ur-*

banikeller, Stempfergasse 1, pleasant atmosphere but the music is canned. For dancing you might try *Tenne,* Sackstr. 27, *Glockenspielkeller,* Glockenspielplatz 8, *Victorian Steak House,* Burggasse 15 (all discothèques) or *Haus Gottinger,* in Strassgang suburb (live music).

HAUS IM ENNSTAL 2,532 ft. By train from Gröbming, 15 minutes.
Hotels *Hauser Kaibling* (2), all rooms with bath or shower, indoor pool. *Gasthof Stiegler* (3) has a good restaurant.

IRDNING In the Enns Valley.
Hotel *Schloss Pichlarn* (L), 134 beds, all rooms with bath, indoor and outdoor pools, riding, fishing, hunting, tennis, 9-hole golf course, excellent restaurant.

KAPFENBERG Hotel *Burghotel Kapfenberg* (2), a castle-hotel in the formidable castle-fortress overlooking the town.

KAPFENSTEIN Hotel *Schloss Kapfenstein* (2), 12 beds, all rooms with bath, a castle-hotel near Bad Gleichenberg in East Styria.

LEIBNITZ At the beginning of the Styrian Wine Road (see p. 361). **Hotel** *Bachner* (2), 50 rooms with bath.

LEOBEN 1,745 ft. Less than 1½ hours by autorail from Graz.
Hotels *Baumann* (2), large, many rooms with bath or shower, excellent dining in quaint and cozy rustic rooms, among them *Alte Mühle,* with old mill decor, and gourmet specialties in *Pferdestall.*
Both (3)—*Kindler,* 80 beds, garni; *Südbahnhof,* with garden restaurant.
Restaurant *Weinstube Sattler* (M) offers fine Styrian food and wine.

MARIAZELL 2,870 ft., sports center and health resort. 3 hours by small local train from St. Pölten on Vienna-Linz railway line; 2½ hours by bus from Bruck an der Mur; 4 hours from Graz; about 4½ hours from Vienna.
Hotels *Mariazellerhof* (1), 15 rooms with bath. Notable for traditional home-made gingerbread.
Feichtegger (2), 160 beds, most rooms with bath or shower, several restaurant rooms, wine tavern and bar, garden café.
All (3), some rooms higher priced—*Goldener Krone,* with fine restaurant; *Grüner Kranz; Goldenes Kreuz,* with attractive restaurant; *Zum Goldenen Ochsen,* grill specialties in its restaurant.
Many colorful old inns (3). Youth Hostel, campsite at Erlaufsee nearby.

MURAU 2,700 ft., 1 hour by bus or small train from Unzmarkt.
Hotels *Lercher* (2), attractive dining rooms, new pension annex, most rooms with bath or shower, sauna, sun terrace, excellent food.
Both (3)—the local brewery-owned *Brauhaus* and *Pension Anny.*
Restaurant *Café Pekari,* terrace overlooking the river, a series of small, attractive rooms, a pleasant place for coffee.

OBDACH Small village below the brow of the pass between Judenburg and Wolfsberg in Carinthia. Excellent center for walking and beginners' skiing. *Groggerhof* is perhaps the most perfect gasthof in Austria. Family run, all rooms with bath/shower, local wines and trout, homebaked cakes and many other delicacies.

PICHL-MANDLING 2,620 ft. train stop on the Salzburg–Graz line.
Hotel *Alpengasthof Pichlmayrgut* (3), 80 beds, indoor pool and sauna.

PRÄBICHL 4,025 ft. 1¼ hours from Leoben by bus, also local railway but slower. Base for mountain climbing in the Eisenerzer Alpen.
Hotel *Hubertushof* (2), 23 rooms, all with bath or shower, celler-bar discothèque, in winter live music, good restaurant, sauna, ski lift. Many more inns and pensions, all (3), including one for children from 3 years of age.

RAMSAU Hotels All (1)—balconied *Matschner*, 150 beds, most rooms with bath, large restaurant, indoor pool; *Alpenkrone; Alpengasthof*, very good restaurant; *Alpengasthof Peter Rosseger*, 16 rooms with bath, attractively furnished, admirable food and regular "candlelight" evenings.
All (2)—*Almfrieden*, smaller, many rooms with bath; *Post*, 144 beds, several apartments, indoor pool; *Ennstalerhof*, fine food; *Pehab*, 55 beds, café, bar and tavern, good restaurant; *Karlwirt*, near the branch-off to the Dachstein cable car.

ROHRMOOS On the southern mountain slopes above Schladming, at about 3,300 ft. **Hotels** All (2)—*Rohrmooserhof*, 20 rooms; *Schütterhof*, 50 rooms; *Waldfrieden*, 39 rooms.
All (3)—*Abelhof; Austria; Gasthof-Pension Sonneck*, 18 rooms, 10 baths; and the older *Moser*, both at the upper end of the Schladming-Rohrmoos chair lift; *Schwaigerhof*, indoor pool; all have view of the Dachstein.

SCHLADMING 2,450 ft., together with Rohrmoos at 3,300 ft., Plainai at about 6,300 ft., and the plateau of Ramsau, averaging about 4,000 ft., under Dachstein the highest peak of Styria. Schladming, the base for mountain climbing the Dachstein and Schladming Tauern, can be reached by autorail from Salzburg in under 2 hours, and from Graz in under 4 hours. Bus service between Schladming and Ramsau.
Hotels *Sporthotel Royer* (1), 60 rooms and apartments, all with bath, radio and safe, kindergarten, indoor pool.
Both (2)—*Alte Post*, with attractive restaurant; and *Haus Barbara*.
Many inns and pensions (2) and (3). Youth Hostel and campsite.
In addition, there are over 50 low-priced inns, pensions and mountain lodges in the Schladming-Rohrmoos-Ramsau area, as well as many guest rooms in private houses.
Restaurants Among the restaurants—the attractive *Rauchkuchl*, with old style timber decor; *Rohrmooser Schlössl*, good wines, own pastries.

SPITAL AM SEMMERING 2,500 ft., together with **Steinhaus** at 2,700 ft., a few km. away on the Styrian side of Semmering.

Hotels All (3)—*Gästehaus Winter; Hirschenhof*, 120 beds, attractive restaurant, in the middle of Spital, country-style; and pension *Onkel Fritz*.

STUBENBERG AM SEE Hotels *Parkhotel* (1), 87 rooms, all with bath, most with southside balcony, opened in 1976 with modern, indoor pool, terrace restaurant, tavern, bar, several public rooms, own bus to lake.

Both (3)—*Seehof Herberstein,* fishing possibilities, dancing at weekends; and *Seepension Erla,* with Styrian dishes in restaurant, garden.

TAUPLITZ Almost 3,000 ft., together with Tauplitzalm, 5,500 ft., located some 6 km. from Bad Mitterndorf, reached in 10 minutes by train. Tauplitz and Tauplitzalm Plateau are linked by a chair lift about 4 km. long. A chair lift connects Tauplitzalm with Lawinenstein at 6,560 ft.

Hotels Both (2)—*Berghotel Tauplitzalm,* best, about 5,500 ft., 40 rooms, all with bath or shower, restaurant, café, wine tavern; *Sporthotel Kirchenwirt,* 46 beds, restaurant, Styrian-style bar, indoor pool.

Both (3)—*Hechl,* 37 beds, good food; and *Zur Sonnenuhr,* some rooms with bath and balcony, restaurant and sun terrace.

SPECIAL EVENTS

AFLENZ KURORT Folklore shows in summer; special folk festival at Easter and on first Sunday in October.

BAD MITTERNDORF Masked processions in *Fasching*.

GRAZ Spring Trade Fair starts last week in April. End Sept. to mid-October, Graz Autumn Fair. Summer music courses at American Institute of Musical Studies. Music, drama and art festival, *Steirischer Herbst* (Styrian Autumn) in Oct. Dec., Christmas crib in Jesuit church is the oldest in Austria.

KINDBERG In May, there's an interesting church feast day.

LEIBNITZ Wine Week in August.

LEOBEN New Year opens with a toboggan race.

MARIAZELL The Three Magi go singing on the eve of Twelfth Night. Masked skiing and carnival procession to mark the end of *Fasching* in Feb.

Numerous ice skating and skiing events, including night jumping; *après ski.* Motorized *Narzissenkorso,* narcissus flower parade, staged 1st Sunday in June. Folk festival and trade exhibition week in Aug.

MURAU Summer brass band concerts in the park, riding (and driving) on the old steam-engined Murtalbahn in summer, Samson procession in August, international ski jumping competitions in winter.

SCHLADMING Masked skiing and carnival procession closes *Fasching* period.

MUSEUMS

GRAZ Joanneum, old buildings, Raubergasse 10, new buildings, Neutorgasse 45. The different buildings have different admission times, so best check with your hotel porter. This, one of the oldest museums in Europe, is really a group of museums. The old buildings contain the natural history museum; a coin collection; and, most important, a prehistoric and antique museum, whose greatest single treasure is probably the sacrificial chariot dating from 700 BC.

The new buildings, in the other half of the same block, contain the picture galleries and the applied art museum. The first shows works from medieval to modern times. Among famous artists represented are Hans von Aachen, Lukas Cranach, Jan Breughel *(Triumph of Death)*, Pieter Breughel *(Peasant Church Fair)*. The *Admont Madonna,* carved in wood in 1315, is Styria's most admired Gothic work of this kind. The other chief treasures are the 14th-century Mühlau crucifix, a 15th-century Madonna from the St. Lambrecht Monastery and the *St. Peter* by the unknown master from Grosslobming, of the same period. In the applied arts museum is the Augsburg Chalice, 16th century, the largest Renaissance chalice in Austria. The wrought-iron work here is particularly admirable.

Styrian Folklore Museum (Steirisches Volkskundemuseum), Paulustorgasse 13, open daily 9–12; Mondays, Tuesdays and Thursdays also 2–5. Among interesting items are: old Styrian folk costumes; garments from Hallstatt and Celtic periods, reconstructed on the basis of early descriptions; ancient spinning wheels; antique rustic furniture and farm utensils; an authentic 16th-century Rauchstube (farmhouse room for smoking meats) with original interior and furnishings; old Styrian handprints, hand embroideries, and musical instruments.

Styrian Armory (Landeszeughaus), located in the Landhaus, entrance from Herrengasse, open every day 9–12, Mondays, Tuesdays and Thursdays also 2–5. This is the original armory built in 1642 and still arranged in the same manner. It contains about 27,000 pieces of armor, weapons, and other military equipment, mostly from the 16th and 17th centuries comprising the actual weapons of the Styrian soldiers, last used at the end of the 17th century, and never out of the armory since: probably the only one of its kind.

City Museum (Stadtmuseum), Sackstrasse 18, open Monday–Saturday 10–5. City history and an apothecary museum.

Schweighofers Schnaps Museum at Bernegg, bus from Bruck–Mur.

SPAS

BAD AUSSEE Noted for its brine waters and treatment of heart and circulation ailments; new (1978) *Kurzentrum.*

BAD GLEICHENBERG This is the most important spa in Styria. The water from its eight carbonic acid springs and hypotonic hydroxide springs, one of them known already to the Romans, is used for the treatment of respiratory, circulatory, heart, and a number of other disorders. Although during the season, lasting from mid-April to the end of Oct., there are daily concerts by the spa orchestra and fencing and dancing tournaments, Bad Gleichenberg is maintained as a quiet spa, intended primarily for healing and rest.

BAD MITTERNDORF The thermal waters and peat baths here are beneficial for rheumatic ailments and general relaxation.

THERME LOIPERSDORF New health resort with thermal waters, indoor and outdoor pools, bio training, diet restaurants.

SPORTS

AFLENZ KURORT Mountain climbing school—*Bergsteigerschule Hochschwab*, A-8623, Aflenz. 1 chair lift. 7 ski lifts, ski school, 2 ski jumps, toboggan run, skating rink, curling facilities, horse sleighs.

ALTAUSSEE Waterskiing on the lake, and swimming in summer. In winter, curling facilities, skating rink, ski school, 5 ski lifts as well as the winter sports installations of Bad Aussee only about 6 km. away.

BAD AUSSEE 9 ski lifts, 2 ski jumps, ski school, 2 skating rinks, 5 toboggan runs, skijoring, horse-drawn sleighs, 8 curling alleys.

BAD GLEICHENBERG Popular center for riding.

BAD MITTERNDORF 4 ski lifts, ski school, 2 ski jumps, with a huge one at Kulm, skijoring, tobogganing, curling rinks, horse sleighs, to game feeding grounds.
The skiing facilities of the Tauplitz area are only some 6 km. away.

DONNERSBACH By toll road or bus service to Planneralp (5,248 ft.) with 4 ski lifts. From Donnersbachwald, deeper in the valley, a chair lift and 3 ski lifts to Riesneralm (6,297 ft.), ski schools, ski tours.

FLADNITZ 7 ski lifts, ski school, ice skating, curling, tobogganing.

HAUS IM ENNSTAL Cable car, 10 ski lifts nearby, ski school, ski jump, 3 toboggan runs, 3 curling rinks, ladies' downhill in Jan.

HOHENTAUERN (Styria), 4,150 ft. Bus from Trieben on Graz-Salzburg railway (about halfway).
Riding lessons are available. 8 ski lifts, ski school, toboggan run.

GRAZ Graz and its environs is an important winter sports complex. *Skiing* terrains exist on the elevations of Ruckerlberg, Platte, Petersberg, Hohe Rannach, Plabutsch, and particularly on Schöckel, called the "ski mountain" of Graz. On Plabutsch is a chair lift and ski lift; on Platte there are 2 ski lifts; on Schökel a cable car from St. Radegung, a chair lift from Semriach, and a ski lift; 1 additional ski lift at St. Radegund and 2 in Semriach. Also available in the area are 2 ski schools, several ski jumps, and *skijoring* facilities.

Ice skating and *curling* are very popular, too; there is a skating stadium at Liebenau, 8 skating rinks (one in St. Radegund) and about 50 curling rinks.

Ice hockey games take place regularly; 8 *toboggan* runs.

The city has about 15 *swimming* establishments. There's an outdoor swimming pool also in St. Radegund.

Tennis courts are available at more than half a dozen places, including St. Radegund.

9-hole *golf* course at Murhof in Frohnleiten, 18 km. north.

Horseback riding and instructors are available at Rechbauerstr. 35 in the suburb of Strassgang; Radegunderstr. 24 in Andritz; and Purbergstr. 54 in Maria-trost. Riding tournaments and *trotting* races are occasionally scheduled on the trotting field.

There is a pistol and air rifle shooting range in nearby Andritz.

Gliding enthusiasts can use the Graz airport, in Thalerhof, south of the city; there is a landing site also on Schöckel plateau. You can get instruction on flying a sports plane at Thalerhof. For information, inquire at Aero-Club-Landesverband, Landhaus, Herrengasse 16, Graz.

GRÖBMING 2,500 ft. Mountain climbing base for the eastern section of the Dachstein group. Center of horsebreeding area. About 2½ hours by fast train from Salzburg and about 4 hours from Graz.

Occasional trotting races.

Gliding school for beginners and experts, located at Niederöblarn nearby, open May to Oct. Rates, including room-and-board, are low, but reserve well in advance. You can take the medical examination in Aigen. Rowboats can be rented here for a trip on the Enns River to Admont.

Cabin car, 4 ski lifts, ski school, skijoring, toboggan run, curling, another ski lift at Michaelerberghaus.

GRUNDLSEE A few km. from Bad Aussee and Altaussee winter sports facilities.

2 ski lifts, ski school; ice skating and curling, on the lake in winter; also sailing school and water skiing.

KINDBERG 1,800 ft. By train from Kapfenberg, 15 minutes.

2 ski lifts, ski school, 5 toboggan runs, 4 curling rinks.

LEOBEN 2 ski lifts, ski jump, toboggan run, 2 skating rinks, ice hockey, 20 curling rinks.

MARIAZELL Cable car, chair lift (5 km. away) 10 ski lifts, 2 ski schools, 2 ski jumps, skijoring, skating rink, ice hockey, 2 curling rinks, 2 toboggan runs, horse sleighs to deer feeding grounds. For the downhill run from Bürgeralpe, if completed under prescribed conditions, you can win the *Mariazell Panther* award.
Swimming in Erlaufsee nearby.
Small airfield for gliders and sports planes.

MURAU Skiing mainly on nearby Frauenalpe, 4 ski lifts, ski school, ski jump, skijoring, 3 toboggan runs, skating rink, curling rinks.

MÜRZZUSCHLAG 2,200 ft 1½ hours by autorail from Graz, 2 hours from Vienna.
2 ski lifts, ski school, 2 ski jumps, skijoring, tobogganing and curling.

PACK 3,650 ft., mountain pass on the main road Graz–Klagenfurt, bus from Köflach.
Together with the village of **Hirschegg,** 15 ski lifts, ski school, ski jump, tobogganing, skating and curling.

PICHL-MANDLING Chair lift, 6 ski lifts, ski school, tobogganing, curling, sleighs.

PRÄBICHL Chair lift, 6 ski lifts, ski school, toboggan run, skating rink, horse sleighs.

RAMSAU Mountain climbing school, *Hochgebirgsschule Steiermark,* A–8972, Ramsau-Kulm. Cable car, 18 ski lifts, schools. Tobogganing, ice skating, ski tours, cross-country skiing, glacier skiing on Dachstein. Riding school.

SCHLADMING Two cable cars, chair lift, 14 ski lifts, ski schools, one for Senior Citizens, cross-country skiing, ski racing run with electronic timing for amateurs on the Planai plateau, ice skating, tobogganing, ski jumps, curling rinks. Glacier all-year-round skiing on Dachstein. Planai men's downhill in Jan.

SPITAL AM SEMMERING In Spital and Steinhaus, 2 chair lifts, 19 ski lifts, floodlit night ski run, tobogganing, 2 skating rinks.

STUBENBERG AM SEE Sailing school, swimming, on Austria's largest dammed lake.

TAUPLITZ There are 12 ski lifts, ski schools, outstanding ski tours with guides available, 2 ski jumps, skijoring, tobogganing, curling, and horse sleighs. The snow usually stays through April. This area is constantly growing in importance as a first class skiing center.

ENTERTAINMENT

GRAZ Opera and operetta—*Opernhaus* at the Opernring. Drama and comed
—at the *Schauspielhaus.* There is an open-air theater on the Schlossberg, whic
gives occasional performances during the summer. There are summer concerts i
the Stadtpark, in the courtyard of the Landhaus and in Schloss Eggenburg. Th
"Styrian Autumn" is a major festival of avant-garde music, theater and art, takin
place in the fall.

SHOPPING

GRAZ The liveliest shopping streets of Graz radiate from the Hauptplatz (mai
square): Sporgasse, Murgasse and particularly Herrengasse, with its side street
and its extension into the section around Jakomini Platz and the Opera. Muc
of this area is a pedestrian mall, one of the most attractive in Austria. The bes
buys in Graz include Styrian dirndls, hats, suits, and other Styrian folk dress an
folklore articles, including handicrafts and lace; leather clothing; hunting gun
and jewelry.

Dirndls and Trachten for Women. *Steirische Kunststube,* Engegasse 1
Mothwurf, Herreng. 6 and Albrechtg. 6. *Steiermärkischer Kunstgewerbeverein*
Landhausgasse 7. *Heimatwerk,* Paulustorgasse 13.

Handicrafts, Gifts and Souvenirs, *Steiermärkischer Kunstgewerbeverein*
Landhausgasse 7. *Steirisches Heimatwerk,* Paulustorgasse 13a (connected with th
folklore museum). *Kölz,* corner of Hauptplatz and Sporgasse (souvenirs).

Men's Hats. *Anton Pichler,* Herrengasse 28, and Südtiroler Platz 9.

Toys. *Koch,* Hauptplatz 10. *Spielzeugschachtel,* Schmiedgasse 16. *Kleinbahn*
Annenstr. 56 (toy trains).

Wrought Iron and Weinhebers. *Kossär,* Jakoministr. 10.

USEFUL ADDRESSES

GRAZ *Fremdenverkehrsbüro,* city tourist information office, Kaiserfeldgasse
25 (tel. 993 76591); *Landesfremdenverkehrsabteilung,* Styrian state tourist department, Landhaus, Herrengasse 16 (tel. 993 831). *Steiermärkisches Landesreisebüro,*
Styrian state travel agency, Hauptplatz 14 (tel. 993 76456), with a money exchange and room reservation office also at the main station.
   Airport. Thalerhof, with sightseeing and taxi flights available.

Car Hire: *Avis,* Humboldtstr. 4; *Hertz,* Annenstr. 42.

ENGLISH–GERMAN VOCABULARY

The most important phrase to know (one that may make it unnecessary to know any others) is: *"Sprechen Sie englisch?"* ("Do you speak English?"). If the answer is, *"Nein,"* then you are referred to the list below.

Conversation	Unterhaltung
Good morning	Guten Morgen
Good afternoon	Guten Tag
Good evening	Guten Abend
Good night	Gute Nacht
Good day	Grüss Gott
How do you do?	Wie geht es Ihnen?
How do you say in German?	Wie sagt man auf deutsch?
Very good!	Sehr gut!
All right	Alles in Ordnung, einverstanden
Good luck!	Viel Glück!
Hello	Hallo
Where is the hotel?	Wo ist das Hotel?
How much is that?	Was kostet das?
How do you feel?	Wie fühlen Sie sich?
I am pleased to meet you	Ich freue mich, Sie kennenzulernen
Permit me to introduce Mr. X	Ich erlaube mir, Herrn X vorzustellen
I like it very much	Es gefällt mir sehr gut
I don't like it	Es gefällt mir nicht
Yes	Ja (yah)
No	Nein (nine)
Many thanks	Vielen Dank
Don't mention it	Bitte sehr! Gern geschehen
I beg your pardon	Verzeihen Sie, entschuldigen Sie
Please	Bitte
Are you ready?	Staben Sie fertig?
I am ready	Ich bin fertig
Welcome	Wilkommen
I am very sorry	Es tut mir sehr leid
What time is it?	Wieviel Uhr ist es? —Wie spät ist es?

I am glad to see you	Ich freue mich, Sie zu sehen
I understand	Ich verstehe
Right	Rechts
Left	Links
Straight ahead	Geradeaus
Whenever it suits you	Wann es Ihnen passt
Please wait	Bitte warten Sie
I shall be a little late	Ich werde mich etwas verspäten
Where is . . .	Wo ist . . .
—the airport?	—der Flugplatz?
—a bank?	—eine Bank?
—the snack bar?	—das Büffet?
—the barber shop?	—ein Friseur?
—the bathroom?	—das Badezimmer?
—the ticket (booking) office?	—der Schalter?
—a chemist's shop (drug store)?	—eine Apotheke?
—the movies (cinema)?	—das Kino?
—the cloakroom?	—die Garderobe?
—the toilet?	—die Toilette?
—the American (British) Consulate?	—das amerikanische (britische) Konsulat?
—the customs office?	—das Zollamt?
—a garage?	—eine Garage?
—a hairdresser?	—ein Friseur?
—the luggage?	—das Gepäck?
—the museum?	—das Museum?
—the police station?	—die Polizei?
—the post office?	—das Postamt?
Have you . . .	Haben Sie . . .
—any American (English) cigarettes?	—amerikanische (englische) Zigaretten?
—a timetable?	—einen Fahrplan?
—a room to let?	—ein Zimmer zu vermieten?
—anything ready (food)?	—etwas fertig?
How long?	Wie lange?
How often?	Wie oft?
I want . . .	Ich brauche . . . Ich möchte . . . Ich bitte um . . . Ich will . . .
—my bill	Ich bitte um meine Rechnung
—to buy	Ich möchte kaufen
—cigars, cigarettes	Ich möchte Zigarren, Zigaretten
—the chambermaid	Ich möchte mit dem Zimmermädchen sprechen

—a dentist	Ich brauche einen Zahnarzt
—a doctor	Ich brauche einen Artz
—a dictionary	Ich brauche ein Wörterbuch
—something to drink	Ich möchte etwas trinken
—something to eat	Ich möchte etwas essen

Border Crossing	**Zollgrenze**
I have nothing to declare	Ich habe nichts zu verzollen
No tobacco	Kein Tabak
No spirits	Keine Getränke
For personal use	Für persönlichen Gebrauch
Worn articles	Gebrauchte Sachen
How much is the customs duty?	Wie hoch ist der Zoll?
Passport	Pass
Identity card	Personal-Ausweis

In the Restaurant	**Im Speisesaal**
Breakfast	Frühstück
Lunch	Mittagessen
Dinner	Abendessen
Bill of fare	Speisekarte
Waiter!	Herr Ober!

For ease of menu-reference, the following items are in German alphabetical order.

Beans	Bohnen
Bread	Brot
Butter	Butter
Ice cream	Eis
Duck	Ente
Peas	Erbsen
Fish	Fisch
Meat	Fleisch
Roast	Gebraten
Boiled	Gekocht
Fried	Geröstet
String Beans	Grüne Bohnen
Lettuce	Grüner Salat
Cucumber	Gurke
Mutton	Hammelfleisch
Hard-boiled egg	Hartgekochtes Ei
Honey	Honig
Chicken	Huhn
Lobster	Hummer
Coffee	Kaffee
Cocoa	Kakao
Veal	Kalbfleisch

Carrots	Karotten
Potatoes	Kartoffeln
Garlic	Knoblauch
Crab	Krabbe
Cake	Kuchen
Salmon	Lachs
Lamb	Lammfleisch
Almonds	Mandeln
Marmalade, jam	Marmelade
Milk	Milch
Clams	Muscheln
Fruit shortcake	Obstkuchen
Olives	Oliven
Omelet	Omelette
Orange juice	Orangensaft
Pepper	Pfeffer
Mushrooms	Pilze, Schwämme
Partridge	Rebhuhn
Radish	Rettich
Beef	Rindfleisch
Red wine	Rotwein
Scrambled eggs	Rühreier
Juice	Saft
Cream	Sahne
Salt	Salz
Sardines	Sardinen
Ham	Schinken
Ham and eggs	Schinken und Eier
Whipped cream	Schlagobers
Chocolate	Schokolade
Pork	Schweinefleisch
Champagne	Sekt
Celery	Sellerie
Mustard	Senf
Sauce	Soβe (Sosse)
Asparagus	Spargel
Bacon	Speck
Fried egg	Spiegelei
Spinach	Spinat
Tea	Tee
Tuna fish	Thunfisch
Turkey	Truthahn
Walnuts	Walnüsse
Water	Wasser
Soft-boiled egg	Weichgekochtes Ei
White wine	Weiβwein (Weisswein)
Sausage	Wurst

Onions	Zwiebeln

Days	**Tage**
Day	Tag
Monday	Montag
Tuesday	Dienstag
Wednesday	Mittwoch
Thursday	Donnerstag
Friday	Freitag
Saturday	Samstag
Sunday	Sonntag
Holiday	Feiertag

Colors	**Farben**
Red	Rot
Blue	Blau
Black	Schwarz
White	Weiβ (Weiss)
Green	Grün
Grey	Grau
Yellow	Gelb
Orange	Orange
Purple	Violett
Brown	Braun

Clothing	**Kleidung**
Hat	Hut
Socks	Socken
Stockings	Strümpfe
Shoes	Schuhe
Dress	Kleid
Skirt	Rock
Blouse	Bluse
Underwear	Unterwäsche
Overcoat	Mantel
Belt	Gürtel
Gloves	Handschuhe
Handkerchief	Taschentuch

The answers to many of the questions you ask will be numbers. Therefore you need to know what they sound like. We suggest you memorize the numbers below, with their pronunciations, given in parentheses.

Numbers (Zahlen)

1 eins (yns)	5 fünf (funf)
2 zwei (tsvy)	6 sechs (sex)
3 drei (dry)	7 sieben (zeeben)
4 vier (fear)	8 acht (ahkt)

 9 neun (noyn)
10 zehn (tzyan)
11 elf (elf)
12 zwölf (tsvulf)
13 dreizehb (drytsayn)
14 vierzehn
15 fünfzehn
16 sechzehn
17 siebzehn (zeeptzayn)
18 achtzehn
19 neunzehn
20 zwanzig (tsvantzig)
21 einundzwanzig
   (ynunstsvantzig)

22 zweiundzwanzig
30 dreissig
40 vierzig
50 fünfzig
60 sechzig
70 siebzig
80 achtzig
90 neunzig
100 hundert (hoondert)
110 hundertzehn
200 zweihundert
1000 tausend (towzent)
1500 fünfzehnhundert

INDEX

The letters H and R indicate Hotel and Restaurant listings.

(See also "Practical Information" sections at the end of each chapter for Sports, Special Events and other useful information.)